AMERICAN
GOVERNMENT
A BRIEF INTRODUCTION

THEODORE J. LOWI Late of CORNELL UNIVERSITY

BENJAMIN GINSBERG JOHNS HOPKINS UNIVERSITY

KENNETH A. SHEPSLE HARVARD UNIVERSITY

STEPHEN ANSOLABEHERE HARVARD UNIVERSITY

W. W. NORTON & COMPANY

Independent Publishers Since 1923

W. W. Norton & Company has been independent since its founding in 1923, when William Warder Norton and Mary D. Herter Norton first published lectures delivered at the People's Institute, the adult education division of New York City's Cooper Union. The firm soon expanded its program beyond the Institute, publishing books by celebrated academics from America and abroad. By mid-century, the two major pillars of Norton's publishing program—trade books and college texts—were firmly established. In the 1950s, the Norton family transferred control of the company to its employees, and today—with a staff of four hundred and a comparable number of trade, college, and professional titles published each year—W. W. Norton & Company stands as the largest and oldest publishing house owned wholly by its employees.

Editor: Laura Wilk
Editorial Assistant: Catherine Lillie
Project Editor: David Bradley
Managing Editor, College: Marian Johnson
Managing Editor, College Digital Media: Kim Yi
Production Manager: Eric Pier-Hocking
Media Editor: Spencer Richardson-Jones
Associate Media Editor: Michael Jaoui
Media Editorial Assistant: Lena Nowak-Laird
Marketing Manager: Ashley Sherwood
Design Director: Rubina Yeh
Book Designer: DeMarinis Design LLC
Photo Editor: Catherine Abelman
Director of College Permissions: Megan Schindel
Composition: GraphicWorld
Manufacturing: Transcontinental

Permission to use copyrighted material is included in the credits section of this book, which begins on page C1.

The Library of Congress has cataloged another edition as follows:

Names: Lowi, Theodore J., author. | Ginsberg, Benjamin, author. | Shepsle,
   Kenneth A., author. | Ansolabehere, Stephen, author.
Title: American government : power and purpose / Theodore J. Lowi, Late of
   Cornell University, Benjamin Ginsberg, Johns Hopkins University, Kenneth
   A. Shepsle, Harvard University, Stephen Ansolabehere, Harvard University.
Description: Sixteenth Edition. | New York : W.W. Norton & Company, [2021] |
   Includes bibliographical references and index.
Identifiers: LCCN 2020051031 | ISBN 9780393427691 (Paperback)
Subjects: LCSH: United States—Politics and government—Textbooks.
Classification: LCC JK276.L69 2021 | DDC 320.473—dc23
LC record available at https://lccn.loc.gov/2020051031

ISBN: 978-0-393-42765-3 (pbk.)

W. W. Norton & Company, Inc., 500 Fifth Avenue, New York, NY 10110
wwnorton.com

W. W. Norton & Company Ltd., 15 Carlisle Street, London W1D 3BS

2 3 4 5 6 7 8 9 0

CONTENTS

14

PREFACE

This Sixteenth Edition continues our endeavor to make *American Government: A Brief Introduction* the most authoritative and contemporary introductory text on the market. This major revision brings a renewed focus to the institutions, processes, and data that illuminate big questions about governance and representation in the United States. Those who have used the book in the past know that we have always emphasized the role of American political institutions. In every chapter we encourage students to think critically and analytically about how well the institutions discussed in that chapter serve the goals of a democratic society. To further support this goal, we have enhanced our in-text pedagogy and digital resource package, including InQuizitive, to help students master the core concepts and ideas in each chapter, and challenge them to apply what they have learned.

This book was written for faculty and students who are looking for a little more than just "nuts and bolts" but prefer a brief-format text. No fact about American government is intrinsically difficult to grasp, and in an open society such as ours, facts abound. The philosophy of free and open media in the United States makes information about the government readily available. The advent of the internet and new communication technologies have further expanded the opportunity to learn about our government. The ubiquity of information in our society is a great virtue. Common knowledge about the government gives our society a vocabulary that is widely shared and enables us to communicate effectively with each other about politics. But it is also important to reach beyond that common vocabulary and to develop a more sophisticated understanding of politics and government.

The sheer quantity of facts in our society can be overwhelming. In a 24/7 news cycle it can be hard to pick out the stories that are important and to stay focused on them. Today, moreover, Americans may choose among a variety of news sources, including broadcast, print, and various digital formats, all clamoring for attention. The single most important task for the teacher of political science is to confront popular ideas and information and to choose from among them the small number of really significant concepts that help us make better sense of the world. This book aims to help instructors and students accomplish this task.

The major changes in this Sixteenth Edition are intended to combine authoritative, concise coverage of the central topics in American politics with smart pedagogical features designed to get students thinking about quantitative data and current issues. Highlights of the revision include the following:

- **New analysis of the 2020 elections**, including data illustrations, walks students through what happened and why. Chapter 10 includes a section devoted to the 2020 elections, as well as updated data, examples, and other information throughout the book.

- **New "Think It Through" questions**, which appear in the margins of each chapter, challenge students to make connections between the concepts and their own lives, while the **new "Check Your Understanding"** end-of-chapter questions help students review the key takeaways from each chapter.

- The revised **"Making Sense of Charts and Graphs" primer**, by Jennifer Bachner (Johns Hopkins University) at the end of Chapter 1 sets students up to understand political data that they encounter in the news and in the course, including in the many new Timeplots and Analyzing the Evidence infographics throughout the book.

- **New coverage of public policy** from contributing author Elizabeth Rigby (George Washington University) is integrated throughout the book, including current coverage of issues like health care, recent legislation to relieve the economic burden during the coronavirus pandemic, the government's role in higher education, and the "hidden welfare state." The economic and social policy chapter (Chapter 13) has been completely revised to reflect updated scholarship.

- **New and revised Timeplot** features use quantitative data to illuminate long-term trends in American politics. New Timeplots explore liberal and conservative outside spending (Chapter 12) and U.S. foreign aid spending as a percentage of GDP (Chapter 14).

- **New Analyzing the Evidence units** written by expert researchers highlight the political science behind the information in the book, while the remaining units have been updated with new data and analysis. Each unit poses an important question from political science and presents evidence that can be used to analyze the question. The new units are

  "How Representative Is Congress?" in Chapter 5, contributed by Leah Stokes (University of California, Santa Barbara)

  "What Motivates Political Engagement among Young People?" in Chapter 11, contributed by David E. Campbell and Christina Wolbrecht (University of Notre Dame)

  "Who's Funding Google's PAC?" in Chapter 12, contributed by Zhao Li (Princeton University)

- **New Policy Principle boxes**, authored by Elizabeth Rigby, highlight the various players and structures that shape current policy debates, including automatic voter registration (Chapter 10) and Trump's border wall proposal (Chapter 6).

This Sixteenth Edition of *American Government: A Brief Introduction* is accompanied by an innovative package of teaching and learning resources to support online and face-to-face classes:

- **InQuizitive**, an adaptive learning tool offers a range of "nuts and bolts" as well as applied and conceptual questions, drawing upon features of the text like the Analyzing the Evidence infographics, to help ensure that students master the material and come to class prepared.

- The **new "Evaluating Sources" InQuizitive module** walks students through the key aspects of identifying and understanding what a source is, how it is used in an argument, and whether it is a valid source or not (such as fake news).

- **New and revised Timeplot exercises** connect quantitative data to the historical development of key aspects of American politics. Each Timeplot exercise offers assessment on the feature, cultivating students' data literacy as well as their understanding of important historical trends in American government.

- **New Weekly News Quizzes** offer students a current news article, video, or podcast plus an assessment, all easily reported into a gradebook. Each Weekly News Quiz promotes media literacy and engagement with an important story concerning American government. The Weekly News Quiz also includes a recommended class activity as well as suggested chapter and topic connections.

- A **comprehensive resource package** to support teaching and learning includes activities that can be assigned through your Learning Management System, a comprehensive test bank, and lecture PowerPoints.

For the Sixteenth Edition we have profited greatly from the guidance of many teachers who have used earlier editions and from the suggestions of numerous thoughtful reviewers. We thank them by name in the Acknowledgments. We recognize that there is no single best way to craft an introductory text, and we are grateful for the advice we have received.

Benjamin Ginsberg
Kenneth A. Shepsle
Stephen Ansolabehere

ACKNOWLEDGMENTS

We note with sadness the passing of Theodore J. Lowi. We miss Ted but continue to hear his voice and to benefit from his wisdom in the pages of this book.

Our students at Cornell, Johns Hopkins, and Harvard have been an essential factor in the writing of this book. They have been our most immediate intellectual community, a hospitable one indeed. Another part of our community, perhaps a large suburb, is the discipline of political science itself. Our debt to the scholarship of our colleagues is scientifically measurable, probably to several decimal points, in the footnotes of each chapter. Despite many complaints that the field is too scientific or not scientific enough, political science is alive and well in the United States. Political science has never been at a loss for relevant literature, and without that literature our job would have been impossible. For this edition, we are grateful for Elizabeth Rigby's continued involvement. She has revised the domestic policy chapter as well as the Policy Principle sections outlined in the preface.

In light of important recent and ongoing discussions, we wanted to note that consistent with our strong commitment to diversity and our belief that all should be treated with respect, we are capitalizing the names of all racial, religious, and ethnic groups.

We are pleased to acknowledge our debt to the many colleagues who had a direct and active role in criticism and preparation of the manuscript. The First Edition was read and reviewed by Gary Bryner, Brigham Young University; James F. Herndon, Virginia Polytechnic Institute and State University; James W. Riddlesperger, Jr., Texas Christian University; John Schwarz, University of Arizona; Toni-Michelle Travis, George Mason University; and Lois Vietri, University of Maryland. We also want to reiterate our thanks to the four colleagues who allowed us the privilege of testing a trial edition of our book by using it as the major text in their introductory American government courses: Gary Bryner, Brigham Young University; Allan J. Cigler, University of Kansas; Burnet V. Davis, Albion College; and Erwin A. Jaffe, California State University, Stanislaus.

For the Second through Seventh Editions, we relied heavily on the thoughtful manuscript reviews we received from J. Roger Baker, Wittenburg University; Timothy Boylan, Winthrop University; David Canon, University of Wisconsin; Victoria Farrar-Myers, University of Texas at Arlington; John Gilmour, College of William and Mary; Mark Graber, University of Maryland; Russell Hanson, Indiana University; Robert Huckfeldt, University of California at Davis; Mark Joslyn, University of Kansas; William Keech, Carnegie Mellon University; Donald Kettl, University of Wisconsin; Anne Khademian, University of Wisconsin; Beth Leech, Rutgers University; James Lennertz, Lafayette College; Allan McBride, Grambling State University; William McLauchlan, Purdue University; Grant Neeley, Texas Tech University; Charles Noble, California State University, Long Beach; and Joseph Peek, Jr., Georgia State University.

For the Eighth Edition, we benefited from the comments of Scott Adler, University of Colorado, Boulder; Scott Ainsworth, University of Georgia; Thomas Brunell, Northern Arizona University; Daniel Carpenter, Harvard University; John Coleman, University of Wisconsin–Madison; Richard Conley, University of Florida; Keith Dougherty, University of Georgia; John Ferejohn, Stanford University; Brad Gomez, University of South Carolina; Paul Gronke, Reed College; Douglas Harris, Loyola College; Marc Hetherington, Bowdoin College; Gregory Huber, Yale University; Brian Humes, University of Nebraska–Lincoln; Jeffrey Jenkins, Northwestern University; Paul Johnson, University of Kansas; Robert Lowry, Iowa State University; Anthony Nownes, University of Tennessee; Andrew Polsky, Hunter College (City University of New York); Mark Richards, Grand Valley State University; Charles Shipan, University of Iowa; Craig Volden, Ohio State University; and Garry Young, George Washington University.

For the Ninth Edition, we were guided by the comments of John Baughman; Lawrence Baum, The Ohio State University; Chris Cooper, Western Carolina State University; Charles Finochiaro, State University of New York at Buffalo; Lisa Garcia-Bellorda, University of California at Irvine; Sandy Gordon, New York University; Steven Greene, North Carolina State University; Richard Herrera, Arizona State University; Ben Highton, University of California at Davis; Trey Hood, University of Georgia; Andy Karch, University of Texas at Austin; Glen Krutz, University of Oklahoma; Paul Labedz, Valencia Community College; Brad Lockerbie, University of Georgia; Wendy Martinek, State University of New York at Binghamton; Nicholas Miller, University of Maryland, Baltimore County; Russell Renka, Southeast Missouri State University; Debbie Schildkraut, Tufts University; Charles Shipan, University of Iowa; Chris Shortell, California State University, Northridge; John Sides, University of Texas at Austin; Sean Theriault, University of Texas at Austin; and Lynn Vavreck, University of California at Los Angeles.

For the Tenth Edition, we were grateful for the detailed comments of Kevin Esterling, University of California at Riverside; Christian Grose, Vanderbilt University; William Hixon, Lawrence University; Martin Johnson, University of California at Riverside; Gregory Koger, University of Miami; Renan Levine,

University of Toronto; Jason MacDonald, Kent State University; Scott Meinke, Bucknell University; Michelle Swers, Georgetown University; and Alan Wiseman, The Ohio State University.

For their advice on the Eleventh Edition, we thank Scott Ainsworth, University of Georgia; Bethany Albertson, University of Washington; Brian Arbour, John Jay College; James Battista, University at Buffalo, State University of New York; Lawrence Becker, California State University, Northridge; Damon Cann, Utah State University; Jamie Carson, University of Georgia; Suzanne Chod, Pennsylvania State University; Michael Crespin, University of Georgia; Ryan Emenaker, College of the Redwoods; Kevin Esterling, University of California at Riverside; Richard Glenn, Millersville University; Brad Gomez, Florida State University; Sanford Gordon, New York University; Christian Grose, Vanderbilt University; James Hanley, Adrian College; Ryan Hurl, University of Toronto; Josh Kaplan, University of Notre Dame; Wendy Martinek, Binghamton University; Will Miller, Southeast Missouri State University; Evan Parker-Stephen, Texas A&M University; Melody Rose, Portland State University; Eric Schickler, University of California at Berkeley; John Sides, George Washington University; and Lynn Vavreck, University of California at Los Angeles.

For the Twelfth Edition we looked to comments from John M. Aughenbaugh, Virginia Commonwealth University; Christopher Banks, Kent State University; Michael Berkman, Pennsylvania State University; Cynthia Bowling, Auburn University; Matthew Cahn, California State University, Northridge; Damon Cann, Utah State University; Tom Cioppa, Brookdale Community College; David Damore, University of Nevada, Las Vegas; Kevin Esterling, University of California at Riverside; Jessica Feezell, University of California at Santa Barbara; Charle J. Finocchiaro, University of South Carolina; Rodd Freitag, University of Wisconsin–Eau Claire; Richard Glenn, Millersville University; Kevin Jefferies, Alvin Community College; Nancy Jimeno, California State University, Fullerton; Gregory Koger, University of Miami; David E. Lewis, Vanderbilt University; Allison M. Martens, University of Louisville; Thomas M. Martin, Eastern Kentucky University; Michael Andrew McLatchy, Clarendon College; Ken Mulligan, Southern Illinois University, Carbondale; Geoffrey D. Peterson, University of Wisconsin–Eau Claire; Jesse Richman, Old Dominion University; Mark C. Rom, Georgetown University; Laura Schneider, Grand Valley State University; Scot Schraufnagel, Northern Illinois University; Ronald P. Seyb, Skidmore College; Martin S. Sheffer, Tidewater Community College; Charles R. Shipan, University of Michigan; Howard A. Smith, Florida Gulf Coast University; Michele Swers, Georgetown University; Charles Tien, Hunter College (City University of New York); Elizabeth Trentanelli, Gulf Coast State College; and Kenneth C. Williams, Michigan State University.

For the Thirteenth Edition we are indebted to Michael M. Binder, University of North Florida; Stephen Borrelli, The University of Alabama; Dan Cassino, Fairleigh Dickinson University; Jangsup Choi, Texas A&M University–Commerce; Martin Cohen, James Madison University; Jeff Colbert, Elon University;

Richard S. Conley, University of Florida; Mark Croatti, American University; David Dulio, Oakland University; Andrew M. Essig, DeSales University; Kathleen Ferraiolo, James Madison University; Emily R. Gill, Bradley University; Brad T. Gomez, Florida State University; Paul N. Goren, University of Minnesota; Thomas Halper, Baruch College; Audrey A. Haynes, University of Georgia; Diane J. Heith, St. John's University; Ronald J. Hrebenar, The University of Utah; Ryan Hurl, University of Toronto Scarborough; Richard Jankowski, State University of New York at Fredonia; Kevin Jefferies, Alvin Community College; Timothy R. Johnson, University of Minnesota; Kenneth R. Mayer, University of Wisconsin–Madison; Mark McKenzie, Texas Tech University; Fiona Miller, University of Toronto Mississauga; Richard M. Pious, Barnard College; Tim Reynolds, Alvin Community College; Martin Saiz, California State University, Northridge; Dante Scala, University of New Hampshire; Sean M. Theriault, University of Texas at Austin; J. Alejandro Tirado, Texas Tech University; Terri Towner, Oakland University; Nicholas Valentino, University of Michigan; Harold M. Waller, McGill University; and Jeffrey S. Worsham, West Virginia University.

We also thank the reviewers who advised us on the Fourteenth Edition: Michael E. Aleprete, Westminster College–Community College of Allegheny County; James Binney, Pennsylvania State University; William Blake, Indiana University–Purdue University, Indianapolis; Eric Boyer, Colby-Sawyer College; Chelsie L. M. Bright, Mills College; Thomas Cioppa, Brookdale Community College; Daniel Coffey, University of Akron; Darin DeWitt, California State University, Long Beach; Scott Englund, University of California at Santa Barbara; Amanda Friesen, Indiana University–Purdue University, Indianapolis; Frank Fuller, Lincoln University; Baogang Guo, Dalton State College; Eric Hanson, State University of New York at Fredonia; Jennifer Haydel, Montgomery College; Peter B. Heller, Manhattan College; Tseggai Isaac, Missouri University of Science and Technology; Vicki Jeffries-Bilton, Portland State University; Nicole Kalaf-Hughes, Bowling Green State University; Ervin Kallfa, Hostos Community College (City University of New York); James Krueger, University of Wisconsin–Oshkosh; Aaron Ley, University of Rhode Island; Christine Lipsmeyer, Texas A&M University; David B. MacDonald, University of Guelph; Samantha Majic, John Jay College (City University of New York); William McLauchlan, Purdue University; Barbara Palmer, Baldwin Wallace University; Hong Min Park, University of Wisconsin–Milwaukee; John Patty, Washington University in St. Louis; John W. Ray, Montana Tech (University of Montana); Michael K. Romano, Georgia Southern University; Eric Sands, Berry College; Kathleen Tipler, Wake Forest University; and David Weaver, Boise State University.

We are grateful for the comments from the reviewers for the Fifteenth Edition: Evelyn Ballard, Houston Community College; Curtis R. Berry, Shippensburg University; Tom Cioppa, Brookdale Community College; Lloyd Crews, Oakland Community College, Royal Oak Campus; Jeffrey Crouch, American University; David Darmofal, University of South Carolina; Paul Djupe, Denison University; Charles J. Finocchiaro, University of Oklahoma; Chris Galdieri,

Saint Anselm College; Ben Gaskins, Lewis & Clark College; Greg Goelzhauser, Utah State University; Jake Haselswerdt, University of Missouri; Michael Herron, Dartmouth College; Krista Jenkins, Fairleigh Dickinson University; Kristin Kanthak, University of Pittsburgh; Peter Kolozi, Bronx Community College; Daniel Levin, The University of Utah; Christine Lipsmeyer, Texas A&M University; Janet M. Martin, Bowdoin College; Robert J. McGrath, George Mason University; Scott Meinke, Bucknell University; Nina M. Moore, Colgate University; Stephen Nichols, California State University, San Marcos; David O'Connell, Dickinson College; Jesse Rhodes, University of Massachusetts; Mark Carl Rom, Georgetown University; Stella Rouse, University of Maryland; Travis S. Smith, Brigham Young University; Jennifer Nicoll Victor, George Mason University; Amber Wichowsky, Marquette University; Geoffrey Willbanks, Tyler Junior College; and Larry Wright, Florida A&M University. We would also like to thank Andie Herrig and Johnathan Romero, students at the Washington University in St. Louis, for identifying two errors in the book. We appreciate your close read.

For their advice on this Sixteenth Edition, we thank George Agabango, Bloomsburg University; Ian G. Anson, University of Maryland—Baltimore County; Michael Bailey, Georgetown University; Josh Berkenpas, Minnesota State University; Nicholas Boushee, San Diego City College; Jonathan N. Brown, Sam Houston State University; Richard S. Conley, University of Florida; Tracy Cooper, University of North Carolina, Pembroke; Murniz A. Coson, California State Polytechnic University, Pomona; Paulina Cossette, Washington College; Evan Crawford, University of San Diego; Kathleen Donovan, St. John Fisher College; Richard Haesly, California State University, Long Beach; George Hawley, University of Alabama; Matthew Dean Hindman, University of Tulsa; Jeneen Hobby, Cleveland State University; Natalie Johnson, Francis Marion University; David Lucander, Rockland Community College; Amber Lusvardi, Millikin University; Domenic Maffei, Caldwell University; Brad Mapes-Martins, University of Wisconsin—Stevens Point; Mary McGrath, Northwestern University; Taneisha N. Means, Vassar College; Rosemary Nossiff, Marymount Manhattan College; Yu Ouyang, Purdue University Northwest; Maxwell Palmer, Boston University; Joseph W. Robbins, Valdosta State University; Samuel VanSant Stoddard, Springfield College; Michael E. Thunberg, Norwich University; Peggy R. Wright, Arkansas State University—Jonesboro. We would also like to thank Alec Alameddine at Washington University in St. Louis for identifying errors in the book. We appreciate your close read.

An important contribution to recent editions was made by the authors of the Analyzing the Evidence units. We are grateful to the authors of the new Analyzing the Evidence units in the Sixteenth Edition, who are named in the preface. In addition, Jennifer Bachner, Jenna Bednar, David E. Campbell, Edward G. Carmines, Jeremiah D. Castle, Rachael Vanessa Cobb, Patrick J. Egan, Robert S. Erikson, Peter D. Feaver, Sean Gailmard, Christopher Gelpi, Martin Gilens, Sanford Gordon, John C. Green, David Konisky, Geoffrey C. Layman, Beth L. Leech, David Lewis, Andrew D. Martin, Kenneth Mayer, Rasmus Kleis Nielsen,

David M. Primo, Kevin M. Quinn, Jason Reifler, Jon Rogowski, Eric R. Schmidt, Matthew S. Shugart, Dara Z. Strolovitch, Steven L. Taylor, and David C. Wilson contributed to this feature in earlier editions, and much of their work is still reflected in this edition.

We would also like to thank our partners at W. W. Norton & Company, who have continued to apply their talents and energy to this textbook. The efforts of Laura Wilk, David Bradley, Catherine Lillie, Eric Pier-Hocking, Spencer Richardson-Jones, and Lena Nowak-Laird kept the production of the Sixteenth Edition and its accompanying resources coherent and in focus. We also thank Ann Shin, Roby Harrington, and Steve Dunn, whose contributions to previous editions remain invaluable.

We are more than happy, however, to absolve all these contributors from any flaws, errors, and misjudgments that this book contains. We wish it could be free of all production errors, grammatical errors, misspellings, misquotes, missed citations, etc. From that standpoint, a book ought to try to be perfect. But substantively we have not tried to write a flawless book; we have not tried to write a book to please everyone. We have again tried to write an effective book, a book that cannot be taken lightly. Our goal is not to make every reader a political scientist. Our goal is to restore politics as a subject of vigorous and enjoyable discourse, releasing it from the bondage of the thirty-second sound bite and the thirty-page technical briefing. Every person can be knowledgeable because everything about politics is accessible. One does not have to be a philosopher to argue about the requisites of democracy, a lawyer to dispute constitutional interpretations, an economist to debate public policy. We will be very proud if our book contributes in a small way to the restoration of the ancient art of political controversy.

Benjamin Ginsberg
Kenneth A. Shepsle
Stephen Ansolabehere

AMERICAN
GOVERNMENT
A BRIEF INTRODUCTION

CHAPTER ONE

INTRODUCTION: GOVERNANCE AND REPRESENTATION

1

In June 2020, protests erupted across America in response to the killing of a handcuffed and unarmed African American man, George Floyd, by a White Minneapolis police officer. In a shocking cell phone video, the officer, Derek Chauvin, could be seen pressing his knee to Floyd's neck for several minutes while Floyd, saying repeatedly that he could not breathe, lost consciousness and died. Chauvin was charged with murder wile three other police officers present at the scene were charged with lesser offenses.

America is a nation that began with protests and demonstrations against British rule, and protests have continued to play an important role in our nation's history. Indeed, antislavery protests, women's suffrage marches, antiwar demonstrations, civil rights protests, and climate change rallies, to name but a few, have changed and shaped the course of American history and will continue to do so. And, unfortunately, protest almost inevitably becomes tinged with violence. Large protests are chaotic and disorderly and in the pandemonium some may seize an opportunity to engage in looting and mayhem.

America's founders certainly understood the importance of public protest. Freedom of assembly is, after all, enshrined in our constitution's First Amendment. Yet, the founders also understood that government by protest was untenable. The eighteenth-century French philosopher Jean-Jacques Rousseau thought that spontaneous political action was the only way the "general will" of the people could be expressed. America's founders, however, thought the will of the people needed to be refined and filtered through representative institutions

to make certain that transient popular impulses and passions expressed, say, through vigilantism and lynch mobs, did not produce injuries and injustice.

The framers were surely right. Government by protest is untenable. And yet, representative institutions can be slow to act, paralyzed by political gridlock, and in need of an occasional nudge or even a shove. Take the matter of police violence. According to the *Washington Post*, the number of *unarmed* individuals, including unarmed Black men like George Floyd, killed by the police has been declining over the past several years. Moreover, according to Samuel Sinyangwe, a data scientist and political activist writing for *FiveThirtyEight*, the overall number of police shootings has especially declined in cities like Los Angeles, Chicago, San Francisco, and Philadelphia, where institutional reforms of police training and practices were undertaken in response to public protests. "Many of these reforms were initiated in response to protests and public outcry over high-profile deaths," Sinyangwe said.

Our's is a government of laws and institutions but protest has its place. It is the nudge that is sometimes very much needed. These concerns point to two of the most fundamental issues of American democracy: governance and representation. **Governance** means making official decisions about a nation's affairs and having the authority to put them into effect. A **government** is the institution or set of institutions that makes such decisions. Governments develop policies and enact laws designed to promote the nation's security and welfare. Some citizens may not agree with particular policies and laws, so governments generally need the power to enforce them.

In a constitutional democracy like the United States, the powers of government are limited (by a constitution) and many perspectives must be taken into account (through democratic institutions). One way that citizens express their perspectives is through protests, which have played an important role in the nation's history, starting with demonstrations against British rule and extending to the present with the massive protests in 2020 against police brutality.

▪ Why do representation and effective governance matter?

governance
The process of governing, which involves making official decisions about a nation's affairs and having the authority to put them into effect.

government
The institutions through which a land and its people are ruled.

representation
An arrangement in which citizens select individuals to express their views when decisions are made.

In some nations, governance is the responsibility of a small group of rulers who are apt to equate the nation's welfare with their own. In a democracy, however, ordinary citizens' voices are heard and taken into account when decisions are made. In modern democracies, citizens influence government by selecting at least some of their leaders. This process is called political **representation**. Generally, when the government makes decisions, the views of the majority as expressed through its representatives prevail. If laws and policies consistently run counter to the will of the majority or favor special interests, the legitimacy of the government—that is, the belief that the government's actions are valid and proper—may be undermined.

The effectiveness and interplay of governance and representation are at the heart of America's constitutional system—and when they are not working effectively, many Americans notice and become concerned. Throughout this book, as we examine the major features of American government, we will see that the themes of representation and effective governance—and how the two do or do not work together—underlie many important questions about today's political system, from calls for a new constitutional convention to lawsuits charging that some states conduct elections in ways that give one party an advantage or deprive minorities of fair representation.

Learning Objectives

- Identify the main purposes of government and the major types of government, including constitutional democracy.

- Define *politics* and explain how representation enables citizens to influence political decisions.

- Describe three reasons why achieving effective governance and meaningful representation can be difficult, even when people agree on these principles.

WHY IS GOVERNMENT NECESSARY?

Before we turn to the particulars of the American political system, let's consider the basic purposes of any government. Government enables a large group of people to live together as peacefully as possible. In the Declaration of Independence, America's founders, influenced by the writings of the British philosopher John Locke (1632–1704), declared that governments were needed to promote "life, liberty and the pursuit of happiness." A modern interpretation of these ideas might say government is necessary for three reasons: to maintain order, to protect property, and to provide public goods.

Maintaining Order.   For people to live together peacefully, law and order are required, and these can be secured only by a government able to use force if needed to prevent violence and lawlessness and maintain citizens' safety. This potential for the use of force may sound like a threat to "life, liberty, and the pursuit of happiness" until you think about the absence of government, or anarchy. According to the British philosopher Thomas Hobbes (1588–1679), anarchy is even worse than the potential tyranny of government because anarchy is characterized by "continual fear, and danger of violent death . . . [where life is] solitary, poor, nasty, brutish and short."[1] Governmental power can be seen as a threat to individual liberty, yet maintaining order and keeping people safe are essential so that we can enjoy that freedom.

Protecting Property.

After the safety of citizens comes the security of their property. Protection of property is almost universally recognized as an important function of government. John Locke wrote that whatever we have created with our own labor is considered our property.[2] But even Locke recognized that although we have the right to own what we produce, that right means nothing if someone with greater power than ours decides to take what we own or trespass on it.

Something we call our own is ours only as long as laws help ensure that we can enjoy, use, consume, trade, or sell it. Property rights, then, can be defined as all the laws against theft and trespass that permit us not only to call something our own but also to make sure our claim sticks.

Providing Public Goods.

Another British philosopher, David Hume (1711–1776), observed that although two neighbors may agree to cooperate in draining a swampy meadow, the more neighbors there are, the more difficult it will be to get the task done. A few neighbors might clear the swamp because they understand the benefits that each of them will receive from doing so. But as the number of neighbors who benefit from the clearing expands, many will realize that they all can get the same benefit if only a few clear the swamp and the rest do nothing.

 think it through

There is always a trade-off between individual liberty, on the one hand, and public safety and order, on the other. Do you see examples of this principle in action in your own life? Safety and order are public goods. From what public goods do you benefit?

One important role of government is to provide public goods, like national defense. National defense may benefit everyone within a country, but without government, no one has an incentive to pay for it on their own.

public good

A good that, first, may be enjoyed by anyone if it is provided and, second, may not be denied to anyone once it has been provided. Also called *collective good*.

free riding

Enjoying the benefits of some good or action while letting others bear the costs.

autocracy

A form of government in which a single individual rules.

oligarchy

A form of government in which a small group of landowners, military officers, or wealthy merchants controls most of the governing decisions.

democracy

A system of rule that permits citizens to play a significant part in government, usually through the selection of key public officials.

constitutional government

A system of rule that establishes specific limits on the powers of the government.

authoritarian government

A system of rule in which the government's power is not limited by law, though it may be restrained by other social institutions.

totalitarian government

A system of rule in which the government's power is not limited by law and in which the government seeks to eliminate other social institutions that might challenge it.

A **public good** (or *collective good*) is a benefit that no member of a group can be prevented from enjoying once it has been provided. The clearing of the swamp is one example; national defense is another. National defense is one of the most important public goods—especially when the nation is threatened by war or terrorism. Enjoying a public good without working for it is called **free riding**. Without government's powers to enforce a policy to build a bridge or create an army, even the richest, most concerned citizens have no incentive to pay for it.

A government provides the processes, procedures, locations, and participants through which these three basic purposes can be fulfilled. Effective governments enact laws and develop policies to maintain order, protect property, and provide essential public goods like defense, public health and sanitation, basic education, and a transportation infrastructure. Governments that do not effectively fulfill these functions are often referred to as "failed states." While we may disagree about how much and what government should do to address these basic purposes, most people agree that government has some role in each area.

FORMS OF GOVERNMENT

Government comes in many different forms, as simple as a tribal council that meets occasionally to advise the chief or as complex as the United States' vast establishment with its forms, rules, governmental bodies, and bureaucracies. Governments vary in structure, size, and operating methods. Two questions are of special importance in determining how they differ: Who governs? And how much governmental control is permitted?

In some nations, political authority is held by a single individual—a system called **autocracy**. When a small group of landowners, military officers, or wealthy merchants controls most of the governing decisions, that government is an **oligarchy**. If many people participate, and the general population has some influence over the choice of leaders and their subsequent actions, the government is called a representative **democracy**.

Governments also vary in how they govern. In the United States and a number of other nations, governments are legally limited in what they control (substantive limits), as well as how they go about controlling it (procedural limits). These are called **constitutional governments**. In other nations—for example, Saudi Arabia—forces that the government cannot fully control, such as a powerful religious organization or the military, may help keep the government in check, but the law imposes few real limits. Such governments are called **authoritarian governments**. In a third group of nations, including the Soviet Union under Joseph Stalin or North Korea today, governments not only lack any legal limits but also seek to eliminate organized social groups or institutions that might challenge their authority. Because these governments attempt to dominate all of a nation's political, economic, and social life, they are called **totalitarian governments**.

Which of these forms of government is best? Representative democracies, limited by constitutions, are not always the most efficient form. Because many voices must be heard, they can be slow to take action. However, citizens generally benefit from a constitution that protects against harsh or arbitrary governmental action, and from rules that require the government to take account of their welfare and views. A trade-off thus exists between efficiency and inclusiveness.

A Brief History of Democratic Government

The government of the United States is a representative democracy and is bound by a constitution that sets limits on what government can do and how it does it. With the possible exception of ancient Athens and several other ancient Greek city-states, such democracies were unheard of before the modern era. Prior to the seventeenth century, governments seldom took into account the opinions of their ordinary subjects. But in the seventeenth century, in a handful of Western nations, important changes began to take place in the character and conduct of government. How did these changes come about? How did we get to where we are today?

The key force behind the imposition of limits on governmental power in Europe was the emergence of a new social class called the *bourgeoisie*, a French word meaning "free residents of the city" (as opposed to landowners and rural residents who were legally required to provide labor to the landowners). The bourgeoisie later came to be thought of as the "middle class" or those engaged in commerce or in industry. To gain a share in the control of government—to join the monarchs and aristocrats who had dominated European governments for centuries—the bourgeoisie tried to change existing governmental institutions, especially parliaments, into ones in which they could actively participate politically.

Parliaments had existed for hundreds of years, controlling governments from the top and not allowing influence from below. The bourgeoisie embraced them as the way to wield their greater numbers and growing economic advantage against aristocratic rivals. The United States was the first nation founded mainly by members of the bourgeoisie, and so, not surprisingly, the first political institution the Founders built in their struggle against the British monarchy was a parliamentary body, the Continental Congress, which provided the collective foundation for colonial opposition to British power.

The bourgeoisie advanced many of the principles that became the central underpinnings of individual freedom for *all* citizens—freedom of speech, of assembly, and of conscience, as well as freedom from arbitrary search and seizure. It is important to note here that the bourgeoisie, including many of America's founders, generally did not favor democracy as such. They advocated political institutions based on elected representatives, but they favored setting conditions such as property requirements for voting and for holding office so as to limit participation to the middle and upper classes. Yet, once the right of non-aristocrats to have a say in government was established, it was difficult in both Europe and America to limit the expansion of that right to the bourgeoisie. Others also wanted voting rights and representation. Indeed, governments found that expanding participation could be a useful way of encouraging citizens to pay their taxes and serve in the military.

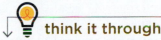

think it through

Many governments believe that citizens who participate in the political process are more willing to accept the result even if it doesn't turn out the way they had hoped. Do you think this is true? Does the chance to participate in political decision making leave you more supportive of the laws that result?

POLITICS: THE BRIDGE BETWEEN GOVERNMENT AND REPRESENTATION

The term *politics* broadly refers to conflicts over the character, membership, and policies of any organizations to which people belong. As the political scientist Harold Lasswell once put it, politics is the struggle over "who gets what, when, how."[3] Although politics exists in any organization, in this book, **politics** refers to conflicts over the leadership, structure, and policies of governments—that is, over who governs and who has power. But politics also involves collaboration and cooperation.

The goal of politics, as we define it, is to have a say in who makes up the government's leadership, how the government is organized, and what its policies will be. Such a say is called power or influence. Most people are eager to have some say in matters that affect them; indeed, over the past two centuries many individuals have risked their lives for voting rights and representation. In recent years, a large number of Americans have become more skeptical about how much "say" they actually have in government, and many do not even bother to vote. This skepticism, however, does not mean that Americans no longer want to have a voice in the governmental process. Rather, many of them doubt that the political system allows them real influence.

In a representative democracy, citizens choose politicians whom they think will promote their interests. This delegation of power gives politicians a level of independence, but elections make them accountable to constituents.

As we will see throughout this book, not only does politics influence government but the character and actions of government also influence a nation's politics. The rules and procedures established by political **institutions** influence the forms that political activity may take. In some nations, the rules of politics limit participation to members of a particular ethnic group, political party, or noble family. In the United States, political participation is open to tens of millions of citizens, though some choose not to take part and others argue that they are improperly deprived of fair voting rights.

Representation

Participation in politics is the key to representation in government. Those who participate have an opportunity to select representatives who will promote their interests when governmental decisions are made. In other words, representative government allows citizens an indirect say over policy through their direct influence on the selection of their representatives. As we will see later, Americans can participate in many forms of politics, including lobbying, working in a campaign, organizing a protest march, or even running for office. Most citizens, however, participate primarily through voting for representatives. The Constitution's framers designed the U.S. Congress to be the nation's chief representative institution. Its members are expected to speak on behalf of the people in their districts, representing the views and interests of numerous constituents when decisions are made in the Capitol.

In ancient Athens, democracy was institutionalized in an assembly, the *ecclesia*, where all citizens might express their views and vote. This sort of assembly was possible within the context of a small city-state. However, one could hardly expect all the citizens of the United States to gather in an amphitheater to engage in political debate. Even today, when technology might permit the construction of an electronic version of the *ecclesia*, could millions of citizens engage in the discussion, deliberation, and compromise needed to produce effective government?

Representation can take many forms. Some citizens prefer that their representatives share their own religious, gender, philosophical, or ethnic identities. This approach, often called **descriptive representation**, hinges on the idea that citizens can be confident in governmental decisions if those decisions are being made by others like themselves.

The framers of the Constitution, in contrast, believed that effective representation was tied to accountability. To the framers, the key to proper representation was the ability of citizens to select and remove—essentially to hire and fire—their representatives. Under the U.S. Constitution, citizens would be able to choose representatives whom they trusted to promote their interests and to depose those who failed to do so. This idea is known as **agency representation**, because representatives serve as the agents of their constituents.

Congress is the United States' chief representative body at the national level, but Americans expect the president and members of the judiciary to

institutions
A set of formal rules and procedures, often administered by a bureaucracy, that shapes politics and governance.

think it through

In a representative democracy, citizens choose leaders who they think will promote their interests. What characteristics do you value in a candidate for office? How do you think those characteristics help ensure your interests will be best represented in government?

descriptive representation
The type of representation in which representatives are trusted to make decisions on their constituents' behalf because they share the religious, gender, philosophical, or ethnic identities of their constituents.

agency representation
The type of representation in which representatives are held accountable to their constituents if they fail to represent them properly. That is, constituents have the power to hire and fire their representatives.

represent their views as well. The president is an elected official and can be held to account by the electorate when running for a second term. The framers deliberately shielded the federal judiciary from the electoral process but, in appointing judges, modern presidents are usually sensitive to the racial, ethnic, and gender composition of the federal courts, since citizens expect the judiciary to be broadly representative of the nation.

CONCLUSION

Why do representation and effective governance matter? Governance means making authoritative decisions; representation means giving citizens a voice in those decisions through their elected representatives. Could anything be simpler? In fact, combining governance with representation produces a number of complications that, taken together, can lead to the impression that the government is "broken." Let's consider three of these problems. Developing a better understanding of these types of issues is precisely what political scientists try to do (see the Analyzing the Evidence section, "Thinking Like a Political Scientist").

Delegating Authority in a Representative Democracy

For over two centuries, voting rights and other forms of political participation in the United States have expanded to the point where citizens, from the time they are roughly the age of the average college freshman to the time they take that final breath, can engage in political activity at various levels of government. Yet it is often convenient for citizens to delegate such activities to others. When we don't pay attention to politics or even register to vote, we leave political decisions entirely to representatives—chiefly legislators and executives—rather than exercising political authority directly. The United States is a representative democracy for very practical reasons. The large number of citizens makes direct democracy almost impossible at the national level; moreover, Americans have lives to live and private concerns to attend to. By delegating political decisions to representatives, they do not have to be specialists and can focus on other matters.

We often think of our political representatives as our agents, whom we "hire" to act on our behalf. In this relationship, citizens are the principals—those with the authority—who delegate some of that authority to politicians, their agents. This **principal-agent relationship**, however, means that citizens don't always get what they want, because, inadvertently or not, they allow agents to pursue their own self-interests or to be influenced unduly by those who care more about political decisions or have more at stake in those decisions. In the

principal-agent relationship
The relationship between a principal (such as a citizen) and an agent (such as an elected official) in which the agent is expected to act on the principal's behalf.

Thinking Like a Political Scientist

American politics often seems disorderly and incomprehensible. How do our institutions work? Do they work as they should? Finding order in political chaos is precisely what political scientists do. We want to identify patterns in all the noise and maneuvering of everyday political life. The discipline of political science, and especially the study of American politics, seeks the answers to two fundamental questions: What do we observe? And why?

What do we observe? Political science aims to identify facts and patterns that are true in the world around us. What strategies do candidates use to capture votes? What decisions do members of Congress make about how to vote on bills? What groups put pressure on the institutions of government? How do the media report politics? What tools are available to the president to achieve policy goals? How do the courts make their decisions? These and many other questions have prompted political scientists to determine what is true about the political world, and we will take each of them up in detail in later chapters.

One important way that political scientists identify facts and patterns is by studying data. At the end of this chapter, we provide a brief guide to "Making Sense of Charts and Graphs" with tips for interpreting the political data that you encounter in this course and beyond.

Why? The second question—why?—is fundamental to any science. We not only would like to know that something is *true* about the world. We also want to know *why* it is true, a question that requires us to create in our minds a theory of how the world works. In this way we not only describe politics; we *analyze* it. One of the most important goals of this book is to provide concepts and tools to help readers critically analyze what they observe in politics and government. In this chapter we cover some fundamental concepts that we hope will clarify why American government works the way it does.

Throughout the rest of this book, we will frequently revisit concepts from this chapter – particularly the ideas related to representation and governance – to better understand some of the fundamental questions about the various institutions and features of American government. Each of the following chapters also includes a two-page "Analyzing the Evidence" section that explains how political science researchers used that data to try to analyze a specific question.

How should government work? We believe that answers to the *what?* and *why?* questions that political scientists study help us formulate better answers to questions about how government and politics *should* work. What rights should citizens have? How should members of Congress vote on the issues before them? How should presidents lead?

In this book, our goal is to help readers identify key facts and patterns of American politics (*what do we observe?*), then to use the core concepts and tools to make sense of those facts and patterns (*why?*), so that readers can develop their own answers to questions about how government should work.

past 25 years, more than two dozen members of Congress have been indicted for official corruption—for using their offices for personal gain rather than for service to constituents.

While outright corruption is one risk, the principal-agent relationship can also be problematic if a representative (legally) helps enact a policy that the majority of constituents oppose, or fails to support a policy that constituents want. According to one recent study, members of Congress vote against the opinions of a majority of their constituents nearly 35 percent of the time.[4] (See the Analyzing the Evidence section in Chapter 5 for an example of this.)

The Tension between Representation and Governance

A second problem in the relationship between representation and governance is that they sometimes contradict one another, each getting in the way of the other. Representation can interfere with effective governance in two ways. First, as mentioned earlier, in a representative democracy many different voices must be heard before decisions are made—a requirement that sometimes produces long delays or even blocks action altogether. Throughout the Obama administration and well into the Trump years, Congress was "gridlocked" and unable to enact legislation on major domestic programs. This inability to legislate stemmed, in part, from the fact that members representing Democratic and Republican districts were pulled in entirely different directions by their constituents. Representation made governance difficult.

Second, groups that are exceptionally influential and well represented may be sheltered from effective governance. Through their representatives in government, they may be able, say, to escape some of the burden of taxation and regulation. The

Groups that are especially well represented may influence government to pass policies that benefit them, at the expense of other groups and the nation as a whole. In 2020, protesters called for an end to interest group influence in Washington, D.C. As a result, several candidates agreed to not accept donations from certain financial and technology companies, and instead focus on grassroots fundraising efforts.

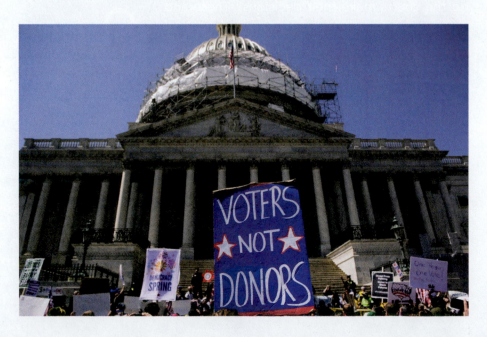

table 1.1

CONDORCET'S PARADOX

	FIRST PREFERENCE	SECOND PREFERENCE	THIRD PREFERENCE
Voter 1	Defense	Health care	Environment
Voter 2	Health care	Environment	Defense
Voter 3	Environment	Defense	Health care

analyzing the evidence

Which is the right policy to pursue when no option has the support of a majority? How might a representative government best address the problem?

pharmaceutical and oil industries, for example, benefit from many tax loopholes (policies that make it possible to avoid paying a tax), so the burden of taxation is passed on to others who are not so well represented. Tactics like these that block action or distort outcomes can put better representation and more effective governance at odds.

The Enigma of Majority Rule

A third problem in the relationship between governance and representation involves the complexity of majority rule. One of the main ideas of representative government is that the will of the majority, as expressed through its representatives, must be respected. But majority rule can trample on minority rights as defined by the Constitution—a problem that will be discussed in Chapters 2 and 4.

There is, in fact, an even more basic problem: sometimes there is no course of action consistent with majority rule. Even if all the agents in a representative body work diligently on behalf of their principals, it is not always easy or even possible to add them up into a collective choice that reflects the will of the majority. This idea was first put forward in 1785 by the Marquis de Condorcet, a French philosopher who presented an example showing that three individuals with equally strong preferences about policies could not achieve a collective choice that would satisfy all of them. This idea, which came to be known as Condorcet's Paradox, is illustrated in Table 1.1.

Suppose that a government is making a choice among three possible spending programs—defense, health care, and protecting the environment—and that there are three voters whose preferences are represented in Table 1.1. If the environment is chosen to receive the funds, it can be argued that health care should win instead, since a majority (voters 1 and 2) prefers health care spending to spending on the environment and only one voter (3) prefers the environment to health care. However, by the same argument and by the same margin, defense spending is preferred to health care spending, and the environment is preferred to defense.

The contradictions at the heart of representative government help to explain why such a government can be inefficient and sometimes seem unfair.

Representatives may fail to work on behalf of their constituents' interests (problem 1). On the other hand, representatives can be too effective and successfully shield their constituents from the costs of public goods—costs that must be borne by others (problem 2). Finally, there may be no course of action that has the support of a majority (problem 3). At times, representative government seems a contradiction in terms, but what alternative would be preferable?

Our goal in this book is to understand the strengths and weaknesses of America's representative government. Can the contradictions be resolved? When can government be part of the solution rather than part of the problem? As we will see in Chapter 2, the framers of the Constitution were well aware of the contradictions at the heart of representative government but thought it was too important to be abandoned because of these imperfections. They hoped that the right institutional design would solve some of these problems.

But before we turn to the Founding and the Constitution, let's put into practice the new critical thinking skills introduced in the "Thinking Like a Political Scientist" on page 11 that will help you think critically about these issues as we move forward. First, look carefully at the questions in the margins. Throughout the book, these "Think It Through" questions will provide opportunities for you to think critically about how these issues and concepts connect to your own life. Second, this chapter's appendix (Analyzing the Evidence on pp. 16–21) provides some insights on how to understand charts and graphs that present empirical data about politics. The political data you encounter in this book—and outside of it—are also an important part of understanding and evaluating politics and government. Political literacy matters. By learning to think critically about concepts, and make sense of data, you will better understand how these issues of governance and representation impact your own life and the important role you play in the American government.

Key Terms

governance 3

government 3

representation 4

public good 6

free riding 6

autocracy 6

oligarchy 6

democracy 6

constitutional government 6

authoritarian government 6

totalitarian government 6

politics 8

institutions 9

descriptive representation 9

agency representation 9

principal-agent relationship 10

Check Your Understanding

1. What are the main purposes of government? What happens when governments do not effectively fulfill these functions?

2. How does representation in a democratic govern-ment, such as the United States, compare to that in an autocracy, oligarchy, and authoritarian government?

3. How do political institutions influence politics?

4. Why was agency representation important to the framers of the Constitution?

5. What are some of the complications that arise from combining governance with representation?

 INQUIZITIVE

Earn a better grade on your test. InQuizitive personalizes your learning path to help you master the concepts from this chapter. In a recent efficacy study of American government students, InQuizitive increased test scores by an average of 17 points (see back cover).

analyzing the evidence

Making Sense of Charts and Graphs

Contributed by **Jennifer Bachner**, *Johns Hopkins University*

Throughout this book, you will encounter graphs and charts that show some of the quantitative data that political scientists use to study government and politics. This section provides three general steps to help you interpret and evaluate common ways data are presented—both in this text and beyond.

1 Identify the Purpose of the Graph or Chart

When you come across a graph or chart, your first step should be to identify its purpose. The title will usually indicate whether the purpose of the graph or chart is to describe one or more variables or to show a relationship between variables. Note that a variable is a set of possible values. The variable "years of education completed" can take on values such as "8," "12," or "16."

Descriptive Graphs and Charts. The title of the graph in Figure A, "Party Identification in the United States, 2020," tells us that the graph focuses on one variable, party identification, rather than showing a relationship

between two or more variables. It is therefore a descriptive graph.

If a graph is descriptive, you should identify the variable being described and think about the main point the author is trying to make about that variable. In Figure A, we see that party identification can take on one of three values ("Republican," "Democrat," or "Independent") and that the author has plotted the percentage of survey respondents for each of these three values using vertical bars. The height of each bar indicates the percentage of people in each category, and comparing the bars to each other tells us that most Americans identified as Independents in 2020. This is one main takeaway from the graph.

Figure A: Party Identification in the United States, 2020

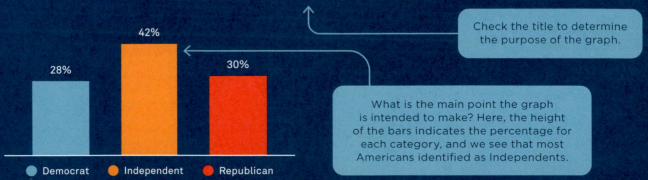

Check the title to determine the purpose of the graph.

What is the main point the graph is intended to make? Here, the height of the bars indicates the percentage for each category, and we see that most Americans identified as Independents.

Graphs and Charts That Show a Relationship. Let's turn to Table A, "Policy Priorities by Age Group." Notice that there are two variables—policy priorities and age—mentioned in the title, which indicates that the chart will compare them. We know, therefore, that the chart will illustrate the relationship between these two variables rather than simply describe them.

The first column in Table A displays the values for age group, which in this case are ranges. The other columns provide data about policy priorities; they display the percentage of survey respondents in each age group who said that Social Security (in the second column) and the environment (in the third column) should be among the government's top priorities. We can compare the columns to determine if there is a relationship between age and policy priorities. We see that a greater percentage of respondents in the higher age ranges said that Social Security should be a top priority; in the oldest age group, 74 percent of respondents would have the government prioritize Social Security compared to 46 percent in the youngest age group. In the lower age groups, more respondents said the environment should be a top priority. This is strong quantitative evidence of a relationship between age and policy priorities, which is the main point.

Table A: Policy Priorities by Age Group
Percent who say that . . . should be a top priority for the government

AGE GROUP	$ SOCIAL SECURITY	∅ THE ENVIRONMENT
18–29	46%	77%
30–49	61%	67%
50–64	70%	57%
65+	74%	55%

Note: Respondents were allowed to pick more than one option.

Does the title mention more than one variable? If so, that usually means the chart or graph is intended to show a relationship between the variables.

By comparing the values for each variable, we can see if there is a relationship between them. Here, we see that the lower age groups were more likely to choose the environment, while the higher age groups were more likely to choose Social Security.

Evaluate the Argument

After you've identified the main point of a graph or chart, you should consider: Does the graph or chart make a compelling argument, or are there concerns with how the evidence is presented? Here are some of the questions you should ask when you see different types of graphs.

Is the Range of the y-Axis Appropriate? For a bar graph or line graph, identify the range of the y-axis and consider whether this range is appropriate for the data being presented. If the range of the y-axis is too large, readers may not be able to perceive important fluctuations in the data. If the range is too small, insignificant differences may appear to be huge.

Median Household Income over Time

Figure B

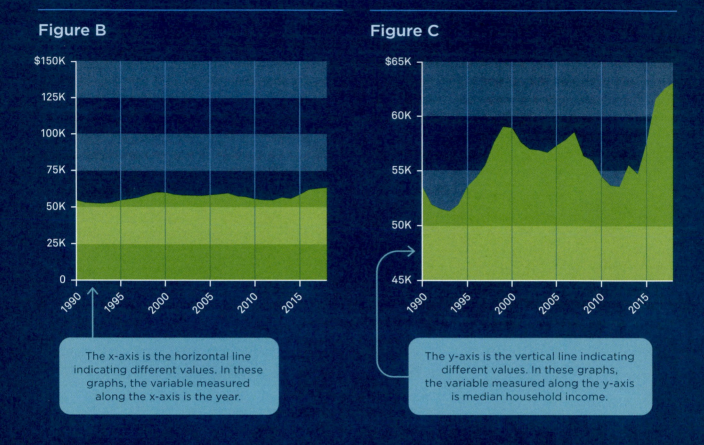

The x-axis is the horizontal line indicating different values. In these graphs, the variable measured along the x-axis is the year.

Figure C

The y-axis is the vertical line indicating different values. In these graphs, the variable measured along the y-axis is median household income.

Figures B and C present exactly the same data but on graphs with very different y-axes. Both graphs plot median U.S. household income from 1990 to 2018. In the first graph, the range of the y-axis is so large that it looks like household income has barely changed over the past 28 years. In the second graph, the range is more appropriate. The second graph highlights meaningful changes in a household's purchasing power over this time period.

Is the Graph a Good Match for the Data?
Different types of graphs are useful for different types of data. A single variable measured over a long period of time is often best visualized using a line graph, whereas data from a survey question where respondents can choose only one response option might best be displayed with a bar graph. Using the wrong type of graph for a data set can result in a misleading representation of the underlying data.

For example, in the months leading up to the 2018 midterm election, pollsters were interested in measuring the importance of various policy issues to voters. Some surveys asked respondents how important each of a series of policy issues would be to their vote decision (for example, "Now for each of those items, please tell me how important each will be in your vote for Congress this year.") Other surveys listed a set of policy issues and asked respondents to select which one of them would be the single *most* important factor in their vote decision. Both approaches captured the importance of different policy issues to vote choice, but they did so in different ways.

Top Policy Priorities, October 2018

Figure D:
A Very Important Policy Issue

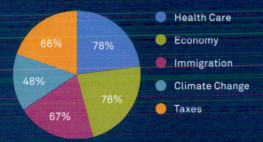

Legend:
- Health Care
- Economy
- Immigration
- Climate Change
- Taxes

78% 66% 48% 67% 76%

Figure E:
The Most Important Policy Issue

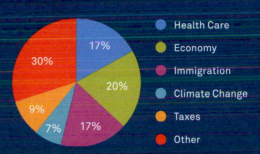

Legend:
- Health Care
- Economy
- Immigration
- Climate Change
- Taxes
- Other

17% 30% 20% 9% 7% 17%

Figures D and E are pie charts that illustrate the data from the two surveys. The difference in how the graphs portray the importance of, say, health care to voters is striking. The first graph, based on the survey in which respondents selected all issues that were very important to them, implies that health care is the most important factor for voters, whereas the second graph indicates that, if respondents can only select one policy issue from the given options, the economy is the single most important issue. Note, however, that 30 percent of respondents in the second graph selected "other" policy issues (such as foreign policy, abortion, and opioid addiction).

This example demonstrates why a pie chart is a poor graph choice for a variable in which the response categories do not add up to 100 percent. In choosing what type of graph to use, researchers and authors have to make thoughtful decisions about how to present data so the takeaway is clear and accurate.

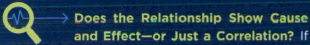 **Does the Relationship Show Cause and Effect—or Just a Correlation?** If a graph or chart conveys a relationship between two or more variables, it is important to determine whether the data are being used to make a causal argument or if they simply show a correlation. In a causal relationship, changes in one variable lead to changes in another. For example, it is well established that, on average, more education leads to higher earnings, more smoking leads to higher rates of lung cancer, and easier voter registration processes lead to higher voter turnout.

Other times, two variables might move together, but these movements are driven by a third variable. In these cases, the two variables are correlated, but changes in one variable do not cause changes in the other. A classic example is the relationship between ice cream consumption and the number of drowning deaths. As one of these variables increases, the other one does too, but not because one variable is causing a change in the other one—both variables are driven by a third variable. In this case, that third variable is temperature (or season). Both ice cream consumption and drowning deaths are driven by increases in the temperature because more people eat cold treats and go swimming on hot days.

There are many examples of data that are closely correlated but for which there is no causal relationship. Figure F displays a line graph of two variables: per capita consumption of mozzarella cheese and the number of civil engineering doctorates awarded in the United States. The two variables are strongly correlated (96 percent), but it would be wrong to conclude that they are causally related. A causal relationship requires theoretical reasoning—a chain of argument linking cause to effect. Distinguishing causal relationships from mere correlations is essential for policy makers. A government intervention to fix a problem will work only if that intervention is causally related to the desired outcome.

Figure F: Per Capita Consumption of Mozzarella Cheese Correlates with Civil Engineering Doctorates Awarded

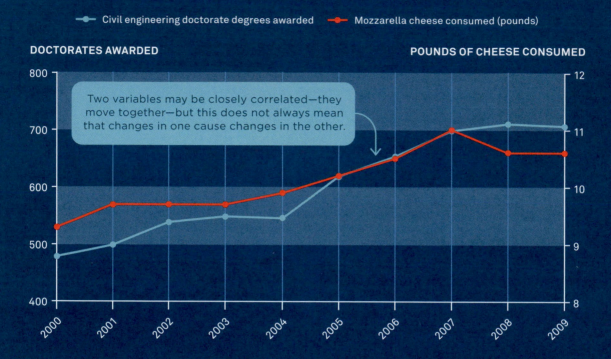

—•— Civil engineering doctorate degrees awarded   —•— Mozzarella cheese consumed (pounds)

Two variables may be closely correlated—they move together—but this does not always mean that changes in one cause changes in the other.

3 Consider the Source

In addition to making sure you understand what a data graphic says, it's important to consider where the data came from and how they were collected.

🔍→ What is the source of the data? Good graphs should have a note citing the source. In the United States, reliable sources include government agencies and mainstream news organizations, which generally gather data accurately and present it objectively. Data from individuals or organizations that have specific agendas, such as interest groups, should be more carefully scrutinized.

🔍→ Is it clear what is being measured? For example, in a poll showing "Support for Candidate A," do the results refer to the percentage of all Americans? The percentage of likely voters? The percentage of Democrats or Republicans? A good data figure should make this clear in the title, in the labels for the variables, and/or in a note.

🔍→ Do the variables capture the concepts we care about? There are many ways, for example, to measure whether a high school is successful (such as math scores, reading scores, graduation rate, or parent engagement). The decision about which variables to use depends on the specific question the researcher seeks to answer.

🔍→ Are survey questions worded appropriately? If the graph presents survey data, do the questions and the answer options seem likely to distort the results? Small changes in the wording of a survey question can drastically alter the results.

→ **Are the data based on a carefully selected sample?** Some data sets include all individuals in a population; for example, the results of an election include the choices of all voters. Other data sets use a sample: a small group selected by researchers to represent an entire population. Most high-quality data sources will include information about how the data were collected, including the margin of error based on the sample size.

Figure G: Voter Registration Rates by Age, 2018

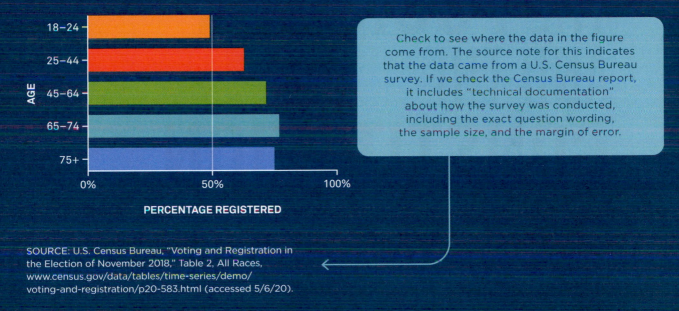

Check to see where the data in the figure come from. The source note for this indicates that the data came from a U.S. Census Bureau survey. If we check the Census Bureau report, it includes "technical documentation" about how the survey was conducted, including the exact question wording, the sample size, and the margin of error.

SOURCE: U.S. Census Bureau, "Voting and Registration in the Election of November 2018," Table 2, All Races, www.census.gov/data/tables/time-series/demo/voting-and-registration/p20-583.html (accessed 5/6/20).

→ **What are several credible sources you can consult for political information?**

SOURCES FOR OTHER FIGURES IN THIS SECTION:

Figure A	Gallup, www.gallup.com/poll/15370/party-affiliation.aspx (accessed 3/3/20).
Table A	Pew Research Center, "As Economic Concerns Recede, Environmental Protection Rises on the Public's Policy Agenda," February 13, 2020, www.people-press.org/2020/02/13/as-economic-concerns-recede-environmental-protection-rises-on-the-publics-policy-agenda (accessed 3/5/20).
Figures B, C	U.S. Census Bureau (via Federal Reserve Bank of St. Louis), https://fred.stlouisfed.org/series/MEHOINUSA672N (accessed 3/3/20).
Figures D, E	PollingReport.com, "Problems and Priorities," www.pollingreport.com/prioriti.htm (accessed 3/3/20).
Figure F	Spurious Correlations, http://tylervigen.com/view_correlation?id=3890 (accessed 3/7/20).

CHAPTER TWO

THE FOUNDING AND THE CONSTITUTION

George Washington, the individual honored as "the father of his country" and chosen to preside over the 1787 convention that adopted the United States Constitution, thought the document produced that hot summer in Philadelphia would probably last no more than 20 years, at which time leaders would have to convene again to come up with something new. That Washington's prediction proved wrong is a testament to the enduring strength of the Constitution. Nonetheless, the Constitution was not carved in stone. It was a product of political bargaining and compromise, formed very much in the same way that political decisions are made today.

The most important issues considered, debated, and resolved through compromises at the Constitutional Convention were questions related to the interplay between governance and representation. To begin with, the delegates hoped to build an effective government—one able to protect citizens' liberties, maintain order, promote prosperity, and defend the nation's interests in the world. The framers were afraid, however, that a government sufficiently powerful to achieve these goals might also become sufficiently powerful to endanger its citizens' liberties.

To guard against this possibility, the framers designed America's government to include the *separation of powers*, which divides the national government's power among different institutions, and *federalism*, which divides power between the national government and state governments. The framers understood that this design could reduce governmental efficiency and effectiveness—produce

At the Constitutional Convention of 1787, the delegates debated and eventually agreed on a set of rules and procedures for American government. The political institutions that they designed shape representation and governance in the United States.

"gridlock," as we might say today—but they were willing to tolerate a bit of gridlock to safeguard liberty.

Most, if not all, of the delegates to the Constitutional Convention also agreed that the interests of ordinary citizens should be represented in the new government. Delegates were concerned, however, that most ordinary Americans had little knowledge of government and politics, could easily be led astray by unscrupulous politicians, and should play only a limited role in the nation's governance.

The institutional design chosen by the framers to reconcile these seemingly contradictory impulses was a system of indirect elections in which citizens would participate in the selection of those who would represent them but would not make the final choice. Senators were to be appointed by the state legislatures, judges appointed by the president with the approval of the Senate, and the president elected by an Electoral College chosen by the state legislatures. All these processes would begin with representative institutions elected popularly by ordinary citizens—the state legislatures—but the final outcomes would be determined and "refined" by members of the political elite, who, the framers hoped, would be somewhat more knowledgeable and wiser in their decisions. In the national institutions of government, only members of the House of Representatives were to be popularly elected, and some framers thought even this concession to direct democracy was a mistake.

> ▪ **How did the framers try to balance effective government with popular representation?**

Today, senators are also popularly elected, as are the members of the Electoral College. Nevertheless, for better or worse, the constitutional system of representation continues to affect governance in the United States. For example, two of America's three most recent presidents—Donald Trump in 2016 and George W. Bush in 2000—joined Rutherford Hayes in 1876 and Benjamin Harrison in 1888 as presidents who were elected by winning majorities in the Electoral College despite losing the popular vote. We will discuss this topic in more detail in Chapter 10.

In this chapter we explore the institutions and procedures established in the Constitution, and how the framers settled on these features of government.

Learning Objectives

- Describe the major political-historical developments that led to the Constitutional Convention of 1787.

- Explain why the Articles of Confederation were not strong enough to provide effective governance.

- Outline the major provisions of the United States Constitution.

- Analyze how the framers attempted to balance representation with effective governance.

- Describe how the amendment process allows the Constitution to evolve over time.

THE FIRST FOUNDING: INTERESTS AND CONFLICTS

Competing ideals often reflect competing interests, and so it was in Revolutionary America. The American Revolution and the American Constitution were outgrowths of a struggle among economic and political forces within the colonies. Five economic sectors of society were important in colonial politics. The first three—(1) New England merchants; (2) southern planters; and (3) the "royalists" (holders of royal lands, offices, and patents, licenses to engage in a profession or business activity)—constituted the colonial elite. The last two groups—(4) shopkeepers, those engaged in skilled crafts such as printers and weavers, and manual laborers; and (5) small farmers—occupied the lower rungs of colonial society.

Throughout the eighteenth century, these groups differed over issues of taxation, trade, and commerce. For the most part, the colonial elite (merchants, planters, and royalists) maintained a political alliance that held in check the more politically radical forces representing shopkeepers, laborers, and small farmers. After 1750, however, British tax and trade policies split the elite, permitting radical forces to expand their political influence and setting off a chain of events that culminated in the American Revolution.[1]

Political Strife and the Radicalizing of the Colonists

The political strife within the colonies was the background for the events of 1773–74. With the Tea Act of 1773, the British government granted the politically powerful East India Company a monopoly on the export of tea from Britain, eliminating a profitable trade for colonial merchants. Together with their southern-planter allies, the merchants called for support from their radical adversaries: shopkeepers, artisans, laborers, and small farmers, all of whom had their own grievances against the established colonial government. The most dramatic result was the Boston Tea Party of 1773, led by Samuel Adams, which played a decisive role in American history.

Although the merchants hoped to force the British government to repeal the Tea Act, they certainly did not seek independence from Britain. By dumping the East India Company's tea into Boston Harbor, however, Adams and other radicals hoped to provoke the British to take actions that would alienate their colonial supporters and pave the way for a rebellion. Their plan succeeded, as a series of acts by the British Parliament closed the port of Boston to commerce, changed the colonial government of Massachusetts, provided for taking colonists accused of crimes to Britain for trial, and added new restrictions on colonists' westward movement (movement that often forced the British military to fight costly skirmishes with Native American tribes)—further alienating the southern planters, who depended on access to new western lands. These acts of retaliation helped radicalize the colonists.

Thus, the Boston Tea Party sparked a cycle of provocation and retaliation that in 1774 resulted in the convening of the First Continental Congress, with delegates attending from all parts of the country. The Congress called for a total boycott of British goods and, under the radicals' prodding, began to consider independence from British rule. The result was the Declaration of Independence.

The Declaration of Independence

In 1776, the Second Continental Congress appointed a committee consisting of Thomas Jefferson of Virginia, Benjamin Franklin of Pennsylvania, Roger Sherman of Connecticut, John Adams of Massachusetts, and Robert Livingston of New York to draft a statement of American independence from British rule. The Declaration of Independence was written by Jefferson, drawing on ideas from the British philosopher John Locke, whose work was widely read in the colonies.

Adopted by the Second Continental Congress, the Declaration was an extraordinary document in both philosophical and political terms. Philosophically, it was remarkable for its assertion (derived from Locke) that governments

think it through

What competing interests do you see active in politics today? Are there events—similar to the Boston Tea Party—that have united disparate groups to work toward a shared goal?

"No taxation without representation" became a rallying cry for American colonists who objected to British tax policies. The 1773 Tea Act, which involved taxes on tea and limits on trade, set off a chain of events—including the Boston Tea Party—that led to the Revolution.

could not deprive citizens of certain "unalienable rights"—including "life, liberty, and the pursuit of happiness." In the world of 1776, in which some kings still claimed they had a God-given right to rule, this was a dramatic statement. Politically, the Declaration was remarkable because it focused on grievances, goals, and principles that might unify the various colonial groups. The Declaration was an attempt to put into words a history and set of principles that might help to forge national unity.[2]

The Revolutionary War

In 1775, even before formally declaring their independence, the colonies had begun to fight the British—most notably at Lexington and Concord, Massachusetts, where colonial militias fought against trained British soldiers. Nevertheless, the task of defeating Britain, then the world's premier military power, seemed impossible. To maintain their hold on the colonies, the British sent a huge force composed of their regular troops and German mercenaries (soldiers hired for foreign service), along with artillery and equipment. To face this force, the colonists relied on inexperienced and lightly armed militias. To make matters worse, the colonists were hardly united in their opposition to British rule. Many saw themselves as loyal British subjects and refused to take up arms against the king. Thousands, indeed, took up arms *for* the king and joined pro-British militias.

The war was brutal and bloody, with tens of thousands of casualties among the colonists, British and German troops, and Native Americans who fought on both sides. Eventually, the revolutionary forces prevailed, mainly because the cost to Britain of a war thousands of miles from home became too great. As colonial militias prevented British forces from acquiring enough food and supplies locally, these had to be brought from Europe at enormous expense. With the eventual help of Britain's enemy, France, the colonists fought until the British had had enough of a seemingly endless war. The conflict ended in 1783 with the signing of the Treaty of Paris, which officially granted the 13 American colonies their independence.

The Articles of Confederation

Having declared independence, the colonies needed to establish a government. In November 1777, the Continental Congress adopted the **Articles of Confederation and Perpetual Union**—the first written constitution of the United States. Although not ratified by all the states until 1781, it served as the country's constitution for more than 11 years, until March 1789. When the Articles were drafted, each of the 13 original colonies was, in effect, an independent nation. While each saw the advantages of cooperating with the others, none of the 13 new governments—now calling themselves *states* to underscore their new nationhood—gave much thought to the idea of surrendering their independence. Accordingly, the Articles established a central government of defined and strictly limited power, with most actual governmental authority left in the hands of the individual states.

The Articles created no executive branch. The central government, such as it was, consisted entirely of the Congress of the Confederacy, which had little power. Execution and interpretation of its laws were left to the individual states, and its members were not much more than ambassadors from the states: they were chosen by state legislatures, paid out of state treasuries, and subject to immediate replacement by state officials. Each state, regardless of size, had only a single vote. Furthermore, amendments to the Articles required the unanimous agreement of the 13 states.

Congress was given the power to declare war and make peace, to make treaties and alliances, to issue currency and borrow money, and to regulate trade with Native Americans. It could also appoint the senior officers of the United States Army. But it could not levy taxes or regulate commerce among the states. Moreover,

Articles of Confederation and Perpetual Union
The United States' first written constitution. Adopted by the Continental Congress in 1777, the Articles were the formal basis for America's national government until 1789, when they were superseded by the Constitution.

the army officers it appointed had no army to serve in because the nation's armed forces were composed of the state militias. An especially dysfunctional aspect of the Articles of Confederation was that the central government could not prevent one state from undermining other states in the competition for foreign commerce.

In brief, the relationship between Congress and the states under the Articles of Confederation was much like the contemporary relationship between the United Nations and its member states—one in which the states retain virtually all governmental powers. It was called a confederation because, as provided under Article II, "each state retains its sovereignty, freedom, and independence, and every power, jurisdiction, and right, which is not by this confederation expressly delegated to the United States, in Congress assembled." Not only was there no executive; there was also no judicial authority, as well as no means of enforcing Congress's will. If there was to be any enforcement, the states would have to do it.[3]

THE SECOND FOUNDING: FROM COMPROMISE TO CONSTITUTION

The Declaration of Independence and the Articles of Confederation were not sufficient to hold the former colonies together as an independent and effective nation-state. From almost the moment of armistice with the British in 1783, moves were afoot to reform the Articles and create a stronger national government.

International Standing, Economic Difficulties, and Domestic Turmoil

Many Americans were concerned about the country's international position. Competition for foreign commerce allowed the European powers to play the states against one another—a dynamic that created problems on both sides of the Atlantic. At one point, John Adams, a leader in the independence struggle, was sent to negotiate a new treaty with the British to cover disputes left over from the war. The British government responded that, since the United States under the Articles of Confederation was unable to enforce existing treaties, it would negotiate with each of the 13 states separately.

At the same time, well-to-do Americans—in particular the New England merchants and southern planters—were troubled by the influence of "populist" forces in the Continental Congress and several state governments. The colonists' victory in the Revolutionary War had not only meant the end of British rule but also significantly changed the balance of political power within the new states. As a result, one key segment of the colonial elite—the holders of royal land, offices, and patents—was stripped of its economic and political privileges.

think it through

What populist issues influence politics today? Do you see any commonalities between these issues and those important in the 1700s?

In fact, many of these individuals, along with tens of thousands of other colonists who considered themselves loyal British subjects, left for Canada after the British surrender.

As the elite was weakened, the radicals gained control in such states as Pennsylvania and Rhode Island, where they pursued policies that threatened established economic and political interests. The central government under the Articles of Confederation was powerless to intervene. Commerce within the states stagnated, and several states borrowed money just to finance the costs they incurred during the Revolutionary War, such as the expense of raising militia forces.

The new nation's weak international position and domestic problems led many Americans to consider whether a new version of the Articles might be necessary. In the fall of 1786, delegates from five states met in Annapolis, Maryland, and called on Congress to send commissioners to Philadelphia at a later time to make adjustments to the Articles. Their resolution gained support as the result of an event the following winter in Massachusetts: Shays's Rebellion, in which Daniel Shays led a mob of farmers protesting foreclosures on their land in a revolt against the state government that climaxed in an attempt to seize a federal armory in Springfield. The state militia dispersed the rebels within a few days, but the incident scared Congress into action. The states were asked to send delegates to Philadelphia to discuss constitutional revision, and eventually every state but Rhode Island did so.

The Constitutional Convention

In May 1787, 29 of a total of 73 delegates selected by the state governments convened in Philadelphia. Recognizing that political strife, international embarrassment, national weakness, and local rebellion were symptoms of fundamental flaws in the Articles of Confederation, the delegates soon abandoned plans for revision and undertook a second founding instead—an ultimately successful attempt to create an accepted and effective national system.

The Great Compromise.   The supporters of a new government fired their opening shot on May 29, 1787, when Edmund Randolph of Virginia offered a resolution that proposed improvements and additions to the Articles of Confederation. Not a simple motion, it provided for virtually every aspect of a new government, and it was in fact the framework for what ultimately became the Constitution.[4]

The part of Randolph's motion that became the most controversial was known as the Virginia Plan, drafted by James Madison. This plan provided for a system of representation in the national legislature based on the population of each state or the proportion of each state's contribution to national tax revenues, or both. Because the states varied enormously in size and wealth, the Virginia Plan appeared heavily biased in favor of the large states, which would have greater representation.

REPRESENTATION IN CONGRESS: STATES' RANKS

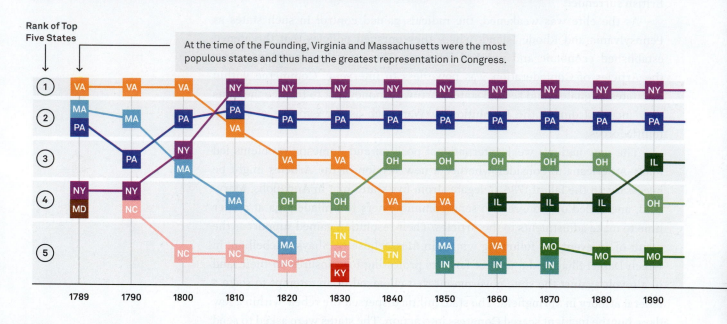

Rank of Top Five States

At the time of the Founding, Virginia and Massachusetts were the most populous states and thus had the greatest representation in Congress.

TIMEPLOT SOURCE: U.S. Census Bureau, www.census.gov/dataviz/visualizations/023 (accessed 2/14/20). The Census is mandated by the Constitution every 10 years, so this apportionment may change with the 2020 results.

Great Compromise
An agreement reached at the Constitutional Convention of 1787 that gave each state an equal number of senators regardless of the size of its population, but linked representation in the House of Representatives to population size. Also called the *Connecticut Compromise.*

While the convention was debating the Virginia Plan, additional delegates arriving in Philadelphia were beginning to mount opposition to it. In particular, delegates from the states with smaller populations, including Delaware, New Jersey, and Connecticut, claimed that the more populous states, such as Virginia, Pennsylvania, North Carolina, and Massachusetts, would dominate the new government if representation were determined by population. The smaller states argued that each state should be equally represented, regardless of its population. Their proposal, called the New Jersey Plan (it was introduced by William Paterson of New Jersey), focused on revising the Articles rather than replacing them. The smaller states' opposition to the Virginia Plan was enough to make the delegates create a committee to rework the competing proposals into a common document.

The outcome was the **Great Compromise**, also known as the Connecticut Compromise. Under its terms, in the first branch of Congress—the House of Representatives—the states would be represented in proportion to the number of their inhabitants, as delegates from the large states wanted. But in the second branch—the Senate—each state would have an equal vote regardless of its population; this arrangement addressed the small states' concerns. In the end, both sides preferred compromise to breakup of the Union, and the plan was accepted. The Timeplot shows the five states with the most representation in Congress from 1789 to today.

timeplot

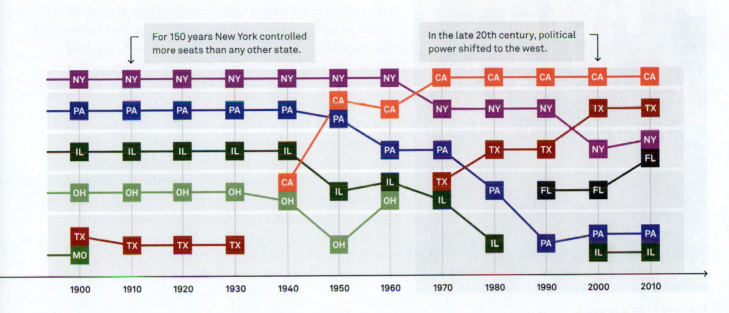

For 150 years New York controlled more seats than any other state.

In the late 20th century, political power shifted to the west.

| 1900 | 1910 | 1920 | 1930 | 1940 | 1950 | 1960 | 1970 | 1980 | 1990 | 2000 | 2010 |

The Question of Slavery: The Three-Fifths Compromise.

Many of the conflicts facing the Constitutional Convention reflected the fundamental differences between the states that allowed slavery (mainly in the South) and the states that prohibited slavery (mainly in the North). Divisions over slavery, in particular, pitted the southern planters and New England merchants against one another. This was the first warning of a conflict that would almost destroy the Republic in later years.

Over 90 percent of all enslaved people lived in five states—Georgia, Maryland, North Carolina, South Carolina, and Virginia—where they accounted for 30 percent of the population. In some places, enslaved people outnumbered free people by as much as 10 to 1. Were they to be counted in determining how many congressional seats a state should have? Whatever individual delegates from the northern states thought of the institution of slavery, most of them opposed including enslaved people in this calculation. But southern delegates made it clear that if the northerners refused to give in, they would never agree to the new government. This conflict was so divisive that many came to question the possibility of creating and maintaining a union of the two regions.

Northerners and southerners eventually reached agreement through the **Three-Fifths Compromise.** The seats in the House of Representatives would be distributed among the states on the basis of a "population" in which only three-fifths of enslaved people would be counted. This arrangement was supported by

Three-Fifths Compromise
An agreement reached at the Constitutional Convention of 1787, stating that for the purpose of distributing congressional seats on the basis of state populations, only three-fifths of enslaved people would be counted.

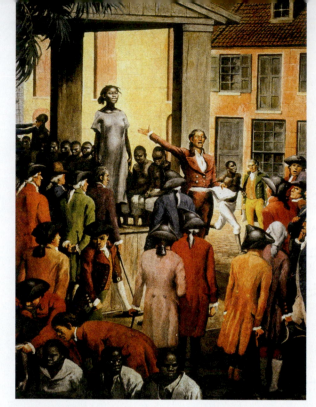

The issue of how to count enslaved people in determining state populations and apportioning congressional seats nearly prevented the passage of the new constitution. Here, enslaved people are auctioned in Charleston, South Carolina, around the time of the Founding.

the slave states, which at the time included some of both the most populous and the least populous states. The Three-Fifths Compromise had a profound effect on American politics in the period before the Civil War. It gave the South an advantage in the Electoral College that led to the election of such presidents as Thomas Jefferson and Andrew Jackson, and additional strength in Congress that prolonged the existence of slavery for another six decades.

The issue of slavery was the most difficult one the framers faced, and it nearly destroyed the Union. Although some delegates considered slavery morally wrong, it was economic and political interests, not moral principle, that caused the framers to support or oppose the Three-Fifths Compromise. White southerners saw slavery as the foundation of their region's prosperity, and a compromise that did not question the legitimacy of slavery was probably necessary to keep the southern states from rejecting the Constitution.

THE CONSTITUTION

The political significance of the Great Compromise and the Three-Fifths Compromise was to restore the alliance of the southern planters and northern merchants. The Great Compromise reassured those of both groups who feared that a new governmental framework would reduce their own local or regional influence, and the Three-Fifths Compromise temporarily defused the rivalry between the groups. Their unity secured, members of the alliance supporting the establishment of a new government moved to fashion a constitutional framework consistent with their economic and political interests.

As we saw in the previous section, the framers sought to establish an effective government, strong enough to maintain order, promote commerce, protect property, and defend the nation from foreign enemies. This goal led the framers to make the presidency a powerful position, to give federal courts and not state courts the last word in judicial decisions, and to establish federal control over commerce and finance. Some framers, however, were concerned that small groups of social and economic elites would seize political power, while others feared that populists and radicals would take control of the government by stirring up mob violence among the lower classes.

To ensure that the government would be unlikely to oppress its citizens, whether on behalf of self-serving elites or of rampaging majorities, the framers embraced such principles as separation of powers, checks and balances (giving each branch of government some power over the others), bicameralism (the division of Congress into two chambers), and federalism—each of which we will examine in the discussion that follows. Though these divisions of power would reduce governmental efficiency and effectiveness, the framers wanted to ensure that governmental power could not be easily abused.

The framers also incorporated popular representation into the new government's framework. Even delegates distrustful of ordinary citizens recognized that without those citizens' consent, the new government would be rejected by the states. Fearing excessive democracy, however, the framers sought to blunt the influence of popular representation through a system of indirect elections and other devices. Some of these rules, such as the appointment of senators and electors by the state legislatures (rather than direct election by the people), have been abandoned in favor of popular voting. Others, such as the Electoral College, remain defining features of the American institutional structure.

Let's now assess the major provisions of the Constitution to see how each affects the interplay of effective governance and representation.

The Legislative Branch

The first seven sections of Article I of the Constitution provided for a Congress consisting of two chambers: a House of Representatives and a Senate. Members of the House of Representatives were given two-year terms in office and directly elected by citizens—though generally, only White males had the right to vote. State legislatures were to appoint members of the Senate for six-year terms (this system was changed in 1913 by the Seventeenth Amendment, providing for direct election of senators), and the terms were staggered so that the appointments of one-third of the senators expired every two years. The Constitution assigned somewhat different tasks to the House and Senate. Though approval by both bodies is required for the enactment of a law, the Senate alone can approve treaties and presidential appointments, and only the House can initiate bills to raise revenue.

The character of the legislative branch reflects the framers' major goals. The House of Representatives was designed to be directly responsible to the people in order to encourage popular support for the new Constitution and to show ordinary citizens that their views would be directly represented in lawmaking. At the same time, to guard against "excessive democracy," the power of the House was checked by the Senate, whose members were to be appointed for long terms rather than elected for short terms.

Staggered terms in the Senate would make that body especially resistant to popular pressure, even if that pressure came indirectly via the state legislatures. Thus, the structure of the legislative branch was designed to contribute to governmental power, promote popular consent for the new government, and at the same time, place limits on the popular political movements that many framers saw as a radical threat to the established economic and social order.

think it through

How large is the state in which you live? Do you think your state benefits from, or is disadvantaged by, the Great Compromise today in terms of representation in Congress?

The Powers of Congress and the States. The issues of power and consent were important throughout the Constitution. Section 8 of Article I specifically listed the powers of Congress, which include the authority to collect taxes, to borrow money, to regulate commerce, to declare war, and to maintain an army and navy. By granting it these powers, the framers indicated clearly that the new government would be far more influential than its predecessor. At the same time, by giving these important powers to Congress rather than to the executive branch, the framers sought to reassure citizens that their views would be fully represented whenever the government exercised its new powers.

As an additional guarantee to the people that the new government would pose no threat, the Constitution implied that any powers *not* listed were not granted to the government at all. This is the doctrine of **expressed powers**: the Constitution grants only those powers specifically *expressed* in its text. But the framers wanted an active and powerful government, so they included the **necessary and proper clause**, sometimes known as the elastic clause, which signified that the expressed powers were meant to be a source of strength to the national government, not a limitation on it. Each power could be used to the fullest extent, although no additional powers could be assumed by the national government without a constitutional amendment. Any power not specifically mentioned was stated to be "reserved" to the states (or the people).

expressed powers
Powers that the Constitution explicitly grants to the federal government.

necessary and proper clause
The last paragraph of Article I, Section 8, which gives Congress the power to make all laws needed to exercise the powers listed in Section 8. Also called the *elastic clause*.

The Executive Branch

The Constitution established the presidency in Article II. As Alexander Hamilton put it, the presidential article aimed at "energy in the Executive." It did so in an effort to overcome the natural stalemate that was built into both the division of the legislature into two chambers and the separation of powers among the legislative, executive, and judicial branches. The Constitution afforded the president a measure of independence both from the people and from the other branches—particularly Congress.

Some of the framers had wanted a multiperson executive or an executive council to avoid the evils that many associated with a monarch. However, Hamilton argued that "energy" required a single rather than a plural executive. While abuse of power should be guarded against by checks and balances and other devices, energy also required that the executive hold "competent powers" to direct the nation's business.[5] These would include the unconditional power to accept ambassadors from—that is, to "recognize"—other countries; the power to negotiate treaties, although their acceptance requires Senate approval; the unconditional right to grant reprieves (temporary delays in criminal punishments) and pardons of those convicted, except in cases of impeachment; and the power to appoint major officials in government departments, to convene Congress in special session, and to veto congressional legislation. (The veto power is not absolute, because Congress can override it by a two-thirds vote. Analyzing the Evidence, on pp. 36–37, explores the various points

at which legislation can be halted in the United States as compared to other countries.)

At the same time, the framers attempted to help the president withstand excessively democratic pressures by filling the office through indirect rather than direct election (through a separate Electoral College). The extent to which the framers' hopes were realized is the topic of Chapter 6.

The Judicial Branch

Article III established the judicial branch. This provision reflects the framers' concern with giving more power to the new national government and checking radical democratic impulses while guarding against potential interference with liberty and property by the government itself.

The framers created a court that was to be literally a supreme court of the United States and not merely the highest court of the national government. The Supreme Court was given the power to resolve any conflicts that might emerge between federal and state laws and to determine which level of government—national, state, or both—could exercise a particular power. In addition, the Court was given jurisdiction over controversies between citizens of different states. The long-term significance of this provision was that as the United States developed a national economy—one based increasingly on commerce between rather than within states—it came to rely more and more on the federal rather than the state courts for resolution of disputes.

Judges were given lifetime appointments to protect them both from pressure by politicians and the public and from interference by the other branches of

Constitutional Engineering: How Many "Veto Gates"?

Contributed by **Steven L. Taylor**, *Troy University*

Matthew S. Shugart, *University of California, Davis*

Any given constitution contains a number of individual elements that interact to produce a specific policy-making environment. These parameters determine how policy decisions are made as well as which political actors can stop them from proceeding through the process. One area of comparative constitutional structures is how many veto gates a system contains. A veto gate is an institution that serves as a point in the legislative process where the progress of a proposal can be halted. This notion conceives of the legislative process as being made up of one or more such gates that have to be opened to allow an idea to "flow" past on its way to becoming law. Each gate, however, is locked and can be opened only by institutional actors who hold the keys.

The simplest possible model of such a system would be an absolute dictator who has to consult only his or her own preferences before acting. Democratic governance, on the other hand, is a system that builds complex (and often multiple) gates and then creates and empowers players to open (or not) those gates.

The exact mix of institutional elements in a given constitution has a profound impact not only on how policy is made but also on what kinds of policies are made. More veto gates and players in a given system will generate more need for negotiation and compromise versus systems with fewer such actors. In counting veto gates, we can ask three questions:

1. **Presidential veto:**
   Is there an elected president who can veto legislation? In parliamentary systems, like the United Kingdom and India, there is no elected presidency at all. Other systems have elected presidents who may be important in some respects but who are not empowered with a veto (for instance, France). The strongest presidents are both elected and have a veto, such as the U.S. president.

2. **Number of legislative chambers:**
   How many legislative chambers are there? Does the government have one chamber (unicameral) or two (bicameral)? If there is only one legislative chamber, as in Costa Rica and Denmark, then obviously there can be only one veto gate among legislative actors—but we need a final question to differentiate different forms of bicameralism.

3. **Symmetry of chambers:**
   If there is a second chamber, are they symmetrical in their powers? Many second chambers are less powerful in their systems than the U.S. Senate, which is fully symmetrical. Some other bicameral legislatures are asymmetrical, meaning the second chamber has minimal powers beyond delaying power, as in Austria, or it has substantial powers in some areas but not others, as with the Canadian Senate and the United Kingdom's House of Lords.

	ELECTED PRESIDENT WITH VETO?	NO. OF LEGISLATIVE CHAMBERS	LEVEL OF CHAMBER SYMMETRY	NUMBER OF VETO GATES
ARGENTINA, BRAZIL, CHILE, COLOMBIA, DOMINICAN REPUBLIC, *MEXICO,* * PHILIPPINES, *UNITED STATES*, URUGUAY	Yes	●●	High	✖✖✖
COSTA RICA,** PANAMA, SOUTH KOREA	Yes	●	Unicameral	✖✖
POLAND	Yes	●●	Low 1 strong chamber 1 weak chamber	✖✖
AUSTRALIA, ITALY, *SWITZERLAND*	No	●●	High 2 strong chambers	✖✖
CANADA, *GERMANY, INDIA*, JAPAN, **NETHERLANDS**, *SOUTH AFRICA*, **UNITED KINGDOM**	No	●●	Medium 1 strong chamber 1 chamber with limitations	✖✖
AUSTRIA, BELGIUM, CZECH REPUBLIC, FRANCE, *SPAIN*	No	●●	Low	✖
BULGARIA, DENMARK, **FINLAND**, GREECE, HUNGARY, IRELAND, ISRAEL, **NEW ZEALAND**, NORWAY, PORTUGAL, SLOVAKIA, **SWEDEN**	No	●	Unicameral	✖

Italicized cases are federal.
Bold cases lack judicial review of legislation.

* Mexico's second chamber has no power over spending bills.

** No veto on budget.

We can see from the table of 40 established democracies that there are multiple ways in which national constitutions can configure the lawmaking process in terms of the type and number of veto gates. Moreover, the United States is not typical. It is only 1 of 9 of these 40 democracies to have three veto gates in the lawmaking process. Most other established democracies have fewer veto gates, although several have multiple veto players—such as frequent coalition governments where political parties have to compromise with one another. This combination of veto gates and veto players directly impacts the policies and may help us understand why policies are different across different democracies.

Beyond the legislative process, there are other constitutional factors that can create veto gates for policy implementation: a federal system may empower states to block the implementation of policy passed at the national level; Supreme Courts or constitutional tribunals may have the ability to declare laws unconstitutional and therefore null and void. All of these factors derive from constitutional design.

SOURCES: Steven L. Taylor, Matthew S. Shugart, Arend Lijphart, and Bernard Grofman, *A Different Democracy: American Government in a Thirty-One-Country Perspective* (New Haven, CT: Yale University Press, 2014); and authors' classifications.

 The United States Congress is often criticized for gridlock preventing it from moving legislation forward. In what countries would you expect to see similar issues? In what countries would you expect it to be easier to pass legislation?

Although the power of judicial review is not mentioned in the Constitution, the courts have assumed this power. The Trump administration's intention to include a question in the 2020 census asking for the citizenship status of respondents was regarded by the Supreme Court as a "contrived" justification that possibly hid the motivation to deport illegal immigrants.

judicial review

The power of the courts to determine whether the actions of the president, Congress, and state legislatures are consistent with the Constitution.

government. To further safeguard judicial independence, the Constitution also prohibited Congress from reducing the salary of any judge while in office. But federal judges would not be totally immune to politics or to the other branches, for the president was to appoint them, and the Senate would have to approve the appointments. Congress would also have the power to create inferior (lower) courts, to change the federal courts' jurisdiction (the geographic area or types of cases over which they had authority), to add or subtract federal judges, and to even change the size of the Supreme Court.

The Constitution does not specifically mention **judicial review**, the power of the courts to render the final decision when there is a conflict over the interpretation of the Constitution or of laws. This conflict could be between the courts and Congress, the courts and the executive branch, or the federal government and the states. Scholars generally feel that judicial review is implicit in the existence of a written Constitution and in the power given to the federal courts over "all Cases . . . arising under this Constitution, the Laws of the United States, and Treaties made, or which shall be made, under their Authority" (Article III, Section 2). The Supreme Court eventually assumed the power of judicial review. Its assumption of this power, as we will see in Chapter 8, was based not on the Constitution itself but on the politics of later decades and the membership of the Court.

National Unity and Power

Various provisions in the Constitution addressed the framers' concern with national unity and power. Article IV provided for comity (recognition of one another's laws and court decisions) among states, which we will discuss in more detail in Chapter 3. Each state was also prohibited from discriminating against the citizens of other states in favor of its own citizens, with the Supreme Court determining in each case whether such discrimination has occurred.

The framers' concern with national supremacy was also expressed in Article VI, in the **supremacy clause**, which provided that national laws and treaties "shall be the supreme law of the land." This meant that all laws made under the "authority of the United States" would be superior to laws adopted by any state or local government, and that the states must respect all treaties made under that authority—a clear effort to keep the states from dealing separately with foreign nations or businesses. The supremacy clause also bound all state and local, as well as federal, officials to take an oath to support the national Constitution if disputes arose between national and state laws.

Constitutional Limits on the National Government's Power

As we have indicated, though the framers wanted a powerful national government, they also wanted to guard against possible misuse of that power. Thus they incorporated two key principles into the Constitution: the **separation of powers** and **federalism** (see also Chapter 3). A third set of limitations, the **Bill of Rights**, was added after its ratification to respond to charges that the Constitution paid too little attention to citizens' rights.

The Separation of Powers.   No principle of politics was more widely shared among literate Americans at the time of the 1787 Founding than the principle that power must be used to balance power. The French political theorist Baron de Montesquieu (1689–1755) believed that this balance was an indispensable defense against tyranny, and his writings "were taken as political gospel" at the Philadelphia Convention.[6] This principle is not stated explicitly in the Constitution, but it is clearly built into Articles I, II, and III, which provide for the following:

1. Three separate branches of government (Figure 2.1), including a legislative branch divided into two chambers—a **bicameral legislature**.

2. Different methods of selecting the top personnel so that each branch is responsible to a different constituency. This arrangement is intended to produce a "mixed regime," in which the personnel of each branch of government will develop very different interests and outlooks on how to govern, and different groups in society will be assured of some access to governmental decision making.

3. **Checks and balances**, with each of the branches given some power over the others. Familiar examples are the presidential veto power over legislation and the requirement that the Senate approve high-level presidential appointments.

In addition to "separation of powers," this system has also been described as "separated institutions sharing power,"[7] thus diminishing the chance that power will be misused.

supremacy clause
A clause of Article VI of the Constitution, stating that all laws and treaties approved by the national government are the supreme laws of the United States and superior to all laws adopted by any state or local government.

separation of powers
The division of governmental power among several institutions that must cooperate in decision making.

federalism
The system of government in which a constitution divides power between a central government and regional governments.

Bill of Rights
The first 10 amendments to the U.S. Constitution, adopted in 1791. The Bill of Rights ensures certain rights and liberties to the people.

bicameral legislature
A legislative body composed of two chambers, or houses.

checks and balances
The ways in which each branch of government is able to influence the activities of the other branches.

figure 2.1

THE SEPARATION OF POWERS

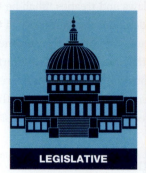

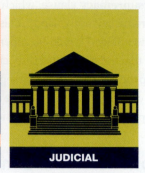

LEGISLATIVE	EXECUTIVE	JUDICIAL
Passes federal laws	Enforces laws	Reviews lower-court decisions
Controls federal appropriations	Serves as commander in chief of armed forces	Decides constitutionality of laws
Approves treaties and presidential appointments	Makes foreign treaties	Decides cases involving disputes between states
Regulates interstate commerce	Nominates Supreme Court justices and federal court judges	
Establishes lower-court system	May pardon those convicted in federal court	

Federalism. Federalism was a step toward greater centralization of power. Aiming to place more power at the national governmental level without completely undermining the power of state governments, the delegates devised a system of two layers of sovereignty, or independent political authority—the states and the nation—with the hope that competition between the two would limit the power of both.

The Bill of Rights. Late in the Philadelphia Convention, a motion was made to include a bill of rights in the Constitution. After a brief debate, it was almost unanimously rejected. Most delegates felt that since the federal government was already limited to its expressed powers, further protection of citizens from it was unnecessary. Many argued that it was the states that should adopt bills of rights, because their greater powers needed greater limitations. But almost immediately after the Constitution was ratified, a movement arose to adopt a national bill of rights. This is why the Bill of Rights, adopted in 1791, is the first 10 amendments to the Constitution rather than part of the body of it. We explore the Bill of Rights further in Chapter 4.

Amending the Constitution

The Constitution established procedures for its own revision in Article V. The amending process is so difficult that it has succeeded only 17 times since 1791, when the first 10 amendments were adopted. Many others have been proposed, but fewer than 40 have even come close to fulfilling the Constitution's requirement of a two-thirds vote in Congress, and only a fraction of those have approached adoption by three-fourths of the states. The Constitution could also be amended by a constitutional convention, but no national convention has been called since the Philadelphia Convention of 1787; Congress has submitted all proposed amendments to the state legislatures for ratification.

Ratifying the Constitution

Rules for ratification of the Constitution of 1787 made up Article VII of the Constitution. This provision actually violated the procedure for constitutional change in the Articles of Confederation. For one thing, it adopted a nine-state requirement for ratification in place of the unanimity required by the Articles. For another, it provided for ratification by special state conventions rather than by state legislatures. All the states except Rhode Island eventually did set up conventions to ratify the Constitution.

The Fight for Ratification

The first hurdle faced by the new Constitution was ratification by 13 conventions of delegates elected by the White, propertied male voters of each state. The struggle for ratification thus included 13 separate campaigns, each influenced by local as well as national considerations. In every state, two sides faced off, calling themselves Federalists and Antifederalists.[8] The **Federalists** supported the Constitution and preferred a strong national government. The **Antifederalists** opposed the Constitution and preferred a more decentralized government, in which state and local needs would come first. The Federalists and Antifederalists had somewhat different views of society. The Antifederalists feared government by elites who would use their power to oppress ordinary citizens. The Federalists feared mob rule that would threaten property rights. Thus, the Antifederalists feared minority tyranny, while the Federalists feared tyranny by the majority.

Under the name Publius, Alexander Hamilton, James Madison, and John Jay wrote 85 articles in New York newspapers supporting ratification of the Constitution. These *Federalist Papers*, as they are known today, defended the principles of the Constitution and sought to dispel the fears of an oppressive national authority.[9] The Antifederalists, however, such as Richard Henry Lee and Patrick Henry of Virginia, and George Clinton of New York, argued that the new Constitution betrayed the Revolution and was a step toward monarchy. They wanted a bill of rights to protect against government.

By the beginning of 1788, the conventions of five states had ratified the Constitution. Delaware, New Jersey, and Georgia approved it unanimously; Connecticut and Pennsylvania approved it by wide margins. Opposition was overcome in Massachusetts by the promise of a bill of rights to be added to the Constitution at

Federalists
Those who favored a strong national government and supported the constitution proposed at the Constitutional Convention of 1787.

Antifederalists
Those who favored strong state governments and a weak national government and who were opponents of the constitution proposed at the Constitutional Convention of 1787.

a later date. Ratification by Maryland and South Carolina followed. In June 1788, New Hampshire became the ninth state to ratify, putting the Constitution into effect. But for the new national government to have real power, Virginia and New York needed to approve it. After impassioned debate and many recommendations for future amendments, especially for a bill of rights, the Federalists mustered enough votes for ratification in Virginia in June and New York in July. North Carolina joined the new government in 1789, after Congress actually submitted a bill of rights to the states for approval, and Rhode Island held out until 1790 before finally voting to become part of the new union.

CHANGING THE FRAMEWORK: CONSTITUTIONAL AMENDMENT

The Constitution has endured for over two centuries as the framework of U.S. government. But it has not endured without change. Without change, the Constitution might have become merely a sacred text, stored under glass.

Amendments: Many Are Called, Few Are Chosen

The framers of the Constitution recognized the need for change, and provisions for amendment were incorporated into Article V. Since 1791, when the first 10 amendments, the Bill of Rights, were added, only 17 amendments have been adopted. And two of them—Prohibition (Eighteenth) and its repeal (Twenty-First)—cancel each other out, so overall, only 15 amendments have been added since 1791, despite vast changes in American society and the American economy.

As Figure 2.2 illustrates, Article V provides for four routes of amendment:

1. Passage in House and Senate by two-thirds vote; then ratification by majority vote of the legislatures of three-fourths (38) of the states.

2. Passage in House and Senate by two-thirds vote; then ratification by conventions called for the purpose in three-fourths (38) of the states.

3. Passage in a national convention called by Congress in response to petitions by two-thirds (34) of the states; ratification by majority vote of the legislatures of three-fourths (38) of the states.

4. Passage in a national convention, as in route 3; then ratification by conventions called for the purpose in three-fourths (38) of the states.

Because no amendment has ever been proposed by national convention, however, routes 3 and 4 have never been employed. And route 2 has been employed only once (for the Twenty-First Amendment, which repealed the Eighteenth, or Prohibition, Amendment). Route 1 has been used for all the other amendments.

figure 2.2

ROUTES OF CONSTITUTIONAL AMENDMENT

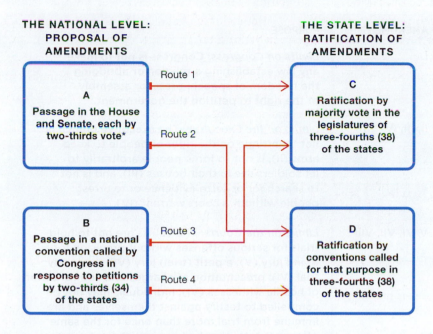

THE NATIONAL LEVEL:
PROPOSAL OF
AMENDMENTS

THE STATE LEVEL:
RATIFICATION OF
AMENDMENTS

A

Passage in the House
and Senate, each by
two-thirds vote*

Route 1

Route 2

C

Ratification by
majority vote in the
legislatures of
three-fourths (38)
of the states

B

Passage in a national
convention called by
Congress in
response to petitions
by two-thirds (34)
of the states

Route 3

Route 4

D

Ratification by
conventions called
for that purpose in
three-fourths (38)
of the states

*For each amendment proposal, Congress has the power to choose the method of ratification, the time limit for consideration by the states, and other conditions of ratification.

**This method of proposal has never been employed. Thus, amendment routes 3 and 4 have never been attempted.

The Twenty-Seven Amendments

The Constitution and its 27 amendments are reproduced in the Appendix. All but two of the amendments are concerned with the structure or composition of the government. This focus is consistent with the concept of a constitution as "higher law," whose purpose is to establish a framework within which government and the process of making ordinary law can take place. A constitution enables the enactment of legislation and public policies, but it should not attempt to determine what that legislation or those policies ought to be.

The purpose of the 10 amendments in the Bill of Rights was to give each of the three branches clearer and more restricted boundaries (Table 2.1). The First Amendment restricts the power of Congress to enact laws regulating religion, speech, the press, and assembly. Indeed, the First Amendment makes this limitation quite explicit by opening with the phrase "Congress shall make no law . . ." The Second, Third, and Fourth Amendments spell out limits on the executive branch as well as on Congress.

The Fifth, Sixth, Seventh, and Eighth Amendments contain some of the most important safeguards for individual citizens against the exercise of governmental power. These amendments regulate court proceedings and outlaw various forms of action by executive branch officials. The Ninth and Tenth Amendments

table 2.1

THE BILL OF RIGHTS: ANALYSIS OF ITS PROVISIONS

AMENDMENT	PURPOSE
I	*Limits on Congress:* Congress is not to make any law establishing a religion or abridging the freedom of speech, press, or assembly or the right to petition the government.
II, III, IV	*Limits on the Executive:* The executive branch is not to infringe on the right of people to keep arms (II), is not to force people arbitrarily to let soldiers live in their houses (III), and is not to search for or seize evidence or to arrest people without a court warrant (IV).
V, VI, VII, VIII	*Limits on the Courts:* The courts are not to hold trials for serious offenses without provision for a grand jury (V); a petit (trial) jury (VII); a speedy trial (VI); presentation of charges and confrontation of hostile witnesses (VI). Individuals may not be compelled to testify against themselves and are immune from trial more than once for the same offense (V). Neither bail nor punishment may be excessive (VIII), and no property may be taken for public use without "just compensation" (V).
IX, X	*Limits on the National Government:* Additional rights exist outside of those enumerated in the Constitution (IX), including those provided in the constitutions of the states, and all powers not enumerated are reserved to the states or the people (X).

think it through

What are your state's voting requirements? Do you think they encourage or discourage people from voting?

reinforce the idea that the Constitution creates a government of limited powers. The Ninth declares that failure to mention a right does not mean it is not possessed by the people, while the Tenth states that powers not granted to the federal government are reserved to the states and the people.

Five amendments adopted since 1791 are concerned with expansion of the electorate, the group of people entitled to vote (Table 2.2).[10] The Founders were unable to agree on uniform national voting qualifications, although they provided in the final draft of Article I, Section 2, that eligibility to vote in a national election would be the same as "the Qualification requisite for Elector of the most numerous branch of the state Legislature." Article I, Section 4, added that Congress could alter state regulations as to the "Times, Places and Manner of holding Elections for Senators and Representatives." But any important expansion of the American electorate would almost certainly require a constitutional amendment.

table 2.2

AMENDING THE CONSTITUTION TO EXPAND THE ELECTORATE

AMENDMENT	PURPOSE	YEAR PROPOSED	YEAR ADOPTED
XIV	Section 1 provided a national definition of citizenship.	1866	1868
XV	Extended voting rights to all races.	1869	1870
XIX	Extended voting rights to women.	1919	1920
XXIII	Extended voting rights to residents of the District of Columbia.	1960	1961
XXIV	Extended voting rights to all classes by abolition of poll taxes.	1962	1964
XXVI	Extended voting rights to citizens ages 18 and over.	1971	1971

Six more amendments are also related to elections, although not concerned directly with voting rights and the expansion of the electorate. These amendments deal with the elective offices themselves or with the relationship between elective offices and the electorate (Table 2.3).

Another five amendments are intended to expand or to limit the powers of the national and state governments (Table 2.4). The Eleventh Amendment protected the states from suits by private individuals and took away from the federal courts any power to hear cases brought by private individuals of one state (or a foreign country) against another state. The next three amendments in Table 2.4 aim to reduce state power (Thirteenth), to reduce state power and expand national power (Fourteenth), and to expand national power (Sixteenth). The Twenty-Seventh limits Congress's ability to raise its members' salaries.

The Eighteenth, or Prohibition, Amendment is the only amendment that the country used to *legislate*, to deal directly with a substantive social problem. And it is the only amendment that has ever been repealed.

table 2.3

AMENDING THE CONSTITUTION TO CHANGE THE RELATIONSHIP BETWEEN ELECTIVE OFFICES AND THE ELECTORATE

AMENDMENT	PURPOSE	YEAR PROPOSED	YEAR ADOPTED
XII	Created separate ballot for the vice presidency in the Electoral College.	1803	1804
XIV	Penalized states for depriving formerly enslaved people of the right to vote.	1866	1868
XVII	Provided direct election of senators.	1912	1913
XX	Shortened the time between the election of a new Congress and president and their inauguration.	1932	1933
XXII	Limited presidential terms.	1947	1951
XXV	Provided presidential succession in case of disability.	1965	1967

Since the Constitution's own ratification, some 11,000 amendments have been proposed and only 27 have been ratified. This low ratification rate reflects not only the many hurdles in the amending process but also a basic rule of political life: long-established institutions and procedures almost always have defenders who, having gained power or political advantage from the established way of doing things, are reluctant to support change.

The Electoral College system, for example, may produce results widely seen as unfair, but it is defended by whichever politicians believe it improves their party's presidential chances. Or take the equality of representation in the Senate created by the Great Compromise. It may seem unfair that the nearly 40 million residents of California have only two senators, while roughly the same number of citizens of the 22 smallest states have 44 senators. It seems highly unlikely, however, that the 22 states would agree to surrender their current advantage. (See the Policy Principle box on p. 48.)

table 2.4

AMENDING THE CONSTITUTION TO EXPAND OR LIMIT THE POWER OF GOVERNMENT

AMENDMENT	PURPOSE	YEAR PROPOSED	YEAR ADOPTED
XI	Limited the jurisdiction of federal courts over suits involving the states.	1794	1795
XIII	Eliminated slavery and the right of states to allow property in persons.	1865	1865
XIV	Established due process of law in state courts for all persons. Was later used to apply the entire Bill of Rights to the states.	1866	1868
XVI	Established the national power to tax incomes.	1909	1913
XXVII	Limited Congress's power to raise its own salary.	1789	1992

CONCLUSION

How did the framers try to balance effective government with popular representation? Although the Constitution was the product of a particular set of political forces, the principles of government that it established have a significance that goes far beyond the interests of its authors.

Creating an Effective Government

The final product of the Constitutional Convention stands as an extraordinary victory for those who wanted a more effective new system of government to replace the Articles of Confederation. In contrast to the relatively weak Articles, the new Constitution laid the groundwork for a national government powerful enough to guard citizens' lives and liberties, to promote trade, to protect property,

the policy principle
THE GREAT COMPROMISE AND POLICY

The way institutions are structured affects the types of laws, programs, and decisions—that is, the types of policies—that are likely to come out of those institutions. Thus, politicians try to create institutions that will help them achieve policy goals they favor and prevent policy outcomes they oppose. For anyone involved in politics, the right institutional arrangements can put them at an advantage, and their opponents at a disadvantage, in conflicts over policy for many years.

This idea is illustrated by the struggles at the Constitutional Convention. Delegates from the states with smaller populations thought that their states had much to gain by creating legislative institutions that gave each state an equal vote regardless of population size. The larger states, however—especially Virginia, Massachusetts, New York, and Pennsylvania—were centers of commerce, and their delegates believed that, over time, the new government's commercial policies would be more likely to serve those states' interests if its legislative institutions reflected their advantage in population size.

Nevertheless, representatives of both groups of states agreed that a new government was likely to produce better policies than those developed under the Articles of Confederation, so they were willing to compromise. They eventually settled, in the Great Compromise, on an institutional arrangement that gave the large states more weight in the House of Representatives (where seats were allocated on the basis of state population size) and the small states equality of representation in the Senate (where each state had the same number of seats).

This Great Compromise has affected policy outcomes throughout American history, giving less populous states disproportionate influence in the legislative process. The political scientist Robert A. Dahl thought that slavery survived longer than it otherwise would have because of the disproportionate influence of small-population southern states. The House of Representatives passed eight antislavery measures between 1800 and 1860, but all died in the Senate. Moreover, the civil rights movement of the mid-twentieth century was slowed by senators representing small-population states.

Today, the 40 million citizens of California, 30 million citizens of Texas, and 20 million citizens of New York are each represented by two senators, just as are the 577,737 inhabitants of Wyoming, 628,000 Vermonters, and 760,000 North Dakotans. This variation means that groups and interests in the smallest states exercise influence in the Senate far out of proportion to their states' populations.

What if representation in the Senate was based on state population?

Greater representation per capita in the Senate is one reason why the smaller states and their public agencies receive more federal aid per capita than do the larger states. In a recent year, residents of Wyoming received $4,180 per capita, while Texans and Californians each received only a bit over $1,700. Also in recent years, bills designed to reform the immigration system, alter U.S. climate policy, and increase the disclosure of campaign spending won the support of senators representing a majority of the population but failed to pass because those senators did not constitute a majority of votes in the Senate. After almost 250 years, the Great Compromise continues to affect public policy in the United States.

think it through

1. How did the Great Compromise give less populous states disproportionate representation in Congress and the policy-making process?

2. If senators from states representing a majority of the population support a certain policy but that policy doesn't pass because those senators do not constitute a majority in the Senate, does that mean American government is not representative? Why or why not?

President Trump's 2016 campaign promise to build a U.S.-Mexico border wall was tested when congressional Democrats refused the requested $1.3 trillion funding for it in the budget. After weeks of negotiations, Trump eventually signed the bill with partial funding to avert a government shutdown.

to defend the nation's interests, to maintain national unity, and to restrain radical state legislatures. Moreover, this new government incorporated internal checks and balances, indirect selection of officeholders, lifetime judicial appointments, and other provisions to guard against abuses of power.

As we saw earlier, the framers gave each of the three branches of government a means of intervening in and blocking the actions of the others. Sometimes checks and balances have seemed to prevent the government from getting things done. During much of President Obama's time in office, Republicans controlled both houses of Congress and blocked most of Obama's initiatives. The media were sharply critical of what members of the press saw as "gridlock."

However, gridlock can become a blessing when checks and balances serve as a safeguard against rash action. During the 1950s, for example, Congress was caught up in a nearly hysterical effort to identify subversive activities in the United States, which might have led to a serious erosion of civil liberties if not for the checks and balances provided by the executive branch and the courts. Thus, a governmental principle that serves as a frustrating limitation on one day, may become a vitally important safeguard the next.

Representing Diverse Interests and Protecting Liberty

The Constitution's framers also recognized the importance of establishing a government that represented a diversity of interests whose support would be needed to make the new government viable. The Great Compromise gave states equal representation in the Senate by assigning each state two senators. The Three-Fifths Compromise satisfied the southern states by partially counting enslaved people in their populations when determining representation in the House of Representatives. To represent ordinary citizens, the Constitution did not impose property qualifications for holding office—a requirement that was common in that era—and it also gave ordinary citizens the right to vote for members of the House.

The Constitution's system of representation was imperfect, leaving out many groups, such as women and African Americans. By today's standards, the Constitution was not a democratic document. Over time, however, many groups unrepresented at first have been able to gain representation. Over time, the United States has become a more democratic nation. How did this come about? The answer is simple: political liberty.

To the framers, a key purpose of government was the protection of citizens' liberties. They hoped that a constitution in which separated powers checked and balanced one another would simultaneously preserve the government's strength and protect liberty. By championing liberty, the framers virtually guaranteed that democracy would sooner or later evolve and expand in the United States. Where they have a measure of liberty, more and more people, groups, and interests will engage in politics and fight to overcome restrictions placed on their participation and representation.

This is precisely what began to take place in the early years of the American Republic. During the Jeffersonian period, political parties formed. During the Jacksonian period, many state voting restrictions were removed, and popular participation greatly expanded. Liberty has given women, African Americans, Latinos, members of the LGBTQ community, and others a chance to seek and win greater representation in governance. The Constitution may not have been a democratic document, but by guaranteeing liberty, its institutional structure promoted more and more democratic representation in America's governance.

Despite the Constitution's brilliant promise, a blight marred America's founding. That, of course, was the institution of slavery. The new nation's population included several hundred thousand enslaved Black persons—individuals who had been transported to America from Africa and their native-born descendants. Indeed, as Thomas Jefferson sat writing the Declaration of Independence, boldly declaring that all men are created equal, he was attended by an enslaved teenage boy who happened to be his wife's half-brother.

The Civil War brought an end to slavery, but in the decades following the War and Reconstruction, African Americans were subject to persecution and vilification. Yet, as they responded the their plight, the descendants of enslaved Africans forced America to live up to its stated ideals and so raised American democracy from an idea to a reality. As a result of two centuries of Black resistance and protest, America was gradually forced to recognize and act in accordance with its declared principles. Black struggles, moreover, paved the way for struggles by other groups, including women, gay people, immigrants, and others to assert their own rights. In this way, the descendants of slaves helped to build American democracy.

Key Terms

Check Your Understanding

1. How did struggles among economic and political forces within the colonies lead to the Boston Tea Party, and ultimately the Declaration of Independence?

2. What was the relationship between the states and the central government in the Articles of Confederation and Perpetual Union? What powers were reserved for the states? What powers were reserved for the central government?

3. What were some of the flaws of the Articles of Confederation and Perpetual Union that led to the Constitutional Convention and the Second Founding?

4. How did the Three-Fifths Compromise affect American politics in the period before the Civil War?

5. How did the framers incorporate into the Constitution the principle that power must be used to balance power?

6. How did the framers account for the need for changes in the Constitution?

⚅ INQUIZITIVE

Earn a better grade on your test. InQuizitive personalizes your learning path to help you master the concepts from this chapter. In a recent efficacy study of American government students, InQuizitive increased test scores by an average of 17 points (see back cover).

CHAPTER THREE

FEDERALISM AND THE SEPARATION OF POWERS

3

After the inauguration of Donald Trump in 2017, several states, including California, and a number of cities declared themselves "sanctuaries" for undocumented immigrants in an attempt to undermine the federal government's efforts to step up deportations. President Trump responded by threatening to curtail federal grants to these states, and the states' attorneys general filed suit against the federal government to block Trump's actions. The cases are still wending their way through the courts.

While the states can sometimes thwart federal efforts, the federal government also has power to block actions by the states. For example, federal courts recently struck down efforts by some states to limit the rights of transgender individuals. These power struggles between federal and state governments are examples of federalism in action.

The Constitution's framers wanted to build a strong government but, at the same time, to ensure that government would not use its strength to oppress citizens. Federalism and the separation of powers are two of the most important ways that the framers hoped to achieve this goal.

Federalism seeks to limit government by dividing it into two levels: the national level and the state level. Often the two levels must cooperate; for example, federal agencies rely on state and local officials, such as police officers, in order to help enforce immigration laws. Yet, as the case of sanctuary cities and states illustrates, each level is also granted sufficient independence to compete with the other, in this way restraining the power of both.

The separation of powers, for its part, seeks to limit the national government's power by dividing government against itself—by assigning the legislative, executive, and judicial branches separate but overlapping functions, thus forcing them to share power. James Madison, the Constitution's chief architect, wrote in *Federalist 51* (reprinted in the Appendix), "The interior structure of the government" must be arranged so "that its several constituent parts may, by their mutual relations, be the means of keeping each other in their proper places." Dividing power might sometimes make government less efficient—promote "gridlock," as we might say today—but the framers thought this was a price worth paying to guard against oppressive governmental action.

As to representation, federalism and the separation of powers are among the building blocks of America's complex system of representative government. State governments are elected by constituencies (groups of voters) that differ from one another and from the constituencies that elect members of the national government. At the national level, each senator, each member of the House, and the president are all elected by different (albeit overlapping) constituencies. This system ensures some form of representation for every nook and cranny of the United States, while virtually guaranteeing that the nation's elected officials, in representing the interests of different constituencies, will seldom see eye to eye.

Both federalism and the separation of powers complicate policy making in the United States. If governmental power were arranged neatly and simply in a

Sanctuary cities, counties, and states shield undocumented immigrants from federal efforts to detain and deport them. Can state and local governments refuse to cooperate with the federal government?

Do federalism and the separation of powers make government more representative? Do they make government more effective?

single hierarchy, decisions could certainly be made more easily and efficiently. But would they be better decisions? The framers thought that although complexity, checks and balances, and institutionalized second-guessing are messy, they would allow more interests within society to have a voice and would eventually produce better results. Along the way, these decision processes would help preserve liberty and prevent tyranny. Although this complexity sometimes seems to make it impossible to get anything done collectively, political decision makers have developed a variety of strategies for overcoming the barriers to policy change. Let's see how this complex system works.

Learning Objectives

- Define federalism and explain how it limits national power.

- Trace how federalism evolved in the United States from the Founding through the twentieth century.

- Describe the shift toward increased national power since 1937 and the major features of American federalism today.

- Identify the major checks and balances among the institutions of government.

- Analyze how federalism and the separation of powers affect representation and governance.

FEDERALISM

federalism

The system of government in which a constitution divides power between a central government and regional governments.

Federalism can be defined as the division of powers between the national government and the state governments. As we saw in Chapter 2, the 13 original states were individual colonies before independence, and for nearly 13 years, each of them functioned as virtually a self-governing unit under the Articles of Confederation. Under the Articles, disorder within states was beyond the reach of the national government, and conflicts of interest between states were not manageable. For example, states made their own trade agreements with foreign countries and companies, which might then play one state against another for special advantages. Some states adopted barriers to foreign commerce that were contrary to the interests of another state.[1] Taxes and other barriers were also erected between states, inhibiting the movement of goods and persons across state borders.[2]

The need for a more effective national government to help solve such problems led directly to the Annapolis Convention in 1786 and the Constitutional Convention in 1787. Even after ratification of the Constitution, however, the states remained more important than the national government. For nearly a century and a half, virtually all of the fundamental policies governing Americans' lives were made by the state legislatures, not by Congress.

Federalism in the Constitution

The United States was the first nation to adopt federalism as its governing framework. With federalism, the framers sought to limit the national government by creating a second layer of **sovereignty**, or independent political authority, in the state governments. The American Constitution recognized the sovereignty of both the national government and the states, and the Bill of Rights reinforced this principle by granting a few expressed (specified) powers to the national government and reserving all the rest to the states. A federal system also allows geographically concentrated groups to wield more power than they can wield in a central system.

The Powers of the National Government. As we saw in Chapter 2, the expressed powers granted to the national government are found in Article I, Section 8, of the Constitution. These 17 powers include the power to collect taxes, to establish a currency, to declare war, and to regulate commerce. Article I, Section 8, also contains another important source of power for the national government: the **implied powers** that enable Congress "to make all Laws which shall be necessary and proper for carrying into Execution the foregoing Powers." Not until several decades after the Founding did the Supreme Court allow Congress to exercise the power granted in this necessary and proper clause, but ultimately the doctrine allowed the national government to expand the scope of its authority. In addition to expressed and implied powers, the Constitution affirmed the national government's power in the supremacy clause (Article VI), which made all national laws and treaties "the supreme Law of the Land."

The Powers of State Governments. One way in which the framers ensured a strong role for the states was through the Tenth Amendment, which says that any powers that the Constitution does not delegate to the national government or deny to the states are "reserved to the States respectively, or to the people." The Antifederalists, who feared that a strong central government would encroach on individual liberty, pressed for such an amendment as a way of limiting national power. Federalists agreed to it because they did not think it would do much harm, given the powers that the Constitution already granted to the national government. The Tenth Amendment is also called the **reserved powers** amendment.

The most fundamental power that is retained by the states is that of coercion—the power to develop and enforce criminal codes, to administer health and safety rules, and to regulate the family via marriage and divorce laws. The states have the power to regulate individuals' livelihoods; if you're a doctor, lawyer, plumber, or barber, you must be licensed by the state. Even more important, the states have the power to define private property, which exists because state laws against trespassing define who is and is not entitled to use a piece of property. If you own a car, your ownership isn't worth much unless the state is willing to enforce your right to possession by making it a crime for anyone else to take your car. Similarly, your "ownership" of a house or piece of land means that the state will enforce your possession by prohibiting others from occupying the property against your will. At the same time, however, under its power

sovereignty
Independent political authority.

implied powers
Powers derived from the necessary and proper clause (Article I, Section 8) of the Constitution. Such powers are not specifically expressed in the Constitution but are implied through the interpretation of delegated powers.

reserved powers
Powers that are not specifically delegated to the national government or denied to the states by the Constitution. Under the Tenth Amendment, these powers are reserved to the states.

The past 89 years—since Franklin Delano Roosevelt's New Deal—have seen an increase in national government power. Today, some Americans question whether the balance has shifted too far toward federal power.

eminent domain
The right of the government to take private property for public use, with reasonable compensation awarded to the owner.

concurrent powers
Authority possessed by both state and national governments, such as the power to levy taxes.

full faith and credit clause
The provision in Article IV, Section 1, of the Constitution, requiring that each state normally honor the governmental actions and judicial decisions that take place in another state.

 **think it through**

In what state was your driver's license issued? How does the full faith and credit clause protect your right to drive in any state in the country regardless of where you took the test?

of **eminent domain**, the state may seize your property (and compensate you) for anything it considers a public purpose.

The coercive power of the states was demonstrated during the coronavirus crisis of 2020. After many citizens ignored recommendations aimed at social distancing, state governors issued executive orders requiring citizens to comply with new public health rules or risk fines. On Sunday, March 15, Ohio governor Mike DeWine was the first state executive to order all restaurants and bars in the state closed. The next day, the governors of Connecticut, New Jersey, and New York ordered the closing of all restaurants, bars, gyms, movie theaters, and casinos in their states to slow the virus's spread. At the same time, DeWine and Governor Larry Hogan of Maryland ordered their states' schools to be closed indefinitely—a decision soon copied by most other states. These state measures produced massive business closings and unemployment, but the governors deemed these consequences to be unavoidable in light of the public health emergency.

In some areas, the states share **concurrent powers** with the national government. The two levels both have some power to regulate commerce and to affect the currency—for example, by being able to establish banks, incorporate businesses, and regulate the quality of products or the conditions of labor. Whenever there has been a direct conflict of laws between national and state levels, the issue has generally been resolved in favor of the national government. However, when the federal government does not set a strong policy in an area of concurrent powers, states can each decide their own policies. Analyzing the Evidence on pp. 58–59 explores the states' varying approaches to renewable energy policies in the absence of a strong national policy.

States' Obligations to One Another. The Constitution also creates obligations among the states. These obligations, spelled out in Article IV, were intended to promote national unity. By requiring the states to recognize actions and decisions taken in other states as legal and proper, the framers aimed to make the states less like independent countries and more like parts of a single nation. Article IV, Section 1, calls for "Full Faith and Credit" among states, meaning that each state is expected to honor the "public Acts, Records, and judicial Proceedings" that take place in any other state. So, for example, if a couple is married in Texas—marriage being regulated by state law—Missouri must also recognize that marriage, even though they were not married under Missouri state law.

This **full faith and credit clause** recently became an important factor in a case involving adoption by a same-sex parent. The state of Alabama had refused to recognize the legal validity of a Georgia adoption involving the same-sex partner of a woman who had conceived a child through artificial insemination. The woman's same-sex partner had legally adopted the child in Georgia but was denied joint custody and visitation when the couple moved to Alabama and then separated. In the 2016 case of *V.L. v. E.L.*, however, the Supreme Court held that the full faith and credit clause required Alabama courts to recognize the Georgia adoption.[3]

Article IV, Section 2, known as the **comity clause**, also promotes national unity. It provides that citizens enjoying the "privileges and immunities" of one state should be entitled to similar treatment in other states; that is, a state cannot discriminate against someone from another state or give special privileges to its own residents. For example, when Alaska passed a law in the 1970s that gave residents preference over nonresidents in obtaining work on the state's oil and gas pipelines, the Supreme Court ruled the law illegal because it discriminated against citizens of other states.[4]

The comity clause also regulates criminal justice among the states by requiring states to return fugitives to the states from which they have fled. For example, in 1952, when an inmate escaped from an Alabama prison and sought to avoid being returned on the grounds that he was subject to "cruel and unusual punishment" there, the Supreme Court ruled that he must be returned according to Article IV, Section 2.[5] There are many exceptions to the comity clause. For example, states may charge out-of-state students a higher tuition rate at state colleges and universities.

This case highlights the difference between the obligations among states and those among different countries. Recently, despite the resumption of diplomatic relations between Cuba and the United States, Cuba declared in 2017 that it would not return several American fugitives, including convicted murderer Joanne Chesimard, who had been granted asylum by the Cuban government. The Constitution clearly forbids states to do something similar.

States' relationships to one another are also governed by the interstate compact clause (Article I, Section 10), which states, "No State shall, without the Consent of Congress . . . enter into any Agreement or Compact with another State." The Supreme Court has interpreted this clause to mean that two or more states may enter into legally binding agreements with one another, subject to congressional approval, to solve a problem that crosses state lines. In the early years of the Republic, states turned to compacts primarily to settle border disputes. Today, compacts are used for a wide range of issues but are especially important in regulating the distribution of river water, addressing environmental concerns, and operating transportation systems that cross state lines.[6]

Local Government and the Constitution.   Local government, including counties, cities, and towns, occupies a peculiar but very important place in the American system. In fact, local government has no status in the American Constitution. *State* legislatures created local governments, and *state* constitutions and laws permit local governments to take on some of the responsibilities of the state governments. Most states amended their own constitutions to give their larger cities **home rule**—a guarantee of noninterference in various areas of local affairs. But local governments enjoy no such recognition in the national Constitution. They have always been mere conveniences of the states. The boundaries of cities and counties can be altered by state governments, and cities and towns can be created or eliminated by state legislatures.[7]

comity clause
Article IV, Section 2, of the Constitution, which prohibits states from enacting laws that treat the citizens of other states in a discriminatory manner.

home rule
The power delegated by a state to a local unit of government to manage its own affairs.

State Policies on Renewable Energy

Contributed by **David Konisky**, *Indiana University*

In a federal system like the United States, laws and policies may vary considerably from state to state. Over the past two decades, many state governments have put in place policies to stimulate the development and use of renewable energy sources such as wind and solar power. One of the key policies that states have employed is the renewable portfolio standard (RPS). An RPS is a mandate that a state's electricity providers generate a specific amount of their power from renewable sources by a particular date.

How do these renewable energy policies differ from state to state, and how does that variation affect outcomes across states? As the map below shows, as of early 2020, 30 states and the District of Columbia had binding RPS policies in place, and an additional 7 states had voluntary RPS goals. States with RPSs are located throughout the country, with the notable exception of the southeastern United States where only North Carolina has a mandatory standard.

State RPSs vary considerably with respect to the target percentage of renewable energy use and the date of expected achievement. States with ambitious targets include Oregon (50 percent by 2040), California (60 percent by 2030), New York (70 percent by 2030), Vermont (75 percent by 2032), and Hawaii (100 percent by 2045).

State Renewable Energy Policies

● Mandatory RPS   ● Voluntary RPS goal   ● None

RPS TARGETS (SELECTED STATES)	
California	60% by 2030
Texas	5880 MW by 2015
New York	70% by 2030
Ohio	8.5% by 2026
Pennsylvania	18% by 2021
Illinois	25% by 2026
Colorado	30% by 2020
North Carolina	12.5% by 2021
Missouri	15% by 2021

SOURCE: NC Clean Technology Center, https://s3.amazonaws.com/ncsolarcen-prod/wp-content/uploads/2019/07/RPS-CES-June2019.pdf (accessed 3/15/20); National Conference of State Legislatures, "State Renewable Portfolio Standards and Goals," April 17, 2020, https://www.ncsl.org/research/energy/renewable-portfolio-standards.aspx (accessed 4/27/20).

Another important way in which RPSs differ is in terms of what counts as renewable energy. Generally, all of the standards include wind and solar power, but some have broader definitions of renewable sources (for example, many include energy efficiency), and several require a portion of the electricity to come from specific sources. For example, the Illinois RPS specifies that 75 percent comes from wind power, and the Maryland RPS requires that 2.5 percent comes from solar power.

Do RPS policies work? The graph below shows how much electricity has been generated from renewable sources since 2000. In states that have mandatory RPSs, electricity generation from non-hydroelectric renewable sources increased by almost 1,500 percent between 2000 and 2018. The use of renewable energy has grown in other states as well, but to a much smaller degree. For this reason, RPSs are often promoted as an effective way to reduce emissions of air pollutants, such as sulfur dioxide, nitrogen oxides, and volatile organic compounds that cause smog, and greenhouse gases like carbon dioxide that contribute to climate change.

Particularly in the absence of a strong national policy on renewable energy, state-level RPS policies have helped start a transition in the U.S. electricity sector toward cleaner, less carbon-intensive sources of energy.

Renewable Energy Generation*

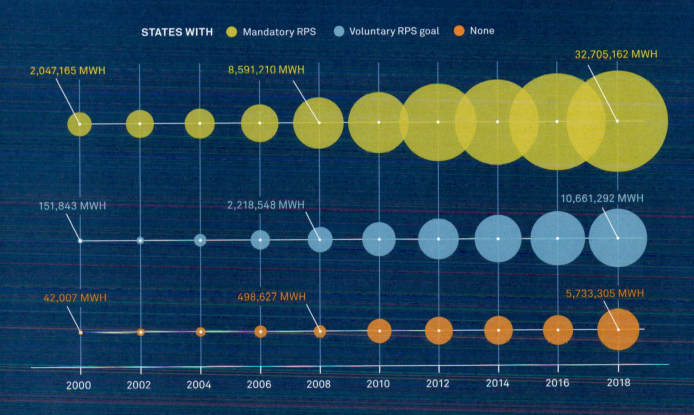

STATES WITH   ● Mandatory RPS   ● Voluntary RPS goal   ● None

2,047,165 MWH   8,591,210 MWH   32,705,162 MWH

151,843 MWH   2,218,548 MWH   10,661,292 MWH

42,007 MWH   498,627 MWH   5,733,305 MWH

2000   2002   2004   2006   2008   2010   2012   2014   2016   2018

* Non-hydroelectric renewable energy measured in megawatt hours.

SOURCE: U.S. Energy Information Administration, https://www.eia.gov/electricity/data/state/ (accessed 3/15/20).

 Given the trends illustrated in these figures, what outcomes might we observe in 2030 if states continue to adhere to such different policies?

Local governments became important in the early Republic because the states had little administrative capability or bureaucracy, so they relied on cities and counties to implement state laws. Today, like the national and state governments, the state and local governments within each state both cooperate and compete with one another, as shown, for example, in the mix of cooperation and rivalry between their police forces.

The Slow Growth of the National Government's Power

dual federalism

The system of government that prevailed in the United States from 1789 to 1937, in which most fundamental governmental powers were shared between the federal and state governments, with the states exercising the most important powers.

Before the 1930s, America's federal system was one of **dual federalism**, a two-layered system—national and state—in which the states and their local governments did most of the governing. We call it the traditional system because almost nothing about it changed during two-thirds of American history. The only exception was the four years of the Civil War, after which the traditional system resumed.

But there was more to dual federalism than merely the existence of two levels of government. As we have seen, the Constitution delegated specific powers to the national government and reserved all the rest to the states. That arrangement left a lot of room for interpretation, however, because of the final "elastic" clause of Article I, Section 8. The three words *necessary and proper* amounted to an invitation to struggle over the distribution of powers between national and state governments. We confront this struggle throughout the book. However, it is noteworthy that federalism remained dual for nearly two-thirds of American history, with the national government remaining steadfastly within a "strict construction" of Article I, Section 8.

The Supreme Court has, at times, weighed in on the debate over the distribution of powers between national and state governments, starting in 1819 with a decision favoring national power, *McCulloch v. Maryland*.[8] The issue was whether Congress had the power to charter a bank—in particular the Bank of the United States (created by Congress in 1791 over Thomas Jefferson's constitutional opposition)—because no power to create banks is mentioned in Article I, Section 8. Chief Justice John Marshall stated that such a power could be "implied" from other powers authorized in Article I, Section 8.

commerce clause

The clause, found in Article I, Section 8, of the Constitution, that delegates to Congress the power "to regulate Commerce with foreign Nations, and among the several States and with the Indian Tribes."

Specifically, Marshall cited the **commerce clause**, which gives Congress the power "to regulate Commerce with foreign nations, and among the several States and with Indian tribes," plus the final necessary and proper clause. Because the power to regulate commerce was expressly granted to Congress by the Constitution and chartering a bank was reasonably related to regulating commerce and not prohibited by the Constitution, Congress's action was deemed constitutionally permissible. Thus, the Court created the potential for significant increases in national governmental power.

The same case raised a second question of national power: whether Maryland's attempt to tax the bank was constitutional. Once again, Marshall and the Supreme Court sided with the national government, arguing that a bank created by a legislature representing all the American people (Congress) could not be taxed out of business by a state legislature (Maryland) representing only a small portion of the people. Here also the Supreme Court reinforced the supremacy clause: whenever a state law conflicts with a federal law, the state law is invalid because "the Laws of the United States . . . shall be the supreme Law of the Land." (For more on federal supremacy, see Chapters 2 and 8.)

This nationalistic interpretation of the Constitution was reinforced by *Gibbons v. Ogden* in 1824. At issue was whether the state of New York could grant a monopoly to a steamboat company to operate an exclusive service between New York and New Jersey. Aaron Ogden had obtained his license from the state, whereas Thomas Gibbons, a former partner of Ogden's, had obtained a competing license from the U.S. government. Chief Justice Marshall ruled that Gibbons could not be kept from competing, because with the commerce clause giving Congress the power "to regulate Commerce . . . among the several States," the state of New York did not have the power to grant this particular monopoly, which affected other states' interests. In his decision, Marshall insisted that the definition of commerce was "comprehensive" but added that the comprehensiveness was limited to "that commerce which concerns more states than one." This opinion gave rise to the legal concept that later came to be called interstate commerce.[9]

Despite the Court's broad interpretation of national power in the Republic's early years, between the 1820s and the 1930s, federal power grew only slowly. Toward the end of the nineteenth century, to be sure, a small number of important federal regulatory agencies, such as the Federal Trade Commission and the Interstate Commerce Commission, were built to establish the groundwork for federal economic management.

However, efforts to expand the national government's power were bitterly contested. During the Jacksonian period, a states' rights coalition developed in Congress. Among its most important members were state party leaders, who often had themselves appointed to the Senate, where they jealously guarded the powers of the states they ruled. Of course, members of Congress from the southern states had a particular reason to support states' rights: as long as the states were powerful and the federal government weak, the South's institution of slavery could not be threatened.

Aside from the interruption by the Civil War, the states' rights coalition dominated Congress and influenced presidential nominations (which were also controlled by the state party leaders) and judicial appointments (which required Senate confirmation) as well. Indeed, the Supreme Court turned away from John Marshall's nationalistic interpretation of the Constitution in favor of a states' rights interpretation—particularly in cases concerning the commerce clause. For many years, any federal effort to regulate commerce so as to discourage such things as fraud, the production of impure goods, the use of child labor, and dangerous working conditions or long hours was declared unconstitutional by the Supreme Court. The factory and the workplace, the Court ruled, were areas inherently local because the goods produced there had not yet passed into

FEDERAL AND STATE/LOCAL SPENDING, 1930-2019

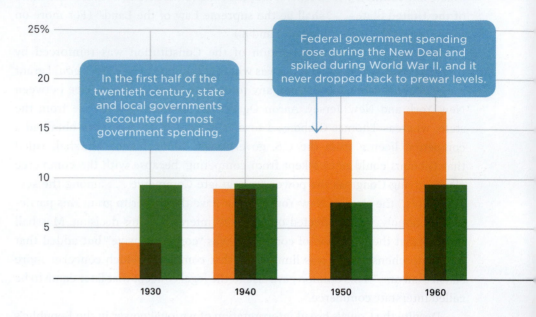

- ■ Federal government spending as a percentage of GDP*

- ■ State and local government spending as a percentage of GDP*

> In the first half of the twentieth century, state and local governments accounted for most government spending.

> Federal government spending rose during the New Deal and spiked during World War II, and it never dropped back to prewar levels.

*TIMEPLOT NOTE: GDP, or gross domestic product, is a measure of the economy as a whole based on the total value of goods and services produced within the country.

commerce and crossed state lines. Therefore, regulation of them constituted police power—a power reserved to the states.

No one questioned the power of the national government to regulate certain kinds of businesses, such as railroads, gas pipelines, and waterway transportation, because by their nature, they involved interstate commerce.[10] But well into the twentieth century, most other efforts by Congress to regulate commerce were blocked by the Supreme Court's interpretation of federalism.

For example, in the 1918 case of *Hammer v. Dagenhart*, the Court struck down a law prohibiting the interstate shipment of goods manufactured with the use of child labor. Congress had been careful to avoid outlawing the production of such goods within states and to prohibit only their interstate shipment. The Court, however, declared that the intent had been to outlaw their manufacture and that the law's language was merely a ruse.[11]

After his election in 1932, President Franklin Delano Roosevelt was eager to expand the power of the national government. His "New Deal" depended on governmental power to regulate the economy and to intervene in every aspect of American society, and it provoked sharp conflicts between the president and the federal courts. After appointing a host of new judges and threatening to expand the size of the Supreme Court, Roosevelt managed to bend the judiciary to his will. Beginning in 1937, the Court issued a series

timeplot

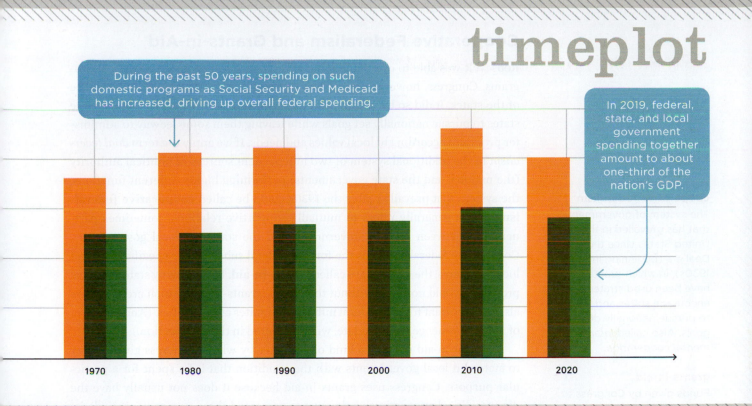

During the past 50 years, spending on such domestic programs as Social Security and Medicaid has increased, driving up overall federal spending.

In 2019, federal, state, and local government spending together amount to about one-third of the nation's GDP.

1970　1980　1990　2000　2010　2020

of decisions that once again made the commerce clause a great engine of national power.

One key case was *National Labor Relations Board v. Jones & Laughlin Steel Corporation*.[12] At issue was the National Labor Relations Act, which prohibited corporations from interfering with the efforts of employees to organize into unions, to bargain collectively over wages and working conditions, and to go on strike and engage in picketing. The newly formed National Labor Relations Board (NLRB) had ordered Jones & Laughlin to reinstate workers fired because of their union activities. The appeal reached the Supreme Court because the steel company had made a constitutional issue over the argument that its man-ufacturing activities, being local, were beyond the government's reach. But the Court ruled that a large corporation with subsidiaries and suppliers in many states was inherently involved in interstate commerce and hence subject to congressional regulation. In other decisions, the Court upheld minimum-wage laws, the Social Security Act, and federal rules controlling how much of any given commodity local farmers might grow.[13] These decisions and other New Deal programs were the beginning of a significant shift toward national govern-ment power. As the Timeplot shows, spending on federal programs surpassed spending by state and local governments after the 1940s and has increased over the past 80 years.

TIMEPLOT SOURCE: Michael Shuyler, "A Short History of Government Taxing and Spending in the United States," https://taxfoundation.org/short-history -government-taxing-and-spending -united-states/; Federal Reserve Economic Data, "Federal Net Outlays as Percent of Gross Domestic Product," https://fred.stlouisfed.org/series /FYONGDA188S and "State and Local Government Current Expenditures," https://fred.stlouisfed.org/series/SLEXPND (accessed 5/6/20).

Cooperative Federalism and Grants-in-Aid

Roosevelt was able to overcome judicial resistance to expansive New Deal programs. Congress, however, forced him to recognize the continuing importance of the states. It did so by crafting some programs in such a way as to encourage states to pursue nationally set goals while leaving them some leeway to administer programs according to local values and needs. If we apply the term *dual federalism* to the traditional system of two independent sources of political authority (the national and the state governments) performing highly different functions, the system that prevailed after the 1930s could be called **cooperative federalism**, which generally refers to mutually supportive relations, sometimes partnerships, between national government and the state and local governments. Cooperative federalism takes the form of federal subsidies for specific state and local programs; these funds are called **grants-in-aid**. In fact, many state and local programs would not exist without the federal grants-in-aid, which are therefore also an important form of federal influence on states and localities. (Another form of federal influence, the mandate, will be covered in the next section.)

A grant-in-aid is really a kind of incentive by which Congress gives money to state and local governments with the condition that it be spent for a particular purpose. Congress uses grants-in-aid because it does not usually have the direct political or constitutional power to command these governments to do its bidding. For example, after passage of the Affordable Care Act (popularly known as Obamacare) in 2010, 26 states challenged its constitutionality. Though the Supreme Court upheld other provisions of the act, it did rule that each state's government had the option to reject the new federal funding for and regulations of Medicaid mandated by the act. Eighteen states subsequently chose to opt out of the expansion of Medicaid eligibility.

Beginning in the late 1930s, Congress set national goals in specific policy categories, such as public housing and assistance to the unemployed, and provided grants-in-aid to meet these goals. The range of categories has expanded greatly over the decades, and the value of **categorical grants-in-aid** increased from $2.3 billion in 1950 to $750 billion in 2020 (Figure 3.1). Sometimes Congress requires the state or local government to match the national contribution dollar for dollar, but for some programs, such as the interstate highway system, the grant-in-aid provides 90 percent of the cost of the program.

For the most part, the categorical grants created before the 1960s simply helped the states perform their traditional functions, such as education and policing.[14] In the 1960s, however, the national role expanded dramatically. For example, during the 89th Congress (1965–66) alone, the number of categorical grant-in-aid programs grew from 221 to 379.[15] The grants authorized during the 1960s announced national purposes much more strongly than did earlier grants, and central among them was to provide opportunities to the poor.

Many of the categorical grants enacted during the 1960s were **project grants**, which require state and local governments to submit proposals to federal agencies.

cooperative federalism
The system of government that has prevailed in the United States since the New Deal era (beginning in the 1930s), in which grants-in-aid have been used strategically to encourage states and localities to pursue nationally defined goals. Also called *intergovernmental cooperation*.

grants-in-aid
Funds given by Congress to state and local governments on the condition that they be used for a specific purpose.

categorical grants-in-aid
Funds given to states and localities by Congress that are earmarked by law for specific policy categories, such as education or crime prevention.

project grants
Grants-in-aid for which state and local governments submit proposals to federal agencies, which provide funding for them on a competitive basis.

figure 3.1

THE HISTORICAL TREND OF CATEGORICAL GRANTS-IN-AID, 1950–2020

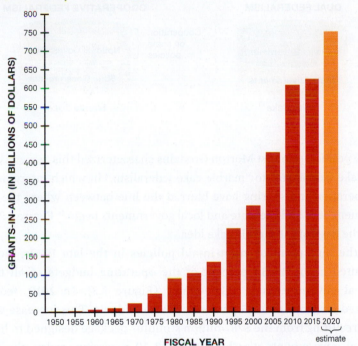

NOTE: Excludes outlays for national defense, international affairs, and net interest.

SOURCE: Office of Management and Budget, Table 12.1, https://www.whitehouse.gov/omb/historical-tables/ (accessed 2/14/20).

analyzing the evidence

Grants-in-aid began to expand dramatically during the 1960s. What political trends might explain this expansion? What are the ramifications of this trend for individuals and for states?

In contrast to the older **formula grants**, which used a formula (composed of such elements as need and state and local capacities) to distribute funds, project grants provided funding on a competitive basis to the proposals that agencies judged to be the best. In this way, the national government gained substantial control over which state and local governments got money, how much they got, and how they spent it. Examples include the Asbestos Hazard Emergency Act of 1986, which requires school districts to inspect for asbestos hazards and remove them from school buildings when necessary, and the Americans with Disabilities Act of 1990, which requires all state and local governments to promote access for the disabled to all government buildings. During his first term, President Trump attempted to exert control over states by threatening to withdraw aid from states and cities that refuse to enforce immigration laws.

A number of judicially developed rules govern federal mandates. In the 1987 Supreme Court decision in the case of *South Dakota v. Dole*, the Court held that mandates must be unambiguous, must not be "coercive," and must not force states to violate the U.S. Constitution.[16] The precise meaning of these stipulations should be clarified when the Supreme Court rules on challenges to President Trump's 2017 executive order withholding federal funds from states adopting sanctuary policies.[17]

formula grants
Grants-in-aid for which a formula is used to determine the amount of federal funds a state or local government will receive.

figure 3.2

TWO HISTORIC VIEWS OF FEDERALISM

DUAL FEDERALISM

National Government

State Governments

Layer Cake

Cooperation on some policies

COOPERATIVE FEDERALISM

National Government

State Governments

Marble Cake

The political scientist Morton Grodzins characterized this move as one from "layer cake federalism" to "marble cake federalism," in which intergovernmental cooperation and sharing have blurred the line between where the national government ends and the state and local governments begin.[18] Figure 3.2 demonstrates the basis of the marble cake idea.

At the high point of grant-in-aid policies in the late 1970s, federal aid contributed about 25–30 percent of the operating budgets of all the state and local governments in the country (Figure 3.3). In 2010, federal aid accounted for more than 35 percent of these budgets. This increase was temporary, resulting from the $787 billion stimulus package designed to help state and local governments weather the 2008–10 recession; today, the figure is 31 percent. Briefly, however, federal aid became the single largest source of state revenue, exceeding sales and property tax revenues for the first time in U.S. history.

Regulated Federalism and National Standards. Developments from the 1960s to the present have moved well beyond marble cake federalism to what might be called **regulated federalism**.[19] In some areas—especially civil rights, poverty programs, and environmental protection—the national government offers grant-in-aid financing to state and local governments for particular policies but threatens to withhold or withdraw it unless their versions of the policies conform to national standards. Such efforts to "set national standards" are also often made in interstate highway use, social services, and education.

The net effect of enforcing standards in this way is that state and local policies are more uniform from coast to coast. In addition, in other programs, the national government imposes obligations on the states without providing any funding at all. These obligations have come to be called **unfunded mandates**.[20]

These burdens became a major part of the rallying cry that produced the Republican Congress elected in 1994 and its Contract with America. One of that Congress's first measures was the Unfunded Mandates Reform Act (UMRA). A triumph of lobbying by state and local governments, UMRA was "hailed as both symbol and substance of a renewed congressional commitment to federalism."[21] Under this law, a point of order raised on the House or Senate floor can stop any

regulated federalism
A form of federalism in which Congress imposes legislation on state and local governments that requires them to meet national standards.

unfunded mandates
National standards or programs imposed on state and local governments by the federal government without accompanying funding or reimbursement.

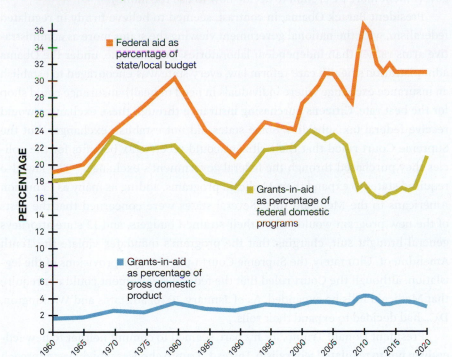

figure 3.3

THE RISE, DECLINE, AND RECOVERY OF FEDERAL AID, 1960–2020

Federal aid as percentage of state/local budget

Grants-in-aid as percentage of federal domestic programs

Grants-in-aid as percentage of gross domestic product

SOURCE: Robert J. Dilger, "Federal Grants to State and Local Governments," Congressional Research Service, 2017; Budget of the U.S. Government Fiscal Year 2020, https://www.whitehouse.gov/wp-content/uploads/2019/03/spec-fy2020.pdf (accessed 2/14/20).

analyzing the evidence

The extent to which state and local governments rely on federal funding has varied a great deal over time. What difference does it make if the states depend fiscally on the federal government?

mandate with an uncompensated state and local cost that the Congressional Budget Office estimates will exceed a certain amount.

This "stop, look, and listen" requirement forced Congress to own up to any mandate and its potential costs. UMRA does not prevent members of Congress from passing unfunded mandates; it only makes them think twice before they do. Moreover, it exempts several areas from coverage, and states must still enforce antidiscrimination laws and meet other requirements to receive federal assistance. Still, UMRA is a serious effort to shift power a bit further toward the state side.

New Federalism and the National-State Tug-of-War

Federalism in the United States is partly a tug-of-war between those seeking more uniform national standards and those seeking more variability from state to state. Even before UMRA, Presidents Richard Nixon and Ronald Reagan called their efforts to reverse the trend toward national standards and reestablish traditional policy making and implementation the "new federalism." They helped craft national policies that would return more discretion to the states. Examples include Nixon's revenue sharing and Reagan's **block grants**, which consolidated a number of categorical grants into one larger category, leaving the state (or local) government more discretion to decide how to use the money.

President Barack Obama, in contrast, seemed to believe firmly in regulated federalism, with the national government viewing the states more as administrative arms rather than independent laboratories. For example, under the Obama administration's health care reform law, every state was encouraged to establish an insurance exchange where individuals in need of health insurance could shop for the best rate. Citizens purchasing insurance through these exchanges would receive federal tax subsidies. Some states did not establish exchanges, but the Supreme Court ruled that their citizens could receive tax benefits for the policies they purchased through the federal government's exchange.[22] The law also required states to expand their Medicaid programs, adding as many as 15 million Americans to the Medicaid rolls. Several states were concerned that the costs of the new program would fall on their strained budgets, and 12 state attorneys general brought suit, charging that the program's mandates violate the Tenth Amendment. Ultimately, the Supreme Court upheld major provisions of the legislation, although the Court ruled that the federal government could not require that Medicaid rolls be expanded. As of January 2020, 36 states and Washington, D.C., had decided to expand their rolls.

President Donald Trump, for his part, seemed to commit neither to new federalism nor to regulated federalism. Instead, Trump chooses whichever approach serves his political goals. For example, in 2017, Trump issued an executive order reducing federal control over K–12 education. As he issued the order, Trump declared, "For too long, the government has imposed its will on state and local governments . . . my administration has been working to reverse this power grab."[23] Trump also gave the states more flexibility in implementing the Affordable Care Act in an effort to water down provisions he was unable to convince Congress to repeal. At the same time, however, in the realm of immigration, Trump seemed to be a champion of regulated federalism and has endeavored to prevent states from opposing his policies by threatening to withhold funds from those that do. Some states have responded by resisting federal directives; pundits have dubbed this action "uncooperative federalism." Several state attorneys general have filed suit against federal immigration and energy directives, among other policies.[24]

The Supreme Court as Referee. For much of the nineteenth century, federal power remained limited. The Tenth Amendment was often cited to support the idea of **states' rights**. Some proponents of this idea claimed that the states did not have to submit to national laws when they believed the national government had exceeded its authority. These arguments in favor of states' rights were voiced less often after the Civil War. But the Supreme Court continued to use the Tenth Amendment to strike down laws that it thought exceeded constitutional limits on national power, including a Civil Rights Act passed in 1875.

Evolution of the Federal System

1789–1834   **Nationalization:** The Marshall Court interprets the Constitution broadly so as to expand and consolidate national power.

1835–1930s   **Dual federalism:** The functions of the national government are very specifically defined. States do much of the fundamental governing that affects citizens' day-to-day lives. There is tension between the two levels of government, and the power of the national government begins to increase.

1930s–1970s   **Cooperative federalism:** The national government uses grants-in-aid to encourage states and localities to pursue nationally defined goals.

1970s–   **Regulated federalism:** The national government sets conditions that states and localities must meet in order to receive certain grants. The national government also sets national standards in policy areas without providing states and localities with funding to meet them.

1980s–2020   **New federalism:** The national government attempts to return more power to the states through block grants to them.

In the early twentieth century, however, the Tenth Amendment appeared to lose its force. Reformers began to press for national regulations to limit the power of large corporations and to preserve the health and welfare of citizens, and the Supreme Court began to uphold many of these laws. By the late 1930s, the Court had approved such an expansion of federal power that the Tenth Amendment appeared irrelevant.

Recent decades have seen a revival of interest in the Tenth Amendment and important Supreme Court decisions limiting federal power. Much of the interest stems from conservatives who believe that a strong federal government threatens individual liberties, and thus power should be returned or "devolved" to the states.

One of the most important Supreme Court rulings in this area came in the 1995 case of *United States v. Lopez*. Stating that Congress had exceeded its authority under the commerce clause, the Court struck down a federal law that barred handguns near schools.[25] Another significant Tenth Amendment decision came in the 1997 case *Printz v. United States* (joined with *Mack v. United States*),[26] in which the Court struck down a key provision of the Brady Bill, enacted in 1993 to regulate gun sales. Under the act, state and local law enforcement officers were required to conduct background checks on prospective gun purchasers. The Court held that the federal government cannot require states to administer or enforce federal regulatory programs. This trend continued with the 2006 *Gonzales v. Oregon* case, in which the Court ruled that the federal government could not use federal drug laws to interfere with Oregon's assisted-suicide law.[27] These rulings signaled a move toward greater independence for the states.

By 2012, however, the Court once again seemed to favor national power in the national-state tug-of-war. In addition to the Obamacare decision cited earlier, the Court struck down portions of an Arizona immigration law, declaring that immigration was a federal, not a state, matter.[28] And in a 2013 decision, it struck down an Arizona law requiring individuals to show documentation of citizenship when registering to vote. The Court ruled that this requirement was preempted by the federal National Voter Registration Act, which requires states to use the official federal registration form.[29] In two other cases, the Court ruled against state legislatures on questions involving congressional-district boundaries.[30]

At the same time, the Court has revived the Eleventh Amendment concept of **state sovereign immunity**. This legal doctrine holds that states are immune from lawsuits by private individuals claiming that the state violated a law enacted by Congress. In a 1996 ruling that prevented Seminole Indians from suing the state of Florida in federal court, the Supreme Court used the Eleventh Amendment to limit the federal government's power over the states. A 1988 law had given tribes the right to sue a state in federal court if the state did not in good faith negotiate issues related to gambling casinos on tribal land. The Court's ruling appeared to signal a much broader limitation on national power by raising new questions about whether individuals can sue a state if it fails to uphold federal law.[31]

The Court, however, shifted direction again in 2018. In the case of *Murphy v. NCAA*, the Court held that a federal law prohibiting the states from authorizing sports gambling constituted a violation of its previous edicts prohibiting the federal government from "commandeering" state executive or legislative authority.[32] And, in a widely discussed 2019 decision, the Supreme Court ruled that the federal courts could not impose their own judgments upon the states when it came to the drawing of legislative district boundaries.[33] Thus, even if state legislatures

state sovereign immunity
A legal doctrine holding that states cannot be sued for violating an act of Congress.

In 2019, the Supreme Court ruled that the federal courts could not weigh in on the drawing of legislative district boundaries, even if state legislatures engaged in partisan gerrymandering. Thus, the court left it up to states and state courts to decide how to handle political questions like gerrymandering.

engaged in partisan gerrymandering, this was beyond the constitutional power of the federal courts to address. The opinion addressed only the issue of partisan gerrymandering designed to help one or the other political party; presumably, racial gerrymandering would still not be allowed. Moreover, partisan gerrymandering complaints could still be brought in the state courts.

Of course, shifting interpretations of the Constitution often reflect underlying struggles for political power, and the political forces controlling the national government generally advocate a jurisprudence of nationalism. Those uncertain of their ability to control Capitol Hill and the White House but more sure of their hold on some states support respect for state power. Until recently, Republicans, who have controlled a majority of the states, have expressed respect for states' rights, while Democrats have sought to increase the power of the federal government. Since Donald Trump's election, however, Democrats have manifested a newfound respect for the states, supporting, for example, the idea that states and even localities can refuse to enforce federal immigration policies and declare themselves to be "sanctuaries" for undocumented immigrants. Democrats also support the right of states like California to continue to abide by the Paris climate accord even though President Trump pulled the federal government out of the agreement in 2017. This idea, in effect, supported the rights of states to conduct their own foreign policies, though the issue of the Paris accord became moot after President Biden announced that the U.S. would rejoin the agreement. Debates over federalism will continue as states and the national government tangle over issues like sanctuary cities, as well as the legalization of marijuana (see the Policy Principle on p. 72).

THE SEPARATION OF POWERS

As we have noted, the separation of powers enables several different federal institutions to influence the nation's agenda, to affect decisions, and to prevent the other institutions from taking action. The Constitution's framers saw this arrangement, although cumbersome, as an essential means of protecting liberty.

In his discussion of the separation of powers, James Madison quoted the originator of the idea, the French political thinker Baron de Montesquieu: "There can be no liberty where the legislative and executive powers are united in the same person . . . [or] if the power of judging be not separated from the legislative and executive powers."[34] Using the same reasoning, many of Madison's contemporaries argued that there was not *enough* separation among the three branches, and Madison had to backtrack to insist that complete separation was not required:

> Unless these departments [branches] be so far connected and blended as to give to each a constitutional control over the others, the degree of separation which the maxim requires, as essential to a free government, can never in practice be duly maintained.[35]

the policy principle
FEDERAL VS. STATE MARIJUANA LAWS

In 2012, the citizens of Colorado and Washington voted to legalize recreational use of marijuana. Similar ballot measures passed soon after in six other states—Alaska and Oregon later in 2012, and then California, Maine, Massachusetts, and Nevada in 2016. Yet, despite clear changes in these states' laws, any form of marijuana use and possession remains illegal under federal law. Specifically, marijuana is included as a Schedule I controlled substance (alongside cocaine, heroin, and other drugs) in the Controlled Substances Act (CSA) enacted by Congress in 1970. As a result, cultivation and distribution of marijuana remains a felony under federal law, regardless of state law, a position that was reinforced by the Supreme Court in 2005.

With federalism, the framers of the Constitution wanted to create an institutional arrangement that would disperse power across the national government and the states, to avoid concentrating power in just a few hands. However, as the case of marijuana laws shows, this institutional arrangement complicates policy on some issues—particularly when federal and state law clearly conflict.

Conflicting state and federal laws regarding marijuana put many people who are following their state law at risk of being charged with a federal crime. Under federal law, individual users of marijuana (charged with possession with no intent to distribute) can be sentenced to up to a year in prison combined with fines of up to $1,000, and people involved in the marijuana business can face steeper fines up to $25,000 and up to five years in prison. It is not only growers and distributors who risk incurring penalties under federal law but any other business that provides goods and services to a marijuana dispensary can be charged with profiting from an illegal drug business. Landlords who rent to marijuana dispensaries risk both fines and federal asset forfeiture, in which the police are allowed to seize money and property simply based on a suspicion that the asset was used to commit a federal crime.

Despite the clear federal law, the federal government has not prioritized the enforcement of federal marijuana law in states that have legalized marijuana. One reason is the federal government depends on cooperation from state and local law enforcement, who are unlikely to help federal agents raid dispensaries that are legal under their own state law. In fact, state legislatures in California and Washington have considered bills that would prohibit a state or local agency from assisting federal agencies in marijuana investigations or enforcement.

A medical marijuana dispensary in Oregon.

This hands-off approach by the federal government was made more explicit in 2013 when the Obama administration issued the Cole Memorandum. This memo—addressed to federal prosecutors—stated that the Justice Department would not enforce federal marijuana laws in states that have legalized use of marijuana, except in cases in which there is harm to the public (for example, cases involving gang operations or selling drugs to children). However, this approach was challenged by President Trump's attorney general Jeff Sessions who emphasized that the federal government retained authority to enforce federal drug laws regardless of state law, rescinding the Cole Memorandum in early 2018, and raising more questions about the appropriate balance of state and federal authority in this policy area.

think it through

1. If marijuana were removed from the federal Controlled Substances Act, what implications would this have for states that have legalized marijuana? What about for states that have not, particularly states like Arizona or Ohio where the public voted "no" on legalization at the state level?

2. Should the federal executive branch be able to determine whether they enforce federal marijuana law in states where it is legal, or should they enforce the federal law equally in all states? Why?

This is the secret of how Americans have made the separation of powers effective: they have made it self-enforcing by giving each branch of government the means to participate in, and partially or temporarily obstruct, the workings of the other branches.

Checks and Balances

The means by which each branch of government interacts with every other branch is known informally as *checks and balances*. The best-known examples are shown in Figure 3.4. The framers tried to guarantee that the three branches would in fact use these checks and balances as weapons against one another by giving each branch a different political constituency—a different group of voters or individuals by which its members are chosen and therefore a different perspective on what the government ought to do. For example, the framers adopted direct, popular election for the members of the House, indirect election of senators through state legislatures (until the Seventeenth Amendment, adopted in 1913), indirect election of the president through the Electoral College, and appointment of federal judges for life. All things considered, the best characterization of the separation-of-powers principle in action is, as we said in Chapter 2, "separated institutions sharing power."[36]

Legislative Supremacy

Although each branch was given adequate means to compete with the other branches, the framers provided for **legislative supremacy** by making Congress the preeminent branch. Legislative supremacy made the provision of checks and balances in the other two branches all the more important.

The most important indication of the intentions of the framers was the provisions in Article I to treat the powers of the national government as powers of Congress. The Founders also provided for legislative supremacy in their decision to give Congress the sole power over appropriations.

Although "presidential government" gradually took the place of legislative supremacy after 1937, the relative power of the executive and legislative branches since that time has varied. The power play between the president and Congress is especially intense during periods of **divided government**, when one party controls the White House and another controls all or part of Capitol Hill.

A recent example of the power play during periods of divided government occurred in 2018 when President Trump declared a national emergency along America's southern border and then issued executive orders diverting funds from the Pentagon's budget to start work on a border wall. Congress reacted sharply. The House of Representatives voted to block the president's emergency declaration and even some GOP lawmakers sharply criticized the president's actions. After the Democrats won control of the House of Representatives later that year, they launched a number of investigations into the activities of President Trump and his aides. Trump responded by ordering White House staffers and other

legislative supremacy
The preeminent position within the national government that the Constitution assigns to Congress.

divided government
The condition in American government in which one party controls the presidency, while the opposing party controls one or both houses of Congress.

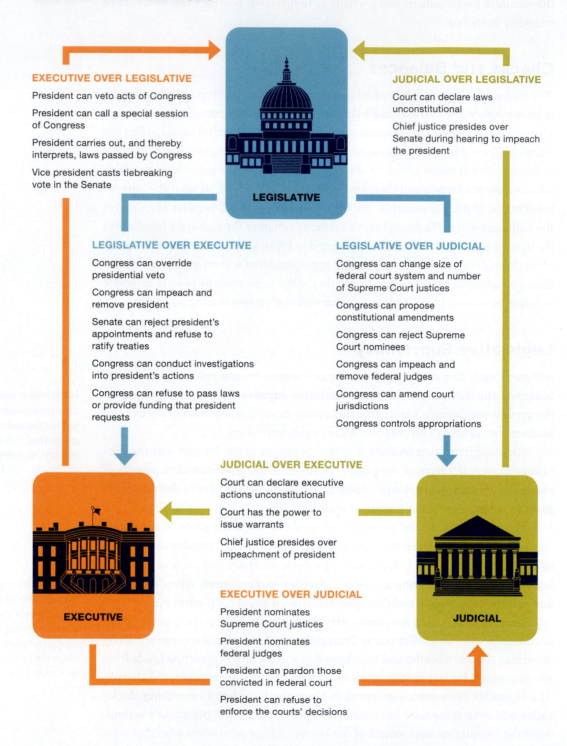

figure 3.4

CHECKS AND BALANCES

EXECUTIVE OVER LEGISLATIVE

President can veto acts of Congress

President can call a special session of Congress

President carries out, and thereby interprets, laws passed by Congress

Vice president casts tiebreaking vote in the Senate

JUDICIAL OVER LEGISLATIVE

Court can declare laws unconstitutional

Chief justice presides over Senate during hearing to impeach the president

LEGISLATIVE

LEGISLATIVE OVER EXECUTIVE

Congress can override presidential veto

Congress can impeach and remove president

Senate can reject president's appointments and refuse to ratify treaties

Congress can conduct investigations into president's actions

Congress can refuse to pass laws or provide funding that president requests

LEGISLATIVE OVER JUDICIAL

Congress can change size of federal court system and number of Supreme Court justices

Congress can propose constitutional amendments

Congress can reject Supreme Court nominees

Congress can impeach and remove federal judges

Congress can amend court jurisdictions

Congress controls appropriations

JUDICIAL OVER EXECUTIVE

Court can declare executive actions unconstitutional

Court has the power to issue warrants

Chief justice presides over impeachment of president

EXECUTIVE OVER JUDICIAL

President nominates Supreme Court justices

President nominates federal judges

President can pardon those convicted in federal court

President can refuse to enforce the courts' decisions

EXECUTIVE

JUDICIAL

officials to refuse to testify before Congress and by asserting executive privilege to deny Congress access to information. This tactic touched off a series of legal battles between the president and the Congress. Some members of Congress declared that the president should be impeached. House Speaker Nancy Pelosi resisted calls for Trump's impeachment, saying that Democrats should focus their energies on defeating Trump in the 2020 national election, but after evidence of Trump withholding congressionally approved defense funding for Ukraine in an attempt to obtain information on a political opponent, he was eventually impeached in the House but ultimately acquitted in the Senate.

think it through

Do the results of the 2020 elections demonstrate divided government? How do you think Congress will react as the president begins implementing his agenda?

The Role of the Supreme Court

The role of the judicial branch in the separation of powers has depended on the power of judicial review, a power not provided for in the Constitution but asserted by Chief Justice Marshall in 1803:

> If a law be in opposition to the Constitution; if both the law and the Constitution apply to a particular case, so that the Court must either decide that case conformable to the law, disregarding the Constitution, or conformable to the Constitution, disregarding the law; the Court must determine which of these conflicting rules governs the case: This is of the very essence of judicial duty.[37]

Review of the constitutionality of acts of the president or Congress is relatively rare. For example, there were no Supreme Court reviews of congressional acts in the 50-plus years between *Marbury v. Madison* (1803) and *Dred Scott v. Sandford* (1857). In the century or so between the Civil War and 1970, 84 acts of Congress were held unconstitutional (in whole or in part), but there were long periods of complete Court deference to Congress, punctuated by flurries of judicial review during periods of social upheaval. The most significant of these periods was 1935–36, when 12 acts of Congress were invalidated, blocking virtually the entire New Deal program.[38]

Then, after 1937, when the Court made its great reversals in upholding New Deal legislation, no significant acts were struck down until 1983, when the Court declared unconstitutional the legislative veto, a practice in which Congress authorized the president to take certain actions but reserved the right to veto those with which it disagreed.[39] The Supreme Court became much more activist (that is, less deferential to Congress) after the elevation of William H. Rehnquist to chief justice (1986–2005), and "a new program of judicial activism"[40]

The system of checks and balances ensures that political power is shared by the separate institutions. Here, President Donald Trump meets with the 116th Congress leadership: Senate Majority Leader Mitch McConnell, Senate Minority Leader Chuck Schumer, and House Speaker Nancy Pelosi.

seemed to be in place. Between 1995 and 2002, at least 26 congressional acts or parts of acts were struck down on constitutional grounds.[41]

The Court has been far more deferential toward the president since the New Deal period, with only five significant confrontations. One was the so-called steel seizure case of 1952, in which the Court refused to permit President Truman to use "emergency powers" to force workers back into the steel mills during the Korean War.[42]

In 1974, the Court declared unconstitutional President Nixon's refusal to respond to a subpoena to make available his tapes of White House conversations as evidence in a criminal prosecution. The Court argued that although the claim of **executive privilege** protected confidentiality of communications between the president and close advisers, this privilege did not extend to data in presidential files or tapes bearing on criminal prosecutions.[43]

During the Trump administration, a number of federal district and circuit courts have ruled against the president, particularly on immigration issues. The Supreme Court, however, has thus far refrained from directly confronting the president. The closest it has come involved the matter of whether a citizenship question could be added to the 2020 census. The administration had sought to ask respondents whether or not they were citizens. Critics charged that the question was designed to reduce legislative representation and federal funding to states with large numbers of undocumented immigrants. Lower federal courts had ruled that the question should be removed and the Supreme Court refused to make a final determination. The Supreme Court ruled that the Commerce Department did not provide adequate justification from including the question in 2020, but might reinstate it in the future.[44]

executive privilege
The claim that confidential communications between a president and close advisers should not be revealed without the consent of the president.

CONCLUSION

Do federalism and the separation of power make government more representative? Do they make government more effective? Federalism and the separation of powers are two of the most important constitutional principles that form the basis of the United States' system of limited government. As we have seen, federalism limits the power of the national government in numerous ways. By its very existence, federalism recognizes the principle of two sources of independent political authority: the national government and the state governments (hence the term *dual federalism*). In addition, the Constitution specifically restrained the power of the national government to regulate the economy.

As a result, the states were free to do most of the fundamental governing for the first century and a half of American government. This situation began to change during and following the New Deal, as the national government began to exert more influence over the states through grants-in-aid and mandates. But even as the powers of the national government grew, so did the powers of the states.

In recent decades, a countertrend to the growth of national power has developed as Congress has opted to devolve some of its powers to the states. But the problem that arises with devolution is that programs that were once uniform across the country (because they were the national government's responsibility) can become highly variable, with some states providing benefits and services not available in other states. To a point, variation can be considered one of the virtues of federalism. But in a democracy, large variations and inequalities in the provision of services and benefits carry inherent dangers.

For example, the Food and Drug Administration has been under attack in recent years. Could the government address the agency's perceived problems by devolving its regulatory tasks to the states? Would people care if drugs required "caution" labels in some states but not in others? Devolution, as attractive as it may seem, is not an approach that can be applied across the board without careful analysis of the nature of the program and of the problems it is designed to solve.

A key puzzle of federalism is deciding when differences across states reflect proper democratic decisions by individual states and when they reflect inequalities that should not be tolerated. Sometimes a decision to eliminate differences is made on the grounds of equality and individual rights, as in the Civil Rights Act of 1964, which outlawed segregation. At other times, a stronger federal role is justified on the grounds of national interest, as in the adoption of a national 55-mile-per-hour speed limit to improve fuel efficiency during the oil shortage in the 1970s.

Advocates of a more limited federal role often point to the value of democracy. Governmental actions can more easily be tailored to fit distinctive state or local desires if states and localities have more power to make policy. Viewed this way, variation across states can be an expression of democratic will.

Another feature of limited government—separation of powers—is shown in our system of checks and balances, in which separate institutions of government share power with each other. Even though the Constitution clearly provided for legislative supremacy, checks and balances have functioned well. Indeed, some would say this system has worked too well. The last 50 years have witnessed long periods of divided government, when one party controls the White House while the other controls one or both houses of Congress. During these periods, the level of conflict between the executive and legislative branches has been particularly severe, resulting in what some analysts derisively call "gridlock."[45]

During President George W. Bush's first six years in office, the separation of powers did not seem to work effectively, as a Congress controlled by the president's fellow Republicans gave Bush free rein in such important matters as the war in Iraq and the war against terrorism. In 2006, Democrats won control of both houses and began to scrutinize the president's actions carefully. With the election of Democrat Barack Obama to the presidency in 2008, Congress and the

From 1974 to 1987, the federal government set a national maximum speed limit at 55 miles per hour to help conserve fuel following the oil shortage of the 1970s. Since 1995, the states have been free to set their own limits, and in some areas of Texas the speed limit is as high as 85 miles per hour.

think it through

Think about how your state differs from neighboring states. Is the economy more dependent on agriculture or global business? What social issues are important to citizens? Does federalism help America deal more effectively with these differences?

presidency were once again controlled by the same party. But Republicans took control of the House of Representatives in 2010, and in 2014 the Senate as well, challenging the president's domestic and foreign policies. At times, the stalemate between Congress and the president nearly paralyzed the government.

In 2016, the Republicans won control of the White House and retained control of both houses of Congress. Though a number of Republican congressional leaders had been lukewarm to Donald Trump's presidential candidacy, all pledged to work with the new president on behalf of a Republican agenda. It seemed that the GOP now had an opportunity to enact legislation supporting its vision of American foreign and domestic policy. Republicans took advantage of this opportunity in December 2017 when Congress enacted and the president signed a major piece of tax reform legislation. Bipartisan cooperation, however, was short lived.

After the 2018 elections gave Democrats control of the House of Representatives, congressional investigators looked into every nook and cranny of the Trump administration and its policies. Many Democrats hoped to find evidence that would lead to the president's impeachment, and they did when a report from a whistle blower surfaced in August of 2019 claiming Trump tried to withhold congressionally approved aid to Ukraine unless that country agreed to investigate his political opponent and future Democratic presidential challenger, Joe Biden. Trump was impeached in the House on accounts of abuse of power and obstruction of Congress, but he was ultimately acquitted by the Senate. For his part, Trump made no secret of his disdain for Congress and its leaders, often referring to House Speaker Nancy Pelosi as "Nervous Nancy" and calling her a "nasty, vindictive, horrible person" in a televised interview with Fox News.

Joe Biden's victory in 2020, along with continued Democratic control of the House of Representatives meant that, for at least two years, House investigators would be unlikely to harass the president. Republicans, however, indicated that if they retained control of the Senate, they would be looking into charges of voter fraud in 2020.

Key Terms

Check Your Understanding

1. Why did the framers adopt federalism in the Constitution? What powers are reserved for the states? What powers are reserved for the national government? What happens if a power isn't clearly delegated to the national government or denied to the states by the Constitution?

2. How has federalism evolved over time in the United States? What are the differences between dual federalism—or the traditional system—and cooperative federalism?

3. How does the Constitution incorporate checks and balances into the legislative, executive, and judicial systems? How does this demonstrate "separated institutions sharing power"?

4. How does legislative supremacy make Congress the preeminent branch of government?

5. What is the significance of *Marbury v. Madison*? How has the role of the judicial branch in the separation of powers depended on the power of judicial review?

INQUIZITIVE

Earn a better grade on your test. InQuizitive personalizes your learning path to help you master the concepts from this chapter. In a recent efficacy study of American government students, InQuizitive increased test scores by an average of 17 points (see back cover).

CHAPTER FOUR

CIVIL LIBERTIES AND CIVIL RIGHTS

The Declaration of Independence states that governments are created to protect "life, liberty, and the pursuit of happiness." American students learn these phrases in school, but we often don't notice that they include a contradiction: a government strong enough and effective enough to protect life might also pose a threat to liberty.

This contradiction often arises in the realm of national security. For example, to protect against the threat of terrorism, over the past decade the U.S. government has expanded its power to eavesdrop on citizens' communications, search people and their homes, and monitor their travels. Most Americans have come to take airport body scanners for granted, and we may joke nervously that the government is tracking our online activity, while some people argue that even stronger measures may be needed in order to keep Americans safe.

The framers of the Constitution would have had concerns about such invasions of privacy. To the framers, political liberty required that citizens be protected from governmental surveillance and from searches into citizens' private affairs. They were concerned that government agents would, in the name of order and safety, search private homes for evidence of political opposition—a British practice that the Founders wanted to prevent in the new United States. This concern lies at the heart of the Constitution's Fourth Amendment, which prohibits "unreasonable searches and seizures."

The fear that strong, effective governance could cross the line and become abusive governance led many, though not all, of the Founders to support the idea of adding a bill of rights to the Constitution. Thomas Jefferson, for example, said that a bill of rights "is what people are entitled to against every government on earth."[1] Note the wording: *against government*. Though effective government was necessary, Jefferson thought citizens always needed protection from the possibility that the government would abuse its power.

The Constitution's first ten amendments are collectively known as the Bill of Rights. The Bill of Rights is the main, but not only, part of the Constitution that addresses two types of checks on the potential abuse of governmental power: civil liberties and civil rights. *Civil liberties* are phrased as negatives (what government *cannot* do). For example, the First Amendment states, "Congress shall make *no* law . . . abridging the freedom of speech, or of the press" (emphasis added).

Civil rights, on the other hand, are obligations (what government *must* do) to guarantee equal citizenship and protect citizens from discrimination. Civil rights regulate *who* can participate in the political process and civil society and *how* they can participate—for example, who can vote, who can hold office, who can have a trial or serve on juries, and when and how citizens can petition the government to take action. Civil rights also define how people are treated in employment, education, and other aspects of American society.

Both civil liberties and civil rights are essential elements of representative government. Without civil liberties such as freedom of speech and of the press, citizens might not be able to make their voices heard in government. Without basic civil rights, there would be no equality of representation. And finally, without representation in governmental decision making, citizens might find it difficult to protect both their liberties and their rights.

To the framers, liberty required that citizens be protected from governmental surveillance and from searches into citizens' private affairs. Do security measures like TSA airport body scanners violate civil liberties?

- **How did the framers of the Constitution view the relationship between liberty and government? How do civil rights promote representation?**

In this chapter, we examine the origins and evolution of civil liberties and civil rights in the United States and see how both contribute to and are in turn strengthened by representative government.

Learning Objectives

- Describe how the civil liberties protections included in the Bill of Rights were gradually applied to state governments, in addition to the federal government.

- Identify the major civil liberties provisions in the Bill of Rights and how Supreme Court cases have shaped today's interpretation of each of them.

- Explain the historical struggle for voting rights and equal protection for women and racial and ethnic minorities.

- Analyze how these movements became models for other groups to press civil rights claims.

- Identify the criteria that the Supreme Court has used in determining whether affirmative action programs are constitutional.

civil liberties

The protections of citizens from improper governmental action.

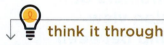

think it through

How does the Bill of Rights factor into our foundational understanding of what it means to be a citizen of the United States? How do debates over these rights—such as the separation of church and state, free speech, the right to bear arms—continue to inspire debate today?

CIVIL LIBERTIES: NATIONALIZING THE BILL OF RIGHTS

Civil liberties protect citizens from improper governmental action. The Bill of Rights includes a series of "thou shalt nots"—limits on *what* the government has the power to do and *how* it acts. For example, the Bill of Rights forbids the government from establishing a state religion, quartering troops in private homes without consent, or seizing private property without just compensation. Other provisions outline the procedures that government must follow when it acts. For instance, the government can arrest and imprison people who violate its criminal laws, but only if it follows the procedures designed to protect the accused.

As we saw in Chapter 2, the Bill of Rights was added to the Constitution in 1791, almost immediately after the Constitution was ratified. In our discussion of civil liberties, we will consider each of the major provisions of the Bill of Rights and how court decisions have shaped today's understanding of those protections. However, we begin with a fundamental question that was left open when the Bill of Rights was adopted: Did it protect citizens from improper action by only the national government, or also by state governments?

The First Amendment says, "Congress shall make no law respecting an establishment of religion . . . or abridging freedom of speech, or of the press; or the right of [assembly and petition]." But this is the only part of the Bill of Rights that specifically addresses the national government. For example, the Second Amendment provides that "the right of the people to keep and bear Arms shall not be infringed." The Fifth Amendment says, among other things, that no person shall "be deprived of life, liberty, or property, without due process of law"; and that private property cannot be taken "without just compensation."[2] The fact that the First Amendment is the only part of the Bill of Rights that explicitly refers to the national government raises a question: Do the remaining parts put limits on state governments or only on the national government?

Dual Citizenship

The question of whether the Bill of Rights also limits state governments appeared to be settled in 1833 in the case *Barron v. Baltimore*, and the facts were simple. In paving its streets, the city of Baltimore had disposed of so much sand and gravel in the water near John Barron's wharf—where ships would load and unload cargo—that the wharf's value was virtually destroyed. Barron took the city to court on the grounds that it had deprived him of his property without just compensation. He argued that, under the Fifth Amendment, this action by the city was unconstitutional.

However, Chief Justice John Marshall, in one of the most significant Supreme Court decisions ever handed down, said,

> The Constitution was ordained and established by the people of the United States for themselves, for their own government, and not for the government of the individual States. Each State established a constitution for itself, and in that constitution provided such limitations and restrictions on the powers of its particular government as its judgment dictated. . . . If these propositions be correct, *the fifth amendment must be understood as restraining the power of the general government, not as applicable to the States.*[3] (emphasis added)

In other words, if the national government had deprived Barron of his property, he would have won his case, because of the provisions of the Fifth Amendment. But if the state constitution of Maryland contained no provision protecting citizens from such action by the state government, then Barron would have had no legal case against the city of Baltimore, an agency of the state of Maryland.

Barron v. Baltimore confirmed the idea of "dual citizenship"—that each American was a citizen of the national government and *separately* a citizen of one of the states. This meant that the Bill of Rights did not apply to decisions or procedures of state (or local) governments. Even slavery could continue, because the Bill of Rights could not protect anyone from state laws treating people as property. This understanding of how the Bill of Rights should be applied lasted for several decades, until the aftermath of the Civil War and the adoption of the Fourteenth Amendment.

The Fourteenth Amendment

After the defeat of the South and the end of the Civil War in 1865, there was more "united" than "states" to the United States. It was clear that secession was not a realistic option for any state. Left unanswered, however, was just how

The Bill of Rights

- **AMENDMENT I: LIMITS ON CONGRESS**
  Congress cannot make any law establishing a religion or abridging freedoms of religious exercise, speech, assembly, or petition.

- **AMENDMENTS II, III, IV: LIMITS ON THE EXECUTIVE**
  The executive branch cannot infringe on the right of people to keep arms (II), cannot arbitrarily take houses for militia (III), and cannot search for or seize evidence or arrest people without a court warrant swearing to the probable existence of a crime (IV).

- **AMENDMENTS V, VI, VII, VIII: LIMITS ON THE JUDICIARY**
  The courts cannot hold trials for serious offenses without provision for a grand jury (V); a trial jury (VII); a speedy trial (VI); presentation of charges and confrontation by the accused of hostile witnesses (VI); immunity from testimony against oneself, and immunity from trial more than once for the same offense (V). Furthermore, neither bail nor punishment can be excessive (VIII), and no property can be taken without "just compensation" (V).

- **AMENDMENTS IX, X: LIMITS ON THE NATIONAL GOVERNMENT**
  Any rights not enumerated are reserved to the states or the people (X), and the enumeration of certain rights in the Constitution should not be interpreted to mean that those are the only rights the people have (IX).

much the states were required to obey the Constitution and, in particular, the Bill of Rights.

Adopted in 1868, the Fourteenth Amendment seemed almost perfectly designed to impose the Bill of Rights on the states and thereby to reverse *Barron v. Baltimore*. Consider the amendment's very first words:

> All persons born or naturalized in the United States, and subject to the jurisdiction thereof, are citizens of the United States and of the State wherein they reside.

This statement provides for a single national citizenship under the U.S. Constitution, which, at a minimum, means that civil liberties should not vary drastically from state to state. This interpretation of the Fourteenth Amendment is reinforced by the next clause:

> No state shall make or enforce any law which shall abridge the privileges or immunities of citizens of the United States; nor shall any state deprive any person of life, liberty, or property, without due process of law.

All of this reads like an effort to extend the entire Bill of Rights to all citizens, no matter which state they reside in.[4] But this was not to be the Supreme Court's interpretation for nearly 100 years. Within five years of ratification of the Fourteenth Amendment, the Court was making decisions as though the amendment had never been adopted.[5]

Table 4.1 outlines the major developments in the history of the Fourteenth Amendment against the backdrop of *Barron*, citing particular provisions of the Bill of Rights as they were "incorporated" by Supreme Court decisions into the Fourteenth Amendment. When we say that a provision from the Bill of Rights is incorporated into the Fourteenth Amendment, we mean that the Supreme Court has ruled that it legally applies to all of the states, not just to the national government.

The only change in civil liberties during the first 60 years after the Fourteenth Amendment came in 1897, when the Supreme Court held that the amendment's due process clause did in fact prohibit states from taking property for public use—a power called eminent domain—without just compensation, as required by the Fifth Amendment.[6] This decision effectively overruled the specific decision in *Barron v. Baltimore*, but the Court had "incorporated" into the Fourteenth Amendment *only* the property protection provision of the Fifth Amendment, leaving aside its other protections of civil liberties.

No further expansion of civil liberties through incorporation occurred until 1925, when the Supreme Court held that freedom of speech is "among the fundamental personal rights and 'liberties' protected by the due process clause of the Fourteenth Amendment from impairment by the states."[7] In 1931, the Supreme Court added freedom of the press to that list; in 1934, it added freedom of religion; and in 1937, freedom of assembly.[8] But that was as far as the Court would go.

The shadow of *Barron v. Baltimore* extended into the mid-twentieth century, despite adoption of the Fourteenth Amendment. At the time of World War II, the Constitution, as interpreted by the Supreme Court, left standing the framework in which the states had the power to determine their own law on numerous fundamental issues. It left states with the power to pass laws segregating the races. It also left them with the power to engage in searches and seizures without a warrant, to indict people accused of a crime without benefit of a grand jury, to deprive citizens of trial by jury, to force people to testify against themselves, to deprive the accused of their right to confront witnesses, and to prosecute people more than once for the same crime—a practice known as double jeopardy.[9] Although few states exercised these powers, they were there for any state whose legislative majority chose to use them.

The Constitutional Revolution in Civil Liberties

Signs of change in the constitutional framework came after 1954 in *Brown v. Board of Education*, when the Court found state segregation laws for schools unconstitutional.[10] Even though *Brown* was not a civil liberties case, it signaled that the Supreme Court would actively review state actions affecting civil rights and civil liberties. The Court indicated that such cases would be subjected to **strict scrutiny**, meaning that the government must show that any law abridging civil rights or civil liberties serves an important larger purpose. Although this constitutional revolution was given a jump-start in 1954 by *Brown v. Board of Education*,

strict scrutiny
The strictest standard of judicial review of a government's actions, in which the government must show that the law serves a "compelling state interest."

table 4.1

INCORPORATION OF THE BILL OF RIGHTS INTO THE FOURTEENTH AMENDMENT

SELECTED PROVISION (AMENDMENT[S])	DATE "INCORPORATED"	KEY CASE
Eminent domain (V)	1897	*Chicago, Burlington and Quincy Railroad v. Chicago*
Freedom of speech (I)	1925	*Gitlow v. New York*
Freedom of the press (I)	1931	*Near v. Minnesota ex rel. Olson*
Freedom of assembly (I)	1937	*De Jonge v. Oregon*
Free exercise of religion (I)	1940	*Cantwell v. Connecticut*
Freedom from unnecessary search and seizure (IV)	1949	*Wolf v. Colorado*
Freedom from warrantless search and seizure ("exclusionary rule") (IV)	1961	*Mapp v. Ohio*
Freedom from cruel and unusual punishment (VIII)	1962	*Robinson v. California*
Right to counsel in any criminal trial (VI)	1963	*Gideon v. Wainwright*
Right against self-incrimination and forced confessions (V)	1964	*Malloy v. Hogan Escobedo v. Illinois*
Right to privacy (III, IV, and V)	1965	*Griswold v. Connecticut*
Right to remain silent (V)	1966	*Miranda v. Arizona*
Right against double jeopardy (V)	1969	*Benton v. Maryland*
Right to bear arms (II)	2010	*McDonald v. Chicago*
Freedom from excessive fines (VIII)	2018	*Timbs v. Indiana*
Right to a unanimous verdict (VI)	2020	*Ramos v. Louisiana*

the results were not apparent until after 1961, when the Court gradually applied all the provisions of the Bill of Rights to the states.

Table 4.1 shows that until 1961, only the First Amendment and one clause of the Fifth Amendment had been clearly incorporated into the Fourteenth Amendment.[11] After 1961, several other important provisions of the Bill of Rights were incorporated. *Gideon v. Wainwright* expanded the Fourteenth Amendment's reach by establishing the right to counsel in a criminal trial.[12] In *Mapp v. Ohio*, the Court held that evidence obtained in violation of the Fourth Amendment ban on unreasonable searches and seizures would be excluded from trial.[13] In *Miranda v. Arizona*, the Court's ruling required that arrested persons be informed of their right to remain silent and to have counsel present during interrogation.[14] By 1969, in *Benton v. Maryland*, the Supreme Court had come full circle regarding the rights of the criminally accused, explicitly reversing a 1937 ruling by incorporating a ban on double jeopardy.[15]

Beginning in the mid-1950s, the Court also expanded another important area of civil liberties: rights to privacy. In 1958, the Court recognized "privacy in one's association" in its decision to prevent the state of Alabama from using the membership list of the National Association for the Advancement of Colored People (NAACP) in the state's investigations.[16] As we will see later in this chapter, legal questions about the right to privacy have come to the fore in more recent cases concerning birth control, abortion, homosexuality, and assisted suicide.

THE BILL OF RIGHTS TODAY

Because every provision in the Bill of Rights is subject to interpretation, the general status of civil liberties can never be considered final and permanent.[17] Although the Supreme Court has the power to expand the Bill of Rights, it also has the power to contract it.[18] In this section, we consider the major provisions of the Bill of Rights and how key court decisions have shaped the way they are understood today.

The First Amendment and Freedom of Religion

The Bill of Rights begins by guaranteeing freedom of religion, and the First Amendment provides for that freedom in two distinct clauses: "Congress shall make no law [1] respecting an establishment of religion, or [2] prohibiting the free exercise thereof." The first clause is called the establishment clause; the second, the free exercise clause.

Separation between Church and State. The **establishment clause** and the idea of "no law" regarding the establishment of religion could be interpreted in several ways. One interpretation, which probably reflects the views of many of

establishment clause
The First Amendment clause that says, "Congress shall make no law respecting an establishment of religion."

the First Amendment's authors, is that the government is prohibited only from establishing an official church. Official state churches, such as the Church of England, were common in the eighteenth century but seemed inappropriate to many Americans. Many colonists had, after all, fled Europe to escape persecution for having rejected official churches.

A second possible interpretation holds that the government may provide assistance to religious institutions or ideas as long as it shows no favoritism among them. The United States accommodates religious beliefs in a variety of ways, from the reference to God on U.S. currency to the prayer that begins every session of Congress. These forms of establishment have never been struck down by the courts.

The third view regarding the establishment clause, the most commonly held today, is that of a "wall of separation" between church and state that the government cannot breach. Despite the absolute sound of the phrase *wall of separation*, there is ample room to disagree on its meaning. For example, the Court has been strict in cases of prayer in public schools, striking down such practices as Bible reading,[19] nondenominational prayer,[20] a moment of silence for meditation or voluntary prayer, and pregame prayer at public sporting events.[21] Yet it has been more willing to allow other forms of officially sanctioned prayer. For example, in 2014 the Court decided that the town of Greece, New York, could permit volunteer chaplains to open legislative sessions with a prayer.[22] Currently, the United States celebrates an officially sanctioned National Day of Prayer. In 2020 it was celebrated on May 7. This event has been challenged in federal court by the Freedom From Religion Foundation. In 1971, after 30 years of cases involving government assistance to religious schools, the Court specified some criteria to guide its decisions and those of lower courts about circumstances in which such aid might be constitutionally acceptable. In *Lemon v. Kurtzman*, a decision invalidating state payments for the teaching of secular (nonreligious) subjects in religious schools, the Court established three criteria, which collectively came to be called the **Lemon** test. Government aid to religious schools would be allowed if (1) it had a secular purpose, (2) its effect was neither to advance nor to inhibit religion, and (3) it did not entangle government and religious institutions in each other's affairs.[23]

In 2004, the question of whether the phrase "under God" in the Pledge of Allegiance violates the establishment clause came before the Court, which ruled that the plaintiff lacked a sufficient personal stake in the case to bring the complaint.[24] This inconclusive decision kept the issue alive for possible resolution in a future case.

In two cases in 2005, the Court also ruled inconclusively on government-sponsored displays of religious symbols, specifically the Ten Commandments. In *Van Orden v. Perry*, the Court ruled that a display of the Ten Commandments in the Texas state capitol did not violate the Constitution.[25] In *McCreary v. ACLU*, however, it found unconstitutional a display of the Ten Commandments inside two Kentucky courthouses.[26] Justice Stephen Breyer, the swing vote in both cases,

Lemon test

A rule, articulated in *Lemon v. Kurtzman*, that says governmental action with respect to religion is permissible if it is secular in purpose, does not lead to "excessive entanglement" of government with religion, and neither promotes nor inhibits the practice of religion. The *Lemon* test is generally used in relation to government aid to religious schools.

Different interpretations of the establishment clause have led to debates about the extent to which church and state must be separated. This World War I monument in the shape of a cross displayed on state land in Maryland was held to be constitutional, but not without controversy.

indicated that the difference had been the purpose of the displays. Most legal observers, though, see little difference between the two and assume that the Court will provide further clarification in future cases. This issue continues to be litigated without a clear conclusion. In 2019, the Court ruled that a World War I memorial in Bladensburg, Maryland, known as the Bladensburg Peace Cross, should be seen as a secular rather than religious symbol.[27] This interpretation seemed to satisfy no one. Some were offended that a government-sponsored religious symbol was allowed to stand while others were offended by the Court's claim that an important religious symbol was merely secular.

Free Exercise of Religion.   The **free exercise clause** protects the right to believe and practice whatever religion one chooses; it also protects the right to be a nonbeliever. Although the Supreme Court has been fairly consistent in protecting the free exercise of religious belief, it has distinguished between beliefs and actions based on those beliefs. The 1940 case of *Cantwell v. Connecticut*, which arose from the efforts of two Jehovah's Witnesses to engage in door-to-door fund-raising, established the "time, place, and manner" rule: Americans are free to hold any religious beliefs, but the time, place, and manner of exercising those beliefs may be regulated in the public interest.[28] So, for example, a claim of free exercise of religion cannot be used to justify what would otherwise be a criminal act. This principle was established by the Supreme Court precedent in the 1878 case of *Reynolds v. U.S.*[29] In this case, Reynolds, a polygamist, had been charged with violating the federal anti-bigamy act. The Court said his prison term was justified even though Reynolds maintained polygamy was sanctioned by his religious beliefs.

In recent years, the principle of free exercise has been strengthened by legislation prohibiting religious discrimination in a variety of realms, including hiring, the treatment of prison inmates, and the enforcement of laws that conflict with religious beliefs. Three recent cases illustrate this point. The first

free exercise clause
The First Amendment clause that protects the right of citizens to believe and practice whatever religion they choose.

involved a Muslim prisoner in an Arkansas jail, who argued that his religious beliefs required him to grow a beard, despite an Arkansas prison policy prohibiting beards. The Court held that the prison's policy violated both the free exercise clause and a federal statute designed to protect the ability of prisoners to worship as they pleased.[30]

In the second case, the Equal Employment Opportunity Commission brought suit against Abercrombie & Fitch for refusing to hire a Muslim woman who wore a head scarf so as to avoid the necessity of accommodating her religious practices.[31] The Court held that the company's actions amounted to religious discrimination in hiring—a violation of federal rules.

The third case involved the owners of the Hobby Lobby chain of craft stores, who claimed that a section of the Affordable Care Act requiring employers to provide their female employees with free contraceptive coverage violated their religious beliefs as protected by the Religious Freedom Restoration Act (RFRA).[32] This law, enacted in 1993, requires the government to prove a "compelling interest" for requiring individuals to obey a law that violates their religious beliefs. In 1997, the Supreme Court found that RFRA could not be applied to the states but allowed its application to the actions of the federal government. The Hobby Lobby case involved a federal statute, so the Court applied RFRA and ruled in favor of Hobby Lobby. In the meantime, a number of states have enacted their own versions of RFRA, leading to concerns, particularly among members of the LGBTQ community, that claims of religious freedom might be used as the basis for discrimination against gay or transgender individuals in hiring or other realms by individuals claiming that such practices violate their own religious beliefs. This concern was heightened in 2018 when the Court ruled in favor of a Colorado baker who refused to create a wedding cake for a same-sex couple, claiming that gay marriage violated his religious beliefs.[33]

In three decisions announced in 2020, the Supreme Court expanded the right of religious exercise and affirmed the special place of religious institutions in American life. Taken together, these decisions seemed to give the free exercise of religion a measure of priority over other political rights in America.

The First Amendment and Freedom of Speech and the Press

Because representative democracy depends on an open political process, freedom of speech and freedom of the press are considered critical. In 1938, freedom of speech (which includes freedom of the press) was given special constitutional status when the Supreme Court promised that any legislation attempting to restrict these fundamental freedoms "is to be subjected to a more exacting judicial scrutiny . . . than are most other types of legislation."[34]

The Court was saying that the democratic political process must be protected at almost any cost. As we noted earlier, this higher standard of judicial review came to be called *strict scrutiny*. Strict scrutiny in this area implies that freedom of speech—at least some kinds of speech—occupies a "preferred" position and will be

Even speech most people find offensive is generally protected under the First Amendment. In 2011, the Supreme Court confirmed the right of the Westboro Baptist Church to display slogans such as "Thank God for Dead Soldiers" outside of military funerals.

protected almost absolutely. In 2011, for example, the Court ruled 8–1 that members of Westboro Baptist Church, a tiny Kansas institution, had a First Amendment right to picket the funerals of American soldiers killed in action while displaying signs reading "Thank God for Dead Soldiers." The church teaches that these deaths represent divine punishment for America's tolerance of homosexuality and other matters. In his opinion, Chief Justice John Roberts wrote, "As a nation we have chosen to protect even hurtful speech on public issues to ensure that we do not stifle public debate."[35]

Political Speech.   Since the 1920s, political speech has been consistently protected by the courts even when it seems "insulting" or "outrageous." In the 1969 case *Brandenburg v. Ohio*, the Supreme Court ruled that as long as speech falls short of actually "inciting or producing imminently lawless action," it cannot be prohibited, even if it is hostile to the government and its policies.[36]

This case involved a Ku Klux Klan leader, Charles Brandenburg, who had been convicted of advocating "revengent" action against the president, Congress, and the Supreme Court, among others, if they continued "to suppress the white, Caucasian race." Although Brandenburg was not carrying a weapon, some members of his audience were. Nevertheless, the Court reversed the state courts and freed Brandenburg while declaring Ohio's Criminal Syndicalism Act unconstitutional because it punished people who "advocate, or teach the duty, necessity, or propriety [of violence] as a means of accomplishing industrial or political reform" or who publish materials or "voluntarily assemble . . . to teach or advocate the doctrines of criminal syndicalism."

The Court argued that the statute did not distinguish "mere advocacy" from "incitement to imminent lawless action." It would be difficult to go much further in protecting freedom of speech. Typically, courts strike down restrictions on speech if they are deemed to be "overbroad," "vague," or lacking "neutrality"—for example, if a statute prohibited the views of the political left but not the political right, or vice versa.

Another area of expansion of political speech—the loosening of limits on spending and donations in political campaigns—was opened up in 1976 with the Supreme Court's decision in *Buckley v. Valeo*.[37] Campaign finance reform laws of the early 1970s, arising out of the Watergate scandal, had put severe limits on campaign spending. But the Court declared a number of important provisions unconstitutional on the basis of a new principle that spending money by or on behalf of candidates is a form of speech protected by the First Amendment (as contrasted with contributions to campaigns, which Congress has more authority to regulate).

The issue arose again in 2003, after passage of a still-stricter campaign finance law, the Bipartisan Campaign Reform Act of 2002 (BCRA). This time, the Court's majority significantly reduced the area of speech protected by *Buckley v. Valeo*, holding that Congress was within its power to limit the amounts that campaign contributors could spend through direct contributions and advertising on behalf of candidates.[38] However, in 2007 the Court struck down a key portion of BCRA, finding that the act's limitations on political advertising violated the First Amendment's guarantee of free speech.[39]

In *Citizens United v. Federal Election Commission*, in 2010, the Court ruled that corporate funding of independent election ads could not be limited under the First Amendment.[40] But, opening the way to higher levels of campaign spending is not entirely a bad thing. In 2020, the two parties together spent more than $10 billion on the presidential, state, and local elections, much of the money raised from wealthy donors. One result was a dramatic increase in voter turnout to levels not seen in the Unites States since the nineteenth century. In this way, campaign spending proved to enhance rather than detract from American democracy.

Symbolic Speech, Speech Plus Action, and the Rights of Assembly and Petition.
The First Amendment treats the freedoms of assembly and petition as equal to the freedoms of religion and political speech. Assembly and petition, including such forms of action as peaceful demonstrations aimed at influencing the government or expressing political views, are closely associated with speech but go beyond it to speech associated with action.

Since at least 1931, the Supreme Court has sought to protect actions that are designed to send a political message. Thus, although the Court upheld a federal statute that made it a crime to burn draft cards to protest the Vietnam War, on the grounds that the government had a compelling interest in preserving draft cards as part of the conduct of the war itself, the Court considered the wearing of black armbands to school a protected form of assembly. In such cases, courts will often use the standard articulated in the draft card case, *United States v. O'Brien*, and now known as the *O'Brien* test.[41] Under this test, a statute restricting expressive or symbolic speech must be justified by a compelling governmental interest and be narrowly tailored toward achieving that interest.

Another example of symbolic speech is the burning of the American flag as a symbol of protest. In 1984, at a rally during the Republican National Convention in Dallas, a political protester burned an American flag in violation of a Texas law

think it through

In recent years, grassroots campaigns built on small, individual donations have grown. Have you ever donated to a political candidate or campaign? How does your donation compete with those of wealthy individuals or corporations? How does this impact the ability of grassroots campaigns to gain traction?

that prohibited desecration of a venerated object. In a 5–4 decision, the Supreme Court declared the Texas law unconstitutional on the grounds that flag burning is expressive conduct protected by the First Amendment.[42] Subsequent efforts in Congress to make flag burning a federal crime were strongly discouraged by the Supreme Court's 2003 decision striking down a Virginia cross-burning statute.[43] In that case, the Court ruled that states could make cross burning a crime only if the statute required prosecutors to prove that the act was intended to intimidate rather than simply to express opinion.

What the framers of the Constitution likely had in mind when they drafted the assembly and petition clause were activities such as picketing, distributing leaflets, and other forms of peaceful demonstration or assembly. Speech accompanied by such actions is known as **speech plus**. Such activities are consistently protected by courts under the First Amendment; state and local laws regulating them are closely scrutinized and frequently overturned. However, restrictions imposed by state or local authorities may be acceptable if properly balanced by considerations of public order.

speech plus
Speech accompanied by activities such as sit-ins, picketing, and demonstrations.

Freedom of the Press.

Freedom of speech includes freedom of the press. With the exception of broadcast media, which are subject to federal regulation, the press is protected under the doctrine prohibiting **prior restraint**. Since 1931,[44] the Supreme Court has held that except under extraordinary circumstances, the First Amendment prohibits the government from seeking to prevent newspapers or magazines from publishing whatever they wish.

The government may prosecute journalists for refusing to reveal their sources and may seek to prosecute individuals who leak information to the press. During the Obama presidency, seven individuals were charged with or prosecuted for disclosing classified information. They included Chelsea Manning, an army intelligence analyst sent to prison for providing classified documents to WikiLeaks, which published many of the documents, and Edward Snowden, an employee of the National Security Agency (NSA) who fled the country to escape arrest after revealing the details of NSA domestic spying operations.

prior restraint
An effort by a government agency to block publication of material by a newspaper or magazine; censorship.

Libel, Slander, Obscenity, and Pornography.

Some speech is not protected at all. If a written statement is made in "reckless disregard of the truth" and is considered damaging to the victim because it is "malicious, scandalous, and defamatory," it can be punished as **libel**. An oral statement of such nature can be punished as **slander**.

Today, most libel cases involve freedom of the press. Historically, newspapers were subject to the law of libel, whereby newspapers that printed false and malicious stories could be compelled to pay damages to those they defamed. Recently, however, American courts have narrowed the meaning of libel and made it extremely difficult, particularly for public figures, to win a libel case against a newspaper.

Cases involving pornography and obscenity can be tricky, because attempts by the courts to define pornography and obscenity have proved impractical. It is

libel
A written statement made in "reckless disregard of the truth" and considered damaging to a victim because it is "malicious, scandalous, and defamatory."

slander
An oral statement made in "reckless disregard of the truth" and considered damaging to a victim because it is "malicious, scandalous, and defamatory."

easy to say that obscenity and pornography fall outside the realm of protected speech, but it is nearly impossible to specify clearly where protection ends and unprotected speech begins. In recent years, the battle against obscene speech has focused on internet pornography, which opponents argue should be banned because of the easy access children have to the internet.

The first significant effort to regulate such content occurred in 1996, when Congress attached to a major telecommunications bill an amendment, the Communications Decency Act (CDA), designed to regulate the online transmission of obscene material. In the 1997 case *Reno v. ACLU*, the Supreme Court struck down the CDA, ruling that it suppressed speech that "adults have a constitutional right to receive."[45] Congress tried again with a 2001 law that required public libraries to install anti-pornography filters on all library computers with internet access. In 2003, the Court upheld this law, asserting that it did not violate library patrons' First Amendment rights.[46]

Other conflicts have focused on the use of children in pornography rather than their access to it. In 2003, Congress outlawed efforts to sell child pornography via the internet. The Supreme Court upheld this act in the 2008 case of *United States v. Williams*.[47]

Student Speech. One category of conditionally protected speech is the free speech of students in public schools. The landmark case in this realm is *Tinker v. Des Moines Independent School District*, decided in 1969.[48] The case involved several students who, in violation of school policy, wore black armbands to school to protest the Vietnam War. The students were suspended and the parents, along with the Iowa Civil Liberties Union, brought suit. When the U.S. Supreme Court eventually heard the case, it declared that the First Amendment applied to public schools. To censor student speech, the Court said, administrators needed to show that the speech in question threatened to substantially disrupt educational activities.

In 1986, however, the Supreme Court backed away from a broad protection of student free speech rights by upholding the punishment of a high school student for making a sexually suggestive speech. The Court held that such speech interfered with the school's goal of teaching students the limits of socially acceptable behavior.[49] Two years later the Court further restricted students' speech and press rights, defining them as part of the educational process and not to be treated with the same standard as adult speech in a regular public forum.[50] A more recent case involving high school students[51] arose from school policies in Juneau, Alaska. In 2002, the Olympic torch relay passed through Juneau on its way to the Winter Olympics. As the torch passed Juneau-Douglas High, a senior, Joseph Frederick, unfurled a banner that read, "Bong Hits 4 Jesus." The school's principal promptly suspended Frederick, who then brought suit, alleging violation of his free speech rights. Like most public schools, Juneau-Douglas High prohibits expressions on school grounds that advocate illegal drug use. Civil libertarians see such policies as restricting students' right to free speech, but the Court ruled that the First Amendment did not require schools to permit students to advocate illegal drug use.

In addition, scores of universities have attempted to develop speech codes to suppress racial or ethnic slurs. The drafting of such codes was encouraged by the Department of Education's Office of Civil Rights (OCR), which interpreted Title IX of the Higher Education Act to require colleges to vigorously prosecute charges involving racial or sexual harassment. However, speech codes at public universities generally have been struck down by federal judges as unconstitutional infringements of speech. In 2018, Education Secretary Betsy DeVos criticized college speech codes and said that she planned to issue new guidelines for colleges and universities. Putting speech codes aside, on a number of campuses protesters have forced the cancellation of controversial speakers such as conservative firebrands Ann Coulter and Milo Yiannopoulos. Some students and professors argue that hateful speech has no place on college campuses, while others assert that colleges should be bastions of free speech even when the speech is offensive.

Efforts to formalize speech guidelines have also been made by large corporations, where many successful complaints and lawsuits have alleged that employers' or supervisors' words create a "hostile or abusive working environment." The Supreme Court has held that "sexual harassment" that creates a "hostile working environment" includes "unwelcome sexual advances, requests for sexual favors, and other *verbal* or physical conduct of a sexual nature"[52] [emphasis added]. A fundamental free speech issue is involved in these regulations of hostile speech.

Fighting Words and Hate Speech. Speech can also lose its protected position when it moves from the symbolic realm toward the sphere of harmful action. "Expressive speech," for example, is protected until it becomes direct incitement of damaging conduct with the use of **fighting words**. In 1942, the Supreme Court upheld the arrest and conviction of a man who had violated a state law forbidding the use of offensive language in public. He had called the arresting officer a "goddamned racketeer" and "a damn Fascist." The Court held that the First Amendment provides no protection for such offensive words because they "are no essential part of any exposition of ideas."[53] Since that time, however, the Court has reversed almost every conviction based on arguments that the speaker used "fighting words." But this is not an absolutely settled area.

Many jurisdictions have drafted ordinances banning forms of expression that assert hatred toward a specific group, be it African Americans, Jews, Muslims, or others. Such ordinances seldom pass constitutional muster. The leading Supreme Court case in this realm is the 1992 decision in *R.A.V. v. City of St. Paul*.[54] Here, a White teenager was arrested for burning a cross on the lawn of a Black family in violation of a municipal ordinance that banned cross burning. The Court ruled that the ordinance was not content neutral, because it prohibited only cross burning—typically an expression of hatred of African Americans. Since a statute banning all forms of hateful expression would be considered

fighting words
Speech that directly incites damaging conduct.

overly broad, the *R.A.V.* standard suggests that virtually all hate speech is constitutionally protected.

Commercial Speech.   Commercial speech, such as newspaper or television advertising, does not have full First Amendment protection, because it cannot be considered political speech. Some commercial speech is still unprotected and therefore regulated. For example, regulation of false and misleading advertising by the Federal Trade Commission is a well-established power of the federal government.[55] However, protection of commercial speech has generally increased in recent years. As the constitutional scholar Louis Fisher explains, "In part, this reflects the growing appreciation that commercial speech is part of the free flow of information necessary for informed choice and democratic participation."[56] For example, in a 2001 case, the Court ruled that a Massachusetts ban on all cigarette advertising violated the tobacco industry's First Amendment right to advertise its products to adult consumers.[57]

The Second Amendment and the Right to Bear Arms

The purpose of the Second Amendment is to provide for militias; they were to be the government's backup for the maintenance of local public order. The framers understood *militia* to be a military or police resource for state governments; militias were distinguished from armies and troops, which were under the jurisdiction of Congress. Some groups, though, have argued that the Second Amendment also establishes an individual right to bear arms.

The United States has a higher gun ownership rate than that of any other developed country (see Figure 4.1 for a comparison with selected countries).

The mass shooting of 17 people—including 14 students—at a high school in Parkland, Florida, in 2018 prompted many young Americans across the country to speak out in favor of gun control at the "March for Our Lives." Opponents of stricter gun laws pointed to the Second Amendment.

figure 4.1

GUN OWNERSHIP IN COMPARISON

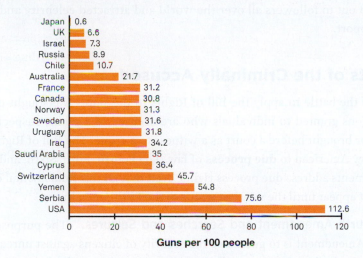

SOURCE: Hugh Morris, "Mapped: The Countries with the Most Guns," *Telegraph,* https://www.telegraph.co.uk/travel/maps-and-graphics/mapped-the-countries-with-the-most-guns/ (accessed 5/15/20).

Within the United States, there is no single national policy, and different state and local governments have very different rules about gun ownership. For instance, Wyoming has no ban on owning any type of gun, no waiting period for purchasing a firearm, and no permit requirement for carrying a concealed weapon. In California, by contrast, the possession of assault weapons is banned, there is a 10-day waiting period to purchase a firearm, and a permit is required to carry a concealed weapon. In Virginia, individuals may practice "open carry" of handguns without a permit but must have a license to carry a concealed weapon.

In a 2008 decision the Supreme Court ruled that the federal government could not prohibit individuals from owning guns for self-defense in their homes.[58] The case involved a District of Columbia ordinance that made it virtually impossible for residents to possess firearms legally. In the majority opinion, Justice Antonin Scalia stated that the decision was not intended to cast doubt on all laws limiting firearm possession, such as the prohibition on gun ownership by felons or the mentally ill. In his dissenting opinion, Justice John Paul Stevens asserted that the Second Amendment protects the right to bear arms only as part of a militia force, not in an individual capacity.

The District of Columbia is a federal district, and the Court did not indicate that its ruling applied to state firearms laws. However, in a 2010 case the Court struck down a Chicago firearms ordinance and applied the Second Amendment to the states as well.[59] Despite these rulings, the debate over gun control continues in American politics today, fueled by frequent mass shootings. In 2018, student-led "March for Our Lives" demonstrations were held in Washington, D.C., and more than 800 other locations to demand that legislators enact gun control legislation. The march was prompted by the February 2018 mass shooting at Stoneman Douglas High School in Parkland, Florida, and drew more than a million participants in the United States. Students used social media to reach out to followers all over the world and attracted celebrity and corporate support.

Rights of the Criminally Accused

Most of the battle to apply the Bill of Rights to the states was fought over the protections granted to individuals who are accused of a crime, suspected of a crime, or brought before a court as a witness to a crime. The Bill of Rights entitles every American to **due process** of law. The Fourth, Fifth, Sixth, and Eighth Amendments address due process rights, even though this fundamental concept does not appear until the very last words of the Fifth Amendment.

The Fourth Amendment and Searches and Seizures.   The purpose of the Fourth Amendment is to guarantee the security of citizens against unreasonable searches and seizures. In 1990, the Supreme Court summarized its understanding of the amendment like this: "A search compromises the individual interest in privacy; a seizure deprives the individual of dominion over his or her person or property."[60]

The **exclusionary rule**, which prohibits evidence obtained during an illegal search from being introduced in a trial, is the most severe restraint imposed by the Constitution and the courts on the behavior of the police. It is a dramatic restriction because it often rules out the evidence that produces a conviction; it sometimes frees people who are *known* to have committed the crime they're accused of. For this reason, in recent years the federal courts have become

due process
The requirement that citizens be treated according to the law and be provided adequate protection for individual rights.

exclusionary rule
The requirement that courts exclude evidence obtained in violation of the Fourth Amendment.

What rights do you have if you are arrested? Due process rights protect individuals who are accused of a crime or brought before a court as a witness.

somewhat more flexible about the exclusionary rule, taking into account the "nature and quality of the intrusion." It is thus difficult to know ahead of time whether a defendant will or will not be protected from an illegal search under the Fourth Amendment.

The Fourth Amendment also applies to electronic searches and governmental surveillance. For example, the Apple Corporation cited its Fourth Amendment rights when it refused to provide the FBI with the information that would have been needed to access an iPhone belonging to Syed Farook, an alleged terrorist who killed 14 of his coworkers in San Bernardino, California, in 2015. In the matter of surveillance, one of the most pressing issues facing the federal courts today is the extent to which the government may eavesdrop on Americans' emails and phone calls as it seeks to prevent terrorist attacks.

The Fifth Amendment.   Under the Fifth Amendment, suspects have the right to have a **grand jury** determine whether a prosecutor has enough evidence to bring criminal charges. Grand juries play an important role in federal criminal cases. However, the provision for a grand jury is the one important civil liberties provision of the Bill of Rights that the Supreme Court has not incorporated into the Fourteenth Amendment and applied to state criminal prosecutions. Thus, some states operate without grand juries: the prosecuting attorney simply files a "bill of information" affirming that sufficient evidence is available to justify a trial.

The Fifth Amendment also provides constitutional protection from double jeopardy, or being tried more than once for the same crime, and the guarantee that no citizen "shall be compelled in any criminal case to be a witness against himself." This protection against self-incrimination led to the *Miranda* case and the **Miranda rule** that police must follow when questioning an arrested criminal suspect.

Another fundamental part of the Fifth Amendment is the *takings clause*, which protects citizens against the taking of private property "without just compensation." As discussed earlier, the power of government to take private property for a public use is called eminent domain. Although the takings clause does not concern protecting persons accused of crimes, it is similar to other Fifth Amendment protections because it deals with an important situation where the government and the citizen may be adversaries.

The Sixth Amendment and the Right to Counsel.   Some provisions of the Sixth Amendment, such as the right to a speedy trial and the right to confront witnesses before an impartial jury, are not very controversial. The *right-to-counsel provision*, however, like the exclusionary rule of the Fourth Amendment and the self-incrimination clause of the Fifth Amendment, is notable for freeing defendants who seem clearly guilty as charged. Under the right to counsel, defendants have the right to be represented by an attorney, and if they are denied that right, their conviction may be overturned.

Gideon v. Wainwright is the perfect case study because it involved a person who seemed patently guilty of the crime for which he was convicted. In and out

grand jury
A jury that determines whether sufficient evidence is available to justify a trial. Grand juries do not rule on the accused's guilt or innocence.

Miranda rule
The requirement, derived from the Supreme Court's 1966 ruling in *Miranda v. Arizona*, that persons under arrest must be informed of their legal rights, including the right to counsel, before undergoing police interrogation.

of jails for most of his 51 years, Clarence Earl Gideon received a five-year sentence in state court for breaking into and entering a poolroom in Panama City, Florida. While serving time, Gideon made his own appeal in a handwritten petition stating that he had been denied access to a defense attorney, as would have been his right in federal court. Gideon eventually won the landmark ruling on the right to counsel in all state court felony cases.[61]

In 1964, the year after the *Gideon* decision, the Supreme Court ruled that suspects have a right to counsel during police interrogations, not just when their cases reach trial.[62] The right to counsel has since been expanded further to encompass the quality of the counsel provided. For example, in 2003 the Court overturned a death sentence on the grounds that the defense lawyer had failed to fully inform the jury of the defendant's history of "horrendous childhood abuse."[63]

The Eighth Amendment and Cruel and Unusual Punishment. The Eighth Amendment prohibits "excessive bail," "excessive fines," and "cruel and unusual punishment." Each of these provisions, including the question of how much bail is "excessive," has provoked a good deal of controversy, but the most intense debates over Eighth Amendment issues have focused on the last of these provisions. One of the greatest challenges in interpreting it consistently is that what is considered "cruel and unusual" varies from culture to culture and from generation to generation. Unfortunately, how this provision is applied also varies by class and race.

In recent years, federal courts have dealt with a number of Eighth Amendment questions. In the case of *Miller v. Alabama*, for example, the Court ruled that mandatory sentences of life without the possibility of parole constituted cruel and unusual punishment for a juvenile offender.[64] The most important questions concerning cruel and unusual punishment are raised by use of the death penalty. Some Americans believe that execution is inherently cruel, but in its consideration of the death penalty the Supreme Court has generally avoided this question. In 1972, the Supreme Court overturned several state death penalty laws not because they were cruel and unusual but because they were being applied in an inconsistent manner.[65] Since 1976, the Court has consistently upheld state laws providing for capital punishment, although it continues to review numerous death penalty appeals each year.

The Right to Privacy

right to privacy
The right to be left alone, which has been interpreted by the Supreme Court to entail individual access to birth control and abortions.

In the mid-1950s and 1960s, the idea of a **right to privacy** gained traction. The Constitution does not specifically mention such a right, but the Ninth Amendment declares that the rights enumerated in the Constitution are not an exhaustive list. In 1958, the Supreme Court recognized "privacy in one's association" in its decision to prevent the state of Alabama from using the NAACP membership list in the state's investigations.

In 1965, the Court ruled that a Connecticut statute forbidding the use of contraceptives violated the right of marital privacy. Justice William O. Douglas, writing for the majority in *Griswold v. Connecticut*, argued that this right of privacy is also grounded in the Constitution because it fits into a "zone of privacy" created by a combination of the Third, Fourth, and Fifth Amendments.[66] The right to privacy was further defined in 1973 in one of the most important Supreme Court decisions in American history: *Roe v. Wade*. This decision established a woman's right to seek an abortion and prohibited states from making abortion a criminal act prior to the point at which the fetus becomes viable.[67] In recent years, a number of states have reinstated restrictions on abortion, including lowering the viability standard to 20 weeks (Texas), 12 weeks (Arkansas), and 6 weeks (North Dakota). However, Arkansas's ban was struck down by a federal appeals court, and North Dakota's ban was blocked by the U.S. Supreme Court. In 2018 and 2019, several states legislated new restrictions prohibiting abortions if a fetal heartbeat could be detected. This comes close to an outright ban on abortion since many women might not even be aware of their pregnancy before modern technology is able to detect a heartbeat.

The *Roe* decision dramatically changed abortion practices in America. It also galvanized and nationalized the abortion debate. Groups opposing abortion, such as the National Right to Life Committee, organized to fight the new liberal standard, while abortion rights groups sought to maintain that protection. The legal standard has shifted against abortion rights supporters in three key Supreme Court cases.

In 1989, in *Webster v. Reproductive Health Services*, the Court narrowly upheld (by a 5–4 majority) the constitutionality of restrictions on the use of public medical facilities for abortion.[68] And in the 1992 case of *Planned Parenthood v. Casey*, another 5–4 majority upheld *Roe* but narrowed its scope. The Court's decision defined the right to an abortion as a "limited or qualified" right subject to regulation by the states as long as the regulation does not constitute an "undue burden."[69] More recently, the Court had another opportunity to rule on what constitutes an undue burden: in 2000, in *Stenberg v. Carhart*, the Court struck down Nebraska's ban on late-term abortions because the law had the "effect of placing a substantial obstacle in the path of a woman seeking an abortion."[70] In 2007, however, the Court upheld a federal ban on late-term abortions, essentially overturning the earlier decision.[71]

In June 2020, the Supreme Court struck down an effort by Louisiana to restrict abortion rights. A state law required that abortion providers have admitting privileges in a nearby hospital if they were to be allowed to perform abortions. In a 5-4 decision the Court ruled that this law, like a similar Texas statute that had been previously overturned, was an impermissible effort to restrict abortion rights.[72]

In recent decades, the right to be left alone began to include the privacy rights of gay men and women. In Atlanta in 1982, Michael Hardwick was arrested by a police officer who discovered him in bed with another man and was charged under Georgia's law against sodomy. Hardwick filed a suit challenging the constitutionality of the law and won his case in the federal court of appeals. The state of Georgia appealed the court's decision to the Supreme Court, whose majority reversed the lower-court decision, holding in 1986 that "the federal Constitution confers [no] fundamental right upon homosexuals to engage in sodomy" and that there was therefore no basis to invalidate "the laws of the many states that still make such conduct illegal and have done so for a very long time."[73]

With *Lawrence and Garner v. Texas* in 2003, however, the Court overturned *Bowers v. Hardwick*, and state legislatures no longer had the authority to make private sexual behavior a crime.[74] The majority opinion maintained, "In our tradition the State is not omnipresent in the home. And there are other spheres of our lives and existence outside the home, where the State should not be a dominant presence." This decision added substance to the idea that the Ninth Amendment allows for the "right to privacy."

Today, technological change has confronted the courts with a number of privacy issues that could not have been foreseen when the Supreme Court wrote its *Griswold* decision a half-century ago. For example, does the right to privacy extend to information stored in a suspect's GPS tracking device?[75] Can the authorities collect DNA from suspects as part of a routine booking procedure?[76] It is certain that new technologies will present additional questions about privacy for the courts to consider in the future.

CIVIL RIGHTS

Civil rights are the rules that government must follow in the treatment of individuals. Some civil rights concern who can be involved in collective decision making such as voting. Other civil rights concern how people are to be treated in society, including who has access to public facilities, such as schools and public hospitals. Increasingly, civil rights have extended to private spheres, including the right to work, the right to marry, and the question of whether clubs and organizations can exclude people on the basis of gender or race. When there is a demand for new civil rights, society must decide whether and how rights should be extended.

Civil rights encompass three features: who, what, and how much. *Who* has a right and who does not? A right to *what*? And *how much* is any individual allowed to exercise that right? Consider the right to vote. The "what," of course, is participating in political decisions through the vote. The "who" concerns which persons are allowed to vote. Today, all U.S. citizens 18 years of age and older are eligible to vote. Some states impose additional criteria, such as requirements that voters show photo IDs, or prohibitions on voting by ex-felons.

The "how much" concerns whether that right can be exercised equally— whether some people's votes count more than others' or whether election laws create greater obstacles for some people than for others. For instance, until the mid-1960s, the California State Senate had one senator from Los Angeles County, with 6 million people, and one senator from Inyo County, with 14,000 people.

The votes of the 14,000 people translated into the same amount of representation in the state senate as the votes of the 6 million people. The U.S. Supreme Court ruled that such arrangements violated the civil rights of those in the more populous counties.

In the course of American history, two principles have emerged that answer the questions of who enjoys civil rights and how much. First, civil rights ought to be universal: all people should enjoy them. Second, they ought to be equal: all people who enjoy a civil right ought to be allowed an equal ability or opportunity to practice that right. However, these principles have not always been applied.

Which civil rights Americans enjoy and who has them are political decisions. The Constitution set forth a small number of civil rights. The Bill of Rights asserted a larger number of legal rights. But many of the civil rights that are protected today were left to Congress and the states to determine. Thus, most civil rights are the result of legislation, litigation, and administration that occurred after the country was founded.

In the following sections, we trace the historical development of civil rights in several key areas, beginning with the fundamental political rights of non-White Americans and women.

The Struggle for Voting Rights

Some of the most profound debates and divisions in American society have concerned *who* has civil rights, because those who already have those rights, such as the right to vote, are asked to extend them to those who do not. At the time of the Founding, most states granted voting rights exclusively to White, male property owners. Many states also imposed religious restrictions, forbidding Catholics or Jews from voting, running for office, and engaging in other public activities. White, male property owners held most political power in 1787 because they had voting rights while no one else did. In order to expand voting rights to other groups, those who had power had to decide to remove property and religious qualifications, extend voting rights to women and non-White people, and loosen other restrictions, such as age.

Property qualifications for voters were the first restrictions to be lifted by the various states. Throughout the first half of the nineteenth century, states began to drop the requirement that people hold property in order to vote or run for office, especially as the economy became more industrial and less agricultural, with many people moving to cities for work and thus becoming less likely to own property. By 1850, virtually all property qualifications had been eliminated. Still, many states had poll taxes well into the twentieth century: voters had to pay a certain amount, such as two dollars, every time they voted. Poll taxes abridged the civil rights of poor people and often also served to discriminate against Blacks, who tended to be poorer. The Twenty-Fourth Amendment to the Constitution eliminated poll taxes in 1964.

The restrictions on the right to vote based on religion and property were removed with relatively little protest. The struggle to extend voting rights to women and to racial and ethnic minorities, however, proved much more contentious, fueling two of the greatest struggles in American political history.

Women's Suffrage.   In the early 1800s, few state or local governments granted women voting rights. It took an entire century of activism, protest, and political maneuvering to guarantee those rights. In the decades prior to the Civil War, attitudes about women's civil rights began to change, in part because of practical problems related to property, inheritance, and settlement in new states and territories.

The United States had adopted laws of inheritance and property from Britain, which granted men control over all property, but those laws proved problematic in a country of settlers rather than established families and classes. It is no coincidence that many of the newer states, such as Indiana and Kentucky, were the first to give women economic rights. Around the same time, American women began to organize to advance their political and social rights, including the right to vote. In 1848, women and men attending the Seneca Falls Convention issued the "Declaration of Sentiments and Resolutions," asserting that women were entitled to rights in every way equal to those of men.

In 1869, the National Woman Suffrage Association (NWSA) was formed and began an effort to amend the U.S. Constitution to allow women to vote. By the 1880s, the issue of voting rights for women was the subject of mass meetings, parades, and protests, and by 1917 the NWSA had 2 million members. By 1918, all of the western states and territories, plus Michigan and New York, had granted women full suffrage. Once a critical mass of states had acted, it was only a matter

It took over a century of activism and protests for women to win the right to vote in national elections. Before the passage of the Nineteenth Amendment in 1920, activists picketed and organized marches, attracting thousands of participants.

of time before federal law followed. In 1919, Congress ratified the Nineteenth Amendment, granting women the right to vote in federal elections.[77] Two months later, the amendment was ratified by the states, and women across the United States voted in the presidential election of 1920.

Black Americans' Right to Vote.   The struggle to extend full voting rights to racial minorities, especially Blacks, reflects deep divisions in American society. It took a full century after the Civil War for Congress to guarantee minorities' voting rights with the Voting Rights Act of 1965, and the battle to protect those rights continues today.

In 1870, the Fifteenth Amendment to the Constitution stated that the right to vote could not be denied on the basis of race, and during Reconstruction the federal government enforced the rights of Black Americans to vote. Following the withdrawal of federal troops from the South after 1876, however, state legislatures and local governments there (and elsewhere) enacted practices that excluded Blacks from elections or weakened their political power. In many states, Blacks were excluded from primary elections, a practice called the *white primary*. Poll taxes, literacy tests, registration list purges, and other tactics were used to keep Blacks from voting.[78] District and municipal boundaries were drawn to place Blacks in jurisdictions in which they had little or no impact on the election of representatives or the approval of public expenditures.[79]

Civil rights advocates had little hope of changing state voting laws because state legislators had benefited electorally from those laws. Congress was also reluctant to pass federal legislation to enforce the Fifteenth Amendment. At last, the Supreme Court intervened. It struck down the white primary in *Smith v. Allwright* in 1944 and asserted the federal government's power to intervene in states' conduct of elections in order to protect Blacks' voting rights.[80] The Court acted again in 1960, ruling that state and local governments could not draw election district boundaries so as to discriminate on the basis of race.[81]

In 1965, Congress finally took action with the Voting Rights Act, sweeping aside many state laws and practices that had discriminated against Blacks. That act has been amended several times to expand who is covered, including Hispanics (1975) and other non-English speakers (1982), and what sorts of activities are prohibited, most notably racial gerrymandering (see Chapter 5).

In 2013, the Supreme Court declared unconstitutional an important section of the Voting Rights Act in *Shelby County v. Holder*. This section—Section 4(b)—required all jurisdictions in Alabama, Alaska, Arizona, Georgia, Louisiana, Mississippi, South Carolina, and Texas, as well as certain cities and counties in some other states, to obtain federal governmental approval of any change in election procedures. Civil rights advocates decried the *Shelby County* decision. Other parts of the act still hold, however, and the *Shelby County* decision shifted the legal battles to those sections on Congress's agenda.[82]

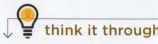
think it through

After the 2020 Census the congressional districts will be redrawn. Look at your district on a voting map. How do today's debates over gerrymandering—the practice of creating custom districts that support one party over another—impact the power of your vote?

equal protection clause

The provision of the Fourteenth Amendment guaranteeing citizens the "equal protection of the laws." This clause has served as the basis for the civil rights of African Americans, women, and other groups.

"separate but equal" rule

The legal principle that public accommodations could be segregated by race but still be equal.

Thus the fight over minority voting rights continues. Administrative procedures, such as laws requiring that voters show a government-issued photo ID and the redrawing of legislative district maps every 10 years, are subject to intense debate. Disputes over these laws and how they affect minorities' voting rights often end up in federal courts. Since the 1960s, the courts—and not legislatures—have become the arena in which minorities, poor people, and many others can argue for the protection of their voting rights.

Racial Discrimination after the Fourteenth Amendment

The Fourteenth Amendment's **equal protection clause** guaranteed equal protection of the laws to all Americans. However, the Supreme Court was initially no more ready to enforce the civil rights aspects of the Fourteenth Amendment than it was to enforce the civil liberties provisions discussed earlier.

Plessy v. Ferguson: "Separate but Equal."

The Court declared the Civil Rights Act of 1875 unconstitutional because it sought to protect Blacks against discrimination by private businesses, whereas the Fourteenth Amendment, according to the Court's interpretation, was intended to protect only against discrimination by *public* officials of state and local governments. In 1896, the Court went further, in the infamous *Plessy v. Ferguson* case, by upholding a Louisiana statute that required racial segregation on trolleys and other public carriers. The Court held that the Fourteenth Amendment's "equal protection of the laws" was not violated by racial distinction as long as the law applied to both races equally.[83] Many people pretended that Blacks were treated equally as long as some accommodation existed. In effect, the Court was saying that it was not unreasonable to segregate and exclude people from public facilities—including schools—on the basis of race. This was the origin of the **"separate but equal" rule** that was not reversed until 1954.

Challenging "Separate but Equal."

The Supreme Court began to change its position regarding racial discrimination before World War II by defining more strictly what counted as equal facilities under the "separate but equal" rule. Notably, in 1938 the Court rejected Missouri's policy of paying the tuition of qualified Blacks to out-of-state law schools rather than admitting them to the University of Missouri Law School.[84] After the war, modest progress resumed. In 1950, the Court rejected the claim by Texas that its new "law school for Negroes" afforded education equal to that of the all-White University of Texas Law School. The Court's decision opened the question of whether *any* segregated facility could be truly equal.[85]

As the Supreme Court was ordering the admission of Blacks to all-White state law schools, it was also striking down the southern practice of White primaries, which excluded Blacks from the process of nominating candidates.[86] And in the 1948 *Shelley v. Kraemer* decision, the Court ruled against the practice of "restrictive covenants," whereby the seller of a home added a clause to the sales

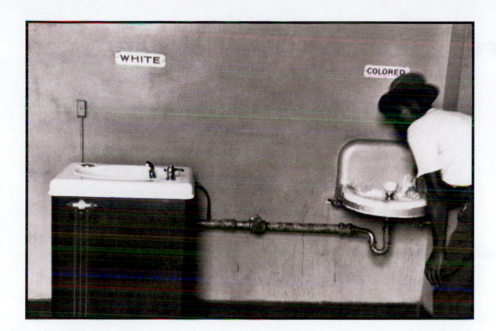

In the infamous 1896 *Plessy* decision, the Supreme Court upheld the "separate but equal" rule that was often used to justify racial segregation. Until the 1960s, laws in many states required separate public facilities—from separate schools to separate drinking fountains—for Blacks and Whites.

contract requiring the buyer to agree not to resell the home to a non-Caucasian, non-Christian, and so on.[87]

Although none of those cases directly confronted "separate but equal" and the principle of racial discrimination as such, they gave civil rights advocates enough encouragement to believe that at last they had an opportunity and enough legal precedent to change the constitutional framework itself. By the fall of 1952, plaintiffs had brought cases to the Supreme Court from Kansas, South Carolina, Virginia, Delaware, and the District of Columbia challenging the constitutionality of school segregation. Of these, the Kansas case became the focal point.

Brown v. Board of Education.   Oliver Brown, the father of three girls, lived in a low-income, racially mixed Topeka, Kansas, neighborhood. Every school-day morning, his daughter Linda took the school bus to a school for Black children about a mile away. In September 1950, however, Brown took Linda to an all-White school closer to their home to enroll her in the third grade in defiance of state law and local segregation rules. When they were refused, Brown took his case to the NAACP, and soon thereafter *Brown v. Board of Education* was born. The case made its way to the Supreme Court.

In deciding the case, the Court, to the surprise of many, rejected as inconclusive all the scholarly arguments about the intent of the Fourteenth Amendment and committed itself to considering only the *consequences* of segregation:

> Does segregation of children in public schools solely on the basis of race, even though the physical facilities and other "tangible" factors may be equal, deprive the children of the minority group of equal educational opportunities? We believe that it does. . . . We conclude that in the field of public education the doctrine of "separate but equal" has no place. Separate educational facilities are inherently unequal.[88]

CAUSE AND EFFECT IN THE CIVIL RIGHTS MOVEMENT

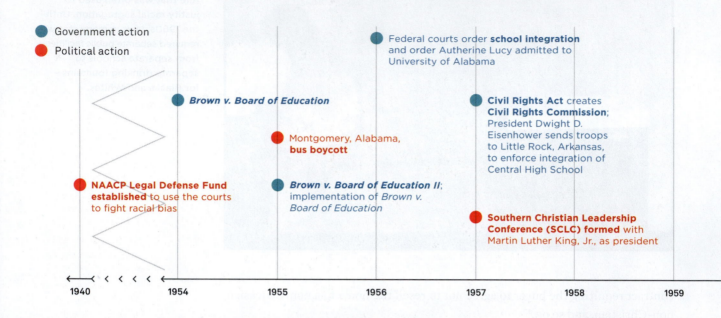

- 🔵 Government action
- 🔴 Political action

🔴 **NAACP Legal Defense Fund established** to use the courts to fight racial bias

🔵 *Brown v. Board of Education*

🔴 Montgomery, Alabama, **bus boycott**

🔵 *Brown v. Board of Education II*; implementation of *Brown v. Board of Education*

🔵 Federal courts order **school integration** and order Autherine Lucy admitted to University of Alabama

🔵 **Civil Rights Act** creates **Civil Rights Commission**; President Dwight D. Eisenhower sends troops to Little Rock, Arkansas, to enforce integration of Central High School

🔴 **Southern Christian Leadership Conference (SCLC) formed** with Martin Luther King, Jr., as president

1940   1954   1955   1956   1957   1958   1959

TIMEPLOT SOURCE: Compiled by authors.

de jure segregation

Racial segregation that is a direct result of law or official policy.

de facto segregation

Racial segregation that is not a direct result of law or governmental policy but a reflection of residential patterns, income distributions, or other social factors.

The 1954 *Brown* decision altered the constitutional framework in two fundamental respects. First, the states no longer had the power to use race as a basis of discrimination in law. Second, the national government now had the power to intervene with strict regulatory policies against the discriminatory actions of state or local governments, school boards, employers, and others in the private sector (see Timeplot).

Civil Rights after *Brown v. Board of Education*.   Although *Brown v. Board of Education* prohibited exclusion on the basis of race, this historic decision was merely a small first step. First, most states refused to cooperate until sued, and many schemes were employed to delay desegregation (such as paying White students' tuition at newly created "private" academies). Second, even as southern school boards began to eliminate their legally enforced (**de jure**) segregation, actual (**de facto**) school segregation persisted in both the North and the South because of racially segregated housing, which *Brown* did not affect. Third, *Brown* did not directly address discrimination in employment, public accommodations, juries, voting, and other areas of social and economic activity.

A decade of frustration after *Brown* showed that the goal of "equal protection" required positive, or affirmative, action by Congress and by government agencies.

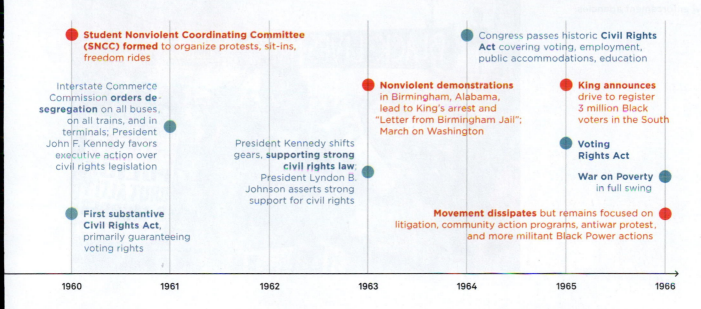

Student Nonviolent Coordinating Committee (SNCC) formed to organize protests, sit-ins, freedom rides

Interstate Commerce Commission **orders de-segregation** on all buses, on all trains, and in terminals; President John F. Kennedy favors executive action over civil rights legislation

President Kennedy shifts gears, **supporting strong civil rights law**; President Lyndon B. Johnson asserts strong support for civil rights

First substantive Civil Rights Act, primarily guaranteeing voting rights

Congress passes historic **Civil Rights Act** covering voting, employment, public accommodations, education

Nonviolent demonstrations in Birmingham, Alabama, lead to King's arrest and "Letter from Birmingham Jail"; March on Washington

King announces drive to register 3 million Black voters in the South

Voting Rights Act

War on Poverty in full swing

Movement dissipates but remains focused on litigation, community action programs, antiwar protest, and more militant Black Power actions

1960   1961   1962   1963   1964   1965   1966

And given massive southern resistance and generally negative national public opinion on racial integration, progress through courts, Congress, or agencies would not be made without intense, well-organized support.

Organized civil rights demonstrations began to mount slowly but surely after *Brown*. Hundreds of thousands of Americans, both Black and White, exercised their right to peaceably assemble and petition the government, demanding that the civil rights guaranteed to White Americans now be recognized and protected for Black Americans too. By the 1960s, the many organizations making up the civil rights movement had accumulated experience and built networks capable of launching massive direct-action campaigns against southern segregationists.

The Southern Christian Leadership Conference, the Student Nonviolent Coordinating Committee, and many other organizations had built a movement across the South that used the media to attract nationwide attention and support. At the massive March on Washington in 1963, the Reverend Martin Luther King, Jr., staked out the movement's moral claims in his "I Have a Dream" speech. Also in the 1960s, images of protesters being beaten, attacked by police dogs, and set on with fire hoses did much to win broad sympathy for the Black civil rights cause and to discredit state and local governments in the South. In these ways,

In recent years, the Black Lives Matter movement has focused on discrimination against African Americans, especially by law enforcement agencies.

the movement created intense pressure for a reluctant federal government to take stronger steps to defend Black civil rights.

The Black Lives Matter Movement.   In recent years, the politics of Black rights has shifted from voting and employment to other arenas, such as discrimination by law enforcement agencies, mass incarceration, and a push to allow ex-felons to vote. Since 2014, a number of protests have focused attention on the disproportionately high rates at which Black men are the victims of police violence. The movement took off in Ferguson, Missouri, after the 2014 shooting of Michael Brown, an unarmed Black teenager, by a White police officer. Known as the Black Lives Matter movement, it spread across the nation as the media carried reports, photos, and videos of police violence against Blacks in Chicago, South Carolina, Baltimore, New York, and other cities. To supporters, the movement highlights the continuing injustice suffered by Blacks at the hands of White authorities—the fact that Black lives seem not to matter. However, some critics embraced a new slogan, "All lives matter," which many advocates of Black civil rights saw as an effort to diminish their concerns.

In 2020, protests erupted when a white Minneapolis police officer was seen on video killing a Black man who had been taken into custody. A video showed another Black man killed by Atlanta, Georgia police who were apparently attempting to arrest him. These killings sparked calls under the banner, "defund the police," for the imposition of major police reforms throughout America. The 2020 protests led to renewed demands for the removal of Confederate statues and other reminders of slavery.

Opportunity in Education

Education has been the focus of some of the most important battles over civil rights, largely because Americans believe that everyone should have an equal chance to succeed. Inequality in educational opportunities was painfully obvious in the 1950s. Poverty rates of Blacks far exceeded those of Whites. Equal access to quality education, it was thought, would reduce and perhaps eliminate those inequities.

School Desegregation. After *Brown v. Board of Education*, the District of Columbia and some school districts in border states responded quickly to court-ordered desegregation, but states in the Deep South responded with delaying tactics. Southern legislatures passed laws ordering school districts to maintain segregated schools and state superintendents to withhold state funding from racially mixed classrooms.

Most of these plans were struck down as unconstitutional by federal courts.[89] But southern resistance went beyond legislation. Perhaps the most serious incident occurred in Arkansas in 1957. On the first day of school, a White mob assembled at Little Rock Central High School to protest integration and block Black students from attending. Governor Orval Faubus ordered the Arkansas National Guard to prevent enforcement of a federal court order to integrate the school. When President Eisenhower deployed U.S. troops and placed the city under martial law, Faubus responded by closing all the city's public high schools. In 1959, the Supreme Court ordered the schools reopened.

As the southern states invented new ways to avoid desegregation, it became clear that the federal courts could not do the job alone. At last, in 1964, Congress passed a new Civil Rights Act that outlawed discrimination against racial, ethnic, and religious minorities and against women. The law allowed federal agencies to withhold grants, contracts, and loans to states and municipalities found to discriminate or obstruct the law's implementation.

Further progress in school desegregation came in the form of busing children across school districts, sometimes for relatively long distances,[90] and reorganizing school attendance zones. Figure 4.2 shows the increase in racial integration in southern schools as a result of such measures. However, continued progress will likely be slow unless the Supreme Court permits federal action against de facto segregation and the varieties of private schools that have sprung up for the purpose of avoiding integration.[91]

A 1995 decision in which the Court signaled to lower courts to "disengage from desegregation efforts" dimmed the prospects for further school integration. In 2007, the Court went further, declaring unconstitutional programs in the Louisville and Seattle school districts that tried to achieve racial diversity by using race as a determining factor in admissions.[92]

Women and Education. Women have also suffered from unequal access to education. Throughout the nineteenth century, relatively few colleges and professional schools admitted them. Even as late as the 1960s, elite universities

**analyzing
the evidence**

What happened in 1964 that
accounts for the upward
trend beginning in 1965?

figure 4.2

PERCENTAGE OF SOUTHERN BLACK CHILDREN ATTENDING SCHOOL WITH WHITES, 1955–1973

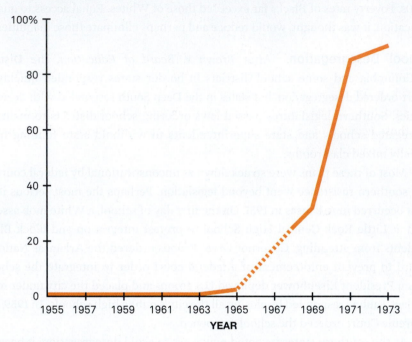

NOTE: Dashed line indicates missing data.

SOURCE: Gerald N. Rosenberg, *The Hollow Hope: Can Courts Bring About Social Change?* (Chicago: University of Chicago Press, 1991), pp. 50–51.

such as Princeton and Yale did not admit women undergraduates, and colleges that did offered women fewer opportunities than men to participate in programs, clubs, and athletics. Congress began to address these inequalities with the Civil Rights Act of 1964, but the most significant federal legislation to guarantee women equal access to education is the 1972 Education Act. Title IX of this act forbids gender discrimination in education. By the mid-1970s, most universities had become fully coed. But enforcing equality was more difficult.

Although the Education Act's enforcement provisions are fairly weak, it has proved effective for litigation. A significant step came in 1992, when the Court ruled that violations of Title IX could be remedied with monetary damages.[93] This ruling both opened the door for further legal action in the area of education and led to stronger enforcement against sexual harassment in educational institutions, as well as gender inequities both in resources (such as lab space, research support for faculty, and athletics) and in staff and faculty compensation. Over the next two years, complaints to the Education Department's Office for Civil Rights about unequal treatment of women's athletic programs nearly tripled. As a result, some universities were ordered to create more women's sports programs; many other colleges and universities have added more women's programs to avoid potential litigation.[94]

Title IX has also played an important role in the area of sexual harassment. During the Obama administration, the Department of Education issued a "Dear Colleague" letter to all of America's colleges and universities declaring that sexual harassment and sexual violence were forms of discrimination outlawed by Title IX. The letter set forward guidelines to be followed when dealing with charges of sexual harassment on campus. Critics asserted that the guidelines offered no protection to men accused of sexual harassment and encouraged false charges. President Trump's Education Secretary, Betsy DeVos, rescinded the Obama era guidelines and issued new instructions designed to enhance legal safeguards for those accused of an offense. Critics of the new guidelines said they would discourage victims from bringing charges.

The Politics of Rights

The Nineteenth Amendment, *Brown v. Board of Education*, the 1964 Civil Rights Act, and the Voting Rights Act helped redefine civil rights in America not just for women and Blacks but for all people. These movements became models for other groups to press civil rights claims, and their strategies have been widely imitated. The principles behind equality in voting and in education have since been applied to many other areas, including employment, housing, immigration, access to public facilities, and athletics. With the push for rights, however, there has also been a push back. Just how far do civil rights extend?

Outlawing Discrimination in Employment. Despite the slow progress of school desegregation, there was some progress in other areas of civil rights during the 1960s and 1970s. Voting rights were established and fairly quickly began to revolutionize southern politics. Service on juries was no longer denied to minorities. But progress in the right to participate in politics and government contrasted with a relative lack of economic progress.

The federal courts and the Justice Department entered the arena of discrimination in employment through Title VII of the Civil Rights Act of 1964, which outlaws job discrimination by all private and public employers, including government agencies (such as fire and police departments), that employ more than 15 workers. As we saw in Chapter 3, the Supreme Court defined "interstate commerce" so broadly that Congress had the constitutional authority to regulate almost any business. This power included outlawing discrimination by virtually any local employer.[95] Title VII made it unlawful to discriminate in employment on the basis of color, religion, sex, or national origin, as well as race.

A potential difficulty with Title VII is that the plaintiff must show that deliberate discrimination caused the failure to get a job or a training opportunity. Employers rarely admit discrimination on the basis of race, sex, or any other illegal factor. For a time, courts allowed plaintiffs to make their case if they could show that hiring practices had the *effect* of exclusion.[96] More recently though, the Supreme Court placed a number of limits on employment discrimination suits. In 2007, for example, it said that a complaint of gender discrimination must be brought within 180 days of the time the discrimination was alleged to have occurred.[97] In 2009, Congress effectively overturned this decision by enacting legislation that greatly extends the time available to workers filing such suits.

Women and Gender Discrimination.   Although women gained voting and property rights long ago, they continue to suffer discrimination in various forms, particularly in employment. Here, women benefited from the civil rights movement and especially from Title VII, which in many ways fostered the growth of the women's movement in the 1960s and 1970s.[98] The first major campaign of the National Organization for Women (NOW) involved picketing the Equal Employment Opportunity Commission (EEOC) for its refusal to ban employment advertisements that classified jobs by gender.

Building on the growth of the women's movement, women's rights activists sought an equal rights amendment (ERA) to the Constitution. The proposed amendment stated that "equality of rights under the law shall not be denied or abridged by the United States or by any State on account of sex." Supporters believed that such a sweeping guarantee of equal rights was necessary to end all discrimination against women and make gender roles more equal. Opponents charged that it would be socially disruptive and would introduce changes—such as unisex restrooms—that most Americans did not want. The amendment easily passed Congress in 1972 and won quick approval in many state legislatures, but it fell three states short of the 38 needed for ratification by the 1982 deadline.[99]

Despite the ERA's failure, gender discrimination expanded dramatically as an area of civil rights law. In the 1970s, the Court helped to establish gender discrimination as a major visible civil rights issue. Although the Court refused to treat gender discrimination as equivalent to racial discrimination,[100] it did make it easier for plaintiffs to file and win gender discrimination suits by applying an "intermediate" level of review to these cases.[101] **Intermediate scrutiny** shifts the burden of justifying a law or policy's use of gender to the government.

The courts have also identified sexual harassment as a form of gender discrimination. In 1986, the Supreme Court held that sexual harassment in the workplace may be illegal even if the employee did not suffer tangible economic or job-related losses from it.[102] In 1993, the Court said harassment may also be unlawful even if the employee did not suffer tangible psychological costs as a result of it.[103] In two cases in 1998, Court further strengthened the law when it said that whether or not harassment results in economic harm to the employee, an employer is liable for it if it was committed by someone with authority over the employee. But the Court also said that an employer may defend itself by showing that it had a sexual harassment prevention and grievance policy in effect.[104]

The development of gender discrimination as an important part of the civil rights struggle has coincided with the rise of women's politics as a discrete movement in American politics. As with the struggle for racial equality, the

intermediate scrutiny
The test used by the Supreme Court in gender discrimination cases, which places the burden of justifying a law or policy's use mainly on the government.

relationship between changes in government policies and political action suggests that changes in government policies to a great degree produce political action. Today the existence of a powerful women's movement derives largely from Title VII of the Civil Rights Act of 1964 and from the Burger Court's application of it to the protection of women. In 2018, cases of sexual harassment involving prominent media and political figures led more and more women to come forward and name those who had victimized them. What came to be called the #MeToo movement revealed the extent to which sexual harassment still pervaded American society. It was founded by New York civil rights activist Tarana Burke but is less an organized movement than a loosely organized expression of concern and outrage directed against sexual violence. The #MeToo movement encourages victims of sexual violence to come forward, share their stories, name their attackers, and thereby give notice that sexual violence will not be tolerated.

Many of the victories won against gender discrimination have, in recent years, been applied to discrimination against transgender and gender-nonconforming individuals. In 2015, President Obama issued an executive order prohibiting federal contractors from discriminating against workers on the basis of their sexual orientation or gender identity. Later that year, the EEOC filed its first-ever lawsuits to protect transgender workers under Title VII of the Civil Rights Act, and Attorney General Eric Holder announced that, going forward, the Justice Department would consider discrimination against transgender people as covered by the Civil Rights Act's prohibition of sex discrimination.[105]

In 2016, the Justice Department declared that a North Carolina law restricting transgender people to the use of public restrooms consistent with the gender stated on their birth certificates constituted a violation of federal civil rights laws. The state government vowed to resist this federal stance. As the legal standoff continued, many companies pulled conventions and other events out of the state, costing North Carolina's economy millions of dollars.

In the midst of this battle, in June 2016, the U.S. military dropped its ban against openly transgender people serving in the uniformed services. But in 2017 President Trump declared that he would reinstate the ban. Trump's move met with opposition from military leaders, who feared disruption and litigation, and it was not clear what effect the president's statement would have. The Policy Principle box on p. 116 looks at changing policy around the transgender movement.

Latinos and Latinas.

The labels "Latino" and "Hispanic" encompass a wide range of groups with diverse national origins and experiences and distinctive cultural identities. The early political experiences of Mexican Americans were shaped by race and region. In 1898, Mexican Americans gained formal political rights, including the right to vote. In many places, however—especially in Texas—they were prevented from voting by such means as the white primary and the poll tax.[106]

the policy principle
TRANSGENDER RIGHTS AND POLICY

The campaign for transgender equality seeks to end discrimination against transgender people in employment, housing, health care, and public accommodations. Roughly 700,000 Americans openly identify as transgender or gender nonconforming, meaning that they do not necessarily identify with the sex they were assigned at birth. The United States' history of rights advocacy on the part of African Americans, women, and other groups blazed a trail for transgender people to follow, demonstrating tactics and offering potential allies for their cause. Earlier victories by these groups established legal principles, laws, and political institutions that transgender advocates could use to develop and implement policies for their own purposes.

For example, in recent years transgender advocates lobbied effectively to achieve court decisions and executive orders that applied to their own cause laws that were originally crafted to protect African Americans and women from workplace discrimination. The federal courts, the Justice Department, and the Equal Employment Opportunity Commission have all agreed that Title VII of the 1964 Civil Rights Act, prohibiting sex discrimination in employment, prohibits discrimination against transgender and gender nonconforming individuals as well. Two executive orders, the first by President Clinton in 1998 and the second by President Obama in 2014, prohibit discrimination in federal employment and in hiring by federal contractors, respectively, based on sexual orientation or gender identity. Thus, favorable federal policies emerged because transgender individuals could channel their policy preferences through an already-existing set of institutions.

The effort to end gender identity–based discrimination in public accommodations has taken a somewhat different path. Discrimination by hotels, restaurants, theaters, and so forth was not a focus for the women's movement, and thus federal antidiscrimination law for public accommodations covers race, religion, national origin, and disability but not gender. As a result, the transgender movement did not inherit an existing legal framework or set of institutions through which to pursue its policy goals. While continuing to work for federal legislation in this area, advocates have made strides at the state and local level to produce the movement's desired policy outcomes: as of 2018, 20 states and a number of localities have expressly

An inclusive restroom that people of any gender identity may use.

prohibited discrimination based on gender identity in public accommodations.

These successes have sometimes proved only temporary, however. In 2015, an antidiscrimination ordinance in Houston was repealed in a referendum. And in 2016, a similar measure in Charlotte, North Carolina, was reversed by the state's legislature, which enacted a bill prohibiting transgender individuals from using bathrooms in schools and other government buildings that correspond to their gender identity. After the federal Department of Justice then warned the state that the law violated the Civil Rights Act, the state and the department filed opposing lawsuits over the issue. In 2017, President Trump declared that the U.S. military would no longer accept transgender troops. However, two federal courts ruled against such a ban and the military leadership was reluctant to implement Trump's order.

 think it through

1. How did earlier rights movements influence the movement for transgender rights?

2. Should policies relating to transgender rights be determined at the federal level or by state and local governments? Why?

In addition, prior to World War II, segregated schools for Mexican Americans were common in Texas and California, along with housing and employment restrictions. In 1947, the League of United Latin American Citizens (LULAC) won a key victory in *Mendez v. Westminster*, which overturned an Orange County, California, policy of school segregation.[107] *Mendez* became an important precedent for *Brown v. Board of Education.*

As LULAC and other Mexican American political organizations worked to fight discrimination after World War II, the first Mexican American was elected to Congress in the late 1950s, and four others followed in the 1960s. In the late 1960s, a new kind of Mexican American political movement was born. Inspired by the Black civil rights movement, Mexican American students boycotted high school classes in Los Angeles, Denver, and San Antonio; students in colleges and universities across California joined in as well. Among their demands were bilingual education, an end to discrimination, and greater cultural recognition. In Crystal City, Texas, which White politicians had dominated despite an overwhelmingly Mexican American population, the newly formed La Raza Unida Party took over the city government by the early 1970s.[108]

In recent years, Latino political strategy has developed along two tracks. One is a traditional ethnic-group path of voter registration and voting along ethnic lines, because Hispanic voter registration rates typically lag far behind those for Whites and Blacks. Helping this strategy is the enormous growth of the Latino population, resulting in part from immigration. The second track is a legal strategy using civil rights laws designed to ensure fair access to the political system. The Mexican American Legal Defense and Educational Fund (MALDEF) has played a key role in designing and pursuing this strategy.

During the Trump presidency, Latino immigration has been a major political issue. President Trump has declared that illegal Latino immigrants represent a serious threat to American safety and security. As a result of Trump's actions, many Latinos have stepped up their political activity, mainly in support of Democratic politicians. Trump's perceived hostility toward Latinos will probably have political repercussions for years to come as America's most rapidly growing population group will see the GOP as a party hostile to its interests.

Asian Americans.   The early Asian experience in the United States was shaped by naturalization laws dating back to 1790, the first of which declared that only White immigrants were eligible for citizenship. Chinese immigrants drawn to California by the gold rush beginning in the 1850s were met with harsh antagonism from Whites, which led Congress in 1870 to declare them ineligible for citizenship. In 1882, the first Chinese Exclusion Act suspended the entry of Chinese laborers.

At the time of the Exclusion Act, the Chinese community in the United States consisted mainly of single male laborers, with few women and children. The few Chinese children in San Francisco were denied entry to public schools until parents of American-born Chinese children pressed legal action; even then, they had to attend a separate Chinese school. In 1898, the Supreme Court ruled that American-born Chinese children could not be denied citizenship.[109] Still, new Chinese immigrants were barred from the United States until 1943; China by then had become a wartime ally, and Congress repealed the Chinese Exclusion Act and permitted Chinese immigrants to become citizens. While Chinese were welcomed during the war, President Roosevelt issued executive orders sending most Japanese Americans on the West Coast to internment camps for the war's duration. Families lost their jobs and property and were forced to live in squalid conditions because they were suspected of sympathizing with Japan after the Japanese empire launched its December 1941 Pearl Harbor attack against the U.S.

Immigration climbed rapidly after the 1965 Immigration and Nationality Act, which lifted discriminatory quotas. Nevertheless, limited English proficiency barred many Asian Americans and Latinos from full participation in American life. Two developments in the 1970s, however, established rights for language minorities. In 1974, the Supreme Court ruled in a suit filed on behalf of Chinese students in San Francisco that school districts must provide education for students whose English is limited.[110] It did not require bilingual education, but it established a duty to provide instruction that students could understand. The 1970 amendments to the Voting Rights Act of 1965 permanently outlawed literacy tests as a prerequisite to register to vote and required bilingual ballots or oral assistance for those who speak Spanish, Chinese, Japanese, Korean, Native American languages, or Inuit languages.

Immigration and Rights.   The United States has always struggled to define the rights of immigrants and the notion of citizenship. Waves of immigration have raised questions as to whether immigrants should enjoy the same civil rights

Immigration laws are a source of debate in American politics. Some people feel that the government should do more to prevent illegal immigration, while others worry that harsher laws violate immigrants' rights and fundamental American values.

as citizens, such as the right to vote and equal access to education, or only a narrower set of rights.

Asian Americans, Latinos, and other groups have long been concerned about the impact of immigration laws on their civil rights. Many Asian American and Latino organizations opposed the Immigration Reform and Control Act of 1986 because it imposes sanctions on employers who hire undocumented workers—sanctions they feared would lead employers to avoid hiring Latinos and Asian Americans. Indeed, a 1990 report by the General Accounting Office found that sanctions had created a "widespread pattern of discrimination" against Latinos and others who appear foreign.[111] Organizations such as MALDEF and the Asian Law Caucus monitor and challenge such discrimination, and as anti-immigrant sentiment has grown in recent years, they have also focused on the rights of legal and illegal immigrants.

The Supreme Court has ruled that undocumented immigrants are eligible for education and medical care but can be denied other social benefits; legal immigrants, however, are to be treated much the same as citizens. But with increased immigration and economic insecurity, many voters nationwide support drawing a sharper line between immigrants and citizens.

The movement to deny benefits to noncitizens began in California, which experienced sharp economic distress in the early 1990s and has the highest levels of immigration of any state. In 1994, Californians voted to deny illegal immigrants all services except emergency medical care. Supporters of the measure hoped to discourage illegal immigration and pressure illegal immigrants already in the country to leave. Opponents argued that denying basic services to illegal immigrants risked creating a subclass whose lack of education and poor health would threaten all Americans. In 1994 and 1997, a federal court affirmed previous rulings that illegal immigrants should be granted public education.

Today, one of the most contentious issues surrounding immigration concerns the nearly one million undocumented immigrants who were brought to the United States as children and were raised and attended school in America. Former president Barack Obama issued an executive order called "Deferred Action for Childhood Arrivals," or DACA, protecting such individuals from deportation. In 2017, President Trump announced that DACA would be discontinued. Trump's action was blocked by a lower federal court decision. In 2020 the Supreme Court ruled that the Trump administration had made a number of procedural errors when it ended the program. This decision, authored by Chief Justice Roberts, gave the 700,000 DACA recipients a reprieve while the administration considered its next steps.

The Constitution begins with the phrase "We the People of the United States"; likewise, the Bill of Rights refers to the rights of *people*, not the rights of citizens. Undocumented immigrants are certainly people, though not citizens. Americans continue to be divided on the question of the rights to which these people are entitled.

Americans with Disabilities.   The concept of rights for people with disabilities emerged in the 1970s as the civil rights model spread to other groups. The seed was planted in a little-noticed provision of the 1973 Rehabilitation Act that outlawed discrimination against individuals on the basis of disabilities. As in many other cases, the law itself helped spark the movement for rights.[112]

Mimicking the NAACP's Legal Defense Fund, the disability movement founded a Disability Rights Education and Defense Fund to press its legal claims. The movement's greatest success has been the passage of the Americans with Disabilities Act (ADA) of 1990, which guarantees people with disabilities equal employment rights and access to public businesses. The law's impact has been far-reaching, as businesses and public facilities have installed ramps, elevators, and other devices to meet its requirements.[113]

Gay Men and Women.   Beginning with street protests in the 1960s, the gay rights movement has grown into a major area of civil rights advocacy.

The 1990s witnessed both the first national anti-gay laws and the first Supreme Court declaration protecting the civil rights of gay men and women. In 1993, in the first months of his presidency, Bill Clinton confronted the question of whether gays should be allowed to serve in the military. As a candidate, he had said he favored lifting the ban on gays in the military, but his administration eventually compromised on a "Don't Ask, Don't Tell" policy, which allowed gay men and women to serve in the military as long as they did not openly proclaim their sexual orientation or engage in homosexual activity. Two years later, gay rights experienced another setback when Clinton signed the Defense of Marriage Act (DOMA), which for the purposes of federal laws, such as those concerning taxes and spousal benefits, recognized a marriage as only the union of one man and one woman.

As with other civil rights movements, it was the Supreme Court that took a major step in protecting gay men and women from discrimination—a step that marked an important departure from its earlier rulings. The first gay rights case that the Court decided, *Bowers v. Hardwick* (1986), had ruled against a right to privacy that would protect consensual homosexual activity. (See "The Right to Privacy" on p. 100.)

Subsequently, the gay rights movement sought suitable legal cases to challenge the constitutionality of discrimination against gay men and women, much as the civil rights movement had done in the late 1940s and 1950s. Among the possibilities were cases stemming from local ordinances restricting gay rights (including the right to marry), from job discrimination, and from family law issues such as adoption and parental rights. In 1996, the Supreme Court explicitly extended fundamental civil rights protections to gay men and women by declaring unconstitutional a 1992 amendment to the Colorado state constitution that prohibited local governments from passing ordinances to protect gay rights.[114] The decision's forceful language highlighted the connection between gay rights and civil rights as it declared discrimination against gay people unconstitutional.

Finally, in 2003 the Court overturned *Bowers* and struck down a Texas statute criminalizing certain sexual conduct between consenting partners of the same sex. The decision extended at least one aspect of civil liberties to sexual minorities: the right to privacy. However, it did not undo various other exclusions that deprived gay men and women of full civil rights. Another important victory came in 2010, when Congress repealed Don't Ask, Don't Tell. After a lengthy study by the Defense Department of the possible consequences of allowing openly gay men and women to serve, Congress voted for the repeal.

The focal point for gay rights soon turned to the right to marry. In 2004, the Supreme Judicial Court of Massachusetts had ruled that under the state's constitution, gay men and women were entitled to marry. The state senate then asked the court to rule on whether a civil union statute (avoiding the word *marriage*) would satisfy the ruling. In response, the Massachusetts court said no, that this approach was too much like the "separate but equal" doctrine that had maintained legalized racial segregation from 1896 to 1954. In the decade between 2004 and 2014, same-sex marriage became legal in 35 states through court order, voter initiative, or legislative enactment. However, these changes faced pushback; in many states, voters and legislatures approved constitutional amendments banning same-sex marriage. Some of these bans were struck down by courts, but in November 2014, same-sex marriage remained illegal in 15 states.

The discrepancy between some state laws, which recognized same-sex marriage, and the federal law under DOMA led to a reevaluation of DOMA. In 2013, the Supreme Court ruled DOMA unconstitutional "as a deprivation of liberty of the person protected by the Fifth Amendment."[115] Finally, in 2015 the Court ruled definitively in *Obergefell v. Hodges* that the right to marry is guaranteed to same-sex couples by the due process clause and the equal protection clause.[116] The decision required all states to issue marriage licenses to same-sex couples and to recognize same-sex marriages performed in other jurisdictions. Despite scattered local resistance, this decision seemed to put an end to the marriage question, though LGBTQ activists continue to fight for equal rights in other arenas. In 2020, LGBTQ and transgender individuals won a significant victory in the Supreme Court. In a 6-3 decision written by Justice Neil Gorsuch, the Court ruled that the 1964 Civil Rights Act prohibited employment discrimination based upon sexual orientation, just as it prohibited employment discrimination based upon race and gender.

Affirmative Action

In the past 50 years, the push for equal opportunity has come to encompass the broader goal of **affirmative action**—action to help overcome the consequences of past discrimination against specific groups by making special efforts to provide members of these groups with access to educational and employment opportunities. In 1965, President Lyndon Johnson issued executive orders promoting minority employment in the federal civil service and in companies doing business with the national government. But affirmative action did not become a prominent goal until the 1970s.

affirmative action
A policy or program designed to correct historical injustices committed against specific groups by making special efforts to provide members of these groups with access to educational and employment opportunities.

As affirmative action spread, the issue of giving preference to minority-group members in college admissions, employment, and other areas began to divide civil rights supporters. In 1974, Allan Bakke, a White man, sued the University of California at Davis School of Medicine on the grounds that in denying him admission, the school had discriminated against him on the basis of his race. That year, the school had reserved 16 of 100 available slots for minority applicants. Bakke argued that his grades and test scores had ranked him well above many students who were accepted and that he had been rejected only because they were Black or Hispanic and he was White.

In 1978, Bakke won his case before the Supreme Court and was admitted to the medical school, but affirmative action was not declared unconstitutional. The Court rejected the medical school's admissions procedures because they included both a quota and a separate admissions system for minorities. The Court agreed with Bakke that racial categorizations are suspect categories that place a severe burden of proof on those using them to show a "compelling public purpose." It went on to say that achieving "a diverse student body" was a compelling public purpose but that the rigid quota of slots assigned on the basis of race was incompatible with the equal protection clause. Thus the Court permitted universities (and other schools, training programs, and hiring authorities) to continue to take minority status into consideration but limited severely the use of quotas.[117]

For nearly a decade after the *Bakke* decision, the Supreme Court was generally permissive about efforts by corporations and governments to experiment with affirmative action programs in employment.[118] But in 1989, it returned to the *Bakke* position, ruling that any "rigid numerical quota" is suspect and that any affirmative action program already approved by federal courts could be challenged by individuals (usually White men) alleging that the program had discriminated against them.[119]

In 1995, another Supreme Court ruling further weakened affirmative action. This decision stated that race-based policies, such as preferences given by the government to minority contractors, must survive strict scrutiny, placing the burden on the government to show that such affirmative action programs serve a compelling governmental interest and are narrowly tailored to address identifiable past discrimination.[120] In 1996, the U.S. Court of Appeals for the Fifth Circuit ruled that race could never be considered in granting admissions and scholarships at state colleges and universities, even as a factor in diversity.[121] The Supreme Court refused to hear a challenge to this decision, which, in the three southern states covered by the Fifth Circuit, effectively rolled back the use of affirmative action permitted by the 1978 *Bakke* case.

In 2003, affirmative action was challenged in two Supreme Court cases arising from the University of Michigan. The first suit alleged that by automatically awarding 20 points (out of 150) on a ranking system to African American, Latino, and Native American applicants, the university's undergraduate admissions policy discriminated unconstitutionally against White students with otherwise equal or superior academic qualifications. The Supreme Court agreed, arguing that something tantamount to a quota was involved.[122]

In a second important case, Barbara Grutter sued the University of Michigan Law School on the grounds that it had discriminated in a race-conscious way against White applicants with grades and law board results equal or superior to those of minority applicants. A 5–4 vote aligned the majority of the Supreme Court with Justice Lewis Powell's opinion in *Bakke* for the first time. Powell had argued that diversity in education is a compelling state interest and that, constitutionally, race could be considered as a positive factor in admissions decisions. In *Grutter v. Bollinger*, the Court reiterated Powell's holding and, applying strict scrutiny to the law school's policy, found that its admissions process was narrowly tailored to the school's compelling state interest in diversity because it gave a "highly individualized, holistic review of each applicant's file," in which race counted but was not used in a "mechanical way."[123] This ruling put affirmative action on stronger ground.

In 2016, the Court affirmed this idea by stating that some intrusion on equal protection, such as considering race in the college admissions process, was warranted by the importance of creating a diverse student body.[124] It seems that race can be one factor in the admissions process but may not be the single or defining criterion for college admission. Public opinion on affirmative action remains somewhat divided, with lower support for programs that help racial minorities than for those that help women. (See the Analyzing the Evidence unit on pp. 124–125.)

Because of America's troubled history of slavery and segregation, we automatically tend to associate discrimination with efforts to exclude African Americans from full participation in American society. Yet, as we have seen, other groups have also faced discrimination in employment and housing. Even today, women face job and salary discrimination, Asian Americans face subtle discrimination in college admissions, and Latinos face severe barriers in winning acceptance and citizenship in the U.S. America's practices often do not live up to our ideals.

CONCLUSION

How did the framers of the Constitution view the relationship between liberty and government? How do civil rights promote representation? As we observed at the beginning of this chapter, the Constitution's Bill of Rights includes both rights and liberties. A liberty is a limit on the government's intrusion into an area such as speech or religious belief. A right, on the other hand, is an obligation imposed on the government. When citizens have a right, such as the right to vote or to a jury trial, the government must not only respect that right but also act vigorously to protect it.

analyzing the evidence

Is the Public Principled or Prejudiced When It Comes to Affirmative Action?

Contributed by **David C. Wilson**, *University of Delaware*

Are opinions about affirmative action based on principled policy positions or prejudices toward beneficiaries? Supporters argue that affirmative action helps redress centuries of prejudice and discrimination that denied certain citizens the opportunity to prosper. They argue that without affirmative action, institutions and employers would be able to discriminate without penalty. Opponents argue that it's a matter of principle: they believe affirmative action grants unfair advantage to racial minorities and other groups at the expense of nonminorities. They claim some people are benefiting from their demographics rather than qualification merits. That is, race and gender unfairly privilege some citizens over others.

In reviewing decades of public opinion research on affirmative action, my colleagues and I discovered that few, if any, studies examined how people's views concerning one targeted beneficiary group (for example, racial minorities) were affected by views concerning another group (such as women). This question bears on the extent to which opinion on affirmative action is based on racial prejudice versus principled reasoning. A principled position would propose that affirmative action is detrimental regardless of what group it benefits, because "special consideration" based on any characteristic is unfair to other individuals who don't receive such consideration. A prejudiced position would mean that people favor some groups over others and the less favored groups are less deserving of the benefits of affirmative action. In theory, principled positions should be consistent across groups, and prejudiced positions should prefer some groups over others.

Using a public opinion experiment embedded in a 2003 Gallup Poll, we assessed whether people's group biases led them to support or oppose affirmative action because of racial or gender cues. In the poll, half the respondents were asked an initial question about affirmative action programs for women and then were asked a follow-up question about affirmative action for racial minorities. The other half were asked the questions in reverse order. The experiment allowed us to determine people's support for each type of affirmative action program when considered in isolation from the other (based on how they responded to whichever question they were asked first), and when considered in the context of the other (based on how they responded to whichever question they were asked second). If context affects opinion, that would mean the public is prejudiced toward one group relative to the other, but if context has no effect on opinion, then the public is principled in their policy positions.

Overall, our results showed that public opinion toward affirmative action is biased by positive beliefs about women and negative beliefs about racial minorities.

SOURCE: David Wilson, David W. Moore, Patrick F. McKay, and Derek R. Avery, "Affirmative Action Programs for Women and Minorities: Support Affected by Question Order," *Public Opinion Quarterly* 73 (2008): 514–22.

The Effect of Context on Opinion toward Affirmative Action

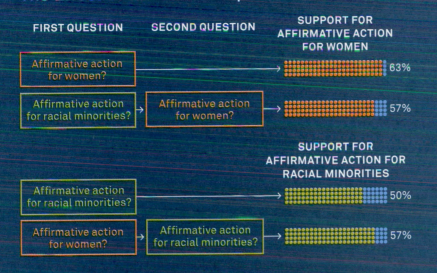

FIRST QUESTION	SECOND QUESTION	SUPPORT FOR AFFIRMATIVE ACTION FOR WOMEN
Affirmative action for women?		63%
Affirmative action for racial minorities?	Affirmative action for women?	57%

FIRST QUESTION	SECOND QUESTION	SUPPORT FOR AFFIRMATIVE ACTION FOR RACIAL MINORITIES
Affirmative action for racial minorities?		50%
Affirmative action for women?	Affirmative action for racial minorities?	57%

We found that the public decreases its support for affirmative action for women (−6 percent) when considered in the context of affirmative action for racial minorities but increases its support for affirmative action for racial minorities (+7 percent) in the context of affirmative action for women.

Support for Affirmative Action for Women

QUESTION ORDER → ● Women → Minorities ◐ Minorities → Women

RESPONDENTS ↓
- White males
- White females
- Black males
- Black females

0% 25% 50% 75% 100%

Separating opinions based on a respondent's race and gender helps us understand where the principles and prejudices lie. Whites, both male and female, decrease their support for affirmative action for women when it is considered in the context of race; however, Blacks are consistent regardless of the beneficiary.

Support for Affirmative Action for Racial Minorities

QUESTION ORDER → ● Women → Minorities ◐ Minorities → Women

RESPONDENTS ↓
- White males
- White females
- Black males
- Black females

0% 25% 50% 75% 100%

White respondents, both male and female, increase their support for affirmative action for racial minorities when it is considered in the context of gender. Once again, Black respondents remain consistent regardless of the beneficiary.

What insights on survey design can we take from this study?
What demographics factors within the groups surveyed, such as age or geographic location, might provide further insights on public opinion on affirmative action?

Rights and liberties are essential elements of representative government in the United States. Without the liberties enjoyed by American citizens, government could become overwhelming. Tyranny could replace governance. Without rights, citizens might not be represented and would not be in a position to protect their liberties. Thus, civil rights and civil liberties are among America's most important promises and aspirations. Perfection is impossible, but we must always strive to be better.

Key Terms

civil liberties 82

strict scrutiny 85

establishment clause 87

Lemon test 88

free exercise clause 89

speech plus 93

prior restraint 93

libel 93

slander 93

fighting words 95

due process 98

exclusionary rule 98

grand jury 99

Miranda rule 99

right to privacy 100

civil rights 102

equal protection clause 106

"separate but equal" rule 106

de jure segregation 108

de facto segregation 108

intermediate scrutiny 114

affirmative action 121

Check Your Understanding

1. What are civil liberties? How was the Bill of Rights developed in order to protect citizens from improper governmental action?

2. Explain how *Brown v. Board of Education* jump-started a constitutional revolution and the role strict scrutiny played in the process.

3. What is the significance of the Supreme Court's decision that any legislation restricting freedom of speech "is to be subjected to a more exacting judicial scrutiny . . . than are most other types of legislation"?

4. How has the idea of right to privacy evolved since the 1950s? How has technological change presented the courts with new questions about privacy in the future?

5. What are civil rights and what are several areas of their concern?

6. How are rights and liberties essential elements of representative government in the United States?

INQUIZITIVE

Earn a better grade on your test. InQuizitive personalizes your learning path to help you master the concepts from this chapter. In a recent efficacy study of American government students, InQuizitive increased test scores by an average of 17 points (see back cover).

CHAPTER FIVE

CONGRESS: THE FIRST BRANCH

In the November 2016 elections, Republicans won control of the White House and both houses of Congress. Since that time, though, only one major piece of legislation—a substantial change in the federal tax code—has been enacted, mainly because members of Congress could not reach agreement on such key matters as health care and infrastructure repair. Congress was again "gridlocked" on policies. After the 2018 midterm elections, the Democrats captured the House of Representatives. With government divided between the parties—a Democratic House and a Republican Senate and president—gridlock intensified. The 2020 elections revealed a still-divided public. The presidency has changed hands, the Republicans continue their control of the Senate, and the House Democratic majority has shrunk.

Most often, gridlock results from sharp divisions between the two parties. During the 115th and 116th Congresses, conflicts within the Republican Party were to blame. All Republicans, for example, had declared themselves opposed to "Obamacare," the health care program developed during the Obama administration. When it came to actually repealing the measure, Republicans could not agree on what, if anything, should replace the program, and some Republicans found that various constituents, including powerful lobby groups like the Pharmaceutical Research and Manufacturers of America (PhARMA), strongly supported keeping Obamacare. The GOP was divided, and the repeal effort ground to a halt.

If gridlock was the culprit for governmental difficulties during this period, then these difficulties were compounded by another culprit: pandemic. Beginning in late January 2020, the COVID-19 virus began spreading throughout the United States. Infections and deaths mounted, creating a national public health crisis. Efforts to fight the coronavirus pandemic produced hardship as economic activity contracted dramatically and unemployment soared to levels not seen since the Great Depression of the 1930s.

The U.S. Congress is the "first branch" of government under Article I of the Constitution, and it is also among the world's most important representative bodies. Most such bodies only confirm and give legal status to decisions actually made by executives like a president, prime minister, or cabinet. The U.S. Congress is one of the few national representative bodies that actually possesses powers of governance. It has a good deal of authority over the two most important powers of any government: the power of force (control over the nation's military forces) and the power over money.

Specifically, according to Article I, Section 8, Congress can "lay and collect Taxes," pay the government's debts and establish national bankruptcy laws, impose duties (taxes on imported or exported goods), borrow and coin (issue) money, and generally control the nation's purse strings. It also can "provide for the common Defence and general Welfare," regulate interstate commerce, undertake public works like roads, acquire and control federal lands, and promote science and "useful Arts" by granting patents and copyrights.

In foreign policy, Congress has the power to declare war, deal with piracy, regulate foreign commerce, and create and regulate the armed forces and military installations. Further, the Senate has the power to decide whether to ratify treaties negotiated by the executive branch (ratification requires a two-thirds vote) and to approve the appointment of ambassadors. Capping these powers, Article I, Section 8, authorizes Congress to make laws "which shall be necessary and proper for carrying into Execution the foregoing Powers, and all other Powers vested by this Constitution in the Government of the United States, or in any Department or Officer thereof."

The framers of the Constitution intended for Congress to be the "first branch" of the national government. Members of Congress are expected to represent the people and to govern through the legislative process.

- **Why does Congress's representative role sometimes seem to interfere with its ability to govern effectively?**

In both the domestic and foreign arenas, Congress competes for power with the president. This competition is consistent with the framers' ideas about the separation of powers. The framers thought that citizens' liberties would be safest if the powers of governance were divided so that no single institution could exercise them on its own.

The fact that Congress is a representative body, however, often complicates its ability to govern. Although it is frequently criticized for being slow and unproductive, procedurally complicated, and uncompromising in its partisan positions, these characteristics stem directly from its representative character. Members of Congress are nominated and elected in a particular state or district rather than as part of a group selected by national party officials, as in many other democracies. Therefore, they are likely to bicker and delay, because they represent a variety of groups and interests that demand to hear their perspectives voiced and have their interests considered when decisions are made. Sometimes, congressional representatives are forced to focus on their constituencies' particular interests rather than on the general good. In this way, Congress can become gridlocked and slow to act, particularly when Americans are themselves deeply divided. The legislative process is complicated because a representative assembly must find ways of balancing minority rights and majority rule, of making decisions while still allowing competing claims to be heard and taken into account.

In essence, Congress is slow to act, cumbersome in its procedures, and contentious in its discussions because it is a representative institution. In this chapter we examine the organization of Congress and the legislative process.

Learning Objectives

- Describe how members of Congress represent their constituents.

- Explain how the electoral system affects who serves in Congress and what they do once in office.

- Identify the major institutional features and rules that shape the legislative process (how a bill becomes a law).

- Summarize three key powers of Congress: oversight of the executive branch, impeachment, and the Senate's "advice and consent" power.

REPRESENTATION

constituency
The citizens who reside in the district from which an official is elected.

Congress is the most important representative institution in American government. The primary responsibility of its members is to their own states or districts—their **constituencies**—not to the congressional leadership, a party, or even Congress itself. Yet views differ about what constitutes fair and effective

figure 5.1

HOW MEMBERS OF CONGRESS REPRESENT THEIR DISTRICTS

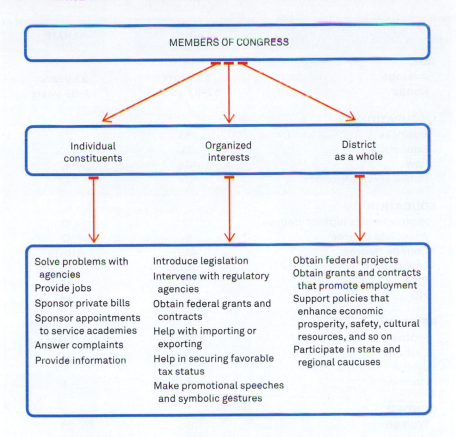

representation and about what demands can be made on representatives. Members of Congress must consider these diverse views and demands as they represent their constituents (Figure 5.1).

Some members see themselves as having been elected to do the bidding of those who elected them, and they act as **delegates**. Others see themselves as having been selected to do what they think is "right," and they act as **trustees**. Most members are a mix of these two types. And all need to survive the next election in order to pursue their chosen role.

Members not only represent others; they may be representative *of* others as well. The latter point is especially significant in terms of gender, sexual orientation, and race, where such representation is symbolically significant at the very least. Women, LGBTQ legislators, and members of minority groups can serve and draw support, both inside their state or district and in the nation at large, from those with whom they share an identity. (See Table 5.1 for a summary of demographic characteristics of members of Congress.)

As discussed in Chapter 1, we think of our political representatives as our agents. Frequent competitive elections are an important means by which constituents hold their representatives to account and keep them responsive

delegates
Legislators who vote according to the preferences of their constituents.

trustees
Legislators who vote according to what they think is best for their constituents.

table 5.1

DEMOGRAPHICS OF MEMBERS OF THE 116TH CONGRESS

	HOUSE	SENATE
AGE*		
Average	58 years	63 years
Range	32–87 years	39–83 years
OCCUPATION†		
Business	183	29
Education	73	20
Law	145	47
Public service/politics	184	47
EDUCATION‡		
High school is highest degree	17	0
Associate degree	6	0
College degree	415	100
Law degree	161	53
PhD	21	24
MD	21	34
RELIGION**		
Protestant	233	60
Catholic	141	22
Jewish	26	8
Mormon	6	4
GENDER		
Women	106	25
Men	332	75
RACE/ETHNICITY††		
White	317	80
African American	55	3
Hispanic/Latino	45	5
Asian/Pacific Islander	17	3
American Indian	4	0
LGBTQ	8	2
CONGRESSIONAL SERVICE		
Number serving in first term	90	9
Average length of service	4.3 terms/ 8.6 years	1.7 terms/ 10.1 years

*Age at beginning of 116th Congress.

†Most members list more than one occupation.

‡Education categories are not exclusive (for example, a representative with a law degree might also be counted as having a college degree).

**About 98 percent of members cite a specific religious affiliation. Other affiliations not listed here include Buddhist, Muslim, Hindu, Greek Orthodox, Unitarian, and Christian Science.

††Some members are in two race categories. Includes Delegates and Resident Commissioners.

SOURCE: Jennifer E. Manning, Membership of the 116th Congress: A Profile, CRS Report for Congress no. R45583 (Washington, DC: Congressional Research Service, 2019).

to constituency views and preferences. The relationship between representative and constituent is similar in some respects to the relationship between client and lawyer or between boss and employee. True, the relationship between a member of the House and 700,000 "bosses" in the district or between a senator and millions of bosses in the state is very different in scale from that between a lawyer and an individual client. But the criteria of performance are comparable.

At the very least, we expect representatives to strive constantly to discover the interests of their constituencies and to speak for those interests in Congress and other centers of government.[1] We expect this because we believe that members of Congress, like politicians everywhere, are ambitious. For many, this ambition is satisfied by maintaining a hold on their present office and advancing up the rungs of power in that legislative body. Some, however, may be looking ahead to the next level—a Senate seat, their state's governorship, or even the presidency.[2] (This means that members of Congress may not be concerned only with their present *geographic* constituency. They may want to appeal to a different geographic constituency, for instance, or seek support from a particular gender, ethnic, or racial community.) In each of these cases, the legislator is eager to serve the interests of constituents, either to enhance the prospects of reelection or to improve the chances of moving to another level.[3]

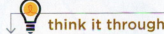

think it through

How do the members of the 116th Congress compare to your community? What groups are overrepresented? What groups are underrepresented? How might these differences impact the representation of your community's needs in Congress?

in brief

Major Differences between Members of the House and the Senate

	House	Senate
Minimum age	25 years	30 years
Minimum length of U.S. Citizenship	7 years	9 years
Length of term	2 years	6 years
Seats at stake in each election	All	One-third
Number	435; distribution based on state populations, with at least 1 per state (approximately 1 per 30,000 people in 1789; 1 per 700,000 today)	100; 2 per state
Constituency	Tends to be local	Both statewide and national

Citizens often feel that officials who share their race, gender, or other demographic characteristics will better represent their interests in government. Linda Sanchez was reelected to the House of Representatives in 2020 with support from women's and Hispanic groups.

bicameral legislature
A legislative body composed of two chambers, or houses.

money bill
A bill concerned solely with taxation or government spending.

House and Senate: Differences in Representation

The framers of the Constitution provided for a **bicameral legislature**, a legislative body consisting of two chambers. As we saw in Chapter 2, the framers intended each chamber to serve a different constituency. Members of the House of Representatives were to be "close to the people," elected by popular vote every two years. Because they saw the House in this way, the framers gave it a special power: all **money bills**—that is, bills authorizing the government to impose new taxes or to spend money for any purpose—were required to originate there. Members of the Senate were to be appointed by state legislatures for staggered six-year terms and were to be attuned more to the interests of elite society and property owners than to those of the general population.

Today, since the Seventeenth Amendment (1913) changed the selection method for senators, members of both chambers are elected directly by the people. The 435 members of the House are elected from districts apportioned (distributed) among the states according to their populations; the 100 members of the Senate are elected by state, with two senators from each.

The House and Senate play different roles in the legislative process. In essence, the Senate is the more deliberative body—the forum in which all ideas can receive a thorough public airing. The House is the more centralized and organized body—better equipped to play a role in the routine governmental process. In part, this difference stems from the different rules governing the two bodies. These rules give House leaders more control over the legislative process and encourage House members to specialize in certain legislative areas. The rules of the much smaller, more freewheeling Senate give its leadership less power and discourage specialization (although in recent years Senate leadership has taken on a more proactive role, much like its counterpart in the House).

Other formal and informal factors contribute to differences between the two chambers. Differences in the length of terms and requirements for holding office lead to differences in how members of each body develop their constituencies and exercise their powers of office. The smaller size and relative economic, social, and cultural uniformity of their districts and the frequency with which they must seek reelection make House members more attuned than senators to local interest groups with specific legislative agendas—used-car dealers seeking relief from regulation, labor unions seeking easier organizing rules, or farmers looking for higher subsidies. This was the intent of the Constitution's drafters—that the House of Representatives be the "people's house" and that its members reflect public opinion in a timely manner.

Senators, in contrast, serve larger and more diverse constituencies. As a result, they are better able than members of the House to be the agents for groups and interests organized on a statewide or national basis. Moreover, with longer terms in office, senators have the luxury of considering new ideas or seeking to bring together new coalitions of interests, rather than simply serving existing ones. This, too, is what the framers intended when they drafted the Constitution.

Ideology: Political Ideas and Beliefs

For much of the late twentieth century, the House displayed more intense divisions than the Senate along the lines of party and ideology. Because of their more diverse constituencies, senators were more inclined to seek compromises than were members of the House, who were more willing to stick to their partisan and ideological guns. Beginning with the presidency of George W. Bush, however, even the Senate grew more partisan and polarized.

During Barack Obama's presidency, many of the president's initiatives dealing with the economic crisis, health care, and other areas received virtually no Republican support. The first two years of the Trump presidency looked like a carbon copy of the Obama experience, with a firmly Republican House and a Senate boasting a bare Republican majority seeking to pass legislation without Democratic participation. The Democrats played an exclusively oppositional role, as in their united disapproval of Neil Gorsuch and Brett Kavanaugh as nominees to the Supreme Court and united opposition to the tax bill enacted on an almost straight party-line vote in 2017. Not a single Democrat voted for the bill, while 12 House Republicans voted against it—not enough to block its passage. Trump's second two years witnessed a more active, Democrat-controlled House; yet its legislative products have mainly died in a Senate still controlled by the Republicans. An important exception, as we discussed in the chapter opener, were the bipartisan coronavirus relief bills. In fact, it took the coronavirus pandemic of 2020 to produce a modicum of bipartisanship as the House and Senate, with support from both parties, passed important health and economic relief measures. But partisan bickering started soon after that.

The Electoral System

In light of their role as agents for various constituencies in their states and districts, and the importance of elections as a mechanism by which principals (constituents) reward and punish their agents, senators and representatives are very much influenced by electoral considerations. Three factors related to the U.S. electoral system affect who gets elected and what that person does once in office. The first factor concerns who decides to run for office and which candidates have an edge over others. The second factor is the advantage that incumbents have in winning reelection. Finally, the way congressional district lines are drawn can greatly affect the outcome of elections.

Running for Office.   Voters' choices are restricted from the start by who decides to run for office. In the past, local party officials decided who would run for a particular office; they might nominate someone who had a record of service to the party, or who was owed a favor, or whose "turn" had come up.

Today, few party organizations have the power to "slate" candidates in that way. Instead, the decision to run for Congress is a more personal choice. One of the most important factors determining who runs for office is individual ambition.[4] Potential candidates may also assess whether they can raise enough money to mount a campaign with a reasonable chance of success using connections to other politicians, interest groups, and the national party organization.

Features distinctive to each congressional district, such as the range of other political opportunities there, also affect its field of candidates. For any candidate, decisions about running must be made early because once money has been committed to already-declared candidates, it is harder for new candidates to break into a race. Thus, the outcome of a November election is partially determined many months earlier, when decisions to run are finalized.[5]

Incumbency.   **Incumbency** plays a key role in the American electoral system and in the kind of representation that citizens get in Washington. Once in office, members of Congress are typically eager to remain in office and make politics a career. And incumbent legislators have created an array of tools that stack the deck in favor of their reelection. Through effective use of these tools, an incumbent establishes a reputation for competence, imagination, and responsiveness—the qualities that most voters look for in a representative.

Perhaps the most important advantage of congressional incumbency is incumbents' opportunity to serve on legislative committees. Doing so enables members to polish their policy credentials, develop expertise, and help constituents, either by sponsoring or supporting legislation or by attempting to influence decisions by agencies and regulatory commissions on their behalf. By serving on committees, incumbents establish a track record of accomplishments that compares favorably with the mere promises of potential challengers.

The opportunity to help constituents—and thus gain support in the district—goes beyond the particular committees on which a member serves. A considerable share of a representative's time and an even greater share of staff members' time is devoted to constituency service, or **casework**, which includes talking to

incumbent
A current office holder.

casework
Efforts by members of Congress to gain the trust and support of constituents by providing personal services. One important type of casework is helping constituents to obtain favorable treatment from the federal bureaucracy.

Alaska's proposed "bridge to nowhere" became an infamous example of pork-barrel legislation after Alaskan members of Congress inserted earmarks for $320 million into a highway bill. The bridge, which would have connected the town of Ketchikan to a sparsely populated island, was never built.

constituents, providing them with minor services, introducing special bills and intervening with the bureaucracy for them, and working with local officials.

One significant way in which members of Congress serve as agents of their constituencies on a larger scale is through **patronage**, direct services and benefits that members provide for their districts, especially making partisan appointments to offices and conferring grants, licenses, or special favors to supporters.

One of the most important forms of patronage is **pork-barrel legislation**, through which representatives seek to capture federal projects and funds for their districts (or states in the case of senators) and thus "bring home the bacon" for their constituents. A common form of pork barreling is the *earmark*, the practice by which members of Congress insert language into otherwise pork-free bills that provides special benefits for their own constituents.[6] Since 2011 Congressional rules have forbidden earmarks, though they are now back in the conversation among members of both parties.[7]

Finally, all of these incumbent benefits are publicized through another incumbency advantage: the *franking privilege*. Under a law enacted by the first U.S. Congress in 1789, members of Congress may send mail to their constituents free of charge to keep them informed of governmental business and public affairs. The franking privilege provides incumbents with a valuable resource for making themselves and their activities visible to voters.

The incumbency advantage is evident in the high rates of reelection: over 90 percent for House members and nearly 90 percent for senators in recent decades (Figure 5.2).[8] The advantage is also evident in what is called *sophomore surge*, the tendency for candidates to win a higher percentage of the vote when seeking their second term than in their initial victory. With their "brand name," incumbents are in a position to raise campaign funds throughout their term, often

patronage
Direct services and benefits that members of Congress provide to their constituents, especially making partisan appointments to offices and conferring grants, licenses, or special favors to supporters.

pork-barrel legislation
Appropriations that members of Congress use to provide government funds for projects benefiting their home district or state.

figure 5.2

THE POWER OF INCUMBENCY, 1964–2020

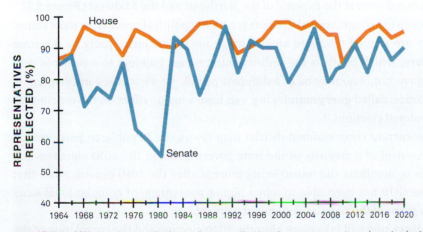

SOURCE: 1964–2018: OpenSecrets, "Reelection Rates over the Years," www.opensecrets.org/overview/reelect.php (accessed 11/7/20). 2020: As of November 7, 2020, several races in the House and Senate were still undecided; the figures for 2020 represent the author's best estimate. .

in quantities that scare off prospective challengers. And even when they draw challengers, incumbents are almost always able to outspend them.[9]

Over the past quarter-century, despite campaign finance regulations seeking to level the playing field, the gap between incumbent and challenger spending has grown (House) or held steady (Senate). Members of the majority party in the House and Senate are particularly attractive to donors who want access to those in power.[10] Potential challengers are often discouraged not only by an incumbent's war chest advantages but also by the fear that the incumbent simply has brought too many benefits to the district or is too well liked or too well known to be defeated.[11]

The role of incumbency also has implications for the social composition of Congress. For example, the incumbency advantage makes it harder for women to increase their numbers in Congress, because most incumbents are men. Women who run for open seats (for which there are no incumbents) are just as likely to win as male candidates.[12] The Women's March in Washington and around the country in January 2017 and the #MeToo movement, among other factors, led to a record number of women running for the House and Senate in primaries and the general election in 2018 and 2020. Supporters of term limits argue that the incumbency advantage and the tendency of legislators to view politics as a career mean that very little turnover will occur in Congress unless limits are imposed on the number of terms a legislator can serve. However, opponents of term limits argue that constant turnover of members would sharply reduce congressional influence vis-à-vis the executive branch.[13]

Congressional Districts.   The final factor that affects who is elected to Congress is the way congressional districts are drawn. Every 10 years, state legislatures must redraw congressional districts to reflect population changes. In 1929, Congress enacted a law fixing the total number of congressional seats at 435. As a result, when states with fast-growing populations gain districts, they do so at the expense of states with slower growth. In recent decades, the South and the West have gained congressional seats at the expense of the Northeast and the Midwest (Figure 5.3).

Redrawing congressional districts is a highly political process: in most states, districts are shaped to create an advantage for the majority party in the state legislature, which controls the redistricting process (subject to a possible veto by the governor, who may be of a different party). As we will see in Chapter 10, this practice, called **gerrymandering**, can have a major effect on the outcome of congressional elections.[14]

The current congressional district map favors the Republican party, which gained control of a majority of the state governments in the 2010 elections and was able to dominate the redistricting process after the 2010 census. Since that time, the GOP has been able to win a higher percentage of congressional seats than its share of the popular vote might warrant.

Redistricting will take place after the 2020 election and the completion of the census (which will determine apportionment of congressional seats among the

gerrymandering
The drawing of electoral districts in such a way as to give advantage to one political party.

figure 5.3

APPORTIONMENT OF HOUSE SEATS BY REGION, 1960 AND 2010

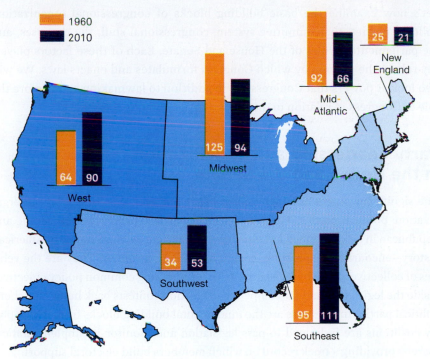

Legend:
- 1960 (orange)
- 2010 (black)

New England: 25 (1960), 21 (2010)
Mid-Atlantic: 92 (1960), 66 (2010)
Midwest: 125 (1960), 94 (2010)
West: 64 (1960), 90 (2010)
Southwest: 34 (1960), 53 (2010)
Southeast: 95 (1960), 111 (2010)

SOURCE: U.S. Census Bureau, www.census.gov/prod/cen2010/briefs/c2010br-08.pdf, table 1 (accessed 5/16/20).

states). Governors and state legislatures in most states oversee this process. The 2018 elections were kind to the Democrats—they picked up a handful of governors; 2020 was not—they lost several state legislatures.

Democrats hope that this time they will be able to turn the tables on the Republicans. Of course, in the case of Senate races, the "districts" are defined by the Constitution. Each state is a district. Accordingly, states with small populations have an advantage over more populous states. The 580,000 residents of Wyoming are represented by two senators, as are the 40 million residents of California.

Since passage of the 1982 amendments to the 1965 Voting Rights Act, race has become a major—and controversial—consideration in drawing voting districts. These amendments, which encouraged the creation of districts in which members of racial minorities form decisive majorities, have greatly increased the number of minority representatives in Congress. After the 2018 and 2020 elections, the House has more minority-group members than ever before. At the same time, however, the growing number of majority-minority districts has meant that the proportions of minority voters in other districts have been reduced, raising the possibility that representatives from these districts will be less responsive to minority policy concerns.

THE ORGANIZATION OF CONGRESS

Let's now examine the basic building blocks of congressional organization: political parties, the committee system, congressional staff, the caucuses, and the parliamentary rules of the House and Senate. Each of these factors plays a key role in the process by which Congress formulates and enacts laws. We will also look at powers that Congress has in addition to lawmaking and explore the role of Congress in relation to the executive.

Party Leadership and Organization in the House and the Senate

One significant aspect of congressional life is not even part of the *official* organization: political parties. The congressional parties—primarily Democratic and Republican in modern times, but also numerous others over the course of American history—encourage cooperation, coalitions, and compromise. They are the vehicles of collective action by legislators, both for pursuing common policy objectives inside the legislature and for competing in election contests back home.[15] In short, political parties in Congress are the fundamental building blocks from which policy coalitions are fashioned to pass legislation and monitor its implementation, thereby providing a track record on which members build electoral support.

Every two years, at the beginning of a new Congress, the parties in each chamber choose leaders. In the House, members gather into partisan groups—called the **party caucus** by the Democrats and the **party conference** by the Republicans—to elect leaders and decide other matters of party policy. The elected leader of the majority party is later proposed to the whole House and is automatically elected to the position of **Speaker of the House**, the chief presiding officer of the House of Representatives, with voting along straight party lines. The House majority caucus or conference then also elects a **majority leader**, the second-in-command to the Speaker. The minority party goes through the same process and selects the **minority leader**. Both parties also elect *whips*, who line up party members on important votes and relay voting intentions to the leaders.

Each member of the House is assigned to several of the chamber's standing committees, as we will discuss shortly. At one time, party leaders strictly controlled committee assignments, using them to enforce party discipline. Today, representatives expect to receive the assignments they want, and they resent leadership efforts to control assignments. But leaders have sought to claw back their control over assignments. Their best opportunities to use committee assignments as rewards and punishments come when more than one member seeks the same seat on a committee.

Generally, representatives seek assignments that will allow them to influence decisions of special importance to their districts. Representatives from farm districts, for example, may request seats on the Agriculture Committee. Seats on powerful committees—such as Ways and Means (responsible for tax legislation)

party caucus or party conference
A nominally closed party meeting to select candidates or leaders, plan strategy, or make decisions regarding legislative matters. Termed a *caucus* in the Democratic Party and a *conference* in the Republican Party.

Speaker of the House
The chief presiding officer of the House of Representatives. The Speaker is elected at the beginning of every Congress on a straight party vote and is the most important party and House leader.

majority leader
The elected leader of the party holding a majority of the seats in the House of Representatives or in the Senate. In the House, the majority leader is subordinate in the party hierarchy to the Speaker.

minority leader
The elected leader of the party holding less than a majority of the seats in the House of Representatives or Senate.

and Energy and Commerce (responsible for health, energy, and regulatory policy)—are especially popular.

Within the Senate, where the vice president is the chief presiding officer, the second-ranking official, the *president pro tempore* (or *pro tem*, for short), exercises mainly ceremonial leadership when the vice president is absent. Usually, the majority party designates its longest-serving member to serve in this capacity. Real power is in the hands of the majority leader and the minority leader, who are each elected by party caucus or conference and together control the Senate's calendar (the agenda for legislation). In addition, the senators from each party elect a whip.

Party leaders reach outside their respective chambers in an effort to enhance their power and the prospects for enacting their party programs. One important external strategy involves fund-raising. In recent years, congressional leaders have frequently established their own political action committees. Interest groups are usually eager to contribute to these "leadership PACs" to curry favor with powerful members of Congress. The leaders, in turn, use these funds to support the various campaigns of their party's candidates and thereby create a sense of obligation to themselves.

In addition to the tasks of organizing Congress, congressional party leaders may seek to set the legislative agenda. Since Roosevelt's New Deal, presidents have taken the lead in creating legislative agendas. (This trend will be discussed in the next chapter.) But in recent years, majority party leaders in each chamber, especially when facing a White House controlled by the opposing party, have attempted to devise their own agendas. They do this by publicizing proposals their members support (positive agenda power) and endeavoring to keep proposals their members oppose off the agenda (negative agenda power).

The Committee System

The committee system provides Congress with its second organizational structure, but it is more a division and specialization of labor than the hierarchy of power that determines leadership arrangements.

Seven fundamental characteristics define the congressional committee system:

1. *The official rules give each* **standing committee** *of the House and Senate a permanent status*, with a fixed size, officers, rules, staff, offices, and—above all—a jurisdiction that is recognized by all other committees and usually by the leadership as well (Table 5.2).

2. *The jurisdiction of each standing committee is defined by the subject matter of the legislation it deals with.* Except for the Rules Committee in the House and the Rules and Administration Committee in the Senate, all the important committees are organized to receive proposals for legislation and to process them into official bills. The House Rules Committee decides the order in which bills come up for a vote and the specific rules that govern the length of debate and the opportunity for amendments. Rules can be used to help or hinder particular proposals.

standing committee
A permanent legislative committee that considers legislation within a designated subject area.

table 5.2

STANDING COMMITTEES OF CONGRESS*

HOUSE COMMITTEES	SENATE COMMITTEES
Agriculture	Agriculture, Nutrition, and Forestry
Appropriations	Appropriations
Armed Services	Armed Services
Budget	Banking, Housing, and Urban Affairs
Education and Labor	Budget
Energy and Commerce	Commerce, Science, and Transportation
Ethics	Energy and Natural Resources
Financial Services	Environment and Public Works
Foreign Affairs	Finance
Homeland Security	Foreign Relations
House Administration	Health, Education, Labor, and Pensions
Judiciary	Homeland Security and Governmental Affairs
Natural Resources	Judiciary
Oversight and Reform	Rules and Administration
Rules	Small Business and Entrepreneurship
Science, Space, and Technology	Veterans' Affairs
Small Business	
Transportation and Infrastructure	
Veterans' Affairs	
Ways and Means	

*These are the committees in the 116th Congress (2019–20). Committee names and jurisdictions change over time, as does the number of committees.

SOURCE: Congress.gov, www.congress.gov/committees (accessed 1/29/20).

3. *Standing committees' jurisdictions usually parallel those of the major departments or agencies in the executive branch.* There are important exceptions, but by and large, the division of labor is designed to parallel executive branch organization.

4. *Bills are assigned to standing committees on the basis of subject matter,* but the Speaker of the House and the Senate's presiding officer have some discretion in the assignment. In some cases, the presiding officer may assign an entire bill to multiple committees, or divide up portions of a bill among several committees. Once assigned to a committee, the committee leadership assigns the bill to one of the committee's subcommittees. Most bills "die in committee"; that is, they are not sent to the full House or Senate for consideration. Ordinarily, this ends a bill's life. There is only one way for a legislative proposal to escape committee processing: a bill passed in one chamber may be permitted to move directly to the calendar of the other chamber. Even here, however, the bill must receive the full committee treatment before passage in the first chamber.

 **think it through**

Given the influence a Congress member can have over specialized areas, as seen in the list in Table 5.2, what committees would you expect to see your representatives on? Are there economic or other issues of importance to your region represented here?

5. *Each standing committee is unique.* No effort is made to compose the membership of any committee to be representative of the total House or Senate membership. Members with a special interest in the subject matter of a committee are expected to seek membership on it. In both the House and the Senate, each party has established a Committee on Committees, which determines the committee assignments of new members and of established members who wish to change committees.

6 *Standing committees are of two types: authorizing and appropriating units.* The authorizing committees deal with substantive issues; their legislation provides the executive and its agencies with authority to act. The appropriations committees, one each in the House and the Senate, provide monies (usually on an annual basis) through 12 appropriations bills that enable agencies to deploy the authority they have been granted. If no money is appropriated for some particular authorized activity, then the agency in question may not be able to act on that authority. There is also a budget committee in each chamber whose joint resolution sets the broad parameters on spending and revenues within which the authorizing and appropriating committees operate.

7. *Traditionally, each standing committee's hierarchy is based on seniority.* **Seniority** is determined by years of continuous service on a particular committee, not by years of service in the House or Senate. In general, each committee is chaired by its most senior member from the majority party. Since the 1970s, committee chairs have been elected by the majority-party members of the full chamber, though normally the most senior committee member of that party is still chosen to assume the chair.

seniority
The priority or status ranking given on the basis of how long an individual has served on a congressional committee.

The Staff System: Staffers and Agencies

A congressional institution second in importance only to the committee system is the staff system. Every member of Congress employs a large number of staff members, whose tasks include handling constituency requests and, to a growing extent, dealing with legislative details and overseeing the activities of administrative agencies. Increasingly, staffers bear the primary responsibility for drafting proposals, organizing hearings, dealing with administrative agencies, and negotiating with lobbyists. Indeed, legislators typically deal with one another through staff rather than through direct, personal contact. Representatives and senators together employ nearly 11,000 staffers in their Washington and home offices.

In addition, Congress employs roughly 2,000 permanent committee staffers. These individuals, attached to every House and Senate committee, stay in their positions regardless of turnover in Congress and are responsible for administering the committee's work, including doing research, scheduling meetings, organizing hearings, and drafting legislation.

Congress has also established three *staff agencies* to provide the legislative branch with resources and expertise and to enhance its capacity to oversee administrative agencies, as well as to evaluate presidential programs and proposals.

- The *Congressional Research Service* performs research for legislators who wish to know the facts and competing arguments relevant to policy proposals or other legislative business.
- The *Government Accountability Office (GAO)* can investigate the financial and administrative affairs of any government agency or program.
- The *Congressional Budget Office (CBO)* assesses the economic implications and likely costs of proposed federal programs.[16]

Informal Organization: The Caucuses

In addition to the official organization of Congress, there is an unofficial organizational structure, consisting of the caucuses, or *legislative service organizations (LSOs)*. Caucuses are groups of senators or representatives who share certain opinions, interests, or demographic characteristics. They include ideological caucuses such as the liberal Democratic Study Group and the conservative Freedom Caucus; a large number of caucuses representing particular economic or policy interests, such as the Travel and Tourism Caucus, the Steel Caucus, and Concerned Senators for the Arts; and caucuses based on shared backgrounds, such as the Congressional Black Caucus, the Congressional Caucus for Women's Issues, and the Hispanic Caucus. All of these caucuses try to advance the interests of specific groups by promoting legislation, encouraging Congress to hold hearings, and pressing administrative agencies for favorable treatment.

RULES OF LAWMAKING: HOW A BILL BECOMES A LAW

The institutional structure of Congress is one key factor that helps to shape the legislative process. Equally important are the rules of congressional procedures. These rules govern everything from introducing a bill through sending it to the president for signing. Not only do they influence the fate of every bill, but they also help determine the distribution of power in Congress (Figure 5.4).

Committee Deliberation

Even if a member of Congress, the White House, or a federal agency has spent months developing a piece of legislation, it does not become a bill until it is submitted officially by a senator or representative to the clerk of the House or

figure 5.4

HOW A BILL BECOMES A LAW

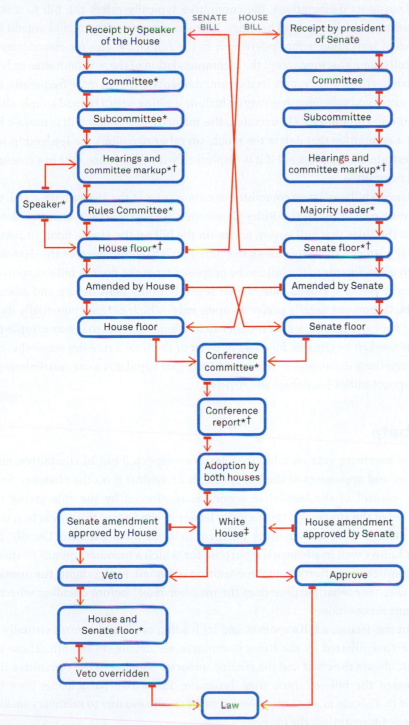

SENATE BILL   HOUSE BILL

Receipt by Speaker of the House	Receipt by president of Senate
Committee*	Committee
Subcommittee*	Subcommittee
Hearings and committee markup*†	Hearings and committee markup*†
Speaker* — Rules Committee*	Majority leader*
House floor*†	Senate floor*†
Amended by House	Amended by Senate
House floor	Senate floor

Conference committee*

Conference report*†

Adoption by both houses

Senate amendment approved by House — White House‡ — House amendment approved by Senate

Veto — Approve

House and Senate floor

Veto overridden

Law

*Points at which the bill can be amended.

†Points at which the bill can die.

‡If the president neither signs nor vetoes the bill within 10 days, it automatically becomes law.

Senate and referred to the appropriate committee for deliberation. No floor action, including discussion or votes on any bill, can occur until the committee with jurisdiction over it has taken all the time it needs to deliberate.

During its deliberations, the committee typically refers the bill to a subcommittee, which may hold hearings, listen to expert testimony, and amend the proposed legislation before referring it to the full committee for consideration. The full committee may accept the recommendation of the subcommittee or hold its own hearings and prepare its own amendments. Or, even more frequently, the committee and subcommittee may do little or nothing with a bill and simply allow it to die in committee.[17] On occasion, the majority leadership will remove a bill from a committee that delays too much; on other occasions the leadership will orchestrate changes in a bill if it is displeased with the version that has emerged from committee.

Once a bill's assigned committee or committees in the House have acted, the bill must pass through the Rules Committee. This powerful committee determines the rules that will govern action on the bill on the House floor. In particular, the Rules Committee allots the time for debate and decides the extent to which amendments to the bill can be proposed from the floor. A bill's supporters generally prefer a **closed rule**, which severely limits floor debate and amendments. Opponents usually prefer an **open rule**, which permits potentially damaging floor debate and makes it easier to add amendments that may cripple the bill or weaken its chances for passage. Most of the time a rule lies somewhere in between these extremes—a "structured" rule that stipulates some restrictions on, and opportunities for, debate and revision.

Debate

Before members vote on a bill that has been reported out of committee, supporters and opponents of the bill speak for or against it on the chamber floor. Party control of the legislative agenda is reinforced by the rule giving the Speaker of the House and the majority leader of the Senate the power to recognize members—or not—in order for them to speak during debate. Usually, the chair knows well in advance the purpose for which a member intends to speak, and spontaneous efforts to gain recognition often fail. For example, the Speaker may ask, "For what purpose does the member rise?" before deciding whether to grant recognition.

In the House, a bill's sponsor and its leading opponent control virtually all of the time allotted by the Rules Committee for debate on the bill. These are almost always the chair and the ranking minority member of the committee that processed the bill—or those they designate. These two participants have the power to allocate most of the debate time in small amounts to members seeking to speak for or against the measure.

In the Senate, other than the power of recognition, the leadership has much less control over the floor debate. Indeed, the Senate is unique among the world's

closed rule
The provision by the House Rules Committee that restricts the introduction of amendments during debate.

open rule
The provision by the House Rules Committee that permits floor debate and the addition of amendments to a bill.

legislative bodies for its commitment to unlimited debate. Once given the floor, a senator may speak for an unlimited time unless a three-fifths majority (60 senators) votes to end debate—a procedure called **cloture**.

Through this tactic of speaking at great length, called the **filibuster**, on a number of memorable occasions a small minority or even one individual in the Senate has successfully prevented action on legislation supported by the majority. During the 1950s and 1960s, for example, opponents of civil rights legislation often tried to block it by filibustering. More recently, it has been employed in the Senate to obstruct a vote on gun control measures and to block legislation restricting immigration. The filibuster remains powerful, though Senate rule changes have reduced its value for blocking the confirmation of executive and judicial appointments.

Votes on cloture and threats of filibuster have increased dramatically in the modern Senate for several reasons. First, senators representing national interests or narrow special interests are prepared to bring the business of the Senate to a halt in order to block legislation they oppose. Second, senators can use the threat of a filibuster to extract concessions. Finally, filibustering brings attention (and possibly campaign support and other forms of gratitude) to senators from outside interests.

On the other hand, much debate is perfunctory because deals have been cut between majority and minority leaders resulting in a bill's passage. Indeed, in some cases a bill is brought forward with virtually no debate—under a unanimous consent agreement in the Senate (requiring unanimous support) or suspension of the rules in the House (requiring two-thirds support)—as a product of bargaining and negotiation by the leaders of the two parties.

Conference Committee: Reconciling House and Senate Versions of a Bill

Getting a bill out of committee and through both houses of Congress is no guarantee that it will be enacted into law. Frequently, bills that began with similar provisions in both chambers emerge from them quite different from one another. For example, a bill may be passed unchanged by one chamber but undergo substantial revision in the other. If the first chamber will not simply accept the other's changes, a **conference committee** composed of the senior members of the committees or subcommittees that initiated the bills in both chambers may be required to iron out differences. On occasion, members representing the party leadership are added to each chamber's conference delegation.

Sometimes, members or leaders will let provisions they find objectionable pass on the floor with the idea that they will be eliminated in conference. Usually, conference committees meet behind closed doors. Agreement requires majority support from both the House and the Senate delegations. Legislation that emerges from a conference committee is more often a compromise than a clear victory by one set of political forces over another.

cloture

A procedure by which three-fifths of the members of the Senate can set a time limit on debate over a given bill.

filibuster

A tactic in which members of the Senate prevent action on legislation they oppose by continuously holding the floor and speaking until the majority abandons the legislation. Once given the floor, senators have unlimited time to speak, and a cloture vote by three-fifths of the Senate is required to end a filibuster.

think it through

Are there issues you are passionate about that you feel Congress hasn't acted on? What might explain some of the barriers in moving legislation forward on these issues?

conference committee

A joint committee created to work out a compromise between House and Senate versions of a bill.

ACTS PASSED BY CONGRESS, 1789-2019

Total acts passed
per Congress

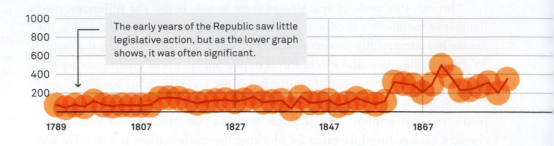

The early years of the Republic saw little legislative action, but as the lower graph shows, it was often significant.

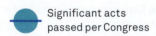
Significant acts
passed per Congress

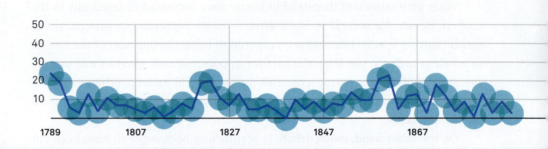

TIMEPLOT SOURCE: George B. Galloway, *History of the United States House of Representatives,* Sidney Wise, ed. (New York: Thomas Y. Crowell, 1976); and The Library of Congress, www.congress.gov/legislation?q=%7B%22-bill-status%22%3A%22law%22%7D (accessed 9/10/20).

veto
The president's constitutional power to reject acts of Congress.

pocket veto
A veto that occurs automatically when Congress adjourns during the 10 days a president has to approve a bill and the president has taken no action on it.

When a bill comes out of conference, it faces one more hurdle. Before it can be sent to the president for signing, the House-Senate conference report embodying the compromise must be approved on the floor of each chamber. Usually, such approval is given quickly. Occasionally, however, opponents use this one last opportunity to defeat a piece of legislation.[18]

Presidential Action

Once adopted by the House and Senate, a bill goes to the president, who may choose to sign the bill into law or veto it. The **veto** is the president's constitutional power to reject a piece of legislation. To veto a bill, the president returns it within 10 days to the chamber of Congress in which it originated, along with a statement of objections to it. The bill is also rejected if Congress adjourns during the 10-day period and the president has taken no action; this outcome is called a **pocket veto**.

The possibility of a presidential veto affects how willing members of Congress are to push for different pieces of legislation at different times. If they think the president is likely to veto a proposal, they might shelve it for a later time. Alternatively, the sponsors of a popular bill opposed by the president might push for passage to force the president to pay the political costs of vetoing it.[19] During

timeplot

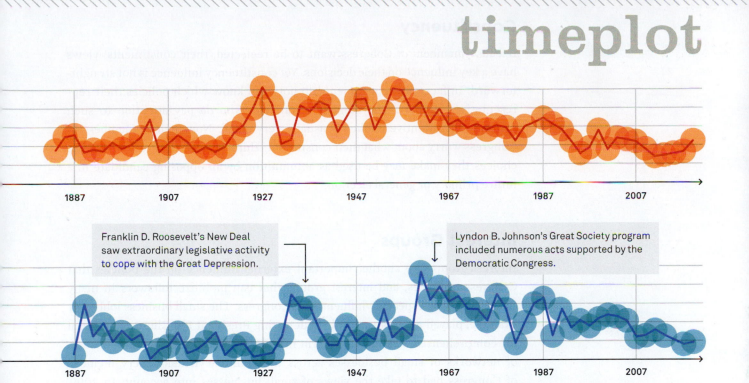

1887   1907   1927   1947   1967   1987   2007

Franklin D. Roosevelt's New Deal saw extraordinary legislative activity to cope with the Great Depression.

Lyndon B. Johnson's Great Society program included numerous acts supported by the Democratic Congress.

1887   1907   1927   1947   1967   1987   2007

periods of divided government, a lot of major legislation is preplanned, with congressional-executive summits held to arrive at an agreement acceptable to both the president and legislative leaders.

A presidential veto may be overridden by a two-thirds vote in both the House and the Senate. A veto override delivers a stinging blow to a president, and presidents will often back down from a veto threat if they believe that Congress will override the veto.

HOW CONGRESS DECIDES

What determines the kinds of legislation that Congress ultimately produces? The process of creating a legislative agenda, drawing up a list of possible measures, and deciding among them is very complex, and a variety of influences from inside and outside government play important roles. External influences include a legislator's constituency and various interest groups. Influences from inside government include party leadership, congressional colleagues, and the president (see Timeplot). Let's examine each of these influences individually and then consider how they interact to produce congressional policy decisions.

Constituency

Because members of Congress want to be reelected, their constituents' views have a key influence on their decisions. Yet constituency influence is not straightforward. In fact, most constituents do not even know which policies their representatives support. The number of citizens who *do* pay attention to such matters—the attentive public—is usually very small. Nonetheless, members of Congress worry about what their constituents think because they realize that the choices they make may be used as ammunition by an opposing candidate in a future primary or general election.[20]

Interest Groups

Interest groups are another important external influence on the policies that Congress produces, and interest groups that can mobilize followers in many districts may be especially influential in Congress. The small business lobby, for example, played an important role in defeating President Bill Clinton's proposal for comprehensive health care reform in 1993–94. Because of the mobilization of networks of small businesses across the country, virtually every member of Congress had to take the views of small businesses into account. In 2009, precisely for this reason, the Obama administration brought small business groups into the early planning process for health care reform.

Today, Republican members of Congress, even though committed to replacing Obamacare, feel pressure from citizen groups, the insurance industry, the pharmaceutical industry, and others who depend on features of the Affordable Care Act to take an "amend it, don't end it" approach. This caused great complications for President Trump and Republican congressional leaders. After failing to "end it" in 2017, Trump dismantled pieces of the Obamacare apparatus by executive order (and doing so at least partly with insurance and small business interests in mind).

In addition to mobilizing voters, interest groups contribute money. In the 2020 election cycle, interest groups and PACs donated many millions of dollars in campaign contributions to incumbent members of Congress and challengers. What does this money buy? A popular conception is that it buys votes—in effect, bribes. Although the vote-buying accusation makes for good campaign rhetoric, it has little factual support. Studies by political scientists show only minimal evidence that contributions from large PACs influence congressional voting patterns.[21]

If contributions don't buy votes, what do they buy? Our claim is that they influence legislative behavior in ways difficult for the public to observe and for political scientists to measure. The institutional structure of Congress and, in particular, the various powers available to members

The National Rifle Association (NRA) is an interest group representing gun owners that has been successful in lobbying Congress against legislation restricting Second Amendment rights. The NRA also endorses or opposes candidates at all levels of government based on their assessment of the candidates' support of gun rights, which directly influences how NRA members vote.

through the committee system offer several different kinds of opportunities for the influence of campaign contributions.

- *Proposal power* enables members of relevant committees to introduce legislation that favors contributing groups.

- *Gatekeeping power* enables them to block legislation that harms such groups. (The *exclusion* of certain provisions from a bill is just as much an indicator of PAC influence as the *inclusion* of others. The difference is that it is hard to measure what you don't see.)

- *Oversight power* enables committee members to intervene in bureaucratic decision making on behalf of contributing groups.

The point is that voting on the floor—the alleged object of campaign contributions, according to the vote-buying hypothesis—is a highly visible public act, one that can easily get members in trouble with their broader electoral constituencies. The committee system, in contrast, provides numerous opportunities for legislators to deliver services to PAC contributors and other donors that are subtler and more hidden from public view. (See Analyzing the Evidence on pp. 152–3 for an example of interest group influence on climate change legislation.) Thus, we suggest that the most appropriate places to look for traces of campaign contribution influence are in the manner in which committees deliberate, mark up proposals, and block legislation from the floor.

In addition to mobilizing voters and contributing campaign funds, interest groups convey information. Although legislators become specialists, gain expertise, and hire skilled staff to assist them, for much of the specialized knowledge they need, especially about how aspects of policy will affect local constituencies, they depend on lobbyists. Informational lobbying is a very important activity in Washington. Interest group spending on lobbying far exceeds that on campaign contributions.[22]

Party Discipline

In both the House and the Senate, party leaders seek to influence their respective members' behavior. This influence, sometimes called *party discipline*, was once so powerful that it dominated the lawmaking process. Because of their control of patronage and the nominating process, party leaders could often command the allegiance of more than 90 percent of their members.

A vote on which 50 percent or more of the members of one party take a particular position while at least 50 percent of the members of the other party take the opposing position is called a **party vote**. At the beginning of the twentieth century, most **roll-call votes** in the House of Representatives were party votes. Today, primary elections have deprived party leaders of the power to decide who receives the party's official nomination. The patronage resources available to the leadership, moreover, have become quite limited. As a result, though leaders continue to exercise some influence, party-line voting today is a matter of shared beliefs within each party more than of leadership power.

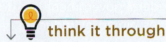

think it through

During the most recent elections, what did you hear in the news about PAC spending? Who were these groups supporting or against? How does this money compete with the influence of individual constituents, including you?

party vote
A roll-call vote in the House or Senate in which at least 50 percent of the members of one party take a particular position and are opposed by at least 50 percent of the members of the other party.

roll-call vote
Voting in which each legislator's yes or no vote is recorded.

How Representative Is Congress?

Contributed by **Leah Stokes**, *University of California, Santa Barbara*

Significant evidence suggests that the public supports action on climate change.[1] Yet the federal government has done little to enact policies aimed at reducing carbon emissions. How can we explain this gap between public support for action and the absence of climate policy?

One hypothesis is that firms that profit from carbon pollution, including fossil fuel companies and electric utilities, have blocked such policies from passing. There are a number of theories for how these companies influence the policy process. Firms can lobby to change the content of bills and their likelihood of passing. Researchers have also found that campaign contributions can facilitate access to politicians.[2]

But just because an individual or group has access, does that mean they will be able to influence public policy?

To try to assess this, I undertook research with Alexander Hertel-Fernandez and Matto Mildenberger.[3] We surveyed the most senior staffers working in Congress and asked them whether they had advised the Congress members for whom they work to change their vote on a bill after meeting with campaign contributors. Knowing that staff were unlikely to admit to being swayed by campaign contributions, we used a questionnaire designed to ensure that respondents didn't just tell us what they thought we wanted to hear.

First, we asked congressional staff to prioritize the opinions that shaped their stance on an issue. As you can see in the figure below, they overwhelmingly reported that constituent opinions and communications from constituents were the most influential factors in how they advised their member of Congress.

Considerations Staffers Reported as Extremely or Very Important in Shaping Their Advice to Their Members, by Staffer Party

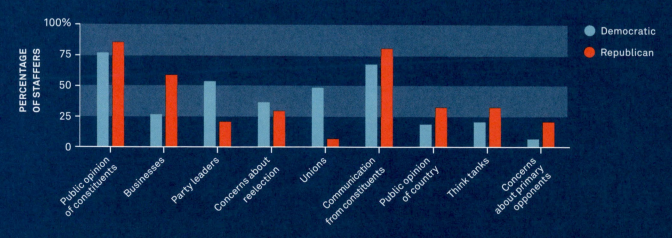

SOURCE: Alexander Hertel-Fernandez, Matto Mildenberger, and Leah C. Stokes, "Legislative Staff and Representation in Congress," *American Political Science Review* 113, no. 1 (2019): 1–18.

Staffer Perceptions of Constituent Preferences

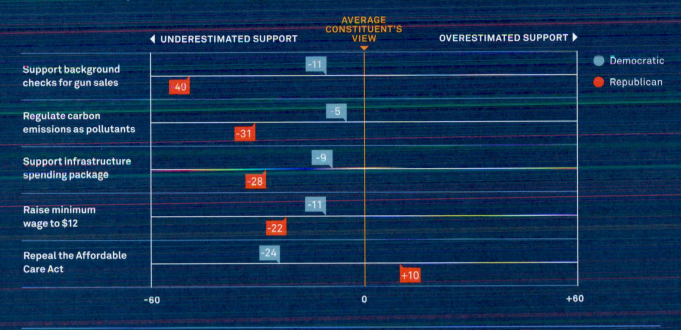

AVERAGE CONSTITUENT'S VIEW

◄ UNDERESTIMATED SUPPORT   OVERESTIMATED SUPPORT ►

● Democratic
● Republican

Support background checks for gun sales
-11
-49

Regulate carbon emissions as pollutants
-5
-31

Support infrastructure spending package
-9
-28

Raise minimum wage to $12
-11
-22

Repeal the Affordable Care Act
-24
+10

-60   0   +60

Next, we asked them what they thought their constituents' preferences were on regulating carbon emissions, among other issues. You can see the results in the above figure. Each row represents the staffers' perceived constituent opinions on an issue. Interestingly, both Republicans and Democrats consistently underestimated their constituents' support for various issues. For regulating carbon emissions, Republicans underestimated support by 31 percent and Democrats by 5 percent.

What accounts for this gap between what constituents want and what congressional staffers think they want? In order to understand this, we examined the role of interest group contact using the questionnaire. We found that 45 percent of staff had changed their minds about a policy after meeting with a campaign contributor. So, the more an office meets with or takes campaign contributions from fossil fuel companies as compared to grassroots environmental groups, the more the office underestimates its constituents' support for climate policy.

Taken together, these studies suggest that fossil fuel companies have been able to block public policy on climate change. Returning to the larger question of representation, one can conclude that the access that comes with campaign contributions has a troubling influence on how attentive representatives are to constituent interests on environmental legislation, as well as other issues.

SOURCE: Alexander Hertel-Fernandez, Matto Mildenberger, and Leah C. Stokes, "Legislative Staff and Representation in Congress," *American Political Science Review* 113, no. 1 (2019): 1–18.

1 Peter D. Howe, Matto Mildenberger, Jennifer R. Marlon, and Anthony Leiserowitz, "Geographic Variation in Opinions on Climate Change at State and Local Scales in the USA," *Nature Climate Change* 5 (2015): 596–603.

2 Joshua L. Kalla and David E. Broockman, "Campaign Contributions Facilitate Access to Congressional Officials: A Randomized Field Experiment," *American Journal of Political Science* 60, no. 3 (2016): 545–58.

3 Alexander Hertel-Fernandez, Matto Mildenberger, and Leah C. Stokes, "Legislative Staff and Representation in Congress," *American Political Science Review* 113, no. 1 (2019): 1–18.

→ Thinking about the data in these figures, as well as the campaign priorities of candidates during the 2020 elections, on what other issues might Congress be underestimating constituent interest?

figure 5.5

PARTY UNITY SCORES BY CHAMBER

analyzing the evidence

Party voting increased in the 1970s and has remained fairly high since then. What contributes to party voting?

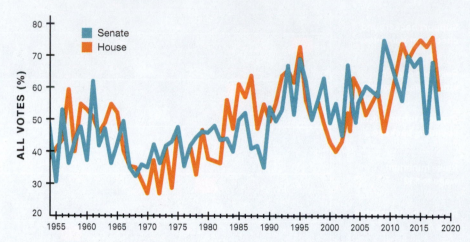

NOTE: The scores represent the percentage of recorded votes on which the majority of one party voted against the majority of the other party.

SOURCES: Voteview, "Party Unity Score," http://voteview.com/Party_Unity.htm (accessed 9/16/13); "2015 Vote Studies: Party Unity Remained Strong," *CQ Weekly*, February 8, 2016; 2016 and 2017 scores compiled by authors. Scores for 2018 found in Jonathan Miller, "Congressional votes take a dive: CQ vote studies," *Roll Call*, February 28, 2019.

Typically, party unity is greater in the House than in the Senate. House rules grant greater procedural control of business to the majority- and minority-party leaders, thus giving them more influence over their members. In the Senate, the leadership has fewer controls over its members. Yet party unity has remained high in both chambers (Figure 5.5).

In the first six years of the Obama administration, party voting in both chambers was strong. Republican votes supporting Obama initiatives were quite rare. After the Republicans won complete control of Congress in the 2014 midterm elections, however, they had to assume some responsibility for governing; a degree of bargaining between them and the minority Democrats emerged as a consequence. In 2016, Republicans maintained their control of both chambers. The 115th Congress (the first two years of the Trump presidency) witnessed continued high party unity in both chambers, and high opposition between them as well, especially in the House. This trend continued during the 116th Congress, after the Democrats took control of the House.

This ideological gap has been especially pronounced since 1980 (Figure 5.6). This gap between majority and minority is known as **polarization**. By the end of President Obama's second term, in 2016, party polarization had produced **gridlock**, a state of affairs in which virtually no legislation could be enacted. These differences certainly help to explain roll-call divisions between the two parties. Ideology and background, however, are only a piece of the explanation of party unity. The other piece has to do with organization and leadership.

polarization
Strong ideological divisions between groups that makes compromise and progress difficult.

gridlock
A situation where legislation cannot move forward, typically resulting from strong polarization between groups.

figure 5.6

THE WIDENING IDEOLOGICAL GAP BETWEEN THE PARTIES

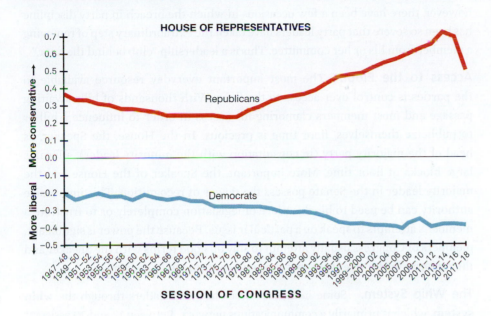

HOUSE OF REPRESENTATIVES

Republicans

Democrats

More conservative ↑   More liberal ↓

SESSION OF CONGRESS

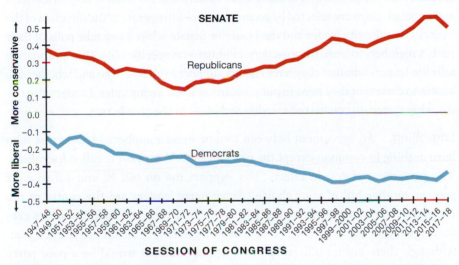

SENATE

Republicans

Democrats

More conservative ↑   More liberal ↓

SESSION OF CONGRESS

SOURCE: Voteview, http://voteview.com/Party_Unity.htm (accessed 5/16/20); 2017–18 updates compiled by author.

Although party organization has weakened over the last century, today's party leaders still have some resources at their disposal: (1) committee assignments, (2) access to the floor, (3) the whip system, (4) logrolling, and (5) the presidency. These resources are often very effective in securing the support of party members.

Committee Assignments.   Leaders can create debts among members by helping them get favored committee assignments. If the leadership goes out of its way to help a member acquire a preferred assignment, this effort is likely to create a bond of obligation that can be called on without any other payments or favors. These assignments are made early in the congressional careers of most members and cannot normally be taken from them if they later resist party discipline. In recent years, however, there have been a few occasions in which the breach in party discipline has been so severe that party leaders have taken the extraordinary step of removing a member from his or her committee. This is a leadership "club behind the door."

Access to the Floor. The most important everyday resource available to the parties is control over access to the floor. With thousands of bills awaiting passage and most members clamoring for access in order to influence a bill or to publicize themselves, floor time is precious. In the House, the Speaker, as head of the majority party (in consultation with the minority leader), allocates large blocks of floor time. More important, the Speaker of the House and the majority leader in the Senate possess the power of recognition. This impressive authority can be used to block a piece of legislation completely or to frustrate a member's attempts to speak on a particular issue. Because the power is significant, members of Congress usually attempt to stay on good terms with the Speaker and the majority leader to ensure that they will continue to be recognized.[23]

The Whip System. Some influence comes to party leaders through the **whip system**, which is primarily a communications network. Between 12 and 20 assistant and regional whips are selected by geographic zones to operate at the direction of the majority or minority leader and the House or Senate whip. They take polls of their party's members to learn the members' intentions on specific bills. This information tells the leaders whether they have enough support to allow a vote and whether the vote is so close that they need to put pressure on a few swing votes. Leaders also use the whip system to convey their wishes and plans to the members.[24]

Logrolling. An agreement between two or more members of Congress who have nothing in common except the need for mutual support is called **logrolling**. The agreement states, in effect, "You support me on bill X, and I'll support you on another bill of your choice." Since party leaders are the center of the communications networks in the two chambers, they can help members create large logrolling coalitions. Hundreds of logrolling deals are made each year. Although there are no official record-keeping books, it would be a poor party leader whose whips did not know who owed what to whom.

The Presidency. Of all the influences that maintain the sharpness of party lines in Congress, the presidency is probably the most important. Indeed, presidential influence is a key feature of party discipline in Congress. Since the late 1940s, under President Truman, presidents each year have identified a number of bills to be considered part of the administration's program. By the mid-1950s, both parties in Congress had begun to look to the president for these proposals, which became the most significant part of Congress's agenda. Support for or opposition to the president's program has become a criterion for party loyalty, and party leaders in Congress are able to use it to rally some members.

Weighing Diverse Influences

Clearly, many factors affect congressional decisions. But at various points in the decision-making process, some factors are more influential than others. For example, interest groups may be more effective at the committee stage, when their expertise is especially valued and their visibility is less obvious. Because committees play a key role in deciding which legislation reaches the floor of the House or Senate, interest groups can often put a halt to bills they dislike, or they can ensure that options that do reach the floor are ones they support. Once legislation reaches the floor and members of Congress are deciding among alternatives in visible roll-call votes, constituent opinion becomes more important.

The influence of the external and internal forces described in the preceding section also varies according to the kind of issue under consideration. On policies of great importance to powerful interest groups—farm subsidies, for example—those groups are likely to have considerable influence. On other issues, members of Congress may be less attentive to narrow interest groups and more willing to consider what they see as the general interest. The Policy Principle box on p. 158 gives an example of how members of Congress, who want to be reelected, are seeking to demonstrate their interest in addressing their constituents' concerns by introducing more bills in response to the growing opioid epidemic.

Party Discipline

The influence that party leaders have over the behavior of their party members is maintained in a number of ways:

- **Committee assignments:** By giving favorable committee assignments to members, party leaders create a sense of obligation.

- **Access to the floor:** The Speaker of the House and ranking committee members of the Senate control the allocation of time for floor debate on bills; legislators want to stay on good terms with these party leaders so that their bills get floor time.

- **Whip system:** The system allows party leaders to keep track of how many votes they can count on for a bill; if the vote is close, they can try to influence members to switch sides.

- **Logrolling:** Party leaders help arrange deals between members to support one another's legislation because each needs the vote.

- **Presidency:** The president's legislative proposals are often the most important part of Congress's agenda. Party leaders use partisan support for or opposition to the president's program to rally members.

the policy principle
CONGRESS AND THE OPIOID EPIDEMIC

Almost 64,000 people died of drug overdoses in 2016, and the majority of those deaths involved opioid drugs such as heroin, prescription pain-killers, and fentanyl (a synthetic opioid). An estimated 2 million Americans suffer from an opioid use disorder.[1] The Centers for Disease Control and Prevention calculated the economic burden of prescription drug misuse (just one part of the opioid epidemic) at nearly $80 billion a year. Among Americans, 43 percent view the use of prescription pain drugs as a very serious or extremely serious problem in their communities, and 37 percent say the same about heroin.[2]

Awareness of this growing opioid epidemic has also reached Capitol Hill. During the 115th Congress (2017–18), members introduced more than 200 separate bills mentioning opioids, and during the 114th (2015–16), 153 such bills were introduced—a very significant increase from the previous two Congresses. In the 113th, only 24 bills even mentioned the word "opioid," and in the 112th there were only four.[3]

One reason for this proliferation of bills addressing the same policy issue is that members of Congress, who want to be reelected, seek to demonstrate their interest in addressing their constituents' concerns. The institutional rules of Congress, specifically the fragmentation of authority between chambers and across numerous committees, have contributed to the fragmented approach.

One concern about Congress's approach to the problem is the use of discretionary spending (common practice in federal policy making), which requires yearly action by the appropriation process to actually allocate any funding to the program. Significant funding to address the opioid crisis was included in the Bipartisan Budget Act of 2018—with $4.6 billion budgeted for law enforcement, prevention, and treatment programs. But because the new funds are discretionary spending rather than mandatory spending (see Chapter 13), it is uncertain whether Congress will continue to fund these efforts at this level in future years.

This congressional response to the opioid epidemic reflects a common pattern described by political scientists

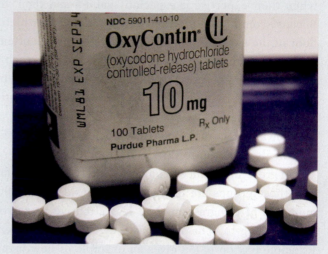

Congress's piecemeal approach to the opioid epidemic has disappointed advocates.

Timothy Conlan, Paul Posner, and David Beam, who identify four common pathways by which policies are inacted.[4] One of their pathways is the "symbolic pathway," which is characterized by the following sequence of events: the public becomes aware of a problem that must be solved, and Congress takes action to respond. However, members of Congress have a greater incentive to respond quickly than to craft comprehensive and substantive legislative solutions. As a result, policies that take shape via the symbolic pathway are often underfunded or poorly coordinated, and therefore less effective on the ground.

think it through

1. Why were so many separate bills related to the opioid epidemic introduced in the 115th Congress? Is this an example of members of Congress representing their constituents effectively?

2. What are the advantages and disadvantages of having so many different congressional committees involved in making policy on this issue?

[1] U.S. Department of Health and Human Services, "The Opioid Epidemic by the Numbers," www.hhs.gov/opioids/sites/default/files/2018-01/opioids-infographic.pdf (accessed 7/17/18).

[2] Associated Press-NORC Center for Public Affairs Research, "Americans Recognize the Growing Problem of Opioid Addiction," *Issue Brief*, April 2018, www.apnorc.org/PDFs/Opioids%202018/APNORC_Opioids_Report_2018.pdf.

[3] Congress.gov, www.congress.gov (accessed 7/17/18).

[4] Timothy J. Conlan, Paul L. Posner, and David R. Beam, *Pathways of Power: The Dynamics of National Policymaking* (Washington, DC: Georgetown University Press, 2014).

BEYOND LEGISLATION: ADDITIONAL CONGRESSIONAL POWERS

In addition to the power to make the law, Congress has a variety of other ways to influence the process of government. As we saw in Chapter 2, the Constitution gives the Senate veto power over treaties and appointments. And Congress has drawn to itself a number of other powers through which it can share with the other branches the capacity to administer the laws.

Oversight

Oversight, as applied to Congress, refers not to something neglected but to the effort to oversee or supervise how the executive branch carries out legislation. Individual senators and members of the House can engage in a form of oversight simply by calling or visiting administrators, sending out questionnaires, or talking to constituents about programs. But in a more formal sense, oversight is carried out by committees or subcommittees of the Senate or House, which conduct hearings and investigations to analyze and evaluate bureaucratic agencies and the effectiveness of their programs. The purpose may be to locate inefficiencies or abuses of power, to explore the relationship between what an agency does and what a law intended, or to change or abolish a program.

Most programs and agencies are subject to some oversight every year during the course of hearings on appropriations—that is, the funding of agencies and governmental programs. Committees and subcommittees have the power to subpoena witnesses, administer oaths, cross-examine, compel testimony, and bring criminal charges for contempt (refusing to cooperate) and perjury (lying). During the 116th Congress, the Democratic majority in the House was especially active in its oversight of the Trump administration, often encountering resistance from the president and his administration colleagues. This has led, in turn, to legal charges of contempt of Congress against recalcitrant Trump officials, and to congressional committees seeking from the court orders to overcome various forms of administrative hindrance. Hearings and investigations resemble each other in many ways, but they differ on one fundamental point: A hearing is usually held on a specific bill, and the questions asked there are usually intended to build a record about that bill. In an investigation, the committee or subcommittee examines a broad area or problem and then concludes its investigation with one or more proposed bills. In the 116th Congress, for example, Democrats in the House conducted investigations of alleged Russian interference (with possible administration complicity) in the 2016 election, treatment of immigrants along the southern border, the President's income tax returns (and alleged financial conflicts of interest), and many other issues.

oversight
The effort by Congress, through hearings, investigations, and other techniques, to exercise control over the activities of executive agencies.

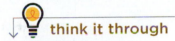

think it through

How does Congressional oversight ensure effective representation and governance? Have you ever spoken with a representative about a particular program?

In 2019, the House Intelligence Committee held hearings as a part of an impeachment inquiry into President Donald Trump. Here a text message exchange between acting Ambassador to Ukraine William Taylor and Gordon Sondland, the U.S. Ambassador to the European Union, is exhibited as Democrats sought to prove President Trump had leveraged U.S. military aid to Ukraine in exchange for political dirt on opponent Joe Biden. Republicans sought to exonerate the president of any quid pro quo.

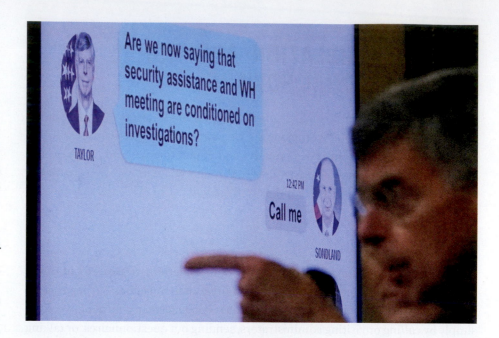

Advice and Consent: Special Senate Powers

The Constitution gives the Senate a special power—one that is not based on law-making. The president has the power to make treaties and to appoint top executive officers, ambassadors, and federal judges—but only "with the Advice and Consent of the Senate" (Article II, Section 2). For treaties, two-thirds of senators present must approve; for appointments, a majority is required.

The Senate only occasionally exercises its power to reject treaties and appointments. For appointments, more common than rejection is a senatorial *hold*, which any senator may place indefinitely on the confirmation of a mid- or lower-level presidential appointment. Sometimes these holds are "principled," but occasionally they aim to wring concessions from the White House on matters unrelated to the appointment. During George W. Bush's administration, Senate Democrats prevented final confirmation votes on a dozen especially conservative judicial nominees. Of course, Republicans had done the same thing to many liberal judicial nominations in the Clinton administration, and they continued the practice in the Obama administration. To counter this most recent GOP obstruction, Democrats changed the rules to make it easier for judicial appointments to move forward. Democrats later had reason to regret this tactic when Republicans changed the rules again to make it impossible for Democrats to block President Trump's appointment of Neil Gorsuch and Brett Kavanaugh to the Supreme Court (see Chapter 8).

Most presidents make every effort to take potential Senate opposition into account in treaty negotiations, and they frequently resort to **executive agreements** with foreign powers instead of treaties when they find the prospects of

executive agreement

An agreement between the president and another country that has the force of a treaty but does not require the Senate's "advice and consent."

Senate consent unlikely. The Supreme Court has held that such agreements are equivalent to treaties, but they do not need Senate approval.[25] However, Congress can refuse to appropriate the funds needed to implement an agreement and in this way, for example, modify or even cancel agreements to provide economic or military assistance to foreign governments. In the past, presidents sometimes concluded secret agreements without informing Congress. In 1972, however, Congress passed the Case Act, which requires that the president inform Congress of any executive agreement within 60 days of its having been reached.

Impeachment

The Constitution also grants Congress the power of **impeachment** over the president, vice president, and other executive officials. To *impeach* means to charge a government official with "Treason, Bribery, or other high Crimes and Misdemeanors," and bring that official before Congress to determine guilt. The procedure is similar to a criminal indictment in that the House of Representatives acts like a grand jury, voting (by simple majority) on whether the accused ought to be impeached. If a majority of the House votes to impeach, the impeachment trial is held in the Senate, which acts like a trial jury by voting whether to convict and remove the person from office. (This vote requires a two-thirds majority.)

Controversy over Congress's impeachment power has arisen over the meaning of "high Crimes and Misdemeanors." A strict reading of the Constitution suggests that the only impeachable offense is an actual crime. But a more commonly agreed-on definition is that an impeachable offense is whatever the majority of the House of Representatives considers it to be at a given time. In other words, impeachment, especially of a president, is a political decision.

During the course of American history, only three presidents have been impeached. In 1867, President Andrew Johnson, a southern Democrat who had battled a congressional Republican majority over Reconstruction, was impeached by the House but saved from conviction by one vote in the Senate. In 1998, President Bill Clinton was impeached for perjury and obstruction of justice arising from his sexual relationship with a White House intern, Monica Lewinsky. At the conclusion of a Senate trial in 1999, Democrats, joined by a handful of Republicans, acquitted Clinton of both charges.

In December 2019 the House impeached President Trump. It voted two articles of impeachment, one on abuse of power and another on obstruction of Congress. The former related to Trump's attempt to induce Ukraine to start an investigation on one of his political rivals and otherwise involve itself in the 2020 elections. The latter accused the president of obstructing the impeachment investigation by denying the House access to documents and witnesses.

impeachment
Charging a government official (president or other) with "Treason, Bribery, or other high Crimes and Misdemeanors," and bringing that official before Congress to determine guilt.

Support for these articles was overwhelmingly partisan, reflecting the fact that impeachment is a *political* decision, not a legal one.

The appearance of partisanship was no different in the Senate, which took up the impeachment charges and conducted a trial starting on January 21, 2020. On February 5, the president was acquitted of both charges by strictly partisan votes. Only one Republican senator (Mitt Romney of Utah) defected on the first impeachment article.

CONCLUSION

Why does Congress's representative role sometimes seem to interfere with its ability to govern effectively? Congress is both a representative assembly and a powerful institution of government. In assessing its effectiveness, we focus on both its representative character and the efficiency with which it is able to get things done.

Consider representation first. A representative claims to act or speak for some other person or group. But how can one person be trusted to speak for another? How do we know that those who call themselves our representatives are actually speaking on our behalf, rather than simply pursuing their own interests?

As we saw earlier in the chapter, legislators vary in the weight they give to personal priorities and to the things desired by campaign contributors and past supporters. Some see themselves as delegates, elected to do the bidding of those who sent them to Congress. Others see themselves as trustees, selected to do what the legislator thinks is "right." Most legislators are mixes of these two types. Frequent, competitive elections are an important means by which constituents hold their representatives to account and keep them responsive to constituency views and preferences.

Indeed, taking care of constituents explains a lot of the legislation that Congress produces. It is not too much of an exaggeration to suggest the following list of individuals whose support is necessary in order to get a measure through Congress and signed into law:

- A majority of the authorizing subcommittees in the House and Senate (probably including the subcommittee chairs)
- A majority of the full authorizing committees in the House and Senate (probably including the committee chairs)
- A majority of the appropriations subcommittees in the House and Senate (probably including the subcommittee chairs)
- A majority of the full appropriations committees in the House and Senate (probably including the committee chairs)
- A majority of the House Rules Committee (including its chair)
- A majority of the full House

- A majority—possibly as many as 60 votes, if needed to shut down a filibuster—of the Senate
- The Speaker and majority leader in the House
- The majority leader in the Senate
- The president

This list includes an extraordinarily large number of public officials. With so many hurdles to clear for a measure to become a law, its benefits must be spread broadly. It is as though a bill must travel on a toll road past a number of tollbooths, each with a collector extending a hand for payment. Frequently, features of the bill are drafted initially or revised so as to be more inclusive, spreading the benefits widely among members' districts. This is the *distributive tendency*.

The distributive tendency is part of the American system of representative democracy. Legislators, in advocating the interests of their constituents, are eager to advertise their ability to deliver for their state or district. They maneuver to put themselves in a position to claim credit for good things that happen there and to duck blame for bad things. Doing so is the way they earn trust back home, discourage strong challengers in upcoming elections, and defeat those who run against them. This job requirement means that legislators must take advantage of every opportunity that presents itself. In some instances, as in our earlier discussion of the pork barrel, the results may seem bizarre. Nevertheless, the distributive tendency is a consequence of how Congress was designed to work.

Another consequence of Congress's design is almost the opposite of the distributive tendency: the tendency toward the status quo. The U.S. Congress has more veto points than any other legislative body in the world. If any of the individuals that we just listed says no, a bill dies. Some celebrate this design because it makes it unlikely that the government will institute changes in response to superficial fluctuations in public opinion. The design of Congress does mean greater representation of minority views in the legislative process (at least to say no to the majority). But it also creates the impression of gridlock, leading some to question Congress's effectiveness.

Critics of Congress want it to be both more representative and more effective. On the one hand, Congress is frequently criticized for failing to reach decisions on important issues, such as Social Security reform. This was one reason why, in 1995, the Republican House leadership reduced the number of committees and subcommittees in the lower chamber. Having fewer committees and subcommittees generally means greater centralization of power and faster, more efficient decision making.

On the other hand, critics want Congress to become more representative of the changing makeup and values of the American population. In recent years, for example, some reformers have demanded limits on the number of terms that any member of Congress can serve. Term limits are seen as a device for producing a more rapid turnover of members and, hence, a better chance for new political and social forces to be represented in Congress. The problem, however, is that although reforms such as term limits and greater internal decentralization of power may make Congress more representative, they may also make it less efficient and effective. By the same token, policies that may make Congress better able to act—such as strong central leadership, fewer committees and subcommittees, and more members with seniority and experience—may make it less representative.

This is the dilemma of congressional reform. Efficiency and representation are often competing principles in our system of government; we must be wary of gaining one at the expense of the other.

Key Terms

Check Your Understanding

1. What is the primary responsibility of a Congress member? What are some of the challenges Congress members face as they balance national policy objectives and interests with the demands of their constituents?

2. What are the basic building blocks of congressional organization? How do these groups influence the process by which Congress formulates and enacts laws?

3. How do the rules of congressional procedures influence the fate of a bill?

4. Who influences the creation of the legislative agenda? How do these different groups limit or increase the representative nature of Congress?

5. How do Congress's oversight abilities demonstrate checks and balances in American government?

 INQUIZITIVE

Earn a better grade on your test. InQuizitive personalizes your learning path to help you master the concepts from this chapter. In a recent efficacy study of American government students, InQuizitive increased test scores by an average of 17 points (see back cover).

CHAPTER SIX

THE PRESIDENCY

Soon after taking office in 2017, President Donald Trump issued dozens of executive orders, including decrees strengthening immigration enforcement and imposing a partial ban on travel from several Middle Eastern countries. These particular orders caused a national furor, with angry critics declaring that the president had no authority to act unilaterally on these issues. Several federal courts ruled against the president's travel ban. The Supreme Court, however, ruled in favor of a scaled-back version. Trump's other orders during this period, which included changes in federal regulatory policy, government contracting, education policy, and financial policy, went unchallenged and simply became the law of the land. A particularly dramatic one occurred in 2019: Trump declared a national emergency at the southern border and redirected appropriated Department of Defense funds for the purpose of paying to build a wall to prevent illegal immigration from Mexico. The courts have allowed this to stand.

In his use of executive orders and other unilateral decrees, President Trump followed squarely in the footsteps of his predecessors. Presidents often see their legislative agendas blocked by Congress but are able to turn to executive orders and presidential "memorandums" to bypass the legislative process. Especially in times of war or other emergencies, such as the coronavirus health crisis of 2020, Americans look for effective governance, particularly from the executive, and are less concerned with representative processes. Later, when the emergency has passed, presidents often find ways to retain the powers they secured during the crisis.

Presidential power begins with Article II of the Constitution, but does it end there? The framers of the Constitution believed that a chief executive was necessary to give the nation effective governance. The framers thought that Congress, a representative body, needed time to hear many points of view and might be too slow to exercise decisive leadership when it was urgently required. The president, they hoped, would give the nation more efficient and effective governance.

Yet the framers knew the risk and worried about what they saw as the tendency of executives to engage in "ambitious intrigues" to enhance their power and prerogatives. The framers hoped that this threat would be reduced by the constitutional system of checks and balances. In recent decades, however, presidents have greatly enhanced the power of the office and built an institution that the framers would hardly recognize.

In this chapter we examine the foundations of the American presidency and assess the origins and character of presidential power today. National emergencies are one source of presidential power, but presidents are also empowered by their ability to control and expand the institutional resources of the office. The courts, to be sure, can sometimes check presidential power, but, as we will see, they rarely do so. And, of course, through its general legislative powers, legislative investigations, and budgetary powers, Congress often opposes and thwarts the president. Nevertheless, presidential power has grown.

A strong presidency may be necessary for effective governance, especially in a time when the nation is threatened by foreign foes and internal disputes. The growth of presidential power, however, may have troubling implications for representative government.

The power of the presidency has grown far beyond what the framers of the Constitution envisioned. Whereas scholars once compared "strong" and "weak" presidents, today every president is strong, because of the powers of the office.

■ **What factors have contributed to the growth of presidential power, and what are the implications for representative government?**

Learning Objectives

- Identify the expressed powers that the Constitution specifically grants to the president.

- Explain how additional presidential powers have been delegated by Congress and claimed by presidents.

- Summarize how the presidency as an institution has changed over the course of American history.

- Describe the resources and tools that modern presidents use to govern.

- Evaluate whether a strong presidency is at odds with representative government.

THE CONSTITUTIONAL ORIGINS AND POWERS OF THE PRESIDENCY

The presidency was established by Article II of the Constitution, which states, "The executive power shall be vested in a President of the United States of America." It goes on to describe the manner in which the president is to be chosen and to define the basic powers of the presidency. By granting executive power to a single official—the president—the framers were emphatically rejecting proposals for collective leadership of the executive branch, most of which aimed to avoid concentration of power in the hands of one individual. Most of the framers were anxious to provide for "energy" in the executive and to have a president capable of taking quick and aggressive action. They believed that a powerful executive would help protect the nation's international interests and promote the federal government's interests relative to those of the states.

Immediately *after* its first sentence, Article II, Section 1, defines the manner in which the president is to be chosen. This odd sequence says something about the difficulty that the delegates to the Constitutional Convention were having over how to give power to the executive and at the same time balance that power with limitations. This conflict reflected the twin struggles etched in the memories of the Founding generation—against the powerful executive authority exercised by King George III and his governors over colonial America, and the low energy of the newly independent American government under the Articles of Confederation.

Some delegates wanted the president to be selected by, and thus responsible to, Congress; others preferred that the president be elected directly by the people. Direct popular elections would create a more independent and more powerful presidency. But by adopting a system of indirect election through an Electoral College, in which the electors would be selected by the state legislatures (and close elections would be resolved in the House of Representatives), the framers hoped to establish a strong presidency responsible to state and national legislators rather than directly to the electorate.

Sections 2 and 3 of Article II outline the powers and duties of the president. These sections identify two sources of presidential power. One source is the specific language of the Constitution. For example, the Constitution states that the president is authorized to make treaties, grant pardons, and nominate judges and other public officials. These specifically defined powers, called the **expressed powers** of the office, cannot be revoked by Congress or any other agency without an amendment to the Constitution. Other expressed powers include the power to receive ambassadors and to command the nation's military forces.

In addition to establishing the president's expressed powers, Article II declares that the president "shall take Care that the Laws be faithfully executed." Since the laws are enacted by Congress, this language implies that Congress is to delegate to the president the power to implement or execute its decisions. Powers given to the president by Congress are called **delegated powers**. As it delegates power to the executive branch, Congress substantially enhances the importance of the presidency. For example, if Congress determines that air quality should be improved, it might delegate to the executive branch the power to determine the best means of improvement, as well as the power to implement the process. These decisions about how to clean the air are likely to have an enormous impact on businesses, organizations, and individuals throughout the nation.

In most cases, Congress delegates power to executive agencies rather than directly to the president. This allows Congress to take advantage of its continuing influence over those agencies (through its power of the purse, for example). As we will see, however, contemporary presidents have found ways to capture a good deal of this delegated power for themselves.

Presidents have claimed a third source of institutional power beyond expressed and delegated powers: **inherent powers**. These powers are not specified in the Constitution or the law but are said to stem from "the rights, duties and obligations of the presidency."[1] They are most often asserted by presidents in times of war or national emergency. For example, after the fall of Fort Sumter and the outbreak of the Civil War, President Abraham Lincoln issued a series of executive orders for which he had no clear legal basis. Without even calling Congress into session, Lincoln combined the state militias into a national volunteer force, called for 40,000 new volunteers, enlarged the regular army and navy, diverted $2 million from other sources to military needs, instituted censorship of the U.S. mail, ordered a blockade of southern ports, suspended the writ of *habeas corpus* in the border states, and ordered the arrest by military police of individuals whom Lincoln deemed guilty of treasonous actions.[2] Lincoln claimed that these extraordinary measures were justified by the president's inherent power to protect the nation.[3]

In this section, we examine the major expressed, delegated, and inherent powers of the presidency.

expressed powers
Powers that the Constitution explicitly grants to the federal government.

delegated powers
Constitutional powers that are assigned to one branch of the government but exercised by another branch with the permission of the first.

inherent powers
Powers claimed by a president that are not expressed in the Constitution but are said to stem from "the rights, duties and obligations of the presidency."

Expressed Powers

The president's expressed powers, as defined by Sections 2 and 3 of Article II, fall into several categories, including military, judicial, diplomatic, executive, and legislative powers.

Military and Domestic Defense Power. The president's military powers are among the most important that the chief executive exercises. The position of **commander in chief** makes the president the highest military officer in the United States, with control of the entire military establishment. The president is also the head of the nation's intelligence hierarchy, which includes not only the Central Intelligence Agency (CIA) but also the National Security Council (NSC), the National Security Agency (NSA), the Federal Bureau of Investigation (FBI), and other security agencies.

The president's military powers include the use of force within the United States. Although Article IV, Section 4, provides that the "United States shall [protect] . . . every State . . . against Invasion . . . and . . . domestic Violence," Congress has made the use of domestic force an explicit presidential power through statutes directing the president, as commander in chief, to discharge these obligations.[4] The Constitution limits this power by providing that a state legislature (or governor when the legislature is not in session) must request federal troops before the president can send them into the state to provide public order. However, presidents are not obligated to deploy national troops merely because the state legislature or governor makes such a request. And more important, presidents may deploy troops without a specific request if they consider it necessary to maintain an essential national service, to enforce a federal judicial order, or to protect federally guaranteed civil rights.

commander in chief
The president's role as commander of the national military and of the state National Guard units (when they are called into service).

In 2020, after the police killing of George Floyd, an unarmed Black man in Minneapolis, massive protests erupted across the country in support of police reform and racial equality. Although they were largely peaceful, President Trump deployed the national guard to several states to help restore order.

One historic example was the decision by President Dwight D. Eisenhower in 1957 to send troops into Little Rock, Arkansas, to enforce court orders to integrate Little Rock's Central High School. He did so only after failed negotiations with the state's governor, who had posted the Arkansas National Guard at the school entrance to prevent the admission of nine Black students. However, in most instances of domestic disorder—whether from human or natural causes—presidents exercise unilateral power by declaring a "state of emergency," thereby making available federal grants, insurance, and direct assistance, as well as troops. President George W. Bush sent various military units to the Gulf Coast in response to Hurricanes Katrina and Rita in 2005, and President Obama sent the Coast Guard and teams from other agencies after the BP *Deepwater Horizon* explosion and oil spill in the Gulf of Mexico in 2010. More recently, as we discussed at the beginning of the chapter, President Trump sent troops to the southern border in 2019 in response to what he felt was an immigration crisis. In 2020, he sent the national guard to states to help restore order during massive protests across the country after the killing of George Floyd, an unarmed Black man, by the police.

Military emergencies related to international threats have also expanded the domestic powers of the executive branch. This was true during World Wars I and II and during the ongoing "war on terrorism" as well. Within a month of the September 11 attacks, the White House drafted and Congress enacted the Patriot Act, expanding the power of government executive agencies to engage in domestic surveillance activities, including electronic surveillance under the Patriot Act, and restricting judicial review of such efforts.

Expressed Powers of the Presidency

The Constitution defines certain specific powers of the presidency. These expressed powers fall into the following categories.

1. **Military.** Article II, Section 2, provides for the power as "Commander in Chief of the Army and Navy of the United States, and of the Militia of the several States, when called into the actual Service of the United States."

2. **Judicial.** Article II, Section 2, also provides the power to "grant Reprieves and Pardons for Offenses against the United States, except in Cases of Impeachment."

3. **Diplomatic.** Article II, Section 3, provides the power to "receive Ambassadors and other public Ministers."

4. **Executive.** Article II, Section 3, authorizes the president to see to it that all laws are faithfully executed; Section 2 gives the chief executive the power to appoint, remove, and supervise all executive officers and to appoint all federal judges.

5. **Legislative.** Article I, Section 7, and Article II, Section 3, give the president the power to participate authoritatively in the legislative process.

The following year, Congress created the Department of Homeland Security, combining offices from 22 federal agencies into one huge, new Cabinet department responsible for protecting the nation from attack. The White House drafted the reorganization plan, but Congress weighed in to make certain that the new agency's workers had civil service and union protections. President Obama signed a four-year extension of the Patriot Act in 2011. In 2015, Congress passed and Obama signed the USA Freedom Act, renewing expiring sections of the Patriot Act but scaling back the domestic surveillance authority of the NSA.

Judicial Power.   The presidential power to grant reprieves, pardons, and amnesties, as well as to "commute" or reduce the severity of sentences, literally gives the president the power of life and death over individuals. Presidents may use this power on behalf of a particular individual, as did Gerald Ford when he pardoned Richard Nixon in 1974 "for all offenses against the United States which he . . . has committed or may have committed." Or they may use it on a large scale, as Jimmy Carter did in 1977 when he declared an amnesty for all Vietnam War draft evaders.

Diplomatic Power.   The president is America's chief representative in dealings with other nations. As "head of state," the president has the power to make treaties for the United States (with the advice and consent of the Senate). When President George Washington received Edmond Genêt as the formal emissary of the revolutionary government of France in 1793, he transformed the power to "receive Ambassadors and other public Ministers" into the power to "recognize" other countries. That power gives the president the authority to review the claims of any new ruling groups to determine whether they indeed control the

The president is the United States' chief representative in dealings with other nations. In 2019, President Trump and Melania Trump hosted Australian Prime Minister Scott Morrison and his wife at an official state dinner at the White House.

territory and population of their country, such that they can commit it to treaties and other agreements.

In recent years, presidents have increasingly used executive agreements to conduct foreign policy.[5] An **executive agreement** is like a treaty because it is a contract between two countries, but it is different because it does not require a two-thirds vote of approval by the Senate. Ordinarily, executive agreements are used to carry out commitments already made in treaties or to address relatively minor matters. But when presidents have decided to use an executive agreement in place of a treaty, Congress has generally not objected.

Executive Power.   The most important basis of the president's power as chief executive is found in the sections of Article II stating that the president must see that all the laws are faithfully executed and that the president will appoint all executive officers and all federal judges. These constitutional provisions focus executive power and legal responsibility on the president. The famous sign on President Truman's desk, "The buck stops here," was not merely an assertion of Truman's personal sense of responsibility. It acknowledged his acceptance of the legal and constitutional responsibility of the president.

The president's executive power is not absolute; many presidential appointments, including ambassadors, cabinet officers and other high-level administrators, and federal judges, are subject to a majority approval by the Senate. But these appointments are made at the discretion of the president. (See Analyzing the Evidence in Chapter 7, pp. 218–9, for more on the president's power to appoint executive branch officials.)

Another component of the president's power as chief executive is **executive privilege**, the claim that confidential communications between a president and close advisers should not be revealed without the president's consent. Presidents have made this claim ever since George Washington refused a request from the House of Representatives to deliver documents concerning negotiations of an important treaty. Washington refused (successfully) on the grounds, first, that the House was not constitutionally part of the treaty-making process and, second, that diplomatic negotiations required secrecy.

Executive privilege became a part of the "checks and balances" between the president and Congress, and presidents have usually succeeded when invoking it. Although many presidents have claimed executive privilege, the concept was not tested in the courts until the Watergate affair of the early 1970s, when President Nixon refused congressional demands that he turn over secret White House tapes that congressional investigators thought would establish his involvement in illegal activities. In *United States v. Nixon*, the Supreme Court ordered Nixon to turn over the tapes.[6] The president complied with the order and resigned from office to avoid impeachment and conviction.

United States v. Nixon is often seen as a blow to presidential power, but actually the Court's ruling recognized for the first time the validity of executive privilege, although it held that the claim did not apply in this instance. Subsequent

executive agreement
An agreement between the president and another country that has the force of a treaty but does not require the Senate's "advice and consent."

executive privilege
The claim that confidential communications between a president and close advisers should not be revealed without the president's consent.

think it through

In what situations do you think executive privilege is necessary? Are there situations in which you think it should not apply? How do you think the lack of clear guidelines make it difficult to assess when this power should be applied as a part of the executive office's "checks and balances" with Congress?

presidents have cited *United States v. Nixon* in support of their claims of executive privilege. Thus, in 2012 the Obama administration cited executive privilege in refusing to comply with a subpoena from the House of Representatives for documents related to "Operation Fast and Furious," a Justice Department program to combat drug trafficking. And more recently President Trump invoked these privileges as justification for refusing to allow members of his cabinet and close advisers to testify in Congress regarding Russian interference during the 2016 election, his businesses and personal finances, and various investigations of his alleged abuses of power.

Legislative Power. Two constitutional provisions are the primary sources of the president's power in the legislative arena. Article II, Section 3, provides that the president "shall from time to time give to the Congress Information of the State of the Union, and recommend to their Consideration such Measures as he shall judge necessary and expedient." This first legislative power has been important, especially since Franklin Delano Roosevelt began to use it to propose specific action in Congress. Roosevelt established the presidency as the primary initiator of legislation.

The second of the president's legislative powers is the **veto**, assigned by Article I, Section 7—the president's constitutional power to reject acts of Congress. This power alone makes the president the most important single legislative leader. No bill vetoed by the president can become law unless both the House and the Senate override the veto by a two-thirds vote. In the case of a **pocket veto**, Congress does not even have the option of overriding the veto, but must reintroduce the bill in the next session.

The president may exercise a pocket veto when presented with a bill during the last 10 days of a congressional session. Usually, if a president does not sign a bill within 10 days, it automatically becomes law. But this is true only while Congress is in session. If a president chooses not to sign a bill presented within the last 10 days that Congress is in session, then the 10-day limit expires while Congress is out of session, and instead of becoming law, the bill is vetoed. Figure 6.1 illustrates the president's veto options.

In 1996, Congress added the **line-item veto**, giving the president the power to strike specific spending items from appropriations bills passed by Congress, unless a two-thirds vote of both the House and the Senate reenacted them. In 1997, President Clinton used this power 11 times to strike 82 items from the federal budget. But in 1998 the Supreme Court ruled that the Constitution does not authorize the line-item veto power.[7] Only a constitutional amendment would give this power to the president.

The Games Presidents Play: The Veto. Use of the veto varies according to the political situation that each president confronts. In President Obama's first term, with Democratic control of both the House and the Senate, he vetoed only two bills. In his second term, during which his party did not control the House and controlled the Senate for only one Congress, Republicans pursued

veto
The president's constitutional power to reject acts of Congress.

pocket veto
A veto that occurs automatically when Congress adjourns during the 10 days that a president has to approve a bill and the president takes no action on it.

line-item veto
The power of the president to veto specific provisions (lines) of a bill passed by the legislature (declared unconstitutional by the Supreme Court in 1998).

figure 6.1

THE VETO PROCESS

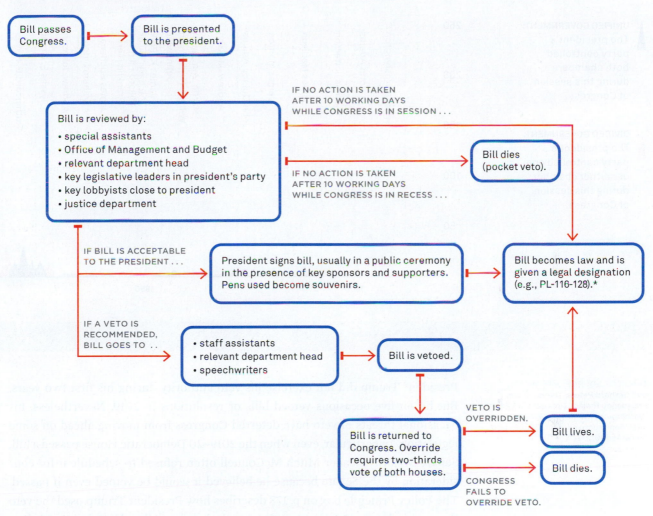

Bill passes Congress. → Bill is presented to the president.

Bill is reviewed by:
- special assistants
- Office of Management and Budget
- relevant department head
- key legislative leaders in president's party
- key lobbyists close to president
- justice department

IF NO ACTION IS TAKEN AFTER 10 WORKING DAYS WHILE CONGRESS IS IN SESSION . . .

IF NO ACTION IS TAKEN AFTER 10 WORKING DAYS WHILE CONGRESS IS IN RECESS . . .

Bill dies (pocket veto).

IF BILL IS ACCEPTABLE TO THE PRESIDENT . . .

President signs bill, usually in a public ceremony in the presence of key sponsors and supporters. Pens used become souvenirs.

Bill becomes law and is given a legal designation (e.g., PL-116-128).*

IF A VETO IS RECOMMENDED, BILL GOES TO . . .
- staff assistants
- relevant department head
- speechwriters

Bill is vetoed.

Bill is returned to Congress. Override requires two-thirds vote of both houses.

VETO IS OVERRIDDEN.

Bill lives.

CONGRESS FAILS TO OVERRIDE VETO.

Bill dies.

*PL stands for *public law*; 116 is the Congress (for example, the 116th Congress was in session in 2019–20); 128 is the number of the law.

the strategy of obstruction, and very little legislation was produced. Obama's vetoes nevertheless increased to the low double digits.

In general, presidents have used the veto to equalize or upset the balance of power with Congress. The politics surrounding the veto is complicated, and it is usually part of an intricate bargaining process between the president and Congress, involving threats of vetoes, repassage of legislation, and second vetoes.[8] As the Timeplot on pp. 176–7 shows, divided government does not necessarily result in more vetoes.

Although presidents veto only a small percentage of laws that are passed by Congress, in many cases the *threat* of a veto is sufficient to make members of Congress alter the content of a bill so that it's more to a president's liking. Thus the veto power can be influential even when the veto pen rests in its inkwell.

PRESIDENTIAL VETOES, 1789–2020

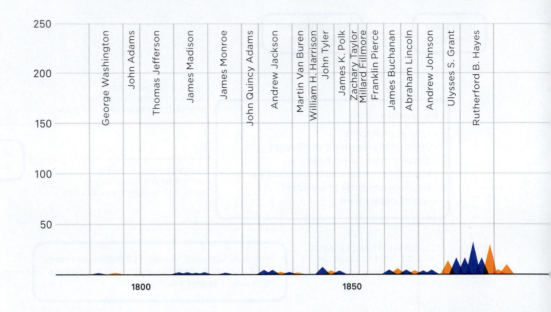

UNIFIED GOVERNMENT: The president's party controlled both chambers during this session of Congress.

DIVIDED GOVERNMENT: The president's party controlled one or neither chamber during this session of Congress.

TIMEPLOT SOURCE: John Woolley and Gerhard Peters, The American Presidency Project, Presidential Vetoes: Washington–Trump, http://www.presidency.ucsb.edu/data/vetoes.php (accessed 10/2/20).

President Trump did not exercise his veto authority during his first two years. But he on five occasions vetoed bills or resolutions in 2019. Nevertheless, his occasional threats of veto have deterred Congress from moving ahead on some legislation. In particular, even when the 2019–20 Democratic House passed a bill, Senate Majority Leader Mitch McConnell often refused to schedule it for consideration by the Senate because he believed it would be vetoed even if passed. The Policy Principle box on p. 178 describes how President Trump used the veto threat to influence Congress's actions on the border wall and immigration policy.

What about the relationship between mass public support for the president and use of the veto? At least for the modern presidency, a crucial resource for the president in negotiating with Congress has been public approval as measured by opinion polls.[9] In some situations, members of Congress pass a bill not because they want to change policy but because they want to force the president to veto a popular bill that he disagrees with in order to hurt his approval ratings.[10] As a result, vetoes may come at a price to the president.

Delegated Powers

Many of the powers exercised by the president and the executive branch come from congressional statutes and resolutions, rather than specific constitutional provisions. Over the past decades, Congress has voluntarily delegated a great

timeplot

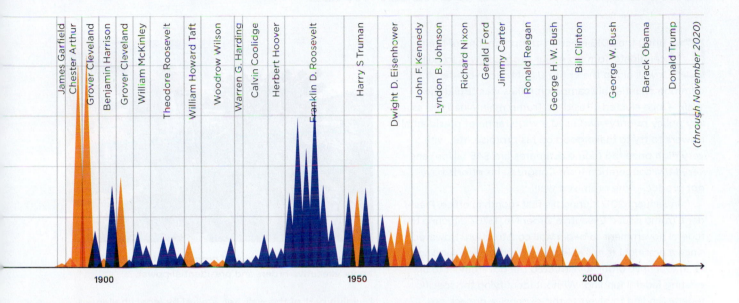

James Garfield · Chester Arthur · Grover Cleveland · Benjamin Harrison · Grover Cleveland · William McKinley · Theodore Roosevelt · William Howard Taft · Woodrow Wilson · Warren G. Harding · Calvin Coolidge · Herbert Hoover · Franklin D. Roosevelt · Harry S Truman · Dwight D. Eisenhower · John F. Kennedy · Lyndon B. Johnson · Richard Nixon · Gerald Ford · Jimmy Carter · Ronald Reagan · George H. W. Bush · Bill Clinton · George W. Bush · Barack Obama · Donald Trump · (through November 2020)

1900   1950   2000

deal of its own legislative authority to the executive branch. To some extent, this delegation is a consequence of the expansion of governmental activity since the New Deal.

Given the vast range of the federal government's responsibilities, Congress cannot execute and administer all the programs it creates and the laws it enacts. It must turn to the hundreds of departments and agencies in the executive branch or, when necessary, create new agencies to implement its goals. Thus, for example, in 1970, when Congress enacted legislation designed to improve the nation's air and water quality, it assigned the task of implementing its goals to the new Environmental Protection Agency (EPA) created by Nixon's executive order. Congress gave the EPA substantial power to set and enforce air- and water-quality standards.

As they implement congressional legislation, federal agencies interpret Congress's intentions, establish thousands of rules aimed at implementing those intentions, and issue thousands of orders to individuals, firms, and organizations who must conform to the law. In the nineteenth and early twentieth centuries, Congress typically wrote laws that provided fairly clear principles and standards to guide executive implementation. At least since the New Deal, however, Congress has tended to give executive agencies broad mandates through legislation that offers few clear standards or guidelines for implementation. The 1972 Consumer Product Safety Act, for example, authorizes the Consumer Product

the policy principle
PRESIDENT TRUMP'S BORDER WALL

During the 2016 election campaign, one of then-candidate Trump's major promises was to build a wall along the entire U.S.-Mexican border. A common chant at his campaign rallies was "Build the Wall." Once elected, President Trump maintained this as a key policy priority—and used a wide range of presidential powers to try to make good on his promise. Yet, with a very high price tag (some estimates are $45 billion) and very little cooperation from Congress, his efforts have not produced the promised wall.

In January 2017, during his first month in office, President Trump issued Executive Order No. 13767 directing the federal government to begin wall construction.[1] However, since a president is not able to appropriate new funding in an executive order, it instructed the government to use existing federal funding. Without identifying the specific federal funding to divert to this expensive project, no construction occurred as a result of the executive order.

In January 2018, the administration released a budget proposal to provide $18 billion in new money to fund a part of the wall. However, this was only a proposal; it was Congress who needed to pass the law and appropriate funding. To put pressure on Congress, the president threatened to veto any spending bill that did not include funding for his wall. The result was a standoff between the president and Congress, resulting in a partial government shutdown that lasted for 35 days. The shutdown ended with Congress providing $1.4 billion in funding for the wall—far less than the president's request.

The president used his other presidential powers to keep his campaign promise. For example, in February 2019, he signed a declaration of national emergency establishing the border situation as a national crisis. President Trump called for a reallocation of federal funding to address the crisis—by building the wall. Then, when Congress voted to overturn this declaration, the president used his veto power to strike back.

President Trump has continued to look for ways to fund the wall. Secretary of Defense Mark Esper (who was appointed by the president and confirmed by the Senate) announced a plan to use $3.6 billion in funds that Congress had allocated to military construction for

President Trump's border wall proposals raised questions about executive orders and presidential power.

building part of the wall. Yet, stalled by legal challenges, the Trump administration instead diverted $3.8 billion in funding that had been designated for the military's antidrug and antiterrorism efforts. Legal challenges to this reallocation of funds continue.

Despite these challenges, the Trump administration has been able to invest $15 billion in wall construction through Customs and Border Protection and the Department of Defense. During the summer of 2020, the Trump administration held a press conference in Yuma, Arizona, to celebrate the completion of nearly 300 miles of the wall.[2] Yet his critics note that this represents a small segment of the nearly 2,000-mile border and that all but 30 miles of this work are constituted of replacement fencing rather than new wall construction.[3]

 think It Through:

1. How does this discussion of President Trump's border wall demonstrate the U.S. system of checks and balances? How were presidential powers checked by Congress?

2. How do checks on presidential power prevent the administration in office from accomplishing its policy agenda?

[1] Donald J. Trump, "Executive Order: Border Security and Immigration Enforcement Improvements," January 25, 2017, https://www.whitehouse.gov/presidential-actions/executive-order-border-security-immigration-enforcement-improvements/ (accessed 9/18/20).

[2] Donald J. Trump, "Remarks by President Trump During Border Wall Construction and Operational Update," August 18, 2020, https://www.whitehouse.gov/briefings-statements/remarks-president-trump-border-wall-construction-operational-update-yuma-az/ (accessed 9/18/20).

[3] Mark Niquette, "The Border Wall That the U.S., Not Mexico, Is Paying For," Bloomberg, September 1, 2020, https://www.bloomberg.com/news/articles/2020-09-01/the-border-wall-that-u-s-not-mexico-is-paying-for-quicktake (accessed 9/18/20).

Safety Commission to reduce unreasonable risk of injury from household products but offers no suggestions of what constitutes reasonable and unreasonable risks or how these are to be reduced.

Inherent Powers

A number of presidential powers are neither expressed explicitly in the Constitution nor delegated by Congress. They are said to be "inherent" powers of a nation's chief executive. The inherent powers claimed by American presidents include powers related to war and protecting the nation, as well as powers related to legislative initiative.

On September 20, 2001, President George W. Bush addressed Congress and the public with a speech declaring a "war on terror." Congress passed a resolution approving the military campaign in Afghanistan (and in 2003, the invasion of Iraq), but Bush insisted he did not need congressional authorization to go to war.

War and Inherent Presidential Power.   The Constitution gives Congress the power to declare war. Presidents, however, have gone a long way toward capturing this power for themselves. Congress has not declared war since December 1941, yet since then, American military forces have engaged in numerous campaigns throughout the world under the orders of the president.

When North Korean forces invaded South Korea in June 1950, Congress was prepared to declare war, but President Harry S Truman decided not to ask for congressional action. Instead, Truman asserted the principle that the president and not Congress could decide when and where to deploy America's military might. He dispatched American forces to Korea without a congressional declaration, and in the face of the emergency, Congress went along with the president's decision. It passed a resolution approving the president's actions, and this became the pattern for future congressional-presidential relations in the military realm. The wars in Vietnam, Bosnia, Afghanistan, and Iraq, as well as a host of smaller-scale conflicts, were all fought without declarations of war.

In 1973, Congress responded to unilateral presidential action by passing the **War Powers Resolution** over President Nixon's veto. This resolution reasserted Congress's power to declare war, required the president to inform Congress of any planned military campaign, and stipulated that forces must be withdrawn within 60 days in the absence of a specific congressional authorization for their continued deployment.

War Powers Resolution
A 1973 resolution by Congress declaring that the president can send troops into action abroad only if Congress authorizes the action or if U.S. troops are already under attack or seriously threatened.

Presidents, however, have generally ignored the War Powers Resolution, claiming inherent executive power to protect the nation. Thus, for example, President George W. Bush responded to the 2001 attacks by Islamic terrorists by organizing a major military campaign to overthrow the Taliban regime in Afghanistan, which had sheltered the terrorists. In 2003, Bush ordered a major American campaign against Iraq, which he accused of posing a threat to the United States. In both instances, Congress passed resolutions approving the president's actions; the War Powers Resolution was barely mentioned on Capitol Hill and was ignored by the White House.

However, tensions stemming from the separation of powers between the president and Congress have not ended. Congress can use its spending powers and investigative powers to restrain the executive. For these reasons, presidents often try to secure congressional approval before they act, but that doesn't always occur. In 2017 and 2018, for example, President Trump authorized U.S. strikes against Syria in response to the Assad regime's alleged use of chemical weapons against civilians. After the attack he notified Congress that he would authorize additional attacks if he thought it necessary for national security. Lawmakers from both parties called on Trump to request permission from Congress before authorizing these attacks and any future attacks. In 2018 and 2019, U.S. troops were sent to Syria on Trump's command. A firestorm of congressional protest arose in 2019 when Trump peremptorily withdrew those troops, deserting America's Kurdish allies. In 2020 the House and Senate, in a measure supported by bipartisan majorities, instructed the president not to engage in military action against Iran without congressional approval.

Legislative Initiative.   Although it is not explicitly stated, the Constitution provides the president with the power of **legislative initiative**, which the framers clearly saw as one of the keys to executive power. *Legislative initiative* refers to the ability of the president and other executive agents to formulate important policy proposals that will then be taken up by the legislative branch. The president, as one individual with a great deal of staff assistance, is able to initiate decisive action more frequently than Congress, whose many members have to deliberate before taking action. Thus it is easier for the president to develop and promote a policy agenda—the set of policies and issues that receive serious attention from the government. Congress is under no constitutional obligation to take up proposals from the president. With some important exceptions, however, Congress counts on the president to set the policy agenda.

For example, in 2009, soon after taking office, President Obama presented Congress with a record-breaking $3 trillion budget proposal that included a host of new programs in such areas as health and human services, transportation, housing, and education. Obama told Congress that he would soon be requesting several hundred billion more for the financial bailout to rescue U.S. banks and revive the nation's credit markets during the Great Recession. Not only was Congress responsive to the president's initiatives, but lawmakers also expected the president to take the lead in responding to the United States' financial emergency and other problems.

The president's initiative does not end with policy making that involves Congress and the "making of laws" in the ordinary sense of the phrase. The president has still another legislative role (in all but name) within the executive branch: the power to issue **executive orders**. The executive order is first and foremost a management tool, the power that virtually any CEO has to make "company policy." Most executive orders of the president provide for the reorganization of structures and procedures or otherwise direct the affairs of the executive branch.

legislative initiative
The president's inherent power to bring a policy agenda before Congress.

executive order
A rule or regulation issued by the president that has the effect of law.

In modern times, however, executive orders have not been "merely administrative," but rather have had the broader effects of legislation—rules with actual policy content—despite avoiding the formal legislative process. We will discuss this tool further in the next two sections.

THE RISE OF PRESIDENTIAL GOVERNMENT

Most of the influence of the modern presidency comes from the powers granted by the Constitution and the laws made by Congress. Presidential power is institutional. Thus, any person properly sworn in as president will possess all of the power held by the strongest presidents in American history. But what variables account for a president's success in exercising these powers? Why are some presidents considered great successes, others colossal failures, and most something in between? The answer relates broadly to the concept of presidential power. Is that power a reflection more of the president's personal attributes or of the political situations that a president encounters?

For many decades, political scientists believed that presidential power depended on personal attributes,[11] but recently scholars have argued that presidential power should be analyzed in terms of the strategic interactions that a president has with other political actors. A bit of historical review will be helpful in understanding how the presidency has risen to its current level of influence.

The Legislative Epoch, 1800–1933

In 1885, a then-obscure political science professor named Woodrow Wilson titled his general textbook *Congressional Government* because American government was just that—government by Congress. There is ample evidence that Wilson's description of the national government was consistent with the intentions of the framers. Within the system of three separate and competing branches, the Constitution clearly makes Congress the preeminent branch.

In the early nineteenth century, some observers saw the president as little more than America's chief clerk. Indeed, most historians agree that between Thomas Jefferson and the beginning of the twentieth century, Andrew Jackson and Abraham Lincoln were the only exceptions to a series of weak presidents. Both Jackson and Lincoln are considered great presidents because they used their power in momentous ways. But it is important in the history of the presidency that neither of them left his powers as an institutional legacy to his successors. That is to say, once Jackson and Lincoln left office, the presidency reverted to its weaker status.

One reason that so few great men became presidents in the nineteenth century is that there was rarely room for greatness in such a weak office.[12] As

Chapter 3 indicated, the national government of that period was not particularly powerful. Another reason is that during this period, the presidency was not closely linked to major national political and social forces. Federalism had fragmented political interests and directed the energies of interest groups toward state and local governments, where most key decisions were made.

The presidency was strengthened somewhat in the 1830s with the introduction of the national convention system of nominating presidential candidates. Until then, presidential candidates had been nominated by their party's members of Congress. The national nominating convention arose in order to provide some representation for a party's voters who lived in districts where they weren't numerous enough to elect a member of Congress. It was seen as a victory for democracy against the congressional elite, and it gave the presidency a base of power independent of Congress. This independence did not transform the presidency into the office we recognize today, though, because Congress was long able to keep tight reins on the president's power. The real turning point came during the administration of Franklin Delano Roosevelt.

The New Deal and the Presidency

The first 100 days of the Roosevelt administration in 1933 have no parallel in U.S. history. The policies proposed by Roosevelt and adopted by Congress during this period dramatically changed the size and character of the national government. But this period was only the beginning. The president's constitutional obligation to see "that the laws be faithfully executed" became, during Roosevelt's presidency, virtually a responsibility to shape the laws before executing them.

An Expanded Role for the National Government.   The New Deal included policies never before tried on a large scale by the national government; it began intervening into economic life in ways that had hitherto been reserved for the states. For example, in the throes of the Great Depression, the Roosevelt administration created the Works Progress Administration, seeking to put the able-bodied back to work; the federal government became the nation's largest employer at this time. The Social Security Act, to give another example, sought to improve the economic condition of the most impoverished segment of the population: the elderly. In other words, the national government discovered that it could directly regulate individuals, as well as provide roads and other services.

The new programs were such dramatic departures from the traditional policies of the national government that their constitutionality was in doubt, and the Supreme Court did, in fact, declare several of them unconstitutional. In 1937, however, a game-changing case—*National Labor Relations Board v. Jones & Laughlin Steel Corporation*—challenged the federal government's authority to regulate relations between businesses and labor unions. The Court's decision affirmed a federal role in regulation of the national economy.[13] Since the end of the New Deal, the Court has never again seriously questioned the legitimacy of interventions of the national government in the economy or society.

think it through

The debate over the right balance of power between state and national government can still be seen in action today. During the most recent election, what sorts of policy proposals did candidates put forth that represented an expansion of the national government? Which policy proposals represented a limitation on national government?

Delegation of Power. The most important constitutional effect of Congress's actions and the Supreme Court's approval of those actions during the New Deal was the enhancement of presidential power. Most major acts of Congress in this period involved significant exercises of control over the economy, but few of them specified the actual controls to be used. Instead, Congress authorized the president, or in some cases a new agency, to determine what the controls would be. Although some of the new agencies were independent commissions responsible to Congress, most of the new agencies and programs were placed in the executive branch directly under presidential authority.

The growth of the national government through acts delegating legislative power tilted the American political system away from a Congress-centered government toward a president-centered government, which has become an established fact of American life.

PRESIDENTIAL GOVERNMENT

Presidents control a variety of formal and informal resources that enable them to govern. Indeed, without these resources, presidents would lack the tools needed to make much use of the power and responsibility given to them by the Constitution and by Congress. Let's first consider the president's formal or official resources (Figure 6.2) and then turn to the more informal ones that affect a president's capacity to govern—in particular, a base of popular support.

Formal Resources of Presidential Power

The formal resources of presidential power include the Cabinet, the White House staff, the Executive Office of the President, and the vice presidency.

The Cabinet. In the American system of government, the **Cabinet** refers to the heads of all the major federal government departments. The Cabinet has only a limited constitutional status. Unlike that of Great Britain or of many other parliamentary countries, where the cabinet *is* the government, the American Cabinet makes no decisions as a group. Each Cabinet appointment must be approved by the Senate, but the person appointed is not responsible to the Senate or to Congress at large.

Presidents typically rely on specialist bodies for policy areas of great national significance, like national security, that often draw on Cabinet personnel. The **National Security Council (NSC)**, established by law in 1947, is composed of the president, the vice president, the secretary of state, the secretary of defense, and other officials invited by the president. It has its own staff of foreign policy specialists run by the special assistant to the president for national security affairs. Presidents have varied in their reliance on the NSC. However, one generalization

Cabinet
The heads of the major departments of the federal government.

National Security Council (NSC)
A presidential foreign policy advisory council made up of the president, the vice president, the secretary of state, the secretary of defense, and other officials invited by the president.

figure 6.2

THE INSTITUTIONAL PRESIDENCY, 2020

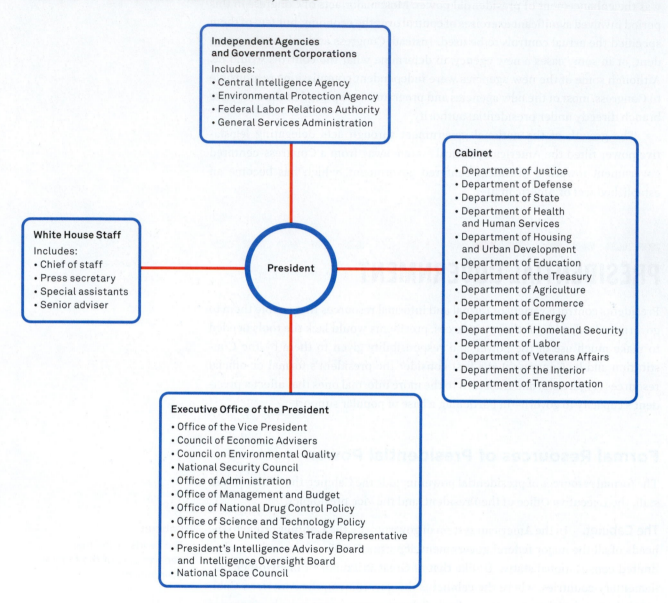

Independent Agencies and Government Corporations

Includes:
- Central Intelligence Agency
- Environmental Protection Agency
- Federal Labor Relations Authority
- General Services Administration

White House Staff

Includes:
- Chief of staff
- Press secretary
- Special assistants
- Senior adviser

President

Cabinet
- Department of Justice
- Department of Defense
- Department of State
- Department of Health and Human Services
- Department of Housing and Urban Development
- Department of Education
- Department of the Treasury
- Department of Agriculture
- Department of Commerce
- Department of Energy
- Department of Homeland Security
- Department of Labor
- Department of Veterans Affairs
- Department of the Interior
- Department of Transportation

Executive Office of the President
- Office of the Vice President
- Council of Economic Advisers
- Council on Environmental Quality
- National Security Council
- Office of Administration
- Office of Management and Budget
- Office of National Drug Control Policy
- Office of Science and Technology Policy
- Office of the United States Trade Representative
- President's Intelligence Advisory Board and Intelligence Oversight Board
- National Space Council

can be made: presidents have increasingly preferred the White House staff to the Cabinet as their means of managing the gigantic executive branch.

The White House Staff. The White House staff is composed mainly of analysts and advisers. Although many of the top White House staffers carry the title *special assistant* for a particular task or sector, the kinds of advice they are supposed to give are generally broader and more political than those that come from the Cabinet departments or from the Executive Office of the President.

The White House staff is a crucial information source and management tool for the president. But it may also insulate the president from other sources of information. Managing this trade-off between in-house expertise and access to independent outside opinion is a major challenge for the president. Sometimes it is botched, as when President George W. Bush depended too heavily on his staff for information about weapons of mass destruction (WMD) in Iraq, leading him to erroneous conclusions.[14]

The Executive Office of the President.

Created in 1939, the Executive Office of the President (EOP) consists of the permanent agencies that perform defined management tasks for the president. The most important and largest EOP agency is the Office of Management and Budget (OMB). Its roles in preparing the national budget, designing the president's legislative proposals, reporting on agency activities, and overseeing regulatory proposals make OMB personnel part of virtually every presidential responsibility. The status and power of the OMB within the EOP has grown in importance from president to president, particularly as it has taken on a greater role in setting the budget guidelines for agencies, as well as for Congress.

The Vice Presidency.

The Constitution created the vice presidency for two purposes: the vice president (1) succeeds the president in the case of a vacancy and (2) presides over the Senate, casting the tiebreaking vote when necessary.[15] The main value of the vice presidency for the president is electoral. Traditionally, a presidential candidate's most important rules for choosing a running mate are that the vice presidential nominee should bring the support of at least one state (preferably a large one) that would otherwise probably not support the ticket and, if possible, should appeal to a subsection of the party differing from the presidential nominee's. For example, it is doubtful that John F. Kennedy would have won in 1960 without the contribution his vice presidential candidate, Lyndon Johnson, made in carrying Texas.

In 2020 the Democratic vice presidential choice, Kamala Harris, targeted two important constituencies for the upcoming election campaign: women and people of color. She made history by becoming the first woman and first person of color to assume the office.

As the executive branch has grown in size and complexity, most recent presidents have sought to use their vice presidents as a management resource after the election. The presidency of George W. Bush resulted in unprecedented power and responsibility for his vice president, Dick Cheney. For the Obama administration, Vice President Joe Biden played important roles as a liaison to Congress and a sounding board on foreign affairs. President Trump, though not one to delegate much to his vice president, nevertheless enlisted Vice President Pence to head his coronavirus task force in 2020.

Presidential candidates often choose their vice presidential running mates to gain a specific electoral advantage. In 2020, Democratic presidential candidate Joe Biden announced Kamala Harris as his running mate after promising to choose a woman and to work toward building an administration as diverse as the citizens of the United States.

The Contemporary Bases of Presidential Power

Generally, presidents can expand their power in three ways: party, popular mobilization, and administration.

Party as a Source of Power.   Presidents may construct or strengthen national party institutions in order to influence the legislative process and implement their programs. All presidents have relied on the members and leaders of their own party to promote their legislative agendas. But the president does not control the party, whose members have considerable autonomy. Moreover, in the U.S. system of separated powers, the president's party may be in the minority in Congress and unable to do much for the chief executive's programs (Figure 6.3). Consequently, although the president's party is valuable, it has not been a fully reliable presidential tool.

The more unified the president's party is behind the president's legislative proposals, the more unified the opposition party is also likely to be. The president often poses as being above partisanship to win "bipartisan" support in Congress. But a bipartisan strategy may make it more difficult to build the party loyalty

figure 6.3

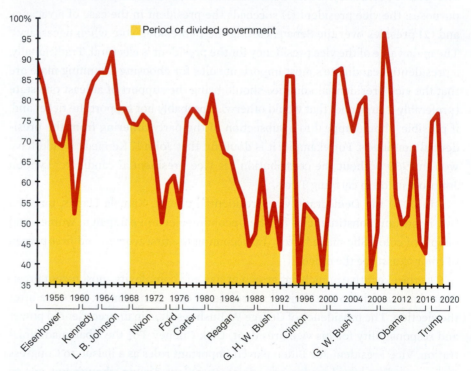

THE PRESIDENTIAL BATTING AVERAGE,* 1953–2019

*Percentage of congressional votes in which the president took the position supported by Congress.

†In 2001, the government was divided for only part of the year.

NOTE: Percentages are based on votes on which presidents took a position.

SOURCES: *Congressional Quarterly Weekly Report*, January 3, 2011, pp. 18–24; and authors' update.

and discipline that would maximize the value of congressional support from the president's own party. This is a dilemma for every president, particularly one with an opposition-controlled Congress.

Going Public. Presidents may also mobilize the public to create a mass base of support for their agendas. Popular mobilization as a technique of presidential power has its historical roots in the presidencies of Theodore Roosevelt and Woodrow Wilson and has become a weapon in the political arsenals of most presidents since the mid-twentieth century. During the nineteenth century, it was considered inappropriate for presidents to engage in personal campaigning on their own behalf or in support of programs and policies. When Andrew Johnson broke this unwritten rule and made a series of speeches vehemently seeking public support for his Reconstruction program, even some of Johnson's most ardent supporters were shocked at what they saw as his lack of decorum.

Franklin Delano Roosevelt was exceptionally effective in appealing to the public.[16] Like Theodore Roosevelt and Wilson, he often embarked on speaking trips around the nation to promote his programs. In addition, Roosevelt made limited but important use of the new electronic medium, the radio, to reach millions of Americans. In his famous "fireside chats," the president, or at least his voice, came into living rooms across the country to discuss programs and policies and generally to assure Americans that he was aware of their difficulties and working diligently toward solutions.

Roosevelt also made himself available for biweekly press conferences, offering candid answers to reporters' questions and making important policy announcements that would provide the reporters with significant stories to file.[17] Roosevelt was especially effective in designating a press secretary, who organized press conferences and made certain that reporters distinguished presidential comments that were off the record from those that could be attributed.

Every president since Roosevelt has sought to craft a public-relations strategy that would emphasize the president's strengths and popular appeal. One innovation under Clinton was to make the White House Communications Office an important institution within the EOP. The Communications Office became responsible not only for responding to reporters' queries but also for developing a coordinated communications strategy—promoting the president's policy goals, developing responses to unflattering news stories, and ensuring that a favorable image of the president would, as much as possible, dominate the news.

Consistent with President Obama's use of social networking in his 2008 election campaign, the Obama administration's Communications Office emphasized social networking techniques to reach news makers and the American people directly. President Trump has innovated on the "going public" strategy with his use of Twitter. Going over the heads not only of his own party but also of the traditional media, Trump communicated directly with his followers, maintaining an almost personal relationship with his political base and attacking his opponents, especially the press, in his frequent tweets. Presidents may also reach out to the

think it through

What types of direct outreach from the president do you think are most effective? Are there situations in which the use of social media is necessary for the president to be able to speak directly to Americans? Are there situations that are better suited to a more formal type of communication, such as a press conference?

figure 6.4

analyzing the evidence

In the nineteenth century, presidents seldom made public speeches or other public appearances. By the end of the twentieth century, the number of times presidents went public had increased dramatically. What accounts for the increase in public appearances? What do presidents hope to accomplish through speeches and other public events? What risks do presidents take when they seek to develop and use popular support as a political tool?

PUBLIC APPEARANCES BY PRESIDENTS

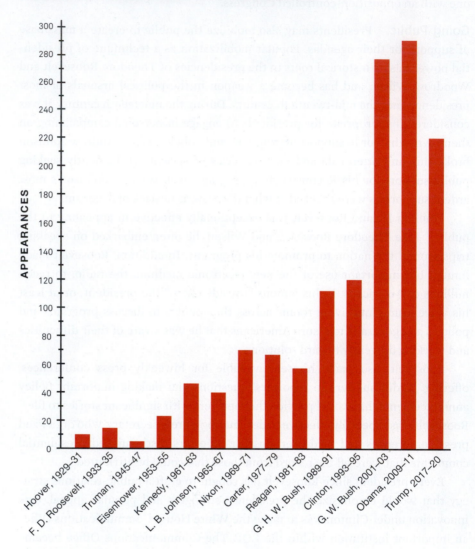

NOTE: Only the first two years of each term are represented, because the last two years include many purely political appearances for the president's reelection campaign.

SOURCES: Kernell, *Going Public*, p. 118; Lyn Ragsdale, *Vital Statistics on the Presidency*, 3rd ed. (Washington, DC: CQ Press, 2009), table 4-9, pp. 202–3; POTUS Tracker, http://projects.washingtonpost.com/potus-tracker (accessed 8/8/11); and authors' updates.

American people through public appearances. President Trump, for example, has become especially reliant on indoor-stadium rallies to rev up supporter enthusiasm (Figure 6.4).

However, popular support has not been a firm foundation for presidential power. To begin with, it is notoriously fickle. President George W. Bush maintained an approval rating of over 70 percent for more than a year after the September 11 terrorist attacks. By 2003, however, his rating had fallen nearly 20 points as American casualties in Iraq mounted, and it steadily declined through the

figure 6.5

PRESIDENTIAL PERFORMANCE RATINGS, 1964–2020

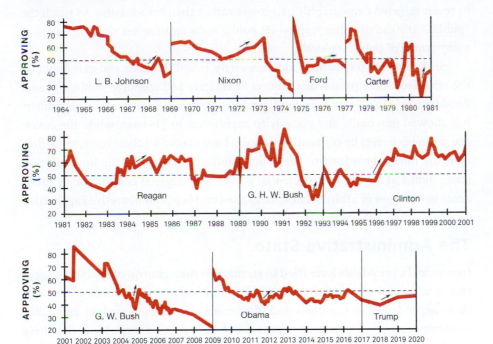

NOTE: Arrows indicate preelection upswings.

SOURCE: Gallup, http://news.gallup.com/interactives/185273/presidential-job-approval-center.aspx?g_source=mn2-us (accessed 4/21/20).

analyzing the evidence

In the presidential performance-rating poll, respondents are asked, "Do you approve of the way the president is handling his job?" The graphs show the percentage of positive responses. What factors help explain changes in presidential approval ratings? Does popular approval really affect presidential power?

rest of his presidency. Barack Obama began his presidency with a high approval rating, but after 2010 it hovered in the 40s and 50s. By the time he left office in 2017, however, it had rebounded dramatically to nearly 60 percent approval. Donald Trump began his presidency with low popular approval; throughout his term it has remained low, hovering in the high 30s to mid-40s, although it did see a temporary spike at the beginning of the coronavirus pandemic.

Declines in popular approval during a president's term in office are nearly inevitable and follow a predictable pattern (Figure 6.5).[18] Presidents generate popular support by promising to undertake important programs that will contribute directly to the well-being of large numbers of Americans, but presidential performance almost inevitably falls short of those promises, leading to a sharp decline in support. Ronald Reagan and Bill Clinton are the exceptions among modern presidents—leaving office at least as popular as when they arrived. Trump is an exception of a different sort, beginning office with very low popular approval, despite promising an active agenda of policy goals.

Technological change has affected the tactics of going public. The growing variety of media outlets—cable stations,

Today, presidents use an array of strategies, including appearances on popular television shows, to reach constituents, shape their images, and attempt to win support for their policies. President Trump has frequently appeared on Fox News, including an interview with anchor Bill Hemmer at the White House.

podcasts, social media such as Facebook and Twitter—and the declining viewership and readership of formerly "mainstream" outlets have fragmented the public. This change has necessitated newly crafted approaches—"narrowcasting" to reach targeted demographic categories rather than broadcasting to reach the "public." Instead of going "capital P" public, new approaches seek to appeal to many "small p" publics (plural).

Shrinking and fragmented audiences have raised the costs and cast doubt on the effectiveness of presidential efforts to educate and mobilize public opinion. President Trump's Twitter strategy stands as a partial exception. The technology has allowed him easily and cheaply to narrowcast to his base, while the coverage given his tweets by conventional media have magnified their impact, in effect allowing him to broadcast to the wider public. Nevertheless, the limitations of going public as a route to presidential power have also led contemporary presidents to make use of a third technique: expanding their administrative capabilities.

The Administrative State

Increasingly, presidents have tried to strengthen their control of executive agencies or to create new administrative institutions and procedures that will reduce their dependence on Congress and give them a more independent capability. Contemporary presidents have done this in two important ways. First, they have sought to increase White House control over the federal bureaucracy. Second, they have expanded the role of executive orders and other instruments of direct presidential governance. Taken together, these components of administrative strategy have given presidents the potential to achieve their goals even when they are unable to secure congressional approval.

regulatory review
The Office of Management and Budget's function of reviewing all agency regulations and other rule making before they become official policy.

Appointments and Regulatory Review.   Presidents have sought to increase their influence through bureaucratic appointments and **regulatory review**. By appointing loyal supporters to top jobs in the bureaucracy, presidents make it more likely that agencies will follow the president's wishes. Through regulatory review, presidents have tried to control rule making by the agencies of the executive branch. Whenever Congress enacts a statute, the agency charged with administering the law must establish hundreds of rules in order to implement it. Some congressional statutes are quite detailed and leave agencies with relatively little discretion. Typically, however, Congress enacts a broad statement of its intentions and delegates to the appropriate agency the power to fill in many important details.[19] In other words, Congress often says to an administrative agency, "Here is the problem. Deal with it."[20]

The discretion that Congress delegates to administrative agencies has provided recent presidents with an important avenue for expanding their power. For example, after President Clinton ordered the Food and Drug Administration (FDA) to develop rules to restrict the marketing of tobacco products to children, White House and FDA staffers prepared nearly a thousand pages of new regulations affecting tobacco manufacturers and vendors.[21] Although Republicans claimed that Bill Clinton had overstepped the powers of the presidency,[22] Presidents George W. Bush and Barack Obama continued the practice of ordering agencies to issue new regulations. President Trump, on the other hand, hit the "pause," even "reverse," button on regulations, instructing his Cabinet and other executive agency heads to pour over current regulations with "reducing red tape" as the objective. In effect, he has eliminated many of the regulatory initiatives of previous administrations.

Executive Orders.   Contemporary presidents have also enhanced their power to govern unilaterally through the use of executive orders and other forms of presidential decrees, including executive agreements, national security findings and directives, proclamations, reorganization plans, signing statements, and others.[23] Presidents cannot use executive orders to issue whatever commands they please. If a president issues an executive order, proclamation, or directive, in principle the decree must fall under powers granted to the president by the Constitution or delegated by Congress, usually through a statute.

When presidents issue such orders, they generally state the constitutional or statutory basis for their actions. For example, when President Truman ordered the desegregation of the armed services, he cited his constitutional powers as commander in chief. In a similar vein, when President Lyndon Johnson issued Executive Order No. 11246 (equal employment opportunity), he asserted that the order was designed to implement the 1964 Civil Rights Act, which prohibited employment discrimination.

Where an executive order has no statutory or constitutional basis, the courts have held it to be void. The most important case illustrating this point is *Youngstown Sheet & Tube Co. v. Sawyer*, the so-called steel seizure case of 1952.[24] Here the Supreme Court ruled that President Truman's seizure of the nation's steel mills during the Korean War had no statutory or constitutional basis and was thus invalid.

A number of court decisions, though, have held that Congress might approve a presidential action after the fact or through "acquiescence"—for example, by not objecting for long periods or by continuing to fund programs established by executive orders. In addition, the courts have indicated that some areas—most notably, military policy—are inherently presidential in character, and so they have allowed presidents wide latitude to make policy by executive decree. Thus, within the very broad limits established by the courts, presidential orders can be important policy tools. Analyzing the Evidence on pp. 192–3 explores how presidents use executive orders and other forms of unilateral action to bypass the legislative process, enabling them to make policy without Congress.

Although all presidents have used the executive order as a policy tool, government by executive order has become an especially common practice since the Clinton presidency, reflecting the growing difficulty of making policy through the legislative process. Divided government and increasing interparty policy differences have raised these costs. Clinton's frequent use of this strategy showed that an

Unilateral Action and Presidential Power

Contributed by **Jon Rogowski**, *Harvard University*

As we've seen in this chapter, Article II of the U.S. Constitution grants the president a limited number of expressed powers, but modern presidents have claimed additional powers and have sometimes used them to act unilaterally on controversial issues. Critics of these unilateral actions express concern that they represent an overreach of presidential power, by allowing presidents to circumvent the legislative process.

But what does research tell us about how and when presidents exercise unilateral powers? Executive orders are perhaps the most prominent examples of unilateral action. Franklin Roosevelt used executive orders to implement parts of the New Deal and to intern Japanese Americans during World War II. More recent presidents have used them to allow warrantless wiretapping by the National Security Administration, to suspend deportation proceedings for some undocumented immigrants, and to deny entry to the United States for people from countries suspected of terrorist connections. However, executive orders are not the only means through which presidents can exercise unilateral powers. Presidents can also use memoranda, proclamations, and other tools to change policies through the executive branch without involving Congress.

The figure below shows how presidents have used these various tools between 1933 and 2016. As the red line illustrates, executive orders have accounted for a relatively small percentage of unilateral actions issued by recent presidents. Since Presidents Kennedy and Johnson issued 510 executive orders in 1963, the most in any year since the conclusion of World War II, the number of executive orders has generally declined.

Types of Unilateral Action, 1933–2016

Legend: Executive orders · Proclamations · Memoranda

Y-axis: NUMBER OF ACTIONS (0, 250, 500, 750)
X-axis: 1935, 1945, 1955, 1965, 1975, 1985, 1995, 2005, 2015

Presidents' declining uses of executive orders, however, should not be taken as evidence that presidents have shied away from unilateral action. We see that presidents have generally made greater use of memoranda, proclamations, and other forms of unilateral action when they issued fewer executive orders. For instance, relatively few memoranda were issued in the 1950s, 1960s, and early 1980s, when the annual number of executive orders was fairly high, but in the 1970s, late 1980s, and 1990s, memoranda generally outnumbered executive orders. Presidents have also made greater use of proclamations, as their number has increased rather steadily from 52 in 1945 to 168 in 2016.

Presidential Unilateral Action, 1933–2016

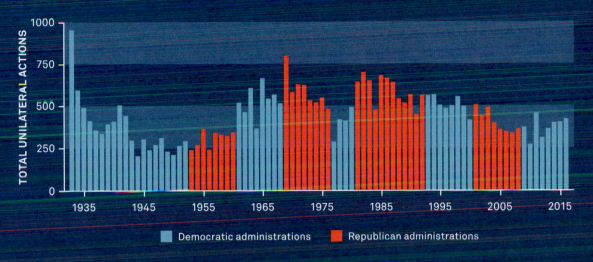

Democratic administrations   Republican administrations

But has the overall use of unilateral action increased in recent years? Combining the various tools of unilateral power, the figure above displays the total number of unilateral actions issued by presidents between 1933 and 2016. Overall, presidents' use of unilateral powers has remained relatively stable over the last seven decades. The red and blue regions of the plot indicate Republican and Democratic presidents, respectively. These data show some partisan differences in how presidents use unilateral powers, with an annual average of 475 for Republicans and 419 for Democrats.

Unilateral Action and Divided Government

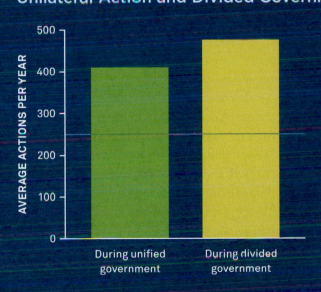

Every president from Nixon to Obama, however, confronted divided government for at least part of their term. During periods of divided government, presidents issued significantly greater numbers of unilateral actions, with an average of 409 per year during unified government compared with 475 during divided government. This finding suggests that contemporary presidents make increased use of unilateral powers when the opposite party controls Congress and presents challenges for a president's legislative agenda.

While the data presented here do not tell us about the content or the policy significance of presidents' unilateral actions, the patterns suggest that unilateral powers may allow presidents to sidestep policy disagreements between the White House and Capitol Hill. The implications of this development merit careful contemplation.

SOURCE: Aaron R. Kaufman and Jon C. Rogowski, "The Unilateral Presidency, 1953–2017." Presented at the Annual Meeting of the American Political Science Association, San Francisco, CA, August 31–September 3, 2017.

 › Given the trends illustrated in these figures, how would you expect to see President Trump's use of unilateral action differ between his first two years in office—during a unified government—and his second two years—during a divided government?

activist president could develop and implement a significant policy agenda without legislation—a lesson that was not lost on his successors. President George W. Bush made aggressive use of executive orders in response to the threat of terrorism; for example, he issued a directive authorizing the creation of military tribunals to try noncitizens accused of involvement in terrorism against the United States.

By the end of his second term, President Obama had issued over 250 executive orders, including a controversial one that would protect some 4 million undocumented immigrants (informally known as "Dreamers") from the threat of deportation. That order spurred a variety of legal challenges and one federal court ruling blocking its implementation. In June of 2016, the Supreme Court sustained the lower-court decision, a major blow to Obama's immigration policy. President Trump issued 33 executive orders in the first 100 days of his administration, more than any of his predecessors over this period. Many of these were aimed at reversing policies of the Obama years.[25] By the end of his first year in office he had issued 65 executive orders, and through 2019 he added 45 additional executive orders. By the end of his presidency, they were nearing a total of 200.

Signing Statements.

The signing statement has become another instrument of presidential power, used frequently by recent presidents to negate congressional actions to which they objected.[26] A **signing statement** is an announcement by the president at the time of signing a bill into law, sometimes presenting the president's interpretation of the law, as well as remarks predicting the benefits it will bring to the nation. Occasionally, presidents have used signing statements to point to sections of the law that they deem improper or unconstitutional or to instruct executive branch agencies how to execute the law.[27]

Presidents have made signing statements throughout American history, though many were not recorded and so did not become part of the official legislative record. Ronald Reagan's attorney general, Edwin Meese, is generally credited with transforming the signing statement into a routine tool of presidential direct action.[28] Reagan used detailed statements—prepared by the Department of Justice—to attempt to reinterpret certain congressional enactments.

Despite subsequent court rulings that the president lacked the power to declare acts of Congress unconstitutional[29] or to "excise or sever provisions of a bill with which he disagrees,"[30] the same tactic of reinterpreting and nullifying congressional enactments was continued by George H. W. Bush and Bill Clinton, and even more so by George W. Bush. The latter Bush challenged more than 800 legislative provisions with his signing statements, including a number of important domestic and security matters, such as a congressional effort to ban the use of torture by American interrogators.

Though he had denounced George W. Bush's use of signing statements while running for president, soon after taking office Barack Obama began to make use of the same tactic. Toward the end of his presidency, by November 2016, Obama had issued 36 signing statements in which he offered his own interpretation of portions of the bills he signed into law. Through 2019, President Trump has issued 51 signing statements. As an illustration of the manner in which presidents use signing statements both to influence interpretation and to promote their

signing statement
An announcement made by the president when signing a bill into law, sometimes presenting the president's interpretation of the law, as well as remarks predicting the benefits it will bring to the nation.

own reputation, Trump, in signing a consolidated appropriations bill in 2019, asserted, "The legislation preserves my authorities to build the wall on our southern border, and it prevents attempts to slash and cap ICE detention beds, as well as efforts to defund and block my administration's successful strategies and use of available law enforcement tools, which have produced dramatic reductions in illegal border-crossings." In recent years, as presidents had hoped, courts have begun giving weight to presidential signing statements when interpreting the meaning of statutes.[31] Still, the legal status of signing statements has not been fully resolved.

President Regan, shown here signing the Deficit Reduction Act of 1984, often issued signing statements to point to elements of the law that he deemed unconstitutional.

The Limits of Presidential Power

Presidents are powerful political actors and have become increasingly powerful during the past century. But there are limits to presidential power. Indeed, presidents have had to resort to strategies like signing statements, executive orders, and public appeals precisely because their official powers are limited. As the framers intended, the separation of powers is a mighty constraint. The president cannot always bend the Congress to his will, though it is an easier task when his party controls the two chambers.

Through the veto power, the president can defeat—but more important, can influence in advance—congressional aspirations. Presidential power is real, but it is tempered by the necessity of bargaining with the legislature and managing the bureaucracy, along with the constraints imposed by rulings of the federal judiciary. The growth in presidential power of the last 100 years has required the acquiescence, if not outright support, of all the other players in the game. In two of its last decisions of the 2019–20 term, the Supreme Court—one of the players in the game—issued significant decisions limiting presidential power. First, they declared in no uncertain terms that the president was not above the law—that he or she could be subpoenaed by a state prosecutor in a criminal case like any other citizen. Second, the Court declared that a president's personal papers—such as his or her tax returns—could be subpoenaed by a congressional committee for a legitimate investigative or legislative purpose.

CONCLUSION

What factors have contributed to the growth of presidential power, and what are the implications for representative government? The framers of the Constitution, as we have seen, granted executive power to a single person because they thought this would make the presidency a more energetic institution. At the same time, they checked the powers of the executive branch by creating a system of separated powers. Did the framers' plan make the presidency a strong or weak institution?

At one time, historians and journalists liked to debate the question of strong versus weak presidents. Some presidents, such as Lincoln and Franklin Delano Roosevelt, were called "strong" for their leadership and ability to guide the nation's political agenda. Others, such as James Buchanan and Calvin Coolidge, were seen as "weak" for failing to develop significant legislative programs and seeming to observe rather than shape political events.

Today, these categorizations of specific presidents have become less meaningful. Despite the limits mentioned in the preceding section, *every president is strong*. This strength is a reflection not so much of individual leadership as of the increasing powers of the institution of the presidency. Of course, as we noted earlier, political savvy in interacting with other politicians and mobilizing public opinion can account for a president's success in exercising these powers. But contemporary presidents all possess a vast array of resources and powers.

The expansion of presidential power over the past century has come about not by accident but as the result of ongoing efforts by presidents to expand the power of the office. Some of these efforts have succeeded, and others have failed. One president, Richard Nixon, was forced to resign, and others have left office under clouds. Most presidents, nevertheless, have sought to increase the office's power. What are the consequences of this development?

As is often noted by the media, popular participation in American political life has declined since the late nineteenth century. Voter turnout in presidential elections barely reaches the 60 percent mark, and hardly a third of eligible voters participate in off-year congressional races. Voter turnout in state and local races is typically even lower. These facts are well known, and they raise concerns about how representative American government is.

Low rates of political participation also have institutional implications that are less obvious. To put the matter briefly, the decline of voting and other forms of popular involvement in American political life reduces congressional influence while enhancing the power of the presidency. Congress is the nation's most representative political institution and remains the only entity capable of placing limits on unwise or illegitimate presidential conduct. The courts have rarely succeeded in thwarting a determined president, especially in the foreign policy realm. However, in the past few decades our nation's undemocratic politics has undermined Congress while paving the way for a more powerful presidency that is capable of acting unilaterally.

The framers of the Constitution created a system of government in which Congress and the executive branch were to share power. In recent decades, however, the powers of Congress have waned while those of the presidency have expanded dramatically. To take one instance of congressional retreat in the face of presidential assertiveness, in October 2002, pressed by President George W. Bush, both houses of Congress voted overwhelmingly to authorize him to use military force against Iraq. The resolution adopted by Congress allowed the president complete discretion to determine whether, when, and how to attack Iraq. Indeed, Bush's legal advisers had pointedly declared that the president did not actually need specific congressional authorization to attack Iraq if he decided such action was in America's interest. Few members of Congress even bothered to object to this apparent rewriting of the U.S. Constitution.

There is no doubt that Congress continues to be able to harass presidents and even, on occasion, to hand the White House a sharp rebuff. In the larger view, however, presidents' occasional defeats—however dramatic—have been temporary setbacks in a gradual shift toward increased presidential power in the twenty-first century. Americans look to their presidents for effective governance, and most think the presidency is a more effective governmental institution than Congress. But what of representation? Can one person claim to represent the American people? The framers sought to create a system of government that was both effective and representative. What would they think of America's government today?

Key Terms

expressed powers 169

delegated powers 169

inherent powers 169

commander in chief 170

executive agreement 173

executive privilege 173

veto 174

pocket veto 174

line-item veto 174

War Powers Resolution 179

legislative initiative 180

executive order 180

Cabinet 183

National Security Council (NSC) 183

regulatory review 190

signing statement 194

Check Your Understanding

1. Explain the difference between expressed, inherent, and delegated powers.

2. How have powers delegated by Congress to the president increased the power of the presidency over the past 70 years?

3. What are the president's formal or official resources? How do presidents use these resources to effectively implement their policy agendas?

4. How do presidents use informal resources—including party, popular mobilization, and administration—to expand their power?

5. Explain how the need for signing statements, executive orders, and public appeals demonstrates the limitations of presidential power.

INQUIZITIVE

Earn a better grade on your test. InQuizitive personalizes your learning path to help you master the concepts from this chapter. In a recent efficacy study of American government students, InQuizitive increased test scores by an average of 17 points (see back cover).

CHAPTER SEVEN

THE EXECUTIVE BRANCH

The Clean Water Act of 1972 gave the federal government broad authority to protect America's navigable water resources from pollution. In 2015, a new set of federal regulations collectively known as the Waters of the United States rule, or WOTUS, greatly expanded the federal government's control over pollution of the nation's rivers, streams, lakes, ponds, and wetlands. While welcomed by environmental groups, WOTUS was greeted with dismay by economic interests, including agriculture, ranching, and construction, that feared they could face billions of dollars in costs for complying with complex new procedures and environmental challenges to their business practices. These opponents lobbied unsuccessfully against the rule and, after its adoption, filed a number of lawsuits that slowed its implementation. In 2017, the Trump administration announced that WOTUS would be reexamined and, in 2019, fulfilled a campaign promise to roll back these regulations.

Most Americans think that in their representative system of government, Congress writes and approves all laws and sends them to the president for a signature. However, WOTUS was never a bill, nor was it enacted by Congress. Instead, it was drafted and implemented by the Environmental Protection Agency (EPA) and the United States Army Corps of Engineers (USACE), two of the hundreds of bureaucratic agencies that make up the executive branch of government.

In fact, Congress enacts only a handful of new laws every year. Federal agencies, on the other hand, write several thousand regulations each year that have the force of law and can have an enormous impact on Americans' lives.

In principle, agency regulations are intended only to clarify and implement the laws enacted by Congress. After a bill is passed by Congress and signed into law by the president, the various federal agencies charged with administering and enforcing the new statute spend months, sometimes years, developing rules

WOTUS rules, established by the EPA and Army Corps of Engineers, expanded the federal government's control over pollution of rivers, streams, lakes, ponds, and wetlands. Here, an EPA employee takes water and soil samples from a Michigan lake.

to implement it. The agencies then continue to write rules under the authority of the statute for decades to come. Over time, these rules can take on a life of their own, modifying or even rewriting the original law. WOTUS, for example, was written under the authority of the 1972 Clean Water Act, governing navigable waterways. With the 2015 rule, the EPA and USACE aimed to extend their authority under the act into *all* waters—a significant expansion of the law's coverage and of the agencies' power.

Effective governance requires Congress to delegate a great deal of power to the agencies of the executive branch. When Congress writes legislation addressing complex issues, members cannot anticipate every problem or question about it that might arise over coming decades, nor can Congress administer the thousands of programs that the legislation creates. Legislators must rely on administrative agencies for these purposes.

- **Does the power of bureaucratic agencies undermine representative government?**

But what about representative government? When an agency writes new rules that effectively change the law, how can we be sure that citizens' views and interests are taken into account? After all, no one elected the thousands of federal officials involved in the rule-making process. Congress addressed this problem in 1946 when it enacted the Administrative Procedure Act (APA), requiring agencies to give public notice of proposed rules, to invite public comment, and to hold public hearings. But as the farmers, ranchers, and builders opposing WOTUS discovered, although the APA requires agencies to invite public comment, it does not require them to revise their proposals in response.

Effective governance requires turning over a great deal of power to federal agencies. Doing so, however, poses challenges to representative government. How can we reconcile these matters? In this chapter we look in detail at the executive branch, examining the government's major administrative agencies, their role in the governmental process, and their political behavior.

Learning Objectives

- Explain what bureaucracies are, and describe how they facilitate effective governance, including their role in making and implementing laws, establishing rules, and settling disputes.

- Describe the structure of the executive branch in the United States.

- Analyze the challenge of keeping bureaucratic agencies accountable to elected officials.

- Evaluate the major proposals for reforming bureaucracy.

HOW DOES BUREAUCRACY WORK?

Despite their tendency to criticize bureaucracy (Figure 7.1), most Americans recognize that maintaining order in a large society is impossible without a large governmental apparatus staffed by professionals with expertise in public administration. When we approve of what a government agency is doing, we give the phenomenon a positive name: "administration"; when we disapprove, we call it "bureaucracy."

Although the terms *administration* and *bureaucracy* are often used interchangeably, it is useful to distinguish between the two. *Administration* is the more general term, referring to all the ways human beings might rationally coordinate their efforts to achieve a common goal, in private as well as public organizations. **Bureaucracy** refers to the actual offices, tasks, rules, and principles of organization that large institutions use to coordinate their work.

bureaucracy
The complex structure of offices, tasks, rules, and principles of organization that large institutions use to coordinate the work of their personnel.

Bureaucratic Organization Enhances Efficiency

The core of bureaucracy is the division of labor; the key to its effectiveness is the coordination of experts performing complex tasks. If each job is specialized to increase efficiency, then each worker must depend on other workers' output, and that dependence requires careful distribution of jobs and resources.

Inevitably, then, bureaucracies become hierarchies, often in the form of a pyramid. At the base of the organization are workers with the fewest skills and specializations; one supervisor can oversee a large number of them. At each

figure 7.1

PUBLIC OPINION ON WASTE IN GOVERNMENT, 1964–2018

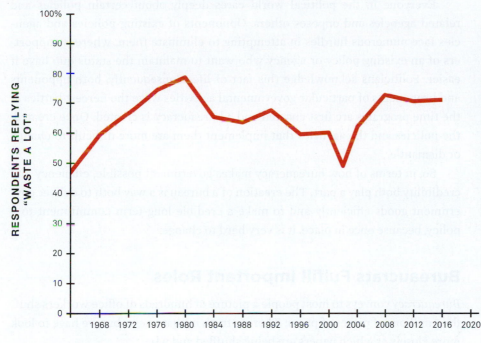

SOURCES: American National Election Studies, https://electionstudies.org/wp-content/uploads/2018/03/anes_timeseries_2016_qnaire_pre.pdf (accessed 6/15/20).

analyzing the evidence

Survey respondents were asked the following question: "Do you think that people in the government waste a lot of the money we pay in taxes, waste some of it, or don't waste very much of it?" What do you, the reader, think? Is the public justified in its belief that the government wastes a lot of money?

higher level, workers are more highly specialized than at the level below, and coordination of work involves fewer workers per supervisor. Toward the top, a handful of executives "manage" the organization, coordinating and overseeing all its tasks, plus distributing supplies to workers and the organization's outputs to the market (if it is a private-sector organization) or to the public.

Bureaucracies Enable Governments to Operate

By dividing up tasks, matching them to a labor force that develops appropriately specialized skills, standardizing procedures, and providing the structure of incentives and supervision to get large numbers of people to operate in a coordinated fashion, bureaucracies accomplish goals more efficiently and effectively than would otherwise be possible. Providing "government goods" as broad as national defense or as narrow as a subsidy to a wheat farmer requires organization, routines, standards, and, ultimately, the authority for someone to cut a check and put it in the mail. Bureaucracies are created to do these things.

Bureaucracy also consolidates programs related to one another and insulates them from opposing political forces. By creating *clienteles*—groups of supporters in Congress, the business sector, or the general public whose interests they serve

 think it through

Think about the bureaucracies that support the institution in which you are currently taking this class: are there loans, subsidies, or programs that are supported or regulated by government agencies? Can you think of other bureaucratic *clienteles* of which you're a part? What are some "government goods" you receive that benefit you?

or represent—a bureaucracy establishes a coalition of supporters, some of whom will fight to keep it in place because they value consistency, predictability, and durability.

Everyone in the political world cares deeply about certain policies and related agencies and opposes others. Opponents of existing policies and agencies face numerous hurdles in attempting to eliminate them, whereas supporters of an existing policy or agency who want to maintain the status quo have it easier. Politicians acknowledge this fact of life. Consequently, both opponents and proponents of particular governmental activities wage the fiercest battles at the time programs are first enacted and a bureaucracy is created. Once created, the policies and the agencies that implement them are more difficult to change or dismantle.

So, in terms of how bureaucracy makes government possible, efficiency and credibility both play a part. The creation of a bureau is a way both to deliver government goods efficiently and to make a credible long-term commitment to a policy, because once in place, it is very hard to change.

Bureaucrats Fulfill Important Roles

Bureaucracy conveys to most people a picture of hundreds of office workers shuffling millions of pieces of paper. There is truth in that image, but we have to look more closely at which papers are being shuffled and why.

Implementing Laws.   Bureaucrats, whether in public or private organizations, communicate with one another to coordinate all the specializations within their

When President Trump declared a nationwide emergency in response to the coronavirus pandemic in March 2020, FEMA, in coordination with the Department of Health and Human Services (HHS), began assisting state, local, tribal, and other eligible entities with health and safety actions, including construction of an emergency hospital at the Javits Center in New York City, as shown here.

organization. This coordination is necessary to carry out the primary task of bureaucracy, which is **implementation**—that is, carrying out the organization's objectives as laid down by its board of directors (if a private company) or by law (if a public agency). In the federal government, the "bosses" are ultimately Congress and the president.

implementation
The development of rules, regulations, and bureaucratic procedures to translate laws into action.

Making and Enforcing Rules. When the bosses—Congress, in particular, when it is making the law—are clear in their instructions to bureaucrats, implementation is fairly straightforward. Bureaucrats translate the law into specific instructions for each of the employees of an agency. But what happens to routine implementation when several bosses disagree as to what the instructions ought to be? This situation requires another job for bureaucrats: interpretation.

Interpretation is a form of implementation, in that the bureaucrats still have to carry out what they see as the intentions of their superiors. But when bureaucrats have to interpret a law before implementing it, they are, in effect, engaging in lawmaking.[1] Congress often deliberately delegates to an administrative agency the responsibility of lawmaking; for example, members conclude that some area of industry needs regulation or some area of the environment needs protection, but they are unwilling or unable to specify just how to do it. In such situations, Congress delegates to the appropriate agency a broad authority within which to make law through the procedures of rule making and administrative adjudication (settling disputes).

Rule making is essentially the same as lawmaking. The rules issued by government agencies provide more detailed indications of what a law actually will mean. For example, the Forest Service is charged with making policies that govern the use of national forests. Just before President Clinton left office in 2001, the agency issued rules that banned new road building and development in the forest—a goal long sought by environmentalists. In 2005, under George W. Bush, the Forest Service relaxed the rules, allowing states to make proposals for building new roads within the national forests. Just as the timber industry had opposed the Clinton rule banning road building, environmentalists challenged the Bush administration's changes and sued the Forest Service in federal court for violating clean-water and endangered-species legislation.

In a similar vein, the Trump administration sought to undo a host of environmental rules developed during the Obama presidency. Environmental groups responded by filing suits in federal court to defend the rules they favored. Some of these suits were successful and some were not. The net result is that by the end of 2019 the Trump administration had rolled back, or was in the process of rolling back, 95 environmental rules.[2]

New rules proposed by an agency take effect only after a period of public comment, and reaction from the people or businesses that will be affected may cause the agency to modify its draft rules. Public participation takes the form of statements filed and testimony given in public forums. The rule-making process is thus highly political. Once rules are approved, they are published in the *Federal Register* and have the force of law.

Settling Disputes. Administrative adjudication is very similar to what courts ordinarily do: applying rules and precedents to specific cases in order to settle disputes. The agency charges the person or business suspected of violating the law, and the ruling applies only to the specific case being considered. Many regulatory agencies use administrative adjudication to make decisions about specific products or practices.

For example, the National Labor Relations Board (NLRB) uses adjudication to decide union certification. When groups of workers seek the right to vote on forming a union as their bargaining agent or on affiliating with an existing union, they are usually opposed by their employers, who assert that relevant provisions of laws protecting union organizing do not apply. The NLRB takes testimony case by case and makes determinations for one side or the other, acting essentially like a court.

Compared with bureaucrats in large private organizations, government bureaucrats operate under far more constraints. They are required to maintain a more thorough paper trail and are subject to more access from the public, such as newspaper reporters. Public access has been vastly facilitated by the Freedom of Information Act (FOIA), adopted in 1966. This act gives ordinary citizens the right of access to agency files and data to determine whether those materials contain derogatory information about them and to learn about what the agency is doing in general.

Bureaucracies Serve Politicians

In principle, Congress could make all bureaucratic decisions itself, writing very detailed legislation each year. In some areas—tax policy, for example—this is, in fact, the way law is made. Tax policy is determined in significant detail by the House Ways and Means Committee, the Senate Finance Committee, and the Joint Committee on Taxation. The agency charged with its implementation, the Internal Revenue Service (IRS), does relatively little rule making compared to many other regulatory and administrative agencies.

The norm is for legislative authority to be delegated, often in vague terms, to the bureaucracy, which is then expected to fill in the gaps. This delegation, however, is not a blank check. The bureaucracy is held to account by congressional monitoring of its performance—a task carried out by the staffs of relevant committees, which also serve as repositories for complaints from affected parties.[3] Poor performance, or making rules or decisions at odds with important members' preferences, risks penalties ranging from the browbeating of senior bureaucrats in public hearings to cutbacks in agencies' budgets and restrictions on their authority.

HOW IS THE EXECUTIVE BRANCH ORGANIZED?

Cabinet departments, agencies, and bureaus are the operating parts of the bureaucratic whole. These parts can be classified into four general types: (1) Cabinet departments, (2) independent agencies, (3) government corporations, and (4) independent regulatory commissions. The heads of Cabinet departments and other major agencies are appointed by the president, subject to confirmation by the Senate. Most other agency employees are career officials or "contractors"—employees hired to perform specific tasks for a specified period of time.

Although Figure 7.2 is an organizational chart of the Department of Agriculture, any other department could serve as an illustration. At the top is the department head, called the secretary of the department. Below the secretary and a deputy secretary are several top administrators, such as the general counsel and the chief economist, whose responsibilities span the various departmental functions and enable the secretary to manage the entire organization. Working alongside these officials are the assistant secretaries and undersecretaries, each with management responsibilities for a group of operating agencies, which are arranged vertically below the undersecretaries.

The next tier, generally called the bureau level, is the highest level of responsibility for specialized programs. These bureau-level agencies are often very well known to the public: the Forest Service and the Food Safety and Inspection Service are examples. Sometimes they are officially called bureaus, such as the Federal Bureau of Investigation (FBI) in the Department of Justice. Within the bureaus are divisions, offices, services, and units.

Not all government agencies are part of Cabinet departments. Some, called independent agencies, are set up by Congress outside the departmental structure, even though the president appoints and directs their heads. Independent agencies usually have broad powers to provide public services that are either too expensive or too important to be left to private initiatives. Some examples are the National Aeronautics and Space Administration (NASA), the Central Intelligence Agency (CIA), and the Environmental Protection Agency (EPA). Government corporations, a third type of government agency, are more like private businesses performing and charging for a market service, such as transporting railroad passengers (Amtrak).

Independent regulatory commissions, which make up a fourth type of agency, are given broad discretion to make rules. The first regulatory agencies established by Congress, beginning with the Interstate Commerce Commission in 1887, were set up as independent regulatory commissions because Congress recognized that regulatory agencies are "mini-legislatures," whose rules are the same as legislation but require the kind of expertise and full-time attention that

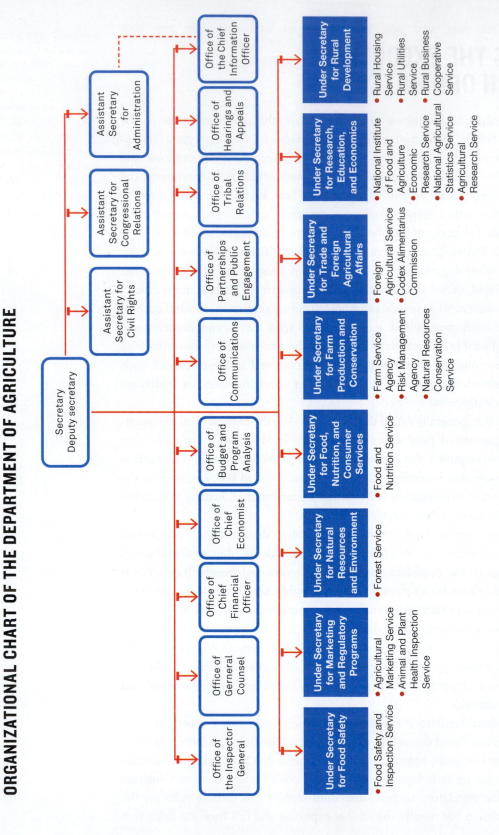

figure 7.2

ORGANIZATIONAL CHART OF THE DEPARTMENT OF AGRICULTURE

Secretary
Deputy secretary

Office of the Inspector General

Office of Gerneral Counsel

Office of Chief Financial Officer

Office of Chief Economist

Office of Budget and Program Analysis

Office of Communications

Office of Partnerships and Public Engagement

Office of Tribal Relations

Office of Hearings and Appeals

Office of the Chief Information Officer

Assistant Secretary for Civil Rights

Assistant Secretary for Congressional Relations

Assistant Secretary for Administration

Under Secretary for Food Safety
• Food Safety and Inspection Service

Under Secretary for Marketing and Regulatory Programs
• Agricultural Marketing Service
• Animal and Plant Health Inspection Service

Under Secretary for Natural Resources and Environment
• Forest Service

Under Secretary for Food, Nutrition, and Consumer Services
• Food and Nutrition Service

Under Secretary for Farm Production and Conservation
• Farm Service Agency
• Risk Management Agency
• Natural Resources Conservation Service

Under Secretary for Trade and Foreign Agricultural Affairs
• Foreign Agricultural Service
• Codex Alimentarius Commission

Under Secretary for Research, Education, and Economics
• National Institute of Food and Agriculture
• Economic Research Service
• National Agricultural Statistics Service
• Agricultural Research Service

Under Secretary for Rural Development
• Rural Housing Service
• Rural Utilities Service
• Rural Business Cooperative Service

SOURCE: U.S. Department of Agriculture, https://www.usda.gov/sites/default/files/documents/usda-organization-chart.pdf (accessed 4/21/20).

As an independent agency, NASA is not part of a Cabinet department but provides public services that are too important to be left to private initiatives. In 2019, a new class of astronauts graduated basic training, including Jessica Watkins, shown here preparing for underwater space-walk training. These graduates will contribute to missions and research that may take them to the International Space Station, to the moon, or to Mars.

is beyond the capacity of Congress. Until the 1960s, most of the regulatory agencies set up by Congress, such as the Federal Communications Commission (1934), were independent regulatory commissions. But beginning in the late 1960s, all new regulatory programs, with only a few exceptions (such as the Federal Election Commission), were placed within existing departments and made directly responsible to the president.

After the 1970s, no major new regulatory programs were established until the financial crisis of 2008–9. The Dodd-Frank Wall Street Reform and Consumer Protection Act of 2010 brought major changes to the regulation of banks and other financial institutions. The act created several new regulatory bodies, including the Financial Stability Oversight Council, the Office of Financial Research, and the Consumer Financial Protection Bureau.

The status of an agency—as one of these four types—defines an agency's powers, its place in the governmental hierarchy, its level of independence, and how its executives are appointed. Agencies also differ from one another in terms of their missions. When it comes to agency missions, the main types are clientele agencies, agencies for revenue and security, regulatory agencies, and redistributive agencies.

Clientele Agencies

Although all administrative agencies have clienteles—economic or other groups whose interests they serve or represent—certain agencies are specifically directed by law to promote the interests of a particular clientele. For example, the Department of Commerce and Labor was founded in 1903 as a single department "to foster, promote, and develop the foreign and domestic commerce, the mining, the manufacturing, the shipping, and fishing industries, and the transportation facilities of the United States."[4] It remained a single department until 1913, when legislation created the two separate departments of Commerce and Labor, with each statute providing for the same obligation: to support and foster their respective clienteles.[5] The Department of Agriculture serves the many farming

Types of Government Agencies

There are four main types of bureaucratic agencies within the U.S. federal government.

- **Cabinet departments:** The largest components of the executive branch. Each of the 15 departments is headed by a Cabinet secretary, and departments encompass related agencies and bureaus.

    Examples: Department of Justice (encompasses more than 50 agencies, including Federal Bureau of Investigation, Office of Tribal Justice, and U.S. Parole Commission)

- **Independent agencies:** Agencies set up by Congress outside the Cabinet departments to provide specific public goods and services, such as protection of the environment or information from space exploration.

    Examples: Environmental Protection Agency (EPA), National Aeronautics and Space Administration (NASA)

- **Government corporations:** Government agencies that perform and charge for a market service, such as transporting rail passengers.

    Examples: Amtrak

- **Independent regulatory commissions:** Agencies given broad discretion to make rules regulating a specific type of activity.

    Examples: Federal Communications Commission (FCC), Financial Stability Oversight Council

---

clientele agency
A department or bureau of government whose mission is to promote, serve, or represent a particular interest.

interests that, taken together, are one of the United States' largest economic sectors. We describe agencies whose mission is to promote, serve, or represent a particular interest as **clientele agencies**.

In most clientele agencies, many of the personnel work in field offices dealing directly with the clientele. A familiar example is the Extension Service of the Department of Agriculture, with its local "extension agents" who consult with farmers to promote farm productivity. These agencies also provide "functional representation"; that is, they learn what their clients' interests and needs are and then operate almost as a lobby in Washington on their behalf. In addition to the Departments of Agriculture, Commerce, and Labor, clientele agencies include the Department of Interior and five of the newest Cabinet departments: Housing and Urban Development (HUD), created in 1966; Transportation (DOT), 1966; Energy (DOE), 1977; Education (ED), 1979; and Health and Human Services (HHS), 1979.[6]

Agencies for Revenue and Security

The Constitution leaves many vital functions of public order, such as the police, to state and local governments. But federal agencies critical to maintaining national cohesion do exist, and they can be grouped into three categories: (1) agencies for collecting government revenue, (2) agencies for controlling conduct defined as a threat to internal national security, and (3) agencies for defending national security from external threats. The most powerful departments in these areas are Treasury, Justice, Defense, State, and Homeland Security.

Revenue Agencies.   The Treasury Department's Internal Revenue Service (IRS) is the most important revenue agency and one of the federal government's largest bureaucracies. Over 75,000 employees are spread through four regions, working in district offices, service centers, and hundreds of local offices.[7]

Agencies for Internal Security.   The United States is fortunate to enjoy national unity maintained by civil law rather than imposed by military force. As long as the country is not in a state of insurrection, most of the task of maintaining the Union involves legal work, and the main responsibility for that lies with the Department of Justice (DOJ). The most important agency in the DOJ is the Criminal Division, which enforces all federal criminal laws except a few assigned to other divisions. Criminal litigation is actually handled by the U.S. attorneys. The president appoints a U.S. attorney for each federal judicial district, who supervises the work of assistant U.S. attorneys.

The work or jurisdiction of the Antitrust and Civil Rights Divisions is described by their official names. The Antitrust Division seeks to prevent monopolistic and other unfair practices by business corporations; the Civil Rights Division investigates and prosecutes activities aimed at promoting political or workplace discrimination. The FBI, another bureau of the DOJ, is the information-gathering agency for all the other divisions.

In 2002 Congress created the Department of Homeland Security (DHS) to coordinate the nation's defense against the threat of terrorism. This department's responsibilities include protecting commercial airlines from would-be hijackers. Most visible to the traveling public are the 50,000 employees of the Transportation Security Administration (TSA), the largest unit of the DHS, who guard airports and rail and bus stations and staff security screening operations.[8]

Agencies for External National Security.   Two departments occupy center stage here: State and Defense. A few key agencies outside State and Defense also have external national security function. Among the most important of these is the Central Intelligence Agency (CIA).

Although diplomacy is generally considered the State Department's primary task, that is only one of its organizational dimensions. The department also includes regional bureaus, concerned with all problems within specific regions of the world; "functional" bureaus, which handle such things as economic and business affairs, intelligence, research, and relationships with international organizations; and bureaus of internal affairs, which handle such areas as security, finance and management, and legal issues.

Despite the State Department's importance in foreign affairs, only a small portion of all U.S. government employees working abroad are directly under its

think it through

One of the government agencies most familiar to Americans is the Internal Revenue Service, or IRS. How does the annual tax return filing process demonstrate how bureaucracies help streamline processes and get large numbers of people to operate in a coordinated fashion?

authority. By far, the largest number of career government professionals working abroad are under the authority of the Department of Defense (DOD). The creation of the DOD between 1947 and 1949 was an effort to unify the two historic military departments—the War Department and the Navy Department—and integrate them with a new department, the Air Force Department.

The United States has experienced relatively mild political problems with its military compared with many other countries, which have struggled to keep their militaries out of the politics of governing. The primary problem is that of pork-barrel politics: defense contracts are often highly lucrative for local districts, so military spending becomes a matter not just of military need but also of narrow political and economic interests. For instance, proposed military-base closings, always a major part of budget cutting, just as inevitably cause a firestorm of opposition from affected members in both parties, even some who otherwise favor slashing the Pentagon budget. Emphasis on jobs rather than strategy and policy means pork-barrel use of the military for political purposes.

Regulatory Agencies

regulatory agency
A department, bureau, or independent agency whose primary mission is to make rules governing a particular type of activity.

The United States has many **regulatory agencies**. Some are bureaus within departments, such as the Food and Drug Administration (FDA) in the Department of Health and Human Services, the Occupational Safety and Health Administration (OSHA) in the Department of Labor, and the Animal and Plant Health and Inspection Service (APHIS) in the Department of Agriculture. Others are independent regulatory commissions—for example, the Federal Trade Commission (FTC).

administrative legislation
Rules made by regulatory agencies that have the force of law.

But whether departmental or independent, an agency or commission is regulatory if Congress delegates to it broad powers over a sector of the economy or a type of commercial activity and authorizes it to make rules governing the conduct of people and businesses within that jurisdiction. Rules made by regulatory agencies have the force of legislation; indeed, such rules are referred to as **administrative legislation**. And when these agencies make decisions or orders settling disputes between parties or between the government and a party, they are acting like courts.

Redistributive Agencies

Fiscal, monetary, and welfare agencies transfer hundreds of billions of dollars annually between the government and private interests. Through such transfers, these agencies influence how trillions of dollars are spent and invested annually. We call them "redistributive agencies" or "agencies of redistribution" because they influence how much money there is in the economy, who has it, who can borrow it, and whether people will invest, save, or spend it.

Fiscal and Monetary Policy Agencies. Governmental activity relating to money includes both fiscal and monetary policy. *Fiscal policy* involves taxing and spending, while *monetary policy* has to do with banks, credit, and currency.

(We will discuss these policies in Chapter 13.) Administration of fiscal policy is primarily a Treasury Department role. Today, in addition to administering and policing income tax and other tax collections (as discussed already), the Treasury manages the enormous federal debt. The Treasury also prints currency, but currency represents only a tiny portion of the entire money economy. Most of the trillions of dollars exchanged in the private and public sectors of the U.S. economy are transferred electronically, not in currency.

Another important agency for both fiscal and monetary policy is the Federal Reserve System, headed by the Federal Reserve Board. The **Federal Reserve System**, or **Fed**, has authority over the lending activities of the nation's most important banks, notably the interest rates they charge. The Fed works to prevent both inflation and deflation of the nation's money and credit. Established by Congress in 1913, it is responsible for adjusting the supply of money to the needs of banks in the different regions and to the needs of commerce and industry in each.

The Fed also ensures that banks do not put themselves at too much financial risk with lending policies that are too liberal. This responsibility was given to the Fed because of fears of a sudden economic scare resulting from too many uncollectible loans that can destabilize the banking system. At its worst, such a shock to the economy could cause another financial crash like the one in 1929 that ushered in the Great Depression. The Federal Reserve Board sits at the top of a pyramid of 12 district Federal Reserve banks, which are "bankers' banks," serving the hundreds of member banks in the national bank system (see also Chapter 13).

Welfare Agencies.   No single agency is responsible for all the programs that make up the "welfare state." The largest agency in this field is the Social Security Administration, which manages the Social Security and Supplementary Security Income programs. The Department of Health and Human Services administers various programs for needy families, including Medicaid, while the Department of Agriculture oversees the food stamp program. With the exception of Social Security, these are means-tested programs, requiring applicants to demonstrate that their annual cash earnings fall below an officially defined poverty line. These public-assistance programs impose a large administrative burden.

Federal Reserve System (Fed)
The system of 12 Federal Reserve banks that facilitates exchanges of cash, checks, and credit; regulates member banks; and uses monetary policy to fight inflation and deflation in the United States.

THE PROBLEM OF BUREAUCRATIC CONTROL

Two centuries, millions of employees, and trillions of dollars after the Founding, we must return to James Madison's observation that "you must first enable the government to control the governed; and in the next place oblige it to control itself."[9] Today the problem is the same, but the form has changed. The problem now is the challenge of keeping the bureaucracy accountable to elected political authorities.

Government agencies depend on Congress to approve their budgets, and bureaucrats work to convince Congress that they are using the funds effectively. In a rare example of bipartisan support for legislation, in March 2020, as the U.S. suffered from the COVID-19 pandemic, Nancy Pelosi signed the $2.2 trillion CARES Act. The stimulus bill, the largest in U.S history, provided economic bailouts and loans to companies and small businesses and included direct payments to individuals.

Bureaucrats' Goals

The economist William Niskanen proposed that a bureau or department of government can be compared to a division of a private firm and that a bureaucrat is like the manager who runs that division.[10] In particular, Niskanen argued that a bureau chief or department head can be thought of as trying to maximize her budget, just as the private-sector manager tries to maximize his division's profits.

Bureaucrats might find many motivations to maximize their budgets. A cynical (though some would say realistic) explanation is that a bureaucrat's own compensation and fringe benefits are often tied to the size of her budget. A second, related motivation is psychological or emotional gratification. An individual enjoys the prestige that comes from running a major enterprise, and her self-esteem and status are boosted by the fact that her bureau has a large budget.

But salary and status are not the only forces driving bureaucrats to gain as large a budget as possible. Many bureaucrats at all levels care deeply about their agency's mission[11] and believe in the importance of serving their country and helping their fellow citizens. As they rise through the ranks and assume management responsibilities, this orientation still drives them. Thus they try to secure as large a budget as possible to succeed in the mission to which they have devoted their professional lives.

Of course, legislators do not have to fork over whatever funds the bureau requests. In making budget allocations, Congress often evaluates a bureau's performance: committees hold hearings, request documentation, assign staff to do research, and question employees. After the fact, the committees engage in oversight, making sure that what Congress was told at the time when policies and appropriations were voted on actually holds in practice.

Budget maximizing is not the only objective that bureaucrats pursue. We must emphasize and reemphasize that bureaucrats are politicians. They spend their professional lives pursuing political goals, bargaining, forming alliances and coalitions, making policy decisions, operating within and interacting with political institutions—in short, doing what other politicians do. Being subject to the oversight and authority of others, bureaucrats must be strategic and forward thinking.

Whichever party wins control of the House, the Senate, and the presidency, whoever becomes chair of the congressional committee with responsibility over their agency, bureau chiefs have to adjust to the prevailing political winds. To protect and expand their authority and resources, bureaucratic politicians seek to insulate themselves from changes in the broader political world, though they don't always succeed.[12] They try to maximize their budgets, to be sure, but they also seek the independence to weather changes in the political atmosphere, and the discretion and flexibility to achieve their goals.

The Bureaucracy and the Principal-Agent Problem

How does the principal-agent problem introduced in Chapter 1 apply to the president's and Congress's control of the bureaucracy? Let's consider a hypothetical "Land Management Bureau" (LMB) created by legislation that requires that new legislation be passed after 10 years to renew the LMB's existence and authority. The issue facing the House, the Senate, and the president in considering renewal involves how much authority to give this bureau and how much money to permit it to spend. Eventually, majorities in the House and Senate and the president agree on a policy reflecting a compromise among their various points of view.

The LMB bureaucrats are not pleased, because the compromise gives them considerably less authority and funding than they had hoped for. If they challenge it by implementing a policy exactly to their liking, they risk the unified anger of the House, the Senate, and the president. Undoubtedly, the politicians would react with new legislation (and the president might also replace the current LMB leadership). However, the leadership might get away with implementing a policy in between its own preferences and those of the politicians—even if it gives way only a little. At the margins, the bureau tilts policy toward its own preferences and possibly away from those of members of Congress or the president, but not so far as to provoke a political response.

Thus we have a principal-agent relationship in which the principals (the president and Congress) formulate policy and create an agent (a bureaucratic agency) to implement its details. The agent, however, has policy preferences of its own and, unless subjected to further controls, will inevitably implement a policy that drifts toward those preferences. (The Policy Principle box on p. 214 looks at a real case in which the EPA and President Obama worked together against a Republican-controlled Congress to expand the agency's authority. In this case, the shift toward the policy preferences of the bureaucratic agents and the president *did* provoke an outcry from members of Congress.)

Controls that might restrict this **bureaucratic drift** include congressional hearings in which bureaucrats may be publicly scolded; funding cutbacks that punish an out-of-control bureau; and watchdog agents, such as the Government Accountability Office (GAO), that may be used to scrutinize a bureau's performance. But these all come after the fact and may be only partially effective threats to the agency.

The most powerful before-the-fact political tool that the president and Congress have in controlling the bureaucracy is the appointment process. Skillful control of a bureau's political stance by the president and the Senate through their joint powers of nomination and confirmation (especially if they can arrange for appointees who share the political consensus on policy) is a way to ensure reliable agent performance.

bureaucratic drift
The tendency of bureaucracies to implement laws in ways that tilt toward the bureaucrats' policy preferences and possibly away from the intentions of the elected officials who created the laws.

the policy principle
THE EPA: REGULATING CLEAN AIR

In 1970, Congress passed the Clean Air Act to provide a platform for policy initiatives focused on reducing air pollution across the United States. It was closely aligned with the National Environmental Policy Act, passed earlier that year, which had created the Environmental Protection Agency. Congress delegated authority to the EPA to regulate substances deemed harmful to air quality. Originally, the list of such substances was limited, including only carbon monoxide, nitrogen oxide, sulfur dioxide, and lead. Over time, as preferences about environmental regulation changed from one presidential administration to another, the federal bureaucracy helped to shape new policies (and reshape old ones) related to air pollution.

On September 20, 2013, more than 40 years after passage of the Clean Air Act, President Obama announced his intention to extend the EPA's authority so that the agency could require polluters to cut their emissions of harmful substances and, in particular, could begin regulating emissions of carbon dioxide (CO_2). Obama's objective was to reduce CO_2 emissions by 30 percent by the year 2030. In 2014, the EPA published its proposed plan to achieve this goal and invited commentary from the general public. By December 1, 2014, the end of a 165-day comment period during which the agency received over 2 million responses, the EPA began writing its regulations.

In addition, President Obama announced plans for his administration to issue other rules governing CO_2 emissions, such as restricting coal-burning power plants directly or engaging states to devise their own plans for carbon dioxide reduction. This is an example of how the powers delegated to the president and a regulatory agency by environmental statutes change in response to a change in an administration's goals (reducing carbon emissions).

Continued pressure to combat greenhouse gases associated with climate change pitted bureaucratic agents in the Obama White House and the EPA against legislators in Congress. Obama sought to leave a legacy of environmental protection, and the EPA wished to interpret its regulatory mandate broadly, but many in Congress were anxious to protect industries in their states and districts that depend on carbon-based fuels. The majority leader in the Senate, Mitch McConnell,

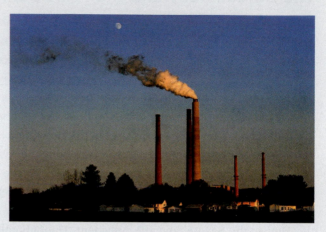

A coal-burning power plant in Ohio.

from coal-rich Kentucky, was eager to prevent the EPA's expanded interpretation of its authority to regulate CO_2. For example, in 2015 he introduced a bill that would block new EPA regulations on carbon emissions from going into effect unless a review by the Labor Department found they would not reduce jobs or the reliability of the electricity supply. Thus, as in many struggles involving the federal bureaucracy, executive, regulatory, and legislative agents all have pressed forward with their respective preferences, producing policy that is never truly settled. Indeed, beginning in 2017, President Donald Trump, who had campaigned on saving jobs in the coal industry, and his first EPA administrator Scott Pruitt, from oil-rich Oklahoma, began systematically to undo many of the Obama-era clean air regulations.

THINK IT THROUGH

1. Why do you think Congress delegated authority to the EPA to regulate substances deemed harmful to air quality instead of including all of the specific regulations in the Clean Air Act?

2. How did the preferences of different presidential administrations influence how the Clean Air Act was implemented? Should bureaucratic agencies adjust how they interpret legislation based on the preferences of the president? Why or why not?

The President as Manager in Chief

In 1937, President Franklin Delano Roosevelt's Committee on Administrative Management gave official approval to an idea that had been growing increasingly urgent: "The president needs help." The national government had grown rapidly during the preceding 25 years, but the structures and procedures necessary to manage the burgeoning executive branch had not yet been established.

The response to the call for help for the president initially took the form of three management policies: (1) all communications and decisions related to executive policy decisions must pass through the White House; (2) to cope with such flow, the White House must have an adequate staff of specialists in research, analysis, legislative and legal writing, and public affairs; and (3) the White House must have additional staff to follow through on presidential decisions—to ensure that those decisions are made, communicated to Congress, and carried out by the appropriate agency.

The story of the modern presidency can be told largely as a series of responses to the plea for managerial help. Indeed, each expansion of the national government into new policies and programs in the twentieth century was accompanied by a parallel expansion of the president's management authority. This pattern began even before Roosevelt's presidency with the policy innovations of President Woodrow Wilson between 1913 and 1920. Congress responded to Wilson's policies with the 1921 Budget and Accounting Act, which conferred on the White House agenda-setting power over budgeting.

The president, in an annual budget message, transmits comprehensive budgetary recommendations to Congress. Because Congress retains ultimate legislative authority, a president's proposals are sometimes said to be dead on arrival on Capitol Hill. Nevertheless, the power to frame deliberations constitutes an important management tool. Each successive president has continued this pattern of setting the congressional agenda, creating what we now know as the "managerial presidency."

For example, with his National Performance Review task force, President Bill Clinton began one of the most systematic efforts to change the way government does business. Heavily influenced by the theories of management consultants who prize decentralization, customer responsiveness, and employee initiative, Clinton tried to introduce these practices into government.[13] Clinton's own management style in the White House was informal and often compared to college bull sessions.

George W. Bush, the first president with a graduate degree in business, followed a standard business school principle: choose skilled subordinates and delegate responsibility to them. Although Bush followed this model closely in appointing highly experienced officials to the executive branch, it was no guarantee of policy success, as doubts emerged about his administration's conduct of the Iraq War and mishandling of relief after Hurricane Katrina.

Barack Obama's administration received high marks for the quality of his appointees but was heavily dependent on a personal staff inexperienced in dealing with Congress and the bureaucracy. The Trump administration has constituted something of an experiment in transferring Donald Trump's business style to Washington: heavy reliance on friends and family with little experience in government, on generals used to giving commands but unused to the give-and-take of Washington politics, and on unconventional personal interventions by the president himself. Early days revealed more disorder than is the norm, not helped at all by staff instability (for example, Trump had four chiefs of staff in three years). As the years progressed, the Trump administration remained error-prone, which was especially apparent in the mishandling of the health crisis brought on by the coronavirus in 2020. Analyzing the Evidence on pp. 218–9 compares recent presidents' approaches to filling appointed positions within the bureaucracy.

Congressional Oversight

Congress is essential to responsible bureaucracy. When a law is passed and its intent is clear, the president knows what to "faithfully execute," and the agency to which responsibility is assigned understands its guidelines. But when Congress enacts vague legislation, everybody, from president to agency to courts to interest groups, gets involved in its interpretation. In that event, to whom is the agency responsible?

The answer lies in **oversight**. The more legislative power Congress delegates to agencies, the more power it seeks to regain through committee and subcommittee oversight of those agencies. The standing-committee system of Congress is well suited for oversight, as most congressional committees and subcommittees focus on areas roughly parallel to one or more executive departments or agencies. The Committee on Agriculture in both the House and Senate have oversight subcommittees, for example, that oversee the operations of programs administered by the Department of Agriculture. Similarly, the House Committee on Ways and Means and the Senate Finance Committee oversee the administration of tax law by the Internal Revenue Service.

However, often the most effective control over bureaucratic behavior is the power of the purse—the ability of the congressional committees and subcommittees that oversee spending to look at agency performance through the microscope of the annual appropriations process. This process makes bureaucrats attentive to Congress because they know that it has an opportunity each year to reduce their funding.[14]

Congress often gives bureaucracies of the executive branch some discretion in determining features of a policy during the implementation phase. Although the complexities of governing a modern industrialized democracy make such discretion necessary, some argue that Congress delegates too much policy-making

oversight
The effort by Congress, through hearings, investigations, and other techniques, to exercise control over the activities of executive agencies.

Some citizens worry that Congress does not engage in sufficient oversight of bureaucratic agencies until after a problem has emerged. Here, citizens of Flint, Michigan, testify before the House Committee on Oversight and Government Reform after it was discovered that drinking water in the city was contaminated.

authority to unelected bureaucrats. By enacting vague laws that give bureaucrats broad discretion, in this view, members give up their constitutionally designated roles and make themselves ineffective.

Others claim that Congress fails to use its tools for effective oversight, since we do not see Congress carrying out much oversight activity.[15] However, political scientists Mathew McCubbins and Thomas Schwartz argue that these critics have missed a type of oversight that benefits members of Congress in their bids for reelection.[16]

McCubbins and Schwartz distinguish between two types of oversight: police patrol and fire alarm. In police-patrol oversight, Congress systematically initiates investigations into agencies' activities. In fire-alarm oversight, Congress waits for citizens or interest groups who are adversely affected by bureaucratic departures from legislative intent to bring them to the attention of the relevant congressional committee. To ensure that such parties bring these violations to members' attention—set off the fire alarm, so to speak—Congress passes laws that help individuals and groups make claims against the bureaucracy, granting them legal standing before administrative agencies and federal courts and giving them access to government-held information through the Freedom of Information Act.

McCubbins and Schwartz argue that fire-alarm oversight is more efficient than the police-patrol variety, given the relative costs and the incentives of elected officials. Why should members spend their scarce resources (mainly time) to initiate investigations without having any evidence that these will enhance their reelection chances? Police-patrol oversight can waste taxpayers' dollars too, because many investigations will not turn up evidence of violations of legislative intent. It is much more cost-effective for members to conserve their resources and then claim credit for fixing the problem after the alarms about it have been sounded.

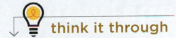

think it through

How do these oversight measures demonstrate how the president and Congress can check the power of the bureaucracy?

REFORMING THE BUREAUCRACY

Many Americans don't like big government because it means big bureaucracy, and promises to cut back bureaucracy are popular campaign appeals. "Cutting out the fat" by reducing the number of federal employees is touted as a surefire way of cutting the deficit.

Yet employment in the federal bureaucracy has hardly grown at all during the past 35 years; it reached its peak post–World War II level in 1968 with 2.9 million civilian employees and 3.6 million military personnel (a figure swollen by the Vietnam War). The number of civilian federal executive branch employees has since remained close to that figure. The size of the federal service is even less imposing when placed in the context of the total workforce and of state and local government employment.

analyzing the evidence

Explaining Vacancies in Presidential Appointments

Contributed by **Sanford Gordon**, *New York University*

The president is the chief executive of a vast bureaucratic apparatus consisting of more than two million men and women. With this in mind, incoming administrations devote considerable resources and attention toward staffing the roughly 1,500 key positions reserved for presidential political appointees.

A surprising number of these appointed positions, however, remain unfilled well into a president's term. While some appointee vacancies reflect a failure of the Senate to act on a nomination submitted by the president, others occur because the president neglects to nominate someone in the first place. Legal scholar Anne Joseph O'Connell describes three negative consequences of appointee vacancies: agency inaction, agency confusion, and a reduction in agency accountability. At the same time, presidents may tolerate vacancies in order to buy time to select the right person for the job, to foster innovation (through high turnover), or to deliberately hobble an agency in the face of uncertainty or political disagreement.[1]

When we look at how presidents negotiate these complicated trade-offs, we would expect to see variation across different administrations as well as variation across agencies within administrations in the tolerance for vacancies. To study these patterns, I gathered data on the total number of available political appointee positions for cabinet-level executive departments and the number of those positions filled in the first seven months of the George W. Bush, Obama, and Trump administrations.

The graph below plots the number of available political appointee positions against the total size of each agency (in terms of full-time civil service employment). The dashed line is one that best fits the data; the fact that it is flat suggests little to no relationship between these two quantities. To the extent that political appointments are seen as a response to the difficulty of controlling a vast civil service, that difficulty is not reducible to the size of the workforce itself.

Agency Size and Appointed Positions, 2016

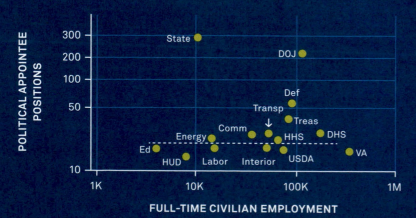

SOURCE: Political appointee data are from *United States Government Policy and Supporting Positions* (Plum Book), 2016, https://www.govinfo.gov/content/pkg/GPO-PLUMBOOK-2016/html/GPO-PLUMBOOK-2016.htm (accessed 6/15/20). Full-time civilian employment data are available from the Office of Personnel Management.

The graph below plots, for each of the three presidents, the percentage of filled appointee positions by department, with the departments ordered according to their reputations for ideological liberalism or conservatism. The data do not show Republican presidents (Bush and Trump) rushing to fill positions in stereotypically left-leaning agencies (as you might expect if they were motivated by mistrust), or a Democratic president (Obama) rushing to fill those in right-leaning ones. In fact, the Bush and Obama lines look fairly similar across the departments. Of greater note is the fact that the line for President Trump lies nearly uniformly below the other two.

Appointed Positions Filled in First 7 Months

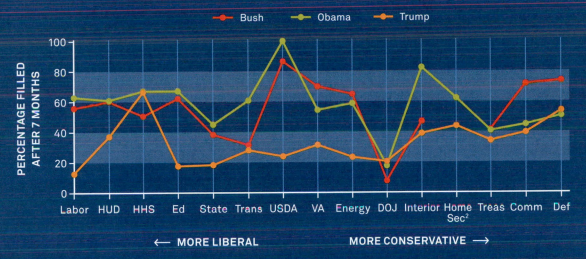

Trump's lower rate of filling appointed positions may reflect his lack of government experience or, alternatively, his lack of political debts to would-be officeholders. The two exceptions to the pattern in Trump's case are the higher percentages of positions filled in the Department of Health and Human Services (HHS) and the Department of Justice (DOJ)—perhaps not surprising, given his priorities related to health care reform and law and order. More surprising is the relatively low percentage of filled appointments for the Department of Homeland Security, given Trump's focus on immigration enforcement (the U.S. Immigration and Customs Enforcement agency is housed in Homeland Security).

1 Anne Joseph O'Connell, "Vacant Offices: Delays in Staffing Top Agency Positions," *Southern California Law Review* 82 (2007): 913–1000.

2 The Department of Homeland Security did not exist during this period of Bush's presidency.

SOURCE: Agency ideological reputation from Joshua D. Clinton and David E. Lewis, "Expert Opinion, Agency Characteristics, and Agency Preferences," *Political Analysis* 16, no. 1 (2008): 3–20. Number of filled positions by agency and administration (numerator of fraction filled) from Jan Diehm, Sergio Hernandez, Aaron Kessler, et al., CNN, www.cnn.com/interactive/2017/politics/trump-nominations (accessed 6/15/20). Total number of political appointments (denominator of fraction filled) from *United States Government Policy and Supporting Positions* (Plum Book), 2016, https://www.govinfo.gov/content/pkg/GPO-PLUMBOOK-2016/html/GPO-PLUMBOOK-2016.htm (accessed 6/15/20).

 Given the trends illustrated in these figures, what appointed positions would you expect to be filled during the first seven months of the Biden administration?

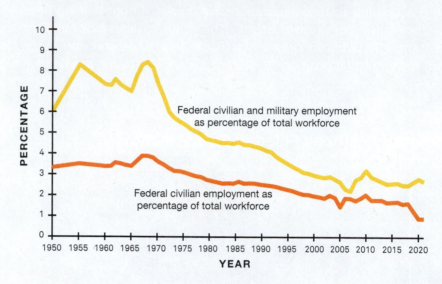

figure 7.3

EMPLOYEES IN THE FEDERAL SERVICE: TOTAL NUMBER AS A PERCENTAGE OF THE WORKFORCE, 1950–2021

NOTE: Workforce includes unemployed persons. 2020 and 2021 numbers reflect OMB estimates.

SOURCES: Tax Foundation, *Facts and Figures on Government Finance* (Baltimore: Johns Hopkins University Press, 1990), pp. 22, 44; Office of Management and Budget, table 17.5, https://www.whitehouse.gov/sites/whitehouse.gov/files/omb/assets/OMB/budget/fy2009/ (accessed 6/17/20); U.S. Bureau of Labor Statistics, table A-1, http://stats.bls.gov/webapps/legacy/cpsatab1.htm (accessed 6/17/20); U.S. Office of Personnel Management, www.opm.gov/policy-data-oversight/data-analysis-documentation/federal-employment-reports/historical-tables/total-government-employment-since-1962 (accessed 6/17/20); 2020 and 2021 data from Congressional Research, "Federal Workforce Statistics Sources: OPM and OMB," March 25, 2020, https://crsreports.congress.gov/product/pdf/R/R43590 (accessed 6/17/20).

As Figure 7.3 indicates, since 1950 the ratio of federal service employment to the total workforce has been relatively steady, declining only slightly. Figure 7.4 offers another useful comparison: although the dollar increase in federal spending shown by the bars looks substantial, the orange line indicates that even here the national government has simply kept pace with the growth of the economy.

To sum up, the federal service has not been growing any faster than the U.S. economy or population. The same is roughly true of state and local public employment. Bureaucracy keeps pace with our society, despite our seeming dislike for it, because we can't operate the control towers, the Social Security system, and other essential elements of government without it. And we could not conduct wars in Iraq and Afghanistan without a gigantic military bureaucracy, or respond to domestic crises like the coronavirus pandemic.

Termination

The only certain way to reduce the size of the bureaucracy is to eliminate programs—a rare occurrence. Most agencies have a supportive constituency: people and groups that benefit from the agency's programs and will fight to reinstate any cuts in them.

figure 7.4

ANNUAL FEDERAL OUTLAYS, 1960–2025

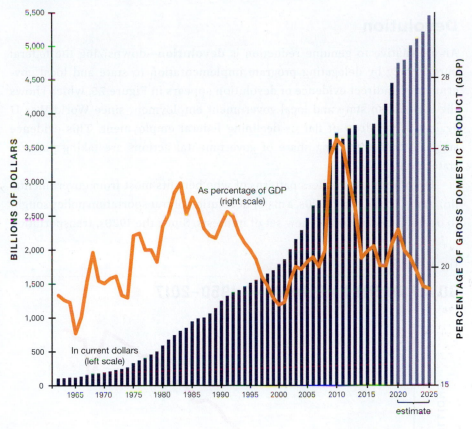

NOTE: Data for 2020–25 are estimated.

SOURCE: Office of Management and Budget, Historical Tables, Table 1.3: Summary of Receipts, Outlays, and Surpluses or Deficits In Current Dollars, Constant Dollars, and Percentage of GDP: 1940–2025, https://www.whitehouse.gov/omb/historical-tables/ (accessed 6/6/20).

analyzing
the evidence

Annual federal outlays have increased steadily over time. So has the size of the U.S. economy (not shown in figure). But the ratio of federal expenditures to annual GDP has varied over time. What might explain these fluctuations, and what might be the consequences when the federal government contributes more or less to the economy?

The overall lack of success in terminating bureaucracy is a reflection of Americans' love/hate relationship with the national government. As antagonistic as Americans may be toward bureaucracy in general, they grow attached to the services and protections offered by particular agencies. A good example was the problem of closing military bases at the end of the Cold War, when the United States no longer needed so many. Since every base is in some congressional member's district, Congress was unable to decide to close any of them. Consequently, between 1988 and 1990, it established a Defense Base Closure and Realignment Commission to make the decisions on which bases to close, taking the matter out of Congress's hands altogether.[17] Even so, the process has been slow and agonizing.

In a more incremental approach to downsizing the bureaucracy, Congress and the president have reduced the budgets of all agencies by small percentages and some less supported ones by larger amounts. Another approach targets highly unpopular regulatory agencies, but these are so small (relatively) that cutting their budgets does virtually nothing to reduce federal spending or employment. This approach, called **deregulation**, simply reduces the number of rules these agencies issue.

Devolution

An alternative to genuine reduction is **devolution**—downsizing the federal bureaucracy by delegating program implementation to state and local governments. Indirect evidence of devolution appears in Figure 7.5, which shows the increase in state and local government employment since World War II against a backdrop of flat or declining federal employment. This evidence suggests that a growing share of governmental actions are taking place at state and local levels.

Devolution often alters patterns of who benefits most from governmental programs. In the early 1990s, a major devolution of transportation policy sought to open up decisions to a new set of interests. Since the 1920s, transportation

figure 7.5

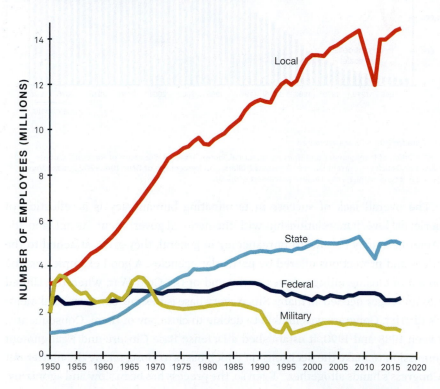

GOVERNMENT EMPLOYMENT, 1950–2017

SOURCES: U.S. Census Bureau, *Statistical Abstract of the United States, 2011* and *Statistical Abstract of the United States, 2012* (Lanham, MD: Bernan Press, 2011, 2012). 2013–2017 State, Federal, and Local employment: Governing, "State and Local Government Employment: Monthly Data," https://www.governing.com/gov-data/public-workforce-salaries/monthly-government-employment-changes-totals.html (accessed 6/17/20). 2013–2017 military employment: Department of Defense, DoD Personnel, "Military and Civilian Personnel by Service/Agency by State/Country," https://www.dmdc.osd.mil/appj/dwp/dwp_reports.jsp (accessed 6/17/20).

policy in both federal and state governments had been dominated by road-building interests—an emphasis that many advocates for cities and many environmentalists believed hurt both cities and the environment. The 1992 reform, initiated by environmentalists, gave more power to metropolitan planning organizations and lifted many federal restrictions on how the money should be spent.

Reformers hoped that these changes would give advocates of alternatives to road building, such as mass transit, bike paths, and walking, more influence over federal transportation spending. Although change has been slow, devolution has indeed brought new voices into decisions about transportation spending, and alternatives to highways have received increasing attention.

Often, devolution is intended to provide more efficient and flexible government services. Yet by its very nature, it entails variation across the states. In some states, government services may improve; in others, services may deteriorate as devolution leads to spending cuts. This has been the effect as aspects of Medicaid authority have devolved to the states through expansion permitted under the Affordable Care Act. This has allowed some states to seek coverage waivers to extend time limits for postpartum care to women, for example, while other states have sought authority to impose work requirements in order to qualify generally for medical care. In short, health coverage for someone with low income would vary considerably, depending on where that person lived.

Privatization

Privatization, another downsizing option, may seem like a synonym for *termination,* but that is true only at the extreme. Most privatization involves private contractors providing goods and services for government under direct governmental supervision. Except for top secret strategic materials, virtually all military hardware, from boats to bullets, is produced by private contractors. And billions of dollars of research services are bought under contract by the government; these private contractors are universities, industrial corporations, and private think tanks.

Privatization simply means that an activity formerly done directly by government employees is picked up under contract by a private company or companies. But such programs are still paid for and supervised by the government. Privatization downsizes the government only in that the workers performing the activity are no longer counted as part of the bureaucracy.

The aim of privatization is to reduce the cost of government. When private contractors can perform a task as well as government does but for less money, taxpayers win. Often, the losers in such situations are the workers. Government workers are generally unionized and therefore receive good pay and benefits. Private-sector workers are less likely to be unionized, and private firms often provide lower pay and fewer benefits. For this reason, public-sector unions have been one of the strongest voices against privatization.

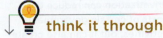

think it through

During the most recent presidential election there were many debates over the appropriate size and role of different government agencies. Which agencies or functions did each candidate want to see expanded or limited? How do these differences demonstrate underlying beliefs regarding the role of the federal government in our daily lives?

privatization
The act of moving all or part of a program from the public sector to the private sector.

Privatization can reduce the costs of certain governmental activities, but it can also create issues of accountability and transparency. In recent years, the practice has become particularly controversial with regard to security contracting in Iraq and Afghanistan.

Other critics observe that private firms are not necessarily more efficient or less costly than government, especially when there is little competition among firms and when public bureaucracies cannot bid in the contracting competition. When private firms have a monopoly on service provision, they may be more expensive than government. Moreover, there are important questions about how private contractors can be held accountable.

CONCLUSION

Does the power of bureaucratic agencies undermine representative government? Bureaucracy is one of humanity's most significant inventions. It is an institutional arrangement that allows for division and specialization of labor, makes use of expertise, and coordinates action for social, political, and economic purposes. It enables governments to exist and perform.

At a theoretical level, public bureaucracy is the concrete expression of abstract policy intentions. Elected politicians have goals: as broad as defending the nation, maintaining public health and safety, or promoting economic growth; as narrow as securing a post office for Possum Hollow, Pennsylvania, or an exit off the interstate for Springfield, Massachusetts. Bureaucracy is the way in which political objectives of elected legislators and executives are transformed from ideas and intentions into the actual "bricks and mortar" of implemented policies.

At a practical level, this transformation depends on the motivations of bureaucratic agents and the institutional machinery that develops around every bureaucratic agency. Elected politicians have their greatest impact at the point when they create and design agencies as institutions. Once an agency is operating,

Americans have complicated feelings toward bureaucracy, and they often disagree about the appropriate role of government agencies. While many people support the EPA's regulation of practices that could harm the environment, others feel that these kinds of regulations go too far when they endanger jobs.

elected officials can only imperfectly control their bureaucratic agents. Institutional arrangements, and simple human nature, provide some insulation to agencies, enabling bureaucrats to march to their own drummers—at least some of the time. Of course, they are not entirely free agents. But controlling them is a constant problem for elected officials.

We cannot live without bureaucracy; it is the most efficient way to organize people to get a large job done. But we can't live comfortably with it either. Bureaucracy requires hierarchy, appointed authority, and professional expertise. Those requirements make it the natural enemy of representation, which requires discussion and mutual influence among equals. The challenge is not to retreat from bureaucracy but to take advantage of its strengths while trying to make it more accountable to the demands that democratic policies and representative government make upon it.

How the Three Branches Regulate Bureaucracy

The President May . . .
- appoint and remove agency heads
- reorganize the bureaucracy (with congressional approval)
- make changes in agencies' budget proposals
- initiate or adjust policies that would alter the bureaucracy's activities

Congress May . . .
- pass legislation that alters the bureaucracy's activities
- abolish existing programs
- investigate bureaucratic activities and force bureaucrats to testify about them

The Judiciary May . . .
- influence presidential appointments of agency heads and other officials
- rule on whether bureaucrats have acted within the law and require policy changes to comply with the law
- force the bureaucracy to respect the rights of individuals through hearings and other proceedings
- rule on the constitutionality of all rules and regulations

Key Terms

Check Your Understanding

1. What is a bureaucracy? How does it help accomplish policy goals more efficiently and effectively than would otherwise be possible?

2. What is the relationship between the bureaucracy and Congress?

3. Describe the relationship between the presidency and the bureaucracy. How does the president shape the agenda of these government agencies and "check" their power?

4. Identify the four types of government agencies. How do the missions of each of these agencies differ?

5. What are the ways in which the bureaucracy can be reduced? What types of issues do politicians encounter when trying to limit the size of these government agencies?

 INQUIZITIVE

Earn a better grade on your test. InQuizitive personalizes your learning path to help you master the concepts from this chapter. In a recent efficacy study of American government students, InQuizitive increased test scores by an average of 17 points (see back cover).

CHAPTER EIGHT

THE FEDERAL COURTS

In June 2017, the Supreme Court at least temporarily upheld President Donald Trump's executive order banning most travelers from six Muslim majority countries. In its decision, not only did the Court overturn the rulings of two lower federal courts, but it did so in a unanimous 9–0 opinion. Many commentators expressed surprise that the Supreme Court's liberal and conservative wings, often depicted as warring factions in black robes, were able to reach agreement on such a contentious issue.

Indeed, ideological and philosophical differences on the Supreme Court do matter, and a number of 5–4 decisions in recent years reflect the Court's longtime balance of five conservative and four liberal justices.[1] Yet despite this ideological division, most Supreme Court decisions are unanimous or near-unanimous, even on controversial matters.[2] This fact tells us a good deal about the place of the judiciary in America's government.

The United States boasts a representative system of government that allows ordinary citizens to choose high-ranking public officials and to hold these officials accountable for their actions. Yet one of the three main branches of this government is the judiciary, an institution designed to be neither representative of nor accountable to citizens. Without the judicial branch, however, neither representation nor governance in America could function effectively.

A central idea of representative government is that citizens' voices must be heard when the law is made. Once the law is made, it then must be interpreted and applied in an impartial and consistent manner. If the law were applied arbitrarily, at the whim of those in power, popular representation when the law was made would be irrelevant. The country would have tyranny rather than representative government. If the law were applied inconsistently, in some instances but not others, people could not know whether their actions would be considered

The federal courts have the power to review the actions of the president and Congress. In 2017 and 2018, the Supreme Court heard arguments related to the Trump administration's "travel ban."

lawful. Eventually, they would likely give up trying to obey the law, and the result would be anarchy rather than effective governance.

Thus, for the health of representative government, when disputes arise among individuals, between individuals and the government, or between parts of the government, an impartial judiciary is needed to help settle the matter. When laws must be enforced, unbiased judges are needed to determine guilt or innocence and—if the accused is found guilty—the appropriate punishment. When questions arise about the meaning of laws, neutral judges must determine what Congress intended and how that intention applies in a given circumstance.

In other words, we expect judges to serve as authorities who are guided by the law rather than by their own beliefs, by the views of competing political forces and interests, or even by public opinion. Of course, judges are human beings who have differing backgrounds,

▪ **What role does an unelected judiciary play in our system of representative government?**

beliefs, and political affiliations that inevitably affect their judgments. Yet judges are also trained to respect the law and to take seriously their responsibility to make judgments according to the law rather than their own beliefs. And federal judges receive lifetime appointments to free them from the need to constantly pay heed to shifting political currents or to cater to the views of the presidents who appointed them. These factors help to explain why most decisions of the U.S. Supreme Court are unanimous or near-unanimous, despite the justices' well-known philosophical differences.

In this chapter we first examine the judicial process, including the types of cases that the federal courts consider. We then assess the structure of the federal court system and consider how judicial review makes the Supreme Court a "lawmaking body." Finally, we examine various influences on the Supreme Court and analyze the role and power of the federal courts in the American political process, looking in particular at the growth of judicial power in the United States.

Learning Objectives

- Outline the basic structure of the court system in the United States and explain the roles of federal courts.

- Explain how the power of judicial review gives the Supreme Court a role in lawmaking.

- Describe the basic procedures of the Supreme Court and the major influences on its decisions.

- Analyze the role of the courts in a representative democracy.

THE COURT SYSTEM

Perhaps the most distinctive feature of the American judiciary is its independence.[3] The Constitution, as it was written and as it has evolved, set up the federal courts as an entity separate from Congress, the presidency, and the states, and insulated them from electoral politics. Four institutional features of the American judiciary ensure a powerful, independent legal system.

1. *Autonomy.* The federal courts are a branch of government separate from Congress and the president.

2. *Hierarchy.* Authority among American courts is hierarchical in two respects. Federal courts may overturn the decisions of state courts, and higher federal courts may reverse the decisions of lower federal courts. The U.S. Supreme Court is the ultimate authority.

3. *Judicial review.* The Supreme Court and other federal courts of appeals can strike down actions of Congress, the president, or states that judges find to be violations of the Constitution.

4. *Lifetime appointment.* Federal judges are appointed for life. They are not subject to the pressures of seeking reappointment or of responding quickly to changes in public opinion.

Court cases in the United States proceed under three broad categories of law: criminal law, civil law, and public law. In cases of **criminal law**, the government

criminal law
Cases arising out of actions that allegedly violate laws protecting the health, safety, and morals of the community.

charges an individual with violating a statute enacted to protect the health, safety, morals, or welfare of the community. In criminal cases, the government is always the plaintiff (the party that brings charges) and alleges that the defendant has committed a crime. Most criminal cases arise in state and municipal courts and involve matters ranging from traffic offenses to robbery and murder. Although the bulk of criminal law is still a state matter, a growing body of federal criminal law deals with such matters as tax evasion, mail fraud, and the sale of narcotics. Defendants found guilty of criminal violations may be fined or sent to prison.

Cases of **civil law** involve disputes among individuals or between individuals and the government where no criminal violation is charged. Unlike the situation in criminal cases, the losers in civil cases cannot be fined or sent to prison, although they may be required to pay monetary damages. In a civil case, the one who brings a complaint is the plaintiff and the one against whom the complaint is brought is the defendant.

The two most common types of civil cases involve contracts and torts. In a typical contract case, an individual or corporation charges that it has suffered because of a violation, by another individual or corporation, of an agreement between the two. For example, Smith Manufacturing Corporation may charge that Jones Distributors failed to honor an agreement to deliver raw materials at a specified time, causing Smith to lose business. Smith asks the court to order Jones to compensate it for the damage allegedly suffered. In a typical tort case, one individual charges that he or she has been injured by what another has done or failed to do. Medical malpractice suits are one example of tort cases.

In deciding civil cases, courts apply statutes (laws) and legal **precedents** (previous decisions). State and federal statutes, for example, often determine the conditions under which contracts are and are not legally binding. Jones Distributors might argue that it was not obliged to fulfill its contract with Smith Manufacturing because actions by Smith, such as the failure to make promised payments, constituted fraud under state law. Attorneys for a physician being sued for malpractice might search for earlier cases in which courts ruled that actions similar to their client's did not constitute negligence.

A civil or criminal case becomes a matter of **public law** when plaintiffs or defendants seek to show that their case involves the powers of government or rights of citizens as defined under the Constitution or by statute. One major form of public law is constitutional law, under which a court determines whether the government's actions conform to the Constitution as it has been interpreted by the judiciary. Thus, what begins as an ordinary criminal case may enter the arena of public law if the defendant in the original case claims that the police violated her constitutional rights.

Another arena of public law is administrative law, which involves disputes over the jurisdiction, procedures, or authority of bureaucratic agencies. Under this type of law, civil litigation between an individual and the government may become a matter of public law if the individual asserts that the government is

civil law
Cases involving disputes among individuals or between the government and individuals that do not involve criminal penalties.

precedents
Past cases whose principles are used by judges as the bases for their decisions in present cases.

public law
Cases involving the powers of government or rights of citizens.

Types of Laws and Disputes

Type of Law	Type of Case or Dispute	Form of Case
Criminal Law	Cases arising out of actions that allegedly violate laws protecting the health, safety, and morals of the community. The government is always the plaintiff.	*U.S. (or state) v. Jones* *Jones v. U.S. (or state)*, if Jones lost and is appealing
Civil Law	"Private law," involving disputes among individuals or between the government and individuals that do not involve criminal penalties. Two general types are contract and tort cases. *Contract cases* are disputes that arise over voluntary actions. *Tort cases* are disputes that arise out of obligations inherent in social life. Negligence and slander are examples of torts.	*Smith v. Jones* *New York v. Jones* *U.S. v. Jones* *Jones v. New York*
Public Law	Cases that involve the powers of government or the rights of citizens. The government is the defendant. *Constitutional law* involves judicial review of the basis of the government's action in relation to specific clauses of the Constitution as interpreted in Supreme Court cases. *Administrative law* involves disputes about the authority, jurisdiction, or procedures of administrative agencies.	*Jones v. U.S. (or state)* *In re Jones*, if the parties have not been identified or the case is uncontested; commonly used in bankruptcy and probate cases *Smith v. Jones*, if a license or statute is at issue in their private dispute

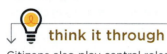

think it through

Citizens also play central roles in the court system, including as witnesses, crime victims, defendants, and most frequently, as members of a jury. Have you served as a member of a jury? If you haven't served, what are the requirements for jury members in your state and county?

violating a statute or abusing its constitutional power. For example, landowners have asserted that federal and state agencies' regulations on land use violate the restrictions that the Fifth Amendment to the Constitution imposes on the government's ability to confiscate private property. In recent decades, the Supreme Court has been sympathetic to such claims, which effectively transform an ordinary civil dispute into a major issue of public law.

Most of the Supreme Court cases we examine in this chapter involve judgments concerning the constitutional or statutory basis of the actions of government agencies. In this arena of public law, the Supreme Court's decisions can have significant consequences for American politics and society.

figure 8.1

THE U.S. COURT SYSTEM

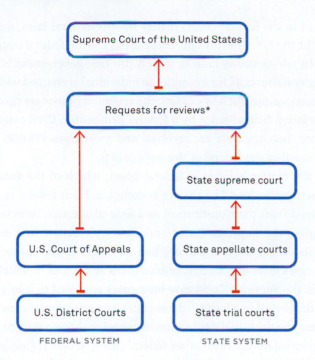

*The U.S. Supreme Court is not required to accept an appeal. This is also true of some state supreme courts.

Types of Courts

In the United States, court systems have been established both by the federal government and by individual state governments. Both systems have several levels (see Figure 8.1), though the one federal system and the 50 state systems are all distinctive in a number of ways. More than 99 percent of all court cases in the United States are heard in state courts. Most criminal cases, for example, involve violations of state laws prohibiting such actions as murder, robbery, fraud, theft, and assault. Cases of state law violation that are brought to trial are heard in a state **trial court**, in front of a judge and sometimes a jury, who will determine whether the defendant violated state law. A defendant who is convicted may appeal the conviction to a higher court, such as a state **court of appeals**, and from there to a state's **supreme court**.

Similarly, in civil cases most litigation is brought in the courts of the state where the activity in question occurred. For example, a patient bringing suit against a physician for malpractice would file the suit in the appropriate court in the state where the alleged malpractice took place. The judge hearing the case would apply state law and state precedent to the matter. (In both criminal and civil matters, however, most cases are settled before trial through negotiated agreements between the parties. In criminal cases, these agreements are called plea bargains.)

trial court
The first court to hear a criminal or civil case.

court of appeals
A court that hears the appeals of lower court decisions. Also called *appellate court*.

supreme court
The highest court in a particular state or in the country.

FEDERAL JURISDICTION

jurisdiction
The types of cases over which a court has authority.

Cases are heard in the federal courts if they involve federal laws, treaties with other nations, or the U.S. Constitution; these areas are the federal courts' official **jurisdiction**. In addition, any case in which the U.S. government is a party is heard in the federal courts. If, for example, an individual is charged with violating a federal criminal statute, such as evading the payment of income taxes, charges are brought before a federal judge by a federal prosecutor. Civil cases in which citizens of more than one state are involved and more than $75,000 is at stake may be heard in either the federal or the state courts.

But even if a matter belongs in federal court, which of the federal courts should exercise jurisdiction? The answer is complex. Each federal court's jurisdiction is derived from the Constitution and federal statutes. Article III of the Constitution gives the Supreme Court appellate jurisdiction (the authority to hear appeals) in all federal cases and original jurisdiction (the authority to hear new cases) in cases involving foreign ambassadors and issues in which a state is a party. That is, the Supreme Court may hear cases appealed to it by a party to a case that was first heard in a lower federal court or a state court (appellate jurisdiction), or it may be the initial destination of cases involving a state or an ambassador (original jurisdiction). In all other federal cases, Article III assigns original jurisdiction to the lower courts that Congress was authorized to establish.

Over the years, as Congress enacted statutes creating the federal judicial system, it specified the jurisdiction of each type of court it established. It has generally assigned jurisdictions on the basis of geography. The nation is currently, by statute, divided into 94 judicial districts, including one court for each of three U.S. territories: Guam, the U.S. Virgin Islands, and the Northern Marianas. Each of the 94 U.S. district courts exercises jurisdiction over federal cases arising within its territorial domain.

The judicial districts, in turn, are organized into 12 regional circuits plus the District of Columbia circuit. Each circuit court exercises appellate jurisdiction over cases heard by the district courts within its region. The circuit court of appeals for the District of Columbia has nationwide jurisdiction to hear appeals in specialized cases, including those arising from actions by federal agencies, and is generally considered to be the nation's second-most-important federal court after the Supreme Court.

Congress has also established specialized courts with nationwide original jurisdiction in certain types of cases. These include the U.S. Court of International Trade, which deals with trade and customs issues, and the U.S. Court of Federal Claims, which handles damage suits against the United States. In addition, the U.S. Court of Appeals for the Federal Circuit has

Cases are heard in federal court if they involve federal law or if the U.S. government is a party in the case. After President Trump's former campaign chairman Paul Manafort was charged with tax evasion and bank fraud, he was tried in federal court. In this courtroom sketch, Paul Manafort and his lawyers (at right), the jury (at left), and the judge (center back) listen to opening arguments in the case.

nationwide appellate jurisdiction; it hears appeals involving patent law and those arising from the decisions of the trade and claims courts.

The federal courts' appellate jurisdiction also extends to cases originating in the state courts. In both civil and criminal cases, a decision of the highest state court can be appealed to the U.S. Supreme Court if a federal issue is raised. Appellants might assert that they were denied the right to counsel or otherwise deprived of the **due process** guaranteed by the federal Constitution, for example, or that important issues of federal law were at stake in the case. The Supreme Court accepts such appeals only if it believes that the matter has considerable national significance. (We return to this topic later in the chapter.)

In addition, in criminal cases, defendants who have been convicted in a state court may request a **writ of *habeas corpus*** from a federal district court. *Habeas corpus* is a court order to authorities to show cause for the incarceration of a prisoner. Generally speaking, state defendants seeking a federal writ of *habeas corpus* must have used up all available possibilities for getting a writ from the state and must raise issues not previously raised in their state appeals. Federal courts of appeals and, ultimately, the U.S. Supreme Court have appellate jurisdiction over *habeas* decisions made in federal district courts.

Although the federal courts hear only a fraction of the civil and criminal cases decided each year in the United States, their decisions are extremely important. It is in the federal courts that the Constitution and federal laws governing all Americans are interpreted and their meaning and significance established. Moreover, it is in the federal courts that the powers and limitations of the increasingly powerful national government are tested. Finally, through their power to review the state courts' decisions, it is ultimately the federal courts that dominate the American judicial system.

Federal Trial Courts

Federal district courts are trial courts of general jurisdiction, and their cases are, in form, indistinguishable from cases in state trial courts.

There are 89 district courts in the 50 states, one each in the District of Columbia and Puerto Rico, and three territorial courts. These courts are staffed by 673 federal district judges,[4] who are assigned to district courts according to the workload; the busiest of these courts may have as many as 28 judges. The procedures of the federal district courts are essentially the same as those of the lower state courts, except that federal procedural requirements tend to be stricter. States, for example, do not have to provide a grand jury or a 12-member trial jury. Federal courts must do both of these things.

Federal Appellate Courts

Roughly 20 percent of all federal lower-court cases, along with appeals from some federal agency decisions, are subsequently reviewed by a federal appeals court. The country is divided into 12 judicial circuits, each of which has a

due process
The requirement that citizens be treated according to the law and be provided adequate protection for individual rights.

writ of *habeas corpus*
A court order demanding that an individual in custody be brought into court and shown the cause for detention. Habeas corpus is guaranteed by the Constitution and can be suspended only in cases of rebellion or invasion.

U.S. Court of Appeals. A thirteenth appellate court, the U.S. Court of Appeals for the Federal Circuit, is defined by subject matter rather than geographic jurisdiction. This court accepts appeals regarding patents, copyrights, and international trade.

Except for cases that the Supreme Court chooses to review, decisions by the appellate courts are final. Because of this finality, certain safeguards have been built into the system. The most important is the provision of more than one judge for every appeals case. Each court of appeals has 3 to 28 permanent judgeships. Although normally three judges hear appealed cases, in some instances a larger number sit *en banc*.

Another safeguard is the assignment of a Supreme Court justice as the circuit justice for each of the 12 circuits. The circuit justice deals with requests for special action by the Supreme Court, most frequently that of reviewing requests for stays of execution when the full Court cannot—mainly during its summer recess.

The Supreme Court

chief justice
The justice on the Supreme Court who presides over the Court's public sessions.

Article III of the Constitution vests "the judicial power of the United States" in the Supreme Court, which is made up of a chief justice and eight associate justices. The **chief justice** presides over the Court's public sessions and conferences. In the Court's actual deliberations and decisions, however, the chief justice has no more authority than his colleagues. Each justice casts one vote. The chief justice, though, always speaks first when the justices deliberate. In addition, if the chief justice has voted with the majority, he decides which justice will write the formal Court opinion. To some extent, the chief justice's influence is a function of his leadership ability. Some chief justices, such as Earl Warren, have led the Court in a new direction; in other instances, a forceful associate justice, such as Felix Frankfurter, is the dominant figure.

Although Franklin Delano Roosevelt attempted to increase the number of justices in 1937, the size of the Supreme Court has remained at nine since 1869. This political cartoon from 1937 reflects the concern that Roosevelt's strategy threatened the independence of the judiciary.

The Constitution does not specify how many justices should sit on the Supreme Court; Congress has the authority to change the Court's size. In the early nineteenth century, there were six justices; later, seven. Congress set the number at nine in 1869, and the Court has remained that size ever since. In 1937, President Franklin Delano Roosevelt, infuriated by several Court decisions that struck down New Deal programs, asked Congress to enlarge the Court so that he could add justices to it—one for every sitting justice above age 70. Although Congress refused, the Court gave in to Roosevelt's pressure and began to view his policy initiatives more favorably. The president, in turn, dropped his efforts to enlarge the Court. The Court's surrender to Roosevelt came to be

To Six of the Nine

known as "the switch in time that saved nine." In light of Republican obstruction in 2016 that denied President Obama the opportunity to fill a vacancy on the Court (by refusing to take up his nominee in the Senate), there is speculation that Democrats will seek congressional action to expand the Court when next they control both houses of Congress and the presidency.

How Judges Are Appointed

The president appoints federal judges. Nominees are typically prominent or politically active members of the legal profession: former state court judges or state or local prosecutors, prominent attorneys or elected officials, or highly regarded law professors. Prior experience as a judge is not necessary. In general, presidents try to appoint judges with legal experience, good character, and partisan and ideological views similar to their own.

During the presidencies of Richard Nixon, Ronald Reagan, George H. W. Bush, and George W. Bush, most federal judicial appointees were conservative Republicans. Bill Clinton's and Barack Obama's appointees, in contrast, tended to be liberal Democrats. George W. Bush made a strong effort to appoint Hispanics. Clinton and Obama appointed many women and African Americans. (See Figure 8.2 for more information on the diversity of court appointees.) Donald Trump's 2017 appointment to the Supreme Court, Neil Gorsuch, was a deeply conservative judge from a lower federal court. Brett Kavanaugh, Trump's 2018 appointment, was a deeply conservative judge of the United States Court of Appeals for the District of Columbia.

The Constitution requires the "advice and consent" of the Senate for federal judicial nominations, thus imposing an important check on the president's influence over the judiciary. Before the president formally nominates someone for a federal district judgeship, senators from the candidate's state must indicate that they support the candidate. This practice is called **senatorial courtesy**.

If one or both senators from a prospective nominee's home state belong to the president's political party, the nomination will almost invariably receive their blessing. Because the president's party in the Senate will rarely support a nominee opposed by a home-state senator from their ranks, these senators hold virtual veto power over federal judicial appointments in their own states. Senators often see this power as a way to reward important allies and contributors. If the state has no senator from the president's party, the governor or members of the state's House delegation may make suggestions for nominees. Senatorial courtesy is less significant for appellate court appointments and plays no role in Supreme Court nominations.

Once the president has formally nominated an individual, the appointment must be approved by the Senate Judiciary Committee and confirmed by a majority vote in the full Senate. The politics and rules of the Senate determine the fate of a president's judicial nominees and influence the types of people who are nominated. There once was the risk of a filibuster, in which closure of debate required an affirmative vote of three-fifths of the senators. This possibility was eliminated

senatorial courtesy
The practice whereby the president, before formally nominating a person for a federal district judgeship, finds out whether the senators from the candidate's state support the nomination.

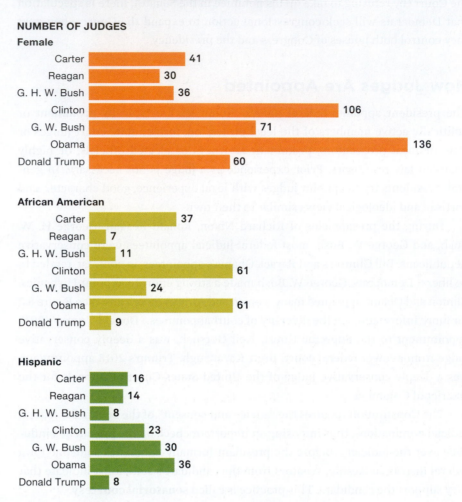

figure 8.2

DIVERSITY OF THE FEDERAL JUDICIARY

NUMBER OF JUDGES

Female

President	Number
Carter	41
Reagan	30
G. H. W. Bush	36
Clinton	106
G. W. Bush	71
Obama	136
Donald Trump	60

African American

President	Number
Carter	37
Reagan	7
G. H. W. Bush	11
Clinton	61
G. W. Bush	24
Obama	61
Donald Trump	9

Hispanic

President	Number
Carter	16
Reagan	14
G. H. W. Bush	8
Clinton	23
G. W. Bush	30
Obama	36
Donald Trump	8

NOTE: Jimmy Carter appointed 261 federal judges; Ronald Reagan, 364; George H. W. Bush, 188; Bill Clinton, 372; George W. Bush, 321; and Barack Obama, 329. As of July 2020, the U.S. Senate has confirmed 189 judges nominated by President Trump.

SOURCE: Federal Judicial Center, www.fjc.gov/history/judges/diversity-bench (accessed 6/27/20); John Gramlich, "Trump has appointed a larger share of female judges than other GOP presidents, but lags Obama," Pew Research Center, http://www.pewresearch.org/fact-tank/2018/10/02/trump-has-appointed- a-larger -share-of-female-judges-than-other-gop-presidents-but-lags-obama/ (accessed 6/27/20); Renee Klahr, "Federal Judge Appointments Tracker (2009–Present)," NPR Politics, https://docs.google.com/spreadsheets /d/1O0ZUPKogqk1PMoJn50_gdbdBwyj54i-RqHUDFQ7Z5E8/edit#gid=1242775320 (accessed 6/7/20).

from Senate rules in 2013 for lower federal judges and in 2017 for Supreme Court justices. The composition of the Senate Judiciary Committee, as well as the Senate as a whole, is critical in determining whether a particular nominee will succeed. Moreover, in recent years the media have intensely scrutinized the most important judicial nominations, thus engaging the broader public in the process.

Before the mid-1950s, the Senate Judiciary Committee rarely questioned nominees on their judicial views, focusing instead on qualifications. Since then, however, judicial appointments have become increasingly partisan and, ultimately,

ideological. Today, the Senate Judiciary Committee subjects nominees to lengthy questioning about issues ranging from gun rights to abortion to federal power under the commerce clause. Senators' support or opposition turns on the nominee's ideological and judicial views as much as on qualifications.

For their part, presidents nominate individuals who share their own political philosophy. Ronald Reagan and George H. W. Bush, for example, looked for appointees who supported the ideological and philosophical positions taken by the Republican Party at that time, particularly opposition to governmental intervention in the economy and to abortion. Not all the Reagan and Bush appointees fulfilled their sponsors' expectations. Bush Supreme Court appointee David Souter, for example, was attacked by conservatives as a turncoat for his decisions on school prayer and abortion rights. Nevertheless, Reagan and Bush did create a far more conservative Supreme Court. Hoping to counteract the influence of their appointees, President Bill Clinton named liberals Ruth Bader Ginsburg and Stephen Breyer to the Court. But George W. Bush's Supreme Court appointees, John Roberts and Samuel Alito, helped bolster the conservative bloc.

Similarly, President Obama hoped that his first two Supreme Court appointees, Sonia Sotomayor and Elena Kagan, would add strong voices to the Court's liberal wing. Sotomayor became the first Supreme Court justice of Hispanic origin and thus made judicial history even before participating in the Court's deliberations. In 2016, after the death of conservative justice Antonin Scalia, Obama nominated U.S. Appeals Court judge Merrick Garland, a moderate Democrat, to take Scalia's place. However, Senate Republicans, who held a majority at the time, refused to take action on the Garland nomination, hoping that the 2016 presidential election would bring a Republican president and a chance to replace Scalia with another conservative.

Left with only eight justices for most of 2016, the Supreme Court tied 4–4 in several important cases. A tie lets stand the lower-court decision. (Table 8.1 gives more information about the current Supreme Court justices.) The Republican

table 8.1

SUPREME COURT JUSTICES, 2020

NAME	YEAR OF BIRTH	PRIOR EXPERIENCE	APPOINTED BY	YEAR OF APPOINTMENT
John G. Roberts, Jr. *Chief Justice*	1955	Federal judge	G. W. Bush	2005
Clarence Thomas	1948	Federal judge	G. H. W. Bush	1991
Stephen G. Breyer	1938	Federal judge	Clinton	1994
Samuel A. Alito, Jr.	1950	Federal judge	G. W. Bush	2006
Sonia Sotomayor	1954	Federal judge	Obama	2009
Elena Kagan	1960	Solicitor general	Obama	2010
Neil Gorsuch	1967	Federal judge	Trump	2017
Brett Kavanaugh	1965	Federal judge	Trump	2018
Amy Coney Barrett	1972	Federal judge	Trump	2020

strategy paid off when Donald Trump was elected and nominated Gorsuch. These fierce struggles over judicial appointments reflect the growing intensity of partisanship today and the critical importance that competing political forces attach to Supreme Court appointments. This was underscored in the contentious and highly visible Judiciary Committee nomination hearings that ultimately led to the narrow confirmation of Brett Kavanaugh. And it was underscored again with the contentious confirmation of Amy Coney Barrett just days before the 2020 election, following the death of Justice Ruth Bader Ginsburg.

Presidents also try to shape the judiciary through their appointments to the lower federal courts. For example, with a combined total of 12 years in office, Reagan and George H. W. Bush were able to exercise a good deal of influence on the composition of the federal district and appellate courts. By the end of Bush's term, he and Reagan together had appointed nearly half of all the federal judges. President Clinton promised to appoint more liberal jurists to the district and appellate courts and to increase the number of women and minorities serving on the federal bench (see Figure 8.2). In 2020, Trump administration officials, together with Republican Senate Majority Leader Mitch McConnell (R-KY), were especially proactive in seeking to shape the judiciary. They approached Republican-appointed judges eligible to retire, urging them to consider retirement before the 2020 election to assure that Republicans could appoint their replacement while still controlling the Senate and presidency.[5]

The increasing role of partisanship or ideology in the nomination process creates a potential danger for the federal court system and the judicial process.

think it through

Do you think it is possible to completely eliminate partisanship or ideology in the nomination process? What attributes do you think would make for a strong candidate?

Because courts derive much of their authority from their position of political independence, the politics of appointments risks tainting judges as little more than extensions of the political views of those who nominate them. Fortunately, the individuals appointed to the federal judiciary tend to have a strong independent sense of themselves and their mission.

JUDICIAL REVIEW

Judicial review is the power of the judiciary to determine whether actions by the legislative and executive branches are consistent with the Constitution and, if not, to invalidate them.

<aside>
judicial review
The power of the courts to determine whether the actions of the president, the Congress, and the state legislatures are consistent with the Constitution.
</aside>

Judicial Review of Acts of Congress

The Constitution does not explicitly give the Supreme Court the power of judicial review of laws enacted by Congress. Among the proposals debated at the Constitutional Convention was one to create a council composed of the president and the judiciary that would share veto power over legislation. Another proposal was to route all legislation through both the Supreme Court and the president; overruling a veto by either would have required a two-thirds vote of the House and the Senate. Those and other proposals were rejected, and no further effort was made to give the Supreme Court review power over the other branches. This history does not prove that the framers opposed judicial review, but it does indicate that, in the words of political scientist C. Herman Pritchett, "if they intended to provide for it in the Constitution, they did so in a most obscure fashion."[6]

Disputes over the framers' intentions were settled in 1803 in *Marbury v. Madison*.[7] In that case, William Marbury sued Secretary of State James Madison for Madison's failure to complete Marbury's appointment to a lower judgeship, an appointment initiated by the outgoing administration of President John Adams. Apart from the details of the case, Chief Justice John Marshall used it to declare a portion of a law unconstitutional. In effect, he stated that although Marbury's request was not unreasonable, the Court's jurisdiction in the matter was based on a section of the Judiciary Act of 1789 that the Court declared unconstitutional.

Although Congress and the president have often been at odds with the Supreme Court, the Court's legal power to review acts of Congress has not been seriously questioned since 1803. One reason is that judicial power has come to be accepted as natural, if not intended. Another reason is that during the early years of the United States, the Supreme Court used its power sparingly, striking down only two pieces of legislation during the first 75 years of its history. In recent years, with the power of judicial review securely accepted, the Court has been more willing to use it.

Between 1980 and 2019, the Supreme Court struck down 58 acts of Congress, in part or in their entirety[8] (see Figure 8.3). In 2013, for example, the Court struck

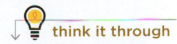

think it through

How does the power of judicial review allow the Supreme Court to "check" the power of Congress?

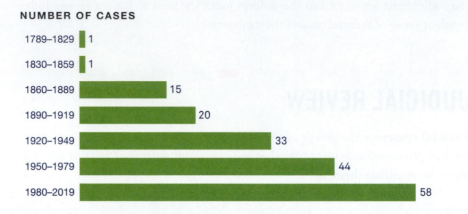

figure 8.3

SUPREME COURT RULINGS INVALIDATING ACTS OF CONGRESS

NUMBER OF CASES

Period	Cases
1789–1829	1
1830–1859	1
1860–1889	15
1890–1919	20
1920–1949	33
1950–1979	44
1980–2019	58

SOURCE: U.S. Government Printing Office, www.congress.gov/constitution-annotated (accessed 3/17/20).

down a portion of the 1965 Voting Rights Act, which had required certain state and local governments to obtain federal pre-clearance before making any changes to their voting rules.[9] Also in 2013, the Supreme Court invalidated the 1996 Defense of Marriage Act, which had denied federal spousal benefits to gay couples.

Judicial Review of State Actions

The power of the Supreme Court to review state legislation or other state action and to determine its constitutionality is neither granted by the Constitution nor inherent in the federal system. But the logic of the **supremacy clause** of Article VI, which declares the Constitution and laws made under its authority to be the supreme law of the land, is very strong. Furthermore, the Judiciary Act of 1789 conferred on the Supreme Court the power to strike down state constitutions and laws whenever they are clearly in conflict with the U.S. Constitution, federal laws, or treaties.[10] This power gives the Court jurisdiction over all the millions of cases handled by American courts each year.

The history of civil rights protections abounds with examples of state laws that were overturned because they violated the Fourteenth Amendment's guarantees of due process and equal protection. For example, in the 1954 case *Brown v. Board of Education*, the Court overturned statutes in Kansas, South Carolina, Virginia, and Delaware that either required or permitted segregated public schools, on the basis that such statutes denied Black schoolchildren equal protection of the law.[11] In 1967, in *Loving v. Virginia*, the Court invalidated a Virginia statute prohibiting interracial marriages.[12] Almost 50 years later, the Court cited the *Loving* case numerous times in its 2015 decision in *Obergefell v. Hodges*, which declared state bans on same-sex marriage unconstitutional (see the Policy Principle box on p. 243).[13]

supremacy clause

A clause of Article VI of the Constitution stating that all laws and treaties approved by the national government are the supreme laws of the United States and superior to all laws adopted by any state or other subdivision.

the policy principle
CHANGING JUDICIAL DIRECTION: GAY MARRIAGE

In 1970, Richard Baker and James McConnell applied for a marriage license in Hennepin County, Minnesota. The county clerk, Gerald Nelson, refused to give them a license because they were both men. The couple sued Nelson, claiming that the Minnesota statute barring them from receiving a marriage license was unconstitutional. They appealed the case all the way to the Minnesota Supreme Court, which held in *Baker v. Nelson* (1971) that "The institution of marriage as a union of man and woman, uniquely involving the procreation and rearing of children within a family, is as old as the book of Genesis." In 1972, the U.S. Supreme Court issued a brief affirmation of the Minnesota ruling.

In the years and decades following this setback, the gay rights movement proceeded down other litigation avenues, bringing a series of lawsuits aimed at changing policies that discriminated against gay men and lesbians. Their collective effort to use the institution of the courts to change policy gradually saw results. A quarter of a century after *Baker v. Nelson,* the U.S. Supreme Court struck down a provision of Colorado state law that denied gay and lesbian residents a variety of privileges that the law labeled "special rights." Justice Anthony Kennedy, writing in the 6–3 majority in *Romer v. Evans* (1996) reversing this view, states, "We find nothing special in the protections [being withheld]. These protections . . . constitute ordinary civil life in a free society."

The *Romer* opinion, written in the same year Congress passed the Defense of Marriage Act (DOMA), limiting marriage to one man and one woman, shows how the Court can turn away from both its own precedents and congressional policy to actively chart a new direction.

Justice Kennedy went on to author opinions on decriminalizing sodomy in *Lawrence v. Texas* (2003), declaring DOMA unconstitutional in *United States v. Windsor* (2013), and eventually establishing a right for gays to marry across the United States in *Obergefell v. Hodges* (2015). Though by the time of *Obergefell,* many states had already legalized gay marriage, the Court was consistently on the front edge of the debate in one of

Gay rights advocates celebrate the Court's 2015 decision.

its most consistent shows of judicial activism in recent times. Kennedy's *Obergefell* opinion was aimed at history, not merely at setting a legal precedent. It showed clearly his intention to shape a policy and enshrine a right, rather than argue over semantics or precedent.

Though public opinion on same-sex marriage has been changing rapidly in its favor, the *Obergefell* decision did not silence dissent. In August 2015, post-*Obergefell,* another county clerk (this time in Kentucky) refused to issue a marriage license to a gay couple. Yet, rather than affirming her action, as had happened in Minnesota four decades earlier, a court held her in contempt and jailed her.

THINK IT THROUGH

1. Read this chapter's section on "Activism and Restraint." In what ways have the Supreme Court's recent decisions on same-sex marriage represented judicial activism?

2. The Obergefell case involved a state law in Ohio, where same-sex marriages were not recognized at the time. Why was a case concerning state law ultimately decided in federal court?

Judicial Review of Federal Agency Actions

Although Congress makes the law, to administer the thousands of programs it has enacted it must delegate power to the president and to a huge bureaucracy. For example, if Congress wishes to improve air quality, it cannot possibly anticipate all the circumstances that may arise with respect to that general goal. Inevitably, Congress must delegate to bureaucrats substantial power to determine the best ways to improve air quality in the face of changing circumstances. Thus, over the years, almost any congressional legislation will result in thousands of pages of discretionary administrative regulations developed by executive agencies.

The issue of delegation of power has led to a number of court decisions over the past two centuries, generally involving the question of the scope of the delegation. Courts have also been called on to decide whether the rules and regulations adopted by federal agencies are consistent with Congress's stated or implied intent.

As presidential power expanded during the New Deal era, one sign of increased congressional subordination to the executive branch was the enactment of laws, often at the president's request, that gave the executive virtually unlimited authority to address a particular concern. For example, the Emergency Price Control Act of 1942 authorized the executive branch to set "fair and equitable" prices without indicating what those terms might mean.[14]

Although the Supreme Court initially challenged these delegations of power, a confrontation with President Franklin Delano Roosevelt caused the Court to retreat from its position. Perhaps as a result, no congressional delegation of power to the president has been struck down as constitutionally too broad in more than 80 years. In the last 30 years in particular, the Court has found that as long as rules and regulations developed by federal agencies are "based upon a permissible construction" or "reasonable interpretation" of the language in a statute, they are acceptable.[15]

In general, the courts defer to administrative agencies as long as those agencies have engaged in a formal rule-making process and have carried out the conditions required by statutes that govern the process. These include the 1946 Administrative Procedure Act, which requires agencies to notify parties affected by proposed rules, as well as to allow them time to comment before the rules go into effect.

Judicial Review and Presidential Power

The federal courts may also review the actions of the president. As we saw in Chapter 6, presidents increasingly make use of unilateral executive powers rather than relying on congressional legislation to achieve their objectives. Often, presidential orders and actions have been challenged in the federal courts by members of Congress and by other individuals and groups. In recent decades, however, assertions of presidential power have generally been upheld and made standard executive practice. We saw one example in Chapter 6 with the 1974 case *United States v. Nixon*, the first case in which the Supreme Court acknowledged the validity of the executive privilege principle.

This pattern of judicial deference to presidential authority also appeared in the Court's decisions regarding President George W. Bush's war on terrorism. Perhaps the most important of these cases was *Hamdi v. Rumsfeld*.[16] In 2004, the Court ruled that Yaser Esam Hamdi, a U.S. citizen captured in Afghanistan and imprisoned in the United States as an "enemy combatant," was entitled to a lawyer and "a fair opportunity to rebut the government's factual assertions." However, the Court affirmed that the president had the authority to declare a citizen an enemy combatant and to order that citizen to be held in federal detention. Several justices hinted that once designated an enemy combatant, a citizen might be tried before a military tribunal, where the normal presumption of innocence would be suspended.

In 2006, however, in *Hamdan v. Rumsfeld*, the Court ruled that the military commissions established to try those designated as enemy combatants and other detainees violated both the Uniform Code of Military Justice and the Geneva Conventions.[17] Thus, the Court did assert that presidential actions were subject to judicial scrutiny, and it placed some constraints on the president's power. But at the same time, it affirmed the president's unilateral power to declare individuals, including U.S. citizens, "enemy combatants" whom federal authorities could detain under adverse legal circumstances.

In June 2016, the Court sustained an appeals court decision blocking President Obama's ambitious program to prevent millions of undocumented immigrants from being deported. At issue was whether Obama had violated the Constitution in formulating immigration policy by using an executive order instead of the legislative and administrative processes. The eight-member Court (in the wake of the death of Justice Antonin Scalia) split 4–4, thereby letting stand the lower-court decision[18] and thwarting an attempt to create new policy through executive action alone.

As noted in the introduction to this chapter, in 2017 President Trump issued an executive order banning travel from a number of primarily Muslim

When President Obama issued an executive order that would shield millions of immigrants from deportation, opponents charged that he did not have the authority to do so. The Supreme Court tied 4–4, calling the legality of his actions into question.

countries. Several federal courts ruled against the order, as well as against revisions of it. A final revised executive order, adding non-Muslim countries, was still ruled unconstitutional by lower federal courts. However, in 2018 the Supreme Court overruled these lower court decisions, allowing the executive order to take effect.

Judicial Review and Lawmaking

Much of the work of the courts involves applying statutes to particular cases. Over the centuries, however, judges have developed a body of rules and principles of interpretation that are not grounded in specific statutes. This body of judge-made law is called common law.

Rulings in the appellate courts can also be considered laws, but ones that govern only the behavior of lower courts. When a court of appeals hands down its decision, it accomplishes two things. First, of course, it decides who wins—the side that won in the lower court or the one that lost there. At the same time, it expresses its decision in a manner that provides guidance to the lower courts for handling future cases in the same area. Appellate judges try to give their rulings and reasons for them in writing so that the "administration of justice" can take place most of the time at the lowest judicial level. They try to make their ruling or reasoning clear so as to avoid confusion, which can produce a surge of litigation at the lower levels.

THE SUPREME COURT IN ACTION

The Supreme Court plays a vital role in government, as it is part of the structure of checks and balances that prevents the legislative and executive branches from abusing their power. The Court also operates as an institution unto itself, with its own internal rules for decision making.

How Cases Reach the Supreme Court

Given the millions of disputes that arise every year, the job of the Supreme Court would be impossible if it were not able to control the flow of cases and its own caseload. The Court has original jurisdiction in a limited variety of cases specified by the Constitution, including (1) cases between the United States and one of the states, (2) cases involving two or more states, (3) cases involving foreign ambassadors or other ministers, and (4) cases brought by one state against citizens of another state or against a foreign country. The most important cases in these categories are disputes between states over land, water, or old debts. Generally, the Court deals with such cases by appointing a "special master," usually a retired judge, who actually hears the case and presents a report. The Court then allows the disputing states to present arguments for or against the master's opinion.[19]

Rules of Access.   Over the years, the federal courts have developed rules for which cases within their jurisdiction they will and will not hear. To be heard, cases must meet certain criteria that are first applied by the trial court but may be reconsidered by appellate courts. These rules of access fall into three major categories: ripeness, standing, and mootness.

Article III of the Constitution and past Supreme Court decisions define judicial power as extending only to "cases and controversies." That is, a case before a court must involve an actual controversy, not a hypothetical one, with two truly adversarial parties. These criteria are called **ripeness**. The courts have interpreted this language to mean that they do not have power to give advisory opinions to legislatures or agencies about the constitutionality of proposed laws or regulations. Furthermore, even after a law is enacted, the courts generally refuse to consider its constitutionality until it is actually applied.

Those seeking to bring a case must also have **standing**; they must have a substantial stake in the outcome. The traditional requirement for standing has been to show injury to oneself; that injury can be personal, economic, or even aesthetic, for example. For a group or class of people to have standing (as in a **class-action suit**, in which a large number of persons with common interests join together to bring or defend a lawsuit), each member must show specific injury. A general interest in the environment, for instance, does not provide a group with sufficient basis for standing.

The Supreme Court also uses a third criterion in determining whether it will hear a case: mootness. In theory, this requirement disqualifies cases that are brought too late: a case may be considered **moot** if the relevant facts have changed or the problem has been resolved by other means. Mootness, however, is subject to the discretion of the courts, which have begun to relax the rules about it, particularly in cases where a situation that has been resolved is likely to recur. In the abortion case *Roe v. Wade*, for example, the Supreme Court rejected the lower court's argument that because the pregnancy had already come to term, the case was moot.[20] The Court agreed to hear the case because no pregnancy was likely to outlast the lengthy appeals process.

Aside from the formal criteria, the Supreme Court is most likely to accept cases that involve conflicting decisions by federal circuit courts, that present important questions of civil rights or civil liberties, or that the federal government is appealing.[21] Ultimately, however, the question of which cases to accept can come down to the justices' preferences and priorities. If several justices believe that the Court should intervene in a particular area of policy or politics, they are likely to look for a case or cases that provide ways of doing so.

For several decades, for example, the Court was not interested in considering challenges to affirmative action or other programs designed to provide particular

ripeness
The requirement that a case must involve an actual controversy between two parties, not a hypothetical one.

standing
The requirement that anyone initiating a court case must show a substantial stake in the outcome.

class-action suit
A lawsuit in which a large number of persons with common interests join together under a representative party to bring or defend a lawsuit.

moot
No longer requiring resolution by the courts, typically because the facts of the case have changed or been resolved by other means.

benefits to minorities. Eventually, however, several conservative justices eager to push back the limits of these programs accepted cases that allowed them to consider such challenges. In 1995, the Court's decision in three cases placed new restrictions on federal affirmative action programs, school desegregation efforts, and attempts to increase minority representation in Congress through the creation of "minority districts." [22]

writ of *certiorari*

A formal request to have the Supreme Court review a decision of a lower court.

Writs.   Most cases reach the Supreme Court through a **writ of *certiorari***, a formal request to have the Court review a lower-court decision. *Certiorari* is an order to a lower court to deliver the records of a particular case to be reviewed for legal errors (Figure 8.4). The term *certiorari* is sometimes shortened to *cert*; cases considered to deserve *certiorari* are referred to as "certworthy."

figure 8.4

REACHING THE SUPREME COURT THROUGH *CERTIORARI*

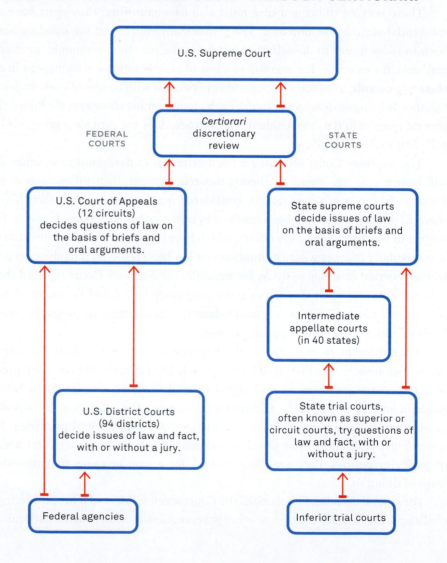

Someone who loses a case in a lower federal court or state court and wants the Supreme Court to review the decision has 90 days to file a petition for a writ of *certiorari* with the clerk of the Court. There are two types of petitions: paid petitions and petitions *in forma pauperis* ("in the form of a pauper"). Paid petitions require payment of filing fees, submission of a certain number of copies, and compliance with numerous other rules. For *in forma pauperis* petitions, usually filed by prison inmates, the Court waives the fees and most other requirements.

Since 1972, most justices have participated in a "*certiorari* pool" in which, throughout the term, their law clerks evaluate the petitions. Each petition is reviewed by one clerk, who writes a memo for all the justices participating in the pool. The memo summarizes the facts and issues in the case and makes a recommendation about whether to grant *certiorari*. Clerks for the other justices add their comments. After the justices review the memos, any justice may place any case on the "discuss list." If a case is not placed on the list, it is automatically denied *certiorari*. Cases placed on the list are considered and voted on during the justices' closed-door conference.

For *certiorari* to be granted, four justices must be convinced that the case satisfies Rule 10 of the Rules of the U.S. Supreme Court: that *certiorari* is to be granted only where there are special and compelling reasons. "Special and compelling reasons" include conflicting decisions by two or more circuit courts or two or more state courts of last resort (the highest-level state courts that consider particular kinds of cases), conflicts between circuit courts and state courts of last resort, decisions by circuit courts on matters of federal law that the Supreme Court should settle, and circuit court decisions on important questions that conflict with Supreme Court decisions.

The Court usually takes action only when there are conflicts among the lower courts about what the law should be, when an important legal question raised in the lower courts has not been definitively answered, or when a lower court deviates from the principles and precedents established by the Supreme Court. In recent years, even though thousands of petitions have been filed (Figure 8.5), the Court has granted *certiorari* to fewer than 90 petitioners each year—about 1 percent of those seeking a Supreme Court review.

A handful of cases reach the Supreme Court through avenues other than *certiorari*. One is the "writ of certification," which can be used when a U.S. Court of Appeals asks the Supreme Court for instructions on a point of law that has never been decided. Another avenue is the "writ of appeal," used to appeal the decision of a three-judge district court.

Controlling the Flow of Cases: The Role of the Solicitor General

If any person has greater influence than individual justices over the work of the Supreme Court, it is the solicitor general of the United States. The solicitor general is third in status in the Justice Department (below the attorney general and

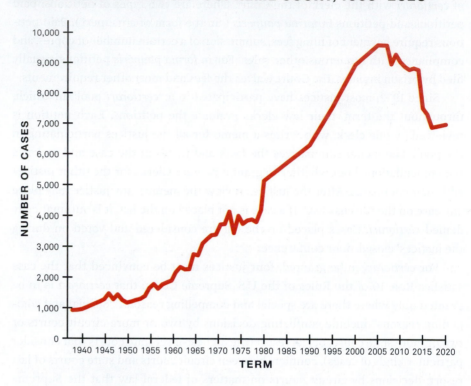

figure 8.5

CASES FILED IN THE U.S. SUPREME COURT, 1938–2020

SOURCES: **Years 1938–69:** successive volumes of U.S. Census Bureau, *Statistical Abstract of the United States*; **1970–79:** Office of the Clerk of the Supreme Court; **1980–2010:** U.S. Census Bureau, www.census.gov/prod/2011pubs/12statab/law.pdf, table 331 (accessed 6/28/20); and U.S. Courts, https://www.uscourts.gov/statistics-reports/analysis-reports/federal-judicial-caseload-statistics (accessed 6/28/20); **2011–2020:** Supreme Court of the United States, www.uscourts.gov/statisticsreports/caseload-statistics-data-tables (accessed 11/1/20).

the deputy attorney general) but is the top government lawyer in almost all cases brought before the appellate courts to which the government is a party. More than half the Supreme Court's total workload consists of cases under the charge of the solicitor general.

The solicitor general exercises especially strong influence by screening cases involving the federal government long before they approach the Supreme Court; the justices rely on the solicitor general to do so. Agency heads may lobby the president or otherwise try to go around the solicitor general, and a few of the independent agencies have a statutory right to make direct appeals, but without the solicitor general's support, these are seldom reviewed by the Court.

The solicitor general can enter a case even when the federal government is not a direct party to it by writing a brief called an ***amicus curiae*** ("friend of the court") brief. A "friend of the court" is not a direct party to a case but has a vital interest in its outcome. Thus, when the government has such an interest, the solicitor general can file an ***amicus curiae*** brief, or the Court can invite such a brief because it wants an opinion in writing. Other interested parties may file briefs as well.

amicus curiae

"Friend of the court," an individual or group that is not a party to a lawsuit but has a strong interest in influencing the outcome.

The Supreme Court's Procedures

Preparation. The Court's decision to accept a case is the beginning of a lengthy and complex process (Figure 8.6). First, attorneys on both sides must prepare **briefs**, written documents explaining why the Court should rule in favor of their client. The document filed by the side bringing the case, called the petitioner's brief, summarizes the facts of the case and presents the legal basis on which the Court is being asked to overturn the lower court's decision. The document filed by the side that won in the lower court, called the respondent's brief, explains why the Court should affirm the lower court's verdict. The petitioner then files another brief, the petitioner's reply brief, that attempts to refute the points made in the respondent's brief. Briefs contain many references to precedents showing that other courts have ruled in the same way that the Supreme Court is being asked to rule.

As the attorneys prepare their briefs, they often ask sympathetic interest groups for help by means of *amicus curiae* briefs. In a case involving separation of church and state, for example, liberal groups such as the American Civil Liberties Union and People for the American Way are likely to file *amicus* briefs in support of strict separation, whereas conservative religious groups are likely to file briefs advocating governmental support for religious causes. Often, dozens of briefs are filed on each side of a major case.

Oral Argument. In the next stage, **oral argument**, attorneys for both sides appear to present their positions before the Court and answer the justices' questions. Each attorney has only a half hour to present a case, including interruptions for questions. Oral argument can be very important to the outcome, for it allows justices to better understand the heart of the case and to raise questions that the opposing sides' briefs do not address. Sometimes justices go beyond the strictly legal issues and ask opposing counsel to discuss the case's implications for the Court and the nation at large.

In oral arguments on the constitutionality of President Obama's executive order on immigration (discussed earlier), Justice Anthony Kennedy expressed

brief
A written document in which an attorney explains—using case precedents—why a court should rule in favor of his or her client.

oral argument
The stage in Supreme Court proceedings in which attorneys for both sides appear before the Court to present their positions and answer questions posed by the justices.

figure 8.6

THE SUPREME COURT'S DECISION-MAKING PROCESS

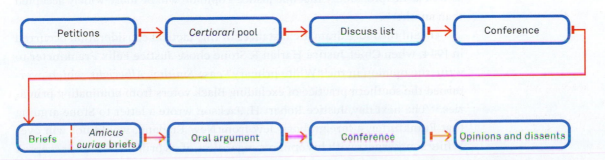

The oral-argument stage of a Supreme Court case is the last opportunity that both sides have to present their positions to the Court. In addition to the immediate legal issues at stake, the attorneys may discuss the larger political and social ramifications of the case.

his concern regarding the administration's understanding of the constitutional separation of powers. Kennedy said, "The briefs go on for pages to the effect that the president has admitted a certain number of people and then Congress approves it. That seems to me to have it backwards. It's as if . . . the president is setting the policy and the Congress is executing it. That's just upside down."[23]

The Conference.   Following oral argument, the Court discusses the case in its Wednesday or Friday conference, attended only by the justices themselves. The chief justice presides and speaks first; the others follow in order of seniority. A decision is reached by a majority vote. In discussing the case, justices may try to influence one another's opinions. This process produces compromise.

Opinion Writing.   After a decision has been reached, one of the members of the majority is assigned to write the **opinion**. This assignment is made by the chief justice or by the most senior justice in the majority if the chief justice is on the losing side. The assignment of the opinion can make a significant difference to the interpretation of a decision, as its wording and emphasis can have important implications for future cases. Thus, the justice assigning an opinion must consider the impression the case will make on lawyers and on the public, as well as the probability that one justice's opinion will be more widely accepted than another's.

One of the more dramatic instances of this tactical consideration occurred in 1944, when Chief Justice Harlan F. Stone chose Justice Felix Frankfurter to write the opinion in the "White primary" case *Smith v. Allwright*, which overturned the southern practice of excluding Black voters from nominating primaries.[24] The next day, Justice Robert H. Jackson wrote a letter to Stone arguing that Frankfurter, a foreign-born Jew from New England, would not win over White southerners with his opinion, regardless of its brilliance. Stone accepted

opinion
The written explanation of the Supreme Court's decision in a particular case.

the advice and substituted Justice Stanley Reed, an American-born Protestant from Kentucky.

Once the majority opinion is drafted, it is circulated to the other justices. If some members of the majority agree with both the outcome and the rationale presented in the majority opinion but wish to highlight a particular point, they draft a concurring opinion for that purpose. In other cases, one or more justices may agree with the majority's decision but disagree with the rationale. These justices may draft a special **concurrence**, explaining their disagreements with the majority.

Dissent. Justices who disagree with the majority decision may publicize the character of their disagreement in the form of a **dissenting opinion**, which is generally assigned by the senior justice among the dissenters. Dissenting opinions can signal to political forces on the losing side in the case that some members of the Court support their position. Ironically, the most dependable way an individual justice can exercise a direct influence on the Court is to write a dissent. Because there is no need to please a majority, dissenting opinions are often more eloquent and less guarded than majority opinions.

The extent of the division on the Court, and the reasons for dissent, are often taken as an indication of the strength of the position and principles expressed by the majority. A large majority—say, seven or more—indicates that it will be hard to overturn a ruling in the future, but the one-vote margin of a 5–4 decision might be hard to sustain in future cases involving a given question. In recent years, the Supreme Court has often split 5–4, with dissenters writing long and detailed opinions that they hope will convince a swing justice to join their side on the next round of cases dealing with a similar topic.

Dissent plays a special role in the work and impact of the Court because it amounts to an appeal to lawyers nationwide to keep bringing cases of the sort at issue. Therefore, an effective dissent influences the flow of cases through the Court, as well as the arguments that will be used by lawyers in later cases.

concurrence
An opinion agreeing with the decision of the majority in a Supreme Court case but with a rationale different from the one provided in the majority opinion.

dissenting opinion
A decision written by a justice who voted with the minority opinion in a particular case, in which the justice fully explains the reasoning behind his or her opinion.

Judicial Decision Making

The judiciary is conservative in its procedures, but its impact on society can be radical. That impact depends on numerous factors, two of which stand out above the rest. The first is the individual members of the Supreme Court, their attitudes, and their relationships with one another. The second is the other branches of government, particularly Congress.

The Supreme Court Justices. The Supreme Court explains its decisions in terms of law and precedent. But ultimately, the Court itself decides what laws mean and what importance precedent will have. Throughout its history, the Court has shaped and reshaped the law.

From the 1950s to the 1980s, the Court took an active role in such areas as civil rights, civil liberties, abortion, voting rights, and police procedures. It was more responsible than any other governmental institution for breaking down America's system of racial segregation. It virtually prohibited states from interfering with a woman's right to seek an abortion, sharply curtailed state restrictions on voting rights, and restricted the behavior of local police and prosecutors in criminal cases.

But since the early 1980s, resignations, deaths, and new appointments have led to many shifts in the mix of ideologies represented on the Court. In a series of decisions between 1989 and 2001, conservative justices appointed by Ronald Reagan and George H. W. Bush were able to swing the Court to a more conservative position on civil rights, affirmative action, abortion rights, property rights, criminal procedure, voting rights, desegregation, and the power of the national government.

However, because the Court was so evenly split during this period, the conservative bloc did not always prevail. Among the justices serving at the beginning of 2005, William Rehnquist, Antonin Scalia, and Clarence Thomas took conservative positions on most issues and were usually joined by Sandra Day O'Connor and Anthony Kennedy. Stephen Breyer, Ruth Bader Ginsburg, David Souter, and John Paul Stevens were reliably liberal. This split produced many 5–4 conservative victories. On some issues, though, O'Connor or Kennedy tended to side with the liberal camp, producing a 5–4 and sometimes a 6–3 victory for liberals.

George W. Bush's appointment of Samuel Alito to replace O'Connor was acknowledged by the media as heralding a shift in a much more conservative direction, but it moved the pivotal vote on the Court only from O'Connor to the ideologically similar Kennedy. During the 2007 term, Kennedy found himself the swing voter on numerous 5–4 decisions. One-third of all cases in 2007 were decided by just one vote. President Obama's appointments of Sonia Sotomayor and Elena Kagan to replace Souter and Stevens did not alter this arithmetic. The death of Justice Antonin Scalia left the Court with a 4–4 liberal-conservative division, but Republican Donald Trump's appointment of Neil Gorsuch in 2017 tipped the balance back in favor of the conservatives. The appointment of Brett Kavanaugh in 2018 bolstered the conservative majority. Analyzing the Evidence on pp. 256–7 looks at ideology in the Court.

We should note that the conservative-liberal bloc structure on the Court does not always predict votes, even in important cases. In *National Federation of Independent Business v. Sebelius*, the 2012 case on the constitutionality of Obama's health care law (the Affordable Care Act), the four liberals voting to uphold the law were joined by Chief Justice John Roberts, a member of the conservative bloc.[25] Similarly, in the 2015 case of *King v. Burwell*, Roberts again sided with the liberal bloc to uphold provisions of the ACA.[26] Dramatically, in 2020 the Court ruled against President Trump in two cases involving the release of his income taxes and other financial documents (to a New York grand jury in one case and to congressional committees in the other). By identical 7-2 votes, these decisions found both of the justices appointed by President Trump voting with the majority against him.

Of course, the meaning of any decision rests not just on which justices vote with the majority but also on the majority's written opinion, which presents the constitutional or statutory rationale for future policy. These options establish the guidelines that govern how federal courts must decide similar cases in the future.

Activism and Restraint.   One element of judicial philosophy is the issue of activism versus restraint. Over the years, some justices have believed that courts should interpret the Constitution according to the framers' stated intentions and defer to the views of Congress when interpreting federal statutes. Felix Frankfurter, for example, advocated judicial deference to legislative bodies and avoidance of the "political thicket" that the Court entangled itself in by deciding questions that were essentially political rather than legal. Advocates of **judicial restraint** are sometimes called "strict constructionists" because they look strictly to the words of the Constitution in interpreting its meaning.

The alternative to restraint is **judicial activism**, which involves going beyond the words of the Constitution or a statute to consider the broader societal implications of court decisions. Activist judges sometimes strike out in new directions, putting forth new interpretations or inventing new legal and constitutional concepts when they consider them socially desirable. For example, Justice Harry Blackmun's opinion in *Roe v. Wade* was based on a constitutional right to privacy that is not found in the words of the Constitution. Blackmun and the other members of the majority in *Roe* argued that other constitutional provisions implied the right to privacy. In this instance of judicial activism, the majority knew the result it wanted to achieve and was not afraid to make the law conform to the desired outcome.

Political Ideology.   The second component of judicial philosophy is political ideology. The liberal or conservative attitudes of justices play an important role in their decisions.[27] Indeed, the philosophy of activism versus restraint is, in part, a smoke screen for political ideology. In the past, liberal judges have often been activists, willing to use the law to achieve social and political change, whereas conservatives have been associated with judicial restraint. In recent years, however, some conservative justices have become activists in seeking to undo some of the work of liberal jurists over the past three decades.

Congress.   At both the national and state levels in the United States, courts and judges are "players" in the game of making policy because of the separation of powers. Essentially, the legislative branch formulates policy; the executive branch implements policy; and the courts, when asked, rule on whether the legislated and executed policy is faithful either to the substance of the statute or to the Constitution itself. The courts, that is, may strike down an administrative action either because it exceeds the authority granted in the relevant statute (statutory rationale) or because the statute itself exceeds the authority granted the legislature or executive by the Constitution (constitutional rationale).

If a court strikes down an administrative action, the majority opinion can impose whatever alternative policy the majority wishes. If the legislature is unhappy with this judicial action, it may either rewrite the legislation (if the rationale for striking it down was statutory)[28] or initiate a constitutional amendment that would permit the legislation (if the rationale was constitutional).

judicial restraint
The judicial philosophy whose adherents refuse to go beyond the text of the Constitution in interpreting its meaning.

judicial activism
The judicial philosophy that the Court should see beyond the text of the Constitution or a statute to consider the broader societal implications of its decisions.

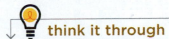 **think it through**

Make an argument for the approach—judicial activism or judicial restraint—for which you would advocate. Are there situations or cases that would change your answer?

Ideological Voting on the Supreme Court

Contributed by **Andrew D. Martin**, *Washington University in St. Louis*

Kevin M. Quinn, *University of Michigan*

Do the political preferences of Supreme Court justices influence their behavior? The starting point for the analysis of the behavior of Supreme Court justices is to look at their votes.[1] For non-unanimous decisions, we can compute agreement scores—the fraction of cases in which a pair of justices vote the same way. We display these agreement scores for the Court's 2018–19 term in the first figure below. If you examine this figure, you will see that two groups of justices emerge. Within each group, the justices agree with one another a lot; in many cases, over 80 percent of the time for justices on both the left and the right. Voting is more structured than we would expect by chance.

One way to represent that structure is by arranging the justices on a line as in the diagram below to the right.[2] Justices who agree a lot should be close to one another; justices who disagree a lot should be far apart.

Does the fact that there are patterns of agreement mean that the justices are deciding based on political ideology? Not necessarily. These patterns are consistent with ideological decision making, but other things might explain the patterns as well. However, when we evaluate the content of particular cases and see who wins or loses, there is a great deal of support for the idea that political ideology influences how justices vote.[3]

	Sotomayor	Ginsburg	Breyer	Kagan	Roberts	Kavanaugh	Gorsuch	Alito	Thomas
Sotomayor	1	.89	.75	.80	.45	.38	.34	.30	.18
Ginsburg	.89	1	.73	.82	.43	.41	.36	.32	.20
Breyer	.75	.73	1	.77	.52	.51	.27	.41	.20
Kagan	.80	.82	.77	1	.52	.51	.45	.41	.34
Roberts	.45	.43	.52	.52	1	.87	.48	.80	.59
Kavanaugh	.38	.41	.51	.51	.87	1	.54	.85	.67
Gorsuch	.34	.36	.27	.45	.48	.54	1	.59	.70
Alito	.30	.32	.41	.41	.80	.85	.59	1	.75
Thomas	.18	.20	.20	.34	.59	.67	.70	.75	1

- ● < 0.35
- ● 0.35–0.44
- ● 0.45–0.54
- ● 0.55–0.64
- ● 0.65–0.74
- ● 0.75–0.99

POSITION

Sotomayor
Ginsburg

Breyer

Kagan

Roberts
Kavanaugh

Gorsuch
Alito

Thomas

Agreement Scores for the 2018–2019 Term

The figure to the left contains the agreement scores for the 2018–19 term of the U.S. Supreme Court for all non-unanimous cases. These scores indicate the proportion of cases when each justice agreed with every other justice. Two justices that always disagreed with each other would get a zero; two justices who always agreed would get a one. Red indicates low agreement scores; green indicates high agreement scores. The policy dimension to the right of the figure is one that best represents the patterns in the agreement scores.

0 = Justices always disagreed
1 = Justices always agreed

This type of analysis can be done for any court, but it becomes more difficult if we are interested in comparing justices across time instead of during just one term. What if we are interested in whether the Supreme Court is becoming more ideologically polarized over time? Or whether individual justices have become more liberal or conservative? Martin-Quinn scores based on a statistical model of voting on the Court help solve this problem.[4]

A number of interesting patterns emerge. Consider the case of Justice Harry Blackmun, who often claimed, "I haven't changed; it's the Court that changed under me."[5] The figure below shows that Justice Blackmun's position did in fact change ideologically over the course of his career. This evidence is consistent with some clear changes in Justice Blackmun's voting behavior, especially in the area of the death penalty.

We can also look at patterns in the positions of chief justices. While the chief's vote counts just the same as the votes of the other justices, he or she plays an important role in organizing the court. Justice William H. Rehnquist was the most conservative justice on the court when he arrived in 1971, but as the figure below shows, after he was elevated to chief justice in 1986, he too drifted more toward the middle. This is what we would expect to see of a justice who was working strategically to build coalitions, as any good chief would.

Ideological Trajectories of Selected Justices

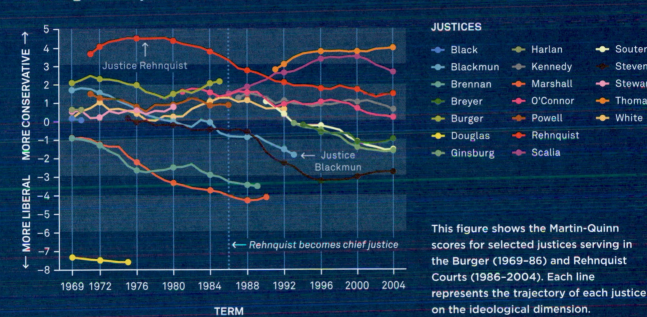

JUSTICES

Black	Harlan	Souter
Blackmun	Kennedy	Stevens
Brennan	Marshall	Stewart
Breyer	O'Connor	Thomas
Burger	Powell	White
Douglas	Rehnquist	
Ginsburg	Scalia	

This figure shows the Martin-Quinn scores for selected justices serving in the Burger (1969–86) and Rehnquist Courts (1986–2004). Each line represents the trajectory of each justice on the ideological dimension.

1 C. Herman Pritchett, *The Roosevelt Court: A Study in Judicial Politics and Values, 1937–1947* (New York: Macmillan, 1948).

2 Glendon A. Schubert, *The Judicial Mind: The Attitudes and Ideologies of Supreme Court Justices, 1946–1963* (Evanston, IL: Northwestern University Press, 1965).

3 Jeffrey A. Segal and Harold J. Spaeth, *The Supreme Court and the Attitudinal Model* (New York: Cambridge University Press, 1993).

4 Andrew D. Martin and Kevin M. Quinn, "Dynamic Ideal Point Estimation via Markov Chain Monte Carlo for the U.S. Supreme Court, 1953–1999," *Political Analysis* 10, no. 2 (2002): 134–53, http://mqscores.lsa.umich.edu (accessed 3/27/20).

5 Linda Greenhouse, *Becoming Justice Blackmun: Harry Blackmun's Supreme Court Journey* (New York: Times Books, 2005).

 → **What impact on the agreement scores would you expect to see after Amy Coney Barrett, who is very conservative, replaces Ruth Bader Ginsburg?**

In reaching their decisions, Supreme Court justices must anticipate Congress's response. As a result, they do not always vote according to their true preferences, because doing so might provoke Congress to overturn their decision by enacting legislation that moves the policy at issue even further away from what the justices prefer. In short, the interactions between the Court and Congress are part of a complex strategic game.[29]

The President. The president's most direct influence on the Court is the power to nominate justices. Presidents typically nominate those who seem close to their policy preferences and close enough to the preferences of a majority of senators, who must confirm the nomination. Yet the efforts by presidents to reshape the federal judiciary are not always successful. Often in American history, judges have surprised and disappointed the presidents who named them to the bench (see Analyzing the Evidence on pp. 256–7).

The president must also confront Congress in shaping the judiciary. By using the filibuster (see Chapter 5), both parties have blocked judicial nominees. In 2013, frustration over Republican blocking of President Obama's judicial nominees led Senate Democrats to eliminate the possibility of a filibuster for most presidential nominees. In 2017, the filibuster was removed by the Senate Republican majority for Supreme Court nominees as well.

Of course, opponents of a nomination may block it in other ways. The Senate Judiciary Committee may refuse to consider the nominee, as in the case of Judge Merrick Garland, Obama's Supreme Court nominee to replace the late Justice Antonin Scalia. As we have seen, the appointment process has subtly tied the judiciary to the executive and, perhaps, helped to upset the constitutional balance of power.

CONCLUSION

What role does an unelected judiciary play in our system of representative government? Over the past 75 years, the place of the judiciary in American politics and society has changed dramatically. Demand for legal solutions has increased, and the judiciary's reach has expanded. Some now call for reining in the power of the courts and the discretion of judges in areas ranging from criminal law and sentencing to property rights to liability and torts. How our society deals with these issues will shape the judiciary's future independence and effectiveness. Even the most conservative justices now seem reluctant to give up their newfound power—authority that has become accepted and thus established.

Federal judges enjoy great freedom because they are not subject to electoral pressures. More than any other politicians in the United States, they can pursue their own ideas about what is right—their own ideologies. They are, however, constrained by rules governing access to the courts, by other courts, by Congress and the president, by their lack of enforcement powers, and most important, by the past in the form of precedent and common law. For much of its history, the federal judiciary acted very cautiously. The Supreme Court rarely challenged laws passed by Congress or actions of the president, and the scope of its decisions was limited to those individuals granted access to the courts.

Two judicial revolutions have expanded the power and reach of the federal judiciary since World War II. The first revolution brought about the liberalization of a wide range of public policies in the United States. As we saw in Chapter 4, in certain policy areas—including school desegregation, legislative apportionment, criminal procedure, obscenity, abortion, and voting rights—the Supreme Court took the lead in bringing about sweeping changes for the role of the U.S. government and, ultimately, the character of American society. The Court put many of these issues before the public long before Congress or the president was prepared to act.

At the same time that the courts were introducing important policy innovations, they were also bringing about a second, less visible revolution. During the 1960s and 1970s, the Supreme Court and other federal courts liberalized the concept of "standing" to permit almost any group seeking to challenge an administrative agency's actions to bring its case before the federal bench. It thus encouraged groups to come to the judiciary to resolve disputes, rather than to Congress or the executive branch.

Complementing this change, the federal courts broadened their scope to permit themselves to act on behalf of broad categories of persons in "class-action" cases, rather than just on behalf of individuals.[30] Finally, they began to use so-called structural remedies, with a court in effect retaining jurisdiction of a case until its ruling had actually been implemented to its satisfaction.[31]

Through these judicial mechanisms, the federal courts paved the way for an unprecedented expansion of national judicial power. Thus, during the 1960s and 1970s, their power expanded through links with constituencies—such as civil rights, consumer, environmental, and feminist groups—that staunchly defended the Supreme Court in its battles with Congress, the executive, or other interest groups.

During the 1980s and early 1990s, the Reagan and George H. W. Bush administrations sought to end the relationship between the Court and liberal political forces. Conservative judges appointed by these Republican presidents modified the Court's position in areas such as abortion, affirmative action, and judicial procedure, though not as completely as some conservative writers and politicians had hoped. Within one week in 2003, for example, the Supreme Court affirmed the validity of affirmative action, reaffirmed abortion rights, strengthened gay rights, offered new protection to individuals facing the death penalty, and ruled in favor of a congressional apportionment plan that dispersed minority voters across several districts—a practice that appeared to favor Democrats.[32] The Court had made these decisions on the basis of the justices' interpretations of precedent and law, not simply their personal beliefs.

Moreover, despite its more conservative ideology in recent decades, there's another sense in which the Court has not become conservative: it has not been eager to surrender the expanded powers carved out by earlier Courts, especially in areas that assert the power of the national government over the states. Indeed, the early opponents to the U.S. Constitution (the Antifederalists discussed in Chapter 2) feared that the independent judiciary would make such an assertion. Over more than two centuries of U.S. history, the reach and authority of the federal judiciary have expanded greatly, and it has emerged as a powerful arm of our national politics. Whatever their policy beliefs or partisan orientations, judges and justices understand the new importance of the courts among the three branches of American government and act not just to interpret and apply the law but also to maintain the power of the courts.

Key Terms

Check Your Understanding

1. Outline the basic structure of the U.S federal court system and the U.S. state court system. What is the process for a case to be appealed to the Supreme Court in each of these systems?

2. Identify the jurisdiction of federal courts. What are several examples of the types of cases they will hear?

3. How are federal judges appointed? How do ideological views influence this process and what challenges does this raise?

4. Explain the significance of judicial review. How was it instituted and how has it shaped the role of the court?

5. What is the jurisdiction of the Supreme Court? How does the Supreme Court determine which cases within this jurisdiction it will hear?

6. Discuss the process of checks and balances as it relates to the Court. How does the Court check the power of Congress? What role does the president play?

 INQUIZITIVE

Earn a better grade on your test. InQuizitive personalizes your learning path to help you master the concepts from this chapter. In a recent efficacy study of American government students, InQuizitive increased test scores by an average of 17 points (see back cover).

CHAPTER NINE

PUBLIC OPINION AND THE MEDIA

Citizens elect representatives to serve as their agents in government, but can we be sure that these representatives pay attention to citizens' views? On the surface, at least, politicians pay a great deal of attention to public opinion. Presidents and members of Congress are avid consumers of poll data and sometimes commission their own surveys to find out what Americans think about important issues and about the performance of their elected officials. President Trump, like his predecessors, received regular briefings on polling related to important issues and from pollsters from his political party about the 2020 presidential election.[1]

On an issue-by-issue basis, public opinion on such matters as health care, climate change, gun control, and tax reform may not seem to have much immediate effect on the government's actions. Most Americans are worried about climate change, but the Trump administration reversed many policies aimed at protecting the environment because the president believed that environmental regulations cost too many American jobs.

A number of studies, however, have identified a relationship between national policy and public opinion over time. In a pathbreaking study, political scientist Alan D. Monroe found that in a majority of cases, changes in public policy followed shifts in public preferences. And, in most cases, if opinion did not change, neither did policy.[2] These findings are certainly supported by the many politicians who claim to be guided by the will of the people in all they do and who poll constituents persistently to find out what that will is.

But do such studies actually show that public opinion is an important force in shaping policy? That there is some consistency between the two does not mean the government's conduct is guided by the public's preferences. In fact, most citizens have no strong preferences about most public issues, and many lack basic

Most Americans are worried about climate change, including most young Americans, but the Trump administration reversed many policies aimed at protecting the environment in favor of protecting jobs these policies might eliminate. Here climate activist Greta Thunberg speaks during the UN Youth Climate Summit in 2019.

information that might help them understand and evaluate policy choices. For example, one survey found that 40 percent of Americans did not know that each state has two senators; 43 percent did not know what an economic recession is; 68 percent did not know that a two-thirds majority in each house is required for congressional override of a presidential veto; and 70 percent did not know that the term of a U.S. House member is two years.[3]

Such findings raise questions about poll data on topics as complicated as the federal debt limit, immigration reform, or economic inequality. Many Americans did not understand all the economic and political implications of plans proposed to address these issues and likely took their cues from politicians they admired or disliked. Many Trump supporters thought the president's ideas about immigration were good ones without really understanding their implications, while many who disliked Trump opposed them because of their source more than their content. To complicate matters more, since few voters have ever met any major politician, they rely for their views on a media "image" fashioned by competing political forces and the media themselves.

Lack of basic political knowledge and accurate information leaves many Americans open to manipulation by politicians and advocates using advertising and other means of messaging. The goal of these politicians and advocates is to develop arguments that will persuade citizens to agree with their own

- **How much does public opinion influence the actions of elected representatives?**
- **What is the role of the media in a representative democracy?**

policy goals.[4] This effort begins with polling. As Bill Clinton's pollster Dick Morris said, "You don't use a poll to reshape a program, but to reshape your argumentation for the program so the public supports it."[5] The effort continues with advertising, publicity, and propaganda that make use of the information gathered from the polls.

Is public opinion the driving force in politics, or is public opinion itself a result of political struggles? In this chapter, we examine further the role of public opinion in American politics. Do Americans know enough to form meaningful opinions about important policy issues? What factors account for differences in opinion? What role do the media play in forming public opinion on political issues?

Learning Objectives

- Define public opinion.

- Identify the major factors that shape an individual's political preferences and beliefs.

- Describe how political leaders and private groups try to influence public opinion.

- Explain the news media's role in the United States and how the media affect political knowledge and public opinion.

- Analyze why government is usually, but not always, responsive to public opinion.

WHAT IS PUBLIC OPINION?

public opinion
Citizens' attitudes about political issues, personalities, institutions, and events.

Public opinion is the collective total of many citizens' views and interests. It includes assessments of those in office, attitudes toward political organizations and social groups, and preferences about whether and how government ought to address important problems. The term sometimes gives the impression that the public has a single opinion on a given matter; however, that is rarely the case.

On some topics, Americans do hold common views on important questions about politics and society. There is consensus on the legitimacy of the U.S. Constitution and trust in the rule of law—that is, the principle that no one is above the law. There is consensus that the United States is a democratic society and that the outcomes of elections determine who governs. These commonly held opinions and values are essential to maintaining a well-functioning democracy in the United States. They ensure peaceful transitions of government after each election and respect for laws produced by a legally chosen government.

There is also wide agreement on fundamental political values, such as liberty, democracy, and equality of opportunity.[6] Nearly all Americans agree that all people should have equal rights, regardless of race, gender, or social standing. Americans hold a common commitment to freedom. People who live in the United States are free to live where they want, travel where they want, work where they want, say what they want, and practice whatever religion they wish, or no religion at all. And Americans have an undying belief in representative democracy—that whenever possible, public officials should be chosen by majority vote.[7] It makes sense to think of the American public as having a single opinion on these elemental questions.

On most matters that come before the government, however, the public does not hold a single view. Usually, opinions are divided between those who support the government or a proposed action and those who do not. Politicians are still attuned to public opinion when it is divided, but what matter most are the balance and direction of opinion. What do the majority of constituents want? Which way is opinion trending? Is it possible to find a popular middle ground?

People express their views to those in power in a variety of ways. Constituents contact their members of Congress, state and local elected officials, people in the bureaucracy, and even the president through letters, phone calls, emails, or even personal visits to members' offices. Indeed, technology has made it so easy for constituents to contact officials that members of Congress and their staff cannot keep up with the volume.[8]

People can also express their opinions more publicly by writing blogs, tweets, letters to newspapers, and op-ed pieces; by talking with others; by displaying lawn signs and bumper stickers; by working on campaigns; by giving money to candidates, groups, and party organizations; and, most simply, by voting.

Expressions of opinion and preferences are not always easy to interpret. If a constituent votes against a member of Congress, is it because the member did something the constituent disliked, or because she decided to vote against all politicians from the member's party? Or for some other reason?

Political scientists and political consultants try to provide more refined and structured descriptions of public opinion using surveys. On any important issue, the government may pursue different policy options. Public opinion on a given issue can often be thought of as the distribution of opinion across the different options. Likewise, public opinion may represent the division of support for a leader or party. Surveys help to gauge where majority support lies and how intensely or firmly citizens across the spectrum hold their views. More and more, politicians rely on opinion polls to anticipate the effects of their decisions, to develop ways to minimize objections to those decisions, and to identify opportunities to change opinions. Answering a survey, then, can also be a form of political action, because it may influence political decisions.

ORIGINS AND NATURE OF PUBLIC OPINION

To understand the meaning and origins of the public's opinions, we must have some sense of the basis for individuals' preferences and beliefs. People's opinions are the products of their personalities, social characteristics, and interests. They mirror who the individuals are, what they want, and how they are related to their family and community, and to the broader economy and society. But opinions are also shaped by institutional, political, and governmental forces that make it more likely that an individual will hold some beliefs and less likely that he will hold others.

Foundations of Preferences

At a foundational level, individual opinion is shaped by several factors, including self-interest, values about what is right and wrong, and the process of socialization.

Self-Interest.   Individuals' preferences about politics and public policy are usually rooted in self-interest. Laws and other governmental actions directly affect people's interests—their income, their safety, and the quality of public services and government benefits they receive, to give just a few examples. It is not surprising, then, that when people express their political opinions, they react to the effects that governmental actions have on them personally.

Economic interests are perhaps the most powerful preferences when it comes to people's opinions. Virtually every American has an interest in the government's role in the nation's economy and strong preferences about tax rates and spending priorities. Given the enormous influence of the federal government in the economy, assessments of the president and the party in power often correspond to how well the economy performs.

Individuals' attitudes toward government reflect other forms of self-interest as well. Laws affect families, civic and religious organizations, and communities. Zoning laws and urban redevelopment programs shape the nature of neighborhoods, including the mix of commercial and residential housing and the density of low-income housing in an area. Family law affects how easy it is for families to stay together, what happens when they break down, and what rights and responsibilities parents have. Proposed changes in such laws bring immediate reaction from those affected.

Values.   Much of what individuals want from their government is rooted in values about what is right or wrong—our philosophies about morality, justice, and ethics. Our value systems originate in many places—from families, religion, education, groups, and so forth—and often determine our preferences in particular circumstances. For example, our values may shape our views on economic justice and preferences about whether and how government redistributes income.

Origins of Individual Opinion

Foundational Factors

- **Self-Interest:** Individuals want government to take actions that will benefit them economically or in terms of their overall well-being.

- **Values:** Individuals have values about what is right and wrong, and these values affect their preferences about governmental policies.

- **Socialization:** Individuals learn opinions and attitudes from their family, their friends, their teachers and religious leaders, and others in their social groups and networks.

Political Ideology

- Most Americans describe themselves as conservative or liberal. These political ideologies include beliefs about the role of government, public policies, and which groups in society should properly exercise power.

Identity Politics

- Individuals identify with groups—including racial, religious, and gender groups. Policies that are beneficial to the group as a whole are viewed as good, and those that are harmful to the group are viewed as bad.

Americans generally believe in equal opportunity, an idea that has driven our society to try to root out discrimination in employment, housing, and education, and to create a universal public education system. In some states, courts have cited this principle of equality to insist that the states try to equalize public school expenditures per pupil across districts.

Values also shape our notions of what is a crime and what is a suitable punishment. One of the most morally significant debates in American history focuses on capital punishment. Does the government have the right to take someone's life if that person has taken the life of someone else? An ancient sense of justice seems to call for exactly that: an eye for an eye. Other ideas of morality speak against capital punishment. In addition, our values about government and its appropriate powers say that people must be protected against unrestrained and unpredictable governmental acts. The possibility of an error has led some to claim that the government should never have the power to take the life of an individual.

Our values also reflect established social norms—customs or principles—of our community. What, for example, is marriage? One might consider it an economic convenience, as defined by laws that tie taxes and inheritance to marital status. Most people, however, hold more complex ideas of marriage, and those principles dictate whether they think that same-sex marriages ought to be allowed. Such norms change over time.

At a societal level, conflicting values are particularly difficult to resolve. Unlike the case with economic interests, it is hard to bargain over differences based on fundamental principles of right and wrong. By the same token, there are many values that unite us. If Americans had few common values or perspectives, it would be very difficult for them to reach agreement on particular issues. Over the past half-century, political philosophers and political scientists have reflected on what those values are and have settled on three important precepts. Americans almost universally agree with (1) the democracy principle (that majority rule is a good decision rule), (2) the equal opportunity principle, and (3) the principle that the best government governs least.

Social Groups.   Another source of political preferences is social groups. People use race, religion, place, language, and many other characteristics to describe and define themselves. These self-identifications are based on fundamental psychological attachments that go beyond self-interest and values, though they are often reinforced by our interests and values.

The process through which our social interactions and social groups affect our perspectives and preferences is called **socialization**. Most 18-year-olds already have definite political attitudes that they have learned from interactions with parents and grandparents, friends, teachers and religious leaders, and others in their social groups and networks. Of course, socialization does not end when one becomes an adult. We continue to learn about politics and what we should think about political questions from our family members, coworkers, and others we see and speak with daily.

socialization
A process in which individuals take on their communities' perspectives and preferences through social interactions.

Membership in a social group may affect individual opinion. For example, Catholics and other religious groups are more likely than the religiously unaffiliated to oppose abortion.

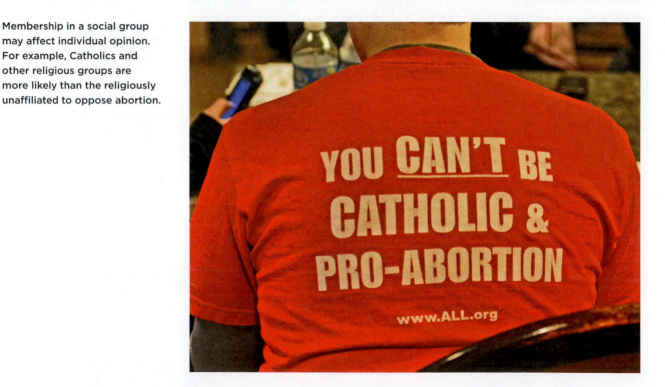

Socialization works in many ways. First, it is a means of providing information about what is going on in the community and even in national politics. Socialization also takes the form of education or instruction. Parents teach their children how to think about a problem, how to decide what is a right or wrong choice or action, and even how to participate in politics. This is how we as humans have learned to survive and adapt. But it means that, by the time we are adults, we have already learned much about what we want government to do, what sorts of people we want in government, and even whether it is worth our while to participate.

Political Ideology

An ideology is a comprehensive way of understanding political or cultural situations. It is a set of assumptions about the way the world and society work that helps us to organize our beliefs, information, and reactions to new situations. It assigns values to different alternatives and helps us balance competing values. In the United States today, people often describe themselves as liberals or conservatives. Liberalism and conservatism are political ideologies that include beliefs about the proper role of government, about appropriate public policies, and about the proper groups to exercise power in society. In earlier times, the terms *liberal* and *conservative* were defined somewhat differently. As recently as the nineteenth century, a liberal was an individual who favored freedom from governmental control, whereas a conservative was someone who supported the use of governmental power and favored the continued rule of elites.

Today, in the United States, the term **liberal** has come to imply support for political and social reform; governmental intervention in the economy; the expansion of federal social services; stronger governmental efforts on behalf of the poor, immigrants, minorities, and women; and greater protections for consumers and the environment. In social and cultural areas, liberals generally support abortion rights and the rights of gay and transgender citizens and oppose governmental involvement with religious institutions and religious expression. In international affairs, liberal positions usually include support for arms control, for aid to poor nations, for limiting the use of American military force, and for the role of international organizations such as the United Nations. Of course, liberalism is not a rigidly unified belief system. For example, many individuals who view themselves as liberal have called for humanitarian intervention in the civil war in Syria, though such action would require the use of American military force.

By contrast, the term **conservative** today is used to describe those who generally support the social and economic status quo and favor markets as solutions to social and economic problems. Conservatives believe that a large and powerful government poses a threat to citizens' freedom, and in the domestic arena they generally oppose the expansion of governmental activity and, in particular, governmental regulation of business. As for social and cultural positions, many conservatives oppose abortion and same-sex marriage, often on religious grounds. In international affairs, conservatism has come to mean support for maintaining

think it through

How do your political preferences and attitudes compare with those of your family members and friends? Who do you think was most influential in shaping your opinions and ideas? Can you imagine a situation in which your attitudes might change based on future experiences or relationships?

liberal
A person who generally believes that the government should play an active role in supporting social and political change and generally supports a strong role for the government in the economy, the provision of social services, and the protection of civil rights.

conservative
A person who generally believes that social institutions (such as churches and corporations) and the free market solve problems better than governments do, that a large and powerful government poses a threat to citizens' freedom, and that the appropriate role of government is to uphold traditional values.

the United States' superpower military status and skepticism about international organizations and diplomacy.

Like liberalism, however, conservatism is far from a rigidly unified ideology. Some conservatives support many governmental social programs, and some oppose efforts to outlaw abortion. An important strain of conservatism has its roots in populism, which generally is isolationist in international affairs, favors limited powers of government, and is suspicious of elites. The real political world is far too complex to be seen in terms of a simple struggle between liberals and conservatives.

Many other ideologies exist besides liberalism and conservatism. Libertarians, for example, seek to expand personal liberty above all other principles and to minimize governmental involvement in all aspects of the economy and society. Other ideologies seek a particular outcome (such as environmental protection) or emphasize certain issues (such as economic growth) and de-emphasize others (such as abortion). Communism and fascism, two ideologies that support governmental control of all aspects of the economy and society, dominated politics in many European countries from the 1920s through the 1940s. Political debate in the United States, however, has revolved around the division between liberals and conservatives for most of the last century.

Political scientists often think of liberal and conservative ideologies as anchors on a spectrum of possible belief systems. Specific values and interests might lead an individual to support many elements of one of these ideologies but not all. The Pew Research Center offers just such a classification in its American Values Survey, conducted annually since 1987.[9] The survey asks respondents about a wide range of political, social, and cultural preferences, behaviors, and beliefs. Classifying people this way, the Pew Research Center finds that most Americans are in fact fairly moderate—having as many conservative views as liberal views, and favoring more centrist, less extreme versions of both kinds.

Identity Politics

Ideology offers one lens through which people can see where their political interests and values lie. Identity provides an alternative simplification of the political world. Political identities are distinctive characteristics or group associations that individuals carry, reflecting their social connections or common values and interests with others in that group. A harm or benefit to any individual with a given identity is viewed as a harm or benefit to all people with that identity. Common identities in politics include race and ethnicity, language, religion, and gender.

Identity politics is often zero-sum: if one group wins, another loses. The term *identity politics* is sometimes used today to refer to groups that have been oppressed and now seek to assert their rights. But the concept is much broader, describing not just the situation of groups that have suffered harm but any group identity. In fact, political identity often has a positive side, as the glue that holds society together and as a basis for collective political action.[10]

Identity politics is quite obvious in the United States today. All citizens, and even many noncitizens, identify themselves as Americans. During international sporting competitions, therefore, we root for athletes representing the United States, and when those athletes win, as Americans we feel happy and proud. We may feel similarly when an American wins a Nobel Prize or makes a significant scientific discovery. The same is true of people from any country, who feel pride in the accomplishments of others from that country.

One of the most powerful political identities in the United States is political party. The authors of *The American Voter* (1960), a now classic work of political science research on the social and psychological foundations of voting behavior in the United States, characterize party identification as a stable psychological attachment usually developed in childhood and carried throughout one's adult life. Party identifications are, of course, shaped by interests and values, as well as by current events, but partisanship also has deep roots in family, local culture, and other factors.

People commonly rely on their partisan identities in filtering information—as in, for example, deciding who won a presidential debate. Party identification also has a unique hold on voting behavior. Even after taking into account self-interest, moral values, and other identities, it remains one of the best predictors of how someone will vote.[11] (See the discussion of party voting in Chapters 10 and 11.) This is not to say that party does not reflect ideological choices or self-interest. It does. But it is certainly also the case that party functions as a social identity.

People who hold a specific identity often express strong affinity for others of the same identity—for example, voting for someone of the same national background or ethnicity quite apart from, or in spite of, the sorts of laws that the particular politician promises to enact. Political scientists call this preference for people of the same identity "descriptive representation," and it is an important subject in the area of race and elections.

The Voting Rights Act tries to protect African Americans, Hispanics, and other minority racial and ethnic groups against discriminatory electoral practices that prevent those voters from electing their preferred candidates. Since the act was passed in 1965, the percentage of members of Congress who are African American or Hispanic has increased from 1 percent (6 in 1965) to 19 percent (101 in 2020). Race, gender, social class, and place all create strong identities that shape voting behavior.

People have a wide range of social, cultural, and political identities. Gender, race, and age or generation are especially obvious because of physical characteristics, but religions, regions of the country, sexual orientations, occupations, and many other distinctive characteristics of people also function as identities. Americans have identities based on who they are, where they live, and how they live, and these identities can have a large impact on individuals' preferences and political behavior.

Race and Ethnicity.

Racial and ethnic identities influence political attitudes. The United States is a racially and ethnically diverse country. Approximately 60 percent of people in the United States are Whites who were born in the country, and within this native-born White population, there are a large variety of ethnic identities, usually tied to the country or culture in Europe of their ancestors—Irish Americans, Italian Americans, Polish Americans, Jewish Americans, and so on. The remaining 40 percent of people in the United States consist of immigrants or of people who identify themselves as non-White or of non-European origin.

One in eight people in the United States was born in another country, and half of those foreign-born individuals are naturalized citizens, meaning they qualified for citizenship by meeting certain legal requirements. Sixty percent of the United States population identify themselves as White, non-Hispanic; 18 percent identify themselves as Hispanic; 13 percent identify themselves as Black or African American; 6 percent identify themselves as Asian; and 1.3 percent identify themselves as Native American or American Indian.[12] The strength of these identities and the relationships among these groups shape political attitudes. The Timeplot on pp. 274–5 shows immigration by continent of origin from the 1820s to the present.

Perhaps the deepest racial fault line in American politics is between Black and White people. The practice of slavery in the colonies and early American states created a deep, lasting divide in society between White and Black Americans. That division is reflected in a staggering number of statistics, from wages and education levels to poverty levels to neighborhood integration to political ideals. For example, Blacks and Whites hold starkly different beliefs about the government's responsibilities for providing shelter, food, and other basic necessities to those in need.[13] The two groups also differ in their views of equality of opportunity in the United States, which can affect their support for policies that address perceived disadvantages (Figure 9.1).

Hispanics, now the largest ethnic or racial group in the United States, also have political opinions and attitudes that are distinctive from those of Whites. For instance, in a 2014 poll, 60 percent of Hispanic voters approved of the Affordable Care Act, while 61 percent of non-Hispanic Whites disapproved.[14] In addition, Hispanic voters routinely identify immigration as one of their top concerns, while the issue ranks lower in priority among non-Hispanic White voters. Many Latinos oppose restrictive immigration laws even if they are not personally affected by them.

Hispanic and Latino political identities are often rooted in particular immigrant communities, such as Mexican Americans, Cuban Americans, and Puerto Ricans,[15] and are strongly tied to particular issues.[16] These

Racial and ethnic identity influences political attitudes. Many Latinos oppose restrictive immigration laws, including the separation of families, even if they are not personally affected by these laws.

figure 9.1

DISAGREEMENT AMONG BLACKS AND WHITES

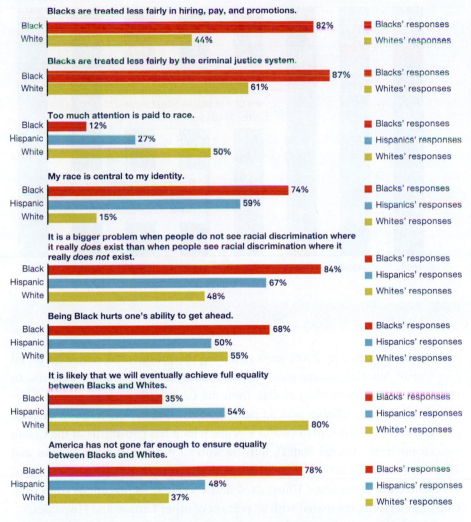

analyzing the evidence

Although America's system of legally mandated racial segregation ended nearly half a century ago, its effects continue to linger. In contemporary America, Blacks and Whites have different perspectives on race relations. Do you think that Black-White differences have increased or decreased in the past few decades? Are these differences of opinion important?

SOURCES: Gallup News, http://news.gallup.com/opinion/polling-matters/193586/public-opinioncontext-americans-race-police.aspx; Pew Research Center, www.people-press.org/2017/10/05/4-race-immigration-and-discrimination; and Pew Research Center, www.pewresearch.org/facttank/2017/09/28/views-about-whether-whites-benefit-from-societal-advantages-split-sharply-along-racial-and-partisan-lines (accessed 5/28/20).

differences have led to a diversity of opinion among Latinos on certain issues. Cuban Americans were long disproportionately Republican, while those of Mexican, Puerto Rican, and Central American descent identify more often as Democrats (Table 9.1).

That difference reflected Cuban Americans' relationship with their homeland—many of them had left Cuba because of the Communist takeover there beginning in 1961—and the long-standing policy differences between the Republicans and Democrats over U.S. relations with Cuba. Interestingly, the difference

IMMIGRATION BY CONTINENT OF ORIGIN

Legend:
- Europe
- Asia
- Americas
- Africa
- Oceania
- Not Specified

The Irish Famine contributed to an increase in immigration to the United States from Europe in the 1840s and 1850s.

The late nineteenth century saw a large wave of mostly White immigrants.

(X-axis: 1820s, 1830s, 1840s, 1850s, 1860s, 1870s, 1880s, 1890s)
(Y-axis: 20, 40, 60, 80, 100%)

TIMEPLOT NOTE: From 1820 to 1867, figures represent alien passenger arrivals at seaports; from 1868 to 1891 and 1895 to 1897, immigrant alien arrivals; from 1892 to 1894 and 1898 to 2014, immigrant aliens admitted for permanent residence; from 1892 to 1903, aliens entering by cabin class were not counted as immigrants. Land arrivals were not completely enumerated until 1908.

had largely vanished by 2008; surveys during the presidential campaign found that Cuban Americans were nearly as Democratic as other Hispanic groups. In the 2016 election, according to data from the Cooperative Congressional Election Study, Hillary Clinton won 52 percent of the Cuban vote nationwide (and just 48 percent of the Cuban vote in Florida, which has two-thirds of the Cuban Americans in the United States). But she won 62 percent of other Latinos and Hispanics nationwide.[17] In 2018, all Hispanic and Latino groups moved toward the Democrats. Democratic House candidates received 58 percent of votes from Cuban Americans, compared with 65 percent of other Latinos and Hispanics.[18]

The fastest-growing racial or ethnic group in the United States is Asian Americans. Over the past two decades the total number of Asian Americans has more than doubled, and since 1980 they have risen from 1 percent of the population to 6 percent. Asian Americans are even more diverse than Hispanics; they come from vastly different cultures and countries—from China to Indonesia, from Japan to Vietnam to India, from Pakistan to the Philippines. These groups are often treated as having a common Asian identity, when in fact they are rooted in many different cultures. They have become part of American culture in their own distinctive ways.[19] As their numbers grow, Asian Americans are assuming a new political identity and voice in U.S. politics.

Gender. Men and women hold differing political opinions as well. Women tend to be less militaristic than men on issues of war and peace and more supportive

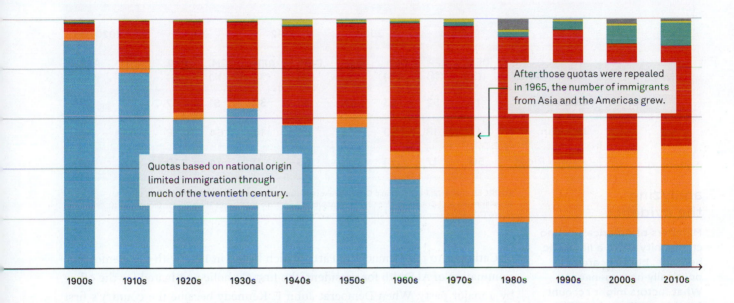

Quotas based on national origin limited immigration through much of the twentieth century.

After those quotas were repealed in 1965, the number of immigrants from Asia and the Americas grew.

| 1900s | 1910s | 1920s | 1930s | 1940s | 1950s | 1960s | 1970s | 1980s | 1990s | 2000s | 2010s |

of measures to protect the environment and of governmental social and health care programs (Table 9.2). Perhaps because of these differences on issues, women are more likely than men to vote for Democratic candidates, whereas men have become increasingly supportive of Republicans.[20]

This tendency for men's and women's voting to differ is called the **gender gap**. The gender gap in voting first became evident in the 1980 election and has persisted, averaging about 8 percentage points. In the 2016 presidential election, Hillary Clinton became the first female major-party candidate. The gender gap was the widest of any presidential election: she won 54 percent of the votes of women, but only 41 percent of the votes of men.

Why the gender gap emerged roughly 40 years ago and persists today is something of a puzzle. Despite speculation that it is rooted in reproductive rights and abortion politics, a Pew Research Center poll from 2019 indicates little or no opinion gap between men and women on the abortion issue.[21] Rather, the gender gap appears more attributable to differences in wages and life experience; to the efforts of Democrats to reach out to women; to other differences between the ways that men and women are treated in the economy and society; and to women's shared objective of ensuring equal treatment for all women.[22]

Religion. Religion shapes peoples' values and beliefs, and thus political ideologies, but it also serves as a strong source of political identity quite apart from the values at play. One of the clearest examples was the decades-long attachment

TIMEPLOT SOURCE: Department of Homeland Security, "Yearbook of Immigration Statistics 2018," https://www.dhs.gov/immigration-statistics/yearbook/2018 (accessed 7/3/20).

gender gap
A distinctive pattern of voting behavior reflecting the differences in views between women and men.

table 9.1

CHANGING PARTY AFFILIATION IN THE LATINO COMMUNITY

BACKGROUND	2004		2008		2012		2016		2020	
	DEM. (%)	REP. (%)	DEM. (%)	REP. (%)	DEM. (%)	REP. (%)	DEM. (%)	REP. (%)	DEM. (%)	REP. (%)
Cuban	17	52	53	20	35	37	51	37	19	54
Mexican	47	18	50	18	43	14	64	18	43	14
Puerto Rican	50	17	61	11	53	11	74	10	53	11

SOURCES: 2004–12: Pew Hispanic Center, www.pewhispanic.org (accessed 11/13/14); 2016: Stephen Ansolabehere and Brian Schaffner, https://dataverse.harvard.edu/dataset.xhtml?persistentId5doi:10.7910/DVN/GDF6Z0 (accessed 1/29/18); 2020 data compiled by authors.

analyzing the evidence

Members of America's Latino community share a linguistic heritage, but they are not politically homogeneous. What factors might account for these differences? Why might so many Cuban Americans have changed their party allegiance between 2004 and 2008?

of Catholics to the Democratic Party, which began in 1928 with the Democrats' nomination of Al Smith for president, the first Catholic nominated for the office by a major party. When Democrat John F. Kennedy became the country's first Catholic president in 1961, that bond was strengthened.[23] The lesson of the Kennedy election is clear: people are much more likely to vote for candidates of their own religion, even after controlling for ideology, party, and other factors. This pattern held true for born-again Christians and Jimmy Carter in 1976, and for Mormons and Mitt Romney in 2012.

Geography. Where we live also molds our sense of identity, affecting characteristics such as how we speak or dress. People in different regions of the country, or even specific states, often strongly identify with others in the same region or state and are thus more likely to trust and to vote for someone from that background. In addition, some people hold negative stereotypes of those from particular regions or states. An unfortunate consequence of the Civil War is a lasting discomfort that many people from the North and South still feel around one another—and that conflict was more than 150 years ago. Many Americans dispute the symbols of the Civil War, asking whether a southern state should have a Confederate battle flag as part of its state's symbol or flying over the statehouse. This issue came to the fore in 2020 during nationwide protests after the killing of George Floyd, an unarmed Black man, by Minneapolis police. In response, institutions including NASCAR prohibited the Confederate battle flag at their events.

Other geographic identities are tied to the type of community one lives in (or prefers to live in). The division between those in urban and rural areas often reflects self-interest; for instance, people from states with predominantly agricultural economies express stronger support for government farm subsidies. But geography also reflects different ways of living, and we tend to identify with people who live like us. Such differences are cultural. Where we shop, what

table 9.2

DISAGREEMENTS AMONG MEN AND WOMEN ON ISSUES OF WAR AND PEACE

GOVERNMENTAL ACTION	APPROVE OF ACTION (%)	
	MEN	WOMEN
Killing of Iranian Major General Qasem Soleimani (2020)	63	43
Sending U.S. ground troops to fight Islamist militants in Iraq and Syria (2015)	52	41
U.S. missile strikes against Syria (2013)	43	30
Use of U.S. troops to attack a terrorist camp (2012)	71	55
Withdrawal of troops from Iraq (2008)	70	52
Use of U.S. troops to intervene in a genocide or civil war (2008)	53	42
Going to war against Iraq (2003)	66	50
Going to war against Iraq (1991)	72	53

SOURCES: Gallup polls, 1991, 1993, and 1999, www.gallup.com/home.aspx; *Washington Post*, 2003, www.washingtonpost.com/politics/polling; Cooperative Congressional Election Study, 2008 and 2012, projects.iq.harvard.edu/cces/home; Langer Research, 2013, www.langerresearch.com; Pew Research Center, 2015, www.people-press.org; ABC News/Washington Post, 2020, www.langerresearch.com/wp-content/uploads/1210a4-Iran.pdf (accessed 3/6/20).

restaurants we go to, what we like to do in our spare time, and so forth—all are aspects of local culture that shape our identification with others of similar backgrounds and ways of living.

Residential segregation can also strengthen other aspects of identity politics. Many Americans tend to live, by choice or not, in neighborhoods separated according to income (which might strengthen social-class identities) and according to race and ethnicity (which reinforces those identities). Those who live in highly segregated neighborhoods have much stronger identification with their own racial groups and also much stronger prejudices against other groups.[24]

Out-groups.   Some groups are defined not by who they are but by who they are not; they are the "out-groups" in society. Often members of an out-group are clearly identifiable, leading to systematic discrimination against or persecution of them. When this treatment is intense and long-lasting, the out-group can develop a distinctive psychology. Social psychologist James Sidanius argues that more numerous groups in all societies systematically discriminate against less numerous groups, whose members therefore develop a common identity and come to see their own situation in the treatment of others of their group.[25] Writing about the psychology of African Americans in the United States, professor and political scientist Michael Dawson calls this perception the "linked fate" of African Americans.[26]

Political, social, and economic discrimination is not limited to race and ethnicity. As we discussed in Chapter 4, the United States has witnessed struggles for equity for many different groups, including women, Catholics, Jews, gays, divorced fathers, and even urban residents. In all of these cases, members of the group had to assert themselves politically to establish or protect their rights to property, to voting, or to equal protection under the laws. Because it is difficult for those without full political rights to work inside the legislative process, these people often had to pursue outsider strategies, including protests, propaganda, and lawsuits. They had been denied rights because they were treated as a class or group, and their identity was the target of discrimination. That same identity, however, served as a source of power, leading these groups to organize and to defend their political rights and identities.

KNOWLEDGE AND INSTABILITY IN PUBLIC OPINION

People are constantly confronted with new political events, issues, and personalities as they watch television, browse the web, talk to friends and family, or read newspapers and magazines. In our democracy, we expect every citizen to have views about how current issues should be addressed and who should be entrusted with political leadership, and we expect people to cast informed votes about what government ought to do. Issues, however, come and go, and people are continually learning about new ones.

Political Knowledge and Democracy

Some Americans know quite a bit about politics, and many hold opinions on a variety of issues. Few Americans, though, devote sufficient time, energy, or attention to politics to really understand or evaluate the many issues that face us. Since the advent of polling in the 1930s, studies have repeatedly found that the average American appears to know little about current events or even basic facts of American government.[27]

Why do people seem to know so little, and how might low levels of information about current events and political institutions affect the long-run health of democracy? Attending to the daily goings-on in Washington or the state capital or city council means spending time, and often money as well, to collect, organize, and digest political information.[28]

Because individuals also anticipate that even political actions they take that are based on being well-informed will rarely make much difference, they may feel it makes more sense to remain ignorant. That is, they may find it more profitable to devote their personal resources—particularly their time—to more narrowly personal matters. Of course, because some kinds of information take little time or money to acquire, such as sound bites from television news shows or tweets from politicians, many people become partially informed. But detailed knowledge is rare.

Precisely because becoming truly knowledgeable about politics requires a substantial investment of time and energy, many Americans gain political information and make political decisions by using shortcuts, labels, and stereotypes, rather than by following current events closely. One "inexpensive" way to become informed is to take cues from trusted others—the local minister, the television commentator or newspaper editorialist, an interest group leader, friends, and relatives.[29] A common shortcut for political evaluation and decision making is to assess new issues and events through the lenses of one's general beliefs and orientation. Thus, if a conservative learns of a plan to expand federal social programs, she might express opposition without needing to pore over the proposal's details.

These shortcuts are handy, but not perfect. Taking cues from others may lead individuals to accept positions that they would reject if they had more information. And general ideological orientations can be imprecise guides to decision making on concrete issues. For example, what position should a liberal take on immigration? Should he favor keeping the United States' borders open to poor people from all over the world, or be concerned that open borders create a pool of surplus labor that permits giant corporations to drive down the wages of American workers? Many other issues defy easy ideological characterization.

Although understandable and perhaps inevitable, widespread inattention to politics weakens American democracy in two ways. First, those who lack political information often do not understand where their political interests lie and thus do not effectively defend them. Second, the large number of politically inattentive or ignorant individuals means that public opinion and the political process can be more easily manipulated by institutions and forces that want to do so.

think it through

Where do you get most of your political information? What are some of the shortcuts you take to become informed? What do you think are some of the advantages of relying on these sources? What about drawbacks?

Instability in Opinion

On most issues and political attitudes, there is great stability to public opinion in the United States. What people want government to do on specific issues and whom they want to have in charge usually changes little from election to election. For example, party identification for a large portion of the American public remains stable for life, as do notions of what is right and wrong, racial and ethnic identities, gender identities, and other cultural identities that are formed early in life. Our occupations and educational levels also shape our economic interests, which tend to be constant throughout our adult lives. Interests, identities, and values, in turn, influence attitudes about when and how government should act.

But at times in history, the majority of Americans' opinions have changed dramatically and rapidly. Between 1945 and 1965, public opinion about federal action to promote racial equality swung from majority opposition to majority support for the Civil Rights Act and the Voting Rights Act, as well as for integration of public schools and transit systems. And since the mid-1990s, there has been a complete about-face in public attitudes toward same-sex marriage. In 1996, Congress passed the Defense of Marriage Act, which, for the purpose of federal benefits, defined marriage as a union between one man and one woman. A CNN/USA Today/Gallup poll in 1996 showed that 68 percent of Americans opposed same-sex marriage and only 27 percent supported it. In 2019, a Pew poll found that those numbers had shifted to 61 percent of Americans *in support* of same-sex marriage and 31 percent in opposition.[30]

In both cases, public attitudes changed greatly within the span of one or two decades. How and why does such dramatic change occur? In part, the answer lies in the evolving positions of the political parties and the public conversations of political elites such as party leaders and candidates, prominent figures in the media, and other celebrities. As elites debate an issue, the public often follows their cues and shifts sides. In the 2020 presidential campaign, for example, which took place shortly after the Black Lives Matter protests, more candidates discussed issues including police reform, racial justice, and reexamining monuments that represent challenging aspects of the nation's history. By putting these issues on the agenda, he caused people to develop opinions about them—or to change or begin to express their previous opinions. As the public learns about an issue, the implications of governmental action or inaction become clearer.

SHAPING OPINION: POLITICAL LEADERS, PRIVATE GROUPS, AND THE MEDIA

The fact that many Americans pay little attention to politics and lack even basic political information creates opportunities to influence how the public thinks. Although direct efforts to manipulate opinion often don't succeed, three forces play especially important roles in shaping opinion. These are the government; private groups, including those backed by politically active billionaires like the Koch brothers and Tom Steyer; and the news media.

Government and Political Leaders

All governments attempt, to a greater or lesser extent, to influence their citizens' beliefs. But the extent to which public opinion is affected by governmental public-relations efforts is probably limited. Despite its size and power, the government is only one source of information in the United States, and very often, its claims are disputed by the media, by interest groups, and at times by opposing forces within the government itself.

Influences on Public Opinion

Government
Political leaders try to present their initiatives and accomplishments in a positive light and to generate positive media coverage. However, their claims are often disputed by the media, interest groups, and opposing forces within the government.

Private Groups
Interest groups work to draw attention to issues and ideas that will further their cause.

The Media
The mass media are Americans' main source of information about government and politics. They influence opinion by bringing attention to particular issues (the agenda-setting effect), priming the public to take a certain view of a political actor, and framing issues and events in a certain way.

Often, too, governmental efforts to manipulate public opinion backfire when the public is made aware of them. Thus, in 1971, such efforts to build popular support for the Vietnam War were hurt when CBS News aired its documentary *The Selling of the Pentagon*, which purported to reveal the techniques, including planted news stories and faked film footage, that had been used to misrepresent the government's activities in Vietnam. These revelations undermined popular trust in the government's claims about the war.

After he assumed office in 2001, President George W. Bush asserted that political leaders should base their programs on the public interest rather than the polls. However, Bush still relied on a low-key polling operation, sufficiently removed from the limelight to allow the president to renounce polling while continuing to make use of survey data.[31] At the same time, the Bush White House developed an extensive public-relations program to bolster popular support for the president's policies and even tried to sway opinion in foreign countries.

President Barack Obama, seeking to maintain the political momentum from his 2008 election campaign, attempted to use social media to generate the same enthusiasm about his legislative agenda. The Obama White House maintained a newsy website, a blog, a YouTube channel, a Facebook page, and a Twitter account, but some criticized the low level of actual engagement with the public. Each of these new media was used like the old media—to talk at people rather than with them, to disseminate information to reporters rather than answer

Social media such as Twitter connect the public with politicians in more direct ways. As a candidate and as president, Trump used Twitter to put his own stamp on the news.

their questions. Indeed, many White House reporters felt that the Obama press office was less accessible than its predecessors'.[32]

Social media, however—especially Twitter—have continued to connect the public with politicians in more direct ways. In the 2016 presidential primary elections, social media proved to be one of Donald Trump's most distinctive campaign advantages over his Republican opponents. By the end of the primary season, Trump had 10.7 million Twitter followers, while Senators Marco Rubio and Ted Cruz each had 1.5 million followers, and Ohio governor John Kasich had only 400,000. Once in office, President Trump continued to rely on Twitter as a way to talk around the mainstream media and put his own stamp on the news.

In 2008, social media was a curiosity. By 2020, it was a political necessity. President Trump mastered the medium as a way to manage the flow of news, and every campaign needed to have a strong social media presence in order to be competitive.[33] The coronavirus pandemic, which began to hit the United States just as the first primaries were being held, created a further need for social media. The campaigns could not hold events and rallies; they could not conduct traditional voter registration drives; they could not send volunteers to towns and cities to canvas door-to-door. The pandemic forced the campaigns to develop virtual events and conventions, to tap social networks to conduct registration drives and canvassing, and, in the case of Democrats, to go all in on vote-by-mail as a way to encourage turnout while preventing the spread of the virus.[34]

Private Groups

The ideas that become prominent in political life are also developed and spread by important economic and political groups seeking to advance their causes. In some instances, private groups espouse values in which they truly believe, in the

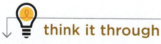

think it through

Do you follow any politicians' social media accounts? If so, how do they use social media to shape their message? Were there posts you found particularly effective in getting out their message? Anything that seemed misleading?

hope of bringing others over to their side—as in the campaign that resulted in the Partial-Birth Abortion Ban Act of 2003, in current federal legislation proposing to ban all abortions after 20 weeks of pregnancy, and legislation in many states proposing further restrictions and even banning abortions.[35] Proponents believed that prohibiting particular sorts of abortions would be a first step toward eliminating all abortions—something they view as a moral imperative.[36]

In other cases, groups promote principles that are designed mainly to further hidden agendas. One famous example is the campaign to outlaw cheap, imported handguns—the so-called Saturday night specials—that was covertly financed by American manufacturers of more expensive firearms. The campaign's organizers claimed that cheap handguns posed a grave risk to the public, but the real goal was to protect the economic well-being of the domestic gun industry. A more recent example is the campaign against the alleged "sweatshop" practices of some American companies that manufacture products in less-developed countries. This campaign is financed mainly by U.S. labor unions seeking to protect their members' jobs by discouraging American firms from manufacturing products abroad.

Typically, ideas are best marketed by groups with access to financial resources and to institutional support. Thus, the development and promotion of conservative ideas in recent years have been greatly facilitated by the millions of dollars that corporations and business organizations, such as the U.S. Chamber of Commerce and the Public Affairs Council, spend each year on public information and "issues management." In addition, businesses have contributed heavily to such conservative research institutions as the Heritage Foundation, the Hoover Institution, and the American Enterprise Institute.[37]

Although they usually lack access to financial assets that match those available to their conservative opponents, liberal intellectuals and professionals have ample organizational skills, access to the media, and practice in communicating and using ideas. During the past four decades, the chief vehicle through which they have advanced their ideas has been public interest groups, organizations that rely heavily on voluntary contributions of time and effort from their members. Such groups include Common Cause, the National Organization for Women, the Sierra Club, Friends of the Earth, the Union of Concerned Scientists, and Physicians for Social Responsibility.[38]

The Policy Principle box on p. 284 explores how political elites in government and business and advocacy groups have influenced public opinion on climate change.

The Media

The communications media are among the most powerful forces operating in the marketplace of ideas. Most Americans say that their primary source of information about public affairs is news media—newspapers, television, radio, and internet news providers. Alternative sources are direct contact with politicians,

the policy principle
PUBLIC OPINION ON CLIMATE CHANGE

The federal government's role in environmental conservation stretches back to the early 1900s, with the creation of the National Park Service and other efforts to preserve natural beauty. In the 1970s, environmental policy become a major component of federal action, with new laws enacted under both Democratic and Republican administrations. Yet in the years since, as new scientific research has provided clearer evidence related to environmental hazards, conflicts have emerged over the government's proper role in protecting the environment.

As scientists have learned more about the effects of human activity on the climate, the issue of climate change has risen on the national agenda—with an expected impact on public opinion as well. According to Gallup polls, in 1997 only 48 percent of Americans agreed that global warming was already occurring, but by 2017, 62 percent of respondents agreed with this statement.[1]

However, this shift in Americans' attitude may seem modest, given the growing scientific consensus on this question. Sociologists Riley E. Dunlap, Aaron McCright, and Jerrod Yarosh emphasize that these modest changes in the aggregate do not tell the whole story. Instead, they call attention to what they refer to as "the political divide on climate change."[2] In 2017, 77 percent of Democrats agreed that climate change was already occurring, compared with only 41 percent of Republicans—a gap of 36 percentage points. In 1997, the gap between Democrats and Republicans on this question was only 4 percentage points. What happened?

Policy makers and researchers have undertaken efforts over the past two decades to inform the public about climate change, but there has been growing skepticism of these messages from the political right, while Democrats are more likely to trust this news than they were in the past. Part of the explanation for this pattern appears to be that polarization on climate change is not really about climate change, but simply reflects the broader trend of party polarization in American politics.

Indeed, despite a history of bipartisanship on environmental issues, elected officials and interest groups today are even more polarized on the issue than the general public is. As elites send a clear signal that climate change is a partisan issue, partisans among the public have shifted their views to align with the elected officials in their party.

Protest against the decision to withdraw from the Paris Agreement in 2018.

The partisan gap in public opinion reached its height following the active involvement of the Obama administration in the 2016 Paris Agreement on climate change, a comprehensive international agreement signed by all 193 United Nations member countries and ratified by 178 as of June 2018. Many Democratic politicians heralded the agreement as a historic achievement, while many Republican elected officials expressed skepticism about the existence of climate change and argued that the treaty imposed unfair burdens on American companies. The issue is no less controversial today: in 2020 the Trump administration completed the complicated, multiyear process of withdrawing the United States from the Paris Agreement.

The case of climate change illustrates some of the limits of public opinion in shaping policy. In fact, the preferences of the American public are often at odds with those of the organized interests that will bear the burdens of governmental regulations. Nowhere have these conflicts been more acute, and the challenges of large-scale collective action more apparent, than in the debate over climate change.

think it through

1. If elites in government and organized groups shape public opinion on climate change (or other issues), what are the implications for representative government?

2. If a majority of Americans (62 percent in 2017) believe that climate change is occurring, is this a good reason for the United States to recommit to the Paris Agreement? Why or why not?

[1] Lydia Saad, "Global Warming Concern at Three-Decade High in U.S.," Gallup, March 14, 2017, http://news.gallup.com/poll/206030/global-warming-concern-three-decade-high.aspx (accessed 6/8/20).

[2] Riley E. Dunlap, Aaron M. McCright, and Jerrod H. Yarosh, "The Political Divide on Climate Change: Partisan Polarization Widens in the U.S.," *Environment: Science and Policy for Sustainable Development* 58, no. 5 (2016): 4–23.

communications from groups and organizations, and conversations with other individuals, such as family members or coworkers. Certainly, few people actually go to Washington to find out what's going on in American politics, and the broad public access to media outlets dwarfs the number of households that receive direct mail from organizations and elected officials. Personal conversation is also an important source of information, but people tend to avoid controversial political topics in casual conversation.

The *mass media*, as the term suggests, can be thought of as mediators. They are the conduits through which information flows. Through newspapers, radio, television, magazines, and the internet, we can learn about what's going on in the world and in our government. As we will see in the following section, providing this opportunity to learn about the world and about politics is the most important way in which the media contribute to public opinion.

THE MEDIA AS AN INSTITUTION

People rely on the media, rather than other sources of information, to find out what's going on in politics and public affairs because it is easy to do so. Almost every community has a newspaper, an increasing number of which appear online in addition to or instead of in print. More households in the United States have a television than have indoor plumbing, and the availability of television news has expanded tremendously in recent decades.

In the 1960s, there were only three television news outlets—CBS, NBC, and ABC. They broadcast evening and nightly national news programs and allowed a half-hour slot for news from local affiliates. The rise of cable television in the 1980s brought a 24-hour news station, Cable News Network (CNN); expanded news programming through the Public Broadcasting System (PBS); and a network devoted exclusively to airing proceedings of Congress and government agencies, C-SPAN. Other important competitors to the "big three" networks eventually emerged, including Fox and the Spanish-language networks Univision and Telemundo. Today there is no shortage of televised news programming available at all hours.[39]

Technological innovations continue to push changes in political communication in the United States. As of 2019, almost 90 percent of Americans use the internet.[40] Traditional media—from the United States and around the world—have moved much of their content online, often providing it for free. The internet has also brought new forms of communication, most notably blogs and Twitter, which provide a platform for anyone to have a say. Several websites, such as Google News and RealClearPolitics, compile and distribute news stories and opinion pieces from many electronic sources. The highly competitive contemporary media environment has radically changed the flow and nature of communication in the United States and the availability of information to the public.

Types of Media

Americans obtain their news from three main sources: broadcast media (radio and television), print media (newspapers and magazines), and, increasingly, the internet. Each of these sources has distinctive institutional characteristics that help to shape the character of its coverage of political events.

Broadcast Media.   Television news reaches more Americans than any other kind of news source. Tens of millions of individuals watch national and local news programs every day. Even in the era of digital news, the most frequented sources of news online are the websites of ABC, CBS, NBC, CNN, and Fox News (with people often going to these sites indirectly via social media). Television news, however, covers relatively few topics and in little depth. More like a series of newspaper headlines connected to pictures, it alerts viewers to issues and events but does little else.

The 24-hour cable news stations, such as CNN, offer more detail and commentary than the networks' evening news shows. In 2003, for example, CNN, Fox, and MSNBC provided 24-hour coverage of the start of the war in Iraq, including on-the-scene reports, expert commentary, and interviews with government officials. In this instance, the depth of coverage by these networks rivaled that of print media. Cable television continues to grow in importance as a news source (Figure 9.2).

Radio news is essentially a headline service without pictures. Usually devoting five minutes per hour to news, radio stations announce the day's major events

figure 9.2

AMERICANS' MAIN SOURCES FOR NEWS, 2019

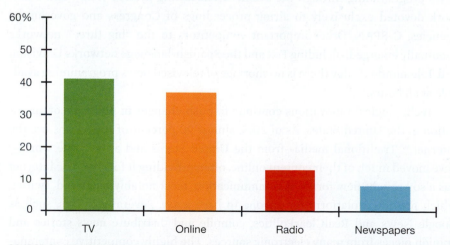

Percentage who often get news on each platform:

SOURCE: Pew Research Center: Journalism and Media, "Nearly As Many Americans Prefer to Get Their Local News Online as Prefer the TV Set," March 26, 2019, www.journalism.org/2019/03/26/nearly-as-many-americans-prefer-to-get-their-local-news-online-as-prefer-the-tv-set (accessed 5/20/20).

with little detail. News stations such as WTOP (Washington, D.C.) and WCBS (New York City) generally repeat the same stories each hour to present them to new listeners.

Radio talk shows have also become important sources of commentary and opinion. Numerous conservative radio hosts, such as Rush Limbaugh, have huge audiences and have helped mobilize support for conservative political causes and candidates. Liberals have had less success in talk radio and complain that biased radio coverage has hurt them in elections.

In recent years, much news content, especially of local news, has shifted away from politics toward "soft news"—focusing on celebrities, health tips, consumer advice, and other topics more likely to entertain than enlighten. Even much political coverage is soft. For example, in the 2016 presidential campaign, when Donald Trump held a press conference in which he promoted one of his golf courses, his winery, "Trump steaks," and "Trump water," he drew significant media attention at the expense of other candidates.

Print Media.   Newspapers remain an important source of news, even though they are not most Americans' primary news source. Also important are magazines of opinion and analysis such as the *Economist*, the *New Republic*, and the *National Review*, whose relatively small readership includes many politically influential Americans. Two other periodicals—the *Hill* and *Roll Call*—are important sources of political news for Washington insiders such as members of Congress, congressional staffers, and lobbyists.

Although the print media have a smaller audience than their cousins in broadcasting have, it is an audience that tends to be influential. The broadcast media rely on leading newspapers such as the *New York Times* and the *Washington Post* to set their news agendas. The broadcast media do very little actual reporting; they primarily cover stories that have been first reported by the print media. One might almost say that if an event is not covered in the *New York Times*, it is not likely to appear on the *CBS Evening News*. An important exception is "breaking" news, which broadcast media can carry as it unfolds or soon after, while the print media must catch up later.

Today, however, the newspaper industry is in serious economic trouble. Online competition has dramatically reduced newspapers' revenues from traditional print advertising, such as retail, "help wanted," and personal ads. Newspaper advertising revenue has dropped by more than 60 percent over the past decade—from $50 billion in 2006 to less than $15 billion in 2018—despite a rise in revenue from papers' own online advertising.[41] Facing serious financial difficulties, some papers have closed (such as the *Rocky Mountain News* in Denver) or switched to an online-only format (such as the *Seattle Post Intelligencer*). And in 2013, the Graham family, which had owned the *Washington Post* for three generations, surprised the industry by announcing the sale of the paper to Jeffrey Bezos, founder and CEO of Amazon.com.

All these changes signal a wider transformation of print media that may leave the country with few or no print newspapers—the traditional "press"—in the future. The great unknowns are whether the newspapers can somehow reverse that trend and whether online venues, such as social media, blogs, or news apps for mobile devices, can adequately replace print newspapers, especially in providing news about state and local politics and public affairs.[42]

The Internet.   The internet combines the depth of print media coverage with the timeliness of television and radio, but it goes much further. Internet news providers have become significant competitors to traditional media outlets, and most daily newspapers and television outlets—such as the *Wall Street Journal* and the *New York Times*, CNN and Fox News—also sponsor websites through which they attract audiences to their traditional media. Viewers see content that resembles a traditional newspaper article or headline news on a television broadcast, but can choose which stories or items to click on for the full content, including video and audio material not available in a print paper.

Unlike a print newspaper, which is wholly new every day, a website can keep important stories up for many days, and most websites focusing on news also contain easily searchable archives. Besides those sponsored by traditional print or broadcast media, other news sites have emerged, some of which function as aggregators, accumulating news on a given topic from many different sources. Perhaps the most powerful aggregator is Google, whose news service compiles information from outlets as different as the *Wall Street Journal* and Al Jazeera, Reuters and the Associated Press, and the *Daily Star* in Lebanon and *Shanghai Daily*.

More specialized sites, like BuzzFeed, Politico, and the Huffington Post—three of the most frequently visited sites for news online—offer a wide range of content, including commentary and analysis in addition to reporting. Some sites provide more focused content. For instance, Slate.com specializes in commentary, and Cook Political Report, in analysis. Podcasts represent one of the fastest-growing ways that people receive programs, including the news. From 2008 to 2019, the percentage of adults in the United States who said they had listened to a podcast in the previous month grew from 8 percent to 32 percent.

Social media have also transformed online provision of the news by changing how news information is distributed, how it is generated, and even what form and format it takes. Both Facebook and Twitter have contributed to political mobilization by creating virtual social networks where groups of like-minded individuals can quickly and easily share information. In 2018, a majority of American adults—68 percent—said they got news on social media.[43] The Analyzing the Evidence section on pp. 290–1 explores where Americans get news about politics.

In addition, social media provide a platform for political candidates, elected officials, and government agencies, which have been quick to adopt Facebook and Twitter as ways to communicate with their supporters or the public without the editorial filters of newspapers or radio or television stations and to provide them with a continuous feed of new information. Obama was the first American president to use social media extensively in his 2008 campaign for president. During the 2012 and 2016 presidential campaigns, the internet was the candidates' medium of choice. In 2016, Hillary Clinton kicked off her presidential campaign with a YouTube video. Both she and Donald Trump made particular use of Twitter, with their campaigns often tweeting multiple times a day. Social media took on new importance during the 2020 presidential race at the height of the coronavirus pandemic. As neither Trump nor Democratic candidate Biden were able to engage directly with voters, they relied heavily on social media to get out their message.

The immediacy of Twitter feeds, in which anyone experiencing an event can provide reactions and reports in real time without editorial filters, is particularly attractive to government offices and politicians seeking to distribute information and commentary. For example, during the coronavirus outbreak in the spring of 2020, Twitter hosted several hashtags for COVID-19-related information, including @COVID19Tracking and #COVID19. Twitter launched a COVID-19 dataset of tweets for approved researchers and developers to improve analysis of the spread of the epidemic.[44]

The internet differs from traditional media outlets in another important way: it enables people to get involved directly. Individual citizens can now more easily help create the news and interpret it. Most news sites provide space for people to post their own photos, videos, and blogs of events, and those at the scene of a crime, natural disaster, or important political event can often provide more coverage of the story (and sometimes even better and faster coverage) than a reporter can.

Regulation of the Media

In most countries, the government controls media content and owns the largest media outlets. In the United States, the government neither owns nor controls the communications networks, but it does regulate content and ownership of the broadcast media.

Broadcast Media. American radio and television are regulated by the Federal Communications Commission (FCC), an independent agency. Radio and TV stations must renew their FCC licenses every five years. Through regulations prohibiting obscenity, indecency, and profanity, the FCC has tried to keep stations from airing explicit material between 6 a.m. and 10 p.m., the hours when children are most likely to be in the audience, though it has enforced these rules haphazardly.

The sheer number of news outlets has ensured that different perspectives are well represented in the media. Popular political commentators such as Sean Hannity and Rachel Maddow, for example, offer clear conservative and liberal viewpoints, respectively.

For more than 60 years, the FCC implemented the Communications Act of 1934 and aimed to regulate and promote competition in the broadcast industry, but in 1996, Congress passed the Telecommunications Act, a broad effort to eliminate most regulations in this area. The act loosened restrictions on media ownership and allowed for telephone companies, cable television providers, and broadcasters to compete for the provision of telecommunications services. Following passage of the act, several mergers between telephone

analyzing the evidence

Where Do Americans Get News about Politics?

Contributed by **Rasmus Kleis Nielsen**, *University of Oxford*

Most of political life is distant from our own personal experience and social circles. Thus, when we know something about a recent international summit, a deal made in Congress, or a war abroad, it is usually because someone covered it as news.

How people get news, however, is changing and varies across generations. Throughout the twentieth century, news media were Americans' number one source of information about politics. Traditionally, newspapers have produced the most detailed and extensive coverage, and television has reached the widest audiences and was for several decades the most important source of news for many.

The development and spread of digital media from the 1990s onward has changed the news media landscape. Newspapers have seen declining readership, make less money, and therefore invest less in news production. Television audiences have been more stable but are increasingly made up of older people. Younger people increasingly get news online.

By 2015, 85 percent of all Americans used the internet and 64 percent had a smartphone.[1] Among people who are online, digital media have now overtaken television as the most important sources of news. In 2015, 43 percent of American internet users named digital sources as their most important sources of news, compared with 40 percent who named television and 5 percent who named printed newspapers.

Main Source of News by Age

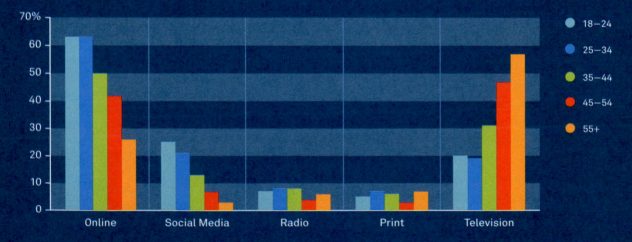

Legend: 18–24, 25–34, 35–44, 45–54, 55+

1 Aaron Smith, "U.S. Smartphone Use in 2015," Pew Research Center, April 1, 2015, www.pewinternet.org/2015/04/01/us-smartphone-use-in-2015 (accessed 6/10/20).

There are clear generational differences in how people get news. Older Americans rely far more on traditional media, such as television, than do younger people, who mostly get news online. For some people, getting news online is about going directly to the websites and apps of news organizations, whether newspapers like the *New York Times*, broadcasters like NBC, or digital-only news sites like HuffPost. But for many, online news is increasingly accessed via digital intermediaries like search engines, messaging apps, and social media. In 2015, 11 percent of American internet users named social media their main sources of news.

Relative Importance of News: Twitter and Facebook Compared

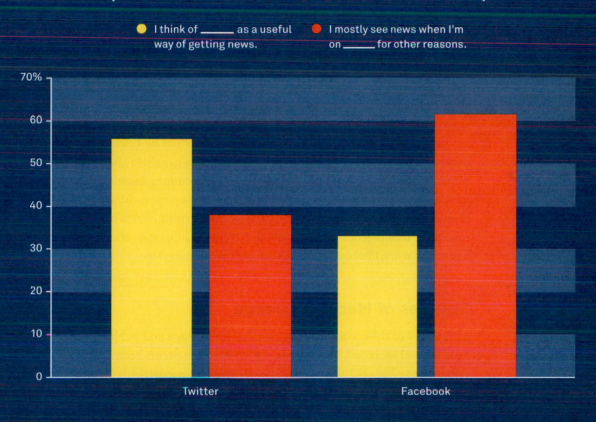

● I think of _____ as a useful way of getting news.

● I mostly see news when I'm on _____ for other reasons.

The graph above shows that some social media, such as Twitter, are often directly linked with news. In contrast, people mostly visit Facebook for other reasons but often stumble upon news when on the site. A changing media environment has sometimes been associated with the rise of "selective exposure," where people seek out information that reflects their existing views. However, the rise of widely used social media like Facebook seems to be associated with a resurgence in "incidental exposure," where people come across news unintentionally.

SOURCE: Surveys of Consumers, www.sca.isr.umich.edu/tables.html (accessed 6/10/20); and author's compilation.

 → Where do you think newer forms of social media frequently used by younger people—including TikTok and Instagram—would appear in the figure above?

and cable companies and among different segments of the entertainment media produced a greater concentration of media ownership.

The federal government has used its licensing power to impose several regulations that can affect the political content of radio and TV broadcasts. The first is the **equal time rule**, under which broadcasters must provide candidates for the same political office equal opportunities to communicate their messages to the public. The second regulation is the **right of rebuttal**, which requires that broadcasters give individuals the opportunity to respond to the airing of personal attacks on them. Beyond these rules, the government does very little to regulate media in the United States.

Freedom of the Press.   Unlike broadcast media, print media are not subject to federal regulation. Indeed, the great principle underlying the federal government's relationship with the press is the prohibition against **prior restraint**, or censorship. Beginning with the landmark 1931 case of *Near v. Minnesota*, the U.S. Supreme Court has held that, except under the most extraordinary circumstances, the First Amendment prohibits government agencies from trying to prevent newspapers or magazines from publishing whatever they wish.[45]

Even though newspapers and magazines may not be restrained from publishing whatever they want, they may be subject to penalties after doing so. Historically, the law of libel has provided that publications found to have printed false and malicious stories can be compelled to pay compensation to those whose reputations they harm. Over time, however, American courts have greatly narrowed the meaning of libel and made it extremely difficult, particularly for public figures, to win a libel case against a newspaper or magazine.

Sources of Media Influence

The power of the media to affect political knowledge and public opinion stems from several sources. Learning through mass media occurs both actively and passively. Active learning occurs when people search for a particular type of program or information: by turning on the television news to find out what has happened in national and international affairs, or by searching the web for information about their member of Congress. But passive learning may be just as important.

For example, many entertainment programs refer to current events and issues, such as social issues or elections, so those who watch a program for entertainment gain information about politics at the same time. One study found that voters learned as much from *Oprah* as from the evening news.[46] Such soft news is particularly important because people who are otherwise not interested in politics get much of their news from soft news sources, and because content containing soft news is far more likely to be distributed over social networks than hard news.[47] Political advertising is perhaps the most common form of passive information. During the final month of national political campaigns, often three or four political advertisements air during one commercial break in a prime-time television program.

equal time rule
An FCC requirement that broadcasters provide candidates for the same political office an equal opportunity to communicate their messages to the public.

right of rebuttal
An FCC requirement that broadcasters give individuals the opportunity to respond to the airing of personal attacks on them.

prior restraint
An effort by a government agency to block publication of material by a newspaper or magazine; censorship.

Mass media are our primary source for information about current affairs. They influence how Americans understand politics, not just through how much information they make available but also through what they present and how they present and interpret it. Editors, reporters, and others involved in preparing the content of the news must ultimately decide which topics to cover, which facts to include, and whom to interview. Journalists usually try to present issues fairly, but it is difficult, perhaps impossible, to be perfectly objective.

Psychologists have identified two potential pathways through which media coverage shapes public opinion. First, it has an **agenda-setting effect**, leading people to think about some issues rather than others; they make some considerations more significant than others. Suppose, for example, that the local television news covers crime to the exclusion of all else. When someone who regularly watches the local news thinks about the mayoral election, crime is more likely to be the primary consideration than it is for someone who does not watch the local news. Psychologists call this phenomenon **priming**.

In addition, news coverage of an issue affects the way the issue is seen in the public mind. Coverage of crime, to continue the example, may include a report on every murder that happens in a large city. Such coverage would likely make it seem that murder occurs much more often than it actually does. This misperception might, in turn, give viewers an exaggerated sense of their risk of violent crime and thus increase their support for tough police practices. **Framing** refers to the media's power to influence how events and issues are interpreted.[48]

Priming and framing are often viewed as twin evils. One can distract us from other important problems, and the other can make us think about an issue or a politician in a biased way. Their combined effects on public opinion depend ultimately on the variety of issues covered by the media and the diversity of perspectives represented. That, after all, is the idea behind the guarantee of a free press in the First Amendment. Free and open communications media make it most likely that people will learn about important issues, learn enough to distinguish good ideas from bad ones, and learn which political leaders and parties can best represent their interests.

In this regard, the most significant framing effects take the form of the balance in the information available to people. Those in politics—elected officials, candidates, leaders of organized groups—work hard to influence what the news covers. A competitive political environment usually translates into a robust flow of information.

However, in some political environments only one view gets expressed and is reflected in the media. Congressional elections are a case in point. Incumbent members today typically raise about three times as much money as their challengers. As a result, House elections often have a significant imbalance in the amount of advertising and news coverage between the campaign of the incumbent and that of the challenger. This imbalance will likely affect public opinion, because voters hear the incumbent's message so much more often.

agenda-setting effect
The power of the media to focus public attention on particular issues.

priming
The use of media coverage to make the public take a particular view of an event or a public figure.

framing
The influence of the media over how events and issues are interpreted.

Similarly, presidential press conferences and events receive much more coverage than do their counterparts featuring leaders of the House or Senate. This imbalance gives the president the upper hand in setting the political agenda, because the public is more likely to hear presidential arguments for a particular policy than congressional challenges to it.

Today, it is easy to learn about public affairs and to hear different opinions—even when we don't want to. Furthermore, the wider variety of media available now has likely made learning easier for people today (compared with prior generations, who relied on a much more limited range of information sources) and reduced some of the biases growing out of priming and framing. No single voice or perspective dominates our multifaceted media environment and competitive political system. And biases in the media often reflect not the lack of outlets or restrictive editorial control but failures of political competition.

CONCLUSION

How much does public opinion influence the actions of elected representatives? What is the role of the media in a representative democracy? In democratic nations, leaders should pay attention to public opinion, and most evidence suggests that they do. Although public policy and public opinion do not always coincide, in general the government's actions are consistent with citizens' preferences. One study found that between 1935 and 1979, in about two-thirds of all cases, significant changes in public opinion were followed within one year by changes in governmental policy consistent with the shift in the popular mood.[49] Other studies have come to similar conclusions about public opinion and governmental policy at the state level.[50]

Do these results suggest that politicians pander to the public? The answer is no. Elected leaders don't always follow the results of public-opinion polls, but instead use polling to sell their policy proposals and thereby shape the public's views.[51] Nevertheless, there are always areas of disagreement between opinion and policy. For example, despite the support of a large majority of Americans for some form of screening of prospective gun owners in the wake of frequent mass shootings in recent years, Congress has not responded. Most Americans are far less concerned with the rights of criminal defendants than the federal courts seem to be. And even though most people say they oppose U.S. military intervention in other nations, interventions continue and often win public approval after the fact.

Several factors contribute to a lack of consistency between opinion and governmental policy. First, those in the majority on a particular issue may not be as intensely committed to their preference as supporters of the minority viewpoint, who may be more willing to commit time, energy, and other resources to backing up their opinions. In the case of gun control, for example, although proponents are in the majority by a wide margin, most do not see the issue as critically important to themselves and make little effort to advance their cause. Opponents, by contrast, are intensely committed, well organized, and well financed; as a result, they usually carry the day.

A second important reason why public policy and public opinion may not coincide has to do with the nature of the American system of government. The framers of the Constitution, as we saw in Chapter 2, aimed to create a system of government that was based on popular consent but did not invariably translate shifting popular sentiments into public policies. As a result, the system includes arrangements such as an appointed judiciary that can produce policy decisions running contrary to prevailing public opinion—at least for a time.

Inconsistencies between opinion and policy might be reduced if the federal government of the United States used ballot initiatives and referenda, as many states do. These processes allow proposals to be enacted into law (or rejected) directly by the voters, bypassing most of the normal machinery of representative government. Among other issues, ballot measures in the states have been used to restrict property tax increases; ban the use of racial or gender preferences in government employment, contracting, and university admissions; enact environmental regulations; legalize marijuana; limit campaign spending; regulate auto insurance; change the rules governing redistricting; and opt out of the Affordable Care Act. Some states even use referenda to pass budget agreements when the legislature does not want to be held responsible for casting unpopular votes.

However, government by initiative and referendum offers little opportunity for reflection and compromise. Voters are presented with a proposition, usually sponsored by a special-interest group and possibly opposed by other groups, and must take it or leave it. Perhaps public opinion on the issue lies somewhere

Ballot initiatives and referenda allow the public to decide issues directly. For example, in 2020, Californians voted on whether or not ride-share apps such as Lyft and Uber should recognize their drivers as employees, rather than independent contractors, making the drivers eligible for sick leave and other benefits.

between the positions held by various interest groups. In a representative assembly, as opposed to a referendum campaign, the outcome might be a compromise measure more satisfactory to more voters than either ballot alternative. This capacity for compromise is one reason the Founders strongly favored representative government rather than direct democracy.

When all is said and done, however, the actions of the American government rarely remain out of line with popular sentiment for very long. A major reason is, of course, the electoral process, to which we turn next.

Key Terms

public opinion 264

socialization 268

liberal 269

conservative 269

gender gap 275

equal time rule 292

right of rebuttal 292

prior restraint 292

agenda-setting effect 293

priming 293

framing 293

Check Your Understanding

1. What is public opinion? Identify the techniques political scientists and political consultants use to try and understand public opinion.

2. What are the factors that shape individual opinion? Identify several examples of each.

3. What are the two main ideologies in the United States? How do political ideologies help people understand political or cultural situations?

4. How might low levels of information about current events and political institutions affect the long-run health of democracy?

5. What are the three main forces that shape public opinion?

6. How has technology changed the media landscape in the United States? How does this impact the type of news available to communities?

 INQUIZITIVE

Earn a better grade on your test. InQuizitive personalizes your learning path to help you master the concepts from this chapter. In a recent efficacy study of American government students, InQuizitive increased test scores by an average of 17 points (see back cover).

CHAPTER TEN

ELECTIONS

The American constitution created a system of frequent, regular elections to allow the public the opportunity to express its will and to change the course of its government when needed. In 2008 and 2016, the U.S. public embraced a new direction, giving one party control of the House, the Senate, and the Presidency. But, in 2010 and again in 2018, Americans used their voice at the midterm elections to rein in a president and Congress that the majority of people felt had pushed public policies that did not reflect what they wanted. In 2020, the public chose a new administration to deal with the coronavirus and its effects on the economy and society. The public initially gave President Trump high marks in dealing with the virus, but as the pandemic spread unabated the public sought a new team to manage the crisis. The public did not, however, embrace the Democrats in Congress. Instead, they chose divided government, hoping that the two parties would come together to address the nation's problems and that no one party would dictate public policy.

Representative government establishes both limits and possibilities for public influence in American political life. On the one hand, citizens are generally limited to choosing representatives through elections. Though several states and municipalities allow voting on some laws and specific decisions, at the federal level Americans cannot directly decide such matters as which laws are enacted, what the nation's tax rates will be, or whether to declare war. On the other hand, representative government makes it possible for citizens to elect the officials who *can* make those decisions. Citizens can elect individuals who they believe will champion their views and interests, and they can send those same officials packing at the next election if they are disappointed.

While this idea seems simple, several problems may arise. One problem is, how do we know that voters are selecting the best people for the job? Voters want to choose people who have the competence to write effective legislation and are attuned to citizens' views and interests. Voters, however, may not have the information or political knowledge (see Chapter 9) to accurately judge which candidates possess those characteristics.

A second problem is that once elected, representatives may believe that their actions cannot easily be monitored and may not do the job for which they were

In 2020, the public chose a new administration to deal with the coronavirus and its effects on the economy and society, electing Joe Biden, the Democratic candidate, as president. The public did not, however, embrace the Democrats in Congress. Instead, they chose divided government, hoping that the two parties would come together to address the nation's problems and that no one party would dictate public policy.

chosen. It is, indeed, very difficult for citizens to know everything officials do in office. Despite media scrutiny, officials may make backdoor deals, fail to pursue constituents' interests, or engage in behind-the-scenes self-serving conduct. Voters, for their part, may not do as much as they could to monitor the actions of their representatives. So, when the official is up for reelection, constituents may not be able to make a fully informed decision.

In addition to the informational problems that may occur in a representative democracy, another possible problem has to do with how the electoral process itself affects society. Voting is part of the glue that holds American institutions and society together. The opportunity to participate in the selection of leaders provides citizens with a sense that the government is responsive to their needs and wishes. The chance to participate in elections can increase popular cooperation with laws, programs, taxes, and military service, because citizens feel that they have had a say in government.

Elections, however, do not always function smoothly and may divide people rather than bringing them together through participation in politics. The framers of the Constitution were concerned that elections could sometimes become so hotly contested that they would be accompanied by "tumult and disorder."[1] Rather than integrating citizens into a shared political process, such elections would "convulse" the community with "violent movements." The elections of 2008, 2016, and 2020 show that the public is willing to embrace change, a new direction, but the elections of 2010 and 2018 reveal that the public will rein in the government when it overreaches.

- **How do electoral rules shape the way citizens are represented in government?**
- **How do voters decide who should represent them?**

In this chapter, we look at how the institutional features of American elections shape the way citizens' goals and preferences are reflected in their government. Then we consider how voters decide among the candidates and questions put before them on the ballot and seek to determine whether voters are able to make wise choices at the polls.

Learning Objectives

- Describe the main rules and procedures of elections in the United States.

- Explain the key factors that influence whether people vote and how they choose between candidates.

- Outline common features of campaign strategy.

- Analyze the 2020 election campaigns and results.

INSTITUTIONS OF ELECTIONS

We have suggested that the relationship between citizens and elected politicians is that of principals and agents. This "agency approach" treats the typical citizen as someone who would much rather spend time and effort on his or her own private affairs than on governance. He or she therefore chooses to delegate governance to agents—politicians—who are controlled through elections. In this approach, citizens' control of their political agents is emphasized. Another possible way to view the citizen-politician relationship, the "consent approach," emphasizes the historical reality that the right of the citizen to participate in his or her own governance, mainly through the act of voting, is designed by those in power to justify and strengthen their own rule. By giving their consent, citizens provide this justification.

Whether seen as a means to control politicians (the agency approach) or to justify governance by them (the consent approach), elections allow citizens to participate in political life on a routine and peaceful basis. Indeed, American voters have the opportunity to select and, if they so desire, remove some of their most important leaders. In this way, they can intervene in and influence the government's policies.

Yet it is important to recall that elections are not spontaneous events, but formal governmental institutions. While giving citizens a chance to participate in politics, they also give the government a good deal of control over which citizens will participate, as well as when, where, and how. Electoral processes are governed by rules and procedures that are a mix of state and federal laws, legal decisions, and local administrative practices. See the Policy Principle section on p. 301 for a discussion on one of these practices, automatic voter registration. These rules provide those in power with significant opportunity to regulate the character—and perhaps also the consequences—of mass political participation.

the policy principle
ELECTION ADMINISTRATION AND AUTOMATIC VOTER REGISTRATION

Efforts to increase voter turnout often point out the two-step process of voting in the United States as a particular problem. Citizens must first register to vote, and only then can they cast a ballot. In most states, there is a waiting period between those two steps that makes registration a significant barrier to voting.

At the time of the 2020 election, 17 states and the District of Columbia had enacted Election-Day registration (sometimes called same-day registration) to make it easier for people who arrived at the polls to register and vote. However, potential voters often do not know that they have that option. In an effort to improve voter turnout, in the last five years, many states have taken a more aggressive step to knock down the registration barrier: automatic voter registration (AVR).

AVR is an automated process in which data on state residents, generally from the Department of Motor Vehicles (DMV), is electronically transferred to state voter registration systems without requiring individuals to fill out paper voter registration forms. These data also allow for regular updates to existing voter rolls as individuals update their addresses with the DMV or other state agencies.

In January 2016, Oregon became the first state to implement AVR. Now, when Oregonians go to the DMV, they are automatically registered to vote. Each individual who is automatically registered receives a mailing letting them know they were registered and giving them 21 days to return a card in order to opt out of their registration. Since Oregon implemented this reform, 14 other states and the District of Columbia have enacted AVR, although the policy details differ a bit between states and states are in different stages of implementation and policy evaluation.

A 2019 study showed that enactment of these policies significantly increases the number of people registered to vote and that a substantial portion of these newly registered individuals actually do vote, although usually at a rate lower than the overall (already registered) population.[1] It is unclear whether this increase in turnout is due to registration itself, or whether the cleaner and more up-to-date voter files allow candidates and parties to do a better job of reaching out to and mobilizing potential voters.

Although AVR is a new electoral reform, it is gaining attention and support; in fact, AVR is often able to secure bipartisan support given its potential to improve both

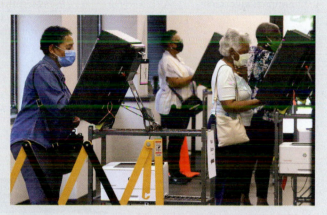

Automatic voter registration initiatives ease obstacles to the ballot.

access to voting (a priority among Democrats) and the integrity of the voting system (a priority among Republicans). Opponents of AVR question whether the opt-out mailing is enough to ensure that an individual has a true choice to register and, thus, whether AVR infringes on citizens' First Amendment rights. Many states have addressed this concern by providing the notification and method of opting out directly to individuals while they are at the DMV. Others express concerns about voter fraud and the privacy needs of particular groups of people who may not want their home addresses to be publicly available on a voter roll (such as victims of domestic violence). And implementation problems in California, among other states, have illustrated the capacity and planning needed to enact any sweeping electoral reform.

With the rapid move to voting by mail in light of the 2020 COVID-19 pandemic, Americans may become more comfortable with significant changes to how we vote. AVR is a reform that would help as many citizens as possible have access to the voting booth.

think it through:

1. What correlation would you expect to see between the use of AVR and voter turnout in the 17 states using this process?

2. In your opinion, what are the most compelling arguments against AVR?

[1] Kevin Morris and Peter Dunphy, "AVR Impact on State Voter Registration," Brennan Center for Justice, 2019, https://www.brennancenter.org/sites/default/files/2019-08/Report_AVR_Impact_State_Voter_Registration.pdf (accessed 9/17/20).

THE GROWTH OF THE U.S. ELECTORATE, 1790–2018

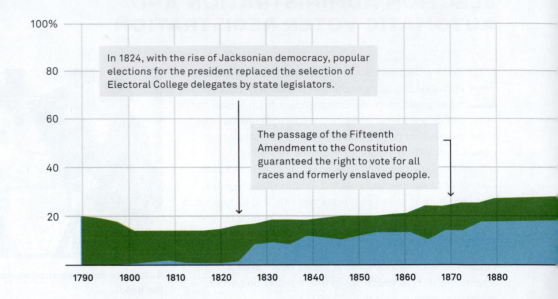

- 🟩 % of population eligible to vote in national elections
- 🟦 % of population that voted in national election

In 1824, with the rise of Jacksonian democracy, popular elections for the president replaced the selection of Electoral College delegates by state legislators.

The passage of the Fifteenth Amendment to the Constitution guaranteed the right to vote for all races and formerly enslaved people.

TIMEPLOT SOURCE: Statistical Abstract of the United States (various years), Bureau of the Census, www.census.gov/library/publications/time-series/statistical_abstracts.html; United States Election Project, "2018 November General Election Turnout Rates," http://www.electproject.org/home/voter-turnout/voter-turnout-data (accessed 5/6/20).

Four features of U.S. election laws deserve particular emphasis:

1. *Who.* The United States provides for universal adult suffrage: all citizens over the age of 18 have the right to vote.[2]

2. *How.* Americans vote in secret and choose among candidates for office using a form of ballot called the Australian ballot.

3. *Where.* The United States selects almost all elected officials through single-member districts that have equal populations.

4. *What* it takes to win. For most offices in the United States, the candidate who wins a plurality—the most votes among all of those competing for a given seat—wins the election, whether or not he or she wins a majority of the total votes cast.

Each of these rules has substantial effects on elections and representation. Before we explore them in more detail, it is important to note that the rules governing elections are not static. The institutions of American elections have evolved over time—through legislation, court decisions, administrative rulings of agencies, and public agitation for electoral reform—to our present system of universal suffrage with secret voting and to the use of single-member districts with plurality rule. But this is only one era, and the future will likely bring further innovations.

timeplot

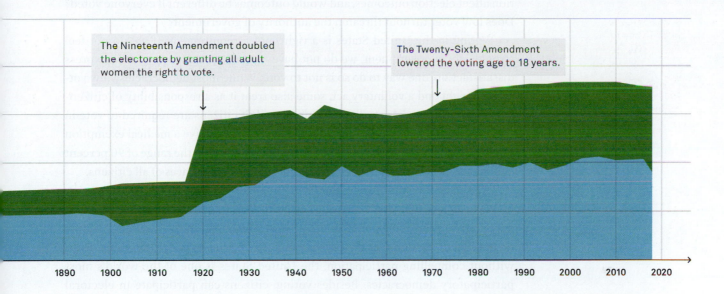

The Nineteenth Amendment doubled the electorate by granting all adult women the right to vote.

The Twenty-Sixth Amendment lowered the voting age to 18 years.

1890 1900 1910 1920 1930 1940 1950 1960 1970 1980 1990 2000 2010 2020

This fluidity raises new issues about secrecy and the form of the ballot; it also provides new opportunities for reform (such as instant runoff voting). Such changes rarely come about through carefully planned federal legislation. Instead, new election institutions typically emerge out of the experiences and experiments of local election officials and state laws. Let's take a closer look at the key institutional features of American elections.

Who Can Vote: Defining the Electorate

Over the course of American history the electorate has expanded greatly. At the beginning of the Republic, voting rights in most states were restricted to White men over 21 years of age, and many states further required that those people own property. Today, all citizens over 18 years of age are allowed to vote, and the courts, the Department of Justice, and activist organizations work to eliminate discrimination in elections.[3] The Timeplot above compares the percentage of the American population eligible to vote with the percentage of the population that has voted in national elections.

While the right to vote is universal, the exercise of this right is not. In a typical U.S. presidential election, approximately 60 percent of those eligible to vote actually do so. In midterm elections for Congress, about 45 percent of the eligible electorate votes. And in local elections, the percentage of people who vote can be quite low; some city elections attract only 10–20 percent of the eligible electorate.[4] Some of the most basic questions about the functioning and health of our democracy concern voting. Who votes and why? How does nonparticipation affect election outcomes, and would outcomes be different if everyone voted? Does low voter turnout threaten the authority of government?

Voting in the United States is a right, not a requirement. If we do not feel strongly about government, we do not have to participate. If we want to express dissatisfaction, one way to do so is not to vote. While most democracies view voting as a right and a voluntary act, some also treat it as a responsibility of citizenship. In Mexico and Australia, for example, adult citizens are required to vote in national elections; those who fail to vote must either receive a medical exemption or pay a fine. That requirement guarantees turnout rates in the range of 90 percent and makes election results a better reflection of the preferences of all citizens.

The idea of compulsory voting is not viewed favorably in the United States, however. Those who don't vote don't want to face a potential fine; those who do may not want the "nonvoters" diluting their power, and most Americans simply do not like the notion that the government can compel us to do something. Even without compelling participation, the United States is one of the world's most participatory democracies. Besides voting, citizens can participate in electoral politics by blogging and posting on social media, speaking with others, joining organizations, giving money, and in many other ways. By nearly all of these measures, Americans participate in politics at much higher rates than do people in nearly every other country.[5]

That said, levels of U.S. voter participation in the second half of the twentieth century were quite low compared with those in other Western democracies[6] and in earlier eras of American history, especially the late nineteenth century (see Figure 10.1).[7] The five decades after World War II saw a steady erosion of voter turnout, with participation in presidential elections falling below 50 percent in 1996. That decline stirred Congress to reform voter registration rules in the mid-1990s. Turnout rates have grown considerably since then, in response both to legal changes and to the recognition by the political parties and candidates that they could influence elections by bringing people back to the polls. In 2016, 61 percent of the adult citizens in the United States voted.[8] In 2018, 48 percent of adult citizens in the United States voted. Such a drop in turnout from the presidential to the midterm elections almost always happens in the United States, as the presidential election attracts the most interest. In 2020, turnout lept. One hundred and fifty million Americans—66.4 percent of the eligible electorate—voted to choose a new president and Congress. The electorate was energized by pressing issues such as the economy, race relations, reproductive rights and, most importantly, COVID.

Who votes and why? The answers lie partly in the motivations and behaviors of individuals and partly in the laws of democracy, which are the institutions of elections. Later in this chapter we will discuss the correlates of voting to understand who chooses to vote. We discuss here the institutions and how they define and limit voting behavior.

figure 10.1

VOTER TURNOUT IN U.S. PRESIDENTIAL ELECTIONS, 1860–2020

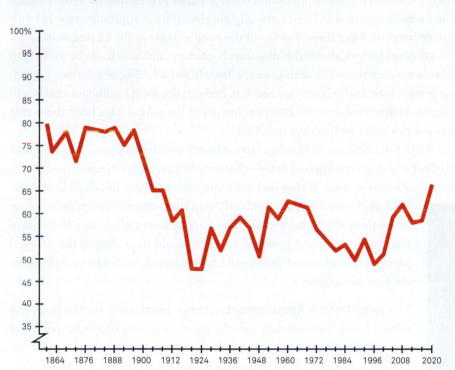

NOTE: Data reflect the population of eligible voters; the percentage of the voting-age population that voted would be smaller.

SOURCES: For 1860–2016, U.S. Census Bureau data. 2020 data reflect author's calculations.

analyzing the evidence

Voter turnout for American presidential elections was significantly higher in the nineteenth century than in the twentieth. What institutional changes caused the sharp decline in turnout between 1890 and 1910? Why did these changes have such a dramatic effect? Did they have any positive outcomes?

Measuring Voter Turnout and the Effects of Restrictions on Voting.
Turnout rate is a term that is simple to define, but some of the details of the definition are important to understand, especially when making comparisons over time or across countries. This rate is the number of people who vote in a given election divided by the number who would have been allowed to vote in it. The first part of the ratio is relatively uncontroversial—the number of individuals who cast ballots.[9] The appropriate baseline, though, is more difficult to define.

Most commonly, the baseline used in turnout rates given for the United States (and other countries) is the entire population old enough to vote (all adults). This voting-age baseline understates the true turnout rate, because it includes noncitizens and people who are incarcerated or (in some states) not allowed to vote because they have been convicted of a felony. Because it is difficult to get reliable population figures for these groups, however, calculating the voting-*eligible* population can be controversial. Following the usual practice, we focus here on the voting-age population.

How big is the U.S. electorate? There are approximately 330 million people in the United States today. But many of them are not allowed to vote; these include

turnout rate
The number of people who vote in a given election divided by the number of people who would have been allowed to vote in it.

children under age 18, noncitizens, and in some states, people currently serving prison sentences. There are approximately 74 million people under age 18, and noncitizenship reduces the eligible electorate by another 13 million adults.[10] Finally, the total ineligible prison and felon population is estimated to be between 3 and 6 million persons.[11] Hence, the eligible electorate is approximately 235 million persons, or about three-fourths of the people living in the United States.

Of course, throughout the nineteenth century and much of the twentieth there were even more constraints on the franchise, including restrictions regarding gender, race, and property ownership. Perhaps the most significant changes in election institutions over the 200-year history of the nation have been those that broke down historical barriers to voting.

To put the changes in election laws into perspective, suppose that the rules in effect 200 years ago applied today—that only White, male citizens over 21 were allowed to vote. If that had been the case in 2020, the eligible electorate would have totaled only about 76 million—about 1 in 4 people. Those restrictions would have made for a very different electorate in terms of interests, values, and preferences; they would have altered the political parties' strategies; and they would have surely resulted in very different election outcomes.

The Registration Requirement. Other restrictions on the franchise relate to how local officials run elections. As Figure 10.1 indicates, voter turnout declined markedly in the United States between 1890 and 1910, years coinciding with two important changes in the institutions of elections. Many states (1) imposed rules such as literacy tests to keep immigrants, Blacks, and other groups from voting; and (2) began to create registration systems so that people had to be on a formal list of eligible voters in order to be allowed to vote on Election Day.

Personal registration was one of several "progressive" reforms begun early in the twentieth century, supposedly to discourage fraud and "corruption"—a category in which reformers included machine politics in large cities, where political parties had organized immigrant and ethnic populations. In fact, such reforms aimed not only to rein in actual corruption but also to weaken urban factions within parties and to keep immigrants and Blacks from voting.

Over the years, voter registration restrictions have been loosened somewhat to make the process easier. In 1993, for example, Congress approved and President Bill Clinton signed the National Voter Registration Act, commonly known as the "motor voter" law, which allows individuals to register when applying for driver's licenses as well as in public-assistance and military-recruitment offices.[12] In some jurisdictions, casting a vote automatically registers the voter for the next election. In most places in the United States, however, citizens still must take some steps in order to be registered to vote. In Europe, by contrast,

People who register to vote are highly likely to turn out and actually vote on Election Day, so getting new voters into the registration system is one way to increase voter participation. Here a Spanish-language message on an electronic billboard in New York encourages people to register to vote.

Determining Who Votes

Manipulation of the electorate's composition is a device used to regulate voting and its consequences. As we saw in Chapter 4, most restrictions on adult voters have been removed.

Past Methods to Limit Voter Participation

- Property ownership and literacy requirements
- Poll taxes
- Race and gender restrictions
- Placement of polls and scheduling of polling hours
- Voter registration rules

Current Limits on Participation

- There are numerous restrictions on the voting rights of convicted felons that vary from state to state. Prison inmates serving a felony sentence are prohibited from voting in 48 states and the District of Columbia.
- There are no other official limits (other than the age requirement), except that a voter must be an American citizen. However, any voter registration rules tend to depress participation by the poor and the uneducated.

voter registration is handled automatically by the government. This is one reason why voter turnout rates there are higher than in the United States.

The mere requirement that people register in order to vote significantly reduces turnout rates. Studies of contemporary voter registration lists find that almost 90 percent of registered voters in fact vote, but only about 70 percent of the eligible electorate is currently registered. In the record-breaking 2020 presidential election, there were an estimated 239 million adult citizens and 158 million registered voters; an estimated 148 million people voted. In other words, the eligible electorate is really only about 160 million people—those who are actually registered to vote. Over 80 million eligible voters have not yet registered—disproportionately those who are ages 18–29. Getting those people into the registration system, and keeping them on the rolls, is an important way to increase the turnout rate. If you are not registered to vote, you cannot vote.[13]

Why, then, have a registration system? Such systems contain a fairly reliable list of all people who are interested in voting. Political campaigns use the lists to communicate with voters about when, where, and how to vote, as well as to prepare grassroots organizing efforts and direct-mail campaigns.

Registration lists also provide the basis for administering elections. Local election offices rely on their registration databases to format ballots, set up precincts, determine which voters should vote in which places, and communicate with those voters about voting places, times, and procedures. Any given area contains many overlapping election jurisdictions, creating many different combinations of offices to vote for, each combination requiring a different ballot. For example, one voter might reside in Congressional District 1, State Senate District 7, State Representative District 3, City Council District 1, and so forth. Variations in district boundaries may mean that voters living a few blocks apart live in entirely different districts. Although they live in the same neighborhood, these voters must vote on different ballots. The first voter is not supposed to vote in Congressional District 2, for instance. Registration lists have become vitally important in sorting out where and on which ballots people should vote.

Efforts to eliminate or reform registration requirements must confront this very practical problem. Twenty-one states allow registration at the polls on Election Day (called same-day registration or Election Day registration). These states have noticeably higher turnout but also must recruit additional poll workers to handle the new registrants in the precincts.[14] Nineteen states have gone even further and will automatically register voters when they renew their driver's licenses or state ID cards.[15] In other states, electronic voting equipment now makes it possible to program many different ballots on a single machine so that each voter just keys in his or her address to get the appropriate ballot and vote. Innovations like these may lead to an election system that does not require or rely heavily on registration before Election Day, but even these systems still require the voter to register.

The past decade has seen a push to create new ways of authenticating voters at the polls. Two-thirds of all states require that voters provide some form of identification when voting, such as a driver's license, and some specifically require that voters provide government-issued photo identification. Such rules have been adopted out of fear of voter fraud. The other states either have no such requirement or prohibit election officials from asking for photographic identification. Legislators and voters there either view the risk of voter fraud as low or view the potential barrier to voting or potential discriminatory effects of such laws as outweighing any possible fraud. Social scientists have tended to find minimal levels of fraud, minimal effects of such laws on voter turnout, and minimal effects on people's confidence in the electoral system.[16]

Laws alone, in any case, cannot explain the variations in turnout. Perhaps the biggest systematic differences in turnout occur between election years. When the president is on the ticket, turnout exceeds 60 percent of the eligible electorate. But in midterm elections, when the president is not on the ticket, turnout drops 10 to 20 points. This pattern of surge and decline in turnout is a function partly of the election calendar, but also of campaign activities and of voter interest in the election outcomes. These are behavioral matters, which we will discuss later in this chapter.

How Americans Vote: The Ballot

The way Americans cast their votes reflects some of our most cherished precepts about voting rights. Most people view voting as a private matter, choosing whether or not to tell others how they voted. Polling places provide privacy and keep an individual's vote secret. In some respects, the secret ballot seems inconsistent with voting, because elections are a very public matter. Indeed, for the first century of the Republic, voting was conducted in the open. Public voting led to vote buying and voter intimidation, however, and at the end of the nineteenth century the secret ballot became widespread in response to such corrupt practices.

With the secret ballot came another innovation, the **Australian ballot**, which lists the names of all candidates running for a given office and allows the voter to select any candidate for each office. This procedure was introduced in Australia in 1851, and in the United States today it is universal. Before the 1880s, some Americans voted in public meetings; others voted on paper ballots printed by the political parties or by slates of candidates. Voters chose which ballot they wished to submit—a Republican ballot, a Democratic ballot, a Populist ballot, a Greenback ballot, and so forth. These ballots were often printed on different-colored paper so that voters could easily distinguish them—and so that local party workers could observe who cast which ballots. With these party ballots, voters could not choose candidates from different parties for different offices; they had to vote the party line.

Under the Australian form, all ballots are identical, making it difficult to observe who votes for which party. More important, voters can choose any candidate for each office, breaking the hold of parties over the vote. The introduction of the Australian ballot gave rise to split-ticket voting, in which voters became able to select candidates from different parties for different offices.[17]

The secret Australian ballot enabled voters to choose candidates as well as parties. The possibility of split-ticket voting also created greater fragmentation in the control of government in the United States. With the party ballot, an opposition party could more easily be swept into power at all levels of government in a given election. A strong national tide toward one of the parties in the presidential election would change not just the presidency but also political control of every state and locality that gave a majority of its votes to that party's presidential candidate. In contrast, because the Australian ballot permitted voters to vote for each office separately, it made the electorate less likely to sweep one party into power and another out at all levels.

One change under way in American electoral rules involves the rise of "convenience voting"—such as voting early or voting by mail. These changes became especially important in 2020 when the coronavirus pandemic made social distancing necessary.

Where Americans Vote: Electoral Districts

Elected officials in the United States represent places, as well as people. Today, the president, representatives, senators, governors, and many other state and local officials are elected on the basis of geographic areas called electoral districts. Generally speaking, the United States employs **single-member districts** with equal populations. This means that the U.S. House of Representatives, almost all state legislatures, and almost all local governments have their own districts and

Australian ballot
An electoral format that presents the names of all the candidates for any given office on the same ballot.

single-member district
An electoral district that elects only one representative—the typical method of representation in the United States.

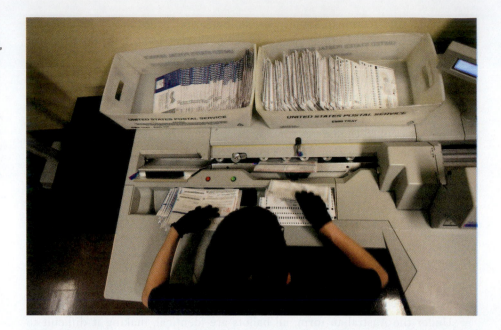

One change under way in American electoral politics is the rise of "convenience voting," such as early voting and voting by mail. This election worker uses a high-speed machine to open vote-by-mail ballots during Super Tuesday in 2020.

Electoral College

An institution established by the Constitution for the election of the president and vice president of the United States. Every four years, voters in each state and the District of Columbia elect electors who, in turn, cast votes for the president and vice president. The candidate receiving a majority of the electoral vote for president or vice president is elected.

elect one representative per district, and that all of the districts for a given legislative body must have equal populations.

Elections for the U.S. Senate and the presidency are the odd cases. In the Senate, the states are the districts, which have multiple (two) members each and unequal populations. In presidential elections, every state is allocated votes in the **Electoral College** equal to its number of U.S. senators (two) plus its number of House members. (The District of Columbia is assigned three votes.) With two exceptions (Maine and Nebraska, which use proportional representation), each state chooses all of its electors in a statewide vote, and the electors commit to casting their votes in the Electoral College for the winner of the popular vote in that state. When the framers of the Constitution established the Electoral College, they mandated that each state's legislature choose its electors, but since the 1860s, all the states have chosen electors by popular vote.

The U.S. Senate and the Electoral College remain the two great exceptions to the requirements of single-member districts with equal populations. Giving an equal number of Senate seats to each state makes that chamber inherently unequal. California's 40 million people have the same number of senators as Wyoming's 600,000. The allocation of Electoral College votes creates a population inequity in presidential elections, with larger states entitled to fewer electors per resident than smaller states get.

In the 1960s, the Supreme Court let stand the unequal district populations in the Senate and the Electoral College because the representation of states in the Senate is specified in the Constitution. The reason lies in the politics of the Constitutional Convention (see Chapter 2), which consisted of delegations of states, each of which held an equal number of votes (one) under the Articles of Confederation. To create a House of Representatives that reflected the preferences of the general population, the large states had to strike a deal with the smaller states, which would have lost considerable power under the initial plan of a single chamber based on population. That deal, the Connecticut Compromise, created the U.S. Senate to balance the representation of people with the representation of states and led to a clause in Article V of the Constitution that guarantees equal representation of the states in the Senate.

Nevertheless, the Senate and the Electoral College share the key feature of elections for the House and for state and local offices: the use of districts to select representatives. All elections in the United States and all elected officials are tied to geographically based constituencies rather than to the national electorate as a whole. Although this is more obvious for the House and Senate, it applies also to presidential elections, in which candidates focus on winning enough states in the Electoral College rather than a majority of the popular vote.

Drawing Electoral Districts.   To ensure that their populations are equal, U.S. House and state legislative districts must be redrawn every decade after the U.S. Census Bureau updates the states' official population data to a fine level of geographic detail. The Census Bureau conducts its count of the population as of April 1st of the census year, and new districts must be created in time for the next congressional elections. In 2020 the Census Bureau conducted its count and released data to the states in the fall, and new districts must be created in 2021 in order to have districts defined before candidates file for office in early 2022. Responsibility for drawing the new boundaries rests, in most states, with the state legislature and the governor, under the supervision of the courts and sometimes with the consultation of a commission (Figure 10.2). The politicians and others with a stake in the outcome use the census data to craft a new district map; ultimately, the legislature must pass and the governor must sign a law defining the new districts. This job is forced on the legislatures by their state constitutions and by the courts.

However, periodic redistricting, although it corrects one problem, invites another. Those in charge may manipulate the new map to increase the likelihood of a particular outcome, such as an electoral majority for one party or interest group. This problem arose with some of the earliest congressional-district maps. In a particularly glaring example, a map of the 1812 Massachusetts House districts, drawn with the approval of Governor Elbridge Gerry, prompted a *Boston Gazette* editorial writer to dub a very strangely shaped district the "Gerry-Mander" because he thought it resembled a salamander. The term stuck, and **gerrymandering** refers broadly to any attempt at creating electoral districts for political advantage.

It is easy to draw an intentionally unfair electoral map, especially with the sophisticated software and data on local voting patterns and demographics that are available today. To facilitate districting, the Census Bureau divides the nation into very small geographic areas, called census blocs, which typically contain a few dozen people. U.S. House districts contain over 760,000 people. Political

gerrymandering
The drawing of electoral districts in such a way as to give advantage to one political party.

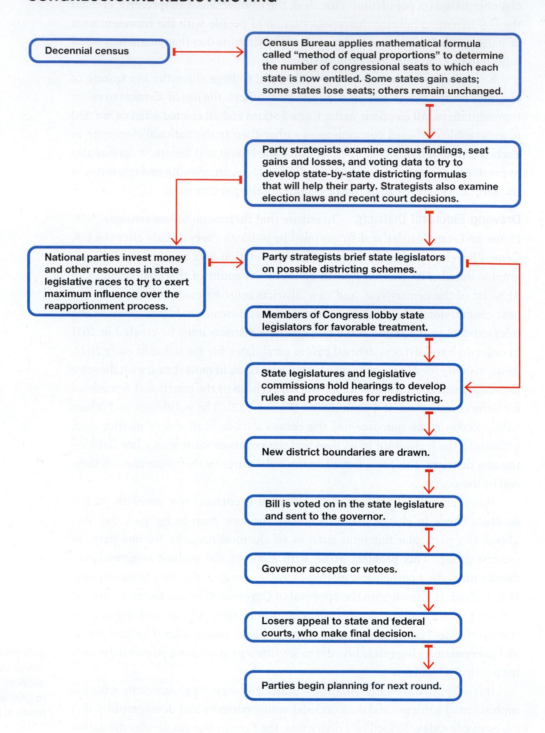

figure 10.2

CONGRESSIONAL REDISTRICTING

Decennial census

→ **Census Bureau applies mathematical formula called "method of equal proportions" to determine the number of congressional seats to which each state is now entitled. Some states gain seats; some states lose seats; others remain unchanged.**

↓ **Party strategists examine census findings, seat gains and losses, and voting data to try to develop state-by-state districting formulas that will help their party. Strategists also examine election laws and recent court decisions.**

National parties invest money and other resources in state legislative races to try to exert maximum influence over the reapportionment process. → **Party strategists brief state legislators on possible districting schemes.**

Members of Congress lobby state legislators for favorable treatment.

State legislatures and legislative commissions hold hearings to develop rules and procedures for redistricting.

New district boundaries are drawn.

Bill is voted on in the state legislature and sent to the governor.

Governor accepts or vetoes.

Losers appeal to state and federal courts, who make final decision.

Parties begin planning for next round.

mapmakers combine various local areas, down to the level of census blocs, to construct legislative districts. Those seeking political advantage try to make as many districts as possible that contain a majority of their own voters, in this way maximizing the number of seats won for a given overall statewide division of the vote. The process does have certain constraints: the district populations must be equal, and all parts of a district must touch (be contiguous). Even so, the number of possible maps that could be drawn for any state's legislative districts is extremely large.[18]

Politicians can use gerrymandering to dilute the strength not only of a party but also of a group. Consider racial minorities. One common strategy has involved redrawing congressional district boundaries so as to divide a Black population that would otherwise constitute a majority within an existing district. This form of gerrymandering was used in Mississippi during the 1960s and 1970s to prevent the election of Black candidates to Congress.

Historically, the state's Black population was clustered along the Mississippi River, in a region called the Delta. From 1882 until 1966, the Delta constituted one congressional district where Blacks were a clear majority, but discrimination in voter registration and at the polls guaranteed the continual election of White congressmen. With passage of the Voting Rights Act in 1965, this district would almost surely have been won by a Black candidate or one favored by the Black majority. To prevent that result, the state legislature drew new House districts that split the Delta's Black population across three districts so that it constituted a majority in none. This gerrymandering helped prevent the election of any Black representative until 1987, when Mike Espy became the first African American since Reconstruction to represent Mississippi in Congress.

Continuing controversies about legislators' involvement in drawing their own districts have raised deep concerns about the fairness of the process. Many states have created commissions or appointed "special masters" to draw the maps. Other states have opened the redistricting process up to input from the public, as new developments in GIS (geographic information system) software and provision of census data enable anyone to draw credible district maps. Opening up the process, it is hoped, will lessen the extent and effect of gerrymandering.

What It Takes to Win: Plurality Rule

The fourth prominent feature of U.S. electoral law is the criterion for winning. Although Americans often embrace majority rule as a defining characteristic of democracy, the real standard is **plurality rule**. The candidate who receives the most votes in the relevant district or constituency wins the election, even if that candidate doesn't receive a majority of votes. Suppose three parties nominate candidates for a seat and divide the vote such that one wins 34 percent and the other two each receive 33 percent of the vote. Under plurality rule, the candidate with 34 percent wins the seat.

plurality rule
A type of electoral system in which victory in an election goes to the individual who gets the most votes, but not necessarily a majority of the votes cast.

There are different types of plurality systems. The system most widely used in the United States combines plurality rule with single-member districts and is called *first past the post*. In choosing electors for the Electoral College, most states use a plurality system—called *winner take all*—in which the presidential candidate who receives the most votes wins all of the state's electors.[19]

In statewide elections, two states, Louisiana and Georgia, require a candidate to receive more than 50 percent of all votes in order to win. This is **majority rule**. If no candidate in an election receives a majority, a runoff election is held about one month later between the two candidates who received the most votes in the first round. Other ways of voting also use plurality-rule and majority-rule criteria. For instance, some city councils still have multimember districts. The top vote-getters win the seats. If there are, say, seven seats to fill, the seven candidates who win the most votes each win a seat.

Plurality rule is often criticized for yielding electoral results that do not reflect the public's preferences. Votes for the losing candidates seem wasted, because they do not translate into representation. Indeed, as the example of the three-candidate race described at the start of this section suggests, it is possible that a majority of voters wanted someone other than the winner.

In overall election results, plurality rule with single-member districts tends to increase the share of seats won by the largest party and decrease the other parties' shares. A striking example of this effect comes from Britain, where in the 2015 election the Conservative Party won 37 percent of the vote but 51 percent of seats, while the Labour Party placed second with 30 percent of the vote and 36 percent of seats. The remainder of the votes and seats were distributed very unevenly among three other parties. For example, the U.K. Independence Party came in third with 13 percent of the vote but won only one seat in the 650-seat House of Commons.

Nevertheless, plurality rule offers certain advantages. It enables voters to choose individuals (not just political parties) to represent them personally, and it picks a definite winner without the need for runoff elections.

Among the world's democracies, the main alternative to plurality rule is **proportional representation**, or **PR**. Under proportional representation, competing parties win legislative seats in proportion to their overall share of the popular vote. For example, if three parties are running and one wins 34 percent of the vote and the other two 33 percent each, the first party receives 34 percent of the seats and the other two 33 percent each.

PR is used rarely in the United States, with the most substantial instances being the Democratic presidential primary elections. During the 1988 primary season, Jesse Jackson routinely won 20 percent of the vote in primaries, but he ended up with only about 5 percent of the delegates to the Democratic National Convention, because the Democratic Party awarded all delegates from each congressional district to the candidate who won a plurality of the vote there. To make the convention and the party more representative of its diverse voting groups, Jackson negotiated with other party leaders to change the rules so that delegates

majority rule

A type of electoral system in which, to win an office, a candidate must receive a majority (50 percent plus one) of all the votes cast in the relevant district.

proportional representation (PR)

A multiple-member district system that awards seats to political parties in proportion to the percentage of the vote that each party won.

Who Wins? Translating Voters' Choices into Electoral Outcomes

Majority System
Winner must receive a simple majority (50 percent plus one).

Plurality System
Winner is the candidate who receives the most votes, regardless of the percentage.

Proportional Representation
Winners are selected to a representative body in proportion to the votes that their party received.

within congressional districts would be allocated on a proportional basis. If a district elects five delegates, a candidate wins one delegate if he or she receives at least 20 percent of the vote in the district, two delegates for winning at least 40 percent, and so forth.

Plurality rule in single-member districts has a very important consequence: the dominance of two-party politics in the United States. Worldwide, countries with plurality rule in single-member districts have far fewer political parties than do other nations. Typically, elections under this system come down to just two major parties that routinely compete for power, with one of them winning an outright majority of legislative seats. Proportional representation systems, on the other hand, tend to have many more than two parties. Rarely does a single party win a majority of seats, and governments form as coalitions of many parties.

How votes are cast and counted, and what it takes to win a seat, then, have substantial consequences for American politics. Plurality rule with single-member districts creates strong pressures toward two-party politics and majority rule in the legislature.

Direct Democracy: The Referendum and Recall

In addition to choosing between candidates, voters in some states also vote directly on proposed laws or other governmental actions through the **referendum** and initiative process. A ballot measure may come about in two ways. First, some state

referendum
A direct vote by the electorate on a proposed law that has been passed by the legislature or on a specific governmental action.

constitutions and laws require that certain types of legislation (such as bonds or property tax increases) be approved by popular vote. When a measure is voted on this way it is called a *referendum*. Second, advocates may get a measure put on the ballot by obtaining enough signatures of registered voters on a petition. This is called an *initiative*. In recent years, for example, voters in several states have voted in referenda to set limits on tax rates, to define marriage, and to prohibit social services for undocumented immigrants.

Although it involves voting, a referendum is not an election. The election is an institution of representative government; through it, voters choose officials to act for them. A referendum or initiative, by contrast, is an institution of direct democracy; it allows voters to act directly.

Like legislative action, however, results of referendums and initiatives are subject to judicial review. If a court finds that the outcome violates the state or national constitution, it can overturn a referendum decision. For example, in 2008, California voters passed Proposition 8, which stated, "Only marriage between a man and a woman is valid or recognized in California." A federal district court ruled Proposition 8 unconstitutional in 2010. The Supreme Court let stand the district court's ruling in 2013, and in 2015 the Court ruled in *Obergefell v. Hodges* that marriage is a fundamental right guaranteed to all people.[20]

Referenda are allowed in 24 states. There are also 24 states that permit various forms of the **initiative**.[21] Whereas the referendum process allows citizens to approve or reject a policy already produced by legislative action, the initiative provides citizens with a way forward in the face of legislative *in*action. They can petition

initiative

A process by which citizens may petition to place a policy proposal on the ballot for public vote.

The initiative process allows voters to make policy directly. For example, 2020 ballots in San Diego, California, asked voters to decide on issues related to new housing construction and affordable housing in their county.

to place a policy proposal (legislation or state constitutional amendment) on the ballot to be approved or disapproved by the electorate. To gain a place on the ballot, a petition must be accompanied by a minimum number of voter signatures—the number varying from state to state—that are certified by the state's secretary of state.

Ballot propositions resulting from initiatives often involve policies that the state legislature cannot (or does not want to) resolve. Like referendum issues, these are often highly emotional and, consequently, not well suited to resolution via popular voting. On the other hand, one of the "virtues" of the initiative is that it may force action: legislative leaders may persuade obstinate colleagues to move ahead on controversial issues by raising the possibility that a worse outcome will result from inaction.[22]

Eighteen states also have legal provisions for **recall** elections, which allow voters to remove governors and other state officials from office before the end of their terms. Federal officials such as the president and members of Congress are not subject to recall. Generally, a recall effort begins with a petition campaign. For example, in California, the site of a tumultuous recall battle in 2003, if 12 percent of those who voted in the most recent general election sign petitions demanding a special recall election, the state board of elections must schedule one.

Such petition campaigns are relatively common, but most fail to garner enough signatures to bring the matter to a statewide vote. In the California case, however, a conservative Republican member of Congress led a successful effort to recall the Democratic governor, Gray Davis. Voters were unhappy about the state's economy and dissatisfied with Davis's performance, blaming him for a $38 billion budget deficit. Davis became the second governor in American history to be recalled by his state's electorate (the first was North Dakota's governor Lynn Frazier, who was recalled in 1921). Under California law, voters in a special recall election also choose a replacement for the official whom they dismiss. Californians in 2003 elected the movie star Arnold Schwarzenegger to be their governor.

recall
The removal of a public official by popular vote.

HOW VOTERS DECIDE

Electoral rules and laws—the institutional side of elections—impose order on the process, but ultimately, elections reflect many millions of people's personal preferences about politics and about whom they want as their representatives and leaders. The voter's decision can be understood as two linked decisions: *whether* to vote and *for whom*. Social scientists have examined both aspects by studying election returns, survey data, and laboratory experiments, as well as field experiments conducted during elections. Generations of research into these questions yield a broad picture of how voters decide.

First, the decision to vote or not is strongly related to individuals' demographic characteristics, especially age and education, but it also depends on the electoral choices and context. An individual who knows nothing about the candidates or dislikes all of them is unlikely to vote. Second, which candidates or party a voter chooses depends primarily on three factors: partisan loyalties, issues, and candidate characteristics. Partisan loyalties are the strongest single predictor of the vote, though party attachments also reflect issues and individuals' experience with candidates.

Voters and Nonvoters

As we saw earlier, turnout in modern American presidential elections is less than two-thirds of the voting-age population. In 2020, 62.7 percent of citizens of voting age turned out; thus, almost 40 percent of those who could have voted did not. Why do so many people not vote?

A general explanation is elusive, but social scientists find that a few demographic characteristics are strong predictors of who votes. Most important are age, education, and residential mobility. Other factors, such as gender, income, and race, also matter, but to a much smaller degree.

According to the 2018 Census Bureau's Current Population Survey, only 36 percent of those under age 29 voted that year; by comparison, 66 percent of those over age 65 voted. The huge difference in participation between these groups surely translates into the interests of retirees being much more likely to receive attention from the government than the interests of people in college or just entering the labor force.

Education shows similarly large differences. More than 65 percent of people with a college education voted, and the rate was 74 percent among those with a professional degree. In contrast, just 27 percent of those without a high school diploma voted, as did 42 percent of those with only a high school diploma.[23]

Finally, consider residency and mobility. Only 55 percent of people who had lived in their current residence less than a year reported voting, compared with 76 percent of people who had lived there at least five years. Those who owned their home or apartment voted at a 63 percent rate, but only 41 percent of those who rented voted.[24] Politicians listen to those who vote, and voters are disproportionately older, better educated, and more rooted in their communities than nonvoters.

As discussed earlier, election laws have historically had a large effect on the size and character of the electorate. The decision to vote itself consists of two steps—registration and turnout. Minimizing registration requirements may increase participation, as the option of Election Day registration has shown. As of 2019, 21 states plus the District of Columbia allow people to register on Election Day at the polls or at a government office. The three states with the longest experience with same-day registration—Minnesota, Wisconsin, and Maine—do have higher turnout than most other states, and most studies suggest that in a typical state, adopting such a law would increase turnout by about 3–5 percent.[25]

Demographics and laws, however, are only part of what accounts for voting and nonvoting. The choices presented to voters are also important. People who do not like the candidates or dislike politics altogether tend not to vote. The top four reasons people say they do not vote are that they are too busy, are sick or disabled, are not interested, or did not like the choices.

Partisan Loyalty

The strongest predictor of how a person will vote is that individual's attachment to a political party. The American National Election Studies (ANES), exit polls, and media polls have found that even in times of great political change, the overwhelming majority of Americans identify with one of the two major political parties and vote almost entirely in accordance with that identity. Researchers determine **party identification** with simple questions along the following lines: "Generally speaking, do you consider yourself to be a Democrat, a Republican, an independent, or what?"[26] Those who choose a party are further classified by being asked whether they identify strongly or weakly with the party, and independents are asked whether they lean toward one party or another.

Party identifications capture voters' inclination toward their party's candidates. Many of these inclinations are rooted in public policies, such as policies on taxes or civil rights. Those long-standing policy positions lead to divisions in party identifications and voting patterns among different demographic groups. Large majorities of African Americans and Hispanics, for example, identify and vote with the Democratic Party.

Women also tend to identify more and vote more with the Democrats than men do. That gap has persisted, averaging 7 percentage points over the past three decades. The 2020 election saw a wide gap between the electoral choice of men and the electoral choice of women. Biden received the vote of 57 percent of women, and 45 percent of the vote of men. He received a higher share of the votes of women than even Hillary Clinton did in 2016. The growing gap between men and women is increasingly significant because women now comprise 52 percent of the electorate.

Although specific features of the choices and context matter as well, party identifications express how voters would likely vote in a "neutral" election. They are extremely good predictors of voting in less prominent elections, such as for state legislature or lower-level statewide offices, about which voters may know relatively little. Even in presidential elections, with their extensive advertising and news coverage, party identifications predict individual voting behavior.

Figure 10.3 displays the percentages of Democratic identifiers, Republican identifiers, and self-described independents who voted for Donald Trump, Joe Biden, or someone else in 2020. Approximately 94 percent of party identifiers voted for their own party's standard-bearer. Independents broke 54 to 41 for Biden. Sometimes the independent vote decides the election. In 2016, for example, Clinton's popular-vote victory was due to Democrats making up the single largest group in the electorate (even though Trump won the Electoral College).

party identification
An individual's attachment to a particular political party, which may be based on issues, ideology, past experience, upbringing, or a mixture of these elements.

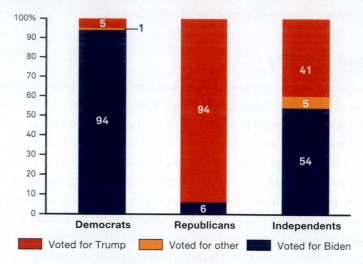

figure 10.3

THE EFFECT OF PARTY IDENTIFICATION ON THE VOTE FOR PRESIDENT, 2020

Legend: Voted for Trump | Voted for other | Voted for Biden

Democrats: 94 (Biden), 5 (Trump), 1 (other)
Republicans: 94 (Trump), 6 (Biden)
Independents: 41 (Trump), 5 (other), 54 (Biden)

SOURCE: CNN, "Exit Polls," https://www.cnn.com/election/2020/exit-polls/president/national-results (accessed 11/11/20). (Note the poll had 15,590 total respondents.)

But party is not the only factor in voting. We consider next how issues and candidates shape voting behavior.

Issues

Voting on issues and policies cuts to the core of our understanding of democratic accountability and electoral control over government. A simple, idealized account of **issue voting** goes as follows. Governments make policies and laws on a variety of issues that affect the public. Voters who disagree with those policies and laws on principle, or who think those policies have failed, will vote against those who made the decisions. Voters who support the policies or like the outcomes will support the incumbent legislators or party.

It is important to note that politicians' choices of which laws to enact and which administrative actions to take are made with the express aim of attracting electoral support. Voters choose the candidates and parties that stand for the policies and laws most in line with voters' preferences. Even long-term factors like party identification are related to voters' policy preferences.

Issue voting usually involves a mix of voters' judgments about the past behavior of competing parties and candidates and their hopes and fears about candidates' future behavior. Political scientists call choices that focus on future behavior **prospective voting** and those that are based on past performance **retrospective voting**. To some extent, whether prospective or retrospective evaluation is more important in a particular election depends on the strategies of competing candidates. Candidates always try to define election issues in terms that will serve their interests.

issue voting
An individual's tendency to base the decision of which candidate or party to vote for on the candidate's or party's position on specific issues.

prospective voting
Voting based on the imagined future performance of a candidate.

retrospective voting
Voting based on the past performance of a candidate or party.

Incumbents running during a period of prosperity, for example, will seek to take credit for the strong economy and define the election as revolving around their record of success. This strategy encourages voters to make retrospective judgments. In contrast, a challenger running against the incumbent's party during a period of economic uncertainty will tell voters that it's time for a change and ask them to make prospective judgments. In 2016, Donald Trump promised dramatic changes in U.S. tax, spending, and trade policies in order to protect Americans' jobs and create new jobs. These policies broke with Democrats on social issues such as health care, but they also ran contrary to the Republican Party on trade and on infrastructure spending. In 2020, as the incumbent during a time of economic instability and uncertainly due to the coronavirus pandemic, Trump focused on his accomplishments in other areas.

Economic voting like this is one way that voters solve a problem that is inherent in representative democracy: their inability to stay informed about every governmental policy. They do, however, have a rough or fundamental way to hold the government accountable: staying the course when times are good and voting for change when the economy sours. Richard Nixon, Ronald Reagan, Bill Clinton, and George W. Bush won reelection easily in the midst of favorable economies. Jimmy Carter in 1980 and George H. W. Bush in 1992 ran for reelection in the midst of economic downturns, and both lost. The Analyzing the Evidence section on pp. 322–3 explores voters' perceptions of the economy in relation to their support for the incumbent party.

The Consumer Confidence Index, calculated on the basis of a public-opinion survey designed to measure citizens' confidence in America's economic future, has proved a fairly accurate predictor of presidential elections. A generally rosy public view of the economy's current state and future prospects, indicated by an index score greater than 100, promises that the party holding the White House will do well. A score of less than 100 suggests that voters are pessimistic about the economy and that incumbents should worry about their job prospects. In October 2020, the Consumer Confidence Index stood at 100.9. That means that the number of people who felt the economy was good was about the same as the number of people who felt that the economy was not good. And the results of the election were mixed. Democrats won the presidential vote by 3 percent, but lost seats in the House and failed to take the Senate.

Candidate Characteristics

Candidates' personal attributes always influence voters' decisions. Some analysts claim that voters prefer tall candidates to short candidates, candidates with shorter names to candidates with longer names, and candidates with lighter hair to candidates with darker hair. Perhaps these rather frivolous criteria do play some role. But the more important candidate characteristics that affect voters' choices are race, ethnicity, religion, gender, geography, and social background. Voters presume that candidates with backgrounds similar to their own are likely to share their views. Moreover, they may be proud to see someone of their background in

Economic Influence on Presidential Elections

Contributed by **Robert S. Erikson**, *Columbia University*

The state of the economy is a key factor in presidential elections. When the United States prospers, the presidential party performs much better than when economic conditions are poor. The economic influence on presidential elections can be seen by predicting the vote based on objective indicators such as GDP growth leading up to the election. The simplest measure, however, is a subjective one—voters' responses when asked in polls whether the economy has been performing well or badly. When survey respondents are asked early in the election year how they plan to vote, candidate and party preferences show little relationship to economic perceptions at that time. By Election Day, however, the national vote falls surprisingly in line with the voters' perceptions of economic performance. In short, the election campaign increases the importance of the economy to voters.

The precise indicator of economic perceptions used here is the average response to the following question, asked regularly by the Survey of Consumers at the University of Michigan in April and November of the election year: "Would you say that at the current time business conditions are better or worse than they were a year ago?"

April Poll Results

The lack of any consistent pattern in the first graph (at left) shows that what voters think about the economy in April of an election year has little bearing on their vote intentions at that time—as if voters had not yet thought about the November election sufficiently to factor in the economy. Especially noteworthy examples are 1980 and 1992 when incumbents Jimmy Carter and George H. W. Bush, respectively, were favored in the early polls, despite being seen as presiding over poor economies. Both lost the general election. John McCain (representing the incumbent Republican Party) was only slightly behind Barack Obama in early 2008, despite an economy that already was almost universally seen as worsening.

The clear pattern in the second graph (below) shows that by November, the vote falls into rough alignment with economic perceptions: the better the average perception of business conditions, the greater the support for the incumbent party. The three weakest economies in terms of perceptions (1980, 1992, 2008) all saw the incumbent party lose.

November Poll Results

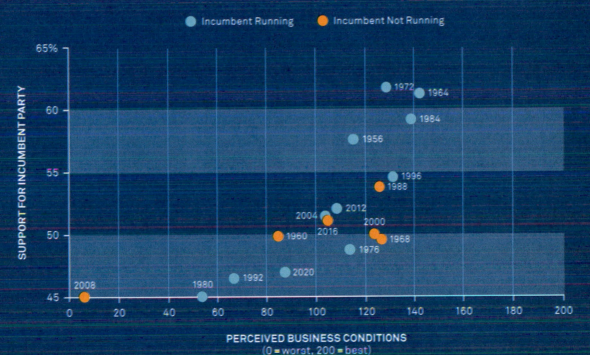

SOURCE: Surveys of Consumers, www.sca.isr.umich.edu/tables.html (accessed 11/11/2020); and author's compilation.

 → How do the trends outlined in these tables help us make sense of the 2020 presidential election results?

How Voters Decide

Partisan Loyalty
Most Americans identify with either the Democratic or the Republican Party and will vote for candidates accordingly. Party loyalty rarely changes and is most influential in less visible electoral contests, such as on the state or local level, where issues and candidates are less well known.

Issues
Voters may choose a candidate whose views they agree with on a particular issue that is very important to them, even if they disagree with the candidate in other areas. It is easier for voters to make choices based on issues if candidates articulate very different positions and policy preferences.

Candidate Characteristics
Voters are more likely to identify with and support a candidate who shares their background, views, and perspectives; therefore, race, ethnicity, religion, gender, geography, and social background are characteristics that influence how people vote. Personality characteristics such as honesty and integrity have become more important in recent years.

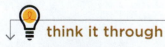

think it through

What characteristics do you consider advantages in a candidate? Do you believe a candidate with a similar background as yours, or one with shared religious beliefs, and so on, will better represent your interests in government?

a position of leadership. This is why politicians have often tried to "balance the ticket" by including members of as many important groups as possible.

Of course, personal characteristics that attract some voters may repel others. Many voters are prejudiced against candidates of certain ethnic, racial, or religious groups. In 2008 and 2016, many people embraced the opportunity to vote for the first African American (Barack Obama) and the first woman (Hillary Clinton) nominated by a major party to be president of the United States. But other people voted against those candidates because they were uncomfortable with having an African American or woman president or because they felt the candidate's race or gender was being used as a campaign gimmick.[27] Nor do voters of specific groups necessarily respond to those with similar characteristics: for example, 61 percent of the Democratic voters on Super Tuesday 2020 were women, but Elizabeth Warren won none of the 14 states up for grabs, including her home state of Massachusetts.[28]

Voters also consider candidates' personality characteristics, such as their competence, honesty, and vigor (or lack thereof), because they figure that politicians with these attributes are likely to produce good outcomes, such as laws that work, fair and honest administration of government, and the ability to address crises. Historically, presidential campaigns build up the reputations and personal images of both major-party candidates. But since the 1980s campaigns have increasingly attacked each other and stressed the personal failings and weaknesses of their opponents. In 2020, the electorate judged between two very familiar politicians, Donald Trump and former vice president Joe Biden. Each had their personal strengths and weaknesses. Trump was viewed as the more energetic of the two candidates, both of whom were in their late 70s. They were viewed as equally courageous. But Biden was seen as more honest, a better role model, even-tempered, and more caring about the needs of ordinary people. In a nation rocked by a pandemic that had killed 300,000 Americans and resulted in a shutdown of the economy, many people wanted steadier and more empathetic leadership.[29]

One of the most distinctive features of American politics is the incumbency advantage, as we saw in Chapter 5. Why this advantage has emerged and grown remains something of a puzzle. Redistricting is almost certainly not the explanation; incumbency effects are as large in gubernatorial elections, where there are no districts, as in House elections. Researchers believe that about half of the incumbency advantage reflects the activities of the politician in office; it is voters rewarding incumbents for their performance. The other half of the advantage evidently reflects the incumbents' opponents.[30] The typical challenger may not have the personal appeal of the typical incumbent, who, after all, has already won office at least once. Moreover, challengers usually lack incumbents' experience in and resources for running a campaign. This critical ability to communicate with voters can give an incumbent the edge in close elections.

While party, issues, and candidate characteristics are perhaps the three most important factors shaping voting decisions, political scientists disagree as to the relative importance of each. Recent scholarship suggests that they have roughly equal weight in explaining the division of the vote in national elections.[31] Part of the difficulty in measuring their importance is that the extent to which they matter depends on the electorate's information levels. In the absence of much information, most voters rely almost exclusively on party cues. A highly informed electorate relies more heavily on issues and candidate characteristics.[32]

CAMPAIGNS: MONEY, MEDIA, AND GRASS ROOTS

American political campaigns are freewheeling events with few restrictions on what candidates may say or do. Candidates in hotly contested House and Senate races spend millions of dollars to advertise on television, radio, and the internet, as well as by direct mail and door-to-door canvassing. Those seeking office are in a race to become as well known and as well liked as possible and to get more of their supporters to vote. Federal laws limit how much an individual or organization may give to a candidate but, with the exception of presidential campaigns, place no restrictions on how much a candidate or party committee may spend.

Adding to the freewheeling nature of campaigns is their organizational structure. Most political campaigns are temporary organizations, formed for the sole purpose of winning the coming elections and disbanded shortly afterward. To be sure, political parties in the United States have permanent, professional campaign organizations that raise money, strategize, recruit candidates, and distribute resources. On the Republican side of the aisle are the Republican National Committee, the National Republican Senatorial Committee, and the National Republican Congressional Committee; on the Democratic side are the Democratic National Committee, the Democratic Senatorial Campaign Committee, and the Democratic Congressional Campaign Committee. These account for roughly one-third of the money in politics and have considerable expertise.

But most campaigns are formed by and around individual candidates, who often put up the initial cash to get the campaign rolling and rely heavily on family and friends as volunteers. Thousands of such organizations are at work during a presidential election year, with relatively little partisan coordination. The two major-party presidential campaigns operate 50 separate state-level organizations, with other campaigns competing for 33 or 34 Senate seats, 435 House seats, dozens of gubernatorial and other statewide offices, and thousands of state legislative seats. All of these organizations simultaneously work to persuade as many people as possible to vote for their candidate on Election Day.

What It Takes to Win.   All campaigns face similar challenges—how to mobilize volunteers, how to raise money, how to coordinate activities, how to decide which messages to emphasize, and how to communicate with the public. Although there is no one best way to run a campaign, there are many tried-and-true approaches, especially building up a campaign from local connections, from the "grass roots." Candidates have to meet as many people as possible and get their friends and their friends' friends to support them.

In-person campaigning becomes increasingly difficult in larger constituencies, however, and candidates continually experiment with new ways of reaching larger segments of the electorate. In the 1920s, radio advertising eclipsed handbills and door-to-door canvassing; in the 1960s, television began to eclipse radio; in the 1980s and 1990s, cable television, phone polling, and focus groups allowed targeting of specific demographic groups. The great innovation of the 2008 Obama campaign was to meld internet networking tools with old-style organizing methods to develop a massive communications and fund-raising network that came to be called a "netroots" campaign. The Clinton campaign in 2016 capitalized on the infrastructure built by Obama and sought the advice of many of the same consultants. The Trump campaign, by contrast, relied heavily on Twitter and media coverage, and ignored the typical organization and mobilization activities considered essential for modern campaigns. The Trump campaign effort established the foundations for the Republican Party's enduring advantage in digital media, which carried through 2018 and 2020.[33] In 2020, the coronavirus pandemic made communication by social media and other digital media essential for both the Trump and Biden campaigns, as traditional campaigning and rallies were impossible due to the need for social distancing.

It has become an assumption of American elections and election law that candidates and parties will mount campaigns that spend millions, even billions of dollars, to persuade people to vote and how to vote. And because of those efforts, voters will understand better the choices they face. In short, campaigns inform voters through competition.

In addition to being costly, American political campaigns are long. Presidential campaigns officially launch a year and a half to two years in advance of Election Day. Serious campaigns for the U.S. House of Representatives begin at least a year ahead and often span the better part of two years. To use the term of the Federal Election Commission, an election is a two-year *cycle*, not a single day or even the period between Labor Day and Election Day loosely referred to as "the general election."

Long campaigns are due largely to the effort required to mount them. There are roughly 330 million people in the United States, and the voting-age population exceeds 250 million. Communicating with all of the voters is expensive and time-consuming. In the 2020 election cycle the Biden campaign and allied committees spent $1.7 billion, and the Trump campaign and allied committees spent $1.1 billion—a combined total of $2.8 billion. Approximately half of that sum purchased airtime for television advertising. The money was raised through personal and political networks that the campaigns and candidates built up over months, even years, of effort.

The campaign season is further extended by the election calendar. American national, state, and local elections proceed in two steps: the party primary elections and the general election. General elections for federal offices are set by the U.S. Constitution to take place on the first Tuesday after the first Monday in November. The first presidential caucuses and primaries come early in January and last through the beginning of June. Primaries for congressional seats and state offices do not follow the same calendar, but most occur in the spring and early summer, with a few states waiting until September. This calendar of elections stretches the campaigns over the entire election year.

Campaign Finance. The expense, duration, and chaos of American campaigns have prompted many efforts at reform, including attempts to limit campaign spending, shorten the campaign season, and restrict what candidates and organizations may say in advertisements. The most sweeping campaign reforms came in 1971, when Congress passed the Federal Election Campaign Act (or FECA). It limited the amounts that a single individual or organization could contribute to a candidate or party to $1,000 per election for individuals and $5,000 for organizations (these limits have since been increased, as Table 10.1 indicates).

The FECA further regulated how business firms, unions, and other organizations could give money, prohibiting donations directly from the organization's treasury and requiring the creation of a separate fund—a **political action committee (PAC)**. It established public funding for presidential campaigns and tied those funds to expenditure limits. And it set up the Federal Election Commission (FEC) to oversee public disclosure of information and to enforce the laws.[34]

Congress has amended the FECA several times, most importantly in the Bipartisan Campaign Reform Act of 2002 (BCRA; also called the McCain-Feingold Act, after senators John McCain and Russell Feingold, its primary sponsors in the Senate). This amendment prohibited unlimited party spending

 think it through

Have you ever donated to a political campaign or party? How do you think rules regarding campaign spending help ensure you have a fair opportunity at having your voice heard?

political action committee (PAC)

A private group that raises and distributes funds for use in election campaigns.

table 10.1

FEDERAL CAMPAIGN FINANCE CONTRIBUTION LIMITS

	TO EACH CANDIDATE OR CANDIDATE COMMITTEE PER ELECTION	TO NATIONAL PARTY COMMITTEE PER CALENDAR YEAR	TO STATE, DISTRICT, AND LOCAL PARTY COMMITTEE PER CALENDAR YEAR	TO EACH PAC (SSF AND NONCONNECTED) PER CALENDAR YEAR*
Individual may give . . .	$2,800[†]	$35,500[†]	$10,000 (combined limit)	$5,000
National party committee may give . . .	$5,000	No limit	No limit	$5,000
State, district, and local party committee may give . . .	$5,000 (combined limit)	No limit	No limit	$5,000 (combined limit)
PAC* (multicandidate) may give[‡] . . .	$5,000	$15,000	$5,000 (combined limit)	$5,000
PAC (not multicandidate) may give . . .	$2,800[†]	$35,500[†]	$10,000 (combined limit)	$5,000
Candidate committee may give . . .	$2,000	No limit	No limit	$5,000

*PAC refers to a committee that makes contributions to other federal political committees. Super PACs may accept unlimited contributions. SSF refers to separate segregated funds.

[†] Indexed for inflation in odd-numbered years.

[‡] A multicandidate committee is a political committee with more than 50 contributors that has been registered for at least six months and, with the exception of state party committees, has made contributions to five or more candidates for federal office.

SOURCE: Federal Election Commission, www.fec.gov/help-candidates-and-committees/candidate-taking-receipts/contribution-limits (accessed 3/20/20).

(called *soft money*) and banned certain sorts of political attack advertisements by interest groups in the final weeks of a campaign. Table 10.1 summarizes some of the rules governing campaign finance in federal elections.

Under the FECA's system of public funding for presidential campaigns, if a candidate agrees to abide by spending limits, that candidate's campaign is eligible for matching funds in primary elections and full public funding in the general election. Until 2000, nearly all candidates bought into the system. George W. Bush chose to fund his 2000 primary election campaign outside this system and spent $500 million to win the Republican nomination. Since 2008, none of the top-tiered candidates in the primaries and no major party candidates in the general election have opted into the public funding system. The amount of money is too little compared to what could be raised, and needs to be raised, to run a competitive national election. The amount allocated for the public funding system has increased with inflation, while the amount of money that people donate to political campaigns has grown at the rate of growth of income or faster. Public funding may be possible still, but the amounts provided to campaigns would need to be much larger.[35]

The FECA originally went much further than the law that survives today. Congress initially passed mandatory limits on spending by House and Senate candidates and prohibited organizations from running independent campaigns (campaigns not coordinated with any candidate) on behalf of or in opposition to a candidate. But James Buckley, a candidate for the U.S. Senate in New York, challenged the law, arguing that the restrictions on spending and contributions limited his rights to free speech and that the FEC had been given excessive administrative power.

In the 1976 landmark case *Buckley v. Valeo*, the U.S. Supreme Court agreed in part.[36] The Court ruled that "money is speech," but that the government also has a compelling interest in protecting elections from corrupt practices, such as bribery through large campaign donations. The justices declared the limits on candidate spending unconstitutional because they violated the free speech rights of candidates and groups. However, the need to protect the integrity of the electoral process led the justices to leave contribution limits in place. The presidential public-funding system was also upheld, because it is voluntary; candidates are not required to participate.

What survived *Buckley* is a system in which candidates, groups, and parties may spend as much as they like to win office, but donations must come in small amounts. This is a more democratic process of campaign finance, but it increases the effort and time needed to construct a campaign.

In 2010, the Court reinforced its reasoning in *Buckley* in the case *Citizens' United v. Federal Election Commission*.[37] Here the justices ruled that the BCRA of 2002 had been wrong in imposing restrictions on independent spending by corporations. It overturned key parts of the law and reversed its ruling in a case that had upheld the law.[38] While striking down limits on independent expenditures from corporate treasuries, the majority opinion kept in place limits on direct contributions from corporations and other organizations to candidates. However, it also strengthened corporations' right to free political speech, equating it with the right to free speech of individuals.

In the wake of this decision, two sorts of organizations formed—501c(4) organizations (which derive their name from the section of the tax code that allows them) and super PACs. Each can raise and spend unlimited amounts on campaigns, though super PACs are subject to more disclosure laws. Super PACs spent approximately $1.2 billion in 2016 and $1.8 billion in 2020. Conservative and liberal super PACs spent about equal amounts.

Congressional Campaigns. Congressional campaigns share a number of important features with presidential campaigns, but they are also distinctive. The two-term limit on the president means that incumbency is a more important advantage for congressional representatives, who have no term limits. In recent decades, the incumbency advantage has grown in both size and importance in U.S. elections. (See Chapter 5 for a full discussion of the incumbency advantage in

Congress.) Today, almost every elective office at the state and federal level exhibits this advantage, ranging from about a 5 percent advantage in state legislative elections to 10 percent for U.S. House and U.S. Senate seats and for governorships. A 10 percent incumbency advantage is a massive electoral edge. It turns a competitive race into a blowout for the incumbent.[39]

Congressional incumbents' advantages arise in spending as well as in votes. Like presidential campaigns, congressional campaigns have witnessed increased spending over time. The average U.S. House incumbent in 2020 raised $2.4 million, while the average House challenger raised $377,000.[40]

Incumbent members of Congress have particular advantages in campaign fund-raising. They have already been tested; they have their campaign organizations in place; and they have connections in their constituencies, as well as in Washington, D.C.

THE 2020 ELECTIONS

2020: A Dynamic Year

The outbreak of the novel coronavirus in February abruptly and radically altered the course of the 2020 election. Early in the year, Donald Trump looked assured to win reelection to the presidency, and Republicans appeared almost certain to hold their Senate majority. The country was prosperous and at peace. During Trump's first three years in office, the number of unemployed persons who were actively seeking work had declined from 8 million, or 5 percent of the workforce, to 6 million, just 3.5 percent of the workforce; the economy was robust and expanding, spurred by Trump's 2017 tax cut and administrative decisions that reduced economic, environmental, and financial regulations. Forecasters predicted continued economic growth throughout 2020.

If anything, it was the Democrats who appeared to be in the more vulnerable political position. Coming into the 2020 election year, they held a 16-seat majority in the House of Representatives following a sweeping electoral victory in the 2018 midterm elections. Thirty-one House Democrats held seats in swing districts where Trump had won a majority of the vote for president in 2016. The Republican Party and allied interest groups planned to capitalize on the good economic times in targeting those 31 Democrats, as well as 24 vulnerable others, in what looked to be a promising year for the Republicans.

Compounding the Democrats' problems was the fact that the Republicans had resisted congressional Democrats' efforts to impeach the president, or at least drag down his popularity with a scandal, in his first term. In 2019, House Democrats wrapped up a three-year investigation into Russian interference in the 2016 election. Those inquiries resulted in convictions for several of Trump's political associates, including his personal lawyer. On December 13, 2019, the

Democratic-controlled House of Representatives voted to levy two articles of impeachment against the president. Within two weeks, the Republican-controlled Senate had rejected those articles. Much to the Democrats' chagrin, public support for the president remained unchanged throughout the investigation; the party's failed gambit thus appeared more likely to hurt them. As with the attempt to remove President Bill Clinton in 1998 following the Monica Lewinsky scandal, the context of a good economy seemed to make the president impervious to attack. By the beginning of February 2020, the dust had settled on the Russia probe and the Democratic primary season was underway. The oddsmakers heavily favored Trump. The headline in one prominent international newspaper read: "Markets have made their prediction: Trump will win the next election."[41]

Then, COVID-19 hit. As the pandemic worsened throughout March and April, Republicans' poll numbers at all levels began to plummet. The president's job approval rating slid, reaching the mid-30s by early summer. The economy shrank quickly, and millions lost their jobs. Of the 160 million Americans in the workforce, 23 million were out of work by April 2020, an unemployment rate of 15 percent. While employment rose slightly over the course of the summer, the unemployment rate was at 8 percent by the beginning of September.[42]

The Trump administration's response to the COVID-19 pandemic was to downplay the virus and even deny that it was a problem, and administration officials expressed the hope that the disease would go away quickly.

As summer began, America confronted yet another crisis: several high-profile incidents of police brutality against African Americans thrust simmering issues of criminal and racial justice into the national consciousness, spurring nationwide protests. The killings were just the latest in a string of police brutality charges and investigations that had gained national attention in recent years. Against the background of the desperation accompanying the COVID-19 outbreak and economic shutdown, these two tragedies for the Black community in the United States felt like the last straw. The deaths sparked nationwide protests against police brutality and calls for criminal justice reform.

The killings and ensuing protests polarized the 2020 candidates. President Trump tweeted that the protesters were "thugs" who must be stopped and that the violence following the protests required a strong "law and order" response.[43] He also claimed to have done more for the Black community in his three years as president than Joe Biden had done in 43 years in Washington.[44] The Democrats hit back with calls for police and criminal justice reform. As the summer carried on, the Floyd and Taylor cases remained in the public eye.

The events of 2020 emerged against a backdrop of economic and demographic shifts in three regions of the country that would turn out to shape the election results. First, the states of the Midwest—Minnesota, Wisconsin, Michigan, and Pennsylvania—had been among the most reliable for the Democratic Party since the election of Bill Clinton in 1992; Hillary Clinton had called them the

"Blue Wall." In recent years, however, these heavily industrial regions had hemorrhaged jobs in the face of foreign competition, especially from China. As a result, the Republican Party had gradually gained strength in the Midwest, and President Trump's aggressive foreign policies toward China and Mexico proved very popular in the region.

Second, the Southwest—Arizona, California, Colorado, Nevada, New Mexico, and Texas—had been moving in the opposite direction, inching away from the Republican Party. The main driver here was the rapid influx of immigrants from Central and South America, especially from Mexico. Latino voters in the region have been trending toward the Democratic Party since the early 1990s, when the Republican Party began to back policies unpopular among Latinos, such as English-only initiatives. Donald Trump's policy focus on building a border wall to limit illegal immigration and his efforts to expel undocumented immigrants pushed many Southwest voters away from the Republicans.

Third, less obvious than the changes in the Midwest and the Southwest, were shifts occurring in the Southeast, especially Florida, Georgia, North Carolina, South Carolina, and Virginia. These states' populations have grown faster than the rest of the nation, and they have increasingly attracted new industries, such as tech, media, and aerospace. Baby-boomer retirees from the Northeast and Midwest have likewise flocked to these states. These new populations tend to have a more centrist or liberal political orientation, and the combination of these "new southerners" with the strongly Democratic minority populations in the region have made these states less reliably Republican.

The Presidential Primaries

The 2020 presidential campaign was as strange as the year. The Democratic field boasted an impressive and diverse set of candidates from a wide range of backgrounds. Two very well-known and prominent candidates in the race, former vice president Joe Biden and Senator Bernie Sanders, had run for the presidential nomination of their party in the past and once again set out to become the Democrats' standard bearer. There were 10 U.S. senators or former senators in the race; in addition to Biden and Sanders, Senators Elizabeth Warren (Massachusetts), Kamala Harris (California), Cory Booker (New Jersey), Amy Klobuchar (Minnesota), Michael Bennet (Colorado), and Kirsten Gillibrand (New York) also ran. The race attracted four governors;[45] five current and former members of the U.S. House of Representatives;[46] five mayors and former mayors;[47] a state senator;[48] an entrepreneur, Andrew Yang; and a self-help author and new age lecturer, Marianne Williamson.

The Democrats spent the better part of 2019 raising funds and developing field organizations in the early primary and caucus states. From June 2019 to February 2020, the Democrats held eight debates, often struggling to find a format that would allow up to 29 contestants on the stage at once. The caucuses and early primaries quickly narrowed the field. In the Iowa caucus on February 3, Bernie

Sanders narrowly defeated the surprise candidate of the season, Pete Buttigieg, a little-known but charismatic mayor from South Bend, Indiana. Elizabeth Warren trailed the two leaders, and Joe Biden posted a distant fourth-place showing. Biden's New Hampshire effort was no better, and his candidacy looked to be on the ropes. The election increasingly seemed to be a two-way race between Warren and Sanders. Biden made his comeback bid in the third primary of the season, in South Carolina. South Carolina's primary electorate is predominantly African American, and Kamala Harris was banking on a win here to keep her candidacy alive. But, on February 29, Biden scored a huge victory in South Carolina, and the race suddenly was Biden versus Sanders and Warren, who were splitting the vote on the left wing of the party.

On the Republican side, President Trump faced opposition from former governor William Weld of Massachusetts, former governor Mark Sanford of South Carolina, and radio talk show host Joe Walsh. But none of these challengers garnered more than small percentages in the polls when put up against President Trump. As a result, many states decided simply to cancel the Republican primary elections rather than spend the cost of running them.

The campaign for the Democratic nomination looked to be following the same pattern as 2016: an insider, establishment candidate (Biden in 2020 and Clinton in 2016) would face off against a candidate representing the left (Sanders in 2016 and Sanders or Warren in 2020). Unlike 2016, President Trump faced no real opposition and he was positioned to use the primary to begin touring the United States with a rousing set of rallies and other events of the sort that had proved incredibly successful four years earlier.

During the week from February 29 to March 3, COVID-19 erupted into the national consciousness. The virus had been spreading throughout the month of February, but serious super-spreader events in Washington State and Boston, Massachusetts, set off alarms among public health officials, and the pandemic began to rule the nightly news. Suddenly, the issues that had dominated the Democratic primaries—health insurance, income inequality, race relations— became secondary concerns. People felt vulnerable, and they wanted experienced leadership to manage the crisis. The shift of the issues away from the economy and equality and to questions of experience and leadership gave Biden a huge boost among the public. It also became impossible to hold campaign events and rallies; even the simple act of voting appeared to be a threat to one's health. Democratic campaigns were forced to take to the airwaves, and that helped Joe Biden secure the nomination, as his campaign emphasized advertising more than events.

The General Election

The events of the spring, however, hinted at the chaos that awaited the election come fall. States that had March and April primaries struggled to conduct voting. They had difficulty recruiting people to be poll workers and finding places to

PRESIDENTIAL DEBATE
TOPIC: THE SUPREME COURT
CNN 9:10 PM ET
CNN FIRST PRESIDENTIAL DEBATE
#Debates2020

During the 2020 general-election campaign, Donald Trump and Joe Biden faced each other in two televised debates. The candidates addressed important issues, such as the economy, but also attacked each other's character and fitness to be president.

hold in-person voting. Many local election offices were unprepared for the surge in absentee balloting, complicating vote counting and creating concerns. Most states were sued to remove barriers to absentee voting in order to accommodate the COVID-19 crisis. States that had late-summer primaries had fewer problems. By fall, it was evident that a significant percentage of the ballots cast in the 2020 election would be absentee by mail or early votes. Several states adopted universal voting by mail, while others relaxed absentee balloting provisions to make it easier for people to cast ballots by mail or early. These seismic changes to the conduct of the election raised the prospect of legal challenges to the counting of ballots, especially absentee ballots received after Election Day, in the event of a close election on November 3.

The polls the week before the election showed a wide lead for Biden overall but tight races in the dozen states essential to winning the Electoral College. Biden held a 7 to 10 percentage point lead in almost every national poll, and most surveys showed that he would win an outright majority of all votes cast. The Electoral College, however, was another matter. In 2016, Trump had nearly completely dismantled Clinton's Midwestern Blue Wall: Michigan, Minnesota, Pennsylvania, and Wisconsin. Those very same states were up for grabs again in 2020. In the Southwest, the rising tide of Latino voters gave the Biden campaign hopes of picking up Arizona and possibly Texas, but the Trump campaign also made a strong bid to move Nevada into the Republican column. In the Southeast, polls showed the candidates to be tied in

Florida, Georgia, and North Carolina. Biden appeared to have more scenarios under which he could put together a majority of the electoral votes needed to win. The near-consensus in January that Trump would win reelection had completely vanished.

Election night was tense. Early returns indicated that Joe Biden captured an outright majority of the vote, but the vote totals for the two candidates were quite close in the dozen states that held the key to the Electoral College (See Figure 10.4). The Democrats won Minnesota and took back Michigan and Wisconsin. Trump held onto Florida, Iowa, Ohio, and Texas. In the days following the election, the returns revealed extremely close contests in Arizona, Georgia, Nevada, and Pennsylvania; all four states went to Biden, giving him the Electoral College win.

Ultimately, the American electorate was energized by the events of 2020 rather than dispirited. Approximately 155 million people voted. Almost two out of every three eligible adults in the United States cast a ballot, far exceeding the high-water mark for turnout over the past 100 years, set in the 2008 election.[49]

The Congressional Elections

Coming into 2020, the Democrats hoped that their fierce challenge of Trump would spread down the ballot to races for the U.S. Senate, U.S. House, and state legislative elections.

At the beginning of the year, the U.S. Senate seemed out of reach for the Democrats. Although there were more Republican seats than Democratic seats on the ballot, almost all of the Republican senators up for reelection came from states that had been reliably Republican in recent years, such as Arizona, Georgia, South Carolina, and Texas, or where there were long-standing Republican incumbents who were relatively popular in their states, such as Susan Collins in Maine. As Trump's electoral fortunes waned, so too did support for Republicans running for the Senate. Eight Republican incumbents—Susan Collins in Maine, David Perdue in Georgia, Kelly Loeffler in Georgia, Thom Tillis in North Carolina, Lindsey Graham in South Carolina, Steve Daines in Montana, Cory Gardner in Colorado, and Martha McSally in Arizona—started the year favored to win reelection. But as the year wore on, they found themselves in increasingly competitive races. By the fall, the Cook Political Report listed all as vulnerable or likely to lose. The Democrats seemed likely to lose only one Senate seat, the one held by Doug Jones in Alabama.[50] Democrats needed to net four seats to win a majority, and by Election Day, that looked more likely than not.

Based on estimates in late November—with two runoffs in Georgia to happen in January 2021—the Democrats look to have come up short. John Hickenlooper defeated Cory Gardner in Colorado and Mark Kelly defeated Martha McSally in Arizona, but the Democrats were unable to tip

figure 10.4

DISTRIBUTION OF ELECTORAL VOTES IN THE 2020 PRESIDENTIAL ELECTION

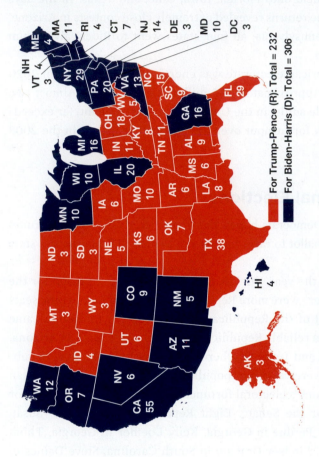

For Trump-Pence (R): Total = 232

For Biden-Harris (D): Total = 306

NOTE: Maine and Nebraska allocate Electoral College votes by congressional district.

SOURCE: Compiled by author. Results reflect projections as of November 11, 2020. *New York Times*, "Presidential Election Results," https://www.nytimes.com/interactive/2020/11/03/us/elections/results-president.html (11/11/2020).

At the beginning of 2020, the U.S. Senate seemed out of reach for the Democrats. But as Trump's electoral fortunes waned, so too did support for Republican's running for the Senate. Seven Republican U.S. Senators—including Susan Collins in Maine—suddenly found themselves in very competitive races. But the Democrats wound up coming up short, and Republicans held onto their majority.

any of the other seats, leaving Republicans to hold onto their majority (see Table 10.2A).

The election for the House of Representatives followed a similar course. At the beginning of the year, it looked likely that the Democrats would lose seats in the November election— possibly even their majority. As 2020 rolled on, the tables gradually turned. On the eve of the election, the Cook Political Report showed no Democratic seats to be leaning or likely to be won by Republicans, but five Republican seats leaned toward or were likely pickups for the Democrats. Another 17 Republican seats and nine Democratic seats were toss ups.[51]

As with the Senate, neither party was able to expand its majority. Based on late-November estimates the Republicans look to ultimately pick up a net of five seats, leaving the House more narrowly split between the two parties (see Table 10.2B).

The State Elections

The year 2020 also saw the election of 11 state governors and more than 5,800 state legislators in 86 state legislative chambers across 44 states. Little change was expected in the gubernatorial elections, as the states holding these elections were solidly Republican or solidly Democratic—with the exception of Montana, where the incumbent Democratic governor was term limited. The state legislatures would be a better indicator of the changing political fortunes of 2020.

table 10.2A

SENATE ELECTION RESULTS, 2000–2020

YEAR	TURNOUT (%)	PARTY RATIO	SEAT SHIFT	DEMOCRATS REELECTED (%)	REPUBLICANS REELECTED (%)
2000	54.2	50 D, 50 R	+5 D	93.3	64.3
2002	39.5	48 D, 51 R	+1 R	83.3	93.3
2004	60.3	44 D, 55 R	+4 R	92.9	100.0
2006	40.2	50 D, 49 R	+6 D	100.0	57.1
2008	61.0	59 D, 41 R	+8 D	100.0	66.7
2010	37.8	53 D, 47 R	+6 R	76.9	100.0
2012	54.0	55 D*, 45 R	+2 D	100.0	71.0
2014	36.4	44 D*, 54 R	+9 R	64.7	100.0
2016	58.0	48 D*, 52 R	+2 D	100.0	90.9
2018	48.5	47 D*, 53 R	+2 R	84.6	87.6
2020	66.4	48 D, 50 R	+1 D	91.7	90.0

*Includes two independents who caucus with the Democrats.

NOTE: Data are based on election results as of 11/11/2020. Senate races in several states remain undecided pending recounts and runoff elections.

SOURCES: 2000-2018: United States Election Project, http://www.electproject.org/home (accessed 11/19/20); 2020 results reflect authors' calculations as of 11/19/20.

Coming into the election, Republicans controlled 58 state legislative chambers (upper or lower house) and Democrats controlled 40. Of those 98 chambers, 19 were in danger of changing from one party's control to the other's.

The biggest implication of the state legislative elections was the extent to which the state legislative and executive branches would end up under the control of a single party or divided between the parties. Divided control forces the parties to negotiate budgets and laws across a wider set of interests than just those represented by any one party, but divided government can also lead to gridlock and ineffectiveness. The state governments are essential in dealing with public health and economic development, two challenges facing all states in 2020, as they manage much of the planning and policy making in these domains, including funding for infrastructure, hospitals, and other vital services. Leading up to the election, Republicans had complete control of the legislature and executive in 21 states, Democrats had complete control in 15 states, and control was divided in 14 states. The situation in 11 states seemed

table 10.2B

HOUSE ELECTION RESULTS, 2000–2020

YEAR	TURNOUT (%)	PARTY RATIO	SEAT SHIFT	DEMOCRATS REELECTED (%)	REPUBLICANS REELECTED (%)
2000	54.2	212 D, 222 R	+1 D	98.0	97.5
2002	39.5	205 D, 229 R	+8 R	97.4	97.5
2004	60.3	201 D, 232 R	+3 R	97.4	99.0
2006	40.2	233 D, 202 R	+30 D	100.0	89.6
2008	61.0	257 D, 178 R	+24 D	97.9	92.1
2010	37.8	193 D, 242 R	+64 R	78.8	98.7
2012	54.0	201 D, 234 R	+8 D	89.0	90.0
2014	36.4	188 D, 247 R	+13 R	94.0	98.9
2016	58.0	194 D, 241 R	+6 D	97.0	95.1
2018	48.5	231 D, 204 R	+37 D	100.0	88.3
2020	66.4	223 D, 212 R	+10 R	93.7	99.5

NOTE: Data are based on election results as of 11/11/2020. House races in several states remain undecided pending recounts and runoff elections.

SOURCES: 2000–2018: United States Election Project, http://www.electproject.org/home (accessed 11/19/20); 2020 results reflect authors' calculations as of 11/19/20.

likely to change with the election. In nearly all cases, the shift was toward divided government.[52]

As with the U.S. House and Senate elections, the 2020 results in the state legislatures returned more of the same. Nearly all of the legislatures remained controlled by the party that had controlled them before the election.

Looking to the Future

The 2020 election was transformed by the extraordinary events surrounding the COVID-19 pandemic. Over 300,000 Americans died as a result of the epidemic between March and November 2020, and the economy experienced the deepest short-term reduction in employment since the Great Depression. The public was concerned first and foremost about the economy and restarting businesses across the United States; they wanted the government to address problems of racial equity; and they wanted the new leadership to get a handle on the pandemic.

According to national exit polls, 34 percent of voters said that the economy was their first concern, 21 percent were most concerned about racial equality, and 18 percent prioritized the coronavirus. These top concerns were followed by issues of crime and safety (11 percent) and health care (11 percent). As a sign of just how much things had changed, in 2018, just two years earlier, health care was the public's number-one concern. Immigration, which was the public's second-highest concern in 2018, did not even make the top-five list in 2020.

The new national and state governments had their work cut out for them. They had to address a pandemic that was again sweeping across the country with a second wave of infections and they had to address the economic dislocations and social unrest sparked by the virus. In addition, difficult questions of racial equity and police reform were now front and center. President-elect Biden wasted no time. The week following the 2020 general election, he established a team of public health experts to begin to address the pandemic.

State governments will also shape the 2021 redistricting process. Following the 2020 census, the United States will reapportion its congressional seats among the states and every congressional district and state legislative district in the country will be redrawn. In nearly every state, the state legislature passes a redistricting law, and the governor may sign the law or veto it. Whoever controls the state legislatures and governorships in 2021, then, will determine the contours of representation in the states and U.S. Congress for the next decade. Following the 2020 election, Republicans controlled the legislature and the governor's office in 23 states; Democrats controlled the legislature and the governor's office in 15 states; and government was divided in 12 states.

The focal point of the 2020 election was surely the presidency. Joe Biden promised to depart from the Trump administration's policies on immigration, climate, energy, health care, racial equity, and, most important, the response to the pandemic. He promised a unity government that would reach out to all constituencies, rather than focusing just on the Democratic Party's base. That promise was more than a posture; it was a political necessity. With Republicans controlling a majority of the Senate and roughly half of all state governments, the Democratic administration would have to reach across the aisle and find common ground in order to deal with the challenges facing the country.

CONCLUSION

How do electoral rules shape the way citizens are represented in government? How do voters decide who should represent them? Elections are not the only form of political action by the public, but they are the most peaceful means of linking citizens and governments—providing governments with popular support and citizens with a measure of influence over government.

The central institutions of American elections—single-member districts and plurality rule—create strong pressures toward a two-party system and majority rule. Even in elections in which one party wins a plurality but not a majority, that party typically wins a majority of legislative seats. The election itself, then, determines the government. Other systems often produce outcomes in which no party wins a majority of seats, resulting in a period of negotiation and coalition formation among the parties to determine who will govern.

Voters' choices depend in no small part on the tendency to vote for a given party as a matter of ingrained personal identity. If that were all there was to voting behavior, then elections might not provide a meaningful way of governing. However, voters' preferences are as strongly rooted in the issues at hand as in the choices themselves: the candidates. Voting decisions reflect individuals' assessments about whether it makes sense to keep public policies on the same track or to change direction, whether those in office have done a good job and deserve to be reelected or have failed and should be replaced. The total of all voters' preferences responds collectively to fluctuations in the economy, to differences in the ideological and policy orientations of the parties, and to the personal attributes of the candidates.

Key Terms

Check Your Understanding

1. Describe how the electorate has expanded since the beginning of the Republic. Which groups of people can now vote who could not at that time?

2. What restrictions are there presently on voting? What are some of the factors that contribute to the low turnout rate in the United States?

3. What are several specific examples of how the United States' electoral laws and institutions differ from those of other democracies throughout the world?

4. How do demographic characteristics like age, education, and geographic location contribute to whether or not an individual decides to vote?

5. Describe the importance of money and the role of the media in campaigns.

6. Given the results of the 2020 elections, what issues do you expect to see at the top of the current administration's policy agenda?

Earn a better grade on your test. InQuizitive personalizes your learning path to help you master the concepts from this chapter. In a recent efficacy study of American government students, InQuizitive increased test scores by an average of 17 points (see back cover).

CHAPTER ELEVEN

POLITICAL PARTIES

Political parties are teams of politicians, activists, and voters whose goal is to win control of the government. They do so by recruiting and nominating candidates to run for office; by accumulating the resources needed to run campaigns, especially people and money; and by pursuing a policy agenda that can appeal to large numbers of voters and win elections. Once in office, parties organize the legislature and attempt to put their stamp on the laws passed by Congress and the president.

We often refer to the United States as a nation with a "two-party system," meaning that since the 1850s, the Democratic and Republican parties have dominated the American political landscape, electing every president and nearly every member of Congress, governor, and state legislator in the country. As we will see, the American electoral system, coupled with voters' loyalties to the two parties, usually dooms third-party or independent candidacies.

The idea of party competition was not always accepted in the United States. In the early years of the Republic, parties were seen as threats to the social order. In his 1796 farewell address, President George Washington warned his countrymen to avoid partisan politics:

> Let me . . . warn you in the most solemn manner against the baneful effects
> of the spirit of party generally. This spirit . . . exists under different shapes
> in all government, more or less stifled, controlled, or repressed, but in
> those of the popular form it is seen in its greater rankness and is truly their
> worst enemy.[1]

Parties, however, play a critical role in making representative government possible. By offering distinctive "brands," the parties simplify the choices that voters must make and help voters to hold officials accountable for their actions. While voters may not know much about individual candidates, they do have a

general idea about the two parties. While they may not know whether a particular individual was an effective representative, they can easily hold the party in power accountable if they are unhappy with the nation's direction.

Parties, moreover, ease the transition from elections to governance. As we will see, they bring together the representatives of diverse constituencies into more coherent coalitions that can work together to govern. Thus, parties help tie elections to governance.

In recent years, the parties' ability to bridge elections and governing has been undermined by ideological polarization. At one time, each party included liberal, moderate, and conservative factions. Today, there are few conservative Democrats and hardly any liberal Republicans. Moreover, within each party, the most ideologically motivated groups are also the most likely to vote, especially in primary elections. This polarization makes it difficult for the parties to achieve agreement on solutions to the nation's problems, thus complicating governance.

In this chapter, we explore the origins and character of the American party system. Political parties are nowhere mentioned in the Constitution and were viewed with suspicion by the country's founders. However, it is difficult to imagine how American government and politics would work without parties.

After the May 2020 killing of George Floyd, an unarmed Black man, by Minneapolis police, Democrats proposed sweeping legislation that would target police misconduct and racial bias. Republicans did not support all of the same proposed measures. In this image, Democrats led by House Speaker Nancy Pelosi and Senate Minority Leader Chuck Schumer observe a moment of silence for victims of police brutality.

▪ **Could representative government be effective without political parties?**

Learning Objectives

- Outline the basic functions of political parties.

- Describe the roles that parties play in government and in the policy-making process.

- Explain how parties organize and influence elections.

- Describe how parties are organized at the national, state, and local levels.

- Trace the historical development of party systems in the United States from the Founding to the present.

FUNCTIONS OF THE PARTIES

Our inability to conceive of democracy without parties is not a failure of our imaginations or an accident of American history. Rather, it reflects a law of democratic politics. Parties form to solve key problems in a democracy. Throughout this chapter, we highlight some of the general functions of parties in any democracy, but we are especially attentive to party politics in the United States.

Why Do Political Parties Form?

political party

An organized group that attempts to control the government by electing its members to office.

Political parties, like interest groups, are organizations seeking influence over government, but ordinarily they can be distinguished from interest groups (which we consider in more detail in Chapter 12) by their purpose. A party seeks to control the entire government by electing its members to office, thereby controlling the government's personnel. Interest groups, through campaign contributions and other forms of assistance, are also concerned with electing politicians—in particular, those who are inclined in the groups' policy directions. But interest groups ordinarily do not sponsor candidates directly, and between elections they usually accept government and its personnel as givens and try to influence governmental policies through them. They are *benefit seekers*, whereas parties are composed largely of *office seekers*.[2]

Parties are involved mainly in nominations and elections: recruiting candidates for office, getting out the vote, and making it easier for citizens to choose their leaders. They also influence the institutions of government—providing the leadership and organization of the various congressional committees. The political parties in the United States were ultimately formed by politicians to serve the politicians' aims. Parties make easier the basic tasks of political life: running for office, organizing one's supporters, and forming a government.

Recruiting Candidates

One of the most important party activities is the recruitment of candidates for office. Each election year, candidates must be found for thousands of state and local offices, as well as congressional seats. Where an incumbent is not seeking reelection or an incumbent in the opposing party appears vulnerable, party leaders identify strong candidates and try to interest them in entering the campaign.

The recruiting season begins early because, in some states, the dates by which candidates must formally declare their candidacy for a November general election come as early as January. Candidate recruitment in the spring shapes each party's message and fortune in November. Over the past decade, the Republicans have been especially successful at recruiting and electing candidates to state legislative seats; once elected, they then become likely prospects to run for the U.S. House and Senate and for statewide offices such as governor and attorney general. But sometimes parties fail to recruit anyone to run for a seat. In 2018, a record number of women ran for U.S. Senate, U.S. House, and governor, in part because of the mobilizing efforts spurred by the Women's Marches in early 2017 and the #MeToo movement. The Democratic Party also had extremely strong recruitment in 2017 and 2018, a fact that many saw as a leading indicator of a strong year for that party or even a wave election.[3] This momentum extended to the 2020 Democratic presidential primary, in which five women initially competed for the nomination. Joe Biden, the Democratic nominee, selected Kamala Harris as his running mate. She would become the first woman, the first child of immigrants, and the first person of color to be elected vice president of the United States.

An ideal candidate will be charismatic, organized, knowledgeable, and excellent at debate; have a scandal-free record; and be able to raise enough money to mount a serious campaign. Party leaders usually do not provide financial backing to candidates who cannot raise substantial funds on their own. For a House seat, candidates typically need to raise between $500,000 and $1 million; for a Senate seat, several million dollars; and for the presidency, upwards of $1 billion.

Nominating Candidates

Nomination is the process of selecting one party candidate to run for each elective office. The nominating process can precede the election by many months, as it does when a large slate of presidential candidates must be pared down through a grueling series of debates and state primaries, conventions, and caucuses until there is only one survivor in each party—that party's nominee. Figure 11.1 summarizes the types of nominating processes that we discuss in this section.

Nomination by Convention.   A nominating convention is a formal meeting of members of a political party that is governed by rules about participation and procedures. Conventions are meetings of delegates elected by party members from the relevant county (county convention) or state (state convention). Delegates to each party's national convention, which nominates the party's presidential and

nomination
The process by which political parties select their candidates for election to public office.

figure 11.1

TYPES OF NOMINATING PROCESSES

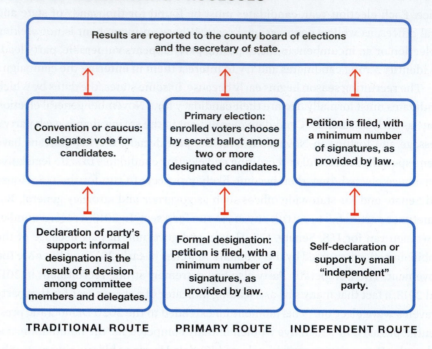

Results are reported to the county board of elections and the secretary of state.

Convention or caucus: delegates vote for candidates.

Primary election: enrolled voters choose by secret ballot among two or more designated candidates.

Petition is filed, with a minimum number of signatures, as provided by law.

Declaration of party's support: informal designation is the result of a decision among committee members and delegates.

Formal designation: petition is filed, with a minimum number of signatures, as provided by law.

Self-declaration or support by small "independent" party.

TRADITIONAL ROUTE   PRIMARY ROUTE   INDEPENDENT ROUTE

vice presidential candidates, are chosen by party members on a state-by-state basis in various ways; there is no single national delegate selection process.

Nomination by Primary Election.   In primary elections, party members select the party's nominees directly rather than choosing delegates to do so. Primaries are the dominant method of nomination in the United States.[4]

Primary elections fall mainly into two categories: closed and open. In a **closed primary**, participation is limited to individuals who have registered their affiliation with the party by a specified time before the primary. In an **open primary**, individuals declare their affiliation at the time of voting in the primary; they simply go to the polling place and ask for the ballot of a particular party. The open primary allows each voter an opportunity to consider candidates and issues before deciding which party's contest they want to participate in. Open primaries, therefore, reduce the power of political parties. But in either case, primaries are more likely than conventions or caucuses to introduce new issues and new types of candidates into parties and political debate.

Nomination by Caucus.   In several states, including Iowa and Nevada, the presidential nominating process begins with local party meetings called caucuses. Voters registered with the party that is holding caucuses are eligible to participate in them. The caucuses involve extensive discussions among those who attend, and the meetings can last several hours. Attendees at local caucuses select delegates to county-level conventions, who in turn select delegates to the state party convention. At the state convention, the party chooses delegates to its national convention.

closed primary

A primary election in which only those voters who have registered their affiliation with the party by a specified time before the election can participate.

open primary

A primary election in which voters can choose on the day of the primary which party's primary to vote in.

Getting Out the Vote

The election period begins immediately after the nominations. An important step in the electoral process is voter registration, which takes place year-round. At one time, party workers were responsible for virtually all registration, but they have been supplemented (and in many states displaced) by civic groups such as the League of Women Voters, unions, and chambers of commerce.

Those who have registered must decide on Election Day whether to go to the polling place, stand in line, and actually vote for the various candidates and referenda on the ballot. Even in states and districts that offer voting by mail, voters have to spend time learning about the issues and candidates. Political parties, candidates, and campaigning can make a big difference in convincing potential voters to vote. Because participating in elections costs voters time and effort, and because many of the benefits that winning parties provide are public goods (that is, parties cannot exclude any individual from enjoying them), people often enjoy the benefits without taking on the costs of electing the party that provided them. Parties help overcome this *free-rider problem* (see Chapter 1) by mobilizing the voters to support the candidates.

In recent years, in addition to the parties themselves, not-for-profit groups have mobilized large numbers of people to vote and have raised millions of dollars for election organizing and advertising. Legions of workers, often volunteers, have used new technologies to build and communicate with networks of supporters—some groups mobilizing Democrats, and others, Republicans. To comply with federal election and tax law, these "netroots" organizations must maintain their independence from the parties,[5] even though they have the same objectives and essentially act as shadow supplements to them. The netroots have become essential to campaign organizations, and these new forms of direct campaigning have produced a noticeable uptick in voter turnout.

Facilitating Electoral Choice

Political parties make the choice much easier for voters. It is often argued that we should vote for the best person regardless of party affiliation. But on any general-election ballot, only a handful of candidates are likely to be well-known to the voters: certain candidates for president, U.S. Senate, U.S. House, and governor. As one moves down the ballot, voters' familiarity with the candidates declines. Without party labels, voters would constantly confront a bewildering array of new choices and have difficulty making informed decisions. Without a doubt, candidates' party affiliations help voters make reasonable choices.

By providing a recognizable "brand name," parties give voters information they need to participate in elections. Without knowing much about a particular candidate, voters can tell from the party label how the candidate will likely behave once elected. In the United States, the Democratic Party is committed to stronger governmental regulation of the economy and a larger public sector; the Republican

Party labels provide a "brand name" and help voters make choices even when they are less familiar with the candidates. Voters can infer from party labels the principles and policies that the candidate is likely to support. Here a campaign sign in Texas emphasized the policy priorities of the Republican party.

Party favors a limited governmental role in the economy and reduced government spending paired with tax reductions. The Democrats favor aggressive protection of civil rights for women and for minorities and a secular approach to religion in public life. The Republicans generally want to ban abortion and favor governmental participation in expanding the role of religion in society.

The parties' positions on the economy were cemented in the 1930s, and their division on social issues emerged during the 1960s and 1970s. The Democratic positions are loosely labeled *liberal*, and those of the Republicans, *conservative*. Party labels also benefit politicians. By having recognizable labels, candidates in most districts and states are spared the expense of educating voters about what they stand for. The labels *Democrat* and *Republican* are usually sufficient.

Influencing National Government

The two major parties are often called "big tents," meaning that they try to bring together as broad a coalition of groups and ideas as possible. Positioning themselves as far-reaching coalitions prevents effective national third parties from emerging and guarantees that the Democrats and Republicans remain the only rivals for control of Congress and for the presidency.

The coalitions that come together in the Democratic and Republican parties shape the parties' platforms on public policy, determining which interests and social groups align themselves with which party and also which issues become politically significant. The Democratic Party today embraces a philosophy of active governmental intervention in the economy, based on the assumption that regulation is necessary to ensure orderly economic growth, prevent the creation of monopolies, and reduce harmful side effects of economic activity, such as pollution, poverty, and unemployment. In addition, the Democratic Party supports the protection and expansion of civil rights, especially for women and racial minorities.

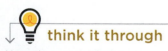

think it through

How do you think the Democrats and Republicans try to appeal to college students such as you? What policies or ideas did each party put forward regarding higher education in an attempt to win this important constituency during the most recent election?

The Republican Party endorses a philosophy of laissez-faire economics and a minimal governmental role in the economy. The coalition that Ronald Reagan built in the late 1970s paired this vision of limited governmental intervention in the economy with expanded governmental support for religion and opposition to affirmative action and abortion—views that continue to represent the party today (see the Policy Principle box on p. 351).

The major U.S. parties appeal to distinctly different core constituencies. The Democratic Party at the national level seeks to unite organized labor, the poor, members of racial minorities, and liberal upper-middle-class professionals. The Republicans, by contrast, appeal to business, to upper-middle-class

the policy principle
PARTY COALITIONS AND ABORTION POLICY

Political action involves merging people's individual preferences in order to pursue some collective purpose. For interest groups, collective action is relatively straightforward: people who share a common policy goal work together to achieve that goal. For political parties, however, collective action is more complicated. Parties hope not only to achieve policy goals but also to capture public offices. In some instances, party leaders find that they must compromise on policy goals in order to enhance the party's overall electoral chances.

To complicate matters, the two major American political parties, the Republican Party and the Democratic Party, are coalitions of various forces and individuals who agree on some things but not on others. The Republican Party, for example, includes economic conservatives who favor lower taxes, social and religious conservatives who oppose abortion and same-sex marriage, libertarians who seek a smaller government, populists who oppose free-trade policies, and a number of other factions.

Every four years the parties write platforms summarizing their core principles and policy positions. Platforms are declarations of collective policy preferences, but the road from collective policy statement to policy action can be complex. Take the case of abortion. In 1973 the Supreme Court affirmed, in the case of *Roe v. Wade*, that women have the right to seek an abortion under the Fourteenth Amendment. Until that time, neither party had mentioned abortion in its platform, but in 1976 the first presidential election following the Court's decision, both parties issued broad statements on the issue. Republicans opposed abortion but called it "a moral and personal issue" on which people might disagree.

Over time, the Republican position hardened. By 1980 the Republican platform stated that the party supported a constitutional amendment protecting "the right to life for unborn children." The 2012 and 2016 Republican Party platforms called for a constitutional amendment to overturn *Roe v. Wade*, opposed the use of public funds for abortion, demanded the prohibition of "partial birth abortion," called on the president to appoint judges who oppose abortion, and demanded an end to federal funding of embryonic-stem-cell research.

On the one hand, Republicans' increasingly staunch opposition to abortion reflected the growing importance

An anti-abortion protest in Washington, D.C., in 2016.

of social conservatives in the electorate and the recognition that the party needed their support in many districts. On the other hand, despite electing three presidents since 1980 and frequently controlling the House, the Senate, or both, Republicans in government have enacted few policies to actually bring an end to abortion.

The explanation for this apparent contradiction between principles and practices is rooted in the nature of the American party system. Anti-abortion rhetoric energizes one faction of the party, but anti-abortion action runs counter to the views of many other Republicans and might offend moderate and independent voters whom the party also needs at the polls. This example illustrates how parties' efforts to appeal to various groups in the electorate may, in fact, make action in the policy arena more difficult.

think it through

1. If parties are "big tents" that claim to represent groups of voters with various preferences, how does this complicate policy making on controversial issues like abortion?

2. Would policy making and governance be easier if numerous smaller parties were represented in Congress? Would voters' preferences be more faithfully represented? Why or why not?

and upper-class people who work in the private sector, to social conservatives, and to working-class conservatives. In 2020, Democrat Joe Biden won 55 percent of the votes of college graduates, and Biden and Republican Donald Trump split the votes of those without a college education evenly, 49 percent to 49 percent. The latter figure, though, masks an important racial difference. Among Whites, Biden won 51 percent of White college graduates and just 32 percent of White non-college graduates.

Often, party leaders try to promote issues and develop programs that will expand their party's base of support while eroding that of the opposition. As noted already, during the 1980s, under President Reagan, the Republicans devised a series of "social issues"—including support for school prayer, opposition to abortion, and opposition to affirmative action—designed to cultivate the support of White southerners. This effort was extremely successful at increasing Republican strength in the once solidly Democratic South. In the 1990s, under President Bill Clinton, the Democratic Party sought to develop new social programs designed to solidify the party's base among working-class and poor voters, along with new, somewhat conservative economic programs aimed at attracting middle- and upper-middle-class voters. President Donald Trump's protectionist policies, especially his promise to withdraw from the Trans-Pacific Partnership and renegotiate NAFTA, played extremely well among working-class voters in the upper Midwest, who had traditionally voted Democratic. We saw these same principles in play in 2020 during the pandemic: President Trump sought to open the economy quickly in order to prevent a recession, while Democrat Joe Biden advocated for a slower opening accompanied by additional public support to Americans to mitigate the effects of unemployment.

Both parties translate their general goals into concrete policies through the members they elect to office. In the 1980s and 1990s, for example, Republicans cut taxes and social spending, increased defense spending, and enacted restrictions on abortion. In the late 1990s, Democrats defended consumer and environmental programs against Republican attacks and sought to expand domestic social programs.

In 2009, through the Affordable Care Act (ACA), President Barack Obama and a Democratic-controlled Congress created a national health insurance system that guarantees all Americans access to health care—a key item on the Democrats' platform since the 1940s. Beginning in 2010, the Republican Party made repeal of the ACA one of its central messages and policy promises, while the Democratic Party doubled down on its support of the act. In 2017 the House of Representatives, with the support of President Trump, passed a bill to repeal large portions of the ACA.

But American political parties are not teams that always work in unison. The repeal effort stalled in the Senate, where it did not go far enough for some conservative Republicans and went too far for some more moderate Republicans. Another example of parties not working in unison occurred in March 2019 when four Republican senators broke with their party to end a partial shutdown of the federal government, triggered when President Trump insisted that Congress appropriate $5.7 billion to build a wall along the US-Mexico border.[6]

PARTIES IN GOVERNMENT

The ultimate test of a political party is its influence on the institutions of government and the policy-making process. Most parties originate inside the government. Political parties form as groups of those who support the government's actions and those who do not; in the United Kingdom these groups are called Government and Opposition.[7] In the American context, parties compete to control both Congress and the presidency.

The Parties and Congress

The two major U.S. political parties have a profound influence on the organization and day-to-day operation of Congress. The Speaker of the House, perhaps the most powerful person in Congress, holds a party office. All House members take part in electing the Speaker, but the actual selection is made by the **majority party**, the party that holds the majority of seats in the chamber. When the majority-party caucus presents a nominee to the entire House, its choice is invariably ratified in a straight party-line vote.

The parties also organize the committee system of both houses of Congress. Although the whole membership of each chamber adopts the rules organizing its committees and defining the jurisdiction of each one, party leadership and party caucuses determine all other features of the committees. For example, each party is assigned a quota of members for each committee, the number depending on the

majority party
The party that holds the majority of seats in a legislative chamber, such as the U.S. House or Senate.

The Speaker of the House, who has enormous influence over committee assignments and other congressional activity, is selected by the majority party. Republican Mitch McConnell served as the Senate Majority leader during the 116th Congress. Democrat Nancy Pelosi was sworn in as Speaker in 2019 for the 116th Congress.

proportion of total seats in the chamber held by the party. On the rare occasions when an independent or third-party candidate is elected, the leaders of the two parties must agree on whose quota this member's committee assignments will count against.

The assignment of individual members to committees is a party decision, as is the choice of the committee chair. Since the late nineteenth century, most appointments of committee chairs have been automatic—based on the length of continuous service on the committee. This seniority system has existed only because of the support of the two parties, and either party can depart from it by a simple vote. During the 1970s, both parties reinstated the practice of reviewing each chair—voting every two years on whether to renew the appointment. In 2001, Republicans limited House committee chairs to three terms. After three terms, chairs are forced to step down but are generally replaced by the next-most-senior Republican member of each committee.

President and Party

The president serves as a symbol for voters of his or her party, whose electoral fortunes rise and fall with the president's success or failure. During midterm congressional elections, when the president is not on the ballot, voters usually hold the president's party accountable for current problems. When the economy does poorly, Americans punish the president's party, even when the opposing party controls Congress.

The president of the United States also relies heavily on fellow party members in organizing the executive branch and passing legislation. Unlike in parliamentary governments, such as that of the United Kingdom, the heads of executive departments are not members of the legislature. With few exceptions, department heads and other key presidential appointees are people loyal to the president and his or her political party: most have served as governors of states, members of Congress, or close advisers of the president in previous offices or campaigns.

The president and White House staff also work closely with congressional party leaders to shepherd legislation through Congress. With few exceptions (such as nominations and treaties), the president cannot introduce legislation and must rely on members of Congress to do so. Nearly all of the president's legislative initiatives begin as bills introduced by fellow party members in the House and Senate. The leadership of the president's party also negotiates with individual members of Congress to build majority support for a White House–sponsored bill. Sometimes even the president will try to persuade individual legislators to support a particular bill.

The president's ability to get bills through Congress depends on which party controls the House and Senate. When the president's party enjoys majorities in both chambers, his or her legislative agenda typically will succeed more than 80 percent of the time. President Obama, during his first year in office, had the

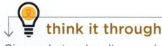

think it through

Given what we've discussed about unified and divided government, how do you expect the results of the 2020 election to impact whether or not the president can achieve his legislative agenda?

highest degree of support for a president since World War II, with a majority of Congress supporting his position 96 percent of the time.[8] When another party controls at least one chamber, however, the president has a much more difficult time. In the 113th Congress (2013–15), Democrats controlled the Senate and Republicans controlled the House. Bills supported by President Obama were passed in the Senate 93 percent of the time and in the House only 15 percent of the time.[9]

PARTIES IN THE ELECTORATE

Political parties are more than just political leaders; they include millions of people and organizations such as labor unions, corporations, and other interest groups. This large-scale membership helps parties organize and influence elections.

Party Identification

As we saw in Chapter 10, individual voters tend to develop **party identification**, a personal attachment to one of the parties. Political scientists have developed three distinct theories of how party identification develops, and they point to very different understandings of its effect on elections.[10] People's identification with a particular party may be based on a psychological attachment formed through their upbringing, on the connection between their ideology and the party's policy positions, on their past experiences with particular politicians, or on a mixture of these influences.

party identification

An individual's attachment to a particular political party, which may be based on issues, ideology, past experience, upbringing, or a mixture of these elements.

Party Identification as Psychological Attachment. First, some scholars view party identification as a psychological attachment that individuals hold, often throughout adulthood, to one of the parties. In this view, such an attachment is shaped by the loyalties of a person's parents and other family members, friends, and local communities, rather than by issues and ideologies. Once an attachment is formed, according to this theory, it is likely to persist and even be handed down to children, unless certain very strong factors convince the individual to reject the party. In some sense, party identification is seen as similar to brand loyalty in the marketplace: consumers choose a brand of automobile for its appearance or mechanical characteristics and stick with it out of loyalty, habit, and unwillingness to reexamine their choices, but they may eventually switch if the old brand no longer serves their interests.

The first few presidential elections that an individual experiences as an adult are also thought to have a particularly profound influence on that person's understanding of the parties and politics. And as new generations encounter politics, their experiences carry forward throughout their lives. Those who were 18 to 24 years old in 1984, for example, identify overwhelmingly with the Republican

Party, because those elections marked the triumph of Ronald Reagan's presidency and political philosophy, the rise of a revitalized Republican Party, and the beginning of the end of the Cold War. Those who were 18 to 24 years old in 2008, in contrast, identify disproportionately with the Democratic Party, because Barack Obama's presidential campaign electrified young voters around a new vision for the future. We will have to wait to see the full effects of Donald Trump's 2016 victory on young people, but Analyzing the Evidence on pp. 358–9 provides some early insights. However it develops, an individual's psychological attachment to a party makes that person want to support it, even when she disagrees with the party on important policies or disapproves of its nominees for office.

Party Identification as Ideological Attachment to Policy Positions.   The Democratic and Republican parties are quite different today from what they were 40 years ago or 80 years ago. On matters of race relations, for example, the Democratic Party has moved during the past century from supporting segregation to spearheading civil rights. The Republican Party before the 1940s promoted protectionist policies intended to shield U.S. companies and workers from foreign competition. Then, from the 1950s to 2016, the party championed free trade. On this issue, change appears to be under way once again for the Republicans, as President Trump questioned the basic principles of free trade, withdrew the United States from the Trans-Pacific Partnership trade agreement, and pursued other policies that restricted imports (and exports) in order to protect U.S. jobs that may be threatened by imports.

Party identities are transmitted from generation to generation, but they also change, especially when new issues arise that disrupt the alignment between the political parties. For example, conflicts over civil rights in the 1950s and 1960s led many traditionally Democratic voters to break away from the Democratic Party in the late 1960s and 1970s. Many became Republicans; others refused to identify with either party. This example and others like it suggest a second explanation of party identification: it reflects the underlying values and ideologies of voters and policy positions of parties.

Parties in government are meaningful organizations for producing public policies. The relatively high degree of party loyalty in Congress and other branches of government means that voters can reasonably anticipate how politicians will act in office, so they identify with the party that pursues public policies more to their liking. For example, a union worker may feel a stronger attachment to the Democratic Party because the Democrats have historically protected union interests. A high-income earner may feel a strong pull toward the Republican Party because that party advocates for lower taxes in general, whereas the Democrats promote higher tax rates for higher-income households.

In this way, the party labels act as brand names and help voters choose the candidates that will best match their preferences. As such, party labels provide an informational shortcut. In part, those who identify with a particular party feel that it represents their interests better than others; hence, they are highly likely

think it through

What role does party label play in your decision to support a candidate? Do you use a candidate's party affiliation as a shortcut to understanding his or her policy platform, or do you still scrutinize a candidate's record and proposals regardless?

to vote for that party without even knowing a candidate's voting record or campaign promises.[11]

However, not all people fit neatly into one ideological camp or another. Some do not think about politics in ideological or policy terms, while others don't have a strong attraction to either major party's ideological position. A significant share of Americans consider themselves centrists and feel that the Democrats are somewhat too liberal and the Republicans somewhat too conservative. Other people feel pulled in different directions by different policy issues and concerns. A union member who strongly opposes abortion, for example, is drawn to both the Democrats' pro-labor policies and the Republicans' anti-abortion policies. Campaigns target such cross-pressured voters, who are often pivotal in elections.[12]

Party Identification as Reaction to Political Experiences.   A third explanation of party identification is that it reflects voters' experiences with political leaders and representatives, especially presidents. Americans hold their presidents and, to a lesser extent, Congress accountable for the country's economic performance and success in foreign affairs. A bad economy or a disastrous military intervention will lead voters to disapprove of the president and to lower their assessment of the president's party's ability to govern.

In this view, parties are teams competing to run the government: they consist of policy experts and leaders who will manage foreign policy, economic policy, and domestic policies such as environmental protection and health care. When things go well, voters conclude that the incumbent party has a good approach to running national affairs; when things go badly, they assume that the party lacks the people needed to run the government competently or the approach needed to produce prosperity, peace, and other desirable outcomes. With each successive presidency and their experience of it, individuals update their beliefs about which party is better able to govern.

As Figure 11.2 shows, most Americans identify with one of the two major political parties. Historically, approximately 7 in 10 Americans have considered themselves to be Republicans or Democrats, and even those who do not choose those labels usually say that they lean toward one of the two parties. Over the past 20 years, however, more and more people have begun to call themselves independents. That category is now consistently the single largest group in opinion polls about party identification, rising to as high as 42 percent in January 2020, an election year.

Party identification gives citizens a stake in election outcomes that goes beyond the race at hand. It is why people who identify strongly with a party are more likely than other Americans to go to the polls and, of course, to support their party. Although identification with a party does not guarantee voting for that party's candidates, "strong identifiers" do so almost always, and "weak identifiers" do so most of the time. For example, according to exit polls, 93 percent of people who called themselves Republicans voted for Donald Trump in 2020, and 94 percent of those who called themselves Democrats voted for Joe Biden.[13]

What Motivates Political Engagement among Young People?

Contributed by **David E. Campbell** and **Christina Wolbrecht**, *University of Notre Dame*

Donald Trump's 2016 victory over Hillary Clinton struck many as a blow against gender equality. Many described Clinton as a role model, but would her defeat discourage the very young women she had hoped to inspire?

To find out, we analyzed a nationally representative survey of 997 adolescents ages 15–18 and their parents, conducted online. Both teens and parents responded to two waves of this survey, the first during the fall 2016 campaign and a follow-up roughly one year later, in the fall of 2017. We asked about their views of American democracy and political engagement. By interviewing the same people both before and after the election, we were able to see whether their attitudes changed.

Here's what we found. First, disillusionment with the political system rose dramatically—but only among girls who identify as Democrats. In the fall of 2016, about a third of Democratic girls said that the political system in America "does not help people with their genuine needs," more or less the same proportion as Democratic boys and Republican girls and boys.[1] One year later, 53 percent of Democratic girls said that U.S. democracy does not help people with their needs—a significant jump, especially compared to the fact that the opinions of the other groups barely budged. (Both Republican boys and girls became slightly less pessimistic, presumably because their candidate won.)

Democratic Girls Become More Disillusioned with U.S. Politics after 2016 Election

Percent saying that the political system DOES NOT help people with their genuine needs

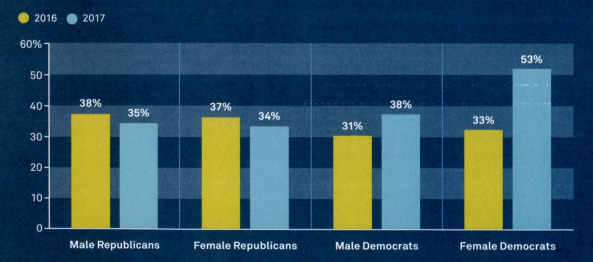

When people are disillusioned with democracy, they often disengage. Why bother getting involved if all is for naught? But Democratic girls who came to doubt American democracy responded quite differently.

After 2016, Democratic girls say they became more politically active—and particularly, they were more likely to say that they are or plan to be engaged in lawful political protest.[2] The biggest spike came among those Democratic girls who became disillusioned. Instead of dampening their enthusiasm for political engagement, their doubts about the state of U.S. politics seem to have increased their desire to be heard.

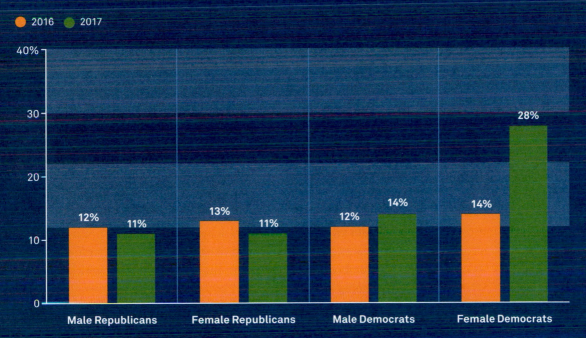

Democratic Girls Become More Interested in Protesting after 2016 Election

Percent saying that they have or will engage in political protest

● 2016 ● 2017

	2016	2017
Male Republicans	12%	11%
Female Republicans	13%	11%
Male Democrats	12%	14%
Female Democrats	14%	28%

Why might Democratic girls in particular become interested in protesting after the 2016 election? We suspect that they're following role models—but not that of just one woman politician. The January 2017 Women's March on Washington, the largest single-day demonstration in U.S. history, protested Trump's inauguration as president and launched a wave of activism.

Across the nation, the majority of activists have been women, many of whom use gendered rhetoric and symbols, such as the famous pink hats.

These protesters provided visible role models to Democratic girls for how to channel their post-2016 political frustration. Many have come to see protest as an important part of their own political repertoire. "The Resistance" is the role model.

1 David E. Campbell and Christina Wolbrecht, "*The Resistance as Role Model: Disillusionment and Protest Among American Adolescents After 2016*," Political Behavior 42 (2020): 1143-1168.

2 Campbell and Wolbrecht, "*Resistance as Role Model.*"

SOURCE: Family Matters Study

 → Looking at the trends illustrated in the second figure, what changes would you expect to see in interest in protesting after the 2020 election?

figure 11.2

AMERICANS' PARTY IDENTIFICATION, 1940–2020

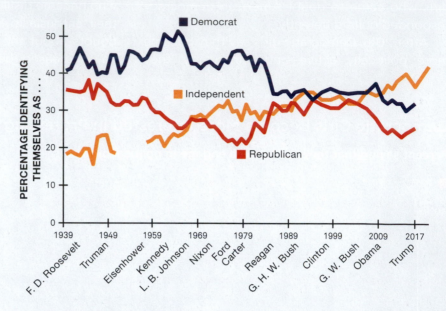

analyzing the evidence

In 1952, Democrats outnumbered Republicans significantly. Since the late 1980s, the two parties appear to have had similar numbers of loyalists. What factors might account for this partisan transformation?

NOTE: Independent data not available for 1951–56.

SOURCES: Pew Research Center, www.people-press.org/interactives/party-id-trend; and Gallup, https://news.gallup.com/poll/15370/party-affiliation.aspx (accessed 4/10/20).

party activist

A person who contributes time and energy beyond voting to support a party and its candidates.

Party activists are strong identifiers who not only vote but also volunteer their time and energy to party affairs. Activists ring doorbells, stuff envelopes, attend meetings, and contribute money to the party—essential work that keeps the organization going.

Group Basis of Politics

One view of political parties, which may be described as a pluralist view, is that they consist of coalitions of many organized groups. The leaders of organizations may choose to side with a party in an effort to influence what government does by influencing the party's policy orientation. A group can offer resources such as campaign workers, contributions, and votes; the party, in exchange, can pursue policies in line with what the group wants. Once a group is aligned with a party, the group's leaders can tell members which candidates they should vote for.

The more disciplined the group and the more resources it can offer, the more power it will have in the party. Party leaders try to build coalitions consisting of many different groups, each seeking a distinct policy or political benefit. The challenge for parties is to build coalitions that can win majorities in elections but not create too many conflicting demands.[14]

Broader social groups are also important. In the United States today, a variety of group characteristics are associated with party identification. These include race and ethnicity, gender, religion, class, and age.

Race and Ethnicity.   Since the 1960s and Democratic support for the civil rights movement, African Americans have been overwhelmingly Democratic in party identification. More than 90 percent of African Americans describe themselves as Democrats and support Democratic candidates in national, state, and local elections. Approximately 25 percent of Democratic votes in presidential races come from African American voters.[15]

Republicans, on the other hand, depend heavily on the support of White voters. Roughly 55 percent of the White electorate has supported the GOP in recent years. In 2020, Donald Trump appealed heavily to White working-class voters on issues of protecting jobs from overseas competition, limiting immigration, and rolling back excessive regulations. He won 58 percent of the votes of Whites overall, and just 26 percent of the votes of non-Whites. Trump won 48 percent of Whites with a college degree, but two thirds of Whites without a college education.[16]

Latino and Hispanic voters include people with ancestry in many different countries and with diverse political orientations. Mexican Americans, the single largest group, have historically aligned themselves with the Democratic Party, as have Puerto Ricans and Central Americans. Historically, Cuban Americans have identified themselves and voted as Republican; recently, however, they have shifted toward the Democrats. Asian Americans have been somewhat divided as well, though more of them support Democrats than Republicans. Japanese, Chinese, Filipino, and Korean communities have been long established in the United States, and their higher-income members tend to be as Republican as higher-income Whites. It is not clear whether newer Asian immigrant groups, such as the Hmong, Vietnamese, Thais, and Indians, will follow the same pattern as the older Asian American communities.

Gender.   Women are somewhat more likely to support Democrats, and men, to support Republicans. This difference is known as the **gender gap**. The 2020 election saw a wide gap between the electoral choice of men and the electoral choice of women. Biden received the vote of 57 percent of women and 45 percent of the vote of men. He received a higher share of the votes of women than even Hillary Clinton did four years earlier. The growing gap between men and women is increasingly significant because women now comprise 52 percent of the electorate.

gender gap
A distinctive pattern of voting behavior reflecting the differences in views between women and men.

Religion.   Protestants comprise 38 percent of the American population; 20 percent are Catholics; 19 percent are "nothing in particular"; 11 percent are atheists and agnostics; and the rest are spread across many different religions, including Judaism, Islam, Buddhism, and Hinduism.[17] Protestants, as a whole, lean toward the Republican Party, and Catholics, toward the Democratic Party. According to the 2018 Cooperative Congressional Election

Study, 41 percent of Protestants identified as Republicans, and 28 percent as Democrats. Among Catholics, 37 percent identified as Democrats, and 31 percent as Republicans.

Jews, Muslims, Buddhists, Hindus, atheists, and agnostics were all strongly Democratic. Jews are among the most strongly Democratic religious groups: 55 percent identified as Democrats, while just 21 percent identified as Republicans. Mormons tend equally strongly toward the Republicans over the Democrats, 49 percent to 16 percent. More religiously conservative Protestant denominations tend to identify with the Republicans, while Protestants who are religiously liberal, such as Unitarians and Episcopalians, tend to identify as Democrats. Evangelical Protestants, in particular, have been drawn to the Republicans' conservative stands on social issues, such as gay marriage and abortion. Of people who identify with any religion (as opposed to atheists, agnostics, or those who are "nothing in particular"), 32 percent identify as Democrats, 35 percent as Republicans, and 33 percent as independents. That said, people who have no affiliation to religious denomination or who are atheists or agnostics are overwhelmingly Democrats: 42 percent identify as Democrats, 14 percent are Republicans, and 44 percent are independents.[18]

Income. Upper-income Americans are likely to affiliate with Republicans, whereas very low-income Americans are likely to identify with Democrats. Middle-class voters split evenly between the two parties, reflecting the differences between the parties on economic issues. In general, Republicans support cutting taxes and social spending—positions that reflect the interests of the wealthy. Democrats favor increased social spending, even if this requires increasing taxes—a position consistent with the interests of less affluent Americans.

Age. Age is also associated with partisanship, mainly because individuals from the same generation likely experienced similar political events during the period when their party loyalties were forming. For example, Americans in their 60s and 70s came of age politically (that is, became aware of political issues and ideas) during the Cold War, the Vietnam War, and the civil rights movement. Apparently, voters of this generation have continued to lean Democratic because they responded more favorably to the actions of Democrats at the time than to those of Republicans. Among young adult Americans in their 20s and 30s, who came of age during an era of political scandals and failures that tainted both parties, most describe themselves as independents.

Figure 11.3 indicates the relationship between party identification and various social criteria. Race, religion, income, and ideology seem to have the greatest influence on Americans' party affiliations, although none of these characteristics is invariably decisive. There are, for example, union Republicans and business Democrats. The general party identifications just discussed are broad tendencies that both reflect and reinforce the issue and policy positions that the two parties take in national and local political arenas. They

figure 11.3

PARTY IDENTIFICATION BY SOCIAL GROUP, 2020

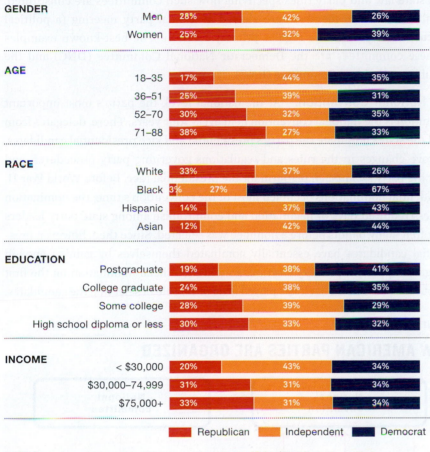

GENDER
- Men: Republican 28%, Independent 42%, Democrat 26%
- Women: Republican 25%, Independent 32%, Democrat 39%

AGE
- 18–35: Republican 17%, Independent 44%, Democrat 35%
- 36–51: Republican 25%, Independent 39%, Democrat 31%
- 52–70: Republican 30%, Independent 32%, Democrat 35%
- 71–88: Republican 38%, Independent 27%, Democrat 33%

RACE
- White: Republican 33%, Independent 37%, Democrat 26%
- Black: Republican 3%, Independent 27%, Democrat 67%
- Hispanic: Republican 14%, Independent 37%, Democrat 43%
- Asian: Republican 12%, Independent 42%, Democrat 44%

EDUCATION
- Postgraduate: Republican 19%, Independent 38%, Democrat 41%
- College graduate: Republican 24%, Independent 38%, Democrat 35%
- Some college: Republican 28%, Independent 39%, Democrat 29%
- High school diploma or less: Republican 30%, Independent 33%, Democrat 32%

INCOME
- < $30,000: Republican 20%, Independent 43%, Democrat 34%
- $30,000–74,999: Republican 31%, Independent 31%, Democrat 34%
- $75,000+: Republican 33%, Independent 31%, Democrat 34%

Legend: Republican — Independent — Democrat

NOTE: Percentages fail to add to 100 because the category "Other/don't know" is omitted.

SOURCE: Pew Research Center, www.people-press.org/2018/03/20/wide-gender-gap-growing-educational-divide-in-voters-party-identification/; U.S. Bureau of Census, "Current Population Survey," www.census.gov/data/tables/time-series/demo/voting-and-registration/p20-583.html (accessed 6/1/20).

analyzing the evidence

The political parties do not draw equal support from members of each social stratum. What patterns in party identification do you see? How might these patterns influence which people are selected as political candidates by political parties and which policies the parties support?

reflect the general tendency of groups—both organized and unorganized—to sort into partisan camps.

PARTIES AS INSTITUTIONS

Political parties in the United States today are not tightly disciplined, hierarchical organizations. Indeed, they never have been. Rather, they are made up of extensive networks of politicians, interest groups, activists, donors, consultants, and, ultimately, voters.

Contemporary Party Organizations

The United States has party organizations at virtually every level of government (Figure 11.4). These are usually committees made up of active party members, with state law and party rules specifying how such committees are constituted. Usually, committee members are elected at a local party meeting (a political **caucus**) or as part of the regular primary election. The best-known examples of these committees are the Democratic National Committee (DNC) and the Republican National Committee (RNC).

The National Convention. At the national level, the party's most important institution is the national convention held every four years. There, delegates from all of the states nominate the party's presidential and vice presidential candidates, approve changes in the rules and regulations governing party procedures, and draft the party's campaign platform for the presidential race. Before World War II, presidential nominations occupied most of the convention's time; the nomination process required days of negotiation and compromise among state party leaders and often many ballots before a nominee was selected. Since then, however, presidential candidates have essentially nominated themselves by gaining enough delegate support in primary elections to win the official nomination on the first ballot. The convention itself has played little or no role in selecting the candidates.

caucus
A meeting of a political or legislative group, normally closed to nonmembers, to select candidates, plan strategy, or make decisions about legislative matters.

figure 11.4

HOW AMERICAN PARTIES ARE ORGANIZED

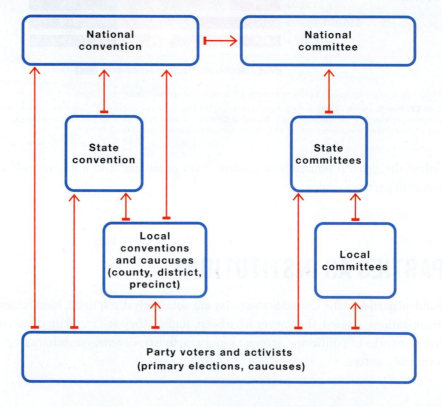

The convention's other two tasks—establishing the party's rules and platform—remain important. Party rules can determine the relative influence of competing factions within the party, as well as the party's chances for electoral success. In the late 1970s, for example, the Democratic National Convention adopted new rules favored by the party's liberal wing, under which state delegations to the convention were required to include women and minority-group members in rough proportion to those groups' representation among the party's membership in that state.

Party platforms are often dismissed as dull documents filled with platitudes that voters seldom read. Furthermore, the parties' presidential candidates make little use of the platforms in their campaigns; usually they promote their own themes. Nonetheless, the platform serves as a "treaty" in which the various factions of the party state their terms for supporting the ticket.

The National Committee.

Between conventions, each party is technically headed by its national committee: the DNC or the RNC. These committees raise campaign funds, head off factional disputes within the party, and try to enhance the party's media image. Since 1972, the number of staff and the amount of money raised have increased substantially for both national committees. The work of each committee is overseen by a chairperson. Other members are generally major party contributors or fund-raisers.

For the party that controls the White House, the national committee chair is appointed by the president. Under a first-term president, the committee focuses on the reelection campaign. The national-committee chair of the party not in control of the White House is selected by the committee itself; this person usually raises money and performs other activities on behalf of the party's members in Congress and state legislatures. For example, in the wake of Hillary Clinton's surprising defeat and the Democrats' disappointing showing in the Senate elections in 2016, the Democratic Party appointed a new chair of the DNC, Thomas Perez, to help unite the party and evaluate what went wrong.

Congressional Campaign Committees.

Each party forms two campaign committees to raise funds for its House and Senate election campaigns. The Republicans call their committees the National Republican Congressional Committee (NRCC) and the National Republican Senatorial Committee (NRSC), respectively. The Democrats call theirs the Democratic Congressional Campaign Committee (DCCC) and the Democratic Senatorial Campaign Committee (DSCC).

Although these organizations also have professional staff devoted to raising and distributing funds, developing strategies, recruiting candidates, and conducting on-the-ground campaigns, they are accountable to the party caucuses inside the House and

Local party organizations are important in conducting voter registration drives and getting out the vote. Here a volunteer at the Orange County, California, Republican headquarters prepares a mailing of campaign literature.

What Parties Do

Parties in Government

- Parties organize in support of and in opposition to governmental actions and policies.

- Parties select leaders in the House and Senate and make committee assignments.

- Politicians who are in the same party often support one another's legislation.

Parties in the Electorate

- Many voters identify with a political party that reflects their views and interests. Once formed, this identification usually persists.

- Voters use parties as a "shortcut" to decide whom to vote for in elections.

- Some people develop strong attachments to a party and become party activists, organizing campaign efforts on behalf of a party's candidates.

Parties as Institutions

- Parties are made up of networks of politicians, activists, interest groups, donors, consultants, and voters.

- Parties recruit candidates to run for office and organize caucuses, primary elections, and conventions to select a candidate to compete against the other party's candidate.

- Parties raise money and perform other activities on behalf of their members in Congress and in state legislatures.

Senate. Their chairs are members of the respective chambers (representatives or senators) and rank high in the party leadership hierarchy. The national committees and the congressional committees are sometimes rivals. Both groups seek donations from the same pool of people but for different candidates: the national committee seeks funds primarily for the presidential race, while the congressional committees focus on House and Senate seats.

State and Local Party Organizations. Each major party has a central committee in each state. The parties traditionally also have county committees and, in some instances, state senate district committees, judicial district committees, and, in larger cities, citywide party committees and local assembly-district "ward" committees. Congressional districts also may have party committees.

These organizations are very active in recruiting candidates and registering voters. Federal law permits them to spend unlimited amounts of money on "party-building" activities such as voter registration and get-out-the-vote drives, with the result that the national party organizations, which are restricted in how much they can spend on candidates, transfer millions of dollars to state and local organizations. The state and local parties, in turn, spend these funds, sometimes called *soft money*, to promote national, as well as state and local, candidates. As local organizations have become linked financially to the national parties, American political parties have grown more integrated and nationalized than ever before. At the same time, the state and local party organizations have come to control large financial resources and play important roles in elections.

The Contemporary Party as Service Provider to Candidates. Party leaders have adapted to the modern age. Parties as organizations are more professional, better financed, and more organized than ever before.[19] Political parties have evolved into "service organizations," without which it would be extremely difficult for candidates to win and hold office. For example, the national organizations of the political parties collect information, ranging from lists of likely supporters and donors in local areas to public-opinion polls in states and legislative districts, and they provide this information directly to their candidates for state and federal offices. They also have teams of experienced campaign organizers and managers who provide assistance to understaffed local candidates.[20]

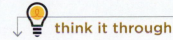

think it through

How do you see state or local party organizations active on your campus or in your social media feeds? Have they helped register students to vote? Or asked you to help in canvassing or other get-out-the-vote initiatives?

PARTY SYSTEMS

Our understanding of political parties would be incomplete if we considered only their composition and roles. The two major parties in the United States compete with each other for offices, policies, and power. Their struggle for control of government shapes the policies that they put forth, the coalitions of interests that they represent, and their ability, indeed the government's ability, to respond to the demands of the times. In short, the fate of each major party is inextricably linked to that of its rival.

Political scientists often call the arrangement of parties that are important at any given moment a nation's party system. The most obvious feature of a party system is the number of major parties competing for power. Usually, the United States has had a two-party system, meaning that only two parties have had a serious chance to win national elections. Of course, we have not always had the same two parties, and minor parties have often put forward candidates.

The term *party system*, however, also refers to the parties' organization, the balance of power between and within party coalitions, the parties' social and institutional bases, and the issues and policies around which party competition is organized. The character of a nation's party system changes as the parties realign their electoral coalitions and alter their public philosophies. Such realignment comes sometimes subtly and sometimes suddenly. Today's American party system is very different from the system of 1950, even though Democrats and Republicans continue to be the major competitors (Figure 11.5).

figure 11.5

HOW THE PARTY SYSTEM EVOLVED

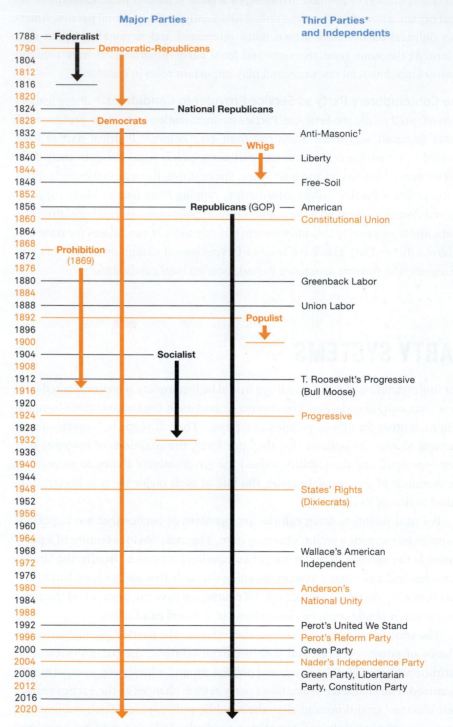

Major Parties

Third Parties* and Independents

1788	Federalist	
1790	Democratic-Republicans	
1804		
1812		
1816		
1820		
1824	National Republicans	
1828	Democrats	
1832		Anti-Masonic†
1836	Whigs	
1840		Liberty
1844		
1848		Free-Soil
1852		
1856	Republicans (GOP)	American
1860		Constitutional Union
1864		
1868		
1872	Prohibition (1869)	
1876		
1880		Greenback Labor
1884		
1888		Union Labor
1892		Populist
1896		
1900		
1904	Socialist	
1908		
1912		T. Roosevelt's Progressive (Bull Moose)
1916		
1920		
1924		Progressive
1928		
1932		
1936		
1940		
1944		
1948		States' Rights (Dixiecrats)
1952		
1956		
1960		
1964		
1968		Wallace's American Independent
1972		
1976		
1980		Anderson's National Unity
1984		
1988		
1992		Perot's United We Stand
1996		Perot's Reform Party
2000		Green Party
2004		Nader's Independence Party
2008		Green Party, Libertarian Party, Constitution Party
2012		
2016		
2020		

*In some cases there was even a fourth party. Most of the parties listed here existed for only one term.

†The Anti-Masonics not only had the distinction of being the first third party but also were the first party to hold a national nominating convention and the first to announce a party platform.

SOURCE: Compiled by authors.

Over the course of American history, changes in political forces and alignments have produced six different party systems, each with distinctive political institutions, issues, and patterns of political power and participation. Of course, some political phenomena persist across party systems—such as conflicts over the distribution of wealth, an enduring feature of American political life. But even such phenomena manifest themselves in different ways during different political eras.

The First Party System: Federalists and Democratic-Republicans

Although George Washington and many other leaders of the time criticized partisan politics, the two-party system emerged early in the history of the new Republic. Competition in Congress between northeastern merchant and southern planter factions led Alexander Hamilton and the northeasterners to form a voting bloc within Congress. The southerners, led by Thomas Jefferson and James Madison, responded by cultivating a popular following to change the balance of power within Congress.

The result of this regional rivalry was the birth of America's first national parties—the Democratic-Republicans, whose primary base was in the South, and the Federalists, whose strength was greatest in New England. The Federalists supported the use of protective tariffs to encourage manufacturers, the assumption by the federal government of responsibility for the states' Revolutionary War debts, the creation of a national bank, and the resumption of commercial ties with England. The Democratic-Republicans opposed these policies, favoring instead free trade, the promotion of farming over commercial interests, and friendship with France.

The primary rationale behind the formation of both parties was that they would create stable voting blocs within Congress around cohesive policy agendas. Although the Federalists and the Democratic-Republicans competed in elections, their ties to the electorate were loose. In 1800, the number of Americans eligible to vote was small, and voters generally followed the lead of local political, religious, and social leaders. Nominations were informal, with no rules of procedure. Local party leaders would simply gather at meetings called caucuses and agree on the person, usually one of the party leaders themselves, who would be the candidate.

In this era, before the secret ballot, many voters were reluctant to defy influential members of their community by publicly voting against them. In this context, the Democratic-Republicans and the Federalists organized political clubs and developed newspapers and newsletters to mobilize elite opinion and draw in more followers. In the election of 1800, Jefferson defeated the incumbent Federalist president, John Adams, and led his party to power. The Federalists continued to weaken and finally disappeared after the pro-British sympathies of some Federalist leaders during the War of 1812 led to charges that the party was guilty of treason.

The Second Party System: Democrats and Whigs

From the collapse of the Federalists until the 1830s, America had only one political party, the Democratic-Republicans. This period of one-party politics is sometimes known as the Era of Good Feeling, to indicate the absence of party competition. Throughout this period, however, there was intense factional conflict within the Democratic-Republican Party, particularly between supporters and opponents of General Andrew Jackson, the great American hero of the War of 1812. Jackson, one of five significant candidates for president in 1824, won the most popular and electoral votes, but a majority of neither, throwing the election into the House of Representatives. His opponents united to deny him the presidency, but he won in 1828 and again in 1832.

Jackson was greatly admired by millions of ordinary Americans living on farms and in villages, and the Jacksonians made the most of the general's appeal to the common people. To bring growing numbers of voters to the polls, they built political clubs and held mass rallies and parades, laying the groundwork for a new and more popular politics. Jackson's vice president and eventual successor, Martin Van Buren, was the organizational genius behind the Jacksonian movement, establishing a central party committee, state party organizations, and party newspapers.

In response to complaints about cliques of party leaders dominating the nominations at caucuses, the Jacksonians also established state and national party conventions as the forums for nominating presidential candidates. The conventions gave control of the presidential nominating process to the new state party organizations that the Jacksonians had created and expected to control.

The Jacksonians, whose party became known as the Democratic Party, were not without opponents, however, especially in New England. During the 1830s, groups opposing Jackson for reasons of personality and politics united to form the Whig Party, thus giving rise to the second American party system. During the 1830s and 1840s, the Democrats and the Whigs built party organizations throughout the nation and sought to enlarge their support by eliminating property restrictions and other barriers to voting—although voting was still limited to White men.

Support for the Whigs was strongest in the Northeast and among merchants; hence, to some extent they were the successors of the Federalists. Many Whigs favored a national bank, a protective tariff, and federally financed "internal improvements" (infrastructure like roads and canals). The Jacksonians opposed all three policies. In 1840, the Whigs won their first presidential election under the leadership of General William Henry Harrison, a military hero. The election marked the first time in American history that two parties competed for the presidency in every state in the Union.

In the late 1840s and early 1850s, conflicts over slavery produced sharp divisions within both parties, despite party leaders' efforts to develop compromises that would bridge the widening gulf between North and South. By 1856, the Whig Party had all but disintegrated under the strain. The Kansas-Nebraska Act of 1854 gave each western territory the right to decide whether to permit slavery. Opposition to this policy led to the formation of a number of antislavery parties, with the Republicans emerging as the strongest.[21] In 1856, the party's first presidential candidate won one-third of the popular vote and carried 11 states.

The early Republican platforms appealed to commercial as well as antislavery interests by supporting grants of federal land to homesteaders, internal improvements, construction of a transcontinental railroad, and protective tariffs. In 1858, the party won control of the House of Representatives; in 1860, the Republican presidential candidate, Abraham Lincoln, was victorious. Lincoln's victory strengthened southern calls for secession from the Union and soon led to civil war.

The Third Party System: Republicans and Democrats, 1860–1896

During the war, President Lincoln depended heavily on Republican governors and state legislatures to raise troops, provide funding, and maintain popular support for a long and bloody conflict. The South's secession had stripped the Democratic Party of many of its leaders and supporters, but the party nevertheless remained politically competitive and nearly won the 1864 presidential election because of war weariness on the part of the northern public.

With the defeat of the Confederacy in 1865, some congressional Republicans tried to convert the South into a Republican region through Reconstruction, a program that enfranchised (gave the vote to) newly freed laborers and provided federal funds for economic recovery and infrastructure rebuilding while disenfranchising many White Democratic voters and disqualifying many White Democratic politicians from holding office. Reconstruction collapsed in the 1870s, however, as a result of divisions among Republicans in Congress and violent resistance by southern Whites.

With the end of Reconstruction, the former Confederate states regained full membership in the Union and full control of their internal affairs. Throughout the South, African Americans were deprived of political rights, including the right to vote, despite post–Civil War constitutional guarantees to the contrary. The postwar South was solidly Democratic, enabling the national Democratic Party to compete with the Republicans on a more or less equal basis. From the end of the Civil War to the 1890s, the Republican Party remained the party of the North, with strong business and middle-class support, while the Democratic Party was the party of the South, with support from working-class and immigrant groups in the North.

The Fourth Party System, 1896–1932

During the 1890s, profound social and economic changes led to the emergence of a variety of protest parties, including the Populist Party, which won the support of hundreds of thousands of voters in the South and West. The Populists appealed mainly to small farmers but also attracted western miners and urban workers. In 1892, the party carried four states in the presidential election and elected governors in eight states.

In 1896, the Democrats in effect adopted the Populist platform and nominated William Jennings Bryan, a Democratic senator with Populist sympathies, for the presidency. The Republicans nominated the conservative senator William McKinley. In the ensuing campaign, northern and midwestern business interests made an all-out effort to defeat what they saw as a radical threat from the Populist-Democratic alliance. When the dust settled, the Republicans had won a resounding victory.

In large urban areas, especially in the Northeast and upper Midwest, workers became convinced that Populist-Democratic policies would threaten the industries that provided their jobs, while immigrants feared the nativist rhetoric of some Populist orators and writers. The Republicans carried the northeastern and midwestern states and confined the Democrats to their strongholds in the South and West.

For the next 36 years, the Republicans were the nation's majority party—very much the party of business, advocating low taxes, high tariffs, and minimal governmental regulation. The Democrats were too weak to offer much opposition. Southern Democrats, moreover, were more concerned with maintaining the region's autonomy on issues of race than with challenging the Republicans on other fronts.

The Fifth Party System: The New Deal Coalition, 1932–1968

The year after the Republican candidate Herbert Hoover won the 1928 presidential election, the nation's economy collapsed. The Great Depression produced economic hardship on a scale never seen before in the United States, and millions of Americans blamed the Republicans for not doing enough to promote recovery. In 1932, voters elected Franklin Delano Roosevelt and a solidly Democratic Congress. Roosevelt's program for economic recovery, the New Deal, led to substantial increases in the size and scope of the national government, which took responsibility for economic management and social welfare to an extent unprecedented in American history.

Roosevelt designed many of his programs specifically to expand the Democratic Party's political base. He rebuilt the party around a nucleus of unionized workers, upper-middle-class intellectuals and professionals, southern farmers, Jews, Catholics, and northern African Americans (few Blacks in the South could vote), making the Democrats the nation's majority party for 36 years. Republicans groped for a response to the New Deal but often wound up supporting its popular programs, such as Social Security, in what was sometimes derided as "me-too" Republicanism.

The New Deal coalition was severely strained during the 1960s by conflicts over President Lyndon Johnson's Great Society initiative, the African American civil rights movement, and the Vietnam War. A number of Great Society programs, targeting poverty and racial discrimination, involved giving power to local groups that were often at odds with city and county governments. These programs touched off battles between local Democratic organizations and the Johnson administration.

For its part, the struggle over civil rights initially divided northern Democrats, who supported the movement, from White southern Democrats, who defended racial segregation. Subsequently, as the movement launched a northern campaign seeking access to jobs and education and an end to racial discrimination in such areas as housing, northern Democrats also split, with blue-collar workers increasingly tending to vote Republican. The Vietnam War divided the Democrats still further, with liberals opposing Johnson's decision to send U.S. forces to Southeast Asia. These divisions within the Democratic Party provided an opportunity for the Republicans to return to power, which they did in 1968 under President Richard Nixon.

The Sixth Party System, 1968–Present

By the 1960s, conservative Republicans, arguing that "me-tooism" was a recipe for continual failure, set out to reposition the party as a genuine alternative to the Democrats. In 1964, Republican presidential candidate Barry Goldwater, author of a book titled *The Conscience of a Conservative*, called for much lower levels of taxation and of government spending and economic regulation, and for the elimination of many federal social programs. Although Goldwater lost to Johnson, the ideas he expressed continue to be major themes of the Republican Party.

It took Richard Nixon's "southern strategy" to end Democratic dominance of the political process. Beginning with his successful 1968 presidential campaign, Nixon appealed to White southerners by promising to reduce federal support for school integration and voting rights. With the help of the independent candidacy of former Alabama governor George Wallace, Nixon sparked the voter shift that eventually gave the once-hated "party of Lincoln" a strong position in all the states of the former Confederacy. In the 1980s, under President Ronald Reagan, Republicans added another important group to their coalition: religious conservatives offended by Democratic support for abortion rights, as well as Democrats' alleged disdain for traditional cultural and religious values.

While Republicans built a political base with economic and social conservatives and White southerners, the Democratic Party maintained support among unionized workers and upper-middle-class intellectuals and professionals. Democrats also appealed strongly to racial minorities. The 1965 Voting Rights Act had greatly increased the participation of Black voters in the South and helped the Democratic Party retain some congressional and Senate seats there. And while the Republicans appealed to social conservatives, the Democrats appealed to voters favoring abortion rights, LGBTQ rights, feminism, environmentalism, and other progressive social causes.

The results have been something of a draw. Democrats have won the presidency 6 out of 14 elections since the passage of the Voting Rights Act, and they have held at least one chamber of Congress for most of that time. That apparent stalemate masked dramatic changes in the parties' regional bases. Republicans surged in the South but lost ground in the Northeast. New England, once the

The most recent party system was initiated by the shift of southern Democrats to the Republican Party. The 1968 campaigns of the Republican Richard Nixon and the independent, Alabama governor George Wallace (right), appealed to disaffected White southerners, cementing this shift.

think it through

What issues or debates do you think could force a realignment of the current party system?

bedrock of the Republican Party, had no Republican U.S. House member (of 22 seats) after the 2020 election.

The electoral realignment that began in 1968 laid the foundations for the political polarization that has come to characterize contemporary politics. As southern Democrats and northeastern Republicans faded, the two parties lost their moderate wings. Southern White Democrats had tended to come from rural areas; they were socially conservative but strongly supported the New Deal. As the rural population in the South declined, and the suburbs grew, these southern Democrats were replaced by suburban Republicans whose constituents are much more economically conservative than their predecessors.

The opposite dynamic was at work in the North. Republicans in places like New York and New England tended to be socially moderate and economically conservative. Social and political shifts in the northeastern states marginalized the Republican Party and led to the emergence of a strong liberal faction within the Democratic Party. As a result, the moderate wings of both parties were substantially reduced, leaving Congress with a more polarized political alignment.

As each political party became ideologically more homogeneous after the 1980s—today there are few liberal Republicans or conservative Democrats—party loyalty in Congress, which had been weak between the 1950s and the 1970s, witnessed a dramatic resurgence. A simple measure of party unity developed by Professor Stuart Rice in the 1920s, and tracked by the *Congressional Quarterly* since the 1950s, is the percentage of bills on which a majority of one party votes against a majority of the other party. Between the 1950s and the 1970s, unity hovered around 70 percent. Since the 1980s it has regularly exceeded 90 percent.[22] But, in 2018 and 2019, party unity plummeted to 59 percent in the House and in the Senate plummeted to 69 percent, members of Congress from swing districts and swing states sought to position themselves closer to their constituencies.[23]

A deep tension runs through the current political system, as both national parties have become more ideologically distinct and have catered more to their base than to the center of the electorate. More and more people are seeking an alternative to the traditional Democratic and Republican formulas—a trend reflected in the rising number of voters calling themselves independents and in the appeal of unconventional candidates such as Bernie Sanders and Donald Trump.

American Third Parties

Although the United States is said to possess a two-party system, it has always had more than two parties. Typically, third parties in this country have represented social and economic protests that were not given voice by the two

table 11.1

PARTIES AND CANDIDATES, 2020

CANDIDATE	PARTY	VOTE TOTAL	PERCENTAGE OF VOTE
Donald Trump	Republican	71,526,505	47.5
Joe Biden	Democrat	76,442,500	50.8
Howie Hawkins	Green	362,588	0.2
Jo Jorgensen	Libertarian	1,764,161	1.2
Others		400,009	0.3

SOURCE: "2020 U.S. Election Results," Associated Press, https://www.ap.org/media-center/understanding-the-election (accessed 11/12/20).

analyzing the evidence

Though the Democrats and the Republicans are the dominant political forces in the United States, many minor parties nominate candidates for the presidency. Why are there so many minor parties? Why don't these parties represent much of a threat to the major parties?

major parties.[24] Such parties have significantly influenced ideas and elections. The Populists of the late nineteenth century and the Progressives, representing the urban middle classes in the late nineteenth and early twentieth centuries, are important examples. Ross Perot, who ran for president in 1992 and 1996 as an independent fiscal conservative, garnered almost 19 percent of the votes in 1992.

The Timeplot on pp. 376–9 shows that although third parties have won entire states in the past, the Democratic and Republican parties have dominated the electoral map in recent decades. Table 11.1 lists all the parties that offered candidates in one or more states in the presidential election of 2020. The third-party and independent candidates won 1.5 million votes in 2020, down from 7 million in 2016. In neither election did they receive any electoral votes. The last third-party candidate to receive any electoral votes was George Wallace of the American Independent party. He won 14 percent of the vote and received 46 electoral votes.

Although it is difficult for third parties to survive, it is worth noting that the two major parties today themselves started as third parties. As we have seen, the Democrats emerged as an alternative to the Federalists and their opponents, loosely, the Antifederalists. The Federalist Party itself gave way to the Whig Party, which was replaced by the Republicans.

In some sense, then, the two major parties today started as alternatives to existing parties, and they have reinvented themselves ideologically to change with the times and to co-opt supporters of emerging third parties. The Democratic Party, for example, became more liberal when it adopted most of the Progressive program early in the twentieth century. In the 1930s, many socialists felt that Roosevelt's New Deal had adopted most of their party's program, including old-age pensions, unemployment compensation, an

PARTIES' SHARE OF ELECTORAL VOTES, 1789–2020

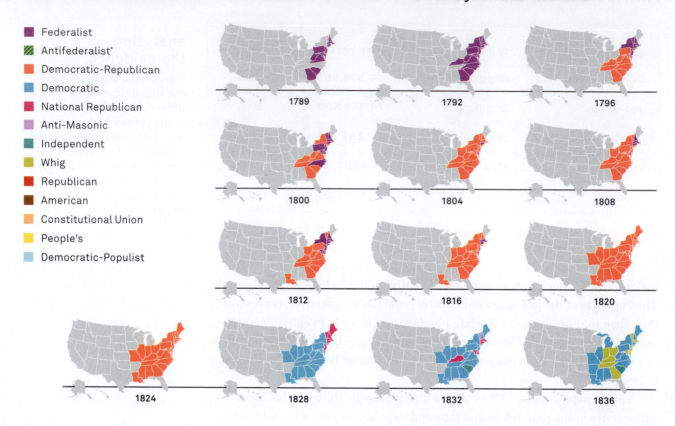

- ■ Federalist
- ▨ Antifederalist*
- ■ Democratic-Republican
- ■ Democratic
- ■ National Republican
- ■ Anti-Masonic
- ■ Independent
- ■ Whig
- ■ Republican
- ■ American
- ■ Constitutional Union
- ■ People's
- ■ Democratic-Populist

1789 1792 1796
1800 1804 1808
1812 1816 1820
1824 1828 1832 1836

*TIMEPLOT NOTE: In the 1792 election, the Anti-Federalist candidates, who ran against Federalists George Washington and John Adams, did not win any states.

agricultural marketing program, and laws guaranteeing workers the right to organize into unions.

The major parties' ability to evolve largely explains the short lives of third parties, whose causes are usually eliminated as the major parties absorb their programs and draw their supporters into the mainstream. An additional reason for the short duration of most third parties is the typical limitation of their electoral support to one or two regions. Populist support, for example, was primarily western and midwestern; the 1948 Progressive Party drew nearly half its votes from New York State; the 1968 American Independent Party, which won the most electoral votes ever polled by a third-party candidate (George Wallace), represented primarily the Deep South.

Moreover, voters usually assume that only the candidates nominated by the two major parties have any chance of winning and thus that a vote cast for a third-party candidate or an independent candidate is wasted. For instance, in

timeplot

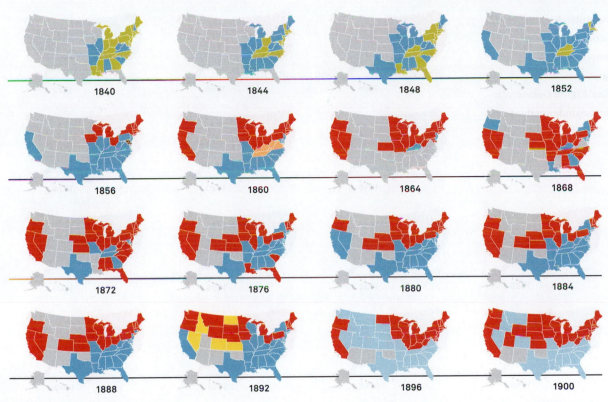

1840 1844 1848 1852

1856 1860 1864 1868

1872 1876 1880 1884

1888 1892 1896 1900

(continued on next page)

the 2000 race between Democrat Al Gore and Republican George W. Bush, the third-party candidate Ralph Nader did better in states where either Bush or Gore was nearly certain of winning and worse in more closely contested states. Third-party candidates must struggle—usually without success—to overcome the perception that they cannot win.

Third-party prospects are also hampered by the United States' single-member-district plurality election system. In many other nations, several individuals are elected to represent each legislative district. With this system of multiple-member districts, weaker parties' candidates have a better chance of winning at least some seats. For their part, voters in multiple-member-district systems are less concerned about wasting ballots and usually more willing than Americans are to support minor-party candidates.

Reinforcing the effects of the single-member district (as noted in Chapter 10), plurality voting rules generally have the effect of setting a high threshold for

TIMEPLOT SOURCE: 270 to Win, www.270towin.com/historical-presidential-elections (accessed 11/13/20).

PARTIES' SHARE OF ELECTORAL VOTES, 1789–2020

(continued from previous page)

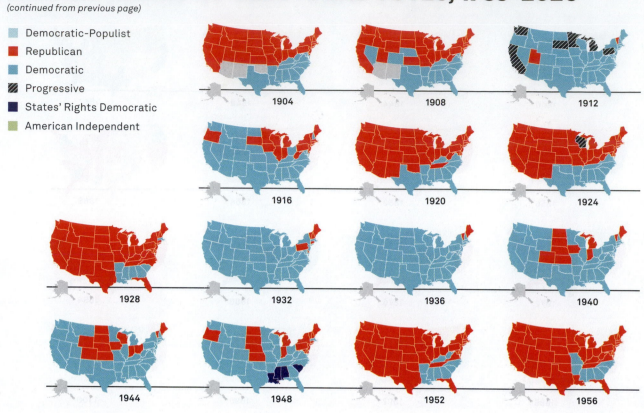

Democratic-Populist
Republican
Democratic
Progressive
States' Rights Democratic
American Independent

1904   1908   1912

1916   1920   1924

1928   1932   1936   1940

1944   1948   1952   1956

victory. To win a plurality race, candidates usually must secure many more votes than they would need under most European systems of proportional representation. For example, to win an American plurality election in a single-member district with only two candidates, a politician must win more than 50 percent of the votes cast. To win a seat in a European multimember district under proportional-representation rules, a candidate may need only 15 or 20 percent of the votes. This high threshold in American elections encourages political factions that might otherwise form minor parties to minimize their differences and remain within the major-party coalitions.[25]

It would nevertheless be incorrect to assert (as some scholars have) that the single-member plurality election system of the United States guarantees that only two parties will compete for power in all regions of the country. All one can say is that American election law depresses the number of parties likely to survive over long periods of time. There is nothing magical about the number two.

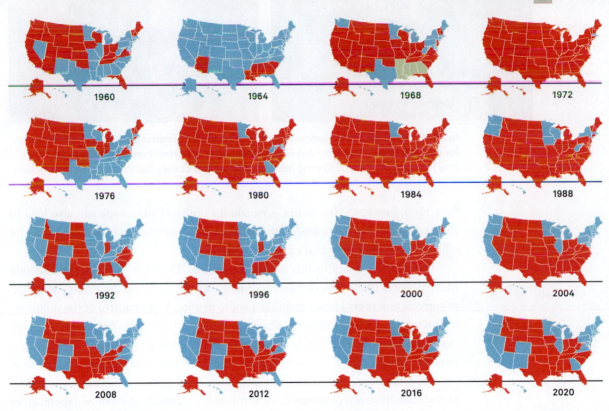

CONCLUSION

Could a representative government be effective without political parties? Political parties help make democracy work. Americans value democracy with broad political participation and an effective government, but these goals are often at odds with each other. Effective government implies decisive action and the creation of well-thought-out policies and programs. Democracy implies an opportunity for all citizens to participate fully in the governmental process. But full participation by everyone is usually inconsistent with getting things done in an efficient and timely manner.

Strong political parties help the United States balance the ideals of representative democracy and efficiency in government. They can both encourage popular involvement and convert participation into effective government. As we

In 2020, candidates from numerous third parties ran for president, including Jo Jorgensen for the Libertarian Party (left) and Howie Hawkins for the Green Party (right). Although they may have little chance of winning national office, minor parties can influence national politics.

have seen, however, the parties' struggle for political advantage can also lead to the type of intense partisanship that cripples the government's ability to operate efficiently and in the nation's best interest.

Parties also simplify the electoral process. They set the electoral agenda through party platforms, recruit candidates, accumulate and distribute campaign resources, and register and mobilize people to vote. Party control of the nominating process and the pressures toward two-party politics in the United States mean that most voters must decide between just two choices in any election. Parties thus facilitate voters' decision making. Voters can reasonably expect what sorts of policies a candidate with a party's endorsement will pursue if elected. Even before a candidate has been nominated, most voters have already determined themselves to be Democratic or Republican and know who they will vote for.

This binary simplification of politics reduces our society's many complex interests to just two competing teams, whose platforms must accommodate the many subtle differences or ideological nuances among groups inside each party. It further reduces politics into warring factions that have little hope of finding common ground. However, the two-party system does give meaning to the vote. It empowers the voter to say, "I want to stay the course with the party in power" or "I want to go in a new direction."

Key Terms

political party 346

nomination 347

closed primary 348

open primary 348

majority party 353

party identification 355

party activist 360

gender gap 361

caucus 364

Check Your Understanding

1. Why do political parties form? Explain how they differ from interest groups.

2. Explain the role of political parties in nominating candidates.

3. How do party labels help voters make choices?

4. In what ways does the majority party control the organization and day-to-day operations in Congress?

5. What factors do political scientists think shape an individual's party identification?

6. What are some of the most influential events that shaped our current party system?

INQUIZITIVE

Earn a better grade on your test. InQuizitive personalizes your learning path to help you master the concepts from this chapter. In a recent efficacy study of American government students, InQuizitive increased test scores by an average of 17 points (see back cover).

CHAPTER TWELVE

GROUPS AND INTERESTS

The statute books of the United States include many laws written to protect special interests rather than the more general interests of Americans. For example, to protect sugar beet growers in Louisiana and Texas, the government imposes quotas on imported sugar. As a result, Americans pay approximately twice as much for sugar as do citizens of other nations.

Or consider that even though 93 percent of Americans favor expanded background checks for gun purchasers,[1] Congress has shown no inclination to require such checks, which gun manufacturers and the NRA oppose.

Or to take a third example, gasoline sold in the United States is required to contain ethyl alcohol that is mainly produced from corn. While farmers benefit from this arrangement, American taxpayers have shelled out tens of billions of dollars in subsidies for a fuel that actually consumes more energy to synthesize than it produces when burned.

What accounts for these curious and expensive arrangements? The answer is simple: lobbying by interest groups. Many such groups are better represented and have better access to the government than do ordinary Americans. Most of the time, elected officials have strong incentives to pay attention to the organized interests that fund their campaigns—and far less attention to ordinary voters. It has been said that politicians follow the political golden rule: those who have the gold make the rules.[2]

Often enough, voters are not aware that their elected officials are giving them the short end of the stick. How many voters understand the intricacies of the laws governing the taxation of profits earned abroad or energy tax credits or Medicare reimbursement rates? In such matters, politicians can serve corporate interests without even considering ordinary citizens, most of whom have no views on these topics. But even on matters that many citizens do care about,

NRA Federal Spending

Citizens United
Decision

2004   2006   2008   2010   2012   2014

#WeThePeople

Interest groups try to influence the policies and actions of the government. For example, the National Rifle Association (NRA) works to promote laws that protect gun rights. Some argue that outside groups such as the NRA have too much influence in government. Here Senate Minority Leader Chuck Schumer (D-NY) presents data showing how much money the NRA has spent to prevent gun control legislation from moving forward. As we'll see later in the chapter, the Supreme Court decision in *Citizens United v. the United States* opened the gates to a flood of money in the political arena.

such as taxes, jobs, and energy costs, politicians will often still favor influential interest groups.

The framers of the Constitution foresaw the power that organized interests could wield and feared that the public good would be "disregarded in the conflict of rival [factions]."[3] Yet they recognized that interest groups thrived because of the freedom that all Americans enjoyed to organize and express their views. To the framers, this problem presented a dilemma: if the government had the power to regulate or forbid efforts by organized interests to interfere in the political process, it would, in effect, have the power to suppress freedom. James Madison suggested a solution to this dilemma:

> Take in a greater variety of parties and interests [and] you make it less probable that a majority of the whole will have a common motive to invade the rights of other citizens. . . . [Hence the advantage] enjoyed by a large over a small republic.[4]

According to Madison's theory, a good constitution encourages many interests so that no single interest can ever dominate the others. The assumption is that competition will produce balance and compromise, with all the interests regulating one another.[5] Today, this principle is called **pluralism**.

Tens of thousands of organized groups in the United States compete to influence every aspect and level of government, but not all interests are fully and equally

- **Do interests make government and policy more representative or less representative of citizens' preferences?**

pluralism
The theory that all interests are and should be free to compete for influence in the government.

represented in the American political process. Generally speaking, small groups, whose members see clear benefits from engaging in political action, have a substantial advantage over large groups, whose individual members see little gain from it. This difference helps to explain why a small number of corn producers earning billions from gasohol can be politically more potent than the tens of millions of people who pay a few pennies more in taxes and gas costs resulting from policies supporting gasohol.

In this chapter, we examine interest group politics in the United States. We analyze the group basis of politics, the challenges that groups face in getting individuals to act collectively, and some solutions to these problems. We discuss the character and balance of the interests promoted through the American political system and the tremendous growth of interest groups in number, resources, and activity in recent decades. Finally, we examine the strategies that groups use to influence politics and whether their influence has become excessive.

Learning Objectives

- Explain which types of groups are most likely to organize successfully to influence governmental policies.

- Describe the strategies that interest groups use to influence policy.

- Analyze the role of interest groups in a representative democracy like the United States.

THE CHARACTERISTICS OF INTEREST GROUPS

interest group
An organized group of people that attempts to influence governmental policies. Also called *lobby*.

An **interest group** is an organized group of people that attempts to influence governmental policies. Individuals form groups to increase the chance that their views will be heard and their interests treated favorably by government. Interest groups may also be referred to as *lobbies*.

Interest groups are sometimes equated with political action committees (PACs; see Chapter 10). However, a PAC focuses narrowly on helping certain candidates win elections. Interest groups' activities are much broader and involve influencing legislative and executive actions. Interest groups also are not political parties, which, as we have said, can be viewed as teams seeking to gain control of the government. Parties are concerned with who is in office, and they may take positions on a wide range of policies for the sake of winning elections. Interest groups concern themselves primarily with the interests of the group and governmental policies that affect those interests. For example, a trade association, such as the Dairy Farmers of America or Associated Builders and Contractors, is concerned with governmental policies that affect the dairy industry or the construction industry.

Enhancing Democracy

Millions of Americans are members of one or more interest groups, at least to the extent of paying dues or attending an occasional meeting. By representing the interests of such large numbers of people and encouraging political participation, organized groups enhance American democracy. They educate their members about issues that affect them, lobby members of Congress and the executive branch, mobilize their own members for elections and grassroots **lobbying**, engage in litigation, and generally represent their members' interests in the political arena. Interest groups also monitor governmental programs to ensure that they do not adversely affect members. In all these ways, organized interests can be said to promote democratic politics. But because not all interests are represented equally, interest group politics works to the advantage of some of them and the disadvantage of others.

lobbying
An attempt by a group to influence the policy process through persuasion of government officials.

Which Interests Are Represented

When most people think about interest groups, they immediately think of groups with a direct economic interest in governmental actions (Table 12.1). Producers or manufacturers in a particular economic sector generally provide the support for these groups, such as the Chamber of Commerce, the American Fuel & Petrochemical Manufacturers, the American Farm Bureau Federation, and the National Federation of Independent Business, which represents small business owners. At the same time that broadly representative groups such as these are active in Washington, specific companies—such as Google, Disney, Shell Oil, IBM, and Microsoft—may be active on issues of particular concern to themselves.

Labor organizations, although fewer in number and more limited in financial resources, are extremely active lobbyists. The AFL-CIO, the United Mine Workers, and the Teamsters union all lobby on behalf of employees in the private sector. More recently, lobbies have arisen to promote the interests of public employees, the most significant being the American Federation of State, County and Municipal Employees (AFSCME).

Professional lobbies such as the American Bar Association and the American Medical Association have been particularly successful in furthering their members' interests in state and federal legislatures. The "gun lobby," including firearms manufacturers and dealers, as well as gun owners, is represented by the National Rifle Association (NRA). The NRA has mobilized furiously to thwart gun control efforts introduced in Congress in the wake of numerous recent mass shootings. Financial institutions, represented by organizations

table 12.1

WHO IS REPRESENTED BY ORGANIZED INTERESTS?

analyzing the evidence

What types of interests are most likely to be represented by interest groups? If interest group politics is biased in favor of the wealthy and the powerful, should we curb group politics?

WORKFORCE STATUS OF THE INDIVIDUAL	U.S. ADULTS (%)	ORGS. (%)	TYPE OF ORG. IN WASHINGTON	RATIO: % OF ORGS. TO % OF ADULTS
Executives	8.5	70.3	Business association	8.27
Professionals	13	23.7	Professional association	1.82
White-collar workers	14	1.1	White-collar union	0.08
Blue-collar workers	22.2	0.4	Blue-collar union	0.02
Farm workers	0.9	1.6	Agricultural workers' organization	1.78
Unemployed	6.2	1.7	Unemployment organization	0.27
Not in workforce	35.3	1.2	Senior citizens' organization, organization for the handicapped, educational organization	0.03

SOURCE: Kay Lehman Schlozman, Sidney Verba, and Henry E. Brady, *The Unheavenly Chorus: Unequal Political Voice and the Broken Promise of American Democracy* (Princeton, NJ: Princeton University Press, 2012), 329. Updated data supplied by Schlozman, Verba, and Brady.

such as the American Bankers Association, are also important in shaping legislative policy.

Recent decades have seen the growth of a powerful "public interest" lobby claiming to represent concerns not addressed by traditional lobbies. Public interest groups have been most visible in consumer protection and environmental policy, although they cover a broad range of issues, from nuclear disarmament to civil rights to abortion. Examples include Americans for Prosperity, the Natural Resources Defense Council, and the Union of Concerned Scientists.

The perceived need for representation on Capitol Hill has also generated a public-sector lobby, including the National League of Cities and a "research" lobby. The latter group includes universities and other institutions, such as the

Brookings Institution and the American Enterprise Institute, that seek government funds for research and support. Indeed, many universities have expanded their lobbying efforts, even as they have reduced faculty positions and course offerings and increased tuition.[6]

Despite the large increase in interest groups, most organizations involved in politics in Washington, D.C., and in the state capitals still represent economic interests. The Policy Principle box on p. 388 gives an example of how the real estate industry and other groups have tried to stop changes to the mortgage interest tax deduction, a policy that is in their own economic interest, even though it is not in the interest of most homeowners.

The Free-Rider Problem

Whether they need individuals to volunteer or merely to send money, all organizations must recruit and retain members. Yet many groups find this task difficult, even with regard to those who agree strongly with the group's goals. The reason, as the economist Mancur Olson explains, is that the benefits of a group's success are often broadly available and cannot be denied to nonmembers.[7] As we saw in Chapter 1, such benefits are called *public goods* (or collective goods). This term is usually associated with certain government benefits, but it can also be applied to beneficial outcomes of interest group activity.

To follow Olson's theory, suppose that a number of private property owners live near a mosquito-infested swamp. Each owner wants the swamp cleared. But if one owner or a few of them were to clear it, their actions would benefit all the other owners as well, without any effort on the others' part. Each of the inactive owners would be **free riding** on the efforts of the one(s) who cleared the swamp. Thus, there is a disincentive for any of the owners to undertake the job alone.

Since the number of concerned owners is small in this particular case, they might eventually be able to organize themselves to share the costs, as well as enjoy the benefits of clearing the swamp. But suppose the common concern is not the neighborhood swamp, but polluted air or groundwater involving thousands of residents in a region, or millions of residents in a whole nation. National defense is the most obvious collective good whose benefits are shared by all Americans, regardless of the taxes they pay or the support they provide.

As the size of the benefited group increases, the free-rider phenomenon becomes more of a problem. Individuals do not have much incentive to become active members and supporters of a group that is already working more or less on their behalf. The group would no doubt be more influential if all concerned individuals were active members—if there were no free riders. But groups will not reduce their efforts just because free riders get the same benefits as dues-paying activists. In fact, groups may work even harder in the hope that the free riders will be encouraged to join in.

free riding
Enjoying the benefits of some good or action while letting others bear the costs.

the policy principle
THE MORTGAGE INTEREST TAX DEDUCTION

When individuals and groups pursue policy goals, players may not have equal access to information and other resources needed to take effective political action. Take the case of the mortgage tax credit. This tax credit benefits the real estate and finance industries and wealthy households. These interests are politically very active, well organized, and well informed, and they have the resources to bring pressure through lobbying.

Under current law, individuals who file itemized personal income tax returns may deduct the interest on as much as $750,000 in mortgage indebtedness from their taxable income. Though the average deduction is only about $1,680 for homeowners who itemize, this law can result in thousands of dollars in savings for an upper-bracket taxpayer with a large mortgage.

Prior to 2017, the mortgage deduction was higher still. Homeowners could deduct the interest on mortgages of up to $1 million, and they could deduct their property taxes entirely. In 2017, Congress reduced the maximum mortgage deduction from interest on $1 million to $750,000 and capped at $10,000 the amount of state and local property taxes that could be deducted. These were highly controversial changes but far less extreme than initial proposals, which would have eliminated the deduction for state and local property taxes entirely and set the mortgage deduction at $500,000.[1]

Proponents of the mortgage interest tax deduction, such as the real estate industry, argue that it benefits the middle class and encourages home ownership, which gives people a stake in the community and the nation, making them better neighbors and citizens. The mortgage interest deduction, in fact, results in a direct savings to many Americans, but it also drives up home prices by allowing purchasers to assume larger mortgages. And the benefits are not universal.

Still, the mortgage interest deduction has long been viewed as politically untouchable—as evidenced by the controversy surrounding the changes in 2017. Wealthy homeowners and the real estate industry fought to keep

A home for sale in Durham, North Carolina.

the policy in place. The availability of a tax deduction encourages wealthier Americans to purchase second homes, to purchase more expensive homes, and to borrow against the value of their homes. From the perspective of the real estate and lending industries, cuts in the mortgage interest deduction would shrink these lucrative markets.

Why, then, did the Trump administration and the Republican leadership in Congress shrink the mortgage deduction in 2017? They reduced the mortgage deduction, over objections from the industry, in order to pay for other tax cuts, especially lowering the marginal tax rates of the wealthiest households. The net effect of the 2017 tax law was to cut the taxes of families with incomes over $730,000 by roughly $50,000. One interest won out at the expense of the other.

think it through

1. Why is it difficult for large groups of ordinary citizens—such as all homeowners—to organize and lobby government? What advantages do narrower interests have?

2. Why does it matter that groups focused on a specific interest are better informed about that topic than the average citizen?

---

[1] Reuben Fischer-Baum, Kim Soffen, and Heather Long, "Republicans Say It's a Tax Cut for the Middle Class. The Biggest Winners Are the Rich," *Washington Post*, updated January 30, 2018, www.washingtonpost.com/graphics/2017/business/what-republican-tax-plans-could-mean-for-you/?utm_term=.a0cfb78de959 (accessed 8/4/20).

Organizational Components

Most interest groups share certain key organizational components. First, they must attract and keep members. Usually, groups appeal to members not only by promoting certain political goals but also by offering direct economic or social benefits.

Thus, for example, AARP (formerly the American Association of Retired Persons), which promotes senior citizens' interests, also offers members insurance benefits and commercial discounts. Similarly, many groups with primarily economic or political goals also seek to attract members through opportunities for social interaction and networking. Thus the local chapters of many national groups provide a congenial social environment while collecting dues that finance the national office's political efforts.

Another kind of benefit involves the appeal of an interest group's purpose. The best examples of such benefits are those of religious groups. The Christian right is made up of various interest groups that offer virtually no material benefits to members—their appeal depending almost entirely on the members' identification with and belief in the group's religious mission. Many religion-based interest groups have arisen throughout U.S. history, such as those that drove the abolition of slavery and Prohibition.

The second component shared by interest groups is that each must build a financial structure capable of sustaining an organization and funding its activities. Most interest groups rely on annual dues and voluntary contributions. Many also sell services such as insurance and vacation tours.

Third, every group must have a leadership and decision-making structure. For some groups, this structure is very simple. For others, it can be quite elaborate and involve hundreds of local chapters melded into a national apparatus.

Last, most groups include an agency that actually carries out the group's tasks. This may be a research organization, a public-relations office, or a lobbying office in Washington or a state capital.

Interest groups may offer their members material benefits. For example, AARP offers its members insurance benefits and commercial discounts. But it also promotes shared political goals, such as lowering the cost of prescription medication. Here AARP members sign a petition to their U.S. senator for affordable access to medication.

The Characteristics of Members

Membership in interest groups is not randomly distributed in the population. People with higher incomes, higher levels of education, and managerial or professional occupations are much more likely to join than are those on lower rungs of the socioeconomic ladder.[8] Well-educated, upper-income people are more likely to have the time, money, and skills needed to play a role in a group. Moreover, for business and professional people, group membership may provide personal contacts and access to information that can help advance their careers. At the same time, corporate entities—businesses and trade associations—usually have ample resources to form or participate in groups that seek to advance their causes.

The result is that interest group politics in the United States has a pronounced upper-income bias. Although many groups do have a working-class or lower-income membership—labor organizations and welfare-rights organizations, for example—the great majority of interest group members are from the middle- and upper-income groups. In general, interest groups serve the interests of society's "haves." When interest groups take opposing positions on issues and policies, the positions usually reflect divisions among affluent groups rather than conflicts between the upper- and lower-income groups.

Even groups associated with a progressive political agenda and support for the rights of the poor tend, in their own membership, to reflect the interests of the middle- and upper middle-income groups. Consider the NAACP and the National Organization for Women (NOW). Both groups advocate for the rights of the poor, but both have a largely middle-income members and focus on issues of concern to primarily that membership: the NAACP on minority access to universities and the professions, and NOW on gender equality in education and women's access to positions in business and the professions.

In general, to obtain adequate political representation, forces low on the socioeconomic ladder must be organized on the massive scale associated with political parties. Indeed, parties can mobilize the collective energies of large numbers of people who, as individuals, may have very limited resources. Interest groups, in contrast, generally organize smaller numbers of the better-to-do. Thus, the relative importance of political parties and interest groups has far-ranging implications for the distribution of political power in the United States.

Response to Changes in the Political Environment

As long as there is government, as long as government makes policies that provide benefits or impose costs, and as long as there is liberty to organize, interest groups will abound. And if government expands, so will interest groups. For example, a spurt of growth in the national government occurred during the 1880s and 1890s, arising largely from early governmental efforts to fight monopolies and regulate some aspects of interstate commerce. In the latter decade, a parallel growth spurt occurred in national interest groups, including the imposing National Association of Manufacturers and other trade associations. Many groups organized around agricultural commodities as well, and this period also saw trade unions begin to expand as interest groups. In the 1930s, interest groups with headquarters and representation in Washington began to grow significantly, reflecting that decade's expansion of the national government.

Recent decades have seen an enormous increase both in the number of interest groups seeking a role in the political process and in the extent of their opportunity to influence that process. As we have noted, today there are tens of thousands of groups at the national, state, and local levels. One indication of the proliferation of their activity is the enormous number of **political action committees (PACs)**, vehicles by which interest group money is spent to influence elections. Nearly

political action committee (PAC)
A private group that raises and distributes funds for use in election campaigns.

The Character of Interest Groups

- **Interests Represented**
  Economic interests (e.g., American Farm Bureau Federation)

  Labor organizations (e.g., AFL-CIO, United Mine Workers, International Brotherhood of Teamsters)

  Professional lobbies (e.g., American Bar Association, American Medical Association)

  Financial institutions (e.g., American Bankers Association)

  Public interest groups (e.g., Common Cause, Union of Concerned Scientists)

  Public-sector lobby (e.g., National League of Cities)

- **Organizational Components**
  Attracting and keeping members

  Fund-raising to support the group's infrastructure and lobbying efforts

  Leadership and decision-making structure

  Agency that carries out the group's tasks

- **Characteristics of Members**
  Interest groups tend to attract members from the middle- and upper middle-income groups because these people are more likely to have the time, money, and inclination to take part in such associations. People from less advantaged socio-economic groups need to be organized on the massive scale of political parties.

four times as many PACs operated in 2020 as in the 1980s, the number increasing during the period in between from fewer than 2,000 to more than 8,000.[9]

A *New York Times* report, for example, noted that during the 1970s, expanded federal regulation of the automobile, oil, gas, education, and health care industries drove each of these interests to substantially increase its efforts to influence the government's behavior. These efforts, in turn, spurred the organization of other groups to support or oppose the activities of the first ones.[10] The rise of PACs reflects one of the most common features of business political activity: businesses are reactive. They are usually drawn into politics to resist regulations, rather than to create a new program. (See the Analyzing the Evidence section on pp. 392–3 for a discussion of Google's PAC.)

Similarly, federal social programs have occasionally sparked (1) political organization and action by groups of beneficiaries seeking to influence the distribution of benefits and, in turn, (2) the organization of groups opposed to the programs or their cost. AARP, perhaps the nation's largest membership organization, emerged because of the creation and expansion of Social Security and Medicare. Once older Americans had guaranteed retirement income and health insurance, they had a clear stake in protecting and expanding these benefits. AARP developed in response to attempts to scale back the program.[11]

Participants in the so-called New Politics of the 1960s, which emphasized environmental, consumer, and civil rights concerns, started or strengthened

analyzing the evidence

Who's Funding Google's PAC?

Contributed by **Zhao Li**, *Princeton University*

Many major companies in the United States set up political action committees (PACs) in order to make campaign contributions to politicians and influence policy making. An underappreciated fact about business PACs is that they are forbidden by law from using their parent companies' treasury accounts to finance their campaign contributions. Instead, business PACs rely entirely on voluntary and limited donations from employees (and other eligible individuals affiliated with the parent companies) for fund-raising.

How do employees' political identities impact business PAC fund-raising and, in turn, PAC spending in the United States more generally? This has become a particularly salient question for tech companies in Silicon Valley, where a company's best interests are often at odds with its employees' own political preferences. When we look at Google, we see an example of the impact—in terms of both PAC fund-raising and spending—that may provide answers to the enduring puzzle of why levels of PAC contributions aren't higher given what's at stake.[1]

Google, as a company, would benefit from supporting Republican legislators who are potential allies of Google's key policy concerns, including antitrust regulations. But, if we look at Google employees' personal campaign donation records (see chart below), we see that Google's workforce is predominantly liberal. As a result, even though giving to Republican lawmakers may generate better "bang for the buck" on PAC contributions, Google's PAC cannot do so without sacrificing fund-raising by alienating its Democratic-leaning donor base. Employees who support the Democratic Party are less willing to donate to their company's PAC when PAC contributions primarily go to Republican candidates, and similarly, Republican-leaning employees are less willing to donate to their company's PAC when PAC contributions primarily end up in the campaign accounts of Democratic candidates.

Google PAC Donors' Inferred Partisan Leanings, 2016

EXCLUSIVE
DEMOCRATIC
DONORS ◄

EXCLUSIVE
REPUBLICAN
DONORS ►

1 Stephen Ansolabehere, John M. de Figueiredo, and James M. Snyder Jr., "Why Is There So Little Money in U.S. Politics?" *Journal of Economic Perspectives* 17, no. 1 (2003): 105–30.

During the 2016 election cycle, roughly 55.7 percent of Google's PAC contributions went to Republican (as opposed to Democratic) candidates. At the same time, Google's PAC raised $1,778,775 in itemized donations from their employees and other eligible donors. Based on estimates derived from my analysis, had Google given all of its PAC contributions to Democratic recipients, it would have raised $2,594,931, representing a 45.9 percent increase relative to the observed fund-raising outcome. Alternatively, if Google had contributed every dollar to Republican politicians, it would have raised $1,140,520, which is a 35.9 percent reduction from the observed fund-raising outcome.

Observed vs. Counterfactual fund-raising by Google's PAC, 2016

- Observed PAC fund-raising

- Counterfactual PAC fund-raising if 100% donations to Democratic recipients

- Counterfactual PAC fund-raising if 100% donations to Republican recipients

$2,594,931
+45.9%

$1,778,775

$1,140,520
-35.9%

How does this type of behavior affect the overall strategic success of business PACs? Since donations to business PACs are required by law to be both voluntary and limited to no more than $5,000 per person per year (this contribution limit applies to all eligible donors, including, for example, corporate executives), business PACs will suffer substantial funding losses if they alienate employees and other eligible donors. As a result, in cases where the legislators that business PACs want to target the most are opposed by employees on partisan grounds, business PACs will be unable to concentrate their campaign contributions on these candidates without sacrificing fund-raising.

This would help us understand why, given what's at stake, these companies contribute much less to campaigns than is legally allowed.

SOURCE: Center for Responsive Politics, https://www.opensecrets.org/bulk-data (accessed 7/8/20).

Based on the counterfactual spending in the second figure, how would you advise Google to move forward in order to maximize their fund-raising and their return on spending in terms of the candidates they support?

public interest groups such as Common Cause, the Sierra Club, the Environmental Defense Fund, Physicians for Social Responsibility, the National Organization for Women, and the various organizations formed by consumer advocate Ralph Nader. These groups were able to influence the media, Congress, and even the judiciary, and enjoyed remarkable success during the late 1960s and early 1970s in getting laws and policies they favored enacted. Activist groups also played a major role in enacting occupational health and safety legislation. More recent social movements include the Tea Party movement (anti-tax) and Black Lives Matter (protesting racial discrimination in policing and the criminal justice system).

Among the factors contributing to the rise and success of public interest groups was technology. Computerized direct-mail campaigns in the 1980s were perhaps the first innovation that allowed organizations to reach out to potential members. Today, Facebook, Twitter, and other social media enable public interest groups to reach hundreds of thousands of potential sympathizers and contributors. Relatively small groups can efficiently identify and mobilize adherents nationwide. Individuals whose perspectives make them a small anonymous minority everywhere can connect and mobilize for national political action through social networking tools unheard of even 30 years ago.

Of course, many individuals who share a common interest do not form interest groups. For example, although college students share an interest in the cost and quality of education, they have seldom organized to demand lower tuition, better facilities, or a more effective faculty. Students could be called a "latent group," of which there are many in American society. Often the failure of a latent group to organize reflects individuals' ability to achieve their goals without joining an organized effort. Individual students, for example, are free to choose among colleges that, in turn, must compete for patronage. Where the market or other mechanisms allow individuals to achieve their goals without joining groups, they are less likely to do so.

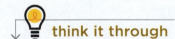

think it through

Why do you think college students haven't formed an interest group? What changes would you advocate for on your campus? On a national level, what changes would you push to see in higher education?

STRATEGIES FOR INFLUENCING POLICY

Interest groups work to make it more likely that all branches and levels of government will hear their policy concerns and treat them favorably. The quest for political influence and power takes many forms, which we can roughly divide into insider strategies and outsider strategies.

Insider strategies include gaining access to key decision makers and using the courts. Of course, influencing policy through traditional political institutions requires understanding how those institutions work. A lobbyist who wishes to address a problem with legislation will seek a sympathetic member of Congress, preferably on a committee with jurisdiction over the problem, and will work directly with the member's staff. Likewise, an organization that decides to file a suit will do so in a jurisdiction where it has a good chance of getting a sympathetic judge or appellate court.

Gaining access is not easy: legislators and bureaucrats have many requests to juggle. Courts, too, have full dockets. Interest groups themselves have limited budgets and staff. They must choose their battles well and map out the insider strategy most likely to succeed.

Outsider strategies include trying to influence public opinion for or against a proposed governmental action and giving contributions, assistance, and endorsements to a campaign or to the opposition. Just as politicians can gain an electoral edge by informing voters, so can groups. A well-planned public-information campaign or targeted campaign activities and contributions can have as much influence as working the corridors of Congress.

Many groups use a mix of insider and outsider strategies. For example, environmental groups such as the Sierra Club lobby members of Congress and key congressional staff, participate in bureaucratic rule making by offering suggestions to agencies on new environmental rules, and bring suits under various environmental laws, such as the Endangered Species Act. At the same time, the Sierra Club attempts to influence public opinion through media campaigns and to influence electoral politics by supporting candidates who share its environmental views and opposing candidates who do not.

Direct Lobbying

The term *lobbying* refers to efforts by individuals or groups to influence the actions of government officials. Traditionally, lobbying was viewed as an effort to influence members of Congress, but lobbying can also be aimed at officials of the executive branch. The First Amendment to the Constitution provides for the right to "petition the Government for a redress of grievances." But as early as the 1870s, *lobbying* became the common term for petitioning.

The 1946 Federal Regulation of Lobbying Act defines a lobbyist as "any person who shall engage himself for pay or any consideration for the purpose of attempting to influence the passage or defeat of any legislation to the Congress of the United States." According to the 1995 Lobbying Disclosure Act, any person who makes at least one lobbying contact with either the legislative or the executive branch in a year, any individual whose service includes more than one lobbying contact, and any individual whose lobbying activities represent 20 percent of his or her time must register as a lobbyist.[12] Lobbyists must report which topics they discussed with the government, though not which individuals or offices they contacted.

Lobbying involves much activity on the part of someone speaking for an interest. Lobbyists pepper legislators, administrators, and committee staff members with facts and claims about pertinent issues, and facts or claims about public support for addressing those issues.[13] Indeed, lobbyists serve a useful purpose in the legislative and administrative process by providing this kind of information.

figure 12.1

HOW INTEREST GROUPS INFLUENCE CONGRESS

analyzing the evidence

Interest groups can influence members of Congress in a variety of ways. They may seek to mobilize popular support in the form of grassroots campaigns, they may try to generate publicity favorable to their cause, they may work through congressional staffers, or they may seek to lobby members of Congress directly. How might these various strategies work together? What pitfalls might an interest group encounter in trying to influence members of Congress?

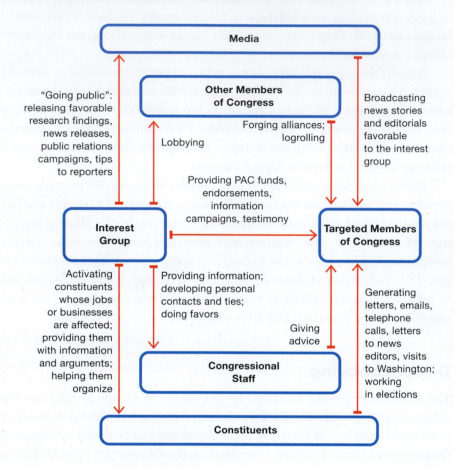

However, within each industry in the economy, for example, the many individuals and organizations involved in lobbying usually do not speak with a common voice. Rather, each advocates for its own interests, often in conflict with other firms in the same industry. What the leading organization or peak association of an industry advocates may be undercut by the activities of individual firms. For example, the Entertainment Software Association likely wants a different set of regulations than does Microsoft or Google.

Lobbying Members of Congress. Interest groups have substantial influence in setting the legislative agenda and helping craft the language of legislation (see Figure 12.1). Today, sophisticated lobbyists win influence by providing information about policies to busy members of Congress, who actually may refuse to meet with them unless they have useful information to offer. But this is only one of the many services that lobbyists perform. They may also testify on their clients' behalf at congressional committee and agency hearings, help clients identify potential allies with whom to build coalitions, draft proposed legislation or regulations to be introduced by friendly lawmakers, and talk to reporters and organize media campaigns. Lobbyists are also important in politicians' fund-raising, directing clients' contributions to congressional and presidential candidates.

Some interest groups go still further. They develop strong ties to individual politicians or policy communities within Congress by hiring former staffers, former members of Congress, or even relatives of sitting members. The frequent rotation of those in positions of power into lobbying jobs, a practice known as revolving-door politics, is driven by the continual turnover of staff, lobbyists, and even political parties in Washington. Because lobbying firms must stay current and connected to Congress to offer the best service to their clients, most large lobbying firms in Washington have strong ties to both the Democrats and the Republicans on Capitol Hill.

Lobbying the President.
So many individuals and groups clamor for the president's attention that only the most skilled and well connected can hope to influence presidential decisions. When running for president, Barack Obama made a bold promise to "free the executive branch from special interest influence." He followed that promise with an executive order tightening rules that prohibited most people who left the government to work as lobbyists for two years. Then-candidate Donald Trump's rhetoric was even more strident, promising to "drain the swamp." These promises proved exceedingly difficult to keep, since many people appointed by Obama and Trump had close ties to lobbyists or worked for lobbying firms.[14]

One of President Obama's first executive orders created an ethics standard and pledge for all executive branch appointments, and the administration imposed further restrictions on those receiving funds from the Emergency Economic Stabilization Act and the American Recovery and Reinvestment Act. Anyone wishing to receive funds from those huge economic stimulus bills had to show that they did not have conflicting interests and were not involved in lobbying the government.[15] Trump also signed an executive order directing each executive branch employee to sign an ethics pledge promising not to engage in lobbying within five years of leaving the government. The Trump order actually weakened the rules regarding stricter prohibitions against revolving-door lobbying created by the Obama administration.

Lobbying the Executive Branch.
Even when an interest group succeeds in getting its bill passed by Congress and signed by the president, full and faithful implementation of that law is not guaranteed. Often, the group and its allies continue their lobbying efforts, directed now toward the executive agency charged with implementation. A study of federal and state lobbying by political scientists

think it through

How do you think these close ties between Congress and interest groups impact how representative Congress is of their constituents' interests? Are there issues—such as climate regulations discussed in the Analyzing the Evidence section in Chapter 5—where Congress might not act on public opinion on an issue because of the influence of these groups?

The most powerful interests can sometimes influence presidential decisions. In 2017, President Donald Trump met with members of the business community to discuss tax reform.

Fred Boehmke, Sean Gailmard, and John Patty found that 45 percent of groups lobby the legislative and administrative agencies, 49 percent lobby only the legislative branch, and 5 percent lobby only administrative agencies.[16]

In some respects, federal law actually promotes interest group access to the executive branch. The Administrative Procedure Act, enacted in 1946 and frequently amended, requires most federal agencies to provide notice and an opportunity for public comment before implementing proposed new rules and regulations. This practice of notice-and-comment rulemaking gives interests an opportunity to publicize their views and participate in implementing legislation that affects them. Since 1990, the Negotiated Rulemaking Act has encouraged administrative agencies to engage in direct and open negotiations with affected interests when developing new regulations. These two laws have played an important role in opening the bureaucratic process to interest group influence. Today, few federal agencies would consider implementing a new rule without consulting affected interests.[17]

Regulation of Lobbying. Concerns that lobbyists have too much influence have led to the adoption of legal guidelines regulating their activities. For example, since 1993, businesses may no longer deduct the cost of lobbying from their taxes. Trade associations must report to members the proportion of their dues that goes to lobbying, and that proportion may not be claimed as a business expense for tax purposes. Most important, the 1995 Lobbying Disclosure Act (amended in 2007) significantly broadened the definition of individuals and organizations that must register as lobbyists. According to the filings under this act, almost 12,000 lobbyists were working the halls of Congress in 2019.[18]

Congress also restricted interest group influence by adopting rules that prohibited members from accepting gifts from registered lobbyists. In addition, congressional rules prohibit members from accepting a gift worth more than $50 from any single source, with a total limit of $100 from any single source during a calendar year. Also banned was the practice of paying honoraria, which special interests had used to supplement congressional salaries. Interest groups can still pay for the travel of representatives, senators, or their spouses or staff members, as long as a trip is related to legislative business and is disclosed on congressional reports within 30 days. The cost of meals and entertainment on these trips does not count toward the gift limit.

In 2007, congressional Democrats adopted ethics rules prohibiting lobbyists from paying for most meals, trips, parties, and gifts for members of Congress. Lobbyists were also required to disclose the amounts and sources of small campaign contributions that they "bundled" into large contributions. And interest groups were required to disclose the funds they used to rally voters for or against legislative proposals.

As soon as the rules were enacted, however, lobbyists and politicians found ways to get around them, and they have had little impact. In the executive branch, in contrast, policies imposed by President Obama in 2009 made it much more difficult for lobbying firms to influence decision making, either directly through lobbying or indirectly by hiring people with direct access to decision makers. President Trump, however, loosened these rules somewhat when he took office.

Using the Courts

Interest groups sometimes turn to the courts to supplement other avenues of access. They can use the courts to affect public policy in at least three ways: (1) by bringing suits directly on behalf of a group; (2) by financing suits brought by individuals; or (3) by filing companion briefs as *amicus curiae* (literally "a friend of the court") to an existing court case (see Chapter 8).

Significant modern uses of the courts by interest groups include those involving the "sexual revolution" and the movement for women's rights. Beginning in the mid-1960s, a series of suits brought in federal courts tried to force them to recognize a right to privacy in sexual matters. The effort began in *Griswold v. Connecticut* with a challenge to state restrictions on obtaining contraceptives for nonmedical purposes; here the Supreme Court held that states could neither prohibit the dissemination of information about contraceptives to, nor prohibit their use by, married couples. In a subsequent case, the Court held that the states could not prohibit the use of contraceptives by single persons. A year later, the Court held, in the 1973 case of *Roe v. Wade*, that states could not impose an absolute ban on voluntary abortions. Each of these cases, as well as others, was part of the Court's definition of a constitutional doctrine of privacy.[19]

Roe v. Wade sparked a controversy that led conservative groups to make extensive use of the courts to narrow the scope of the privacy doctrine. They obtained rulings, for example, that upheld a prohibition on the use of federal

Political movements often make use of the courts to advance policy preferences. In the past 30 years, pro- and anti-abortion groups have frequently brought lawsuits related to abortion policies.

funds to pay for voluntary abortions. And in 1989, the *Roe v. Wade* decision was significantly undermined in the case of *Webster v. Reproductive Health Services*, which allowed states to place some restrictions on abortion.[20]

Another significant use of the courts as a strategy for political influence is found in the history of the NAACP. The most important of these cases was *Brown v. Board of Education of Topeka, Kansas* (1954), in which the Supreme Court held that legal segregation of public schools was unconstitutional.[21]

Business groups are also frequent users of the courts, because so many governmental programs apply to them, notably in such areas as taxation, antitrust cases, interstate transportation, patents, and product quality and standardization. Major corporations and their trade associations pay tremendous fees each year to prestigious Washington law firms. Some of this money is spent in gaining access, but much of it serves to keep the firms' most experienced lawyers prepared to represent the corporations in court or before administrative agencies.

The new political movements that arose beginning in the 1960s made significant use of the courts to advance their goals during the following decades. Facilitated by changes in the legal rules governing access to the courts, the agenda of these groups was visible in decisions handed down in several key policy areas. For example, they forced federal agencies to pay attention to environmental issues, even when the agencies' activities were not directly related to environmental quality.

By the 2000s, the courts often were the battleground on which these movements waged their fights. Perhaps most dramatic was a string of lawsuits spanning 30 years (1986–2016) in which pro- and anti-abortion organizations, such as Pro-Life Action Network, Operation Rescue, and NOW, repeatedly sued state and local governments, and sometimes each other, to establish the rules governing protests near abortion clinics. Ultimately, the Supreme Court sided with the anti-abortion groups, but not before deciding three separate cases on the matter, at extremely high cost to both sides.[22]

Mobilizing Public Opinion

going public
Trying to influence public opinion for or against some proposed action by the government.

Organizations also try to pressure politicians by mobilizing public opinion—a strategy known as **going public**. When groups go public, they try to persuade large numbers of people to pay attention to their concerns in the hope that greater visibility and public support will make those in power see those concerns as important. Increased use of this strategy is traced to the rise of modern advertising at the beginning of the twentieth century. As early as the 1930s, political analysts distinguished between the "old lobby" of group representatives attempting to influence Congress directly and the "new lobby" of public-relations professionals addressing the public in order to reach Congress indirectly.[23]

A casual scan of major newspapers, magazines, and websites will reveal an abundance of expensive, well-designed ads by major companies and industry associations, such as those from the oil and gas, automobile, and health and pharmaceutical industries. Such ads often highlight what the firms or industries do for the country, not merely the products or services they offer. Their purpose is to create and maintain a positive association between the advertiser and the community at large, in the hope that the community's favorable feelings can be drawn on in political controversies later.

Sometimes groups advertise expressly to shift public opinion on a question. One of the most famous such campaigns was run by the Health Insurance Association of America in 1993 and 1994 in opposition to President Bill Clinton's proposed national health insurance plan. These ads featured a couple, Harry and Louise, sitting at their kitchen table disparaging the bureaucratic problems they would face under Clinton's plan. These ads are widely credited with turning public opinion against Clinton's plan, which never got off the ground in Congress.

A decade later, when President Barack Obama proposed an extensive overhaul of the health insurance industry, a trade group representing drug makers remade the Harry-and-Louise spot using the same actors, but this time to support the administration's plan. Louise concludes the new ad by saying, "A little more cooperation, a little less politics, and we can get the job done this time."[24]

A second strategy for going public, **grassroots lobbying**, entails many of the same organizing methods used in political campaigns: developing lists of supporters and having them voice their concern about an issue and recruit others to do so as well. It is common practice today to send direct mail or email that includes a draft message about a particular bill or controversy for recipients to adapt and then send to their members of Congress. A grassroots campaign can cost anywhere from $40,000 to try to sway the votes of one or two crucial members of a committee or subcommittee, to millions of dollars to mount a national effort aimed at Congress as a whole. Such grassroots campaigns are often organized around controversial, prominent legislation or appointments, such as Supreme Court nominees.

Grassroots lobbying has become more prevalent in recent decades because congressional rules limiting gifts to members have made traditional lobbying more difficult. But has it reached an intolerable extreme? One case in particular illustrates the extremes of what has come to be known as "Astroturf" lobbying (a play on the brand name of an artificial grass used on many sports fields). Beginning in 1992, 10 giant companies in the financial services, manufacturing, and high-tech industries spent millions of dollars over three years on a grassroots campaign to influence a decision in Congress to limit investors' ability to sue for fraud. Retaining an expensive consulting firm, these corporations paid for the use of specialized computer software to persuade Congress that there was "an outpouring of popular support for the proposal." Thousands of letters about the issue flooded Capitol Hill. Many came from people who sincerely believed that investor lawsuits are often frivolous and should be curtailed, but much of the mail was artificial, generated by the consultants, and came from people who had no strong feelings or even no opinion at all about the issue.

Astroturf campaigns have increased in frequency as members of Congress have grown more skeptical of Washington lobbyists and far more concerned about

grassroots lobbying
Mobilizing an interest group's membership to contact government officials in support of the group's position.

Protests, including marches, rallies, and sit-ins, are the oldest means of going public. Organized protests, like this Black Lives Matter demonstration in Philadelphia, raise awareness of issues. After the May 2020 police killing of George Floyd, an unarmed Black man, in Minneapolis, protests extended across the country demanding police reform.

whether their constituents support or oppose a particular issue. Interestingly, after the firms in the sue-for-fraud campaign spent millions of dollars and generated thousands of letters, they came to the somber conclusion that "it's more effective to have 100 letters from your district where constituents took the time to write and understand the issue," because "Congress is sophisticated enough to know the difference."[25]

Protests, including marches, rallies, and sit-ins, are the oldest means of going public. Those who lack money, contacts, and expertise can always resort to protest to bring attention to an issue or pressure on the government. Indeed, the right to assembly is protected in the First Amendment to the Constitution.

Protests may have many different consequences, depending on how they are managed. One basic consequence of a successful protest is that it attracts attention. Organized protests also create a sense of community among the protesters and raise the consciousness of others about the issue involved. In addition, protests often attempt to impose costs on others by disrupting traffic or commerce, thereby forcing people to bargain with the protesters. In 2020, for example, after the police killing of George Floyd, an unarmed Black man, Black Lives Matter protesters took to the streets worldwide to demonstrate against police brutality and systemic racism and to demand policy reform.

Using Electoral Politics

In addition to attempting to influence members of Congress and other officials, interest groups use the electoral process to try to elect the "right" legislators in the first place and to ensure that those elected will owe them a debt of gratitude for their support. To put matters into perspective, groups invest far more resources in lobbying than in electoral politics. Nevertheless, financial support and campaign activism can be important tools for organized interests.

Political Action Committees. By far the most common electoral strategy that interest groups use is that of giving financial support to political parties or candidates. But because such support can easily cross the threshold into outright bribery, Congress has occasionally tried to regulate it. For example, the Federal Election Campaign Act of 1971 (FECA; amended in 1974) limits campaign contributions and requires that each candidate or campaign committee provide comprehensive information about each donor who contributes more than $100.

These provisions have been effective up to a point, considering the large number of embarrassments, indictments, resignations, and criminal convictions in the aftermath of the Watergate scandal of the early 1970s. This scandal was triggered by Republican workers breaking into the office of the Democratic National Committee in Washington. But an investigation revealed numerous violations of campaign finance laws, involving millions of dollars passed from corporate executives to President Richard Nixon's reelection committee.

Reaction to Watergate produced further legislation on campaign finance, but the effect has been to restrict individual rather than interest group campaign activity. Individuals may now contribute no more than $2,800 to any candidate for federal office in any primary or general election. A PAC, however, can contribute $5,000, provided it contributes to at least five different federal candidates each year. Beyond this, the laws permit corporations, unions, and other interest groups to form PACs and to pay the costs of soliciting funds for them from individuals.

Electoral spending by interest groups has increased steadily despite these reforms: total PAC contributions increased from nearly $260 million in the 2000 election cycle to $1.8 billion in the 2020 cycle. (See the Timeplot on pp. 404–5 for a comparison of liberal and conservative spending over time.)

Interest groups focus their direct contributions on Congress, especially the House. Because of the enormous cost of running modern political campaigns (see Chapter 10), most politicians are eager to receive PAC contributions. Half of the campaign money that a typical U.S. House incumbent receives comes from interest groups. There is little evidence that donations actually buy roll-call votes or other favors from members of Congress, but they do help to keep in office those who are sympathetic to groups' interests.[26]

The potential influence of interest group campaign donations has prompted frequent calls to abolish PACs or limit their activities. The challenge is how to regulate groups' participation without violating their members' rights to free speech and free association. In 1976, the Supreme Court weighed in on this matter in terms of the constitutionality of the 1971 Federal Election Campaign Act, which had been amended in 1974.[27] In its decision to let the act stand, the majority on the Court ruled that donors' rights of expression were at stake, but that these had to be weighed against the government's interest in limiting corruption, or the perception of it. The Court has repeatedly upheld the key aspects of this decision: that (1) money is a form of speech but (2) speech rights must be weighed against concerns about corruption.

TOTAL OUTSIDE SPENDING, LIBERAL VS. CONSERVATIVE, 1990–2020

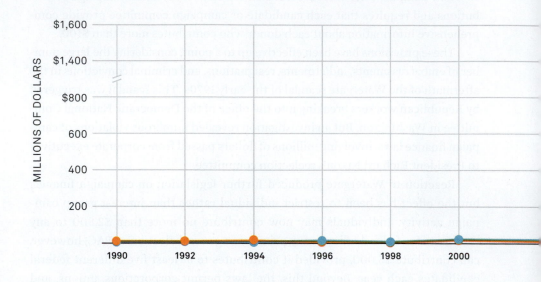

■ Conservative spending

■ Liberal spending

TIMEPLOT SOURCE: Center for Responsive Politics, "Total Outside Spending by Election Cycle, Excluding Party Committees," https://www.opensecrets.org/outsidespending/cycle_tots.php (accessed 11/5/20).

As we saw in Chapter 10, Congress in 2002 imposed significant limits on independent campaign expenditures in the Bipartisan Campaign Reform Act (BCRA). BCRA restricted donations to nonfederal (for example, state party) accounts in order to limit corruption, and it imposed limits on the types of campaign commercials that groups could air within 60 days of an election. It also raised the limits on direct campaign contributions to compensate for the effect of inflation.

In 2010, the Supreme Court struck down the restrictions on campaign commercials.[28] The case involved a political movie, created by an organization called Citizens United, that was critical of then-senator and presidential candidate Hillary Clinton. The movie aired on cable television inside the blackout period for independent political advertising stipulated by BCRA. A 5–4 majority on the Court ruled that such blackout dates restricted the rights to free speech of corporations and other associations.

This decision firmly established the right of corporations and labor unions to engage in political advocacy and opened the gates to the flood of money in the political arena. This flood was evident during the 2018 midterms, when the total was $1.1 billion, as well as during the 2020 national elections, in which independent expenditures amounted to some $2.6 billion (Figure 12.2).

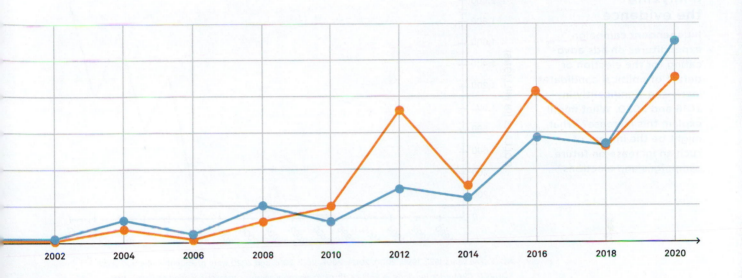

2002 2004 2006 2008 2010 2012 2014 2016 2018 2020

Campaign Activism. Financial support is not the only way in which organized groups seek influence through the electoral process. Sometimes activism can be even more important. In perhaps the most notable example, labor unions have regularly launched massive get-out-the-vote drives on behalf of Democratic Party candidates. The largest such activities are those of the Service Employees International Union (SEIU), which represents workers ranging from hotel and restaurant employees to clerical staff, and the United Automobile Workers (UAW). Other sorts of groups routinely line up behind the Democratic or Republican campaigns. The NRA, for example, routinely seeks to mobilize its millions of members on behalf of candidates who pledge to support Second Amendment rights.

The cumulative effect of such independent campaign activism is difficult to judge, but an important research initiative within political science is trying to measure the effectiveness of direct campaign contact in getting people to vote. In field experiments where campaigns agree to conduct direct activity randomly in some neighborhoods but not others, political scientists Alan Gerber and Donald Green have been able to measure the marginal effect of each additional piece of mail, each additional personal visit, or each additional phone call. In a typical election context, it costs about $40 to get an additional voter to the polls. Professors Gerber and Green

figure 12.2

INDEVENDENT EXPENDITURES PER ELECTION CYCLE, 1990–2020

analyzing the evidence

Independent campaign expenditures on ads advocating for the election or defeat of political candidates increased significantly in 2016 and 2020. What might explain this increase? What might be the impact of such an increase on future campaigns and elections?

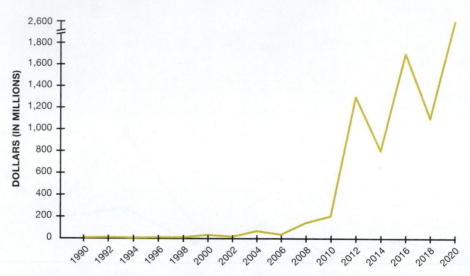

NOTE: The years 1992, 1996, 2000, 2004, 2008, 2012, 2016, and 2020 were presidential election years.

SOURCE: Center for Responsive Politics, https://www.opensecrets.org/outsidespending/cycle_tots.php?cycle=2020&view=Y&chart=A#viewpt (accessed 11/7/20).

also found that an initial contact can make a big difference in persuading people to vote. The effectiveness of each additional contact after the first tends to diminish, however, and after a potential voter has been contacted unsuccessfully six times, additional contacts have no effect and campaign workers might as well give up.

This research has given campaigns and reformers some sense of the effectiveness of campaign activism in stimulating turnout and possibly influencing elections. Especially in low-turnout elections, such as those for city councils or state legislatures, interest groups' get-out-the-vote activities can significantly affect the outcome. But as other money enters the scene, especially candidates' own campaign expenditures, the effects of such activities become muted.[29]

The Initiative.   Another political tactic that interest groups sometimes use is to sponsor ballot initiatives at the state level. The **initiative** allows laws proposed by citizens through petitions to be submitted directly to the state's voters for approval or rejection, bypassing the state legislature and governor. Perhaps the most famous initiative was Proposition 13 in California in 1978, which limited property tax increases and forever changed how that state finances education.

The initiative was originally promoted by late-nineteenth-century Populists, who saw it as a way to counteract interest group influence in the legislative process. Ironically, most initiative campaigns today are actually sponsored by interest groups seeking to get around legislative opposition to their goals. In recent years, for example, the insurance industry, trial lawyers' associations, and tobacco companies have often sponsored initiatives.[30] The role of interest groups in initiative campaigns is no surprise, because such campaigns can cost millions of dollars.

initiative

A process by which citizens may petition to place a policy proposal on the ballot for public vote.

in brief

Interest Group Strategies

- **Lobbying**
  Influencing the passage or defeat of legislation

- **Gaining Access**
  Developing close ties to decision makers on Capitol Hill and bureaucratic agencies

- **Litigation**
  Taking action through the courts, usually in one of three ways:

  - Filing suit against a specific government agency or governmental program

  - Financing suits brought by individuals against the government

  - Filing companion briefs as *amicus curiae* (friend of the court) to existing court cases

- **Going Public**
  Especially by advertising and grassroots lobbying; also by organizing boycotts, strikes, rallies, marches, and sit-ins; generating positive news coverage

- **Electoral Politics**
  Giving financial support to a party or candidate. Congress passed the Federal Election Campaign Act of 1971 to try to regulate this practice by limiting the amount that interest groups can contribute to campaigns.

CONCLUSION

Do interests make government and policy more representative or less representative of citizens' preferences? A clear answer is difficult to find among the mountains of research on this question. A survey of dozens of studies of campaign contributions and legislative decision making found that in only about 1 in 10 cases was there evidence of a correlation between contributors' interests and legislators' roll-call voting.[31]

Earmarks are a good case in point. Earmarks are appropriations to fund particular projects in specific districts or states, and they are usually included in a bill late in the legislative process to help gain enough votes for passage. Millions of dollars in earmarks are written into law every year. In a study of lobbyists' effectiveness in obtaining earmarks for college and university clients, lobbying was found to have a limited impact. The more money schools spent on lobbying activities, the more earmarked funds they received; however, the size of the effect depended greatly on other factors. A few cases showed exceedingly high returns. Schools in states with a senator on the Senate Appropriations Committee received $18 to $29 in earmarks for every $1 spent on lobbying. Schools in congressional districts whose representative served on the House Appropriations Committee received between $49 and $55 for every $1 spent. Having a legislator on the relevant committee, then, explains most of the observed influence.[32]

These results suggest that institutions and politics are profoundly related. Schools without access to influential members of Congress cannot gain much from lobbying. Schools with such access still need to lobby to maximize the potential gain that it can give them. But if they do so, the return is substantial. Political scientists conducted a comprehensive assessment of lobbying efforts on 98 different policy issues over a 20-year span. On 60 percent of the issues, policies moved opposite to the efforts of the lobbying groups, but when the groups did succeed the policy changes often aligned with what the public wanted or with the agenda of the majority party.[33]

The institutions of American government embrace an open and democratic process to ensure that government is responsive to the public's preferences and needs. The Bill of Rights provides for free speech, freedom of the press, and freedom of assembly. The nation's laws have further cemented this commitment, requiring open meetings of many governmental bodies, citizen advisory commissions, lobbying, direct contact between legislators and constituents, financial contributions to candidates and causes, trials open to the public, protests, and many other routes through which individuals and groups may advocate for their interests.

Through these many points of access, legislators and other government officials learn how their decisions affect the public. Politics is the arena in which many interests compete for the attention and support of government. Indeed, tens of thousands of organizations compete for political influence in the United States, and countless other movements and coordinated efforts of citizens rise and fall as issues come and go. This is pluralism at work, and it aligns closely with the sort of politics the Founders envisioned.

But this system of government is hardly perfect. The policies and laws that the U. S. government enacts are often thought to favor those who are organized. The American interest group system creates opportunities for *those who can use their resources* to represent their interests before the government. Individuals and organizations that can muster the most money or manpower can best make their case before the legislature, executive branch agencies, the courts, and even the voters.

Problems of collective action and free riding prevent many latent interests from developing permanent political organizations capable of bringing concerted pressure on the government. Businesses, unions, and professional and industry associations—groups that exist for some other reason than just to gain political influence—usually have less trouble providing the financial resources and overcoming the obstacles to organization and group maintenance that volunteer associations face. Consequently, interest group politics in Washington, D.C., and state governments tends to reflect the interests of and conflicts among those engaged in economic activity.

Even economically based groups do not necessarily succeed in the political arena. Unlike economic activity, politics involves power derived from the ability to vote on proposals, introduce legislation or rules, or block actions from happening. Interest groups are outsiders that can do none of these things directly. Nonetheless, these organizations can seek support in the appropriate institutions, such as a court with a sympathetic judge or a congressional subcommittee with a sympathetic chair. Often, groups succeed not by bringing pressure but by providing expertise to the government and by learning from those in office about the impact of new rules and regulations.

Interest group politics today does not neatly fit stereotypical notions of political power and influence. There are as many lobbyists as ever, but the backroom dealings of the "old lobby" are no longer typical of their activity and influence. Interest group politics spans all branches of government and involves many interests vying for attention in an increasingly crowded field. Moreover, competing interests may very well cancel out a given organization's efforts.

In addition, the activities of all groups constitute just one aspect of the deliberations of legislators, judges, and executive branch officials. Those who must ultimately make political decisions and be held accountable weigh other voices as well, especially those of legislators' constituents. Perhaps a better contemporary characterization is that the organized and disorganized interests participating in politics today are really contributing to a much broader sphere of political debate. That debate takes place inside the institutions of government—Congress, courts, executives, and elections.

Key Terms

pluralism 384

interest group 384

lobbying 385

free riding 387

political action committee (PAC) 390

going public 400

grassroots lobbying 401

initiative 406

Check Your Understanding

1. How do interest groups differ from parties? How do they differ from political action committees (PACs)?

2. How do the issues represented by the rise of a "public interest" lobby in recent decades compare to those of more traditional interest groups?

3. Who is more likely to be a member of an interest group in the United States? How does this influence the type of issues raised and publicized?

4. How do interest groups use insider and outsider strategies to influence policy?

5. How has Congress tried to control the financial support that interest groups provide candidates and parties?

InQuizitive

Earn a better grade on your test. InQuizitive personalizes your learning path to help you master the concepts from this chapter. In a recent efficacy study of American government students, InQuizitive increased test scores by an average of 17 points (see back cover).

CHAPTER THIRTEEN

ECONOMIC AND SOCIAL POLICY

The passage of the Affordable Care Act (ACA) into law on March 23, 2010, represented the culmination of a nearly hundred-year push to establish a federal health care policy in the United States. Earlier attempts began in 1912, when Theodore Roosevelt ran for president (as a third-party candidate for the Bull Moose Party), with a federally guaranteed right to health insurance as a key demand in his party platform. A few decades later, Franklin Delano Roosevelt gave in to pressure to exclude health insurance from the 1935 Social Security Act in order to secure enough votes for its passage.

In 1965, President Lyndon B. Johnson was able to enact Medicare and Medicaid—programs that provide health insurance for specific groups: the elderly and the poor, respectively. But efforts to offer broader coverage did not gain traction. In the early 1970s, President Richard Nixon proposed a universal comprehensive health insurance plan that looked a lot like the ACA, but his proposal was blocked by Democrats who wanted a broader program. Over the subsequent decades, efforts to enact federal health care reform, including Bill Clinton's high-profile proposal, also collapsed.

These failed efforts to develop a national health care policy are not surprising when we consider the unique nature of American political institutions. In many countries, the leadership of the executive branch is chosen by the legislature, making it easier to agree on and pass laws. In the United States, the separation of the executive and legislative branches put these presidents in a more difficult position: proposing national health insurance but relying on Congress to make something actually happen. Moreover, as we saw in Chapter 10, the electoral system in the United States—especially the use of plurality rule and single-member districts—makes members of Congress more beholden to their particular constituents than to a national party and its policy objectives, limiting both parties'

HAPPENING TODAY:
AFFORDABLE CARE ACT
Application & Enrollment Help

Westside Family Healthcare
We treat you well.

ChooseHealth
DELAWARE
Your guide to the health insurance marketplace

ability to craft and enact broad national policy solutions. As we will see in this chapter, multiple institutions and players are involved in making and implementing public policy in the United States.

Public policy is a law, a rule, a statute, a regulation, or an order that expresses the government's goals. Public policies often incorporate rewards and punishments as incentives to influence people's behavior and accomplish the government's goals. Public policy is the point at which representation and governance meet and sometimes collide. In principle, Americans are represented when Congress enacts the nations' policies. Once policies are written into law, representation ends and governance begins. Some people find themselves forced to obey laws they may not like. For example, many Republicans objected to the requirements imposed under the ACA. Every governmental program is touted by its proponents as serving the public interest, but when Americans are deeply divided on an issue, it can be difficult to enact a policy that will be satisfactory to everyone.

Another concern about policy making and representation is that some public programs may benefit narrow groups at the expense of the broader public. Policy makers can be driven by self-interest, partisanship, institutional concerns, and the demands of powerful groups. As we saw in Chapter 12, well-organized groups with substantial resources and a high stake in a particular policy are more likely than ordinary individuals to make successful efforts to pressure officials into enacting

The ACA represented the culmination of a nearly hundred-year push to establish a federal health care policy. But once the policy was written into law, some people found themselves forced to obey a law whose requirements they didn't like, while others fought to protect their new coverage.

> ▪ **How do representation and governance meet and sometimes collide when it comes to issues of public policy?**

public policy
A law, rule, statute, or edict that expresses the government's goals and often incorporates rewards and punishments to incentivize their attainment.

the policies they favor.[1] In this chapter, we consider two broad areas of public policy: economic policy and social policy. We consider the goals and major programs in each area, as well as the players and politics involved in policy making.

Learning Objectives

■ Explain the conditions required for a functioning market economy and the role of government in providing them.

■ Identify the goals of public policy and the tools that the federal government uses to accomplish them.

■ Describe how Americans' differing views and priorities influence economic and social policy.

■ Explain how economic and social policy work hand in hand.

ECONOMIC POLICY

economic policy
A governmental policy aimed at improving economic performance and outcomes.

Economic policy is governmental action aimed at improving economic performance and outcomes. Few Americans realize how much of their economic freedom they owe to such governmental action. Americans often point with pride to their "free-market" economy and view governmental institutions and policies as intrusions on the freedom of the marketplace. Yet the very existence of what we regard as a free market depends heavily on public policies and institutions. And our increasingly global economy depends on cooperation among national governments and their economic institutions.

HOW DOES GOVERNMENT MAKE A MARKET ECONOMY POSSIBLE?

There are many ways in which governments at all levels in our federal system undergird, manage, protect, and sometimes undermine economic activity. In this section, we explore the conditions required for a functioning market economy and the role of government in providing them.

Conditions Required for a Market Economy

A market economy is a complex set of arrangements that government can support and protect. Let's consider the conditions that constitute this support system.

Establishing Law and Order. The first condition necessary for a market economy is inherent in the very idea of government. There must be at least a minimal degree of predictability about the basic rules of interaction; there must be a system of law and order. Market participants must be able to assume not only that they can get to the market safely—that they won't be robbed on the way—but also that the people they deal with will behave predictably and be bound by calculable laws.

Defining Rules of Property and Its Exchange. The second condition that encourages people to participate in the market involves defining and dealing with property. If exchanges of ownership—buying and selling property—are part of the market, there must be clear laws about what constitutes property. Property may be many things—your labor or your ideas or the bed you sleep in—but the very concept of property is inconceivable without laws that define what you can call your own.

Something is not our own unless we can be reasonably certain that someone else cannot walk away with it or lay claim to it. Before we can enter a market and participate in buying and selling, we must be able to expect that others will respect our claim of ownership. In this sense, private property has a public component.

Enforcing Contracts. A third prerequisite for a market economy is to have rules for the enforcement of contracts. In the broadest sense, contracts facilitate exchanges of property. A contract is a voluntary agreement between two or more people that governs future conduct. Although the agreement is private, it has a public component: a contract must be enforceable under the law, or it is meaningless. If contracts were meaningless, the economy would grind to a halt. Businesses would not sell goods to one another if they could not count on the other's promise to provide the agreed-on goods or payment; lenders would not offer loans to home buyers without a legally binding promise from the buyers to repay the loan. What makes these contracts "enforceable" is the courts' role in arbitrating disputes between the parties involved. If a homeowner fails to repay her home loan as agreed to in the contract, for instance, the lender can follow a legal procedure to demand payment or take possession of the house.

Setting Market Standards. The fourth condition necessary for the modern free market is related to defining property and the conditions for its exchange. When people engage in exchanges that are not face-to-face—where they can't point to a good and say, "I want that tomato"—both parties must have some way of understanding exactly what goods they are bargaining over. To that end, terminology must be standardized, and one of government's essential functions is to establish standard weights and measures.

Providing Public Goods. A fifth condition necessary to the operation of a market economy is the provision of **public goods** (or *collective goods*). As we saw in Chapter 1, public goods are facilities or services that the government may

public good
A good that, first, may be enjoyed by anyone if it is provided and, second, may not be denied to anyone once it has been provided. Also called *collective good*.

↓ 💡 **think it through**

What public goods do you benefit from on a regular basis? How does your state or local government help support those public goods so that everyone can take advantage of them?

A lighthouse is a classic example of a public good: its benefits can be enjoyed by everyone and cannot be denied to anyone. By providing public goods, the government helps make a market economy possible.

monopoly

A situation in which a single firm dominates a market, controlling the supply of a particular good or service; the absence of competition.

provide because no single individual or organization can afford to or is willing to provide them. The provision of public goods may include (1) establishing the physical marketplace itself (like the common in nineteenth-century New England towns or the souk in North Africa and the Middle East), (2) building and maintaining transportation infrastructure to facilitate the distribution of goods and people, and (3) enforcing laws and keeping order (as noted earlier).

Public goods are essential to market operation, and how government provides those goods affects the market's character. In the United States, public goods related to transportation have been particularly important in promoting economic development. From the first canal systems that spread commerce into the country's interior to the contemporary public role in supporting and regulating air transportation, government has created the conditions for reliable and efficient business activity. In some cases, government supplies a public good and then allows private companies to take over. The federal government brought electricity to rural areas in the 1930s to promote economic development, but over time, private companies have taken over the provision of electricity.

Creating a Labor Force. A sixth condition necessary for a market economy is a labor force. Every society has provisions that enable and encourage, or sometimes force, people to work. Consider education: one reason children are required to attend school is so that they can learn the skills necessary to function in the market. Long before education laws, however, the United States had poorhouses, vagrancy laws, and other more police-oriented means of forcing people to work; these rules meant that people might starve or suffer punishment if they failed to earn their own keep. Under our welfare system today, government periodically adjusts the system to ensure that the support given is uncomfortable enough that people will prefer working to the low income they get from welfare.

Promoting Competition. Once markets emerge, they must be maintained. Thus, it should be reasonably easy for a producer to enter and freely compete in the market. If this is not the case, as when one company has a **monopoly**, the market's efficiency and the equitable distribution of its benefits are threatened. For many years in the twentieth century, a single company (AT&T) provided telecommunications products and services. Antitrust action brought to a conclusion by the Reagan administration broke up the company and lowered the barriers to competition against it. As a result, more telecommunications companies entered the market, providing more options to consumers and competing for their business. The government functions as a watchdog over potential monopoly control and moves against monopolies when they emerge.

THE GOALS OF ECONOMIC POLICY

Government intervenes not only to buttress the conditions for a market economy but also to achieve other concrete goals. The first goal is to promote economic stability, the second is to stimulate economic growth, the third is to promote business development, and the fourth is to protect employees and consumers.

Promoting Stable Markets

One of the central reasons for governmental involvement in the economy is to protect the welfare and property of individuals and businesses. Governments seek to maintain a measure of stability and predictability in the marketplace so that investors, lenders, and consumers will feel confident in engaging in economic activity.

Businesses also need access to new sources of capital in order to grow. The federal government promotes reliable access to new investment through its regulation of financial markets, such as stock exchanges. The most important federal agency in this regard is the **Securities and Exchange Commission (SEC)**, created after the stock market crash of 1929. The SEC requires companies to disclose information about the securities (such as stocks and bonds) that they are selling, inform buyers of the investment risks, and protect investors against fraud. In this way, the SEC helps maintain investor confidence and a strong supply of capital for American business.

The SEC faced harsh criticism during the 2008–9 financial crisis when analysts pointed to weak SEC oversight and regulation as an important factor in driving the financial sector to the brink of collapse. Congressional critics called for tougher SEC regulation of Wall Street. In 2010, passage of the Dodd-Frank Wall Street Reform and Consumer Protection Act was aimed at providing precisely such regulation.

Securities and Exchange Commission (SEC)
The agency charged with regulating the U.S. securities industry and stock exchanges.

Promoting Economic Prosperity

Although the idea that government should stimulate economic growth can be traced back to Alexander Hamilton's views about promoting industry, it was not until the twentieth century that the federal government assumed a central role in promoting economic growth. There had long been a suspicion of centralized political power, and during the nineteenth century, state and local governments were more likely than the federal government to engage with the private economy. By the late nineteenth century, circumstances had begun to change because the states could not deal with the massive growth in interstate economic activity. There are many aspects to the national government's role in economic growth and prosperity.

analyzing the evidence

The rates of GDP growth have varied over time. In 2008, growth slowed as the economy went into recession. What pattern of growth characterized the last six presidential-election years?

figure 13.1

CHANGES IN REAL GROSS DOMESTIC PRODUCT, 1995–2020*

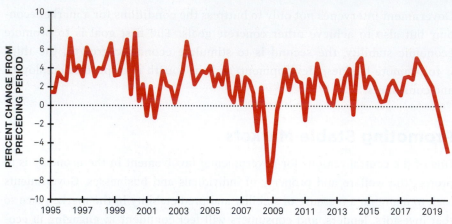

*Estimate as of July 2020.

SOURCE: U.S. Department of Commerce, www.bea.gov/national (accessed 7/9/20).

gross domestic product (GDP)
The total value of goods and services produced within a country.

Measuring Economic Growth. Since the 1930s, the federal government has carefully tracked national economic growth in several different ways. The two most important measures are the gross national product (GNP), which is the market value of goods and services produced in the economy, and the **gross domestic product (GDP)**, the same measure but excluding income from foreign investments.

In the late 1990s, the GDP grew at a rate of over 4 percent a year—a high rate by modern standards (Figure 13.1). Growth fell to 0.5 percent during the recession in 2001. It briefly rose but began to fall again (to a modest 2.2 percent in 2007). During 2008 and 2009—crisis years—the economy actually shrank. But since 2010, annual GDP growth has been positive, ranging between 1.5 (2016) and 4.0 (2018). In first quarter of 2020, during the global coronavirus pandemic, the GDP decreased 5 percent. Estimates for the rest of the year suggested more than a 30 percent decline as a result of the crisis.

Full Employment. Before the 1930s, neither the federal nor the state governments sought to promote full employment, in which all those willing and able to work were able to find a job. Excessive unemployment was considered an unfortunate occurrence that government could do little to alter. The New Deal response to the prolonged and massive unemployment of the Great Depression changed that view. The federal government put millions of people back to work on public projects sponsored by such programs as the Works Progress Administration (WPA) and the Civilian Conservation Corps (CCC). The bridges, walkways, and buildings they constructed can still be seen across the country today.

Federal policy again placed an emphasis on achieving full employment during the 1960s. Economists in the Council of Economic Advisers convinced President John F. Kennedy to enact the first tax cut designed to stimulate the economy and promote full employment.[2] The policy was widely considered a success, and the unemployment rate declined to a low of 3.4 percent in 1968.

As the economy fell into recession in 2008, unemployment began once again to climb, reaching about 10 percent. Over the following decade, unemployment declined steadily until it was under 4 percent at the beginning of 2020. Yet, after the onset of the Covid-19 pandemic, by April 2020 the unemployment rate had spiked to 14.7 percent due to widespread layoffs and business closures associated with emergency shutdowns.

Today, the federal government also supports the development of a productive workforce with programs related to higher education (educational grants, tax breaks, and loans), as well as job-training programs that focus primarily on low-skilled workers.

Low Inflation. During the 1970s and early 1980s, **inflation** (an increase in the general level of prices) was a highly vexing problem. The rate at which the level changed from year to year often exceeded 10 percent. There was much disagreement over what to do about it. The first effort, beginning in 1971, involved strict controls over wages, prices, dividends, and rents—that is, authorizing an agency in the executive branch to place limits on what wage people could be paid for their work, what rent their real estate could bring, and what interest they could get on their money.

inflation
A consistent increase in the general level of prices.

After two years, these policies were deemed unsuccessful. Because soaring oil prices had become a major source of inflation in the late 1970s, President Jimmy Carter imposed licensing of oil imports from the Middle East, tariffs and excise taxes on unusually large oil profits made by producers, and sales taxes at the pump to discourage casual consumption of gasoline. Carter also attempted to reduce consumer spending by raising income taxes, especially Social Security taxes.

In the 1980s, the Reagan administration supported Federal Reserve policies of pushing up interest rates (see the next section), which limited the amount of credit in the economy. These policies had the effect of reducing the number of dollars chasing goods—the culprit in inflation—which thus put downward pressure on prices. Inflation was finally reduced from its historic highs of over 10 percent. From 1983 until the beginning of the Great Recession of 2008–9, the inflation rate rarely exceeded 4.5 percent each year and rarely dipped below 2 percent. Since 2009, inflation has been even lower, in some periods actually turning negative (deflation).

Promoting Business Development

Since the Founding, the national government has been a promoter of markets. National roads and canals were built to tie states and regions together. National tariff policies supported domestic markets by restricting imported goods. (A tariff is a tax on an import, which raises its price, weakens its ability to compete with similar domestic products, and thus discourages its entry into the domestic market.)

The national government also heavily subsidized the railroad system, particularly in the second half of the nineteenth century. Subsidies promote business by making it cheaper for firms to produce their goods. Agriculture remains highly subsidized. In the first two decades of the twenty-first century, about 40 percent of farms in the United States received subsidies. The total over this period ranged between $10 billion and $30 billion.

The federal government also supports other specific business sectors with direct subsidies, grants, loans, and tax breaks. Since September 11, 2001, the federal government has heavily promoted technological innovation related to national security. For example, to promote its access to the latest technology, the Department of Defense ran a billion-dollar program that funds the early stages of research and development for innovative small firms and high-tech start-ups.

These targeted efforts complement ongoing efforts of the federal government to spur innovation more broadly. One of the most important is through the National Science Foundation (NSF). Created in 1950, the NSF supports basic research across a range of scientific fields. The aim is to advance fundamental knowledge that may be useful in many different applications.[3] In addition, research sponsored by the military has long been an important source of innovation for the U.S. economy. Radar and nuclear power stemmed from military research, as did the technology for the twenty-first century with ARPANET, the precursor of the internet.

Protecting Employees and Consumers

Stable relations between business and labor are important elements of a productive economy. For most of American history, the federal government did little to regulate relations between business and labor. In 1935, Congress passed the National Labor Relations Act, which established a new framework for industrial relations. The law created a permanent agency, the National Labor Relations Board (NLRB), to oversee union elections and collective bargaining between labor and industry. The federal government further supported organized labor in 1938 when it passed the Fair Labor Standards Act, which created the minimum wage.

Economic policies also protect consumers. The Food and Drug Administration (FDA), for example, was created in 1927. Today, the FDA regulates many areas of food and drug production. The movement for consumer protection experienced new momentum in the 1960s. The first response was the 1966 National Traffic and Motor Vehicle Safety Act, which made the Department of Transportation responsible for ensuring vehicle safety. Federal responsibility for consumer safety expanded in 1972 when Congress created the Consumer Product Safety Commission (CPSC), an independent agency that informs consumers about product hazards and works with industry to set product standards. In cases where safety concerns are severe, the commission sees to it that the products are recalled.

Through the CPSC, the Department of Transportation, and the FDA, the federal government continues to protect the public from unsafe products. For example, in July 2020 the FDA released a public warning about hand sanitizer

think it through

Look at several of your household products or toiletries. Some will have warnings and others will have notes that they have not been approved by the FDA. How does the FDA promote the safety of consumers through requiring this messaging?

products containing wood alcohol (methanol) typically used to create fuel and antifreeze, which are toxic if absorbed through the skin and life-threatening when ingested.[4] The FDA provided a list of products containing methanol, as well as others listing their ingredients as ethanol but found to contain methanol when tested, and it worked with manufacturers and distributors to recall dangerous products whether produced in the United States or imported through any U.S. border.

Other federal statutes aimed at consumer protection include the Fair Credit Reporting Act and the Truth in Lending Act, designed to discourage rapacious lending practices (see discussion about regulating payday lenders in the Policy Principle section on p. 420). In 2010, Congress created the Consumer Financial Protection Bureau to regulate financial products and services, such as credit cards, used by Americans on a daily basis.

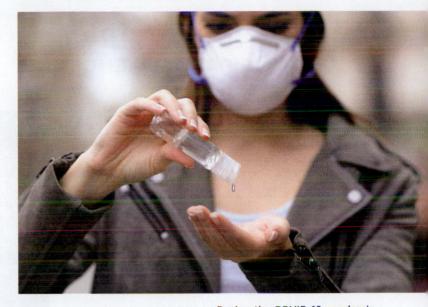

During the COVID-19 pandemic in 2020, when hand sanitizer was in great demand, the FDA issued a warning for several new brands that suddenly appeared on the market containing lethal ingredients, including methanol. These warnings demonstrate how the FDA protects consumers from unsafe or dangerous products.

THE TOOLS OF ECONOMIC POLICY

The current state and structure of the U.S. economy are the result of policies that have expanded American markets and sustained massive economic growth. As it works to meet the multiple goals of economic policy outlined in the previous sections of this chapter, the federal government relies on a broad set of tools that has evolved over time.

Monetary Policy

Monetary policy entails regulation of the economy through manipulation of the supply of money, the price of money (interest rates), and the availability of credit. With few exceptions, U.S. banks are privately owned and locally operated. Until well into the twentieth century, banks were regulated, if at all, by state legislatures. Each bank was granted a charter, giving it permission to issue loans, hold deposits, and make investments within that state. Today, state-chartered banks are less important than they used to be in the overall financial picture because the most important banks now are members of the federal banking system.

Early in its history, the national government sought to develop institutions that could implement monetary policy. The Federalist majority in Congress, led

monetary policy
Regulation of the economy through manipulation of the supply of money, the price of money (interest rates), and the availability of credit.

the policy principle
REGULATING PAYDAY LENDERS

In response to the 2009 financial crisis, Congress enacted the Dodd-Frank Wall Street Reform and Consumer Protection Act of 2010, a set of policies designed to make banking and other consumer financial markets work better for the public and to protect consumers from predatory lending practices. Many of the act's provisions focused on banks—imposing stricter rules that limited their ability to engage in risky activities. But another important change was the establishment of a new federal agency: the Consumer Financial Protection Bureau (CFPB).

The CFPB is an independent agency with broad powers to oversee consumer lending and financial services, including the practices of credit card companies, payday lenders, auto dealers, and debt collectors. Its institutional structure design makes it more independent and less political than most federal agencies.

Supporters of the CFPB say that it has benefited consumers by increasing transparency in financial services and by holding companies that break the law accountable. However, critics accuse the CFPB of suffocating businesses and costing jobs by overregulating the financial services sector.

These conflicting views are particularly clear in the reactions to the CFPB's efforts to regulate payday loans. Across the United States there are nearly 20,000 payday lenders, who offer small loans designed to be repaid when the borrower receives the next paycheck. The loans typically come with very high interest rates and substantial fees for extending the repayment date. Although payday loans were intended to be used mainly for emergencies, they are often used for routine expenses by low-wage workers who have few other credit options. Moreover, borrowers are typically unable to repay the loan on time and end up extending the loan. A 2013 report showed that on a payday loan of $375, the average borrower takes five months to repay the loan and incurs fees of $520 that must be paid in addition to the original $375.[1]

Before the 2010 Dodd-Frank legislation, regulation of payday loans was primarily a state-level responsibility. States adopted different positions on the issue, and 15 states had outlawed payday lenders entirely. Once the CFPB was created, it established limits on how much customers can borrow in payday loans and also began

Do the benefits provided by payday lenders outweigh the risks associated with the loans?

fining lenders who engage in deceptive practices. The payday loan industry has pushed back against these regulations and has challenged the negative characterization of payday loans. Since most people who take out payday loans are unable to get credit or financing in other ways, they may depend on payday lenders to avoid being evicted, having their car repossessed, or suffering other serious consequences of unpaid bills.

Under the Trump administration, the CFPB has taken a less aggressive stance on payday lending, and it has backed off from new regulations and enforcement actions begun under the Obama administration. Although the CFPB was designed to be less political than other agencies, the right amount of regulation of the financial services industry remains a controversial political issue.

think it through

1. Consider the general goals of economic policy discussed in this chapter. Which broad goals are at stake in the debate over regulating the payday loan industry? Explain your answer.

2. What are some of the possible benefits of designing the CFPB to be relatively independent of Congress and the presidency? What are some of the possible drawbacks?

[1] Pew Charitable Trusts, "Payday Loans Explained," May 8, 2013, www.pewtrusts.org/en/research-and-analysis/video/2013/payday-loans-explained (accessed 7/25/20).

by Alexander Hamilton, established a Bank of the United States in 1791. Federalists hoped that a national bank would help the new nation create a sound currency and stabilize the nation's credit. The bank, however, was vigorously opposed by the nation's agricultural interests, led by Thomas Jefferson, who feared that urban, industrial capitalists would dominate such a bank. The 20-year charter of the Bank of the United States was not renewed in 1811. The Second Bank of the United States was created in 1816 to deal with the financial chaos following the War of 1812. But as with its predecessor, its charter was terminated, this time during Andrew Jackson's administration, in 1836.

The Federal Reserve System. The fear of a central bank lingered eight decades later, when Congress in 1913 established an institution—the **Federal Reserve System** (the **Fed**)—to manage the supply of money and credit in the economy. The core of the Federal Reserve System comprises 12 Federal Reserve banks, each located in a major commercial city. These are not ordinary banks; they are bankers' banks that make loans to other banks, clear checks, supply the economy with currency and coins, and seek to prevent both inflation and deflation. The Fed also regulates the activities of the commercial banks that are members of the Federal Reserve System, each of which must follow national banking rules. State-chartered banks and savings and loan associations may also join if they accept national rules.

At the top of the system is the Federal Reserve Board, made up of seven members appointed by the president (with Senate confirmation) for 14-year terms. The board's chairperson is selected by the president from among the board members for a four-year term. In all other concerns, the Fed is an independent agency; the president's executive power does not extend to it or its policies. Nonetheless, in recent years the Fed chair has been a politically visible figure, occasionally receiving political pressure from elected officials who wish to claim credit for economic growth, which may be slowed by Fed policies aiming for price stability, controlling inflation, or other beneficial economic outcomes. For example, observers charged longtime Fed chairman Alan Greenspan with being attentive to politics in his endorsement of President George W. Bush's tax cuts. In his 2005 confirmation hearings to head the Fed, economist Ben Bernanke promised Congress that he would be "strictly independent of all political influences."[5] Nevertheless, a few years later Bernanke played a significant, visible role during the financial crisis, closely coordinating the response of the Fed with the actions of the Treasury Department. Despite this history, the most recent Fed chairman, Jerome Powell, emphasized his commitment to maintaining the Fed's independent, impartial, and nonpartisan status. During his Senate confirmation hearing, he stressed his independence from the Trump administration,[6] and given the complaints from President Trump about his performance and decision-making,[7] it seems that Powell maintained his independent approach, which is essential for long-term steering of U.S. economic policy in our current politicized fiscal policy environment.

Federal Reserve System (Fed)

The system of 12 Federal Reserve banks that facilitates exchanges of cash, checks, and credit; regulates member banks; and uses monetary policy to fight inflation and deflation in the United States.

At the beginning of the COVID-19 pandemic in 2020, the Federal Reserve took emergency action by lowering the interest rates to near zero in order to keep the financial markets moving and to prevent the same sort of crash that occurred during the 2009 recession.

reserve requirement
The minimum amount of liquid assets and ready cash that the Federal Reserve requires banks to hold in order to meet depositors' demands for their money.

open-market operations
The buying and selling of government securities (such as bonds) by the Federal Reserve System to help finance governmental operations and to reduce or increase the total amount of money circulating in the economy.

Banks in the Federal Reserve System are able to borrow from the system. This arrangement enables them to expand their loan operations continually, as long as there is demand for loans in the economy. However, it is this very access of member banks to the Federal Reserve System that gives the Fed its power: the ability to expand and contract the amount of credit available in the United States.

The Fed affects the total amount of credit through a number of regulations on bank lending and through the interest it charges (called the *discount rate*) on the loans it extends to member banks. If the Fed significantly decreases the discount rate, it can boost a sagging economy by making it easier to borrow and spend money. For example, as the economy began to sag in late 2007, all eyes were on the Fed to reduce interest rates. By March 2008, the Fed had cut rates six times; by 2009, the discount rate had dropped nearly to zero in an effort to stimulate recovery from the deepest recession since the Great Depression of the 1930s. The rate remained there for several years but began to rise again in 2018. But during the pandemic in 2020, it reversed course, cutting rates to almost zero. If the Fed raises the discount rate, it can put a brake on the economy because the higher discount rate also increases the general interest rates charged by leading private banks to their customers.

Although the Federal Reserve helps ensure high employment when it keeps interest rates low to stimulate the economy, it is also responsible for controlling inflation. During the late 1970s and early 1980s, with inflation at record high levels, Fed chairman Paul Volcker aggressively raised interest rates to dampen inflation. His actions provoked a sharp recession, but they also raised the Fed's stature, demonstrating its ability to manage the economy.

Beyond its ability to influence interest rates and the availability of credit, a second power of the Fed is control over the **reserve requirement**—the amount of cash and securities that every bank must have available to cover withdrawals and checks written by its depositors. When the Fed decides to increase the reserve requirement, it can significantly decrease the amount of money that banks have to lend; conversely, if the Fed lowers the reserve requirement, banks can be more liberal in extending loans.

A third power of the Fed is **open-market operations**, whereby the Fed buys and sells government securities (such as bonds) to fund governmental activities and to increase or decrease the supply of money in the economy. When the Fed buys government securities in the open market, it increases the amount of money available to consumers to spend or invest; when it sells securities, it reduces the money supply.

Finally, a fourth power is derived from one of the Federal Reserve System's important services: the opportunity for member banks to borrow from one another. One of the original reasons for creating a Federal Reserve System, this power enables banks in a growing region, facing great demand for credit, to borrow money from banks in regions where the demand is much lower. This exchange is called the "federal funds market," and the interest rate charged by one bank to another, the **federal funds rate**, can be manipulated just like the discount rate, to expand or contract credit.

The federal government also provides insurance to foster credit and encourage private investment. The Federal Deposit Insurance Corporation (FDIC) insures bank deposits up to $250,000. Another important promoter of investment is the federal insurance of home mortgages through the Department of Housing and Urban Development (HUD). By guaranteeing mortgages, the government can reduce the risks that banks run in making such loans, thereby promoting lower interest rates and making such loans more affordable to middle- and lower-income families.

federal funds rate
The interest rate on loans between banks; the Federal Reserve Board uses its powers to influence this rate.

Fiscal Policy

Fiscal policy includes the government's taxing and spending powers. On the tax side, personal and corporate income taxes raise most of the U.S. government's revenues. Although the direct purpose of a tax is to raise revenue, each tax has a different impact on the economy, and government can attempt to plan for that impact. How the federal government decides to spend this revenue is one of the most consequential aspects of economic policy. Decisions about how much to spend affect the overall health of the economy, as well as every aspect of American life, from the distribution of income to the availability of different modes of transportation to the level of education in society.

fiscal policy
Regulation of the economy through taxing and spending powers.

Given the high stakes of fiscal policy making, it is not surprising that the fight for control over taxing and spending decisions is one of the most contentious in Washington, as interest groups and politicians struggle to shape economic policy. A good deal of this debate centers on the federal **budget deficit**, which is the gap between what the government collects from taxes or other revenue sources and how much it spends (called *outlays*). The size of the deficit is assessed relative to general levels of economic growth (typically as a percentage of GDP). For example, the budget deficit for fiscal year 2019 was $9,846 billion (an increase of $205 billion from the previous year).[8] This deficit represented 4.6 percent of the GDP (the highest share of GDP since 2012). The deficit is expected to reach $1 trillion in 2020.

budget deficit
The amount by which government spending exceeds government revenue in a fiscal year.

The **national debt** is the total amount owed by the U.S. government. Each year's budget deficit is added to those outstanding from previous years for a total value of accumulated annual surpluses and deficits over time, which is called the national debt. In 1980 the national debt was a mere $710 billion, or about 31 percent of the GDP. But by mid-2020, it had risen to $26.5 trillion—or more than eighty thousand dollars for every single person in America.[9]

national debt
The accumulation of each year's budget deficits or surpluses; the total amount owed by the U.S. government.

figure 13.2

U.S. BUDGET DEFICITS AND SURPLUSES, 1962–2021*

The federal deficit grew during the 1980s under President Ronald Reagan. During the 1990s the budget deficit declined significantly, but then it grew dramatically in the 2000s. When was the last time the federal budget showed a surplus? Why did the budget deficit grow so much after 2007? Given the events discussed in this chapter, what do you think it will look like for 2020?

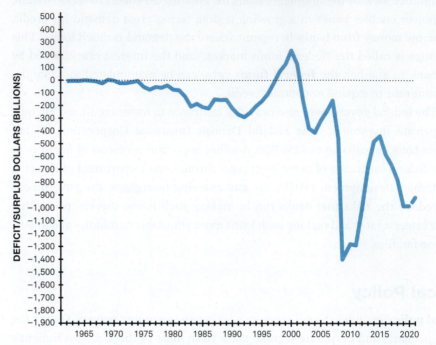

NOTE: Positive values indicate governmental surpluses, while negative values indicate deficits. *2020–2021 are estimates.

SOURCE: Office of Management and Budget, Table 1.3, www.whitehouse.gov/omb/historical-tables/ (accessed 7/9/20).

think it through

Future public spending must cover the country's debt and interest, making the national debt a flashpoint for contemporary political debate. In what situations do you think the government needs to spend without concern for this debt? Are there times when you think the government should instead slash spending?

In any year that the United States runs a budget deficit, the national debt increases, while a surplus (in which more money is taken in than is spent) reduces the national debt. When spending exceeds revenue, the government ordinarily covers the deficit either by raising taxes or by borrowing. Because the first option is naturally unpopular with voters, Congress usually turns to borrowing—especially during wars or severe economic downturns, when increased public spending aids in recovery. As a result, part of future public spending must go toward paying back that debt or, at the very least, paying the interest on the borrowed funds.

Since the 1990s, political debates over budget deficits, the national debt, and the debt ceiling have become more intense and central to federal policy making. Deficits persisted throughout President George W. Bush's second term—a result of both earlier massive tax cuts and spending increases. The Bush administration and Republican congressional leadership pushed the view that lower taxes would stimulate the economy and thereby generate more revenue. Government revenues did rise during this period, but so did spending.[10] As Figure 13.2 shows, deficits diminished for several years (2004–6) but then dramatically increased. Thus, despite the growth of revenues, political leaders could not agree on where in the budget to restrain spending, so they didn't, exacerbating the deficit.

In 2011, the nation's growing budget deficit produced a political crisis. The newly elected Republican Congress was unwilling to allow an increase in the debt ceiling. Republicans demanded that President Obama slash spending instead. Without an increase in the debt ceiling, however, the United States would be unable to pay its creditors, and a financial calamity would be the likely result. After months of negotiations, the president and Congress reached an agreement that raised the debt ceiling and reduced increases in future expenditures. However, debates over the federal budget and the deficit continue every year.

Taxation. The revenue side of fiscal policy is overseen primarily by the Treasury Department, specifically the Internal Revenue Service (IRS). The work of the IRS has expanded greatly as the size and complexity of government have grown. During the nineteenth century, the federal government received most of its revenue from one source, the **tariff**, a tax on imported goods. It also relied on excise taxes levied on specific products, such as tobacco and alcohol (see the Timeplot on pp. 426–7).

As federal activities expanded in the 1900s, the federal government added new sources of tax revenue. Most important was the income tax, proposed as a constitutional amendment by Congress in 1909, ratified by the states, and added to the Constitution in 1913 as the Sixteenth Amendment. The income tax is levied on both individuals and corporations. With the creation of the Social Security system in 1935, social insurance taxes became an additional source of federal revenue.

Before World War II, individual income taxes accounted for only 14 percent of federal revenues.[11] But as the need to raise revenue for the war made the income tax more important, Congress expanded the tax's base, so that after World War II, most Americans paid income taxes. There have been several notable shifts in taxes since 1960. Social insurance taxes now make up a much greater share of federal revenues, and receipts from corporate income taxes have declined over the same period. The share of the federal individual income tax has grown; it was 44 percent in 1960 and 49 percent in 2020.

A key feature of the income tax is that it is a **progressive tax**, or *graduated tax*, in which the heaviest burden is carried by those most able to pay. The U.S. income tax is a progressive tax because the proportion of income paid in taxes goes up with each higher income bracket. For example, in 2019, someone filing with head-of-household status would be taxed 10 percent on the first $9,525 of income but 37 percent of any income earned above $500,000.

Although the primary purpose of the income tax is to raise revenue, a second objective is to collect revenue in such a way as to reduce the disparities of wealth between the lowest and the highest income brackets. We call this policy **redistribution**.

In contrast to progressive taxation, a **regressive tax** is one applied uniformly, such that the proportion of income that people in lower income brackets pay toward the tax is higher than that paid by people in higher income brackets.

tariff
A tax on imported goods.

progressive tax
A tax in which the proportion of income paid goes up as income goes up. Also called *graduated tax*.

redistribution
A tax or spending policy that changes the distribution of income, usually to create greater equality between the rich and the poor in a society.

regressive tax
A tax that is applied uniformly, such that people in low income brackets pay a higher proportion of their income toward the tax than do people in high income brackets.

GOVERNMENT REVENUE BY SOURCE, 1790–2020

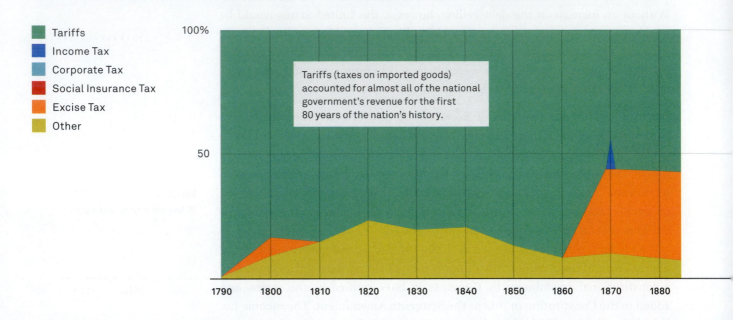

- Tariffs
- Income Tax
- Corporate Tax
- Social Insurance Tax
- Excise Tax
- Other

Tariffs (taxes on imported goods) accounted for almost all of the national government's revenue for the first 80 years of the nation's history.

100%

50

1790 1800 1810 1820 1830 1840 1850 1860 1870 1880

TIMEPLOT NOTE: For 1920, income and corporate tax are estimates.

TIMEPLOT SOURCES: U.S. Bureau of the Census, www.census.gov/library/publications (1790–1950); Office of Management and Budget, www.whitehouse.gov/omb/historical-tables (1960–2020) (accessed 5/7/20).

tax expenditure

A benefit to an individual or business in the form of relief from taxes that would otherwise be owed to the government.

For example, a sales tax is considered regressive because lower-income individuals spend a larger proportion of their income on consumption covered by a sales tax than higher-income individuals pay; thus, the share of their income that goes to paying sales tax is higher than the share paid by richer people (even though the sales tax rate is the same for everybody).

Another policy objective of the income tax is encouragement of the capitalist economy by rewarding investment. The tax laws allow individuals or companies to deduct from their taxable income any money they can justify as an investment or a "business expense." This deduction gives individuals and companies an incentive to spend money to expand their production, their advertising, or their staff, and it reduces the income taxes that businesses must pay.[12]

Supporters of such deductions call them "incentives"; others call them "loopholes." Analysts for the Treasury Department call them **tax expenditures** because, like much of government spending, they provide cash or another benefit to encourage a particular activity. But unlike government spending, tax expenditures do not show up in the budget as a category of spending.

Tax expenditures extend beyond incentivizing business investment, and they make up a substantial part of the federal budget. The largest category of tax expenditures relates to employer-paid health insurance and medical payments. Specifically, the payments that employers make to provide health insurance to

timeplot

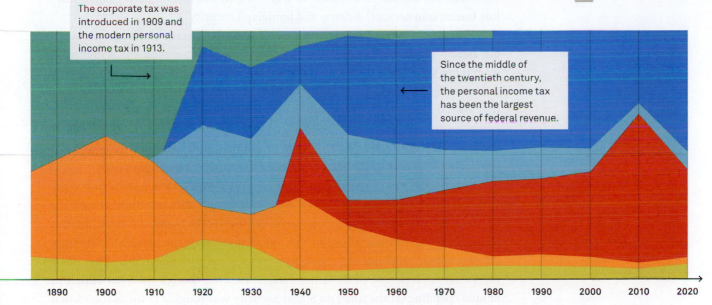

The corporate tax was introduced in 1909 and the modern personal income tax in 1913.

Since the middle of the twentieth century, the personal income tax has been the largest source of federal revenue.

1890 1900 1910 1920 1930 1940 1950 1960 1970 1980 1990 2000 2010 2020

their employees are excluded from the employees' gross income (and therefore not taxed). The Office of Management and Budget (OMB) estimates that between 2017 and 2026, the medical insurance exemption will amount to $2.9 trillion of lost tax revenue.

Another significant tax expenditure, estimated to cost the Treasury more than $1.2 trillion over this decade, is the home mortgage interest deduction (HMID), which allows taxpayers to pay less in taxes by subtracting the amount they pay in interest on loans taken out to purchase or remodel homes from the estimate of their taxable income. As Congress considered major tax reforms in 2017, a bipartisan set of experts was calling for an end to the HMID because of concerns that it does more to subsidize the real estate and home-building market than to help low- or middle-income families buy homes, particularly by artificially inflating home prices (see the Policy Principle box in Chapter 12, p. 390). The recent tax reform kept the HMID in place, although it did limit the deduction to mortgages of less than $750,000, rather than $1 million, and it eliminated the deduction for interest on second homes.

As Congress considered major tax reforms in 2017, Senator Elizabeth Warren (D-Mass.) spoke at a rally outside the U.S. Capitol building in opposition to the Republican tax plan that offered tax breaks to the wealthy.

Spending and Budgeting. How does the government spend the revenue it collects through taxes? Former undersecretary of the treasury Peter Fisher described the federal government as "a gigantic insurance company (with a sideline business in national defense and homeland security)."[13]

Fisher was speaking about the government's budgetary challenges in 2002, but nearly two decades later, that characterization of government spending is even more true. More than half of the $4.45 trillion federal budget in fiscal year 2019 was spent on Social Security, Medicare, and health programs alone, and that statistic rises to 70 percent of the total budget if Medicaid, unemployment compensation, and veterans' benefits are included. Another 15 percent of federal spending in 2019 ($686 billion) went to national defense, with an additional 8 percent ($375 billion) devoted to paying interest on our national debt.[14]

This breakdown of spending is often misunderstood by the American people. In 2014, the Pew Research Center asked Americans this question: On which of these activities does the U.S. government currently spend the most money: Social Security, transportation, foreign aid, or interest on the national debt? Only 20 percent of respondents chose the correct answer: Social Security. Most respondents chose one of the other categories, even though the $773 billion in annual spending (at the time) on Social Security was roughly 17 times the annual spending on foreign aid, eight times larger than the transportation budget, and nearly four times more than the net interest on the national debt.

A very large and growing proportion of the annual federal budget goes to **mandatory spending**, consisting of expenditures that are, in the words of the OMB, "relatively uncontrollable." Interest payments on the national debt, for example, are determined by the actual size of the national debt and the cost of borrowed funds. Legislation has mandated payment rates for such programs as retirement under Social Security, retirement for federal employees, unemployment assistance, Medicare, and farm price supports (see Figure 13.3). These payments increase as the cost of living rises, as the average age of the population goes up, and as national and world agricultural surpluses increase. In 1970, 38.5 percent of the total federal budget was made up of uncontrollables; in 1975, 52.5 percent fell into that category; and by 2019, nearly 70 percent was in the uncontrollable category.[15]

All this means that the national government now has very little money for **discretionary spending**—that is, funding for transportation, parks, education, public safety, and other services that the public demands and governments typically supply. As mandatory spending eats up more of government revenues, managing the budget will require higher taxes, cuts to services, or (most likely) a combination of both of those budget-balancing strategies.

Budget Process and Politics. The budget process involves both the president and Congress. Each branch has created institutions and procedures designed to fulfill its budgetary responsibilities and to assert control over the budget process. The president and Congress use their budgetary institutions to promote their

mandatory spending
Federal spending that is made up of "uncontrollables," budget items that cannot be controlled through the regular budget process.

discretionary spending
Federal spending on programs that are controlled through the regular budget process.

figure 13.3

COMPONENTS OF MANDATORY SPENDING AS A PERCENTAGE OF FEDERAL SPENDING, 1970–2025

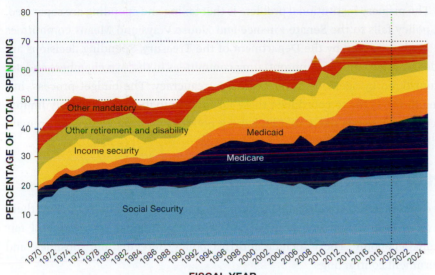

FISCAL YEAR

NOTE: Future values are estimates (to the right of the dotted line).

SOURCE: Congressional Research Service, *Present Trends in the Evolution of Mandatory Spending*, January 23, 2017, https://www.everycrsreport.com/files/20170131_R44763_ed8bc2f1bd6981381b238b779afdd4e3ddec2bd6.pdf (accessed 7/9/20).

analyzing the evidence

Spending on mandatory programs has grown considerably over the past four decades. By 2025, these popular programs are expected to make up almost 70 percent of government expenditures. Which programs are driving this increase in spending? How does mandatory spending affect the attempts by government to control its budget and budget deficit?

own budget preferences and priorities. The OMB in the Executive Office of the President is responsible for preparing the president's budget, which contains the president's spending priorities and estimated costs of policy proposals. It is the starting point for the annual debate over the budget.

Congress has its own budgetary institutions. It created the Congressional Budget Office (CBO) in 1974 so that it could have reliable information about the costs and economic impact of the policies it considers. At the same time, Congress created a budget process to establish spending priorities and to consider individual expenditures in light of the entire budget. A key element of the process is the annual budget resolution, which designates broad targets for spending.

By estimating the costs of policy proposals, Congress hoped to control spending and reduce deficits. When the congressional budget process proved unable to hold down deficits in the 1980s, Congress established stricter measures, including spending caps on some types of programs. Even these stricter restrictions have proved ineffective. For one thing, when actual spending bills arrive on the legislative floor in violation of spending caps, appropriators seek—and often are granted—waivers of the restriction, permitting the out-of-compliance measure to be taken up. Whether legislators will entertain more dramatic reform is an open question.

As discussed earlier in the chapter, budgetary politics is increasingly controversial and partisan. Politicians and citizens alike want to reduce the deficit and avoid taking on more debt, but they also say, "Don't cut my project" or "Don't close my military base" or "Don't reduce money for student loans (or hospital subsidies, job-training programs, scientific research, or food and drug inspection)."

The primary institutional problem is that taxing and spending are separated. Tax policy falls to the Senate Finance and House Ways and Means committees and is administered by the Department of the Treasury. Spending decisions are made by authorizing and appropriating committees in the two chambers and are administered by agencies in the federal bureaucracy. The budget process, initiated in the 1970s to coordinate these far-flung activities, has had only limited success, so it seems likely that budgetary politics and fiscal policy will remain challenging areas.

Other Economic Policy Tools

Although monetary and fiscal policy are the core tools of economic policy, there are other policy approaches aimed at promoting a stable, growing, and fair national economy. These include antitrust policy, deregulation, subsidies, and government contracting.

Antitrust Policy. Americans have long been suspicious of concentrations of economic power. Federal economic regulation aims to protect the public against potential abuses by concentrated economic power in two ways. First, the government can establish conditions that regulate the operation of big businesses to ensure fair competition. For example, it can require businesses to make information about their activities and account books available to the public. Second, the government can force a large business to break up into smaller companies if the business has established a monopoly. This is called **antitrust policy**. In addition to economic regulation, the federal government engages in social regulation. Social regulation establishes conditions on businesses in order to protect workers, the environment, and consumers.

antitrust policy
Governmental regulation of large businesses that have established monopolies.

Deregulation. Historically, federal regulatory policy was a reaction to public demands. As the economy prospered throughout the nineteenth century, some companies grew so large that they were recognized as possessing "market power": they could eliminate competitors and impose conditions on consumers rather than cater to consumer demand. Small businesses, laborers, farmers, and consumers all began to clamor for protective regulation. They faced problems in organizing, however, and thus were always at a disadvantage against better-organized corporate interests.

Nevertheless, the states had been regulating businesses in one way or another all along. Local interest groups turned to Washington and national political entrepreneurs as economic problems grew beyond the reach of individual state governments. If markets were national and commerce frequently crossed state lines, there would have to be national regulation.

The first national regulatory policy was the Interstate Commerce Act of 1887, which created the first national independent regulatory commission, the Interstate Commerce Commission (ICC), designed to control the railroads' monopolistic practices. About two years later, the Sherman Antitrust Act extended regulatory power to cover all monopolistic practices, including "trusts" or any other agreement between companies to eliminate competition. This power was strengthened in 1914 with the Federal Trade Commission Act (creating the Federal Trade Commission, or FTC) and the Clayton Antitrust Act.

The modern era of comprehensive national regulation began in the 1930s. Most of the regulatory programs of the 1930s sought to regulate the conduct of companies within specifically designated sectors of American industry. For example, the jurisdiction of one agency was the securities industry; the jurisdiction of another was the radio (and eventually television) industry. Still other agencies regulated banking, coal mining, and agriculture. At this time, Congress also set the framework of American labor regulation, including the rules for collective bargaining and the minimum wage.

When Congress turned again to regulatory policies in the 1970s, it moved beyond a focus on specific industries. Instead, it targeted cross-industry problems, worker safety, consumer safety, and environmental protection under the jurisdiction of new agencies: the Occupational Safety and Health Administration (OSHA), the Consumer Product Safety Commission (CPSC), and the Environmental Protection Agency (EPA), respectively.

Businesses complained about the burden of new regulations, and many economists saw excessive regulation as hurting the economy. In the late 1970s, Congress and the president responded with a wave of **deregulation**. President Carter presided over the deregulation of the airlines in the late 1970s. In a more sweeping manner, President Reagan exercised "presidential oversight" in giving the OMB authority to review all executive branch proposals for new regulations. In this way, Reagan significantly reduced the total number of regulations issued by federal agencies.

More recently, calls for the creation of new regulatory authority spiked again, especially for the financial services industry, when weaknesses in the subprime mortgage business triggered a worldwide crisis of confidence leading to the Great Recession. Such an overhaul, the Dodd-Frank Act, was enacted by Congress and signed into law by President Obama in 2010, subjecting banks to tighter regulation and prohibiting them from engaging in a number of risky activities. Some of the Dodd-Frank rules were rolled back by Congress in 2018. The law also established a consumer protection agency to oversee consumer lending and the practices of credit card issuers, though in 2018 President Trump worked to curtail the agency's power.

Subsidies.   **Subsidies** are government grants of cash or other valuable commodities, such as land. Subsidies are a key "carrot" used in economic policy. They encourage people to either do something they might not otherwise do or else do more of what they are already doing.

deregulation
The policy of reducing the number of rules issued by federal regulatory agencies.

subsidy
A government grant of cash or other valuable commodities, such as land, to an individual or an organization. Subsidies are used to promote activities desired by the government, to reward political support, or to buy off political opposition.

Subsidies were the dominant form of public policy of the national government and the state and local governments throughout the nineteenth century. Under later policy makers, subsidies in the form of land grants were given to farmers and to railroad companies to encourage western settlement. Substantial cash subsidies have traditionally been given to shipbuilders to develop the commercial fleet and to guarantee the use of their ships as military personnel carriers in wartime.

Policies using the subsidy technique continued in the twentieth and twenty-first centuries. For example, crop subsidies for farmers, direct from the federal government, amounted to approximately $24 billion in 2019. This money was distributed to more than 700,000 farmers by the U.S. Department of Agriculture, with the bulk going to large corporate farming operations, rather than small family farmers. Politicians have always favored subsidies, because their benefits can be spread widely in response to many demands that might otherwise produce profound political conflict.

Contracting.   Government agencies often purchase goods and services by contract. The law requires open bidding for many of these contracts because they are extremely valuable to private-sector businesses and because the opportunities for abuse are very great. But contracting is more than a method of buying goods and services. It is also an important policy tool, because government agencies are often authorized to use their **contracting power** as a way of helping to build up whole sectors of the economy and of encouraging certain desirable goals or behavior, such as equal employment opportunity. For example, the infant airline industry of the 1930s was nurtured by the national government's lucrative contracts to carry airmail. A more recent example is the use of government contracting to encourage industries, universities, and other organizations to engage in research and development on a wide range of issues in basic and applied science.

contracting power
The power of government to set conditions on companies seeking to sell goods or services to government agencies.

WHO INFLUENCES ECONOMIC POLICY?

Decisions about economic policy represent real choices among the various goals of economic policy. For example, policy makers often face trade-offs between minimizing unemployment and limiting inflation, between protecting workers and incentivizing investment in new technology, or between raising taxes and cutting government services. The consequence of these choices is governmental policy that produces winners and losers in the economic sphere. Not surprisingly, these are fiercely fought political debates in which Americans hold differing views and priorities—based on their own economic self-interest, as well as their ideological orientation, partisan affiliation, and other political beliefs.

A 2017 Pew Research poll showed clear differences in economic policy positions between Democrats and Republicans. For example, Democrats are more likely to support spending on areas such as education (78 percent, compared with only 52 percent of Republicans), Social Security (53 percent, compared with 36 percent of Republicans), and assistance for the unemployed (44 percent, compared with only 13 percent of Republicans). However, Republicans were more likely to support increasing spending on military defense (71 percent in support, compared with only 31 percent of Democrats).[16] Given these differences, it is not surprising that research examining a wide range of economic policy issues has found greater government spending under Democratic Party control at the federal, state, and local levels.

We also see differences in the policy preferences held by richer and poorer Americans. This imbalance has important implications for policy decisions, since wealthier Americans tend to be more conservative on many economic policy issues—supporting cuts in taxes and reductions in social spending—than are poorer Americans.

The interest groups that influence decisions about economic policy are as wide-ranging as the objectives of policy. Consumer groups, environmentalists, businesses, and labor all attempt to shape economic policy. Of these groups, organized labor and business most consistently weigh in across the spectrum of economic policies. In the past, organized labor was much more important in influencing economic policy than it is today. At the height of their strength in the 1950s, unions represented some 35 percent of the labor force. Today, they are much less influential, representing only a tenth of the labor force.

Business organizations are the most consistently powerful actors in economic policy. Organizations such as the U.S. Chamber of Commerce (which represents small business), and the Business Roundtable and National Association of Manufacturers (which represent big business), have actively worked to roll back governmental regulation and reduce corporate taxes over the last few decades. These organizations, and myriad industry-specific groups, have an even greater impact on policy because of the *Citizens United* case decided in 2010 by the Supreme Court, which removed many constraints on their capacity to make campaign contributions.

A study of nearly two thousand policy issues found that the policy position adopted by business groups and the economic elites they represent is a key predictor of which policies the government enacts.[17] The opinion held by the average citizen or by other interest groups had little or no influence on the policy outcomes included in the study.

Today, policy makers from both sides of the aisle are coming together to enact response legislation to address our current financial crisis—and its particular impact on unemployed workers, small businesses, and local governments. This political response to economic crisis illustrates how closely interwoven American political and economic institutions are as well as how central economic policy is to both systems.

It is clear that economic policy making must acknowledge a key reality that was hit home by the 2008 meltdown and rapid global economic crisis during the

think it through

Do you think outside groups have too much say in economic policy decisions? Are there powerful business organizations active in your city that lobby for or against government regulations and policy changes?

COVID-19 pandemic in 2020: we are operating in a global economy. Neither our political institutions nor those of any other government have autonomy in the economic policy world. Trade and economic interactions within and between countries have huge implications for citizens of other nations. Creating economic policies that work well across a large and diverse nation is challenging enough, given the institutional fragmentation and intense partisan polarization that often leads to gridlock and inconsistent policy approaches. Doing so in an internationalized context will likely require new policy ideas and coalition building across a range of economic policy issues.

SOCIAL POLICY

Economic policy and social policy work hand in hand. A well-designed social policy can improve a nation's economy by creating opportunities for otherwise disadvantaged individuals to succeed and by addressing issues, such as health care, education, and housing, that affect the well-being of the nation's workforce. At the same time, social policy can provide a safety net for the elderly, poor, and infirm, who can be left behind in a market economy.

social policy
Governmental social insurance, welfare, health, and education programs aimed at protecting against risk and insecurity, reducing poverty, and/or expanding opportunity.

The term **social policy** refers to programs promoting three broad public goals. The first is to provide social insurance protecting against the risks and insecurities that most people face during their lives, including illness, disability, temporary unemployment, and the reduced earning capacity of old age. Most spending on social welfare in the United States goes to programs for the elderly, such as Social Security and Medicare. Widely regarded as successful, these programs are the least controversial areas of social spending, although debates about funding Social Security reveal that even widely agreed-on policies can generate conflict.

The second goal of social policy—to alleviate poverty—is more controversial, particularly because it often calls on government to redistribute income from wealthier to poorer individuals and families. Americans take pride in a strong work ethic, and they value self-sufficiency. In keeping with these values, many people in the United States worry that the able-bodied poor will not try to support themselves if they are offered "too much" assistance or the wrong kind. Yet there is also recognition that poverty may be the product of unequal opportunity in the past.

A third goal of social policy is to promote equality of opportunity. Although Americans generally admire the ideal of equal opportunity, there is no general agreement about what government should do to address inequalities: groups that have suffered from past inequality generally support more extensive governmental action to promote equality of opportunity than do others. Yet most Americans favor some governmental action, especially in the areas of preschool, K–12 education, and higher education policy.

THE HISTORICAL DEVELOPMENT OF U.S. SOCIAL POLICY

In his January 2013 inaugural address launching his second term in office, Barack Obama declared that the beneficiaries of social programs were not "takers" who weakened the nation by undermining Americans' sense of initiative. Instead, said Obama, social programs like Social Security, Medicare, Medicaid, and his own Affordable Care Act (ACA) "strengthen us," by ensuring that all have an opportunity to share in the country's prosperity.

This assertion presents a view of social policy at odds with the traditional American perspective. Unlike people in many other western democracies, Americans do not have a long history of taking public responsibility for economic inequality. This history has, as always, made some courses of action more likely and others less likely for Americans to follow. The United States was one of the last western democracies to enter this realm of social policy, for several reasons.

First, Americans' faith in individualism was extremely strong. Second, that faith was long fed by the existence of the frontier, which was so enticing that poverty was considered a temporary condition that could be alleviated by moving westward. Third, Americans conceived of poverty in two separate classes: the "deserving poor" and the "undeserving poor." The deserving poor were widows, orphans, and others rendered dependent by some misfortune beyond their control, such as national disaster, injury during honest labor, or the effects of war. The undeserving poor were able-bodied persons unwilling to work, transients, or others of whom the community disapproved.

Until the late nineteenth century, governmental involvement in what we today call *social policy* was slight, with the expectation that the deserving poor would be taken care of by religious, charitable, and other private efforts in their local community.

The traditional approach began to crumble in the face of the Great Depression. During the depression, misfortune became widespread and private wealth shrank so drastically that private charity was not robust enough to meet the growing need. The depression proved that poverty could result from imperfections in the economic system instead of from individual irresponsibility.

Once poverty and economic insecurity were accepted as inherent in the economy, a large-scale public-policy approach became practical. There was no longer any question about whether the national government would assume a major responsibility for poverty; from that time forward, it was a matter of how generous or restrictive the government would be about the welfare of the poor.

However, Americans never truly lost their historic discomfort with social policy, and the United States still spends a far lower percentage of its wealth on social programs than do other western governments. In the United States, social spending amounts to less than 20 percent of gross domestic product (GDP). In many

The Great Depression helped establish the ideas that unemployment and poverty reflected problems with America's economic system, not just individual irresponsibility, and that the government should take an active role in shaping fiscal and social policy.

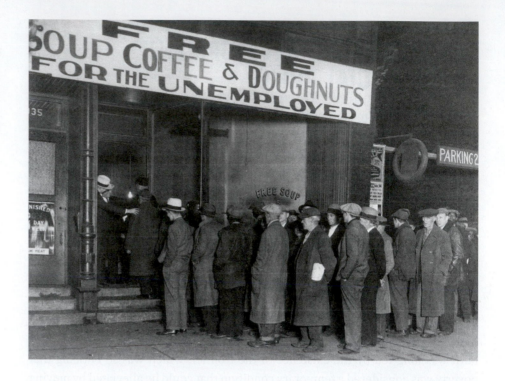

countries in the European Union—those with more robust welfare states—social spending accounts for nearly 30 percent of the national GDP (see Figure 13.4).

What is most distinctive about the U.S. approach to the welfare state is how much of the nation's social spending is focused on providing assistance to the broad middle class in dealing with life's risks and misfortunes (rather than subsidies to the poor). Although social programs such as Social Security, Medicare, and public education provide benefits to all Americans, and although some poor families benefit from them, the poor are not the *primary* beneficiaries of significant government social spending in these realms. The upper and middle classes are more likely to enjoy the benefits of such programs.

The poor, moreover, have not benefited to the same degree from a set of policies that are often called "America's hidden welfare state."[18] Today, the hidden **welfare state** consists of about $1 trillion in annual tax savings from various tax credits and deductions. As we saw earlier, these so-called tax expenditures, such as the deductibility of home mortgage interest or of donations to charity, were designed to promote desirable causes and practices, but their immediate benefits flow mainly to wealthier Americans, who are more likely to be able to buy a home or make a charitable contribution in the first place. In contrast to these hidden benefits, most social policies are more visible, and those who benefit from them are more likely to be stigmatized as "takers."

We turn now to the most important policies that constitute the welfare state. In the following section, we examine efforts by the government to expand opportunity for all Americans.

welfare state
A set of national public policies by which the government takes a central role in promoting the social and economic well-being of its citizens.

figure 13.4

GOVERNMENT SOCIAL SPENDING AS A PERCENTAGE OF GDP, 2018

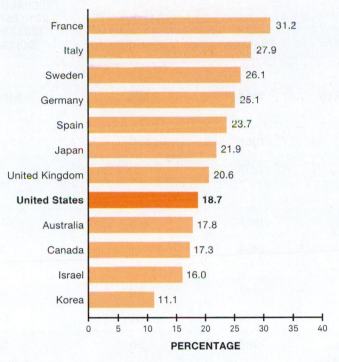

Country	Percentage
France	31.2
Italy	27.9
Sweden	26.1
Germany	25.1
Spain	23.7
Japan	21.9
United Kingdom	20.6
United States	**18.7**
Australia	17.8
Canada	17.3
Israel	16.0
Korea	11.1

PERCENTAGE

SOURCE: Organisation for Economic Co-Operation and Development, https://data.oecd.org/socialexp/social-spending.htm (accessed 7/9/20).

analyzing the evidence

Although the American welfare state has grown significantly over the past century, the United States spends less on social programs than do many other advanced democracies. How does the country's history help explain Americans' discomfort with social spending?

THE FOUNDATIONS OF THE SOCIAL WELFARE STATE

The foundations of the American welfare state were established by the Social Security Act of 1935. Programs like Social Security that guarantee benefits to certain groups of people, according to categories established by federal law, are known as **entitlement programs**. These programs generally fall into two categories: contributory programs and noncontributory programs. Table 13.1 outlines key entitlement programs in the United States.

Social Security

Social Security is the nation's most important **contributory program** and is financed by taxation. As the program was originally enacted, employer and employee were required to pay equal amounts, which in 1937 were set at 1 percent

entitlement program
A social program that guarantees benefits to a category of people defined by law.

Social Security
A contributory welfare program into which working Americans must place a percentage of their wages and from which they receive cash benefits after retirement.

contributory program
A social program financed in whole or in part by taxation or other mandatory contributions by its present or future recipients. The most important example is Social Security, which is financed by a payroll tax.

table 13.1

ENTITLEMENT PROGRAMS IN THE UNITED STATES

	YEAR ENACTED	FEDERAL OUTLAYS, 2017 (BILLIONS OF DOLLARS)	FEDERAL OUTLAYS, 2020 ESTIMATE (BILLIONS OF DOLLARS)
CONTRIBUTORY			
Old-age, survivors, and disability insurance (Social Security)	1935	939	1,108
Medicare	1965	690	796
Unemployment compensation	1935	31	31
NONCONTRIBUTORY			
Medicaid	1965	375	363
Supplemental Nutrition Assistance Program (SNAP; formerly food stamps)	1964	70	51
Earned income tax credit (EITC)	1975	60	58
Supplemental Security Income (SSI)	1974	52	54
Temporary Assistance for Needy Families (TANF; family-support payment to states)	1996	20	20

SOURCE: Office of Management and Budget, table 11.3, www.whitehouse.gov/omb/historical-tables (accessed 7/17/20).

of the first $3,000 of wages, to be deducted from the employee's paycheck and matched by the employer. This percentage has increased over the years; in 2020, the total employee contribution was 6.2 percent on the first $137,700 of income for the Social Security program, plus 1.45 percent on all earnings for Medicare. Individuals must pay an additional 0.9 percent on earnings over $200,000 for Medicare. Employers pay another 6.2 percent for Social Security and 1.45 percent for Medicare.[19]

Retirees enrolled in the Social Security system receive benefits based on the number of years they have worked, the amount they have contributed, and the age at which they choose to retire. Individuals begin to be eligible for benefits at age 62, but the monthly amount they receive increases substantially, the longer they wait to begin collecting payments (until age 70). Spouses and children of deceased enrollees are also often entitled to benefits, as are—under the Social Security Disability Insurance (SSDI) program—workers who become disabled before retirement.

Social Security has some characteristics of an insurance program, but it operates a bit differently from private insurance. Worker contributions do not accumulate in a personal account as, say, a private annuity does. Consequently, contributors do not receive benefits in proportion to their contributions, so there is some redistribution of wealth. In brief, contributory Social Security mildly redistributes wealth from higher- to lower-income people, and it significantly redistributes wealth from younger workers to older retirees.

The Politics of Reforming Social Security.   In 2019, nearly 65 million Americans received about $1 trillion in Social Security benefits. For more than half of all American workers, Social Security is their only pension plan. And without Social Security, half of all senior citizens would be living below the poverty line.

Clearly, the Social Security program makes a real difference to many people's lives. The program, however, has faced demographic pressure as the ratio between contributing workers and retirees has declined, from a comfortable 16 contributors to one retiree in the 1950s downward toward three contributors to one retiree today. With the record-breaking retirement of baby boomers continuing, this ratio is expected to drop further—estimated to reach only two workers for each retiree by 2030—stoking concern that contributions will not pay for the retirements of tomorrow if the system is not reformed (see Analyzing the Evidence on pp. 440–1).

Worker contributions are deposited in a Social Security trust fund, which officially earns interest at the average level for U.S. government securities. But that "official" description is a myth. The U.S. Treasury regularly borrows money from the trust fund and leaves IOUs to soften the impression of the nation's true national debt. Thus, the Social Security system, under successive Democratic and Republican administrations, has become a pay-as-you-go program in which today's youth take care of today's aged. That is what we mean when we say that Social Security provides for the redistribution of some wealth from the young to the elderly.

Most experts believe that Social Security taxes must be increased and the retirement age raised to maintain the program's solvency. When Social Security was introduced in 1935, a retirement age of 60 seemed reasonable. Indeed, American workers' average life expectancy was barely 60. Today, Americans can expect to live longer and healthier lives than their forebears, so increasing the retirement age may be a viable approach.

Unemployment Insurance

The federal Social Security Act of 1935 also created a federal unemployment insurance program designed to help workers whose jobs have been terminated through no fault of their own. By providing unemployment payments for a short period, the program gives workers time to find a new job or shift into a sector or geographic area with greater job opportunities without being forced to take a job for which they are overqualified or to turn to the welfare system.

Although it is a federal policy, unemployment insurance is jointly administered by the national government and each of the state governments. Both federal and state taxes on employers fund the program, and a combination of federal and state laws determine which employees are eligible for compensation, how much

Fixing Social Security?

Contributed by **Rachael Vanessa Cobb**, *Suffolk University Boston*

Every month, millions of elderly and disabled Americans receive a check from the U.S. government. These funds are designed to provide a safety net—income for retirement and assistance to those with disabilities. When the Social Security Act passed both houses of Congress and was signed into law by President Franklin D. Roosevelt in 1935, 50 percent of elderly Americans were living in poverty. By the 1950s, that number had fallen to 35 percent. Today, only 10 percent of elderly Americans live in poverty.

However, the number of retired Americans is rising because of an increase in life expectancy and because of a growing population of elderly Americans. In 2010, 54 million people received Social Security. In 2035, a projected 91 million people will receive Social Security. In 1960, the number of workers per beneficiary was five. That number is projected to decline to two by 2035. Thus Social Security faces the challenge of remaining solvent for future generations. Left unchanged, full benefits are possible only through 2033, according to a 2012 report from the Trustees of the Social Security Trust Fund. The figure below, from 2010, shows the projected divergence of program cost and tax revenue over time. More recent analyses have reached similar conclusions.

Social Security Cost vs. Expected Tax Revenue*

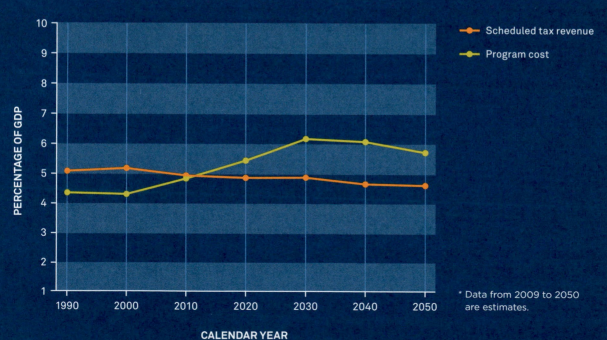

Legend:
- Scheduled tax revenue
- Program cost

Y-axis: PERCENTAGE OF GDP (1 to 10)
X-axis: CALENDAR YEAR (1990, 2000, 2010, 2020, 2030, 2040, 2050)

* Data from 2009 to 2050 are estimates.

Policy solutions aimed at preserving Social Security fall into three broad categories: raising payroll taxes, reducing benefits to future retirees, or changing eligibility requirements. Currently, 6.2 percent of a person's paycheck is deducted for Social Security, but only on wages and salaries up to $127,200 per year. That means that any income someone earns above $127,200 per year is not deducted. As earnings inequality has increased, the share of earnings that is taxed for Social Security has declined. This is because, according to the Congressional Budget Office, "a greater share of income is above the taxable maximum."[1] Policy makers could lift the ceiling on which payroll taxes are paid, or the tax rate of 6.2 percent could be increased. Finally, the retirement age could be raised from 65 or overall benefits could be cut.

As the figures below show, a 2015 Economist/YouGov poll found that 55 percent of Americans support taxing income above the 2015 threshold, which was $118,500, while only 23 percent oppose it. A 2012 Pew Research Study found that 66 percent of Americans favored raising payroll taxes on high income earners. At the same time, a majority of Americans has reliably opposed increasing the age of eligibility or reducing benefits.

Percentage of Americans Who:

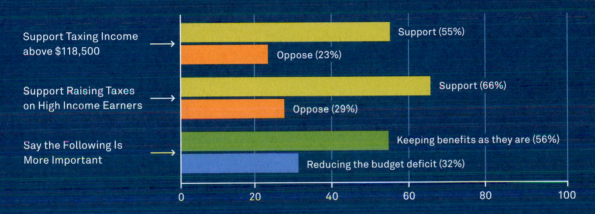

- Support Taxing Income above $118,500 → Support (55%); Oppose (23%)
- Support Raising Taxes on High Income Earners → Support (66%); Oppose (29%)
- Say the Following Is More Important → Keeping benefits as they are (56%); Reducing the budget deficit (32%)

Social Security is a broadly popular program. Since 1984, the National Opinion Research Center at the University of Chicago has asked Americans whether they think too much, too little, or just the right amount of money is being spent on Social Security. In every survey, 90 percent or more of the public said too little or just the right amount.[2] Americans support Social Security and also demonstrate support for policy changes that would preserve it and its goals.

1 Noah Meyerson and Sheila Dacey, "How Does Social Security Work?" Congressional Budget Office, September 19, 2013, www.cbo.gov/publication/44590 (accessed 6/12/20).

2 Fay Lomax Cook and Rachel L. Moskowitz, "What Americans Think About the Future of Social Security," Scholars Strategy Network, 2012, www.scholarsstrategynetwork.org/brief/what-americans-think-about-future-social-security (accessed 6/12/20).

SOURCES: Steven C. Goss, www.ssa.gov/policy/docs/ssb/v70n3/v70n3p111.html (accessed 6/12/20); Economist/YouGov Poll, https://d25d2506sfb94s.cloudfront.net/cumulus_uploads/document/5bfxk1yh2f/econTabReport.pdf (accessed 6/12/20); and Kim Parker, www.pewsocialtrends.org/2012/12/20/the-big-generation-gap-at-the-polls-is-echoed-in-attitudes-on-budget-tradeoffs (accessed 6/12/20).

 If the government decided to increase the taxable income threshold, as the survey suggests a majority of citizens would support, how would you expect the estimates for scheduled tax revenue and program costs to changes in the graph at left by 2050?

In an effort to address the economic hardships brought by the COVID-19 pandemic, Congress passed several pieces of bipartisan legislation, including the Coronavirus Aid, Relief, and Economic Security (CARES) Act, which was signed into law by President Trump in March 2020. This act extended unemployment benefits to workers who normally not would receive these benefits; it also extended the length of benefits for all recipients.

money they receive, and how long the benefits are paid. The standard time period is 26 weeks (about six months), although the federal government has extended this timeline during economic downturns. During the recent Great Recession, for example, unemployment benefits were extended to 73 weeks. More recently, in March 2020, the Coronavirus Aid, Relief, and Economic Security (CARES) Act expanded unemployment benefits for those impacted by the COVID-19 pandemic from 26 to 39 weeks; it also provided an additional $600 per week to current unemployment insurance payments through July 2020. Another significant feature of the CARES Act is that it temporarily expanded eligibility to many more workers impacted by the COVID-19 pandemic, including independent contractors and those working in the "gig economy" who are not typically eligible for unemployment insurance.

Major Health Programs

Medicare
National health insurance for the elderly and the disabled.

Medicare.   The creation of **Medicare** was the biggest expansion in contributory programs after 1935. Established in 1965, it aimed to provide substantial medical insurance for elderly persons who are already eligible to receive old-age, survivors, and disability insurance through their contributions under the original Social Security system. Like Social Security, Medicare is not means tested. In other words, beneficiaries receive Medicare benefits without regard to personal wealth and income. (Means-tested noncontributory programs are discussed in the next section.)

Today, nearly 60 million senior citizens are covered by Medicare. However, the spectacular increase in the program's cost is only partly attributable to the growing number of participants; much of the increase is due to the rising cost of health care and to the 2003 drug benefit championed by the George W. Bush administration.

The Affordable Care Act. As discussed in the chapter introduction, in 2010 the Obama administration initiated a major expansion of federal health care policy. The Patient Protection and Affordable Care Act, popularly known as "Obamacare," was designed to ensure that tens of millions of Americans who could not afford health insurance would have access to at least basic coverage. Among other things, the act required individuals to maintain health insurance and required the states to establish insurance exchanges or use federal exchanges through which individuals and small employers could obtain low-cost and, in some cases, federally subsidized health insurance policies. The act also expanded Medicaid (though the Supreme Court later ruled that states could opt not to do this) and children's health insurance programs, and imposed regulations on providers aimed at cutting costs. The administration claimed that the new law would ultimately lower health care costs by imposing greater efficiencies on providers and reducing fraud.

The act passed despite vehement and unanimous Republican opposition in Congress, and by 2015, nearly 10 million Americans had used the state and federal insurance exchanges to purchase health insurance. During the 2016 presidential campaign, Donald Trump promised to repeal Obamacare. And this was a key priority during his first 100 days in office, as Congress advanced a number of different repeal proposals. Yet each of these repeal bills was unsuccessful. Despite this failure at a clean repeal of the Affordable Care Act, the Trump administration was successful in repealing one of the act's least popular provisions—the individual mandate—as part of its 2017 tax reform legislation. In addition, through executive orders, administrative guidance, and regulatory policies, the Trump administration has been successful in weakening many other aspects of the ACA (see Chapter 6).

Income Support Programs

Programs to which beneficiaries do not have to contribute—**noncontributory programs**—are also known as public-assistance programs, often referred to as "welfare" despite the more narrow focus on income support rather than the broad scope of social benefits considered part of the welfare state. Until 1996, the most important noncontributory program was Aid to Families with Dependent Children (AFDC; originally called Aid to Dependent Children, or ADC), which was founded in 1935 by the original Social Security Act. In 1996, Congress replaced AFDC with the **Temporary Assistance for Needy Families (TANF)** block grant. Eligibility for public assistance is determined by **means testing**, a procedure that requires applicants to show a financial need for assistance. Between 1935 and 1965, the government also created programs to provide housing assistance, school lunches, and food stamps to needy Americans.

As early as the 1960s, public-opinion polls consistently showed that Americans disliked welfare more than any other governmental program, and that the public viewed welfare beneficiaries as "undeserving." Underlying that judgment was the belief that welfare recipients did not want to work. These negative opinions were amplified by racial stereotypes.[20] By 1973, approximately 46 percent of

noncontributory program
A social program that assists people on the basis of demonstrated need rather than contributions they have made. Also called *public-assistance program.*

Temporary Assistance for Needy Families (TANF)
Federal cash assistance for children in families that fall below state standards of need.

means testing
A procedure that determines eligibility for governmental public-assistance programs. A potential beneficiary must show need as well as income and assets below a defined level.

Medicaid

A federally financed, state-operated program for medical services to low-income people.

Supplemental Nutrition Assistance Program (SNAP)

An in-kind benefits program that provides eligible individuals and families with debit cards that can be used to buy food at most retail stores.

in-kind benefits

Goods and services provided to eligible individuals and families by the federal government, as contrasted with cash benefits.

earned income tax credit (EITC)

A tax benefit that is designed to supplement the earnings of lower-income workers. The EITC lowers the total taxes the worker must pay—providing a cash refund on most recipients' tax returns.

analyzing the evidence

Welfare caseloads dropped dramatically after 1994. Why? What are the positive and negative consequences of the policy change that reduced welfare rolls?

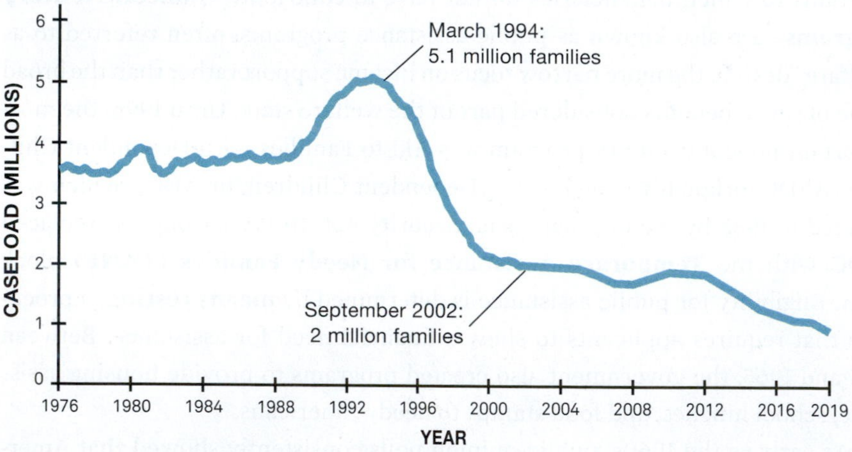

welfare recipients were African American. Although most recipients were White, media portrayals promoted the perception that the vast majority were Black.

Despite public opposition to welfare, reform proved difficult. Congress added modest work requirements in 1967, but little changed in the program's administration. A more significant reform in 1988 imposed stricter work requirements and also provided additional support services, such as child care and transportation assistance. These reforms had barely been implemented, when welfare rolls rose again with the recession of the early 1990s, reaching an all-time high in 1994. Sensing continuing public frustration, presidential candidate Bill Clinton vowed to "end welfare as we know it"—but found it difficult to design a plan that would provide an adequate safety net for recipients who were unable to find work.

Congressional Republicans proposed a more dramatic reform, and Clinton, after initially vetoing two earlier versions, and with a looming reelection campaign in 1996, signed the TANF legislation. In place of the individual entitlement to assistance, the new law created block grants to the states and allowed states more discretion in designing cash assistance programs for needy families. While many of these programs, especially Medicaid, have grown, cash assistance for poor families under TANF has shrunk to about 2 million families—representing only 22 percent of families in poverty. TANF grants have not been indexed for inflation and have not increased since 1996—making fewer and fewer families eligible each year (see Figure 13.5).

Like contributory programs, noncontributory public-assistance programs made their most significant advances in the 1960s and 1970s. The year 1965 saw

figure 13.5

NUMBER OF AFDC/TANF FAMILIES, 1976–2019

SOURCES: **Years 1976–2013:** Congressional Research Service, 2016; https://fas.org/sgp/crs/misc/R43187.pdf; **2014–17:** U.S. Department of Health & Human Services, https://aspe.hhs.gov/report/indicators-welfare -dependence-annual-report-congress-2009-2013/temporary-assistance-needy-families-tanf-and-aid-families -dependent-children-afdc; **2018:** U.S. Department of Health & Human Services, Office of Family Assistance, www.acf.hhs.gov/sites/default/files/ofa/2018tanf_totalfamilies_03252019_508.pdf; **2019:** U.S. Department of Health & Human Services, Office of Family Assistance, www.acf.hhs.gov/sites/default/files/ofa/fy2019_tanf _caseload.pdf (all accessed 7/9/20).

the establishment of **Medicaid**, a program that provides extensive medical services to all low-income persons who have established eligibility through means testing under TANF. Another transformation in the 1970s was the level of benefits provided. Besides being means tested, noncontributory programs are administered by the states; grants-in-aid are provided by the national government to the states as incentives to establish the programs (see Chapter 3).

Thus, from the beginning there were considerable differences in benefits from state to state. The national government sought to address differences in levels of benefits in 1974 by creating Supplemental Security Income (SSI) to augment benefits for the aged, the blind, and the disabled. SSI provides uniform minimum benefits nationwide. States may be more generous, but no state is permitted to provide benefits below the minimum level set by the national government.

The TANF program is also administered by the states, and benefit levels vary widely from state to state. For example, in 2019 the states' monthly TANF benefits for a family varied from $170 in Mississippi and $185 in Tennessee to $923 in Alaska and $1,066 in New Hampshire. Even the most generous TANF payments fall well below the federal poverty line. In 2018, the poverty level for a family of three was $21,720, or $1,810 a month.[21]

The number of people receiving AFDC benefits expanded in the 1970s, in part because new welfare programs had been established in the mid-1960s: Medicaid (discussed earlier) and food stamps (now called the **Supplemental Nutrition Assistance Program**, or **SNAP**, with the stamps replaced by debit cards, which are used to buy food at most retail stores). Medicaid and SNAP provide what are called **in-kind benefits**—noncash goods and services that would otherwise have to be paid for in cash by the beneficiary.

The **earned income tax credit (EITC)** is a tax benefit that supplements the take-home pay for lower-income workers and their families. When eligible workers file their tax returns, they can claim a credit that helps cover their federal taxes, and they may also receive a cash refund. Today, one in five taxpayers (about 25 million people) claims the EITC—receiving an average credit of about $2,000. Often called America's "stealth poverty program," the EITC lifts about 6 million people out of poverty each year, about half of them children. In approximately half the states, the effect of the EITC is further enhanced by the addition of a state-level credit.

The Supplemental Nutrition Assistance Program (SNAP), formerly known as food stamps, helps people in need buy food. Today, recipients use government-provided debit cards to make their purchases.

think it through

TANF payments vary from state to state. What is the average TANF payment in your state? How does this compare with the cost of living in your state?

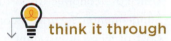

HOW CAN GOVERNMENT CREATE OPPORTUNITY?

In the United States, social programs not only supply a measure of economic security but also seek to broaden opportunity. Americans' belief in equality of opportunity makes such programs particularly important in providing a way to keep people from falling into poverty and in offering a hand up to the poor.

table 13.2

GROWTH OF THE WELFARE SYSTEM

WELFARE	EDUCATION	HEALTH AND HOUSING
STATE ERA (1789–1935)		
Private and local charity State child labor laws State unemployment and injury compensation State mothers' pensions	Northwest Ordinance (1787, federal) Local academies Local public schools State compulsory education laws Morrill Act (1862) for land-grant colleges (federal)	Local public health ordinances
FEDERAL ERA (1935–PRESENT)		
Social Security Disability Insurance Volunteers in Service to America (later folded into AmeriCorps); Office of Economic Opportunity Supplemental Security Income Cost-of-living adjustment (indexing)	GI Bill (of Rights) (1944) National Defense Education Act (1958) Elementary and Secondary Education Act (1965) Higher Education Act (1965) School desegregation Head Start No Child Left Behind Act (2001) Every Student Succeeds Act (2015)	Public housing Hospital construction School lunch program Food stamps Medicare Medicaid Patient Protection and Affordable Care Act

SOURCE: Compiled by the author.

Elementary and Secondary Education Policy

Most primary and secondary education programs in the United States are provided by the public policies of state and local governments. Though the federal role has been growing in recent years, of the nearly $700 billion spent on public K–12 education each year, less than 10 percent consists of federal spending. These education policies are a key force in the distribution and redistribution of opportunity in America.

Compared with state and local efforts, national education policy pales. With a few exceptions, the national government did not involve itself in education during the United States' first century (Table 13.2). The first two exceptions preceded the Constitution—the Land Ordinance of 1785, followed by the Northwest Ordinance of 1787. These two acts provided for a survey of all public lands in the Northwest Territory and required that certain sections in each township be reserved for public schools and their maintenance. Not until 1862, with the Morrill Act, did Congress take a third step, establishing land-grant colleges and universities. Later, more federal programs targeted the education of farmers and other rural residents.

The most important national education policies came after World War II: the GI Bill of 1944, the National Defense Education Act (NDEA) of 1958, the Elementary and Secondary Education Act (ESEA) of 1965, and various youth and adult vocational training acts since 1958. But because the GI Bill almost exclusively addressed postsecondary schooling, the national government did not really enter the field of elementary education until after 1957.[22]

What finally brought the national government into elementary education was embarrassment over the Soviets beating the United States into space with *Sputnik*. National policy under the NDEA specifically targeted improving education in science and mathematics. General federal aid for education did not come until 1965, with ESEA, which allocated funds to school districts that had a substantial number of children whose families were unemployed or earning less than $2,000 a year.

The federal role was substantially increased by President George W. Bush's No Child Left Behind Act, signed in 2002, which created stronger federal requirements for testing and school accountability. It required that every child in grades 3 through 8 be tested yearly in math and reading. Schools were judged on the basis of their students' performance on these tests. Parents whose child was in a failing school had the right to transfer the child to a better school and to access special funds for tutoring and summer programs. The states were responsible for setting standards and devising appropriate tests.

Although there was bipartisan support for the program, the act was difficult to implement for several reasons. First, many states were unable to move to a new system of standards and testing. Second, education experts viewed yearly test results as too volatile to adequately measure school performance and warned that failing schools would become weaker as parents transferred their children

President Obama signed into law Every Student Succeeds, which gave states more flexibility in rating school performance and in deciding how best to support struggling students. Here, students, educators, and lawmakers take photos of the signed law.

out of them.[23] Third, and most important, the federal government was demanding major improvements without providing funding to pay for them.

Several states, along with the National Education Association, sued the federal government on the grounds that Congress had not provided enough money to pay for the required testing and other services, and in 2011, the Obama administration gradually began to allow the states to opt out of the requirements.

In 2015, a bipartisan group in Congress undertook the task of rewriting No Child Left Behind and enacted a new law to replace it called Every Student Succeeds. This act gave the states more latitude in rating school performance and in deciding whether and how to intervene to help schools whose students seem to be struggling. The Every Student Succeeds Act represented a retreat by the federal government in efforts to regulate public education.

Higher Education Policy

Although much of the higher education system in the United States consists of public institutions run by state or local governments, as well as private colleges and universities, the federal government has played an increasingly important role. A major focus of federal higher education policy has been to help students access and afford higher education through a range of federal grants and loan programs. Today, funds from the federal government make up more than 75 percent of the total student financial aid provided in the United States.

Foreshadowing its current role, the federal government became involved in subsidizing individual students as a result of the 1944 GI Bill, which provided veterans returning from the Second World War with a voucher they could use to pay for higher education at the institution of their choice. Nearly two decades later, the federal government stepped into a broader role with the 1965 Higher Education Act (HEA). The act provided financial assistance as part of an effort to increase enrollment rates, particularly among lower-income and minority populations. Through a series of reauthorizations, the HEA has been expanded in scope and funding levels—now providing about $80 billion in spending on student grants, loans, and tax credits to students and their families.

One of the most significant expansions to the HEA occurred during the 1972 reauthorization, which created the Pell Grant program. Pell Grants provide up to $6,095 (as of 2019) toward undergraduate tuition and expenses to students from low- and moderate-income families (nearly half of all undergraduate students). Since 1972, spending on the Pell Grant program has increased, and the number of individuals receiving grants has too. Yet increases in the size of the grants awarded have not kept up with rising tuition prices. In fact, Pell Grants now cover only about 30 percent of the cost of attending college at a public university—a significant decrease from the 1970s, when they covered about 80 percent of a public university education (Figure 13.6). Although there

figure 13.6

SHARE OF COLLEGE COSTS COVERED BY PELL GRANTS

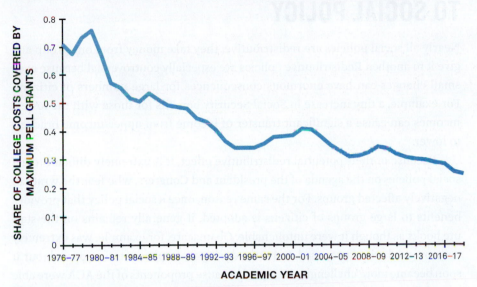

*Attendance costs are the average undergraduate tuition, fees, room, and board rate for public four-year institutions.

SOURCE: College Board, https://research.collegeboard.org/pdf/2019-trendsinsa-figs20a-20b-21a-21b.pdf (accessed 7/9/20).

seems to be increasing bipartisan support for increasing the Pell Grant, legislation for doing so failed to move forward after Congressional attention turned to the COVID-19 crisis.

In addition to direct spending, the federal government helps subsidize the cost of higher education through the tax code. The largest education-related tax credit is the American opportunity tax credit (AOTC), which provides a tax cut of $2,500 a year for up to four years of each student's postsecondary education. This indirect aid through the AOTC accounts for more than $20 billion in foregone revenue that the government would collect were it not for the tax credit—an amount close to the total spent on direct aid through the Pell Grant program.

In addition to offering grants and tax credits, the federal government plays a key role in making student loans available for career training and undergraduate and graduate education. Unlike private loans offered by banks or credit unions, federal loans offer low interest rates, income-based repayment plans, loan forgiveness for certain types of employment, and the ability to postpone payments for various reasons. Federal student loans are typically available to all borrowers and do not require a credit check. Private banks would not be able to offer such good terms to borrowers without going out of business. In fact, the Congressional Budget Office has estimated that the federal government loses a lot of money on the student loan program—a loss that is expected to amount to about $170 billion over the next decade.[24]

SUPPORT FOR AND OPPOSITION TO SOCIAL POLICY

Nearly all social policies are redistributive: they take money from one group and give it to another. Redistributive policies are especially controversial because even small changes can have enormous consequences for large numbers of citizens. For example, a tiny increase in Social Security benefits for those with the lowest incomes can cause a significant transfer of income from upper-income brackets to lower.

Because of their potential redistributive effect, it is extremely difficult to get social policies on the agenda of the president and Congress, who fear the wrath of negatively affected groups. For the same reason, once a social policy that provides benefits to large groups of citizens is adopted, it generally remains on the stat-ute books as though it were untouchable. Obamacare, for example, was extremely controversial when proposed and even during its implementation period, but it soon became more challenging to repeal because proponents of the ACA were able to mobilize those who were benefiting from the bill and publicize their stories.

Conflicting views about whether and how the government should help citizens have a significant effect on the nature of the social policies we have today. In an effort to respond to calls both to limit government and to expand the pro-vision of social benefits, politicians often design indirect—and often inefficient—policies that seem to minimize the role for government while actually increas-ing the size and complexity of governmental social policy. By delivering benefits through the tax code, delegating authority to the states or local governments, and relying on government contractors or the private sector to provide government

Once a social policy that provides benefits to a large group of citizens (like Medicare and Medicaid) is adopted, it generally remains in place and becomes untouchable, as repre-sentatives fear the wrath of their constituents if they take it away.

benefits, policy makers expand social benefits in ways that simply add to the complexity and fragmentation of the social policy landscape in the United States. Further, these indirect policy designs produce programs that are hard to target to areas of greatest need or to coordinate with other governmental programs. This approach also makes these social programs very hard to administer, implement, evaluate, or hold accountable for outcomes.

In the end, much of public support or opposition to social programs comes down to the question of who is deserving—in other words, whom the government should help. When program beneficiaries are viewed as earning their benefits—by working and paying payroll taxes, or by serving in the military—there is generally broad support for programs to benefit them, such as Social Security and the GI Bill. Yet for many other social programs—particularly means-tested, noncontributory programs—the recipients are often viewed as undeserving and untrustworthy. Programs such as TANF and SNAP are often criticized for providing the wrong incentives to recipients.

Benefits for wealthier Americans, such as the home mortgage interest deduction, are easy to access, and recipients are trusted to use the benefits wisely. By contrast, more meager welfare benefits are subject to burdensome application and renewal processes, reviews of income and asset documentation, work requirements, and persistent concerns about waste, fraud, and abuse. Further, these notions of who deserves welfare benefits are often tied in with implicit bias and racial resentment in ways that decrease support for social programs that are viewed as benefiting African Americans and other minority-group members.

CONCLUSION

How do representation and governance meet and sometimes collide when it comes to issues of public policy? Many Americans are deeply suspicious of government. However, without government to maintain law and order, to define rules of property, to enforce contracts, and to provide public goods, no market economy could function. Without government to provide a safety net for the elderly, poor, and sick, ours would become a brutal society in which we would all be diminished. Without government to provide for the nation's defense, Americans would be vulnerable to foreign foes.

Yet, too much or poorly fashioned governmental intervention—in the form of burdensome regulations, badly designed monetary and fiscal policies, and public policies serving private interests at the public's expense—can stifle a market economy and undermine representative democracy. Inappropriate social policies can bankrupt the Treasury and wreck communities without promoting public welfare. Poorly conceived national security policies can leave us constantly at war without protecting our safety.

What is the proper balance between governmental intervention and free enterprise, between social spending and wasteful extravagance, between defense and militarism? There is no single answer to these questions. In the United States, as in other liberal democracies, we have a political process designed to allow every citizen to weigh in. If this process sometimes seems stalemated, perhaps it is because Americans have not reached any consensus and hope they can have both strong government and maximum individual freedom.

Key Terms

public policy 411

economic policy 412

public good 413

monopoly 414

Securities and Exchange Commission (SEC) 415

gross domestic product (GDP) 416

inflation 417

monetary policy 419

Federal Reserve System (Fed) 421

reserve requirement 422

open-market operations 422

federal funds rate 423

fiscal policy 423

budget deficit 423

national debt 423

tariff 425

progressive tax 425

redistribution 425

regressive tax 425

tax expenditure 426

mandatory spending 428

discretionary spending 428

antitrust policy 430

deregulation 431

subsidy 431

contracting power 432

social policy 434

welfare state 436

entitlement program 437

Social Security 437

contributory program 437

Medicare 442

noncontributory program 443

Temporary Assistance for Needy Families (TANF) 443

means testing 443

Medicaid 445

Supplemental Nutrition Assistance Program (SNAP) 445

in-kind benefits 445

earned income tax credit (EITC) 445

Check Your Understanding

1. What is public policy? Explain how public policy represents the convergence of representation and governance.

2. What types of actions does government take to influence economic activity? How do these actions conflict or support the perception of America having a "free-market" economy?

3. What are the goals of economic policy? What tools does government employ to promote them?

4. What are the goals of social policy? How does a well-designed social policy also help improve the nation's economy?

5. What is an entitlement program? Who benefits from these social programs?

6. What is a contributory program? Who benefits from these social programs?

 INQUIZITIVE

Earn a better grade on your test. InQuizitive personalizes your learning path to help you master the concepts from this chapter. In a recent efficacy study of American government students, InQuizitive increased test scores by an average of 17 points (see back cover).

CHAPTER FOURTEEN

FOREIGN POLICY

In January 2020, President Donald Trump authorized a drone strike that killed Iranian general Qasem Soleimani, commander of Iran's Quds Force, a unit of Iran's Revolutionary Guard responsible for clandestine international operations. The United States believed that Soleimani was the mastermind responsible for dozens of attacks against American forces in the Middle East, and viewed his death as a blow to the Iranian military. Iran threatened harsh reprisals for the American attack. The United States, which had already imposed severe economic sanctions on Iran, promised to respond with force against any Iranian retaliation for Soleimani's death. When the Iranians made a relatively minor retaliatory gesture the White House largely ignored it, and diplomatic efforts were set in motion to defuse the crisis. Military force, economic sanctions, and diplomacy are all tools of foreign policy and are often used in combination to achieve national objectives.

The term *foreign policy* refers to the programs and policies that determine a country's relations with other countries and foreign entities. Of course, foreign policy and domestic policy are closely intertwined. Consider security policy. Defending the nation requires the design and manufacture of tens of billions of dollars' worth of military hardware. The manufacture and procurement of this equipment involve numerous economic policies, and paying for it shapes the United States' fiscal policies.

Foreign policy—especially security policy—is traditionally an area in which the nation's leaders act without consulting public opinion. Indeed, foreign policy is often made in secrecy. Would greater transparency bring about better policy—that is, policy more representative of citizens' preferences—or would it harm the nation's interests and make effective governance impossible in this realm?

Much recent public debate has centered on the effectiveness of current U.S. foreign policy and whether government actually can—and should attempt to—end violence elsewhere in the world. Some Americans believe that our government is itself too quick to make use of armed violence and should seek peaceful means of solving international differences.

Often, citizens and politicians denounce the use of force by some groups or nations while casting a tolerant eye at its use by others. Politically progressive Americans typically denounce military actions by the United States and other Western nations, but tend to be more accepting of the use of violence by those they regard as oppressed groups, such as the Palestinians and Tibetans. Most progressive politicians strongly oppose the use of force against North Korea and, for that matter, Iran, saying that diplomacy is the only way to deal with international differences.

Politically conservative groups generally take the opposite view, sharply criticizing revolutionary movements for their use of violence. And, in the cases of North Korea and Iran, some conservatives, most notably President Trump's former national security adviser, John Bolton, say that the United States should be ready to use military force against these hostile regimes. The moral implications of American foreign policy are further complicated by important concerns about national security and interests, and by the difficult reality that not intervening abroad with violent force may mean effectively condemning some peoples to live under tyranny.

How should the government respond to international violence? Are there peaceful means of solving problems? We need to remember that many current international threats—climate change, disease, energy shortages—do

President Trump employed the various tools of foreign policy—threat of military force, economic sanctions, and diplomacy—in dealings with Iran. His actions didn't always align with public opinion on the issue, highlighting the challenge of reconciling the need for decisive action in certain situations to ensure the safety of the country with the obligation to reflect the will of the people in a representative democracy.

- **Does effective governance in the realm of foreign policy require decisive and sometimes secret action by the executive branch, or would U.S. foreign policy be improved if more views were represented when policies were made?**

not seem solvable by military means. Other pressing foreign policy issues have to do with the country's economic goals in an age of globalization.

In this chapter, we consider the goals and tools of American foreign policy, as well as the various makers and shapers of foreign policy decisions. Finally, we will turn to the question of the United States' role in the world today.

Learning Objectives

■ Describe the general goals of American foreign policy, including security, economic prosperity, and—to a lesser extent—humanitarian objectives.

■ Identify the domestic actors—such as the president, the bureaucracy, Congress, and interest groups—who shape U.S. foreign policy.

■ Explain how economic, diplomatic, institutional, and military means are used strategically to implement foreign policy and further the interests of the United States.

■ Analyze how the ideals of American democracy may come into conflict with the United States' international interests.

THE GOALS OF FOREIGN POLICY

Although U.S. foreign policy has a number of purposes, three main goals stand out: security, prosperity, and the creation of a better world. These goals are closely intertwined.

Security

To many Americans, the chief purpose of the nation's foreign policy is the protection of U.S. security in an often hostile world. Traditionally, the United States has been concerned about threats posed by other nations, such as Nazi Germany during the 1940s and then the Soviet Union until its collapse in the late 1980s. Today, American security policy addresses not only the actions of other nations but also those of terrorist groups and other hostile **non-state actors**.[1] To protect against foreign threats, the United States has built an enormous military apparatus and a complex array of intelligence-gathering institutions, such as the Central Intelligence Agency (CIA), charged with evaluating and anticipating challenges from abroad.[2] While all nations are concerned with security, American power and global commitments give U.S. foreign policy a unique focus on security issues.

Security is a broad term. First, policy makers must be concerned with Americans' physical security. The September 11 terrorist attacks killed and injured thousands of Americans; the government constantly fears that new attacks could

non-state actor
A group, other than a nation-state, that attempts to play a role in the international system.

be even more catastrophic. Second, policy makers must weigh such matters as the security of food supplies, transportation infrastructure, and energy supplies. Many U.S. foreign policy efforts in the Middle East, for example, have been aimed at protecting American access to vital oil fields. Third, in recent years cyberspace has become a new security concern, as the government must be alert to efforts by hostile governments, groups, or even individual hackers to damage computer networks.

Isolationism. During the eighteenth and nineteenth centuries, the nation's security was based on its geographic isolation. Separated by two oceans from European and Asian powers, many Americans thought that national security would be best preserved by keeping out of international power struggles. This policy was known as **isolationism**. In his 1796 farewell address, President George Washington warned against permanent alliances with foreign powers, and in 1823 President James Monroe warned foreign powers not to meddle in the Western Hemisphere. Washington's warning and what came to be called the Monroe Doctrine were the cornerstones of U.S. isolationism until the late nineteenth century. The United States saw itself as the dominant power in the Western Hemisphere and believed that its "manifest destiny" was to expand from sea to sea. The rest of the world, however, should remain at arm's length.

In the twentieth century, technology made oceans less of a barrier to foreign threats, and the world's growing economic interdependence meant that the United States could no longer ignore events abroad. Early in the twentieth century, the United States entered World War I on the side of Great Britain and France when the Wilson administration concluded that a German victory would adversely affect U.S. economic and security interests. In 1941, the United States was drawn into World War II when Japan attacked the Americans' Pacific fleet anchored at Pearl Harbor, Hawaii. Even before the attack, President Franklin Delano Roosevelt's administration had concluded that the United States must act to prevent a victory by the German-Japanese-Italian Axis alliance. Until Pearl Harbor, Roosevelt had been unable to overcome arguments that national security was best served by avoiding foreign conflicts. However, the Japanese attack proved that the Pacific Ocean could not protect the United States from foreign foes and that isolationism was no longer a real option.

Containment and Deterrence. After World War II, the United States developed a new security policy, known as **containment**, to limit the Soviet Union's growing power. This policy stressed the need for the United States to contain the Soviets by patiently applying counterpressure wherever the Soviets sought to expand their influence.

By the late 1940s, the Soviets had built a huge empire and enormous military forces. Most threatening were their nuclear weapons and intercontinental bombers capable of attacking the United States. The United States was committed to maintaining its own military might as a means of **deterrence**, to discourage the Soviets from attacking America or its allies. Containment and deterrence

isolationism
The desire to avoid involvement in the affairs of other nations.

containment
A policy designed to limit the political and military expansion of a hostile power.

deterrence
The development and maintenance of military strength as a means of discouraging attack.

preventive war
The policy of striking first when a nation fears that a foreign power is contemplating hostile action.

appeasement
The effort to avoid war by giving in to the demands of a hostile power.

Cold War
The period of struggle between the United States and the Soviet Union, occurring from the late 1940s to about 1990.

remained the cornerstone of American policy toward the Soviet Union throughout the Cold War. Some Americans argued that the United States should attack the Soviets before it was too late—a policy known as **preventive war**. Others said that the United States should show its peaceful intentions and attempt to accommodate Soviet demands—a policy called **appeasement**.

The policies that the United States actually adopted—deterrence and containment—stand midway between preventive war and appeasement. A nation pursuing deterrence, on the one hand, signals peaceful intentions, but on the other hand indicates willingness and ability to fight if attacked. Thus, during the era of confrontation with the Soviets, known as the **Cold War**, the United States frequently stated that it had no intention of attacking the Soviet Union. At the same time, however, the United States built a huge military force, including nuclear weapons and intercontinental missiles, and made clear that if the Soviets attacked, the United States had the ability to respond with overwhelming force. The Soviet Union announced that its nuclear weapons were also intended for deterrent purposes. Eventually, the two sides possessed such enormous arsenals that each potentially had the ability to destroy the other completely.

During the 1962 Cuban missile crisis, the United States and the USSR came to the brink of war when President John F. Kennedy threatened to use force if the Soviets refused to remove their nuclear missiles from Cuba. After several extremely tense weeks, the crisis was defused by a compromise in which the Soviets agreed to remove the missiles in exchange for a U.S. guarantee not to invade Cuba. The two superpowers had come so close to nuclear war that the leaders of both nations sought ways of reducing tensions. This effort eventually led to a period of reduced hostilities in which a number of arms control agreements were signed and the threat of war was reduced.

The Soviet Union finally collapsed in 1991, partly because its huge military expenditures had undermined its economy. The new post-Soviet nation of Russia, though still a significant power, seemed to pose less of a threat to the United States. Americans celebrated the end of the Cold War and believed that the enormous expense of the United States' own military forces might be reduced. Within a few years, however, new security threats emerged, requiring new policy responses.

New Security Threats. The September 11, 2001, terrorist attacks demonstrated a new type of threat: that non-state actors and so-called rogue states—nations with unstable, ideologically or religiously driven leaders—might acquire significant military capabilities, including nuclear weapons, and not be affected by American policies of deterrence. To counter this possibility, the George W. Bush administration shifted from a policy of deterrence to one of **preemption**, a willingness to strike first in order to prevent an enemy attack. The United States declared that if necessary, it would disable terrorist groups and rogue states before they could do us harm. The Bush administration's "global war on terror" reflected this notion of preemption, as did the U.S. invasion of Iraq in 2003.

preemption
The willingness to strike first in order to prevent an enemy attack.

The United States has also refused to rule out the possibility that it would attack North Korea or Iran if it deemed those nations' nuclear programs an imminent threat to American security interests.

The Obama administration took a different tone, declaring that it would endeavor to establish constructive dialogues with North Korea, Iran, and other hostile states. However, President Obama did not renounce all of the Bush-era policies. He did not immediately withdraw American troops from Iraq and Afghanistan, as many Democrats had expected. Instead, he initially stepped up the United States' military effort in Afghanistan and kept U.S. forces in Iraq. This policy was finally reversed, and by 2014 the United States had begun to withdraw from both countries.

However, both regions remained unstable. In 2014, for example, the military success of the terrorist group the Islamic State of Iraq and Syria (ISIS) led Obama to send troops back to Iraq to help defend its government, and in 2015 he announced that some American forces would remain in Afghanistan indefinitely. In addition, American air power was deployed against ISIS in Syria, special-forces teams struck at ISIS in Iraq, and the United States armed groups such as Kurdish forces to battle ISIS throughout the region.

U.S. foreign policy makers also continued to express concern over Iran and North Korea. In 2013, when the North Korean regime began to test missiles that might soon be able to reach U.S. shores, the Obama administration positioned additional antimissile batteries to protect America's West Coast. In 2015, the North Koreans pledged to use all means necessary to repel what they called America's aggressive designs and continued testing ever-more-sophisticated missiles.

For its part, as Iran continued to work toward the development of nuclear weapons, the West responded with economic sanctions. In 2015, the United States and Iran reached an agreement designed to halt the Iranian nuclear program in exchange for the lifting of U.S. economic sanctions. Critics, however, feared that the Iranians would not truly end their efforts to build nuclear bombs. During his 2016 campaign Donald Trump promised to abrogate the agreement, and he officially withdrew from the Iran nuclear deal in 2018.

The Trump Doctrine: America First.   When he took office in 2017, President Donald Trump was sharply critical of Barack Obama's foreign policies, which he declared had not focused enough on the United States' national interests. Trump said that he planned to put "America first," a phrase that had not been uttered in official Washington since its use by pre–World War II isolationists who opposed going to war against Nazi Germany. By "America first," Trump meant that he would expect U.S. allies to pay a larger share of collective defense costs and that the United States would be reluctant to make trade concessions to foes or friends. Trump also promised to revisit the Iran treaty and to bring an end to North Korea's nuclear weapons program. He also seemed to favor better relations with Russia, while working to reduce the United States' trade imbalance with China, as well as countering China's growing influence in the Pacific Rim.

Donald Trump's "America first" policy echos the pre–World War II isolationists who opposed the country's going to war against Nazi Germany.

While many feared that Trump's aggressive statements would spark international hostilities, by 2018 Trump was engaged in active diplomatic efforts with Russia, China, and North Korea designed to identify mutual interests and reduce the threat of conflict. Unlike his predecessors, Trump, who saw himself as a deal-maker, seemed to favor personal meetings with world leaders, diminishing the roles of secretaries of state and national security advisers. Trump met with North Korean leader Kim Jong-un in June 2018 and with Russian president Vladimir Putin in July 2018. Trump expressed satisfaction with both meetings but was criticized for achieving no concrete results with Kim and for accepting Putin's claims that Russia had not interfered in the 2016 American election.

Economic Prosperity

A second major goal of U.S. foreign policy is promoting a strong American economy. U.S. international economic policies seek to expand employment domestically, to maintain access to foreign energy supplies at a reasonable cost, to promote foreign investment in the United States, and to lower the prices that Americans pay for goods and services.

Trade policy, which seeks to promote American goods and services abroad, is one key element of U.S. international economic policy. This effort involves a complex arrangement of treaties, **tariffs**, and other mechanisms. For example, the United States has a long-standing policy of granting **most favored nation status** to certain countries; that is, it offers to another country the lowest tariff rate that it offers any of its trading partners, in return for trade (and sometimes other) concessions. In 1998, to avoid any suggestion that "most favored nation" implied some special relationship with an undemocratic country (China, for

tariff
A tax on imported goods.

most favored nation status
The status that a country bestows on a trading partner in which it offers that partner the lowest tariff rate that it offers any of its trading partners.

A goal of U.S. foreign policy is to reduce American dependence on foreign imports and promote a strong American economy. This issue came to the fore during the 2020 coronavirus pandemic when the United States did not have access to sufficient crucial medical supplies, including masks and nasal swabs that were largely manufactured outside the country. Here, a National Guard member manages the distribution of scarce supplies from China during the pandemic.

example), President Bill Clinton changed the official term from "most favored nation" to "permanent normal trade relations," or PNTR.[3]

The most important international organization for promoting free trade is the **World Trade Organization (WTO)**, established in 1995. The WTO grew out of the General Agreement on Tariffs and Trade (GATT), which, after World War II, brought together a wide range of nations for regular negotiations designed to reduce barriers to trade. Such barriers, many believed, had contributed to the breakdown of the world economy in the 1930s and helped to cause World War II. The WTO has 161 members worldwide, including the United States. Similar policy goals are pursued in regional arrangements, such as the **North American Free Trade Agreement (NAFTA)** among the United States, Canada, and Mexico. In 2018 the Trump administration renegotiated NAFTA, resulting in a three-nation agreement that retained NAFTA's basic structure with some revised terms the administration saw as more favorable to the United States. The new agreement is called the **United States-Mexico-Canada Agreement**.

For over a half century, the United States has led the world in supporting free trade as the best route to growth and prosperity. Yet the U.S. government has also tried to protect domestic industry from international pressures. Subsidies have long boosted American agriculture, artificially lowering the price of American products on world markets.

In 2015, the Obama administration proposed a free-trade agreement between the United States and 11 Pacific Rim nations. The Trans-Pacific Partnership (TPP) lowered tariffs and other trade barriers throughout the Pacific region. During the 2016 presidential campaign, however, Donald Trump charged that U.S. trade policies had led to a loss of American jobs, and he called for placing limits on free trade. Trump specifically condemned the TPP, which he said would send even

World Trade Organization (WTO)

The international trade agency that promotes free trade. The WTO grew out of the General Agreement on Tariffs and Trade (GATT).

North American Free Trade Agreement (NAFTA)

An agreement by the United States, Canada, and Mexico to lower and eliminate tariffs among the three countries.

United States-Mexico-Canada Agreement

Renegotiated free-trade agreement between the United States, Mexico, and Canada that was signed in 2020.

 think it through

Reconciling the costs and benefits of trade agreements is challenging. Think about the industries in your state. In what ways would trade agreements help these industries? How would they potentially hurt them?

more American jobs to Asia, and after his election he withdrew the United States from the agreement.

International Humanitarian Policies

A third goal of American policy is to make the world a better place for all its inhabitants—an aim addressed mainly by international environmental policy, international human rights policy, and international peacekeeping efforts. The United States' wealth makes it a major source of funding for such endeavors. The nation also contributes to international organizations that support global humanitarian goals. However, humanitarian policies often come second to the other goals of American foreign policy: security and economic strength. Moreover, although the United States spends billions annually on security policy and hundreds of millions on trade policy, it spends relatively little on environmental, human rights, and peacekeeping efforts. Some critics charge that the United States has the wrong priorities, spending far more to make war than to protect human rights and the global environment. Nevertheless, many American foreign policy efforts do seek, at least in part, to make the world a better place.

United States–backed international efforts to protect the environment include the United Nations Framework Convention on Climate Change (an agreement to study and address harmful changes in the global environment) and the Montreal Protocol (an agreement by more than 150 countries to limit the production of substances potentially harmful to the Earth's ozone layer). Other nations have criticized the United States for withdrawing from the 1997 Kyoto Protocol (an agreement setting limits on industrial countries' emissions of greenhouse gases), on the grounds that it would harm American economic interests. The Kyoto Protocol expired in 2012, but 37 countries then signed the so-called Doha Amendment, which renewed their commitment to reduce greenhouse gas emissions.

The United States continued objecting to the mandatory emission limits and refrained from signing this new agreement as well. In 2016, however, the United States joined the Paris Agreement to reduce greenhouse gas emissions. Each signatory country agreed to reduce dangerous emissions but would set its own contribution to the effort. Many Republicans, including Donald Trump, opposed the agreement, and in 2017, President Trump withdrew the United States from it.

The same national priorities seem apparent in human rights policy. The United States has a long-standing commitment to human rights and has joined many major international agreements about human rights, including the International Covenant on Civil and Political Rights, the International Convention on the Elimination of All Forms of Racial Discrimination, and various agreements to protect children around the world. The State Department's Bureau of Democracy, Human Rights, and Labor works cooperatively with international organizations to investigate and focus attention on human rights abuses. In 1998, the United

States approved the International Religious Freedom Act, which calls on all governments to respect religious freedom and lists sanctions that signatories may use to punish nations that violate the act. The United States has also signed a number of UN resolutions promoting women's and LGBTQ rights.

Backing up such commitments, however, receives a lower priority in American foreign policy than does safeguarding security and economic interests. Thus, the United States usually overlooks human rights violations by its major trading partners, such as China, and its allies, such as Saudi Arabia. Nevertheless, it does take concrete actions to defend human rights concerns. For example, since 2007 the United States has made available several million dollars annually in small grants to pay medical and legal expenses incurred by victims of retaliation in their own countries for working against their governments' repressive practices.

U.S. foreign policy also often includes support for international peacekeeping and other humanitarian efforts. At any given time, border wars, civil wars, and guerrilla conflicts flare somewhere in the world—usually in its poorer regions—and generate humanitarian crises in the form of casualties, disease, and refugees. In cooperation with international agencies and other nations, the United States funds efforts to keep the peace in volatile regions and address conflict-related health and refugee problems. In 2015, for example, the United States provided nearly $2 billion in humanitarian assistance to refugees displaced by the civil war in Syria. By the beginning of 2018, the United States had donated nearly $7.7 billion to the cause.[4] And in 2020, the United States extended its commitment by pledging another $397 million as part of the Regional Refuge and Resilience Plan.[5]

European nations, who responded to the Syrian refugee crisis by admitting more than a million refugees to their countries, charged that the United States, which admitted fewer than ten thousand refugees, was not doing enough to deal

One way the United States promotes humanitarian goals is by providing assistance to nations facing crises and emergencies. Although the U.S. has donated billions of dollars to support Syrians displaced by the civil war in their country, far fewer Syrian refugees were admitted into the United States than were admitted into European nations.

with the crisis. In 2017, President Trump, citing fears of terrorism, placed sharper restriction on admitting refugees from Syria and other Middle Eastern countries to the United States.

In 2019, the Trump administration announced that foreign aid policies would be aimed at helping poor countries achieve a level of economic development that would end their need for American aid and reduce the number of refugees seeking to enter the United States. This initiative was labelled the "Journey to Self-Reliance." Critics charged that this program was designed to legitimate American efforts to cut foreign aid and admit fewer refugees.

WHO MAKES AND SHAPES FOREIGN POLICY?

Domestic policies are made by governmental institutions but influenced by interest groups, political movements, and even the mass media. In the case of foreign policy, governmental institutions have much more autonomy, but interest groups and the media continue to play a role.

The President

The president exercises substantial control over the nation's diplomatic and military institutions, and thus is the most important voice determining with whom, when, and how the United States will engage in the international arena. Since World War II, for example, American military forces have fought numerous engagements throughout the world—Korea, Vietnam, the Middle East, Kosovo, Panama, and others.

In every instance, the decision to commit troops to battle was made by the president, often with little or no consultation with Congress. When, following the September 11 terrorist attacks, President George W. Bush ordered American troops into Afghanistan and later Iraq, Congress voiced approval, but the president made clear that he did not believe he needed Congress's permission. And when President Barack Obama ordered special-operations soldiers to attack Osama bin Laden's compound in Pakistan, Congress learned of the operation and bin Laden's death from news broadcasts—just like other Americans did. Similarly, in 2015 Obama ordered air strikes to combat ISIS in Syria and Iraq without seeking congressional approval. Furthermore, presidents have often made use of private military contractors to pursue their own policy preferences without having to defer to Congress (see the Policy Principle box on p. 465). President Trump declared that the United States would no longer serve as the "world's policeman," and began to reduce American forces in the Middle East. Trump also demanded that the nation's NATO allies increase their own defense spending and reduce their reliance on the United States.

the policy principle
THE USE OF PRIVATE MILITARY CONTRACTORS

Since the earliest years of the Republic, Congress and the president have vied for control of American foreign and military policy. The Constitution gives Congress the power to declare war but makes the president commander in chief of American military forces. In the realm of foreign and military policy, presidents have worked to develop institutions and procedures that help implement their own preferences rather than those of Congress. One such procedure is the use of private military contractors—rather than regular military forces—to implement presidential decisions.

George W. Bush relied heavily on private contractors in Iraq in 2003–4 and in Afghanistan during the next several years to provide security and other services for U.S. operations. The use of these private soldiers was brought to the attention of the American public in 2004 when four employees of Blackwater USA, a North Carolina security firm, were ambushed and killed in the Iraqi town of Fallujah and their bodies dragged through the streets. The horrific event gave rise to questions about the regulation and accountability of private companies. Critics worried that private soldiers show a lack of discipline and a lack of commitment to the interests of the states that employed them. To take one example, in 2014, several Blackwater soldiers were found guilty of having murdered 14 innocent Iraqi civilians, including women and children, in 2007.

These concerns have not seemed to deter presidents from employing private military contractors. The ability of private firms to deploy heavily armed professional soldiers has given presidents access to military capabilities outside the scope of public or congressional scrutiny. Indeed, several recent presidents have employed private military contractors to engage in activities that Congress has expressly forbidden U.S. military forces to undertake.

For example, when Congress authorized assistance to Colombia in the War on Drugs in the 1990s, it prohibited U.S. forces from engaging in counterinsurgency efforts and providing assistance to Colombian military units with poor human rights records. The Clinton administration, however, believed that drug gangs and antigovernment insurgents were difficult to distinguish and that it would be hard to identify Colombian military units with unblemished human rights records. Accordingly, the administration employed private military contractors to avoid what it saw as burdensome congressional restrictions. Military Professional Resources Inc. was given a contract

An American private military contractor in Afghanistan.

to develop the Colombian government's overall military plan, and another contractor, Northrop Grumman, was engaged to provide technical specialists for such tasks as staffing radar sites. Two additional firms provided what amounted to fully equipped combat troops. The use of private contractors allowed the administration to claim it was following the letter of the law regarding the role of U.S. soldiers and, at the same time, offered "deniability" and political cover if military plans went awry.

In this and other instances, military contractors have provided presidents with the means to pursue their own policy goals without having to defer to congressional views and priorities. In 2017, continuing this tactic, President Trump and his advisers met with three major military contractors to discuss the possibility of "privatizing" the United States' war in Afghanistan. By 2020, nearly 6,000 private military contractors worked for the United States in Afghanistan.

think it through

1. How does the president's use of private military contractors to engage in activities that Congress expressly forbids the U.S. military from undertaking jeopardize the idea of checks and balances in American democracy?

2. What consequences does the United States face in moving forward other foreign policy goals in the face of concerns about the action of these private military contractors?

The president's foreign policy powers, particularly in the military realm, are far greater than the Constitution's framers intended. The framers gave the power to declare war to Congress and made the president the nation's top military commander if and when Congress chose to go to war.[6] Today, presidents command the troops and also decide when to go to war.

The Bureaucracy

The major foreign policy players in the bureaucracy are the secretaries of the departments of State, Defense, and the Treasury; the Joint Chiefs of Staff (JCS), especially the chair of the JCS; and the director of the CIA. A separate unit in the bureaucracy comprising these people and a few others is the National Security Council (NSC). The NSC includes the president, the vice president, the secretary of defense, and the secretary of state, plus others that each president has the authority to add.

After the profound shake-up of September 11, two additional players were added. The first was the secretary of the new Department of Homeland Security (DHS), made up of 22 agencies relocated from the executive branch on the theory that their expertise could be better coordinated and more efficient in a single organization designed to fight international terrorism and domestic natural disasters. The second was introduced during the war in Iraq: a director of national intelligence to coordinate intelligence from multiple sources and to report to the president on a daily basis.

The president's power in the realm of foreign policy has increased since World War II, especially in recent administrations. For example, the 2011 attack on Osama bin Laden's compound in Pakistan was initiated by President Obama without broad congressional consultation.

In addition to top cabinet-level officials, key lower-level staff members have policy-making influence as strong as—and sometimes even stronger than—that of the cabinet secretaries. These include the two or three specialized advisers in the White House, the staff of the NSC (headed by the president's national security advisers), and a few other career bureaucrats in the departments of State and Defense. Within the Executive Office of the President, the Office of the United States Trade Representative coordinates trade policy and helps conduct trade negotiations.

Congress

For most of American history, the Senate was the only important congressional foreign policy player because of its constitutional role in reviewing and approving treaties. The treaty power is still an important way that the Senate can shape foreign policy. In recent decades, however, presidents have chosen to avoid the use of treaties and turned instead to **executive agreements** as the basic instruments of American foreign policy. This practice has reduced congressional influence. Executive agreements have the force of treaties but do not require prior approval by the Senate. Although the president has become the dominant actor in foreign policy, Congress as a whole has remained influential because most foreign policies require financing, which requires approval from both the House of Representatives and the Senate.

There are two types of executive agreements. The first, a *sole executive agreement*, entails only presidential action and does not require congressional approval. While they provide presidents with maximum flexibility, sole executive agreements have limited usefulness because they cannot go against existing law and Congress is not required to provide funding to implement them. The second form of executive agreement is called an *executive-congressional agreement*. Such an agreement is negotiated by the president and then submitted to Congress for approval. Approval consists of a majority vote of both houses rather than a supermajority in the Senate. This approval requirement generally represents a lower hurdle than the constitutional two-thirds vote in the Senate that would be required for a treaty.

Other congressional players are the foreign policy, military policy, and intelligence committees. In the Senate, these are the Foreign Relations Committee, the Armed Services Committee, and the Homeland Security and Governmental Affairs Committee; in the House, they are the Foreign Affairs Committee, the Armed Services Committee, and the Homeland Security Committee. Usually, a few members of these committees with extensive experience in foreign affairs become influential makers of foreign policy. In fact, several members of Congress have left to become key foreign-affairs cabinet members, including the secretary of state during Obama's second term, John Kerry.[7]

executive agreement
An agreement between the president and another country that has the force of a treaty but does not require the Senate's "advice and consent."

Interest Groups

Interest groups that have at least a partial focus on foreign policy are important nonofficial players. Economic interest groups have a reputation for wielding the most influence, yet myths about their influence far outweigh the realities. The actual influence of organized economic interest groups in foreign policy varies enormously from issue to issue and year to year.

Most are *single-issue* groups, who are most active when their particular issue is on the agenda. On many broader and more sustained issues, such as NAFTA, TPP, or the general question of American involvement in international trade, the larger interest groups have difficulty getting their many members to speak with a single voice. For example, some business groups represent industries dependent on exports, and others are threatened by imports; hence, "business" has more than one view on trade policy. Most successful in influencing foreign policy are the single-issue groups, such as the tobacco industry (which prevented heavy restrictions on international trade in and advertising of tobacco products) and the computer hardware and software industries (which have hardened the American attitude toward Chinese piracy of intellectual property rights).

Another type of interest group with significant influence on foreign policy consists of people who strongly identify with their country of origin. For example, Jewish Americans with family in and emotional ties to Israel wield great influence. In 2015, many, though not all, Jewish groups lobbied heavily but ultimately unsuccessfully against the Obama administration's agreement with Iran, which they argued posed a threat to both the United States and Israel. Similarly, some Americans of Irish heritage, despite having lived in the United States for generations, still maintain vigilance about American policies toward Ireland and Northern Ireland, while Americans of Armenian descent frequently lobby Congress to condemn Turkey for its actions in Armenia in 1915. Many other ethnic and national interest groups also exert influence over American foreign policy.

A third type of interest group, increasingly prominent in recent decades, focuses on human rights. Instead of having self-serving economic or ethnic interests in foreign policy, such groups are concerned about the welfare of people worldwide—particularly those who suffer under harsh political regimes. An example is Amnesty International, whose exposés of human rights abuses have altered the practices of many regimes.

Related are the ecological or environmental groups with fast-growing influence that are sometimes called the "greens." Groups of this nature often depend more on demonstrations than on lobbying and electoral politics. Demonstrations in strategically located areas can have significant influence on American foreign policy. In recent years, environmental activists staged major protests at the 2009 London and 2010 Toronto international economic summits, and at the 2015 Paris environmental summit. In 2019, as many as 6 million protestors around the world joined demonstrations demanding that governments act to address climate change.

think it through

What types of interest-group ads do you see on television or in your social media? Are there particular issues that appear to have a lot of support or opposition?

Makers and Shapers of Foreign Policy

Makers

- The president
- The bureaucracy (secretaries of State, Defense, and the Treasury; the Joint Chiefs of Staff; the director of the Central Intelligence Agency; the president's national security adviser; the head of the National Security Agency; and the director of Homeland Security)
- Congress (Senate approves treaties; both chambers vote on financing; foreign policy and military policy committees in each chamber hold hearings and write legislation)

Shapers

- Interest groups (economic groups, cultural/ethnic groups, human rights groups, environmental groups)
- The media

Putting It Together

Who really makes American foreign policy? First—except for the president, who influences virtually every area of foreign policy—the key players vary from case to case. Second, because the one constant is the president's centrality, it is useful to evaluate other actors and factors as they interact with the president.[8] Third, influence varies from case to case because each case involves not only different conditions but also different time constraints: for issues that arise and are resolved quickly, the opportunity for influence is limited. Fourth, foreign policy experts often disagree about the level of influence that any player or type of player has on policy making.

But we can make some tentative generalizations. When an important foreign policy decision must be made under conditions of crisis, the influence of the presidency is strongest. Within those time constraints, access to the decision-making process is limited almost exclusively to the officially and constitutionally designated participants of the "foreign policy establishment," the collection of institutions and leaders that normally direct American foreign policy. In other words, in a crisis, the foreign policy establishment works as it is supposed to.[9]

As time becomes less restricted, the arena of participation expands to include more government players and more nonofficial, informal players—the most concerned interest groups and the most important journalists. In other words, the arena becomes more pluralistic and therefore less distinguishable from the politics of domestic policy making.

THE INSTRUMENTS OF MODERN AMERICAN FOREIGN POLICY

Any government uses certain tools in implementing its foreign policy. While there have been many instruments of American foreign policy, here we discuss those that have been most important in the era since World War II: diplomacy, the United Nations, the international monetary structure, economic aid and sanctions, collective security, military force, and dispute arbitration.

Diplomacy

diplomacy
The representation of a government to other foreign governments.

Diplomacy is the representation of a government to other foreign governments. Its purpose is to promote national values or interests by peaceful means.

The first effort to create a modern diplomatic service in the United States was the Rogers Act of 1924, which established the initial framework for a professional foreign service staff. But it took World War II and the Foreign Service Act of 1946 to forge the foreign service into a fully professional diplomatic corps.

Although diplomacy is a powerful tool of foreign policy, by its very nature it is overshadowed by spectacular international events and dramatic initiatives. The traditional American distrust of diplomacy continues today, though in weaker form. Impatience with or downright distrust of diplomacy has been built into not only all the other instruments of foreign policy but also the modern presidential system itself.[10] So much personal responsibility has been heaped on the presidency that it is difficult for presidents to entrust any of their authority or responsibility in foreign policy to professional diplomats in the State Department and other bureaucracies.

In 2008, both major parties' presidential candidates criticized the George W. Bush administration for having failed to use diplomacy to secure greater international support for the Iraq War. Both promised to revitalize American diplomacy. President Obama appointed Hillary Clinton as his secretary of state in part to underline the importance he attached to diplomacy by appointing such a prominent figure as the United States' chief diplomat. Two of the Obama administration's biggest diplomatic achievements took place in 2015. The United States and Iran signed a nuclear deal, discussed earlier, and the United States and Cuba reestablished diplomatic relations that had been severed in 1961. Though the immediate impact was small, over time, Cuba was expected to benefit greatly from economic relations with the United States.

As we saw earlier, Donald Trump was sharply critical of Obama's foreign policies and promised a new direction that he called "America first." In 2018, President Trump met with North Korean leader Kim Jong-un in an attempt to reduce tensions on the Korean Peninsula. Trump also met with Russian president

Vladimir Putin, though in the aftermath of the meeting Trump was severely criticized for failing to take a stronger position with Putin on Russian meddling into American politics. In 2019–20, Trump engaged in extensive negotiations with Chinese president Xi Jinping to avert a trade war between the two nations.

The United Nations

The **United Nations (UN)** has been a useful instrument of American foreign policy, even though it is a large, unwieldy institution with few powers and no armed forces to implement its rules and resolutions. Its supreme body is the UN General Assembly, comprising one representative from each of the 193 member states; each representative has one vote, regardless of the size of the country. Important decisions require a two-thirds-majority vote of the General Assembly, and its annual session runs only from September to December. The General Assembly has little organization that can promote effective decision making, with only six standing committees, few tight rules of procedure, and no political parties to provide priorities and discipline. The UN's defenders assert that although it lacks armed forces, it relies on the power of world opinion, and that should not be taken lightly.

The UN's powers reside mainly in its Security Council, which alone has the real authority to make decisions that member states are obligated to implement. The Security Council may be called into session at any time, and each member's representative (or a designated alternate) must be present at UN Headquarters in New York at all times. It has 15 members: five are permanent (the victors of World

United Nations (UN)

An organization of nations founded in 1945 to be a channel for negotiation and a means of settling international disputes peaceably.

Kelly Craft (center), the U.S. ambassador to the United Nations, addressed the Security Council about the situation in Yemen in 2020. The UN, which is made up of representatives of 193 member nations, has been a useful tool of American foreign policy.

War II—the United States, United Kingdom, France, Russia, and China), and 10 are elected by the General Assembly for two-year, nonrepeatable terms. Each of the 15 members has one vote, and a nine-vote majority is required on all substantive matters. But each of the five permanent members also has veto power, and one veto is sufficient to reject any substantive proposal.

The UN can be a useful forum for international discussions and an instrument for multilateral action. Most peacekeeping efforts to which the United States contributes, for example, are undertaken under UN auspices.

The International Monetary Structure

Fear of a repeat of the economic devastation that followed World War I brought the United States together with its allies (except the USSR) at Bretton Woods, New Hampshire, in 1944 to create a new international economic structure for the post–World War II world. The result was the creation of two institutions: the International Bank for Reconstruction and Development (commonly called the World Bank) and the International Monetary Fund.

The World Bank was set up to finance long-term projects, chiefly development aid to poor countries. Wealthier nations took on the obligation of contributing funds to enable the World Bank to make loans; the U.S. quota has been about one-third of the total.

The **International Monetary Fund (IMF)** was set up to provide for the short-term flow of money. After World War II, the U.S. dollar replaced gold as the chief means by which the currency of one country is "changed into" that of another for purposes of international transactions. The IMF lends dollars or other appropriate currencies to help needy member countries overcome temporary trade deficits and thereby enables them to make purchases and investments.

For many years after World War II, the IMF, along with U.S. foreign aid, constituted the only international medium of exchange. During the 1990s, the IMF took on enhanced importance through its efforts to reform the finances of some of the largest debtor nations and formerly communist countries so as to bring them more fully into the global capitalist economy. Often the IMF requires "structural adjustment" on the part of aid recipients, which generally means these countries must adopt more market-oriented, free-trade policies as a condition for loans. Structural readjustment has been criticized as an instrument through which rich nations impose their own views and trade interests on poor nations, but poor nations often have little choice but to accept IMF terms.

Although the IMF, with tens of billions of dollars contributed by its members, has more money to lend poor countries than do its leading shareholders—the United States, Europe, western European states, and Japan—individually, the IMF makes policy decisions in ways generally consistent with those shareholders' interests.[11] For example, two weeks after September 11, 2001, the IMF approved a $135 million loan to economically troubled Pakistan, a key player in the war against the Taliban government of Afghanistan because of its strategic

International Monetary Fund (IMF)

An institution, established in 1944, that provides loans and facilitates international monetary exchange.

location. Turkey was likewise put back in the IMF pipeline at that time.[12] In 2010 and again in 2015, the IMF organized multibillion-dollar loan packages to save the Greek government from defaulting on its debt, which the United States and major European governments feared might spark a worldwide economic crisis.

The future of the IMF, the World Bank, and all other private sources of international investment will depend in part on the extension of more credit to developing countries, because credit means investment and productivity. But the future may depend even more on reducing the debt that exists already from previous extensions of credit.

Economic Aid and Sanctions

The issue of economic aid rose to the surface of American political debate when President Trump was accused of withholding congressionally appropriated military funding to Ukraine, which prompted Trump's impeachment in 2020. Every year, the United States provides nearly $50 billion in economic assistance to other nations. Some aid has a humanitarian purpose, such as helping to provide health care, shelter for refugees, or famine relief. Much of it, however, seeks to promote American security or economic concerns, or both. For example, the United States provides military assistance to various allies in the form of advanced weapons or loans to purchase such weapons. These arrangements came to the fore in 2019 when President Trump was accused of leveraging payment of promised military support funds to Ukraine in an attempt to obtain politically damaging information on his chief Democratic presidential rival Joe Biden. Generally, loan recipients must purchase the weapons from American firms. In this way, the United States hopes to bolster its security and economic interests with one grant. For years, the two largest recipients of such military assistance have been Israel and Egypt, American allies that have fought two wars against each other. The United States believes that its military assistance allows both to feel sufficiently secure to remain at peace with each other. (See Timeplot on p. 474–5 for spending on foreign aid over time.)

Aid is an economic carrot. Sanctions are an economic stick. Economic sanctions that the United States employs against other nations include trade embargoes, bans on investment, and efforts to prevent the World Bank or other international institutions from extending credit to nations against which the United States has a grievance. Sanctions are most often used when the United States seeks to weaken a hostile regime or to compel particular action by another regime. Thus, for example, to weaken Fidel Castro's communist government in Cuba, the United States long prohibited American firms from doing business there. The United States has maintained economic sanctions against North Korea to try to prevent that nation from pursuing nuclear weapons programs, and in 2014 it imposed economic sanctions against Russia in response to its annexation of Crimea, which the United States regards as part of Ukraine.

Unilateral sanctions by the United States typically have little effect, since the target countries can usually trade elsewhere, sometimes even with foreign affiliates

FOREIGN AID: ECONOMIC AND MILITARY ASSISTANCE, 1980–2018

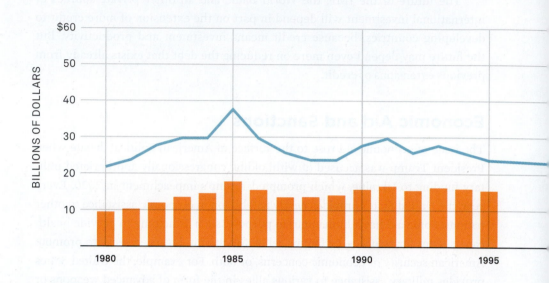

- 🟧 Foreign Aid Spending
- 🔵 Foreign Aid Spending as % of GDP

TIMEPLOT SOURCES: USA Facts, Foreign aid obligations," https:// usafacts.org/data/topics/security -safety/national-defense-and-foreign -aid/foreign-affairs-and-aid/foreign -aid-obligations/? (accessed 5/14/20); USA Facts, "GDP," https://legacy .usafacts.org/topics/42?adjustment =Inflation&metric=116535 (accessed 5/14/20).

of U.S. firms. If allies can be convinced to cooperate, sanctions have a better chance of success. International sanctions applied to Iran, for example, influenced that regime's decision to begin negotiations with the United States that culminated in the nuclear weapons deal of 2015 (which President Trump subsequently voided in favor of renewed sanctions). The Trump administration maintained that its tough sanctions policy was instrumental in convincing North Korea to participate in talks in 2018, although the talks failed to produce a conclusive result.

Collective Security

In 1947, most Americans hoped that the United States could meet its world obligations through the UN and economic structures alone. But when drafting the UN Charter, most foreign policy makers anticipated future military entanglements by insisting on language that recognized the right of all nations to provide for their mutual defense independently of the UN. And almost immediately after enactment of the Marshall Plan, an aid program designed to promote European economic recovery, the White House and a parade of State and Defense department officials urged Congress to ratify and finance treaties providing for mutual-defense alliances.

Initially reluctant to approve such collective-security treaties, the Senate ultimately agreed with the executive branch. The first collective security agreement

timeplot

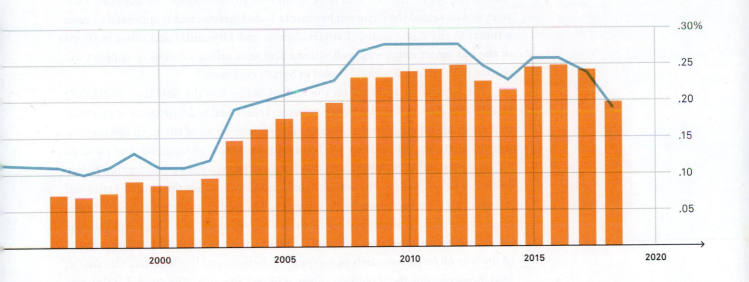

was the Rio Treaty (in 1947), which created the Organization of American States (OAS). It anticipated all succeeding collective security treaties by providing that an armed attack against any OAS member "shall be considered as an attack against all the American States," including the United States.

A more significant break with U.S. tradition against peacetime entanglements came with the North Atlantic Treaty (signed in April 1949), which created the **North Atlantic Treaty Organization (NATO)**. ANZUS, a treaty tying Australia and New Zealand to the United States, was signed in September 1951. Three years later, the Southeast Asia Collective Defense Treaty created the Southeast Asia Treaty Organization (SEATO). In addition to these multilateral treaties, the United States entered into a number of **bilateral treaties**—treaties between two countries.

It is difficult to evaluate collective security or particular treaties as instruments of foreign policy, because their purpose is prevention, and success must be measured in terms of what did *not* happen. Critics have argued that U.S. collective security treaties posed a threat of encirclement to the Soviet Union, forcing it to ensure its own collective security, particularly through creation of the Warsaw Pact.[13] Nevertheless, no one can deny the counterargument that more than 80 years have passed without a world war.

In 1998, NATO expanded with the inclusion of former Warsaw Pact members Poland, Hungary, and the Czech Republic. Most of Washington embraced this

North Atlantic Treaty Organization (NATO)
A treaty organization comprising the United States, Canada, and most of western Europe, formed in 1949 to address the perceived threat from the Soviet Union.

bilateral treaty
A treaty made between two nations.

expansion as the true end of the Cold War, and the U.S. Senate, with a resounding 80–19 vote, inducted the three former Soviet satellites into NATO. After the collapse of the Soviet Union, the importance of NATO as a military alliance seemed to wane. Beginning in 2014, however, the resurgence of Russian military aggression forced NATO members to once again look to one another for support. That year, Russia seized the Crimean Peninsula from Ukraine, and it appeared to pose a threat to the Baltic states (Estonia, Latvia, and Lithuania) and other portions of the old Soviet empire as well. Russia also sent military forces to support the regime of President Bashar al-Assad in Syria's civil war.

The September 11 attack on the United States was the first time in NATO's history that Article 5 of the North Atlantic Treaty had to be invoked; it provides that an attack on one member country is an attack on all of them. In fighting the war on terrorism, the George W. Bush administration recognized that no matter how preponderant American power was, some aspects of U.S. foreign policy could not be achieved without multilateral cooperation. Yet the United States did not want to be constrained by its alliances. The global coalition initially forged after September 11 numbered more than 170 countries. Not all joined the war effort in Afghanistan, but most provided some form of support for some aspect of the war on terrorism, such as economic sanctions and intelligence. The war in Iraq, however, put the "coalition of the willing" to a test. The Bush administration was determined not to make its decision to go into Iraq subject to the UN or NATO or any other international organization; the breadth of the U.S. coalition was deemed secondary to this consideration. As a result, no major power except Britain supported the Iraq War.

Military Force

The most visible instrument of foreign policy is military force. The Trump Doctrine calls for reducing America's direct military involvement and led to the departure of American forces from Syria. Nevertheless, the United States has the world's most imposing military—with army, navy, marine, and air force units stationed across the globe—and spends more on military might than any other nation spends (Figure 14.1). The famous Prussian military strategist Carl von Clausewitz called war "politics by other means." He meant that nations use force not simply to demonstrate their capacity for violence; rather, force or the threat of it sometimes serves to achieve foreign policy goals. Military force may be needed to protect a nation's security interests and economic concerns. Ironically, it may also be needed to achieve humanitarian goals. For example, in 2014 and 2015, international military force was required to protect tens of thousands of Yazidi refugees threatened by ISIS forces in Iraq. Without it, humanitarian assistance to the Yazidis would have been irrelevant.

Military force is generally seen as a last resort and avoided if possible, because of problems associated with its use. First, of course, it is extremely costly in both human and financial terms. In the past 50 years, tens of thousands of Americans

figure 14.1

SHARES OF WORLD MILITARY EXPENDITURES
BY 10 LARGEST SPENDERS, 2018

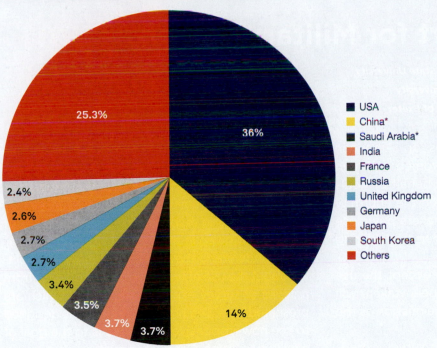

USA 36%
China* 14%
3.7%
3.7%
3.5%
3.4%
2.7%
2.7%
2.6%
2.4%
Others 25.3%

- USA
- China*
- Saudi Arabia*
- India
- France
- Russia
- United Kingdom
- Germany
- Japan
- South Korea
- Others

NOTE: Total world military spending in 2018: $1.822 trillion.

*China and Saudi Arabia represent estimates by the Stockholm International Peace Research Institute.

SOURCE: Nan Tian, Aude Fleurant, Alexandra Kuimova, Pietrer D. Wexeman, and Siemon T. Wezeman, "Trends in World Military Expenditure, 2018," Stockholm International Peace Research Institute, April 2019, https://reliefweb.int/sites/reliefweb.int/files/resources/fs_1904_milex_2018.pdf (accessed 4/20/20).

**analyzing
the evidence**

Although U.S. military spending is much greater than that of any other country, the United States also has the world's biggest economy. Why does the United States spend so much on its military? What roles do external security concerns and domestic political factors play in the budget process?

have been killed and hundreds of billions of dollars spent in U.S. military operations. Before using military force to achieve national goals, policy makers must be certain that achieving these goals is essential and that other means are unlikely to succeed.

Second, the use of military force is inherently fraught with risk. However carefully policy makers and generals plan for military operations, results can seldom be fully anticipated. Variables ranging from the weather to unexpected weapons and tactics deployed by opponents may turn carefully calculated operations into costly disasters, or maneuvers expected to be quick and decisive into long, drawn-out struggles. For example, American policy makers expected to defeat the Iraqi army quickly and easily in 2003—and they did. They did not anticipate, however, that American forces would still be struggling years later to defeat the insurgency that arose in the war's aftermath.

Finally, any democratic government that addresses policy problems through military means is almost certain to encounter political difficulties. Generally speaking, the American public will support relatively short and decisive military engagements. If a conflict drags on, however, producing casualties and expenses with no clear outcome, the public loses patience, and opposition politicians decry

Public Support for Military Action

Contributed by Christopher Gelpi, *Ohio State University*

Peter D. Feaver, *Duke University*

Jason Reifler, *University of Exeter*

One of the most fateful steps an American president can take is to order women and men into battle, to risk their lives on behalf of goals decided by political leaders. Given the enormity of these commitments, policy makers pay close attention to public opinion when considering military action.

When is the public willing to accept the use of force? And once action has been taken, will the public continue to support the mission as the conflict continues?

In recent years, innovations in survey experiments have enabled scholars to understand these topics better. In these experiments, respondents typically read a short vignette and then answer follow-up questions. Note that respondents are randomly assigned to receive vignettes that differ in small but important ways (for example, they might vary in terms of the likelihood that a mission will succeed or the number of expected casualties). Researchers then ask follow-up questions and compare the answers to see how support for a war changes in response to different pieces of information given in the various vignettes.

To understand the factors that influence opinion about the use of force, we examined data from a series of survey experiments, two of which are presented here. The first experiment was designed to see how responsive the public is to the goal of a military mission. Conducted relatively soon after the September 11 terrorist attacks, this experiment shows that the public was strongly supportive of missions that targeted terrorist bases but was much less supportive of using the military to serve humanitarian goals and, perhaps surprisingly, to maintain access to Middle Eastern oil resources.

Support for Military Intervention in Yemen, 2001, Depending on Goal

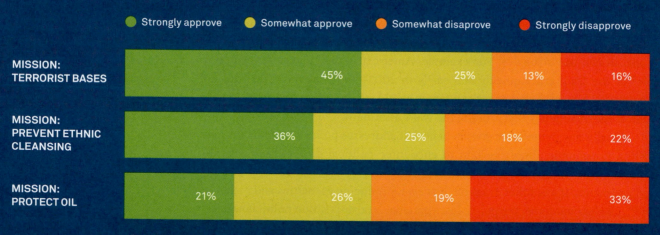

Legend: Strongly approve · Somewhat approve · Somewhat disapprove · Strongly disapprove

	Strongly approve	Somewhat approve	Somewhat disapprove	Strongly disapprove
MISSION: TERRORIST BASES	45%	25%	13%	16%
MISSION: PREVENT ETHNIC CLEANSING	36%	25%	18%	22%
MISSION: PROTECT OIL	21%	26%	19%	33%

Yet, there is more to shaping support for the use of military force than just the goal of the mission. Some research has shown that support for a war declines as casualties increase. This idea has intuitive appeal: as the cost of something increases, the desirability of that thing should decrease. However, in reality, the relationship between casualties and support for war is more complicated. Perceptions of whether a war is likely to succeed also influence opinion. To compare how casualties and expectations of success matter, we asked people about a hypothetical military mission and varied military leaders' expectations of success and the number of casualties.

Using data from the Iraq War, we then examined this idea more closely. What we find is that when a military mission is making progress toward its goal, as was the case in the early stages of the Iraq War as well as during the movement toward the first Iraqi elections in March 2005, mounting casualties are not associated with declines in support. However, once a war starts going poorly and it looks like the war might be headed to failure,

as appeared to be the case in Iraq between May 2003 and June 2004 and again from March 2005 through late 2006 when the data end, then even modest numbers of casualties can be highly corrosive of support.

Approval for Military Force Depending on Expected Casualties and Success

Iraq War Casualties and Presidential Approval

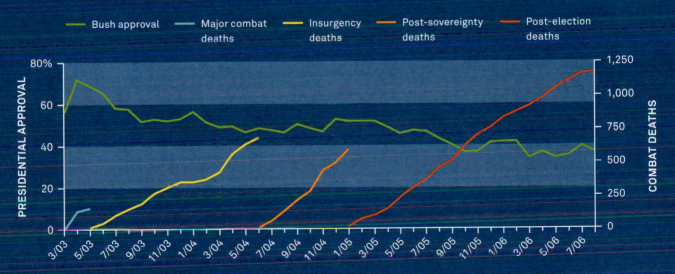

SOURCE: Christopher Gelpi, Peter D. Feaver, and Jason Reifler, *Paying the Human Costs of War: American Public Opinion and Casualties in Military Conflicts* (Princeton, NJ: Princeton University Press, 2009).

 → Based on the trends outlined in the Presidential Approval figure above, where would have expected President Trump's approval to be before the 2020 elections, given the "America first" doctrine discussed in this chapter?

think it through

In what situations do you do think military action is warranted? Have there been recent military engagements abroad in which the United States could have better achieved the desired result using a different foreign policy tool, such as diplomacy or economic sanctions?

International Court of Justice (ICJ)
The UN's chief judicial agency, located in The Hague, Netherlands. The ICJ settles legal disputes submitted by UN member states.

the government's lies and ineptitude. The wars in Korea, Vietnam, and Iraq are all examples of protracted conflicts whose domestic repercussions included dissipating public support.

Military force remains a major foreign policy tool, and the United States currently possesses military capabilities more powerful and effective than those of any other nation. Nevertheless, the use of military force is fraught with risk and is not to be undertaken lightly. Analyzing the Evidence on pp. 478–9 takes a closer look at when and under what circumstances the American public is likely to support the use of military force.

Arbitration

In dispute arbitration, an international disagreement is referred to a neutral third party for resolution. Arbitration is sometimes seen as a form of "soft power," as distinguished from military force, economic sanctions, and other coercive foreign policy instruments. The United States occasionally turns to international tribunals to resolve disputes with other countries. For example, in 2008 the U.S. government asked the **International Court of Justice (ICJ)** to resolve a long-standing dispute with Italy over American property the Italian government had confiscated more than 40 years earlier.

More important, the United States relies heavily on arbitration panels to maintain the flow of international trade on which the nation's economy depends. American firms would hesitate to do business abroad if they could not be certain that their property and contractual rights would be honored by other nations. Arbitration helps produce that certainty. Almost every international contract contains an arbitration clause requiring that disputes between the parties be resolved by impartial arbitral panels accepted by both sides.

By the terms of the New York Convention of 1959, virtually every nation in the world has agreed to accept and enforce arbitral verdicts. The United States has incorporated the terms of the New York Convention into federal law, and U.S. courts vigorously enforce arbitral judgments. The United States may not be happy with the outcome of every proceeding, but the arbitral system is essential to the country's economic interests.

CONCLUSION

Does effective governance in the realm of foreign policy require decisive and sometimes secret action by the executive branch, or would U.S. foreign policy be improved if more views were represented when policies were made? The nineteenth-century British statesman Lord Palmerston famously said, "Nations have no permanent friends or allies; they only have permanent interests." Palmerston's comment illustrates the "realist" view of foreign policy, which holds that foreign policies should be guided by the national interest—mainly security and economic interest—and that policy makers should be prepared to make decisions that might seem cold and ruthless, as long as those decisions serve the nation's interests.

Although public officials have tended to denounce such views—especially while running for office—many have become realists once in power. Every one of the United States' post–World War II presidents—liberals and conservatives, Democrats and Republicans alike—have been willing to order young Americans into battle and to visit death and destruction on the citizens of foreign states if they believed the national interest required it.

The harsh reality of foreign policy often clashes with the United States' history and ideals. Our democratic and liberal traditions lead us to hope for a world in which ideals rather than naked interests govern foreign policy. The ideals that Americans have historically supported (though not always lived by) assert that our foreign policies should have a higher purpose than the pursuit of interest and that America should use force only as a last resort. Since the realities of our foreign policy often clash with these ideals, our policy makers struggle to explain their actions and avoid admitting to motivations that don't embody those ideals.

Must the United States always choose between its ideals and its interests? The Founders believed that America would be different from other nations—that its ideals would be its source of power, allowing it to inspire and lead others as a "shining beacon." If, in the interest of national power and security, our political leaders always choose narrow interests over transcendent ideals, might they be robbing the United States of its true source of international power and global security?

What should the United States' role be in world politics? American foreign policy is often controversial both within the United States and around the world. These "America first" protesters demonstrate the conflict between America's ideals and its interests.

Key Terms

Check Your Understanding

1. What are the main goals of American foreign policy?

2. Who makes and shapes foreign policy in the United States? Identify the main actors and the different roles they play.

3. How has American attitude about foreign policy evolved since the founding? How do attitudes prior to World War II compare with those now?

4. What are the different tools of American foreign policy deployed now?

 INQUIZITIVE

Earn a better grade on your test.   InQuizitive personalizes your learning path to help you master the concepts from this chapter. In a recent efficacy study of American government students, InQuizitive increased test scores by an average of 17 points (see back cover).

APPENDIX

THE **DECLARATION** OF **INDEPENDENCE**

IN CONGRESS, JULY 4, 1776

When in the course of human events, it becomes necessary for one people to dissolve the political bands which have connected them with another, and to assume among the Powers of the earth, the separate and equal station to which the Laws of Nature and of Nature's God entitle them, a decent respect to the opinions of mankind requires that they should declare the causes which impel them to the separation.

We hold these truths to be self-evident, that all men are created equal, that they are endowed by their Creator with certain unalienable rights, that among these are Life, Liberty, and the pursuit of Happiness. That to secure these rights, Governments are instituted among Men, deriving their just powers from the consent of the governed. That whenever any Form of Government becomes destructive of these ends, it is the Right of the People to alter or to abolish it, and to institute new Government, laying its foundation on such principles and organizing its powers in such form, as to them shall seem most likely to effect their Safety and Happiness. Prudence, indeed, will dictate that Governments long established should not be changed for light and transient causes; and accordingly all experience hath shown, that mankind are more disposed to suffer, while evils are sufferable, than to right themselves by abolishing the forms to which they are accustomed. But when a long train of abuses and usurpations, pursuing invariably the same Object evinces a design to reduce them under absolute Despotism, it is their right, it is their duty, to throw off such Government, and to provide new Guards for their future security.—Such has been the patient sufferance of these Colonies; and such is now the necessity which constrains them to alter their former Systems of Government. The history of the present King of Great Britain is a history of repeated injuries and usurpations, all having in direct object the establishment of an absolute Tyranny over these States. To prove this, let Facts be submitted to a candid world.

He has refused his Assent to Laws, the most wholesome and necessary for the public good.

He has forbidden his Governors to pass Laws of immediate and pressing importance, unless suspended in their operation till his Assent should be obtained; and when so suspended, he has utterly neglected to attend to them.

He has refused to pass other Laws for the accommodation of large districts of people, unless those people would relinquish the right of Representation in the Legislature, a right inestimable to them and formidable to tyrants only.

He has called together legislative bodies at places unusual, uncomfortable, and distant from the depository of their public Records, for the sole purpose of fatiguing them into compliance with his measures.

He has dissolved Representative Houses repeatedly, for opposing with manly firmness his invasions on the rights of the people.

He has refused for a long time, after such dissolutions, to cause others to be elected; whereby the Legislative powers, incapable of Annihilation, have returned to the People at large for their exercise; the State remaining in the mean time exposed to all dangers of invasion from without, and convulsions within.

He has endeavored to prevent the population of these States; for that purpose obstructing the Laws of Naturalization of Foreigners; refusing to pass others to encourage their migrations hither, and raising the conditions of new Appropriations of Lands.

He has obstructed the Administration of Justice, by refusing his Assent to Laws for establishing Judiciary powers.

He has made Judges dependent on his Will alone, for the tenure of their offices, and the amount and payment of their salaries.

He has erected a multitude of New Offices, and sent hither swarms of Officers to harass our People, and eat out their substance.

He has kept among us, in times of peace, Standing Armies without the Consent of our legislature.

He has affected to render the Military independent of and superior to the Civil Power.

He has combined with others to subject us to a jurisdiction foreign to our constitution, and unacknowledged by our laws; giving his Assent to their Acts of pretended Legislation:

For quartering large bodies of armed troops among us:

For protecting them, by a mock Trial, from Punishment for any Murders which they should commit on the Inhabitants of these States:

For cutting off our Trade with all parts of the world:

For imposing taxes on us without our Consent:

For depriving us in many cases, of the benefits of Trial by jury:

For transporting us beyond Seas to be tried for pretended offences:

For abolishing the free System of English Laws in a neighboring Province, establishing therein an Arbitrary government, and enlarging its Boundaries so as to render it at once an example and fit instrument for introducing the same absolute rule into these Colonies:

For taking away our Charters, abolishing our most valuable Laws, and altering fundamentally the Forms of our Governments:

For suspending our own Legislatures, and declaring themselves invested with Power to legislate for us in all cases whatsoever.

He has abdicated Government here, by declaring us out of his Protection and waging War against us.

He has plundered our seas, ravaged our Coasts, burnt our towns, and destroyed the lives of our people.

He is at this time transporting large armies of foreign mercenaries to compleat the works of death, desolation, and tyranny, already begun with circumstances of Cruelty & perfidy scarcely paralleled in the most barbarous ages, and totally unworthy the Head of a civilized nation.

He has constrained our fellow Citizens taken Captive on the high Seas to bear Arms against their Country, to become the executioners of their friends and Brethren, or to fall themselves by their Hands.

He has excited domestic insurrections amongst us, and has endeavored to bring on the inhabitants of our frontiers, the merciless Indian Savages, whose known rule of warfare, is an undistinguished destruction of all ages, sexes, and conditions.

In every stage of these Oppressions We have Petitioned for Redress in the most humble terms: Our repeated Petitions have been answered only by repeated injury. A Prince, whose character is thus marked by every act which may define a Tyrant, is unfit to be the ruler of a free people.

Nor have We been wanting in attention to our British brethren. We have warned them from time to time of attempts by their legislature to extend an unwarrantable jurisdiction over us. We have reminded them of the circumstances of our emigration and settlement here. We have appealed to their native justice and magnanimity, and we have conjured them by the ties of our common kindred to disavow these usurpations, which, would inevitably interrupt our connections and correspondence. They too must have been deaf to the voice of justice and of consanguinity. We must, therefore, acquiesce in the necessity, which denounces our Separation, and hold them, as we hold the rest of mankind, Enemies in War, in Peace Friends.

WE, THEREFORE, the Representatives of the United States of America, in General Congress, Assembled, appealing to the Supreme Judge of the world for the rectitude of our intentions, do, in the Name, and by Authority of the good People of these Colonies, solemnly publish and declare, That these United Colonies are, and of Right ought to be Free and Independent States; that they are Absolved from all Allegiance to the British Crown, and that all political connection between them and the State of Great Britain, is and ought to be totally dissolved; and that as Free and Independent States, they have full Power to levy War, conclude Peace, contract Alliances, establish Commerce, and to do all other Acts and Things which Independent States may of right do. And for the support of this Declaration, with a firm reliance on the Protection of Divine Providence, we mutually pledge to each other our Lives, our Fortunes, and our sacred Honor.

The foregoing Declaration was, by order of Congress, engrossed, and signed by the following members:

John Hancock

NEW HAMPSHIRE
Josiah Bartlett
William Whipple
Matthew Thornton

MASSACHUSETTS BAY
Samuel Adams
John Adams
Robert Treat Paine
Elbridge Gerry

RHODE ISLAND
Stephen Hopkins
William Ellery

CONNECTICUT
Roger Sherman
Samuel Huntington
William Williams
Oliver Wolcott

NEW YORK
William Floyd
Philip Livingston
Francis Lewis
Lewis Morris

NEW JERSEY
Richard Stockton
John Witherspoon
Francis Hopkinson
John Hart
Abraham Clark

PENNSYLVANIA
Robert Morris
Benjamin Rush
Benjamin Franklin
John Morton
George Clymer
James Smith
George Taylor
James Wilson
George Ross

DELAWARE
Caesar Rodney
George Read
Thomas M'Kean

MARYLAND
Samuel Chase
William Paca
Thomas Stone
Charles Carroll,
of Carrollton

VIRGINIA
George Wythe
Richard Henry Lee
Thomas Jefferson
Benjamin Harrison
Thomas Nelson, Jr.
Francis Lightfoot Lee
Carter Braxton

NORTH CAROLINA
William Hooper
Joseph Hewes
John Penn

SOUTH CAROLINA
Edward Rutledge
Thomas Heyward, Jr.
Thomas Lynch, Jr.
Arthur Middleton

GEORGIA
Button Gwinnett
Lyman Hall
George Walton

Resolved, That copies of the Declaration be sent to the several assemblies, conventions, and committees, or councils of safety, and to the several commanding officers of the continental troops; that it be proclaimed in each of the United States, at the head of the army.

THE **ARTICLES** OF **CONFEDERATION**

AGREED TO BY CONGRESS NOVEMBER 15, 1777;
RATIFIED AND IN FORCE MARCH 1, 1781

To all whom these Presents shall come, we the undersigned Delegates of the States affixed to our Names send greeting. Whereas the Delegates of the United States of America in Congress assembled did on the fifteenth day of November in the Year of our Lord One Thousand Seven Hundred and Seventy seven, and in the Second Year of the Independence of America agree to certain articles of Confederation and perpetual Union between the States of Newhampshire, Massachusetts-bay, Rhodeisland and Providence Plantations, Connecticut, New-York, New-Jersey, Pennsylvania, Delaware, Maryland, Virginia, North-Carolina, South-Carolina and Georgia in the Words following, viz. "Articles of Confederation and perpetual Union between the states of Newhampshire, Massachusetts-bay, Rhodeisland and Providence Plantations, Connecticut, New-York, New-Jersey, Pennsylvania, Delaware, Maryland, Virginia, North-Carolina, South-Carolina and Georgia.

Art. I. The Stile of this confederacy shall be "The United States of America."

Art. II. Each state retains its sovereignty, freedom and independence, and every Power, Jurisdiction and right, which is not by this confederation expressly delegated to the United States, in Congress assembled.

Art. III. The said states hereby severally enter into a firm league of friendship with each other, for their common defence, the security of their Liberties, and their mutual and general welfare, binding themselves to assist each other, against all force offered to, or attacks made upon them, or any of them, on account of religion, sovereignty, trade, or any other pretence whatever.

Art. IV. The better to secure and perpetuate mutual friendship and intercourse among the people of the different states in this union, the free inhabitants of each of these states, paupers, vagabonds and fugitives from Justice excepted, shall be entitled to all privileges and immunities of free citizens in the several states; and the people of each state shall have free ingress and regress to and from any other state, and shall enjoy therein all the privileges of trade and commerce, subject to the same duties, impositions and restrictions as the inhabitants thereof respectively, provided that such restriction shall not extend so far as to prevent the removal of property imported into any state, to any other state of which the Owner is an inhabitant; provided also that no imposition, duties or restriction shall be laid by any state, on the property of the united states, or either of them.

If any Person guilty of, or charged with treason, felony, or other high misdemeanor in any state, shall flee from Justice, and be found in any of the united states, he shall upon demand of the Governor or executive power, of the state from which he fled, be delivered up and removed to the state having jurisdiction of his offence.

Full faith and credit shall be given in each of these states to the records, acts and judicial proceedings of the courts and magistrates of every other state.

Art. V. For the more convenient management of the general interests of the united states, delegates shall be annually appointed in such manner as the legislature of each state shall direct, to meet in Congress on the first Monday in November, in every year, with a power reserved to each state, to recall its delegates, or any of them, at any time within the year, and to send others in their stead, for the remainder of the Year.

No state shall be represented in Congress by less than two, nor by more than seven Members; and no person shall be capable of being a delegate for more than three years in any term of six years; nor shall any person, being a delegate, be capable of holding any office under the united states, for which he, or another for his benefit receives any salary, fees or emolument of any kind.

Each state shall maintain its own delegates in a meeting of the states, and while they act as members of the committee of the states.

In determining questions in the united states, in Congress assembled, each state shall have one vote.

Freedom of speech and debate in Congress shall not be impeached or questioned in any Court, or place out of Congress, and the members of congress shall be protected in their persons from arrests and imprisonments, during the time of their going to and from, and attendance on congress, except for treason, felony, or breach of the peace.

Art. VI. No state without the Consent of the united states in congress assembled, shall send any embassy to, or receive any embassy from, or enter into any conference, agreement, or alliance or treaty with any King, prince or state; nor shall any person holding any office or profit or trust under the united states, or any of them, accept of any present, emolument, office or title of any kind whatever from any king, prince or foreign state; nor shall the united states in congress assembled, or any of them, grant any title of nobility.

No two or more states shall enter into any treaty, confederation or alliance whatever between them, without the consent of the united states in congress assembled, specifying accurately the purposes for which the same is to be entered into, and how long it shall continue.

No state shall lay any imposts or duties, which may interfere with any stipulations in treaties, entered into by the united states in congress assembled, with any king, prince or state, in pursuance of any treaties already proposed by congress, to the courts of France and Spain.

No vessels of war shall be kept up in time of peace by any state, except such number only, as shall be deemed necessary by the united states in congress assembled, for the defence of such state, or its trade; nor shall any body of forces be kept up by any state, in time of peace, except such number only, as in the judgment of the united states, in congress assembled, shall be deemed requisite to garrison the forts necessary for the defence of such state; but every state shall always keep up a well regulated and disciplined militia, sufficiently armed and accoutred, and shall provide and constantly have ready for use, in public stores, a due number of field pieces and tents, and a proper quantity of arms, ammunition and camp equipage.

No state shall engage in any war without the consent of the united states in congress assembled, unless such state be actually invaded by enemies, or shall have received certain advice of a resolution being formed by some nation of Indians to invade such state, and the danger is so imminent as not to admit of a delay, till the united states in congress asssembled can be consulted; nor shall any state grant commissions to any ships or vessels of war, nor letters of marque or reprisal, except it be after a declaration of war by the united states in congress assembled, and then only against the kingdom or state and the subjects thereof, against which war has been so declared, and under such regulations as shall be established by the united states in congress assembled, unless such state be infested by pirates; in which case vessels of war may be fitted out for that occasion, and kept so long as the danger shall continue, or until the united states in congress assembled shall determine otherwise.

Art. VII. When land-forces are raised by any state for the common defence, all officers of or under the rank of colonel, shall be appointed by the legislature of each state respectively by whom such forces shall be raised, or in such manner as such state shall direct, and all vacancies shall be filled up by the state which first made the appointment.

Art. VIII. All charges of war, and all other expences that shall be incurred for the common defence or general welfare, and allowed by the united states in congress assembled, shall be defrayed out of a common treasury, which shall be supplied by the several states, in proportion to the value of all land within each state, granted to or surveyed for any Person, as such land and the buildings and improvements thereon shall be estimated according to such mode as the united states in congress assembled, shall from time to time direct and appoint. The taxes for paying that proportion shall be laid and levied by the authority and direction of the legislatures of the several states within the time agreed upon by the united states in congress assembled.

Art. IX. The united states in congress assembled, shall have the sole and exclusive right and power of determining on peace and war, except in the cases mentioned in the sixth article—of sending and receiving ambassadors—entering into treaties and alliances, provided that no treaty of commerce shall be made whereby the legislative power of the respective states shall be restrained from imposing such imposts and duties on foreigners, as their own people are subjected to, or from prohibiting the exportation of any species of goods or commodities whatsoever—of establishing rules for deciding in all cases, what captures on land or water shall be legal, and in what manner prizes taken by land or naval forces in the service of the united states shall be divided or appropriated—of granting letters of marque and reprisal in times of peace—appointing courts for the trial of piracies and felonies committed on the high seas and establishing courts for receiving and determining finally appeals in all cases of captures, provided that no member of congress shall be appointed a judge of any of the said courts.

The united states in congress assembled shall also be the last resort on appeal in all disputes and differences now subsisting or that hereafter may arise between two or more states concerning boundary, jurisdiction or any other cause whatever; which authority shall always be exercised in the manner following. Whenever the legislative or executive authority or lawful agent of any state in controversy with another shall present a petition to congress stating the matter in question and praying for a hearing, notice thereof shall be given by order of congress to the legislative or executive authority of the other state in controversy, and a day assigned for the appearance of the parties by their lawful agents, who shall then be directed to appoint by joint consent, commissioners or judges to constitute a court for hearing and determining the matter in question: but if they cannot agree, congress shall name three persons out of each of the united states, and from the list of such persons each party shall alternately strike out one, the petitioners beginning, until the number shall be reduced to thirteen; and from that number not less than seven, nor more than nine names as congress shall direct, shall in the presence of congress be drawn out by lot, and the persons whose names shall be so drawn or any five of them, shall be commissioners or judges, to hear and finally determine the controversy, so always as a major part of the judges who shall hear the cause shall agree in the determination: and if either party shall neglect to attend at the day appointed, without shewing reasons, which congress shall judge sufficient, or being present shall refuse to strike, the congress shall proceed to nominate three persons out of each state, and the secretary of congress shall strike in behalf of such party absent or refusing; and the judgment and sentence of the court to be appointed, in the manner before prescribed, shall be final and conclusive; and if any of the parties shall refuse to submit to the authority of such court, or to appear to defend their claim or cause, the court shall nevertheless proceed to pronounce sentence, or judgment, which shall in like manner be final and decisive, the judgment or sentence and other proceedings being in either case transmitted to congress, and lodged among the acts of congress for the security of the parties concerned: provided that every commissioner, before he sits in judgment, shall take an oath to be administered by one of the judges of the supreme or superior court of the state, where the cause shall be tried, "well and truly to hear and determine the matter in question, according to the best of his judgment, without favour, affection or hope of reward:" provided also that no state shall be deprived of territory for the benefit of the united states.

All controversies concerning the private right of soil claimed under different grants of two or more states, whose jurisdictions as they may respect such lands, and the states which passed such grants are adjusted, the said grants or either of them being at the same time claimed to have originated antecedent to such settlement of jurisdiction, shall on the petition of either party to the congress of the united states, be finally determined as near as may be in the same manner as is before prescribed for deciding disputes respecting territorial jurisdiction between different states.

The united states in congress assembled shall also have the sole and exclusive right and power of regulating the alloy and value of coin struck by their own authority, or by that of the respective states—fixing the standard of weights and measures throughout the united states—regulating the trade and managing all affairs with the Indians, not members of any of the states, provided that the legislative right of any state within its own limits be not infringed or violated—establishing and regulating post-offices from one state to another, throughout all the united states, and exacting such postage on the papers passing thro' the same as may be requisite to defray the expences of the said office—appointing all officers of the land forces, in the service of the united states, except regimental officers—appointing all the officers of the united states—making rules for the government and regulation of the said land and naval forces, and directing their operations.

The united states in congress assembled shall have the authority to appoint a committee, to sit in the recess of congress, to be denominated "A Committee of the States," and to consist of one delegate from each state; and to appoint such other committees and civil officers as may be necessary for managing the general affairs of the united states under their direction—to appoint one of their number to preside, provided that no person be allowed to serve in the office of president more than one year in any term of three years; to ascertain the necessary sums of Money to be raised for the service of the united states, and to appropriate and apply the same for defraying the public expences—to borrow money, or emit bills on the credit of the united states, transmitting every half year to the respective states an account of the sums of money so borrowed or emitted,—to build and equip a navy—to agree upon the number of land forces, and to make requisitions from each state for its quota, in proportion to the number of white inhabitants in such state; which requisition shall be binding, and thereupon the legislature of each state shall appoint the regimental officers, raise the men and cloath, arm and equip them in a soldier like manner, at the expence of the united states, and the officers and men so cloathed, armed and equipped shall march to the place appointed, and within the time agreed on by the united states in congress assembled: But if the united states in congress assembled shall, on consideration of circumstances judge proper that any state should not raise men, or should raise a smaller number than its quota, and that any other state should raise a greater number of men than the quota thereof, such extra number shall be raised, officered, cloathed, armed and equipped in the same manner as the quota of such state, unless the legislature of such state shall judge that such extra number cannot be safely spared out of the same, in which case they shall raise, officer, cloath, arm and equip as many of such extra number as they judge can be safely spared. And the officers and men so cloathed, armed and equipped, shall march to the place appointed, and within the time agreed on by the united states in congress assembled.

The united states in congress assembled shall never engage in a war, nor grant letters of marque and reprisal in time of peace, nor enter into any treaties or alliances, nor coin money, nor regulate the value thereof, nor ascertain the sums and expences necessary for the defence and welfare of the united states, or any of them, nor emit bills, nor borrow money on the credit of the united states, nor appropriate money, nor agree upon the number of vessels of war, to be built or purchased, or the number of land or sea forces to be raised, nor appoint a commander in chief of the army or navy, unless nine states assent to the same: nor shall a question on any other point, except for adjourning from day to day be determined, unless by the votes of a majority of the united states in congress assembled.

The congress of the united states shall have power to adjourn to any time within the year, and to any place within the united states, so that no period of adjournment be for a longer duration than the space of six Months, and shall publish the Journal of their proceedings monthly, except such parts thereof relating to treaties, alliances or military operations as in their judgment require secresy; and the yeas and nays of the delegates of each state on any question shall be entered on the Journal, when it is desired by any delegate; and the delegates of a state, or any of them, at his or their request shall be furnished with a transcript of the said Journal, except such parts as are above excepted to lay before the legislatures of the several states.

Art. X. The committee of the states, or any nine of them, shall be authorised to execute, in the recess of congress, such of the powers of congress as the united states in congress assembled, by the consent of nine states, shall from time to time think expedient to vest them with; provided that no power be delegated to the said committee, for the exercise of which, by the articles of confederation, the voice of nine states in the congress of the united states assembled is requisite.

Art. XI. Canada acceding to this confederation, and joining in the measures of the united states, shall be admitted into, and entitled to all the advantages of this union: but no other colony shall be admitted into the same, unless such admission be agreed to by nine states.

Art. XII. All bills of credit emitted, monies borrowed and debts contracted by, or under the authority of congress, before the assembling of the united states, in pursuance of the present confederation, shall be deemed and considered as a charge against the united states, for payment and satisfaction whereof the said united states and the public faith are hereby solemnly pledged.

Art. XIII. Every state shall abide by the determinations of the united states in congress assembled, on all questions which by this confederation are submitted to them. And the Articles of this confederation shall be inviolably observed by every state, and the union shall be perpetual; nor shall any alteration at any time hereafter be made in any of them; unless such alteration be agreed to in a congress of the united states, and be afterwards confirmed by the legislatures of every state.

AND WHEREAS it hath pleased the Great Governor of the World to incline the hearts of the legislatures we respectively represent in congress, to approve of, and to authorize us to ratify the said articles of confederation and perpetual union. KNOW YE that we the undersigned delegates, by virtue of the power and authority to us given for that purpose, do by these presents, in the name and in behalf of our respective constituents, fully and entirely ratify and confirm each and every of the said articles of confederation and perpetual union, and all and singular the matters and things therein contained: And we do further solemnly plight and engage the faith of our respective constituents, that they shall abide by the determination of the united states in congress assembled, on all questions, which by the said confederation are submitted to them. And that the articles thereof shall be inviolably observed by the states we respectively represent, and that the union shall be perpetual. In Witness whereof we have hereunto set our hands in Congress. Done at Philadelphia in the state of Pennsylvania the ninth Day of July in the Year of our Lord one Thousand seven Hundred and Seventy-eight and in the third year of the independence of America.

THE CONSTITUTION OF THE UNITED STATES OF AMERICA

ANNOTATED WITH REFERENCES
TO *FEDERALIST PAPERS*

Federalist Paper
Number (Author)

[PREAMBLE]

84 (Hamilton)

We the People of the United States, in Order to form a more perfect Union, establish Justice, insure domestic Tranquility, provide for the common defence, promote the general Welfare, and secure the Blessings of Liberty to ourselves and our Posterity, do ordain and establish this Constitution for the United States of America.

ARTICLE I

Section 1

[LEGISLATIVE POWERS]

10, 45 (Madison)

All legislative Powers herein granted shall be vested in a Congress of the United States, which shall consist of a Senate and House of Representatives.

Section 2

39, 45, 52–53, 57 (Madison)

[HOUSE OF REPRESENTATIVES, HOW CONSTITUTED, POWER OF IMPEACHMENT]

The House of Representatives shall be composed of Members chosen every second Year by the People of the several States, and the Electors in each State shall have the Qualifications requisite for Electors of the most numerous Branch of the State

52 (Madison)

Legislature.

60 (Hamilton)

No Person shall be a Representative who shall not have attained to the Age of twenty-five Years, and been seven Years a Citizen of the United States, and who shall not, when

54, 58 (Madison)

elected, be an inhabitant of that State in which he shall be chosen.

Representatives and *direct Taxes*[1] shall be apportioned among the several States which may be included within this Union, according to their respective Numbers, *which shall be determined by adding to the whole Number of free Persons, including those bound to Service for a Term of Years,* and excluding Indians not taxed, *three-fifths of all other Persons.*[2] The actual Enumeration shall be made within three Years after the first Meeting of the Congress of the United States, and within every subsequent

55–56 (Madison)

Term of ten Years, in such Manner as they shall by Law direct. The Number of Representatives shall not exceed one for every thirty Thousand, but each State shall have at

---

1   Modified by Sixteenth Amendment.
2   Modified by Fourteenth Amendment.

Least one Representative; *and until such enumeration shall be made, the State of New Hampshire shall be entitled to chuse three, Massachusetts eight, Rhode-Island and Providence Plantations one, Connecticut five, New-York six, New Jersey four, Pennsylvania eight, Delaware one, Maryland six, Virginia ten, North Carolina five, South Carolina five, and Georgia three.*[3]

When vacancies happen in the Representation from any State, the Executive Authority thereof shall issue Writs of Election to fill such Vacancies.

The House of Representatives shall chuse their Speaker and other Officers; and shall have the sole Power of Impeachment.

79 (Hamilton)

Section 3
[THE SENATE, HOW CONSTITUTED, IMPEACHMENT TRIALS]

The Senate of the United States shall be composed of two Senators from each State, *chosen by the Legislature thereof,*[4] for six Years; and each Senator shall have one Vote.

39, 45 (Madison)
60 (Hamilton)

Immediately after they shall be assembled in Consequence of the first Election, they shall be divided as equally as may be into three Classes. The Seats of the Senators of the first Class shall be vacated at the Expiration of the second Year, of the second Class at the Expiration of the fourth Year, and of the third Class at the Expiration of the sixth Year, so that one third may be chosen every second Year: *and if vacancies happen by Resignation, or otherwise, during the Recess of the Legislature of any State, the Executive thereof may make temporary Appointments until the next Meeting of the Legislature, which shall then fill such Vacancies.*[5]

62–63 (Madison)
59, 68 (Hamilton)

No person shall be a Senator who shall not have attained to the Age of thirty Years, and been nine Years a Citizen of the United States, and who shall not, when elected, be an Inhabitant of that State for which he shall be chosen.

62 (Madison)
64 (Jay)

The Vice-President of the United States shall be President of the Senate, but shall have no Vote, unless they be equally divided.

The Senate shall chuse their other Officers, and also a President pro tempore, in the Absence of the Vice-President, or when he shall exercise the Office of President of the United States.

The Senate shall have the sole Power to try all Impeachments. When sitting for that Purpose, they shall be on Oath or Affirmation. When the President of the United States is tried, the Chief Justice shall preside: And no Person shall be convicted without the Concurrence of two-thirds of the Members present.

39 (Madison)
65–67, 79 (Hamilton)

Judgment in Cases of Impeachment shall not extend further than to removal from Office, and disqualification to hold and enjoy any Office of honor, Trust or Profit under the United States: but the Party convicted shall nevertheless be liable and subject to Indictment, Trial, Judgment and Punishment, according to Law.

84 (Hamilton)

Section 4
[ELECTION OF SENATORS AND REPRESENTATIVES]

The Times, Places and Manner of holding Elections for Senators and Representatives, shall be prescribed in each State by the Legislature thereof; but the Congress may at any time by Law make or alter such Regulations, except as to the Places of chusing Senators.

59–61 (Hamilton)

---

3   Temporary provision.

4   Modified by Seventeenth Amendment.

5   Modified by Seventeenth Amendment.

The Congress shall assemble at least once in every Year, and such Meeting shall be on the first Monday in December, unless they shall by Law appoint a different Day.[6]

Section 5
[QUORUM, JOURNALS, MEETINGS, ADJOURNMENTS]

Each House shall be the Judge of the Elections, Returns and Qualifications of its own Members, and a Majority of each shall constitute a Quorum to do Business; but a smaller Number may adjourn from day to day, and may be authorized to compel the Attendance of absent Members, in such Manner, and under the Penalties as each House may provide.

Each House may determine the Rules of its Proceedings, punish its Members for disorderly Behavior, and, with the Concurrence of two-thirds, expel a Member.

Each House shall keep a Journal of its Proceedings, and from time to time publish the same, excepting such Parts as may in their Judgment require Secrecy; and the Yeas and Nays of the Members of either House on any questions shall, at the Desire of one-fifth of the present, be entered on the Journal.

Neither House, during the Session of Congress, shall, without the Consent of the other, adjourn for more than three days, nor to any other Place than that in which the two Houses shall be sitting.

Section 6
[COMPENSATION, PRIVILEGES, DISABILITIES]

55 (Madison)
76 (Hamilton)

The Senators and Representatives shall receive a Compensation for their Services, to be ascertained by Law, and paid out of the Treasury of the United States. They shall in all Cases, except Treason, Felony and Breach of the Peace, be privileged from Arrest during their Attendance at the Session of their respective Houses, and in going to and returning from the same; and for any Speech or Debate in either House, they shall not be questioned in any other Place.

No Senator or Representative shall, during the time for which he was elected, be appointed to any civil Office under the authority of the United States, which shall have been created, or the Emoluments whereof shall have been encreased during such time; and no Person holding any Office under the United States, shall be a Member of either House during his Continuance in Office.

Section 7
[PROCEDURE IN PASSING BILLS AND RESOLUTIONS]

66 (Hamilton)

All Bills for raising Revenue shall originate in the House of Representatives; but the Senate may propose or concur with Amendments as on other Bills.

69, 73 (Hamilton)

Every Bill which shall have passed the House of Representatives and the Senate, shall, before it become a Law, be presented to the President of the United States; if he approve he shall sign it, but if not he shall return it, with his Objections to that House in which it shall have originated, who shall enter the Objections at large on their Journal, and proceed to reconsider it. If after such Reconsideration two-thirds of that House shall agree to pass the Bill, it shall be sent, together with the Objections, to the other House, by which it shall likewise be reconsidered, and if approved by two-thirds of that House it shall become a Law. But in all such Cases the Votes of both Houses shall be determined by Yeas and Nays, and the Names of the Persons voting for and against

---

6   Modified by Twentieth Amendment.

the Bill shall be entered on the Journal of each House respectively. If any Bill shall not be returned by the President within ten Days (Sundays excepted) after it shall have been presented to him, the Same shall be a Law, in like Manner as if he had signed it, unless the Congress by their Adjournment prevent its Return, in which Case it shall not be a Law.

Every Order, Resolution, or Vote to which the Concurrence of the Senate and House of Representatives may be necessary (except on a question of Adjournment) shall be presented to the President of the United States; and before the Same shall take Effect, shall be approved by him, or being disapproved by him, shall be repassed by two-thirds of the Senate and House of Representatives, according to the Rules and Limitations prescribed in the Case of a Bill.

69, 73 (Hamilton)

Section 8
[POWERS OF CONGRESS]

The Congress shall have Power

To lay and collect Taxes, Duties, Imposts and Excises, to pay the Debts and provide for the common Defence and general Welfare of the United States; but all Duties, Imposts and excises shall be uniform throughout the United States;

30–36 (Hamilton)
41 (Madison)

To borrow Money on the Credit of the United States;

To regulate Commerce with foreign Nations, and among the several States, and with the Indian Tribes;

56 (Madison)
42, 45, 56 (Madison)

To establish an uniform Rule of Naturalization, and uniform Laws on the subject of Bankruptcies throughout the United States;

32 (Hamilton)

To coin Money, regulate the Value thereof, and of foreign Coin, and fix the Standard of Weights and Measures;

42 (Madison)

To provide for the Punishment of counterfeiting the Securities and current Coin of the United States;

42 (Madison)

To establish Post Offices and post Roads;

To promote the Progress of Science and useful Arts, by securing for limited Times to Authors and Inventors the exclusive Right to their respective Writings and Discoveries;

42 (Madison)
42, 43 (Madison)

To constitute Tribunals inferior to the supreme Court;

81 (Hamilton)

To define and Punish Piracies and Felonies committed on the high Seas, and Offences against the Law of Nations;

42 (Madison)

To declare War, grant Letters of Marque and Reprisal, and make Rules concerning Captures on Land and Water;

41 (Madison)

To raise and support Armies, but no Appropriation of Money to that Use shall be for a longer Term than two Years;

23, 24, 26 (Hamilton)

To provide and maintain a Navy;

41 (Madison)

To make Rules for the Government and Regulation of the land and naval forces;

To provide for calling for the Militia to execute the Laws of the Union, suppress Insurrections and repel Invasions;

29 (Hamilton)

To provide for organizing, arming, and disciplining, the Militia, and for governing such Part of them as may be employed in the Service of the United States, reserving to the States respectively, the Appointment of the Officers, and the Authority of training the Militia according to the discipline prescribed by Congress;

29 (Hamilton)
56 (Madison)

To exercise exclusive Legislation in all Cases whatsoever, over such District (not exceeding ten Miles square) as may, by Cession of particular States, and the Acceptance of Congress, become the Seat of the Government of the United States, and to exercise

32 (Hamilton)
43 (Madison)

like Authority over all Places purchased by the Consent of the Legislature of the State in which the Same shall be, for the Erection of Forts, Magazines, Arsenals, dock-Yards, and other needful Buildings;—And

29, 33 (Hamilton)
44 (Madison)

To make all Laws which shall be necessary and proper for carrying into Execution the foregoing Powers, and all other Powers vested by this Constitution in the Government of the United States, or in any Department or Officer thereof.

Section 9
[SOME RESTRICTIONS ON FEDERAL POWER]

42 (Madison)

The Migration or Importation of such Persons as any of the States now existing shall think proper to admit, shall not be prohibited by the Congress prior to the Year one thousand eight hundred and eight, but a Tax or Duty may be imposed on such Importation, not exceeding ten dollars for each Person.[7]

83, 84 (Hamilton)

The privilege of the Writ of *Habeas Corpus* shall not be suspended, unless when in Cases of Rebellion or Invasion the public Safety may require it.

84 (Hamilton)

No Bill of Attainder or ex post facto Law shall be passed.

No Capitation, or other direct, Tax shall be laid, unless in Proportion to the Census or Enumeration herein before directed to be taken.[8]

No Tax or Duty shall be laid on Articles exported from any State.

32 (Hamilton)

No Preference shall be given by any Regulation of Commerce or Revenue to the Ports of one State over those of another; nor shall vessels bound to, or from, one State, be obliged to enter, clear, or pay Duties in another.

No Money shall be drawn from the Treasury, but in Consequence of Appropriations made by Law; and a regular Statement and Account of the Receipts and Expenditures of all public Money shall be published from time to time.

39 (Madison)
84 (Hamilton)

No Title of Nobility shall be granted by the United States: And no Person holding any Office of Profit or Trust under them, shall, without the Consent of the Congress, accept of any present, Emolument, Office or Title, of any kind whatever, from any King, Prince, or foreign State.

Section 10
[RESTRICTIONS UPON POWERS OF STATES]

33 (Hamilton)
44 (Madison)

No State shall enter into any Treaty, Alliance, or Confederation; grant Letters of Marque and Reprisal; coin Money; emit Bills of Credit; make any Thing but gold and silver Coin a Tender in Payment of Debts; pass any Bill of Attainder, ex post facto Law, or Law impairing the Obligation of Contracts, or grant any Title of Nobility.

32 (Hamilton)
44 (Madison)

No State shall, without the Consent of the Congress, lay any Imposts or Duties on Imports or Exports, except what may be absolutely necessary for executing its inspection Laws: and the net Produce of all Duties and Imposts, laid by any State on Imports or Exports, shall be for the Use of the Treasury of the United States; and all such Laws shall be subject to the Revision and Control of the Congress.

No State shall, without the Consent of Congress, lay any Duty of Tonnage, keep Troops, or Ships of War in time of Peace, enter into any Agreement or Compact with another State, or with a foreign Power, or engage in War, unless actually invaded, or in such imminent Danger as will not admit of Delay.

---

7   Temporary provision.
8   Modified by Sixteenth Amendment.

ARTICLE II

Section 1

[EXECUTIVE POWER, ELECTION, QUALIFICATIONS OF THE PRESIDENT]

The executive Power shall be vested in a President of the United States of America. *He shall hold his Office during the Term of four years and, together with the Vice-President, chosen for the same Term, be elected, as follows:*[9]

39 (Madison)
70, 71, 84 (Hamilton)

Each State shall appoint, in such Manner as the Legislature thereof may direct, a Number of Electors, equal to the whole Number of Senators and Representatives to which the State may be entitled in the Congress: but no Senator or Representative, or Person holding an Office of Trust or Profit under the United States, shall be appointed an Elector.

68, 69, 71, 77 (Hamilton)
39, 45 (Madison)

The electors shall meet in their respective States, and vote by ballot for two Persons, of whom one at least shall not be an Inhabitant of the same State with themselves. And they shall make a List of all the Persons voted for, and of the Number of Votes for each; which List they shall sign and certify, and transmit sealed to the Seat of the Government of the United States, directed to the President of the Senate. The President of the Senate shall, in the Presence of the Senate and House of Representatives, open all the Certificates, and the Votes shall then be counted. The Person having the greatest Number of Votes shall be the President, if such Number be a Majority of the whole Number of Electors appointed; and if there be more than one who have such Majority and have an equal Number of Votes, then the House of Representatives shall immediately chuse by Ballot one of them for President; and if no person have a Majority, then from the five highest on the List the said House shall in like Manner chuse the President. But in chusing the President, the Votes shall be taken by States, the Representation from each State having one Vote; A quorum for this Purpose shall consist of a Member or Members from two-thirds of the States, and a Majority of all the States shall be necessary to a Choice. In every Case, after the Choice of the President, the person having the greatest Number of Votes of the Electors shall be the Vice-President. But if there should remain two or more who have equal vote, the Senate shall chuse from them by Ballot the Vice-President.[10]

66 (Hamilton)

The Congress may determine the Time of chusing the Electors, and the Day on which they shall give their Votes; which Day shall be the same throughout the United States.

No Person except a natural born Citizen, or a Citizen of the United States, at the time of the Adoption of this Constitution, shall be eligible to the Office of President; neither shall any Person be eligible to that Office who shall not have attained to the Age of thirty-five Years, and been fourteen Years a Resident within the United States.

64 (Jay)

In Case of the Removal of the President from Office, or his Death, Resignation, or Inability to discharge the Powers and Duties of the said Office, the same shall devolve on the Vice-President, and the Congress may by Law provide for the Case of Removal, Death, Resignation, or Inability, both of the President and Vice-President, declaring what Officer shall then act as President, and such Officer shall act accordingly, until the Disability be removed, or a President shall be elected.

The President shall, at stated Times, receive for his Services, a Compensation, which shall neither be encreased nor diminished during the Period for which he shall have been elected, and he shall not receive within that Period any other Emolument from the United States, or any of them.

73, 79 (Hamilton)

---

9 Number of terms limited to two by Twenty-Second Amendment.

10 Modified by Twelfth and Twentieth Amendments.

Before he enter on the Execution of his Office, he shall take the following Oath or Affirmation:—"I do solemnly swear (or affirm) that I will faithfully execute the Office of President of the United States, and will to the best of my Ability, preserve, protect and defend the Constitution of the United States."

Section 2
[POWERS OF THE PRESIDENT]

69, 74 (Hamilton)

The President shall be Commander in Chief of the Army and Navy of the United States, and of the Militia of the several States, when called into the actual Service of the United States; he may require the Opinion, in writing, of the principal Officer in each of the executive Departments, upon any Subject relating to the Duties of their respective Offices, and he shall have Power to grant Reprieves and Pardons for Offences against the United States, except in Cases of Impeachment.

42 (Madison)
64 (Jay)
66, 69, 76, 77
(Hamilton)

He shall have Power, by and with the Advice and Consent of the Senate, to make Treaties, provided two-thirds of the Senators present concur; and he shall nominate, and by and with the Advice and Consent of the Senate, shall appoint Ambassadors, other public Ministers and Consuls, Judges of the Supreme Court, and all other Officers of the United States, whose Appointments are not herein otherwise provided for, and which shall be established by Law: but the Congress may by Law vest the Appointment of such inferior Officers, as they think proper, in the President alone, in the Courts of Law, or in the Heads of Departments.

67, 76 (Hamilton)

The President shall have Power to fill up all Vacancies that may happen during the Recess of the Senate, by granting Commissions which shall expire at the End of their next Session.

Section 3
[POWERS AND DUTIES OF THE PRESIDENT]

69, 77, 78 (Hamilton)
42 (Madison)

He shall from time to time give to the Congress Information of the State of the Union, and recommend to their Consideration such Measures as he shall judge necessary and expedient; he may, on extraordinary Occasions, convene both Houses, or either of them, and in Case of Disagreement between them, with Respect to the Time of Adjournment, he may adjourn them to such Time as he shall think proper; he shall receive Ambassadors and other public Ministers; he shall take Care that the Laws be faithfully executed, and shall Commission all the Officers of the United States.

Section 4
[IMPEACHMENT]

39 (Madison)
69 (Hamilton)

The President, Vice-President and all civil Officers of the United States shall be removed from Office on Impeachment for, and Conviction of, Treason, Bribery, or other high Crimes and Misdemeanors.

ARTICLE III

Section 1
[JUDICIAL POWER, TENURE OF OFFICE]

65, 78, 79, 81, 82
(Hamilton)

The judicial Power of the United States, shall be vested in one supreme Court, and in such inferior Courts as the Congress may from time to time ordain and establish. The Judges, both of the supreme and inferior Courts, shall hold their Offices during good Behavior, and shall, at stated Times, receive for their Services, a Compensation, which shall not be diminished during their Continuance in Office.

Section 2

[JURISDICTION]

The judicial Power shall extend to all Cases, in Law and Equity, arising under this Constitution, the Laws of the United States, and Treaties made, or which shall be made, under their Authority;—to all Cases affecting Ambassadors, other public Ministers and Consuls;—to all Cases of admiralty and maritime Jurisdiction;—to Controversies to which the United States shall be a party;—to Controversies between two or more States;—*between a State and Citizens of another State;*—between Citizens of different States,—between Citizens of the same State claiming Lands under Grants of different States, *and between a State,* or the Citizens thereof, *and foreign States, Citizens or Subjects.*[11]

80 (Hamilton)

In all Cases affecting Ambassadors, other public Ministers and Consuls, and those in which a State shall be Party, the supreme Court shall have original Jurisdiction. In all the other Cases before mentioned, the supreme Court shall have appellate Jurisdiction, both as to Law and Fact, with such Exceptions, and under such Regulations as Congress shall make.

81 (Hamilton)

The Trial of all Crimes, except in Cases of Impeachment, shall be by Jury; and such Trial shall be held in the State where the said Crimes shall have been committed; but when not committed within any State, the Trial shall be at such Place or Places as the Congress may by Law have directed.

83, 84 (Hamilton)

Section 3

[TREASON, PROOF, AND PUNISHMENT]

Treason against the United States, shall consist only in levying War against them, or in adhering to their Enemies, giving them Aid and Comfort. No Person shall be convicted of Treason unless on the Testimony of two Witnesses to the same overt Act, or on Confession in open Court.

43 (Madison)
84 (Hamilton)

The Congress shall have Power to declare the Punishment of Treason, but no Attainder of Treason shall work Corruption of Blood, or Forfeiture except during the Life of the Person attained.

43 (Madison)
84 (Hamilton)

ARTICLE IV

Section 1

[FAITH AND CREDIT AMONG STATES]

Full Faith and Credit shall be given in each State to the public Acts, Records, and judicial Proceedings of every other State. And the Congress may by general Laws prescribe the Manner in which such Acts, Records and Proceedings shall be proved, and the Effect thereof.

42 (Madison)

Section 2

[PRIVILEGES AND IMMUNITIES, FUGITIVES]

The Citizens of each State shall be entitled to all Privileges and Immunities of Citizens in the several States.

80 (Hamilton)

A person charged in any State with Treason, Felony or other Crime, who shall flee from Justice, and be found in another State, shall on Demand of the executive Authority of the State from which he fled, be delivered up to be removed to the State having Jurisdiction of the Crime.

---

11 Modified by Eleventh Amendment.

No person held to Service or Labour in one State, under the Laws thereof, escaping into another, shall, in Consequence of any Law or Regulation therein, be discharged from such Service or Labour, but shall be delivered up on Claim of the Party to whom such Service or Labour may be due.[12]

Section 3
[ADMISSION OF NEW STATES]

43 (Madison)   New States may be admitted by the Congress into this Union; but no new State shall be formed or erected within the Jurisdiction of any other State; nor any State be formed by the Junction of two or more States, or Parts of States, without the Consent of the Legislatures of the States concerned as well as of the Congress.

43 (Madison)   The Congress shall have Power to dispose of and make all needful Rules and Regulations respecting the Territory or other Property belonging to the United States; and nothing in this Constitution shall be so construed as to Prejudice any Claims of the United States, or of any particular State.

Section 4
[GUARANTEE OF REPUBLICAN GOVERNMENT]

39, 43 (Madison)   The United States shall guarantee to every State in this Union a Republican Form of Government, and shall protect each of them against Invasion; and on Application of the Legislature, or of the Executive (when the Legislature cannot be convened) against domestic Violence.

ARTICLE V
[AMENDMENT OF THE CONSTITUTION]

39, 43 (Madison)
85 (Hamilton)   The Congress, whenever two-thirds of both Houses shall deem it necessary, shall propose Amendments to this Constitution, or, on the Application of the Legislatures of two-thirds of the several States, shall call a Convention for proposing Amendments, which, in either Case, shall be valid to all Intents and Purposes, as Part of this Constitution, when ratified by the Legislatures of three-fourths of the several States, or by Conventions in three-fourths thereof, as the one or the other Mode of Ratification may be proposed by the Congress; *Provided that no Amendment which may be made prior to the Year One thousand eight hundred and eight shall in any Manner affect the first and fourth Clauses in the Ninth Section of the first Article;*[13] and that no State, without its Consent, shall be deprived of its equal Suffrage in the Senate.

ARTICLE VI
[DEBTS, SUPREMACY, OATH]

43 (Madison)   All Debts contracted and Engagements entered into, before the Adoption of this Constitution, shall be as valid against the United States under this Constitution, as under the Confederation.

27, 33 (Hamilton)
39, 44 (Madison)   This Constitution, and the Laws of the United States which shall be made in Pursuance thereof; and all Treaties made, or which shall be made, under the Authority of the United States, shall be the supreme Law of the Land; and the Judges in every State shall be bound thereby, any Thing in the Constitution or Laws of any State to the Contrary notwithstanding.

---

12 Repealed by Thirteenth Amendment.

13 Temporary provision.

The Senators and Representatives before mentioned, and the Members of the several State Legislatures, and all executive and judicial Officers, both of the United States and of the several States, shall be bound by Oath or Affirmation, to support this Constitution; but no religious Test shall be required as a Qualification to any Office or public Trust under the United States.

27 (Hamilton)
44 (Madison)

ARTICLE VII
[RATIFICATION AND ESTABLISHMENT]

The Ratification of the Conventions of nine States, shall be sufficient for the Establishment of this Constitution between the States so ratifying the Same.[14]

39, 40, 43 (Madison)

Done in Convention by the Unanimous Consent of the States present the Seventeenth Day of September in the Year of our Lord one thousand seven hundred and Eighty seven and of the Independence of the United States of America the Twelfth. *In Witness* whereof We have hereunto subscribed our Names,

G:⁰ WASHINGTON—
*Presidt, and Deputy
from Virginia*

NEW HAMPSHIRE
John Langdon
Nicholas Gilman

MASSACHUSETTS
Nathaniel Gorham
Rufus King

CONNECTICUT
Wm Saml Johnson
Roger Sherman

NEW YORK
Alexander Hamilton

NEW JERSEY
Wil: Livingston
David Brearley
Wm Paterson
Jona: Dayton

PENNSYLVANIA
B Franklin
Thomas Mifflin
Robt Morris
Geo. Clymer
Thos. FitzSimons
Jared Ingersoll
James Wilson
Gouv Morris

DELAWARE
Geo Read
Gunning Bedfor Jun
John Dickinson
Richard Bassett
Jaco: Broom

MARYLAND
James McHenry
Dan of St Thos Jenifer
Danl Carroll

VIRGINIA
John Blair—
James Madison Jr.

NORTH CAROLINA
Wm Blount
Richd Dobbs Spaight
Hu Williamson

SOUTH CAROLINA
J. Rutledge
Charles Cotesworth
Pinckney
Charles Pinckney
Pierce Butler

GEORGIA
William Few
Abr Baldwin

---

14 The Constitution was submitted on September 17, 1787, by the Constitutional Convention, was ratified by the conventions of several states at various dates up to May 29, 1790, and became effective on March 4, 1789.

THE CONSTITUTION OF THE UNITED STATES OF AMERICA   A21

AMENDMENTS TO THE CONSTITUTION

PROPOSED BY CONGRESS AND RATIFIED BY THE LEGISLATURES OF THE SEVERAL STATES, PURSUANT TO ARTICLE V OF THE ORIGINAL CONSTITUTION

Amendments I–X, known as the Bill of Rights, were proposed by Congress on September 25, 1789, and ratified on December 15, 1791. *The Federalist Papers* comments, mainly in opposition to a Bill of Rights, can be found in number 84 (Hamilton).

AMENDMENT I
[FREEDOM OF RELIGION, OF SPEECH, AND OF THE PRESS]

Congress shall make no law respecting an establishment of religion, or prohibiting the free exercise thereof; or abridging the freedom of speech, or of the press; or the right of the people peaceably to assemble, and to petition the Government for a redress of grievances.

AMENDMENT II
[RIGHT TO KEEP AND BEAR ARMS]

A well regulated Militia, being necessary to the security of a free State, the right of the people to keep and bear Arms, shall not be infringed.

AMENDMENT III
[QUARTERING OF SOLDIERS]

No Soldier shall, in time of peace be quartered in any house, without the consent of the Owner, nor in time of war, but in a manner to be prescribed by law.

AMENDMENT IV
[SECURITY FROM UNWARRANTABLE SEARCH AND SEIZURE]

The right of the people to be secure in their persons, houses, papers, and effects, against unreasonable searches and seizures, shall not be violated, and no Warrants shall issue, but upon probable cause, supported by Oath or affirmation, and particularly describing the place to be searched, and the persons or things to be seized.

AMENDMENT V
[RIGHTS OF ACCUSED PERSONS IN CRIMINAL PROCEEDINGS]

No person shall be held to answer for a capital, or otherwise infamous crime, unless on a presentment or indictment of a Grand Jury, except in cases arising in the land or naval forces, or in the Militia, when in actual service in time of War or in public danger;

nor shall any person be subject for the same offence to be twice put in jeopardy of life or limb; nor shall be compelled in any Criminal Case to be a witness against himself, nor be deprived of life, liberty, or property, without due process of law; nor shall private property be taken for public use, without just compensation.

AMENDMENT VI
[RIGHT TO SPEEDY TRIAL, WITNESSES, ETC.]

In all criminal prosecutions, the accused shall enjoy the right to a speedy and public trial, by an impartial jury of the State and district wherein the crime shall have been committed, which district shall have been previously ascertained by law, and to be informed of the nature and cause of the accusation; to be confronted with the witnesses against him; to have compulsory process for obtaining Witnesses in his favor, and to have the Assistance of Counsel for his defence.

AMENDMENT VII
[TRIAL BY JURY IN CIVIL CASES]

In suits at common law, where the value in controversy shall exceed twenty dollars, the right of trial by jury shall be preserved, and no fact tried by a jury shall be otherwise re-examined in any Court of the United States, than according to the rules of the common law.

AMENDMENT VIII
[BAILS, FINES, PUNISHMENTS]

Excessive bail shall not be required, nor excessive fines imposed, nor cruel and unusual punishments inflicted.

AMENDMENT IX
[RESERVATION OF RIGHTS OF PEOPLE]

The enumeration in the Constitution, of certain rights, shall not be construed to deny or disparage others retained by the people.

AMENDMENT X
[POWERS RESERVED TO STATES OR PEOPLE]

The powers not delegated to the United States by the Constitution, nor prohibited by it to the States, are reserved to the States respectively, or to the people.

AMENDMENT XI
[Proposed by Congress on March 4, 1794; declared ratified on January 8, 1798]
[RESTRICTION OF JUDICIAL POWER]

The Judicial power of the United States shall not be construed to extend to any suit in law or equity, commenced or prosecuted against one of the United States by Citizens of another State, or by Citizens or Subjects of any Foreign State.

AMENDMENT XII
[Proposed by Congress on December 9, 1803; declared ratified on September 25, 1804.]
[ELECTION OF PRESIDENT AND VICE-PRESIDENT]

The Electors shall meet in their respective states, and vote by ballot for President and Vice-President, one of whom, at least, shall not be an inhabitant of the same state with themselves; they shall name in their ballots the person voted for as President, and in distinct ballots the person voted for as Vice-President, and they shall make distinct lists of all persons voted for as President, and of all persons voted for as Vice-President, and of the number of votes for each, which lists they shall sign and certify, and transmit sealed to the seat of the government of the United States, directed to the President of the Senate;—The President of the Senate shall, in presence of the Senate and House of Representatives, open all the certificates and the votes shall then be counted;—The person having the greatest number of votes for President, shall be the President, if such number be a majority of the whole number of Electors appointed; and if no person have such majority, then from the persons having the highest numbers not exceeding three on the list of those voted for as President, the House of Representatives shall choose immediately, by ballot, the President. But in choosing the President, the votes shall be taken by states, the representation from each state having one vote; a quorum for this purpose shall consist of a member or members from two-thirds of the states, and a majority of all states shall be necessary to a choice. And if the House of Representatives shall not choose a President whenever the right of choice shall devolve upon them, before the fourth day of March next following, then the Vice-President, shall act as President, as in the case of the death or other constitutional disability of the President. The person having the greatest number of votes as Vice-President, shall be the Vice-President, if such a number be a majority of the whole number of Electors appointed, and if no person have a majority, then from the two highest numbers on the list, the Senate shall choose the Vice-President; a quorum for the purpose shall consist of two-thirds of the whole number of Senators, and a majority of the whole number shall be necessary to a choice. But no person constitutionally ineligible to the office of President shall be eligible to that of Vice-President of the United States.

AMENDMENT XIII
[Proposed by Congress on January 31, 1865; declared ratified on December 18, 1865]

Section 1
[ABOLITION OF SLAVERY]

Neither slavery nor involuntary servitude, except as a punishment for crime whereof the party shall have been duly convicted, shall exist within the United States, or any place subject to their jurisdiction.

Section 2
[POWER TO ENFORCE THIS ARTICLE]

Congress shall have power to enforce this article by appropriate legislation.

AMENDMENT XIV
[Proposed by Congress on June 13, 1866; declared ratified on July 28, 1868]

Section 1
[CITIZENSHIP RIGHTS NOT TO BE ABRIDGED BY STATES]

All persons born or naturalized in the United States, and subject to the jurisdiction thereof, are citizens of the United States and of the State wherein they reside. No state shall make or enforce any law which shall abridge the privileges or immunities of citizens of the United States; nor shall any State deprive any person of life, liberty, or property, without due process of law; nor deny to any person within its jurisdiction the equal protection of the laws.

Section 2
[APPORTIONMENT OF REPRESENTATIVES IN CONGRESS]

Representatives shall be apportioned among the several States according to their respective numbers, counting the whole number of persons in each State, excluding Indians not taxed. But when the right to vote at any election for the choice of electors for President and Vice-President of the United States, Representatives in Congress, the Executive and Judicial officers of a State, or the members of the Legislature thereof, is denied to any of the male inhabitants of such State, being twenty-one years of age, and citizens of the United States, or in any way abridged, except for participation in rebellion, or other crime, the basis of representation therein shall be reduced in the proportion which the number of such male citizens shall bear to the whole number of male citizens twenty-one years of age in such State.

Section 3
[PERSONS DISQUALIFIED FROM HOLDING OFFICE]

No person shall be a Senator or Representative in Congress, or elector of President and Vice-President, or hold any office, civil or military, under the United States, or under any State, who, having previously taken an oath, as a member of Congress, or as an officer of the United States, or as a member of any State legislature, or as an executive or judicial officer of any State, to support the Constitution of the United States, shall have engaged in insurrection or rebellion against the same, or given aid or comfort to the enemies thereof. But Congress may by a vote of two-thirds of each House, remove such disability.

Section 4
[WHAT PUBLIC DEBTS ARE VALID]

The validity of the public debt of the United States, authorized by law, including debts incurred for payment of pensions and bounties for services in suppressing insurrection or rebellion, shall not be questioned. But neither the United States nor any State shall assume or pay any debt or obligation incurred in aid of insurrection or rebellion against the United States, or any claim for the loss or emancipation of any slave; but all such debts, obligations and claims shall be held illegal and void.

Section 5
[POWER TO ENFORCE THIS ARTICLE]

The Congress shall have power to enforce, by appropriate legislation, the provisions of this article.

AMENDMENT XV
[Proposed by Congress on February 26, 1869; declared ratified on March 30, 1870]

Section 1
[NEGRO SUFFRAGE]

The right of citizens of the United States to vote shall not be denied or abridged by the United States or by any State on account of race, color, or previous condition of servitude.

Section 2
[POWER TO ENFORCE THIS ARTICLE]

The Congress shall have power to enforce this article by appropriate legislation.

AMENDMENT XVI

[Proposed by Congress on July 12, 1909; declared ratified on February 25, 1913]

[AUTHORIZING INCOME TAXES]

The Congress shall have power to lay and collect taxes on incomes, from whatever source derived, without apportionment among the several States, and without regard to any census or enumeration.

AMENDMENT XVII

[Proposed by Congress on May 13, 1912; declared ratified on May 31, 1913]

[POPULAR ELECTION OF SENATORS]

The Senate of the United States shall be composed of two Senators from each State, elected by the people thereof, for six years; and each Senator shall have one vote. The electors in each State shall have the qualifications requisite for electors of the most numerous branch of the State Legislature.

When vacancies happen in the representation of any State in the Senate, the executive authority of such State shall issue writs of election to fill such vacancies: Provided, That the Legislature of any State may empower the executive thereof to make temporary appointment until the people fill the vacancies by election as the Legislature may direct.

This amendment shall not be so construed as to affect the election or term of any Senator chosen before it becomes valid as part of the Constitution.

AMENDMENT XVIII

[Proposed by Congress December 18, 1917; declared ratified on January 29, 1919]

Section 1

[NATIONAL LIQUOR PROHIBITION]

After one year from the ratification of this article the manufacture, sale, or transportation of intoxicating liquors within, the importation thereof into, or the exportation thereof from the United States and all territory subject to the jurisdiction thereof for beverage purposes is hereby prohibited.

Section 2

[POWER TO ENFORCE THIS ARTICLE]

The Congress and the several states shall have concurrent power to enforce this article by appropriate legislation.

Section 3

[RATIFICATION WITHIN SEVEN YEARS]

This article shall be inoperative unless it shall have been ratified as an amendment to the Constitution by the legislatures of the several states, as provided in the Constitution, within seven years from the date of the submission hereof to the states by the Congress.[15]

AMENDMENT XIX

[Proposed by Congress on June 4, 1919; declared ratified on August 26, 1920]

[WOMAN SUFFRAGE]

The right of the citizens of the United States to vote shall not be denied or abridged by the United States or by any state on account of sex.

Congress shall have power to enforce this article by appropriate legislation.

---

15 Repealed by Twenty-First Amendment.

AMENDMENT XX

[Proposed by Congress on March 2, 1932; declared ratified on February 6, 1933]

Section 1

[TERMS OF OFFICE]

The terms of the President and Vice-President shall end at noon on the 20th day of January, and the terms of the Senators and Representatives at noon on the 3rd day of January, of the years in which such terms would have ended if this article had not been ratified; and the terms of their successors shall then begin.

Section 2

[TIME OF CONVENING CONGRESS]

The Congress shall assemble at least once in every year, and such meeting shall begin at noon on the 3rd day of January, unless they shall by law appoint a different day.

Section 3

[DEATH OF PRESIDENT-ELECT]

If, at the time fixed for the beginning of the term of the President, the President-elect shall have died, the Vice-President-elect shall become President. If a President shall not have been chosen before the time fixed for the beginning of his term, or if the President-elect shall have failed to qualify, then the Vice-President-elect shall act as President until a President shall have qualified; and the Congress may by law provide for the case wherein neither a President-elect nor a Vice-President-elect shall have qualified, declaring who shall then act as President, or the manner in which one who is to act shall be selected, and such person shall act accordingly until a President or Vice President shall have qualified.

Section 4

[ELECTION OF THE PRESIDENT]

The Congress may by law provide for the case of the death of any of the persons from whom the House of Representatives may choose a President whenever the right of choice shall have devolved upon them, and for the case of the death of any of the persons from whom the Senate may choose a Vice-President whenever the right of choice shall have devolved upon them.

Section 5

[AMENDMENT TAKES EFFECT]

Sections 1 and 2 shall take effect on the 15th day of October following ratification of this article.

Section 6

[RATIFICATION WITHIN SEVEN YEARS]

This article shall be inoperative unless it shall have been ratified as an amendment to the Constitution by the legislatures of three-fourths of the several States within seven years from the date of its submission.

AMENDMENT XXI

[Proposed by Congress on February 20, 1933; declared ratified on December 5, 1933]

Section 1

[NATIONAL LIQUOR PROHIBITION REPEALED]

The eighteenth article of amendment to the Constitution of the United States is hereby repealed.

Section 2
[TRANSPORTATION OF LIQUOR INTO "DRY" STATES]

The transportation or importation into any State, Territory, or Possession of the United States for delivery or use therein of intoxicating liquors, in violation of the laws thereof, is hereby prohibited.

Section 3
[RATIFICATION WITHIN SEVEN YEARS]

This article shall be inoperative unless it shall have been ratified as an amendment to the Constitution by conventions in the several States, as provided in the Constitution, within seven years from the date of the submission hereof to the States by the Congress.

AMENDMENT XXII
[Proposed by Congress on March 21, 1947; declared ratified on February 26, 1951]

Section 1
[TENURE OF PRESIDENT LIMITED]

No person shall be elected to the office of President more than twice, and no person who has held the office of President or acted as President for more than two years of a term to which some other person was elected President shall be elected to the Office of the President more than once. But this Article shall not apply to any person holding the office of President when this Article was proposed by the Congress, and shall not prevent any person who may be holding the office of President, or acting as President, during the term within which this Article becomes operative from holding the office of President or acting as President during the remainder of such term.

Section 2
[RATIFICATION WITHIN SEVEN YEARS]

This Article shall be inoperative unless it shall have been ratified as an amendment to the Constitution by the legislatures of three-fourths of the several states within seven years from the date of its submission to the States by the Congress.

AMENDMENT XXIII
[Proposed by Congress on June 21, 1960; declared ratified on March 29, 1961]

Section 1
[ELECTORAL COLLEGE VOTES FOR THE DISTRICT OF COLUMBIA]

The District constituting the seat of Government of the United States shall appoint in such manner as the Congress may direct:

A number of electors of President and Vice-President equal to the whole number of Senators and Representatives in Congress to which the District would be entitled if it were a State, but in no event more than the least populous State; they shall be in addition to those appointed by the States, but they shall be considered, for the purposes of the election of President and Vice-President, to be electors appointed by a State; and they shall meet in the District and perform such duties as provided by the twelfth article of amendment.

Section 2
[POWER TO ENFORCE THIS ARTICLE]

The Congress shall have power to enforce this article by appropriate legislation.

AMENDMENT XXIV

[Proposed by Congress on August 27, 1963; declared ratified on January 23, 1964]

Section 1
[ANTI-POLL TAX]

The right of citizens of the United States to vote in any primary or other election for President or Vice-President, for electors for President or Vice-President, or for Senator or Representative of Congress, shall not be denied or abridged by the United States or any State by reasons of failure to pay any poll tax or other tax.

Section 2
[POWER TO ENFORCE THIS ARTICLE]

The Congress shall have power to enforce this article by appropriate legislation.

AMENDMENT XXV

[Proposed by Congress on July 7, 1965; declared ratified on February 10, 1967]

Section 1
[VICE-PRESIDENT TO BECOME PRESIDENT]

In case of the removal of the President from office or his death or resignation, the Vice-President shall become President.

Section 2
[CHOICE OF A NEW VICE-PRESIDENT]

Whenever there is a vacancy in the office of the Vice-President, the President shall nominate a Vice-President who shall take the office upon confirmation by a majority vote of both houses of Congress.

Section 3
[PRESIDENT MAY DECLARE OWN DISABILITY]

Whenever the President transmits to the President pro tempore of the Senate and the Speaker of the House of Representatives his written declaration that he is unable to discharge the powers and duties of his office, and until he transmits to them a written declaration to the contrary, such powers and duties shall be discharged by the Vice-President as Acting President.

Section 4
[ALTERNATE PROCEDURES TO DECLARE AND TO END PRESIDENTIAL DISABILITY]

Whenever the Vice-President and a majority of either the principal officers of the executive departments, or of such other body as Congress may by law provide, transmit to the President pro tempore of the Senate and the Speaker of the House of Representatives their written declaration that the President is unable to discharge the powers and duties of his office, the Vice-President shall immediately assume the powers and duties of the office as Acting President.

Thereafter, when the President transmits to the President pro tempore of the Senate and the Speaker of the House of Representatives his written declaration that no inability exists, he shall resume the powers and duties of his office unless the Vice-President and a majority of either the principal officers of the executive departments, or of such other body as Congress may by law provide, transmit within four days to the President pro tempore of the Senate and the Speaker of the House of Representatives their written declaration that the President is unable to discharge the powers and duties of his office. Thereupon Congress shall decide the issue, assembling within 48 hours for that purpose if not in session. If the Congress, within 21 days after receipt of the latter written declaration, or, if Congress is not in session, within 21 days after Congress is required to assemble, determines by two-thirds vote of both houses that the President is unable to discharge the powers and duties of his office, the Vice-President shall continue to discharge the same as Acting President; otherwise, the President shall resume the powers and duties of his office.

AMENDMENT XXVI

[Proposed by Congress on March 23, 1971; declared ratified on June 30, 1971]

Section 1

[EIGHTEEN-YEAR-OLD VOTE]

The right of citizens of the United States, who are eighteen years of age or older, to vote shall not be denied or abridged by the United States or by any State on account of age.

Section 2

[POWER TO ENFORCE THIS ARTICLE]

The Congress shall have power to enforce this article by appropriate legislation.

AMENDMENT XXVII

[Proposed by Congress on September 25, 1789; ratified on May 7, 1992]

No law varying the compensation for the services of the Senators and Representatives shall take effect until an election of Representatives shall have intervened.

FEDERALIST PAPERS

NO. 10: MADISON

Among the numerous advantages promised by a well-constructed Union, none deserves to be more accurately developed than its tendency to break and control the violence of faction. The friend of popular governments never finds himself so much alarmed for their character and fate as when he contemplates their propensity to this dangerous vice. He will not fail, therefore, to set a due value on any plan which, without violating the principles to which he is attached, provides a proper cure for it. The instability, injustice, and confusion introduced into the public councils have, in truth, been the mortal diseases under which popular governments have everywhere perished, as they continue to be the favorite and fruitful topics from which the adversaries to liberty derive their most specious declamations. The valuable improvements made by the American constitutions on the popular models, both ancient and modern, cannot certainly be too much admired; but it would be an unwarrantable partiality to contend that they have as effectually obviated the danger on this side, as was wished and expected. Complaints are everywhere heard from our most considerate and virtuous citizens, equally the friends of public and private faith and of public and personal liberty, that our governments are too unstable, that the public good is disregarded in the conflicts of rival parties, and that measures are too often decided, not according to the rules of justice and the rights of the minor party, but by the superior force of an interested and overbearing majority. However anxiously we may wish that these complaints had no foundation, the evidence of known facts will not permit us to deny that they are in some degree true. It will be found, indeed, on a candid review of our situation, that some of the distresses under which we labor have been erroneously charged on the operation of our governments; but it will be found, at the same time, that other causes will not alone account for many of our heaviest misfortunes; and, particularly, for that prevailing and increasing distrust of public engagements and alarm for private rights which are echoed from one end of the continent to the other. These must be chiefly, if not wholly, effects of the unsteadiness and injustice with which a factious spirit has tainted our public administration.

By a faction I understand a number of citizens, whether amounting to a majority or minority of the whole, who are united and actuated by some common impulse of passion, or of interest, adverse to the rights of other citizens, or to the permanent and aggregate interests of the community.

There are two methods of curing the mischiefs of faction: the one, by removing its causes; the other, by controlling its effects.

There are again two methods of removing the causes of faction: the one, by destroying the liberty which is essential to its existence; the other, by giving to every citizen the same opinions, the same passions, and the same interests.

It could never be more truly said than of the first remedy that it was worse than the disease. Liberty is to faction what air is to fire, an aliment without which it instantly expires. But it could not be a less folly to abolish liberty, which is essential to political life, because it nourishes faction than it would be to wish the annihilation of air, which is essential to animal life, because it imparts to fire its destructive agency.

The second expedient is as impracticable as the first would be unwise. As long as the reason of man continues fallible, and he is at liberty to exercise it, different opinions will be formed. As long as the connection subsists between his reason and his self-love, his opinions and his passions will have a reciprocal influence on each other; and the former will be objects to which the latter will attach themselves. The diversity in the faculties of men, from which the rights of property originate, is not less an insuperable obstacle to a uniformity of interests. The protection of these faculties is the first object of government. From the protection of different and unequal faculties of acquiring property, the possession of different degrees and kinds of property immediately results; and from the influence of these on the sentiments and views of the respective proprietors ensues a division of the society into different interests and parties.

The latent causes of faction are thus sown in the nature of man; and we see them everywhere brought into different degrees of activity, according to the different circumstances of civil society. A zeal for different opinions concerning religion, concerning government, and many other points, as well of speculation as of practice; an attachment to different leaders ambitiously contending for pre-eminence and power; or to persons of other descriptions whose fortunes have been interesting to the human passions, have, in turn, divided mankind into parties, inflamed them with mutual animosity, and rendered them much more disposed to vex and oppress each other than to co-operate for their common good. So strong is this propensity of mankind to fall into mutual animosities that where no substantial occasion presents itself the most frivolous and fanciful distinctions have been sufficient to kindle their unfriendly passions and excite their most violent conflicts. But the most common and durable source of factions has been the various and unequal distribution of property. Those who hold and those who are without property have ever formed distinct interests in society. Those who are creditors, and those who are debtors, fall under a like discrimination. A landed interest, a manufacturing interest, a mercantile interest, a moneyed interest, with many lesser interests, grow up of necessity in civilized nations, and divide them into different classes, actuated by different sentiments and views. The regulation of these various and interfering interests forms the principal task of modern legislation and involves the spirit of party and faction in the necessary and ordinary operations of government.

No man is allowed to be judge in his own cause, because his interest would certainly bias his judgment and, not improbably, corrupt his integrity. With equal, nay with greater reason, a body of men are unfit to be both judges and parties at the same time; yet what are many of the most important acts of legislation but so many judicial determinations, not indeed concerning the rights of single persons, but concerning the rights of large bodies of citizens? And what are the different classes of legislators but advocates and parties to the causes which they determine? Is a law proposed concerning private debts? It is a question to which the creditors are parties on one side and the debtors on the other. Justice ought to hold the balance between them. Yet the parties are, and must be, themselves the judges; and the most numerous party, or in other words, the most powerful faction must be expected to prevail. Shall domestic manufacturers be encouraged, and in what degree, by restrictions on foreign manufacturers? are questions which would be differently decided by the landed and the manufacturing classes, and probably by neither with a sole regard to justice and the public good. The apportionment of taxes on the various descriptions of property is an act which seems to require the most exact impartiality; yet there is, perhaps, no legislative act in which greater opportunity and temptation are given to a predominant party to trample on the rules of justice. Every shilling with which they overburden the inferior number is a shilling saved to their own pockets.

It is in vain to say that enlightened statesmen will be able to adjust these clashing interests and render them all subservient to the public good. Enlightened statesmen will not always be at the helm. Nor, in many cases, can such an adjustment be made at all without taking into view indirect and remote considerations, which will rarely prevail over the immediate interest which one party may find in disregarding the rights of another or the good of the whole.

The inference to which we are brought is that the *causes* of faction cannot be removed and that relief is only to be sought in the means of controlling its *effects*.

If a faction consists of less than a majority, relief is supplied by the republican principle, which enables the majority to defeat its sinister views by regular vote. It may clog the administration, it may convulse the society; but it will be unable to execute and mask its violence under the forms of the Constitution. When a majority is included in a faction, the form of popular government, on the other hand, enables it to sacrifice to its ruling passion or interest both the public good and the rights of other citizens. To secure the public good and private rights against the danger of such a faction, and at the same time to preserve the spirit and the form of popular government, is then the great object to which our inquiries are directed. Let me add that it is the great desideratum by which alone this form of government can be rescued from the opprobrium under which it has so long labored and be recommended to the esteem and adoption of mankind.

By what means is this object attainable? Evidently by one of two only. Either the existence of the same passion or interest in a majority at the same time must be prevented, or the majority, having such coexistent passion or interest, must be rendered, by their number and local situation, unable to concert and carry into effect schemes of oppression. If the impulse and the opportunity be suffered to coincide, we well know that neither moral nor religious motives can be relied on as an adequate control. They are not found to be such on the injustice and violence of individuals, and lose their efficacy in proportion to the number combined together, that is, in proportion as their efficacy becomes needful.

From this view of the subject it may be concluded that a pure democracy, by which I mean a society consisting of a small number of citizens, who assemble and administer the government in person, can admit of no cure for the mischiefs of faction. A common passion or interest will, in almost every case, be felt by a majority of the whole; a communication and concert results from the form of government itself; and there is nothing to check the inducements to sacrifice the weaker party or an obnoxious individual. Hence it is that such democracies have ever been spectacles of turbulence and contention; have ever been found incompatible with personal security or the rights of property; and have in general been as short in their lives as they have been violent in their deaths. Theoretic politicians, who have patronized this species of government, have erroneously supposed that by reducing mankind to a perfect equality in their political rights, they would at the same time be perfectly equalized and assimilated in their possessions, their opinions, and their passions.

A republic, by which I mean a government in which the scheme of representation takes place, opens a different prospect and promises the cure for which we are seeking. Let us examine the points in which it varies from pure democracy, and we shall comprehend both the nature of the cure and the efficacy which it must derive from the Union.

The two great points of difference between a democracy and a republic are: first, the delegation of the government, in the latter, to a small number of citizens elected by the rest; secondly, the greater number of citizens and greater sphere of country over which the latter may be extended.

The effect of the first difference is, on the one hand, to refine and enlarge the public views by passing them through the medium of a chosen body of citizens, whose wisdom may best discern the true interest of their country and whose patriotism and love of justice will be least likely to sacrifice it to temporary or partial considerations. Under such a regulation it may well happen that the public voice, pronounced by the representatives of the people, will be more consonant to the public good than if pronounced by the people themselves, convened for the purpose. On the other hand, the effect may be inverted. Men of factious tempers, of local prejudices, or of sinister designs, may, by intrigue, by corruption, or by other means, first obtain the suffrages, and then betray the interests of the people. The question resulting is, whether small or extensive republics are most favorable to the election of proper guardians of the public weal; and it is clearly decided in favor of the latter by two obvious considerations.

In the first place it is to be remarked that however small the republic may be the representatives must be raised to a certain number in order to guard against the cabals of a few; and that however large it may be they must be limited to a certain number in order to guard against the confusion of a multitude. Hence, the number of representatives in the two cases not being in proportion to that of the constituents, and being proportionally greatest in the small republic, it follows that if the proportion of fit characters be not less in the large than in the small republic, the former will present a greater option, and consequently a greater probability of a fit choice.

In the next place, as each representative will be chosen by a greater number of citizens in the large than in the small republic, it will be more difficult for unworthy candidates to practise with success the vicious arts by which elections are too often carried; and the suffrages of the people being more free, will be more likely to center on men who possess the most attractive merit and the most diffusive and established characters.

It must be confessed that in this, as in most other cases, there is a mean, on both sides of which inconveniencies will be found to lie. By enlarging too much the number of electors, you render the representative too little acquainted with all their local circumstances and lesser interests; as by reducing it too much, you render him unduly attached to these, and too little fit to comprehend and pursue great and national objects. The federal Constitution forms a happy combination in this respect; the great and aggregate interests being referred to the national, the local and particular to the State legislatures.

The other point of difference is the greater number of citizens and extent of territory which may be brought within the compass of republican than of democratic government; and it is this circumstance principally which renders factious combinations less to be dreaded in the former than in the latter. The smaller the society, the fewer probably will be the distinct parties and interests composing it; the fewer the distinct parties and interests, the more frequently will a majority be found of the same party; and the smaller the number of individuals composing a majority, and the smaller the compass within which they are placed, the more easily will they concert and execute their plans of oppression. Extend the sphere and you take in a greater variety of parties and interests; you make it less probable that a majority of the whole will have a common motive to invade the rights of other citizens; or if such a common motive exists, it will be more difficult for all who feel it to discover their own strength and to act in unison with each other. Besides other impediments, it may be remarked that, where there is a consciousness of unjust or dishonorable purposes, communication is always checked by distrust in proportion to the number whose concurrence is necessary.

Hence, it clearly appears that the same advantage which a republic has over a democracy in controlling the effects of faction is enjoyed by a large over a small republic—is enjoyed by the Union over the States composing it. Does this advantage consist in the substitution of representatives whose enlightened views and virtuous sentiments render them superior to local prejudices and to schemes of injustice? It will not be denied that the representation of the Union will be most likely to possess these requisite endowments. Does it consist in the greater security afforded by a greater variety of parties, against the event of any one party being able to outnumber and oppress the rest? In an equal degree does the increased variety of parties comprised within the Union increase this security? Does it, in fine, consist in the greater obstacles opposed to the concert and accomplishment of the secret wishes of an unjust and interested majority? Here again the extent of the Union gives it the most palpable advantage.

The influence of factious leaders may kindle a flame within their particular States but will be unable to spread a general conflagration through the other States. A religious sect may degenerate into a political faction in a part of the Confederacy; but the variety of sects dispersed over the entire face of it must secure the national councils against any danger from that source. A rage for paper money, for an abolition of debts, for an equal division of property, or for any other improper or wicked project, will be less apt to pervade the whole body of the Union than a particular member of it, in the same proportion as such a malady is more likely to taint a particular county or district than an entire State.

In the extent and proper structure of the Union, therefore, we behold a republican remedy for the diseases most incident to republican government. And according to the degree of pleasure and pride we feel in being republicans ought to be our zeal in cherishing the spirit and supporting the character of federalist.

PUBLIUS

NO. 51: MADISON

To what expedient, then, shall we finally resort, for maintaining in practice the necessary partition of power among the several departments as laid down in the Constitution? The only answer that can be given is that as all these exterior provisions are found to be inadequate the defect must be supplied, by so contriving the interior structure of the government as that its several constituent parts may, by their mutual relations, be the means of keeping each other in their proper places. Without presuming to undertake a full development of this important idea I will hazard a few general observations which may perhaps place it in a clearer light, and enable us to form a more correct judgment of the principles and structure of the government planned by the convention.

In order to lay a due foundation for that separate and distinct exercise of the different powers of government, which to a certain extent is admitted on all hands to be essential to the preservation of liberty, it is evident that each department should have a will of its own; and consequently should be so constituted that the members of each should have as little agency as possible in the appointment of the members of the others. Were this principle rigorously adhered to, it would require that all the appointments for the supreme executive, legislative, and judiciary magistracies should be drawn from the same fountain of authority, the people, through channels having no communication whatever with one another. Perhaps such a plan of constructing the several departments would be less difficult in practice than it may in contemplation appear. Some difficulties, however, and some additional expense would attend the execution of it. Some deviations, therefore, from the principle must be admitted. In the constitution of the judiciary department in particular, it might be inexpedient to insist rigorously on the principle: first, because peculiar qualifications being essential in the members, the primary consideration ought to be to select that mode of choice which best secures these qualifications; second, because the permanent tenure by which the appointments are held in that department must soon destroy all sense of dependence on the authority conferring them.

It is equally evident that the members of each department should be as little dependent as possible on those of the others for the emoluments annexed to their offices. Were the executive magistrate, or the judges, not independent of the legislature in this particular, their independence in every other would be merely nominal.

But the great security against a gradual concentration of the several powers in the same department consists in giving to those who administer each department the necessary constitutional means and personal motives to resist encroachments of the others. The provision for defense must in this, as in all other cases, be made commensurate to the danger of attack. Ambition must be made to counteract ambition. The interest of the man must be connected with the constitutional rights of the place. It may be a reflection on human nature that such devices should be necessary to control the abuses of government. But what is government itself but the greatest of all reflections on human nature? If men were angels, no government would be necessary. If angels were to govern men, neither external nor internal controls on government would be necessary. In framing a government which is to be administered by men over men, the great difficulty lies in this: you must first enable the government to control the governed; and in the next place oblige it to control itself. A dependence on the people is, no doubt, the primary control on the government; but experience has taught mankind the necessity of auxiliary precautions.

This policy of supplying, by opposite and rival interests, the defect of better motives, might be traced through the whole system of human affairs, private as well as public. We see it particularly displayed in all the subordinate distributions of power, where the constant aim is to divide and arrange the several offices in such a manner as that each may be a check on the other—that the private interest of every individual may be a sentinel over the public rights. These inventions of prudence cannot be less requisite in the distribution of the supreme powers of the State.

But it is not possible to give to each department an equal power of self-defense. In republican government, the legislative authority necessarily predominates. The remedy for this inconveniency is to divide the legislature into different branches; and to render them, by different modes of election and different principles of action, as little connected with each other as the nature of their common functions and their common dependence on the society will admit. It may even be necessary to guard against dangerous encroachments by still further precautions. As the weight of the legislative authority requires that it should be thus divided, the weakness of the executive may require, on the other hand, that it should be fortified. An absolute negative on the legislature appears, at first view, to be the natural defense with which the executive magistrate should be armed. But perhaps it would be neither altogether safe nor alone sufficient. On ordinary occasions it might not be exerted with the requisite firmness, and on extraordinary occasions it might be perfidiously abused. May not this defect of an absolute negative be supplied by some qualified connection between this weaker branch of the stronger department, by which the latter may be led to support the constitutional rights of the former, without being too much detached from the rights of its own department?

If the principles on which these observations are founded be just, as I persuade myself they are, and they be applied as a criterion to the several State constitutions, and to the federal Constitution, it will be found that if the latter does not perfectly correspond with them, the former are infinitely less able to bear such a test.

There are, moreover, two considerations particularly applicable to the federal system of America, which place that system in a very interesting point of view.

First, In a single republic, all the power surrendered by the people is submitted to the administration of a single government; and the usurpations are guarded against by a division of the government into distinct and separate departments. In the compound republic of America, the power surrendered by the people is first divided between two distinct governments, and then the portion allotted to each subdivided among distinct and separate departments. Hence a double security arises to the rights of the people. The different governments will control each other, at the same time that each will be controlled by itself.

Second. It is of great importance in a republic not only to guard the society against the oppression of its rulers, but to guard one part of the society against the injustice of the other part. Different interests necessarily exist in different classes of citizens. If a majority be united by a common interest, the rights of the minority will be insecure. There are but two methods of providing against this evil: the one by creating a will in the community independent of the majority— that is, of the society itself; the other, by comprehending in the society so many separate descriptions of citizens as will render an unjust combination of a majority of the whole very improbable, if not impracticable. The first method prevails in all governments possessing an hereditary or self-appointed authority. This, at best, is but a precarious security; because a power independent of the society may as well espouse the unjust views of the major as the rightful interests of the minor party, and may possibly be turned against both parties. The second method will be exemplified in the federal republic of the United States. Whilst all authority in it will be derived from and dependent on the society, the society itself will be broken into so many parts, interests and classes of citizens, that the rights of individuals, or of the minority, will be in little danger from interested combinations of the majority. In a free government the security for civil rights must be the same as that for religious rights. It consists in the one case in the multiplicity of interests, and in the other in the multiplicity of sects. The degree of security in both cases will depend on the number of interests and sects; and this may be presumed to depend on the extent of country and number of people comprehended under the same government. This view of the subject must particularly recommend a proper federal system to all the sincere and considerate friends of republican government, since it shows that in exact proportion as the territory of the Union may be formed into more circumscribed Confederacies, or States, oppressive combinations of a majority will be facilitated; the best security, under the republican forms, for the rights of every class of citizen, will be diminished; and consequently the stability and independence of some member of the government, the only other security, must be proportionally increased. Justice is the end of government. It is the end of civil society. It ever has been and ever will be pursued until it be obtained, or until liberty be lost in the pursuit. In a society under the forms of which the stronger faction can readily unite and oppress the weaker, anarchy may as truly be said to reign as in a state of nature, where the weaker individual is not secured against the violence of the stronger; and as, in the latter state, even the stronger individuals are prompted, by the uncertainty of their condition, to submit to a government which may protect the weak as well as themselves; so, in the former state, will the more powerful factions or parties be gradually induced, by a like motive, to wish for a government which will protect all parties, the weaker as well as the more powerful. It can be little doubted that if the State of Rhode Island was separated from the Confederacy and left to itself, the insecurity of rights under the popular form of government within such narrow limits would be displayed by such reiterated oppressions of factious majorities that some power altogether independent of the people would soon be called for by the voice of the very factions whose misrule had proved the necessity of it. In the extended republic of the United States, and among the great variety of interests, parties, and sects which it embraces, a coalition of a majority of the whole society could seldom take place on any other principles than those of justice and the general good; whilst there being thus less danger to a minor from the will of a major party, there must be less pretext, also, to provide for the security of the former, by introducing into the government a will not dependent on the latter, or, in other words, a will independent of the society itself. It is no less certain than it is important, notwithstanding the contrary opinions which have been entertained, that the larger the society, provided it lie within a practicable sphere, the more duly capable it will be of self-government. And happily for the *republican cause,* the practicable sphere may be carried to a very great extent by a judicious modification and mixture of the *federal principle.*

PUBLIUS

ENDNOTES

CHAPTER 1

1 Thomas Hobbes, *Leviathan, or The Matter, Forme and Power of a Commonwealth, Ecclesiasticall and Civil* (1651; repr., New York: Macmillan, 1947), p. 82.

2 John Locke, *Second Treatise of Government* (New York: Dover, 2002).

3 Harold Lasswell, *Politics: Who Gets What, When, How* (New York: Meridian, 1958).

4 Asher Schechter, "Study: Politicians Vote against the Will of Their Constituents 35 Percent of the Time," *ProMarket* (blog), June 16, 2017, https://promarket.org /study-politicians-vote-will-constituents-35-percent-time.

CHAPTER 2

1 The social makeup of colonial America and some of the social conflicts that divided colonial society are discussed in Jackson Turner Main, *The Social Structure of Revolutionary America* (Princeton, NJ: Princeton University Press, 1965).

2 See Carl Becker, *The Declaration of Independence* (New York: Vintage, 1942).

3 See Merrill Jensen, *The Articles of Confederation* (Madison: University of Wisconsin Press, 1963).

4 There is no verbatim record of the debates, but James Madison's notes are included in Max Farrand, ed., *The Records of the Federal Convention of 1787*, rev. ed., 4 vols. (New Haven, CT: Yale University Press, 1966).

5 *Federalist*, no. 70 (Alexander Hamilton).

6 Max Farrand, *The Framing of the Constitution of the United States* (New Haven, CT: Yale University Press, 1962), p. 49.

7 Richard E. Neustadt, *Presidential Power: The Politics of Leadership* (New York: Wiley, 1960), p. 33.

8 For an excellent analysis of the ratification campaigns, see William H. Riker, *The Strategy of Rhetoric: Campaigning for the American Constitution* (New Haven, CT: Yale University Press, 1996).

9 *Federalist*, esp. nos. 10 and 51 (James Madison).

10 The Fourteenth Amendment is included in Table 2.2, as well as in Tables 2.3 and 2.4, because it seeks not only to define citizenship but seems to intend also that this definition of citizenship included, along with the right to vote, all the rights of the Bill of Rights, regardless of the state in which the citizen resided. A great deal more is said about this in Chapter 4.

CHAPTER 3

1 For a good treatment of these conflicts of interests between states, see Forrest McDonald, *E Pluribus Unum—The Formation of the American Republic, 1776–1790* (Boston: Houghton Mifflin, 1965), chap. 7, esp. pp. 319–38.

2 See David O'Brien, *Constitutional Law and Politics* (New York: Norton, 1997), vol. 1, pp. 602–3.

3 *V.L. v. E.L.*, 577 U.S. __ (2016)

4 *Hicklin v. Orbeck*, 437 U.S. 518 (1978).

5 *Sweeny v. Woodall*, 344 U.S. 86 (1953).

6 Patricia S. Florestano, "Past and Present Utilization of Interstate Compacts in the United States," *Publius* 24 (Fall 1994): 13–26.

7 A good discussion of the constitutional position of local governments is in York Y. Willbern, *The Withering Away of the City* (Bloomington: Indiana University Press, 1971). For more on the structure and theory of federalism, see Thomas R. Dye, *American Federalism: Competition among Governments* (Lexington, MA: Lexington Books, 1990), chap. 1; and Martha Derthick, "Up-to-Date in Kansas City: Reflections on American Federalism," *PS: Political Science & Politics* 25 (December 1992): 671–5.

8 *McCulloch v. Maryland*, 4 Wheaton 316 (1819).

9 *Gibbons v. Ogden*, 9 Wheaton 1 (1824).

10 In *Wabash, St. Louis, and Pacific Railway Company v. Illinois*, 118 U.S. 557 (1886), the Supreme Court struck down a state law prohibiting rate discrimination by a railroad. In response, Congress passed the Interstate Commerce Act of 1887, creating the Interstate Commerce Commission (ICC), the first federal regulatory agency.

11 *Hammer v. Dagenhart*, 247 U.S. 251 (1918).

12 *National Labor Relations Board v. Jones & Laughlin Steel Corporation*, 301 U.S. 1 (1937).

13 *Wickard v. Filburn*, 317 U.S. 111 (1942).

14 Kenneth T. Palmer, "The Evolution of Grant Policies," in *The Changing Politics of Federal Grants*, by Lawrence D. Brown, James W. Fossett, and Kenneth T. Palmer (Washington, DC: Brookings Institution, 1984), p. 15.

15 Palmer, "Evolution of Grant Policies," p. 6.

16 *South Dakota v. Dole*, 483 U.S. 203; Brian T. Yeh, "The Federal Government's Authority to Impose Conditions on Grant Funds," Congressional Research Service, 2017.

17 Congressional Research Service, "Unfunded Mandates Reform Act: History, Impact and Issues," 2017.

18 Morton Grodzins, "The Federal System," in *Goals for Americans: The President's Commission on National Goals* (Englewood Cliffs, NJ: Prentice Hall, 1960), p. 265.

19 The concept and the best discussion of this modern phenomenon can be found in Donald F. Kettl, *The Regulation of American Federalism* (Baltimore: Johns Hopkins University Press, 1987), esp. pp. 33–41.

20 See John Dilulio, Jr., and Donald F. Kettl, *Fine Print: The Contract with America, Devolution, and the Administrative Realities of American Federalism* (Washington, DC: Brookings Institution, 1995), p. 41.

21 Paul Posner, "Unfunded Mandate Reform: How Is It Working?" *Rockefeller Institute Bulletin*, 1998, p. 35.

22 *King v. Burwell*, 576 U.S. __ (2015).

23 S.A. Miller, "Trump to Pull Feds Out of K-12 Education," *Washington Times*, April 26, 2017. https://www.washingtontimes.com/news/2017/apr/26/donald-trump-pull-feds-out-k-12-education/.

24 *King v. Burwell*, 576 U.S. __ (2015).

25 *United States v. Lopez*, 514 U.S. 549 (1995).

26 *Printz v. United States*, 521 U.S. 898 (1997); *Mack v. United States*, 117 S. Ct. 2365 (1997).

27 *Gonzales v. Oregon*, 546 U.S. 243 (2006).

28 *Arizona v. United States*, 567 U.S. 387 (2012).

29 *Arizona et al. v. Inter Tribal Council of Arizona, Inc.*, 570 U.S. __ (2013).

30 *Alabama Legislative Black Caucus v. Alabama*, 575 U.S. __ (2015); *Arizona State Legislature v. Arizona Independent Redistricting Commission*, 576 U.S. __ (2015).

31 *Seminole Indian Tribe v. Florida*, 517 U.S. 44 (1996).

32 *Murphy v. NCAA*, 584 U.S. __ (2018).

33 *Rucho v. Common Cause*, 18–422 (2019).

34 Clinton L. Rossiter, ed., *The Federalist Papers; Alexander Hamilton, James Madison, and John Jay* (New York: New American Library, 1961), no. 47 (James Madison), p. 302.

35 Rossiter, *Federalist Papers*, no. 48 (James Madison), p. 308.

36 Richard E. Neustadt, *Presidential Power: The Politics of Leadership* (New York: Wiley, 1960), p. 33.

37 *Marbury v. Madison*, 1 Cranch 137 (1803).

38 C. Herman Pritchett, *The American Constitution* (New York: McGraw-Hill, 1959), pp. 180–86.

39 *Immigration and Naturalization Service v. Chadha*, 462 U.S. 919 (1983).

40 Cass R. Sunstein, "Taking Over the Courts," *New York Times*, November 9, 2002, p. A19.

41 Sunstein, "Taking Over the Courts."

42 *Youngstown Sheet & Tube Co. v. Sawyer*, 343 U.S. 579 (1952).

43 *United States v. Nixon*, 418 U.S. 683 (1974).

44 *Department of Commerce v. New York*, 18–966 (2019).

45 For a good evaluation of divided government, see David Mayhew, *Divided We Govern: Party Control, Law Making and Investigations, 1946–1990* (New Haven, CT: Yale University Press, 1991). See also Charles O. Jones, *Separate but Equal Branches—Congress and the Presidency* (Chatham, NJ: Chatham House, 1995).

CHAPTER 4

1 "From Thomas Jefferson to James Madison, 20 December 1787," *Founders Online*, National Archives, https://founders.archives.gov/documents/Jefferson/01-12-02-0454.

2 For a spirited and enlightening essay on the extent to which the entire Bill of Rights was about equality, see Martha Minow, "Equality and the Bill of Rights," in *The Constitution of Rights: Human Dignity and American Values*, ed. Michael J. Meyer and William A. Parent, pp. 118–28 (Ithaca, NY: Cornell University Press, 1992).

3 *Barron v. Mayor and City of Baltimore*, 32 U.S. 243 (1833).

4 The Fourteenth Amendment also seems designed to introduce civil rights. The final clause of the all-important Section 1 provides that no state can "deny to any person within its jurisdiction the equal protection of the laws." It is not unreasonable to conclude that the purpose of this provision was to obligate state governments, as well as the national government, to take *positive* actions to protect citizens from arbitrary and discriminatory actions, at least those based on race. This question will be explored in the second half of the chapter.

5 *Slaughter-House Cases*, 16 Wallace 36 (1873); *Civil Rights Cases*, 109 U.S. 3 (1883).

6 *Chicago, Burlington and Quincy Railroad Company v. Chicago*, 166 U.S. 266 (1897).

7 *Gitlow v. New York*, 268 U.S. 652 (1925).

8 *Near v. Minnesota*, 283 U.S. 697 (1931); *Hague v. C.I.O.*, 307 U.S. 496 (1939).

9 All of these were implicitly identified in *Palko v. Connecticut*, 302 U.S. 319 (1937), as "not incorporated" into the Fourteenth Amendment as limitations on the powers of the states.

10 *Brown v. Board of Education of Topeka, Kansas*, 347 U.S. 483 (1954).

11 The one exception was the right to public trial (Sixth Amendment), but a 1948 case (*In re Oliver*, 33 U.S. 257) did not actually mention the right to public trial as such; this right was cited in a 1968 case (*Duncan v. Louisiana*, 391 U.S. 145) as a precedent establishing the right to public trial as part of the Fourteenth Amendment.

12 *Gideon v. Wainwright*, 372 U.S. 335 (1963); Anthony Lewis, *Gideon's Trumpet* (New York: Random House, 1964).

13 *Mapp v. Ohio*, 367 U.S. 643 (1961).

14 *Miranda v. Arizona*, 384 U.S. 436 (1966).

15 *Benton v. Maryland*, 395 U.S. 784 (1969).

16 *NAACP v. Alabama ex rel. Patterson*, 357 U.S. 449 (1958).

17 This section is taken from Benjamin Ginsberg, Theodore J. Lowi, Margaret Weir, and Caroline J. Tolbert, *We the People: An Introduction to American Politics*, 9th ed. (New York: Norton, 2013).

18 For a lively and readable treatment of the possibilities of restricting provisions of the Bill of Rights without actually reversing prior decisions, see David G. Savage, *Turning Right: The Making of the Rehnquist Supreme Court* (New York: Wiley, 1992).

19 *Abington School District v. Schempp*, 374 U.S. 203 (1963).

20 *Engel v. Vitale*, 370 U.S. 421 (1962).

21 *Wallace v. Jaffree*, 472 U.S. 38 (1985).

22 *Town of Greece v. Galloway*, 52 U.S. __ (2014).

23 *Lemon v. Kurtzman*, 403 U.S. 602 (1971).

24 *Elk Grove Unified School District v. Newdow*, 542 U.S. 1 (2004).

25 *Van Orden v. Perry*, 545 U.S. 677 (2005).

26 *McCreary v. ACLU*, 545 U.S. 844 (2005).

27 *The American Legion v. American Humanist Association*, 588 U.S. __ (2019).

28 *Cantwell v. Connecticut*, 310 U.S. 296 (1940).

29 *Reynolds v. U.S.*, 98 U.S. 145 (1878).

30 *Holt v. Hobbs*, 574 U.S. __ (2015).

31 *Equal Employment Opportunity Commission v. Abercrombie & Fitch Stores*, 575 U.S. __ (2015).

32 *Burwell v. Hobby Lobby*, 573 U.S. __ (2014).

33 *Masterpiece Cake Shop v. Colorado Civil Rights Commission*, 584 U.S. __ (2018).

34 *United States v. Carolene Products Company*, 304 U.S. 144 (1938). This footnote is one of the Court's most important doctrines. See Alfred H. Kelly, Winfred A. Harbison, and Herman Belz, *The American Constitution: Its Origins and Development*, 7th ed. (New York: Norton, 1991), vol. 2, pp. 519–23.

35 *Snyder v. Phelps*, 562 U.S. 443 (2011).

36 *Brandenburg v. Ohio*, 395 U.S. 444 (1969).

37 *Buckley v. Valeo*, 424 U.S. 1 (1976).

38 *McConnell v. Federal Election Commission*, 540 U.S. 93 (2003).

39 *Federal Election Commission v. Wisconsin Right to Life*, 551 U.S. 449 (2007).

40 *Citizens United v. Federal Election Commission*, 558 U.S. 310 (2010).

41 *United States v. O'Brien*, 391 U.S. 367 (1968).

42 *Texas v. Johnson*, 491 U.S. 397 (1989).

43 *Virginia v. Black*, 538 U.S. 343 (2003).

44 *Near v. Minnesota* (1931).

45 *Reno v. ACLU*, 521 U.S. 844 (1997).

46 *United States v. American Library Association*, 539 U.S. 194 (2003).

47 *United States v. Williams*, 553 U.S. 285 (2008).

48 *Tinker v. Des Moines Independent School District*, 393 U.S. 503 (1969).

49 *Bethel School District No. 403 v. Fraser*, 478 U.S. 675 (1986).

50 *Hazelwood School District v. Kuhlmeier*, 484 U.S. 260 (1988).

51 *Morse v. Frederick*, 551 U.S. 393 (2007).

52 *Meritor Savings Bank v. Vinson*, 477 U.S. 57 (1986).

53 *Chaplinsky v. State of New Hampshire*, 315 U.S. 568 (1942).

54 *R.A.V. v. City of St. Paul*, 506 U.S. 377 (1992).

55 *Capital Broadcasting Company v. Acting Attorney General*, 405 U.S. 1000 (1972).

56 Louis Fisher, *American Constitutional Law*, 7th ed. (Durham, NC: Academic Press, 2007), vol. 2, p. 546.

57 *Lorillard Tobacco v. Reilly*, 533 U.S. 525 (2001).

58 *District of Columbia v. Heller*, 554 U.S. 570 (2008).

59 *McDonald v. Chicago*, 561 U.S. 3025 (2010).

60 *Horton v. California*, 496 U.S. 128 (1990).

61 For a full account of the story of the trial and release of Clarence Earl Gideon, see Lewis, *Gideon's Trumpet*.

62 *Escobedo v. Illinois*, 378 U.S. 478 (1964).

63 *Wiggins v. Smith*, 539 U.S. 510 (2003).

64 *Miller v. Alabama*, 567 U.S. 460 (2012).

65 *Furman v. Georgia*, 408 U.S. 238 (1972).

66 *Griswold v. Connecticut*, 381 U.S. 479 (1965).

67 *Roe v. Wade*, 410 U.S. 113 (1973).

68 *Webster v. Reproductive Health Services*, 492 U.S. 490 (1989), which upheld a Missouri law that restricted the use of public medical facilities for abortion. The decision opened the way for other states to limit the availability of abortion.

69 *Planned Parenthood v. Casey*, 505 U.S. 833 (1992).

70 *Stenberg v. Carhart*, 530 U.S. 914 (2000).

71 *Gonzales v. Carhart*, 550 U.S. 124 (2007).

72 *June Medical Services v. Russo* 18–1323, 591 U.S. __ (2020).

73 *Bowers v. Hardwick*, 478 U.S. 186 (1986). The dissenters were quoting an earlier case, *Olmstead v. United States*, 277 U.S. 438 (1928), to emphasize the nature of their disagreement with the majority in the *Bowers* case.

74   *Lawrence and Garner v. Texas*, 539 U.S. 558 (2003).

75   *United States v. Jones*, 565 U.S. 400 (2012).

76   *Maryland v. King*, 569 U.S. __ (2013).

77   Wikisource, s.v. "Woman Suffrage," *Collier's New Encyclopedia* (1921), http://en.Wikisource.org/wiki /Collier%27s_New_Encyclopedia_%281921%29 /Woman_suffrage.

78   V. O. Key, *Southern Politics in State and Nation* (New York: Knopf, 1949).

79   Bernard Taper, *Gomillion v. Lightfoot: The Tuskegee Gerrymander Case* (New York: McGraw-Hill, 1962).

80   *Smith v. Allwright*, 321 U.S. 649 (1944).

81   *Gomillion v. Lightfoot*, 364 U.S. 339 (1960).

82   *Shelby County v. Holder*, 570 U.S. 529 (2013).

83   *Plessy v. Ferguson*, 163 U.S. 537 (1896).

84   *Missouri ex rel. Gaines v. Canada*, 305 U.S. 337 (1938).

85   *Sweatt v. Painter*, 339 U.S. 629 (1950).

86   *Smith v. Allwright*, 321 U.S. 649 (1944).

87   *Shelley v. Kraemer*, 334 U.S. 1 (1948).

88   *Brown v. Board of Education* (1954).

89   For example, *Griffin v. Prince Edward County School Board*, 337 U.S. 218 (1964), forced all the schools of that Virginia county to reopen after five years of being closed to avoid desegregation.

90   *Swann v. Charlotte-Mecklenberg Board of Education*, 402 U.S. 1 (1971).

91   For a good evaluation, see Gary Orfield, *Must We Bus? Segregated Schools and National Policy* (Washington, DC: Brookings Institution, 1978), pp. 144–46. See also Bob Woodward and Scott Armstrong, *The Brethren: Inside the Supreme Court* (New York: Simon & Schuster, 1979), pp. 426–27; and J. Anthony Lukas, *Common Ground* (New York: Random House, 1986).

92   *Parents Involved in Community Schools v. Seattle School District No. 1*, 551 U.S. 701 (2007).

93   *Franklin v. Gwinnett County Public Schools*, 503 U.S. 60 (1992).

94   Jennifer Halperin, "Women Step Up to Bat," *Illinois Issue* 21 (September 1995): 11–14.

95   See especially *Katzenbach v. McClung*, 379 U.S. 294 (1964).

96   *Griggs v. Duke Power Company*, 401 U.S. 24 (1971).

97   *Ledbetter v. Goodyear Tire and Rubber Co.*, 550 U.S. 618 (2007).

98   This and the next five sections are drawn in part from Ginsberg et al., *We the People*.

99   See Jane J. Mansbridge, *Why We Lost the ERA* (Chicago: University of Chicago Press, 1986); and Gilbert Steiner, *Constitutional Inequality* (Washington, DC: Brookings Institution, 1985).

100 See *Frontiero v. Richardson*, 411 U.S. 677 (1973).

101 See *Craig v. Boren*, 423 U.S. 1047 (1976).

102 *Meritor Savings Bank v. Vinson*, 477 U.S. 57 (1986).

103 *Harris v. Forklift Systems*, 510 U.S. 17 (1993).

104 *Burlington Industries v. Ellerth*, 524 U.S. 742 (1998); *Faragher v. City of Boca Raton*, 524 U.S. 775 (1998).

105 Claire Zillman, "Barnes & Noble Is Latest Retailer to Face Transgender Discrimination Lawsuit," *Fortune*, May 7, 2015, http://fortune.com/2015/05/07 /barnes-noble-transgender-lawsuit.

106 New Mexico had a different history because not many Anglos settled there initially. (*Anglo* is the term for a non-Hispanic White of European background.) Mexican Americans had considerable power in territorial legislatures between 1865 and 1912. See Lawrence H. Fuchs, *The American Kaleidoscope* (Hanover, NH: University Press of New England, 1990), pp. 239–40.

107 *Mendez v. Westminster*, 161 F2d 744 (Ninth Cir., 1947).

108 On the La Raza Unida Party, see Carlos Muñoz, Jr., and Mario Barrera, "La Raza Unida Party and the Chicano Student Movement in California," in *Latinos and the Political System*, ed. F. Chris Garcia, pp. 213–35 (Notre Dame, IN: University of Notre Dame Press, 1988).

109 *United States v. Wong Kim Ark*, 169 U.S. 649 (1898).

110 *Lau v. Nichols*, 414 U.S. 563 (1974).

111 Dick Kirschten, "Not Black and White," *National Journal*, March 2, 1991, p. 497.

112 See the discussion in Robert A. Katzmann, *Institutional Disability: The Saga of Transportation Policy for the Disabled* (Washington, DC: Brookings Institution, 1986).

113 For example, after pressure from the Justice Department, one of the nation's largest car rental companies agreed to make special hand controls available to any customer requesting them. See "Avis Agrees to Equip Cars for Disabled," *Los Angeles Times*, September 2, 1994, p. D1.

114 *Romer v. Evans*, 517 U.S. 620 (1996).

115 *United States v. Windsor*, 570 U.S. 744 (2013). That same day, the Court also cleared the way for the legalization of same-sex marriage in California in the case *Hollingsworth v. Perry*, 570 U.S. 639 (2013).

116 *Obergefell v. Hodges*, 576 U.S. __ (2015).

117 *Regents of the University of California v. Bakke*, 438 U.S. 265 (1978).

118 *United Steelworkers of America v. Weber*, 443 U.S. 193 (1979); *Fullilove v. Klutznick*, 448 U.S. 448 (1980).

119 *Martin v. Wilks*, 490 U.S. 755 (1989).

120 *Adarand Constructors, Inc. v. Pena*, 515 U.S. 200 (1995).

121 *Hopwood v. State of Texas*, 78 F3d 932 (Fifth Cir., 1996).

122 *Gratz v. Bollinger*, 539 U.S. 244 (2003).

123 *Grutter v. Bollinger*, 539 U.S. 306 (2003).

124 *Fisher v. University of Texas*, 579 U.S. __ (2016).

CHAPTER 5

1 The classic treatment is Richard F. Fenno, Jr., *Home Style: House Members in Their Districts* (Boston: Little, Brown, 1978). A more recent examination is Daniel M. Butler and David W. Nickerson, "Can Learning Constituency Opinion Affect How Legislators Vote? Results from a Field Experiment," *Quarterly Journal of Political Science* 6 (1) (2011): 55–83.

2 For more on political careers generally, see John R. Hibbing, "Legislative Careers: Why and How We Should Study Them," *Legislative Studies Quarterly* 24 (1999): 149–71. See also Cherie D. Maestas, Sarah Fulton, L. Sandy Maisel, and Walter J. Stone, "When to Risk It? Institutions, Ambitions, and the Decision to Run for the U.S. House," *American Political Science Review* 100, no. 2 (May 2006): 195–208.

3 Constituents are not a legislative agent's only principals. Agents may also be beholden to party leaders and special interests, as well as to members and committees in the chamber. On this, see Forrest Maltzman, *Competing Principals* (Ann Arbor: University of Michigan Press, 1997). For a more general consideration, see David R. Mayhew, *Congress: The Electoral Connection* (New Haven: Yale University Press, 1974).

4 For historical background, see Linda L. Fowler and Robert D. McClure, *Political Ambition: Who Decides to Run for Congress* (New Haven, CT: Yale University Press, 1989); and Alan Ehrenhalt, *The United States of Ambition: Politicians, Power, and the Pursuit of Office* (New York: Times Books, 1991). A more recent treatment is Danielle M. Thomsen, "Ideological Moderates Won't Run: How Party Fit Matters for Partisan Polarization in Congress," *Journal of Politics* 76 (3) (2014): 786–797. We await the new work that will bring into focus the great success of women candidates in the 2018 elections.

5 On the thesis of "strategic candidacy," see Gary C. Jacobson and Jamie L. Carson, *The Politics of Congressional Elections*, 9th ed. (New York: Pearson Longman, 2016).

6 See Diana Evans, *Greasing the Wheels: Using Pork-Barrel Projects to Build Majority Coalitions in Congress* (New York: Cambridge University Press, 2004); and Steven J. Balla, Eric D. Lawrence, Forrest Maltzman, and Lee Sigelman, "Partisanship, Blame Avoidance, and the Distribution of Legislative Pork," *American Journal of Political Science* 46 (3)(2002): 515–525. However, recent research has shown the limitations placed on benefits of committees for acquiring the pork for their constituents: Christopher R. Berry and Anthony Fowler, 2016. "Cardinals or Clerics? Congressional Committees and the Distribution of Pork," *American Journal of Political Science* 60 (3) (2016): 692–708.

7 See John Hudak, "Congress in 2019: Why the First Branch Should Bring Back Earmarks," https://www.brookings.edu/blog/fixgov/2018/12/27/congress-in-2019-why-the-first-branch-should-bring-back-earmarks/ (December 27, 2018).

8 Norman J. Ornstein, Thomas E. Mann, and Michael J. Malbin, *Vital Statistics on Congress, 1995–1996* (Washington, DC: CQ Press, 1996), pp. 60–61 (see also subsequent editions); Robert S. Erikson and Gerald C. Wright, "Voters, Candidates, and Issues in Congressional Elections," in *Congress Reconsidered*, ed. Lawrence C. Dodd and Bruce I. Oppenheimer, 5th ed. (Washington, DC: CQ Press, 1993), p. 99; John R. Alford and David W. Brady, "Personal and Partisan Advantage in U.S. Congressional Elections, 1846–1990," in *Congress Reconsidered*, ed. Dodd and Oppenheimer, pp. 141–57. For 1997–2018, see the Center for Responsive Politics, www.opensecrets.org (accessed 11/10/18). Recent research shows a decrease in the incumbency advantage since the late 1990s, however: Gary C. Jacobson, "It's Nothing Personal: The Decline of the Incumbency Advantage in US House Elections," *The Journal of Politics* 77, no. 3 (July 2015): 861–873.

9 Stephen Ansolabehere and James Snyder, "Campaign War Chests and Congressional Elections," *Business and Politics*, no. 2 (2000): 9–34.

10 Gary W. Cox and Eric Magar, "How Much Is Majority Status in the U.S. Congress Worth?" *American Political Science Review* 93, no. 2 (June 1999): 299–309.

11 Kenneth Bickers and Robert Stein, "The Electoral Dynamics of the Federal Pork Barrel," *American Journal of Political Science* 40 (1996): 1300–1326; and Pamela Ban, Elena Llaudet, and James M. Snyder Jr., "Challenger Quality and the Incumbency Advantage," *Legislative Studies Quarterly* 41(1) (2016).

12 Richard L. Fox, "Congressional Elections: Where Are We on the Road to Gender Parity?" in *Gender and Elections*, eds. Susan J. Carroll and Richard L. Fox, pp. 97–116 (New York: Cambridge University Press, 2006). There was a major uptick in women running for Congress in 2018, and succeeding, in part as a response to the 2017 Women's March on Washington.

13 It should be noted that the incumbency advantage, though still a factor for all the reasons just given, has eroded. It is now back to levels not seen since the mid-1960s, a response to the nationalization and polarization of politics. This argument is developed in Gary C. Jacobson, "It's Nothing Personal: The Decline of the Incumbency Advantage in US House Elections," *Journal of Politics* (2015).

14 In a 5–4 decision the Supreme Court ruled in its 2018–19 term that redistricting involving even extreme partisan gerrymandering cannot be reversed through judicial remediation (unless an issue of racial discrimination is involved). The Court left it to the state legislatures to oversee the redistricting process.

15 See John H. Aldrich, *Why Parties? The Origin and Transformation of Political Parties in America* (Chicago: University of Chicago Press, 1995); John H. Aldrich, *Why Parties? A Second Look* (Chicago: University of Chicago Press, 2011); and Gary W. Cox and Mathew D. McCubbins, *Legislative Leviathan: Party Government in the House* (Berkeley: University of California Press, 1993).

16 For some legislation, a CBO "score" is required before the legislation may be taken up by the House or Senate.

17 A member introduces a bill not only in the hope it becomes law, but also in order to burnish his or her reputation as a policy specialist and to claim credit from relevant constituents and interest groups for fighting their fight. A member may know a bill has no chance of passage but introduces it anyway for these alternate purposes. It is no surprise, therefore, that many bills are hopeless exercises and die in committee.

18 In recent years the conference procedure has fallen into relative disuse, reserved mainly for major bills. Instead, party leaders in each chamber themselves negotiate a compromise between House and Senate versions and bring this to their respective chambers for final passage votes.

19 John Gilmour, *Strategic Disagreement* (Pittsburgh: University of Pittsburgh Press, 1995).

20 See Kenneth W. Kollman, *Outside Lobbying: Public Opinion and Interest Group Strategies* (Princeton, NJ: Princeton University Press, 1998).

21 See Janet M. Grenke, "PACs and the Congressional Supermarket: The Currency Is Complex," *American Journal of Political Science* 33, no. 1 (February 1989): 1–24. More generally, see Jacobson, *Politics of Congressional Elections*. See also Stephen Ansolabehere, John M. de Figueiredo, and James M. Snyder, Jr., "Why Is There So Little Money in U.S. Politics?" *Journal of Economic Perspectives* 17, no. 1 (Winter 2003): 105–30.

22 See Sven E. Feldmann and Morten Bennedsen, "Informational Lobbying and Political Contributions," *Journal of Public Economics* 90 (2006): 631–56.

23 An analysis of how floor time is allocated is found in Gary W. Cox and Mathew D. McCubbins, *Setting the Agenda: Responsible Party Government in the U.S. House of Representatives* (New York: Cambridge University Press, 2005).

24 The structure of the whip system varies—over time, between chambers, and between parties. See Barbara Sinclair, *Unorthodox Lawmaking: New Legislative Processes in the US Congress* (Washington, DC: CQ Press, 2017).

25 *United States v. Pink*, 315 U.S. 203 (1942). For a good discussion of the problem, see James W. Davis, *The American Presidency* (New York: Harper & Row, 1987), chap. 8.

CHAPTER 6

1 *In re Neagle*, 135 U.S. 1 (1890).

2 James G. Randall, *Constitutional Problems under Lincoln* (New York: Appleton, 1926), chap. 1.

3 Edward S. Corwin, *The President: Office and Powers*, 4th rev. ed. (New York: New York University Press, 1957), p. 229.

4 These statutes are contained mainly in Title 10 of the U.S. Code, Sections 331, 332, and 333.

5 In *United States v. Pink*, 315 U.S. 203 (1942), the Supreme Court ruled that an executive agreement is the legal equivalent of a treaty, despite the absence of Senate approval.

6 *United States v. Nixon*, 418 U.S. 683 (1974).

7 *Clinton v. City of New York*, 524 U.S. 417 (1998).

8 Charles M. Cameron, *Veto Bargaining: Presidents and the Politics of Negative Power* (New York: Cambridge University Press, 2000). See also David W. Rohde and Dennis Simon, "Presidential Vetoes and Congressional Response: A Study of Institutional Conflict," *American Journal of Political Science* 29 (1985): 397–427.

9 Theodore J. Lowi, *The Personal President: Power Invested, Promise Unfulfilled* (Ithaca, NY: Cornell University Press, 1985).

10 Timothy Groseclose and Nolan McCarty, "The Politics of Blame: Bargaining before an Audience," *American Journal of Political Science* 45 (2001): 100–119.

11 Richard Neustadt, *Presidential Power: The Politics of Leadership* (New York: Wiley, 1960).

12 For related appraisals, see Jeffrey Tulis, *The Rhetorical Presidency* (Princeton, NJ: Princeton University Press, 1988); Stephen Skowronek, *The Politics Presidents Make: Presidential Leadership from John Adams to George Bush* (Cambridge, MA: Harvard University Press, 1993); and Robert Spitzer, *President and Congress: Executive Hegemony at the Crossroads of American Government* (New York: McGraw-Hill, 1993).

13 *National Labor Relations Board v. Jones & Laughlin Steel Corporation*, 301 U.S. 1 (1937).

14 See George Krause, "The Secular Decline in Presidential Domestic Policymaking: An Organizational Perspective," *Presidential Studies Quarterly* 34 (2004): 779–92. On the general issue, see James P. Pfiffner, ed., *The Managerial Presidency*, 2nd ed. (College Station: Texas A&M University Press, 1999).

15 Article I, Section 3, provides that the vice president "shall be President of the Senate, but shall have no Vote, unless they be equally divided."

16 Sidney M. Milkis, *The President and the Parties* (New York: Oxford University Press, 1993), p. 97.

17 Samuel Kernell, *Going Public: New Strategies of Presidential Leadership*, 3rd ed. (Washington, DC: CQ Press, 1997), p. 79.

18 Lowi, *Personal President*.

19 The classic critique of this process is Theodore J. Lowi, *The End of Liberalism*, 2nd ed. (New York: Norton, 1979).

20 Kenneth Culp Davis, *Administrative Law Treatise* (St. Paul, MN: West, 1958), p. 9.

21 Elena Kagan, "Presidential Administration," *Harvard Law Review* 114 (2001): 2265.

22 For example, Douglas W. Kmiec, "Expanding Power," in *The Rule of Law in the Wake of Clinton*, ed. Roger

Pilon, pp. 47–68 (Washington, DC: Cato Institute Press, 2000).

23 A complete inventory is provided in Harold C. Relyea, *Presidential Directives: Background and Review*, CRS Report for Congress no. 98–611 (Washington, DC: Congressional Research Service, 2001).

24 *Youngstown Sheet & Tube Co. v. Sawyer*, 343 U.S. 579 (1952).

25 See Avalon Zoppo, Amanda Proença Santos, and Jackson Hodgins, "Here's the Full List of Donald Trump's Executive Orders," NBC News, October 17, 2017, www.nbcnews.com/politics/white-house /here-s-full-list-donald-trump-s-executive-orders -n720796 (accessed 4/24/20).

26 Mark Killenbeck, "A Matter of Mere Approval: The Role of the President in the Creation of Legislative History," *University of Arkansas Law Review* 48 (1995): 239.

27 Philip J. Cooper, *By Order of the President: The Use and Abuse of Executive Direct Action* (Lawrence: University Press of Kansas, 1998), p. 201.

28 Cooper, *By Order of the President*, p. 201.

29 *Ameron, Inc. v. U.S. Army Corps of Engineers*, 610 F. Supp. 750 (D.N.J. 1985).

30 *Lear Siegler, Inc. v. Lehman*, 842 F. 2nd 1102 (1988).

31 Kristy Carroll, "Whose Statute Is It Anyway? Why and How Courts Should Use Presidential Signing Statements When Interpreting Federal Statutes," *Catholic University Law Review* 46 (1997): 475. For a comprehensive list of presidential signing statements, see Presidential Signing Statements, 2001–present, http://www.coherentbabble.com/listDJTall.htm (accessed 4/20/20).

CHAPTER 7

1 When bureaucrats engage in interpretation, the result is what political scientists call "bureaucratic drift." Bureaucratic drift occurs because, as we've suggested, the "bosses" (in Congress) and the "agents" (within the bureaucracy) don't always share the same purpose.

2 Nadja Popovich, "95 Environmental Rules Being Rolled Back Under Trump." *New York Times*, December 21, 2019, https://www.nytimes.com/interactive/2019 /climate/trump-environment-rollbacks.html (accessed 4/20/20).

3 See Mathew D. McCubbins and Thomas Schwartz, "Congressional Oversight Overlooked: Police Patrols versus Fire Alarms," *American Journal of Political Science* 28 (1984): 165–79.

4 Establishment of the US Department of Commerce and Labor, 15 USC 1501 (1903).

5 For a detailed account of the creation of the Department of Commerce and Labor and its split into two separate departments, see Theodore J. Lowi, *The End of Liberalism*, 2nd ed. (New York: Norton, 1979), pp. 78–84.

6 Until 1979, the Department of Education and the Department of Health and Human Services were joined in a single department, the Department of Health, Education, and Welfare (HEW), which was established by Congress in 1953.

7 Internal Revenue Service, "IRS Budget and Workforce," March 19, 2020, https://www.irs.gov/statistics/irs -budget-and-workforce (accessed 4/20/20).

8 Transportation Security Administration, "FactSheet: TSA by the Numbers," February 4, 2020, https://www .tsa.gov/sites/default/files/resources/tsabythenumbers _factsheet.pdf (accessed 4/20/20).

9 Clinton L. Rossiter, ed., *The Federalist Papers; Alexander Hamilton, James Madison, and John Jay* (New York: New American Library, 1961), no. 47 (James Madison).

10 William A. Niskanen, *Bureaucracy and Representative Government* (Chicago: Aldine, 1971).

11 John Brehm and Scott Gates, *Working, Shirking, and Sabotage: Bureaucratic Response to a Democratic Public* (Ann Arbor: University of Michigan Press, 1997). For detailed insight about the motivations for government service combining the personal and the patriotic, consider the case of Henry Paulson, who became George W. Bush's treasury secretary. Paulson's story is described well in Andrew Ross Sorkin, *Too Big to Fail* (New York: Viking, 2009), chap. 2.

12 For an expanded view of bureaucratic autonomy and insulation with historical application to the U.S. Department of Agriculture and the Post Office Department (predecessor of the U.S. Postal Service), see Daniel P. Carpenter, *The Forging of Bureaucratic Autonomy: Reputations, Networks, and Policy Innovation in Executive Agencies, 1862–1928* (Princeton, NJ: Princeton University Press, 2001).

13 See John Micklethwait, "Managing to Look Attractive," *New Statesman*, November 8, 1996, p. 24.

14 See Aaron Wildavsky, *The New Politics of the Budgetary Process*, 2nd ed. (New York: HarperCollins, 1992), pp. 15–16.

15 Morris S. Ogul, *Congress Oversees the Bureaucracy: Studies in Legislative Supervision* (Pittsburgh: University of Pittsburgh Press, 1976); and Peter Woll, *American Bureaucracy*, 2nd ed. (New York: Norton, 1977).

16 See McCubbins and Schwartz, "Congressional Oversight Overlooked."

17 Public Law 101-510, Title XXIX, Sections 2,901 and 2,902 of Part A (Defense Base Closure and Realignment Commission).

CHAPTER 8

1 For example, the Court split 5-4 in a 2018 decision that made permanent the Court's 2017 temporary ruling allowing President Trump's travel ban. But the story does not even end there: in 2020 the Court of Appeals for the 4th Circuit heard new arguments on the constitutionality of the ban.

2 Max Bloom, "The Supreme Court Still Knows How to Find a Consensus," *National Review*, June 29, 2017, www.nationalreview.com/article/449088/unanimous-supreme-court-decisions-are-more-common-you-think (accessed 4/19/20).

3 The administration of President Trump, possibly more than any other in the history of the Republic, has pushed the envelope on judicial independence both by intervening in the management of justice by the U.S. Department of Justice and by insulating Trump and others in his administration from legal probes by the federal courts.

4 Federal Judicial Center. Also see https://en.wikipedia.org/wiki/List_of_current_United_States_district_judges (accessed 4/27/20) and https://en.wikipedia.org/wiki/List_of_current_United_States_circuit_judges (accessed 4/27/20).

5 Carl Hulse, "McConnell Has a Request for Veteran Federal Judges: Please Quit." *New York Times*, March 16, 2020, www.nytimes.com/2020/03/16/us/politics/mcconnell-judges-republicans.html (accessed 4/19/20).

6 C. Herman Pritchett, *The American Constitution* (New York: McGraw-Hill, 1959), p. 138.

7 *Marbury v. Madison*, 1 Cranch 137 (1803).

8 For an analysis of the Court's use of judicial review to nullify acts of Congress, see Ryan Emenaker, "Constitutional Interpretation and Congressional Overrides: Changing Trends in Court–Congress Relations" (paper, Annual Meeting of the Western Political Science Association, Hollywood, CA, March 28–30, 2013). For comprehensive information on invalidated laws, see Constitution Annotated: Analysis and Interpretation of the U.S. Constitution, "Table of Laws Held Unconstitutional in Whole or in Part by the Supreme Court." https://constitution.congress.gov/resources/unconstitutional-laws/ (accessed 4/19/20).

9 *Shelby County v. Holder*, 570 U.S. 2 (2013).

10 This review power was affirmed by the Supreme Court in *Martin v. Hunter's Lessees*, 1 Wheaton 304 (1816).

11 *Brown v. Board of Education of Topeka, Kansas*, 347 U.S. 483 (1954).

12 *Loving v. Virginia*, 388 U.S. 1 (1967).

13 *Obergefell v. Hodges* 576 U.S. __ (2015).

14 Pub. L. No. 421, 77th Cong. 2d Sess. (January 30, 1942).

15 *Chevron v. Natural Resources Defense Council*, 467 U.S. 837 (1984).

16 *Hamdi v. Rumsfeld*, 542 U.S. 507 (2004).

17 *Hamdan v. Rumsfeld*, 548 U.S. 557 (2006).

18 *United States v. Texas*, 579 U.S. __ (2016).

19 Walter F. Murphy, "The Supreme Court of the United States," in *Encyclopedia of the American Judicial System*, ed. Robert J. Janosik (New York: Scribner's, 1987).

20 *Roe v. Wade*, 410 U.S. 113 (1973).

21 Gregory A. Caldeira and John R. Wright, "Organized Interests and Agenda Setting in the U.S. Supreme Court," *American Political Science Review* 82 (1988): 1109–27.

22 *Adarand Constructors, Inc. v. Peña*, 515 U.S. 200 (1995); *Missouri v. Jenkins*, 515 U.S. 70 (1995); *Miller v. Johnson*, 515 U.S. 900 (1995).

23 Mark Joseph Stern, "The Supreme Court Looks Poised to Block Obama's Immigration Actions Indefinitely," *Slate*, April 18, 2016, https://slate.com/news-and-politics/2016/04/texas-v-united-states-supreme-court-could-block-obamas-immigration-executive-actions.html (accessed 4/27/20).

24 *Smith v. Allwright*, 321 U.S. 649 (1944).

25 *National Federation of Independent Business v. Sebelius*, 567 U.S. 519 (2012). Also see Adam Liptak, "Supreme Court Upholds Health Care Law, 5–4, in Victory for Obama," *New York Times*, June 28, 2012, www.nytimes.com/2012/06/29/us/supreme-court-lets-health-law-largely-stand.html (accessed 4/27/20).

26 *King v. Burwell*, 576 U.S. 988 (2015).

27 C. Herman Pritchett, *The Roosevelt Court* (New York: Macmillan, 1948).

28 William N. Eskridge, Jr., "Overriding Supreme Court Statutory Interpretation Decisions," *Yale Law Journal* 101 (1991): 331–55.

29 A full strategic analysis of the maneuvering among the legislative, executive, and judicial branches in the separation-of-powers arrangement choreographed by the U.S. Constitution may be found in William N. Eskridge, Jr., and John Ferejohn, "The Article 1, Section 7 Game," *Georgetown Law Review* 80 (1992): 523–65.

30 See "Developments in the Law: Class Actions," *Harvard Law Review* 89 (1976): 1318.

31 See Donald Horowitz, *The Courts and Social Policy* (Washington, DC: Brookings Institution, 1977).

32 David Van Drehle, "Court That Liberals Savage Proves to Be Less of a Target," *Washington Post*, June 29, 2003, p. A18.

CHAPTER 9

1 Maggie Haberman and Annie Karni, "Polls Had Trump Stewing, and Lashing Out at His Own Campaign," *New York Times*, April 29, 2020, www.nytimes.com/2020/04/29/us/politics/trump-campaign-reelection-polls.html (accessed 5/28/20).

2 Alan D. Monroe, "Consistency between Public Preferences and National Policy Decisions," *American Politics Quarterly 7* (1979): 3–19. Subsequent research has found similarly high degrees of agreement between public opinion and policy decisions. See Stuart N. Soroka and Christopher Wlezien, *Degrees of Democracy: Politics, Public Opinion, and Policy* (New York: Cambridge University Press, 2009).

3 Carol Glynn, Susan Herbst, Garret O'Keefe, Robert Shapiro, et al., *Public Opinion*, 2nd ed. (Boulder, CO: Westview, 2004), p. 293.

4 Lawrence R. Jacobs and Robert Y. Shapiro, *Politicians Don't Pander* (Chicago: University of Chicago Press, 2000), p. xv.

5 Dick Morris, *Behind the Oval Office* (Los Angeles: Renaissance, 1999), quoted in Jacobs and Shapiro, *Politicians Don't Pander*, p. xv.

6 See Louis Hartz, *The Liberal Tradition in America: An Interpretation of American Political Thought Since the Revolution* (New York: Harcourt, Brace, 1955).

7 Richard Wike, Katie Simmons, Bruce Stokes, and Janell Fetterolf, "Globally, Broad Support for Representative and Direct Democracy," *Pew Research Center*, October 2017, www.pewglobal.org/2017/10/16/democracy -widely-supported-little-backing-for-rule-by-strong -leader-or-military/pg_2017-10-16_global-democracy _2-01 (accessed 5/28/20).

8 Klint Finley, "Apps Make Pestering Congress So Easy That Politicians Can't Keep Up," *Wired*, January 29, 2017, www.wired.com/2017/01/apps-make-pestering -congress-easy-cant-keep/ (accessed 5/28/20).

9 The American Values Survey is available at www .people-press.org/values-questions (accessed 6/10/20).

10 Rawi Abdelal, Yoshiko M. Herrera, Alastair Iain Johnston, and Rose McDermott, "Identity as a Variable," *Perspectives on Politics* 4, no. 4 (2006): 695–711.

11 Angus Campbell, Philip E. Converse, Warren E. Miller, and Donald E. Stokes, *The American Voter* (New York: Wiley, 1960).

12 United States Census, "Quick Facts," www.census.gov /quickfacts/fact/table/US (accessed 6/24/20).

13 Pew Research Center, "The Black and White of Public Opinion," October 31, 2005, www.people-press .org/2005/10/31/the-black-and-white-of-public -opinion/ (accessed 5/28/20).

14 Pew Research Center, "Wide Partisan Differences over the Issues That Matter in 2014," September 12, 2014, www.people-press.org/2014/09/12/wide -partisan-differences-over-the-issues-that-matter -in-2014/ (accessed 5/28/20).

15 Gabriel R. Sanchez, "The Role of Group Consciousness in Latino Public Opinion," *Political Research Quarterly* 59, no. 3 (2006): 435–46; Pamela Johnston Conover, "The Influence of Group Identifications on Political Perception and Evaluation," *Journal of Politics* 46, no. 3 (1984): 760–85.

16 Taeku Lee, "Race, Immigration, and the Identity-to-Politics Link," *Annual Review of Political Science* 11 (2008): 457–78.

17 Computed by the authors from the 2016 Cooperative Congressional Election Study. Stephen Ansolabehere and Brian F. Schaffner, 2017, "CCES Common Content, 2016," https://doi.org/10.7910/DVN/GDF6Z0 (accessed 6/12/20).

18 Computed by the authors from the 2018 Cooperative Congressional Election Study. Brian Schaffner, Stephen Ansolabehere, and Samantha Luks, 2019, "CCES Common Content, 2018," https://doi.org/10.7910 /DVN/ZSBZ7K (accessed 6/12/20).

19 Jennifer C. Lee and Samuel Kye, "Racialized Assimilation of Asian Americans," *Annual Review of Sociology* 24 (2016): 253–73.

20 For data, see Center for American Women and Politics, Eagleton Institute of Politics, Rutgers, State University of New Jersey, www.cawp.rutgers.edu/facts/voters /turnout (accessed 5/28/20).

21 Pew Research Center, "Public Opinion on Abortion: Views on Abortion, 1995–2019," August 29, 2019, www .pewforum.org/fact-sheet/public-opinion-on-abortion (accessed 5/28/20).

22 See Ebonya Washington, "Female Socialization: How Daughters Affect Their Legislator Fathers' Voting on Women's Issues," *American Economic Review* 98 (2008): 311–32.

23 Campbell et al., *American Voter*.

24 Rene R. Rocha and Rodolfo Espino, "Racial Threat, Residential Segregation, and the Policy Attitudes of Anglos," *Political Research Quarterly* 62, no. 2 (2009): 415–26.

25 James Sidanius, *Social Dominance: An Intergroup Theory of Social Hierarchy and Oppression* (Cambridge University Press, 1999). Being a numerical majority is not necessary. For over a century, blacks in South Africa were oppressed by Afrikaners, even though the white population accounted for only about 10 percent of all people in the country.

26 Michael C. Dawson, *Behind the Mule: Race and Class in African-American Politics* (Princeton, NJ: Princeton University Press, 1995).

27 Philip E. Converse, "The Nature of Belief Systems in Mass Publics," in *Ideology and Discontent*, ed. David E. Apter (New York: Free Press, 1964).

28 Anthony Downs, *An Economic Theory of Democracy* (New York: Harper & Row, 1957).

29 For a discussion of the role of information in democratic politics, see Arthur Lupia and Mathew D. McCubbins, *The Democratic Dilemma: Can Citizens Learn What They Need to Know?* (New York: Cambridge University Press, 1998).

30 Pew Research Center, "Attitudes on Gay Marriage," May 14, 2019, www.pewforum.org/fact-sheet/changing -attitudes-on-gay-marriage (accessed 5/28/20).

31 Joshua Green, "The Other War Room," *Washington Monthly*, April 2002.

32 Michael Calderone, "White House News Strategy Causes Concerns about Access," February 15, 2011, http://news.yahoo.com/s/yblog_thecutline/20110215 /bs_yblog_thecutline/white -house-media-strategy -causes-concerns-about -access (accessed 5/28/20).

33 Emily Glazer, "Presidential Candidates Take to Social Media," *Wall Street Journal*, December 19, 2019, www .wsj.com/articles/presidential-candidates-take-to -social-media-11574942401 (accessed 5/28/20).

34 Jeff Greenfield, "How Coronavirus Will Blow Up the 2020 Campaign," Politico, April 12, 2020, www.politico.com/news/magazine/2020/04/12/coronavirus-2020-campaign-178487 (accessed 5/28/20).

35 Sabrina Tavernise, "'The Time Is Now': States Are Rushing to Restrict Abortion, or to Protect It," New York Times, May 15, 2019, www.nytimes.com/2019/05/15/us/abortion-laws-2019.html (accessed 5/28/20).

36 Cynthia Gorney, "Gambling with Abortion," Harper's Magazine, November 2004, pp. 33–46.

37 See David Vogel, "The Power of Business in America: A Reappraisal," British Journal of Political Science 13 (January 1983): 19–44.

38 See David Vogel, "The Public Interest Movement and the American Reform Tradition," Political Science Quarterly 96 (Winter 1980): 607–27.

39 See Stephen Ansolabehere, Roy Behr, and Shanto Iyengar, The Media Game (New York: Macmillan, 1993).

40 Monica Anderson, Andrew Perrin, Jingjing Jiang, and Madhumitha Kumar, "10% of Americans Don't Use the Internet. Who Are They?," Pew Research Center, April 22, 2019, www.pewresearch.org/fact-tank/2019/04/22/some-americans-dont-use-the-internet-who-are-they/ (accessed 5/28/20).

41 Michael Barthel, "Newspapers Fact Sheet," in State of the News Media 2015, Pew Research Center, April 2015, pp. 24–31, www.journalism.org/2015/04/29/newspapers-fact-sheet (accessed 5/28/20).

42 "The 10 Most Endangered Newspapers in America," Time, March 9, 2009, http://content.time.com/time/business/article/0,8599,1883785,00.html (accessed 6/12/20).

43 Jeffrey Gottfried and Elisa Shearer, "News Use across Social Media Platforms 2016," Pew Research Center, May 26, 2016, www.journalism.org/2016/05/26/news-use-across-social-media-platforms-2016 (accessed 5/28/20).

44 Sarah Perez, "Twitter Launches a COVID-19 Data Set for Tweets for Approved Developers and Researchers," Techcrunch, April 29, 2020, https://techcrunch.com/2020/04/29/twitter-launches-a-covid-19-dataset-of-tweets-for-approved-developers-and-researchers/ (accessed 5/28/20).

45 Near v. Minnesota, 283 U.S. 697 (1931).

46 See Matthew Baum, Soft News Goes to War (Princeton, NJ: Princeton University Press, 2006).

47 Bente Kalsnes and Anders Olof Larsson, "Understanding News Sharing across Social Media," Journalism Studies 19 (2018): 1669–1688.

48 The seminal work on priming and framing in public policy and politics is Shanto Iyengar and Donald Kinder, News That Matters (Chicago: University of Chicago Press, 1987).

49 Benjamin I. Page and Robert Y. Shapiro, "Effects of Public Opinion on Policy," American Political Science Review 77, no. 1 (March 1983): 175–90.

50 Robert S. Erikson, Gerald C. Wright, and John P. McIver, Statehouse Democracy: Public Opinion and Democracy in the American States (New York: Cambridge University Press, 1994).

51 The results of separate studies by the political scientists Lawrence Jacobs, Robert Shapiro, and Alan Monroe were reported in Richard Morin, "Which Comes First, the Politician or the Poll?" Washington Post National Weekly Edition, February 10, 1997, p. 35.

CHAPTER 10

1 Edward Earle, ed., The Federalist (New York: Random House, 1954), no. 48 (Alexander Hamilton), p. 442.

2 In addition, there is the restriction that those currently serving sentences for felonies cannot vote; some states also prohibit ex-felons from voting.

3 Some states have further restrictions that prohibit ex-felons from voting and impose residency requirements.

4 Drew Desilver, "U.S. Trails Most Developed Countries in Voter Turnout," Pew Research Center, May 21, 2018, www.pewresearch.org/fact-tank/2018/05/21/u-s-voter-turnout-trails-most-developed-countries/ (accessed 5/26/20).

5 Sidney Verba, Kay Lehman Schlozman, and Henry E. Brady, Voice and Equality: Civic Voluntarism in America (Cambridge, MA: Harvard University Press, 1995).

6 See Walter Dean Burnham, "The Changing Shape of the American Political Universe," American Political Science Review 59, no. 1 (March 1965): 7–28. It should be noted that other democracies, such as India and Switzerland, have even lower turnout rates, as do some of the new democracies in eastern Europe.

7 See statistics of the U.S. Census Bureau and the Federal Election Commission. For voting statistics covering 1960–2014, see Infoplease, "National Voter Turnout in Federal Elections: 1960–2004," www.infoplease.com/ipa/A0781453.html (accessed 5/28/20).

8 Thom File, Voting in America: A Look at the 2016 Presidential Election, Census Bureau Report, May 10, 2017, www.census.gov/newsroom/blogs/random-samplings/2017/05/voting_in_america.html (accessed 5/28/20).

9 Not all states report such figures in their certified tally of the vote. In fact, 11 states do not report the number of ballots cast, and researchers must substitute the total votes for all candidates for the presidency or another office on the top of the ballot. Since nearly all voters who turn out do vote on the races at the top of the ticket, counting those totals is a reasonably accurate substitute for official turnout records.

10 These figures exclude undocumented immigrants, which are estimated to make up another 12 million people.

11 The United States Elections Project estimates the number of disenfranchised felons in the United States to be 3.1 million. See "2018 November General Election Turnout Rates," December 14, 2018, http://www.electproject.org/2018g. The Sentencing Project puts that figure at 6.1 million people. See Christopher

Uggen, Ryan Larson, and Sarah Shannon, "6 Million Lost Voters: State-Level Estimates of Felony Disenfranchisement, 2016," October 6, 20116, https://www.sentencingproject.org/publications/6-million-lost-voters-state-level-estimates-felony-disenfranchisement-2016/ (accessed 6/12/20).

12 Helen Dewar, "'Motor Voter' Agreement Is Reached," *Washington Post*, April 28, 1993, p. A6.

13 Stephen Ansolabehere and Eitan Hersh, "Validation: What Big Data Reveal about Survey Misreporting and the Real Electorate," *Political Analysis* 20, no. 4 (Autumn 2012): 437–59.

14 National Conference of State Legislatures, "Same Day Voter Registration." June 28, 2019, www.ncsl.org/research/elections-and-campaigns/same-day-registration.aspx (accessed 5/28/20).

15 National Conference of State Legislatures, "Automatic Voter Registration," April 14, 2020, www.ncsl.org/research/elections-and-campaigns/automatic-voter-registration.aspx (accessed 5/28/20).

16 Nathaniel Persily and Stephen Ansolabehere, "Vote Fraud in the Eye of the Beholder," *Harvard Law Review* 121 (2008): 1737; Stephen Ansolabehere, "Effects of Identification Requirements on Voting: Evidence from the Experiences of Voters on Election Day," *PS: Political Science & Politics* (January 2009): 127–130.

17 Jerold G. Rusk, "The Effect of the Australian Ballot Reform on Split Ticket Voting, 1876–1908," *American Political Science Review* 64, no. 4 (December 1970): 1220–38.

18 For definitions of these units, see U.S. Census Bureau, "Geographic Areas Reference Manual," www.census.gov/programs-surveys/geography/guidance/geographic-areas-reference-manual.html (accessed 5/28/20).

19 For an excellent analysis of voting systems and a complete classification, see Gary W. Cox, *Making Votes Count: Strategic Coordination in the World's Electoral Systems* (Cambridge: Cambridge University Press, 1997).

20 *Hollingsworth v. Perry*, 570 U.S. 693 (2013); *Obergefell v. Hodges*, 576 U.S. 644 (2015).

21 National Conference of State Legislatures, "Initiative, Referendum and Recall," www.ncsl.org/research/elections-and-campaigns/initiative-referendum-and-recall-overview.aspx (accessed 5/28/20).

22 This point is developed in Mordon Bennedsen and Sven Fledmann, "Lobbying Legislatures," *Journal of Political Economy* 110, no. 4 (August 2002).

23 Jordan Misra, "Voter Turnout Rates Among All Voting Age and Major Racial and Ethnic Groups Were Higher Than in 2014," United States Census Bureau, April 23, 2019, https://www.census.gov/library/stories/2019/04/behind-2018-united-states-midterm-election-turnout.html (accessed 5/26/20).

24 The most reliable source of information about the demographics of voting is the Current Population Survey, conducted by the United States Census Bureau. For these and other statistics see "Voting and Registration in the Election of November 2018," https://www.census.gov/data/tables/time-series/demo/voting-and-registration/p20-583.html (accessed 5/28/20).

25 "Same Day Voter Registration," National Conference of State Legislatures, June 28, 2019, https://www.ncsl.org/research/elections-and-campaigns/same-day-registration.aspx (accessed 5/26/20).

26 This is the wording used by the Gallup poll. Others ask "In politics today . . ." or offer "or another party" instead of "or what."

27 See Michael Tesler and David Sears, *Obama's Race* (Chicago: University of Chicago Press, 2010); John Sides and Lynn Vavrek, *The Gamble* (Princeton, NJ: Princeton University Press, 2014).

28 *Washington Post*, "Live Results: Super Tuesday 2020," March 3, 2020, www.washingtonpost.com/elections/election-results/super-tuesday/ (accessed 5/28/20).

29 Donald Trump, "Sleepy Joe has been in politics for 40 years, and did nothing. Now he pretends to have the answers. He doesn't even know the questions. Weakness will never beat anarchists, looters or thugs, and Joe has been politically weak all of his life. LAW & ORDER!" June, 2, 2020, 3:56 PM; https://twitter.com/realDonaldTrump/status/1267907954537312256 (accessed 8/1/20).

30 The partitioning of the incumbency effect into office-holder advantages and challenger qualities begins with the important work of Gary C. Jacobson; see, for example, his excellent text *The Politics of Congressional Elections* (7th ed., New York: Pearson Longman, 2008). Estimating exactly what fraction of the incumbency effect is due to officeholder benefits is tricky. See Stephen Ansolabehere, James M. Snyder, Jr., and Charles H. Stewart III, "Old Voters, New Voters, and the Personal Vote: Using Redistricting to Measure the Incumbency Advantage," *American Journal of Political Science* 44, no. 1 (2000): 17–34.

31 See Stephen Ansolabehere, Jonathan Rodden, and James M. Snyder, Jr., "The Strength of Issues: Using Multiple Measures to Gauge Preference Stability, Ideological Constraint, and Issue Voting," *American Political Science Review* 102, no. 2 (May 2008): 215–32.

32 The classic study showing this is Philip E. Converse, "The Nature of Belief Systems in Mass Publics," in *Ideology and Discontent*, ed. David Apter (New York: Free Press, 1964).

33 Kiran Stacey, "U.S. Election: Democrats Try to Blunt Trump's Digital Edge," *Financial Times*, February 10, 2020, www.ft.com/content/02fc42b2-3072-11ea-9703-eea0cae3f0de (accessed 5/28/20).

34 The FEC's website is an excellent resource for those interested in U.S. campaign finance: www.fec.gov.

35 Sean McMinn and Alyson Hurt, "Tracking the Money Race Behind the Presidential Primary Campaign," National Public Radio, April 21, 2020, www.npr.org/2019/04/16/711812314/tracking-the-money-race-behind-the-presidential-campaign (accessed 5/28/20).

36 *Buckley v. Valeo*, 424 U.S. 1 (1976).

37 *Citizens United v. Federal Election Commission*, 558 U.S. 310 (2010).

38 *McConnell v. Federal Election Commission*, 540 U.S. 93 (2003).

39 See Stephen Ansolabehere and James M. Snyder, Jr., "The Incumbency Advantage in U.S. Elections: An Analysis of State and Federal Offices, 1942–2000," *Election Law Journal* 1 (2002): 315–38.

40 OpenSecrets, "Incumbent Advantage," https://www .opensecrets.org/elections-overview/incumbent -advantage (accessed 11/11/2020).

41 Ian McGugan, "Markets Have Made Their Verdict: Donald Trump Will Win the Next Election," *Globe and Mail*, February 6, 2020, www.theglobeandmail.com /investing/markets/inside-the-market/article-wall -street-bullish-on-trumps-growing-re-election-momentum (accessed 11/17/20); see also Adam Goodman, "Don't Watch Opinion Polls to Predict Trump's Fate. Watch the Stock Market," *Tampa Bay Times*, August 9, 2019, www .tampabay.com/opinion/2019/08/09/dont-watch -opinion-polls-to-predict-trumps-fate-watch-the -stock-market-adam-goodman (accessed 11/17/20).

42 U.S. Bureau of Labor Statistics, "Unemployment Rate Rises to Record High 14.7 Percent in April 2020," May 13, 2020, www.bls.gov/opub/ted/2020/unemployment -rate-rises-to-record-high-14-point-7-percent-in-april -2020.htm (accessed 11/17/20).

43 Donald J. Trump, "These THUGS are dishonoring the memory of George Floyd, and I won't let that happen. Just spoke to Governor Tim Walz and told him that the Military is with him all the way. Any difficulty and we will assume control but, when the looting starts, the shooting starts. Thank you!," Twitter, May 29, 2020, 12:53 a.m., https://twitter.com/realDonaldTrump/ status/1266231100780744704 (accessed 11/18/20).

44 Katelyn Burns, "Trump's Latest Tweets Are from an Alternate Reality Where the Protests Are out of Control," Vox, June 3, 2020, www.vox.com/policy-and -politics/2020/6/3/21279088/trump-tweets-alternate -reality-george-floyd-protests (accessed 11/17/20).

45 Deval Patrick (Massachusetts), Steve Bullock (Montana), Jay Inslee (Washington), and John Hickenlooper (Colorado).

46 Tulsi Gabbard (Hawaii), John Delaney (Maryland), Seth Moulton (Massachusetts), Beto O'Rourke (Texas), and Eric Swalwell (California).

47 Pete Buttigieg (South Bend, Indiana), Julián Castro (San Antonio), Bill de Blasio (New York City), Michael Bloomberg (New York City), and Wayne Messam (Miramar, Florida).

48 Richard Ojeda (West Virginia).

49 The modern era for measuring turnout began with the expansion of the franchise to women in 1920.

50 "Ratings," Cook Political Report, https://cookpolitical .com/ratings (accessed 11/17/20).

51 "Ratings," Cook Political Report, https://cookpolitical .com/ratings (accessed 11/17/20).

52 Nathaniel Rakich, "Could Democrats Win Full Control of More State Governments Than Republicans?" FiveThirtyEight, October 20, 2020, https:// fivethirtyeight.com/features/could-democrats-win -full-control-of-more-state-governments-than -republicans (accessed 11/17/20).

CHAPTER 11

1 "Washington's Farewell Address 1796," Avalon Project, http://avalon.law.yale.edu/18th_century/washing.asp (accessed 6/11/20).

2 This distinction comes from John H. Aldrich, *Why Parties? The Origin and Transformation of Party Politics in America* (Chicago: University of Chicago Press, 1995).

3 For an excellent analysis of the parties' role in recruitment, see Paul S. Herrnson, *Congressional Elections: Campaigning at Home and in Washington* (Washington, DC: CQ Press, 1995).

4 For a discussion of some of the effects of primary elections, see Peter F. Galderisi and Benjamin Ginsberg, "Primary Elections and the Evanescence of Third-Party Activity in the United States," in *Do Elections Matter?* ed. Benjamin Ginsberg and Alan Stone, pp. 115–30 (Armonk, NY: M. E. Sharpe, 1986).

5 If a group coordinates its activities with a political party, it is subject to additional reporting requirements and contribution limits, and political action can violate the conditions for the tax-exempt status of nonprofits.

6 "Democrats may have votes to block Trump's border emergency in U.S. Senate," Reuters, March 3, 2019, www .reuters.com/article/us-usa-trump-congress/democrats -may-have-votes-to-block-trumps-border-emergency-in -us-senate-idUSKCN1QK0OP (accessed 6/3/20).

7 Maurice Duverger, *Political Parties: Their Organization and Activity in the Modern State*, trans. Barbara North and Robert North (New York: Wiley, 1954).

8 Don Gonyea, "CQ: Obama's Winning Streak on Hill Unprecedented," NPR, January 11, 2010, www.npr .org/templates/story/story.php?storyId=122436116 (accessed 6/11/20).

9 Shawn Zeller, "Running on Empty," *CQ Weekly*, March 15, 2015, pp. 26-36, library.cqpress.com/cqweekly/file .php?path=/files/wr20150316-2014_Presidential.pdf (accessed 6/11/20).

10 For an excellent treatment of the meanings of party identification, and analysis of the implications of different theories, see Donald Green, Bradley Palmquist, and Eric Schickler, *Partisan Hearts and Minds* (New Haven, CT: Yale University Press, 2002).

11 For a detailed assessment of the political use of information-economizing devices such as party labels, see Arthur Lupia and Mathew D. McCubbins, *The Democratic Dilemma: Can Citizens Learn What They Need to Know?* (New York: Cambridge University Press, 1998).

12 For a more in-depth discussion of independent voters, policy indifference, and cross-pressure, see Sunshine Hillygus and Todd Shields, *The Persuadable Voter: Wedge Issues in Presidential Campaigns* (Princeton, NJ: Princeton University Press, 2008).

13 "National Election Polls: How Different Groups Voted," *New York Times*, https://www.nytimes.com/interactive/2020/11/03/us/elections/exit-polls-president.html (accessed 11/12/20).

14 For a recent formulation of the pluralist model of parties, see Kathleen Bawn, Martin Cohen, David Karol, Seth Masket, et al., "A Theory of Political Parties: Groups, Policy Demands, and Nominations in American Politics," *Perspectives on Politics* 10 (2012): 571–97.

15 CNN Politics, "Exit Polls," updated November 23, 2016, http://edition.cnn.com/election/results/exitpolls (accessed 12/17/17).

16 "National Election Polls: How Different Groups Voted," *New York Times*, https://www.nytimes.com/interactive/2020/11/03/us/elections/exit-polls-president.html (accessed 11/12/20).

17 Ansolabehere, Stephen, Brian Schaffner, and Samantha Luks, 2017, Guide to the 2016 Cooperative Congressional Election Study, https://dataverse.harvard.edu/file.xhtml?persistentId=doi:10.7910/DVN/GDF6Z0/RK0ONG&version=4.0, page 42 (accessed 6/11/20).

18 Stephen Ansolabehere, Samantha Luks, and Brian Schaffner, Cooperative Congressional Election Study, 2018. https://dataverse.harvard.edu/dataset.xhtml?persistentId=doi%3A10.7910/DVN/ZSBZ7K (accessed 6/11/20).

19 See Aldrich, *Why Parties? The Origin and Transformation of Party Politics in America*, chap. 8.

20 See Paul S. Herrnson, *Party Campaigning in the 1980s* (Cambridge, MA: Harvard University Press, 1988).

21 See William E. Gienapp, *The Origins of the Republican Party, 1852–1856* (New York: Oxford University Press, 1987).

22 See David W. Rohde, *Parties and Leaders in the Postreform House* (Chicago: University of Chicago Press, 1991). An elaboration of this argument is presented in Gary W. Cox and Mathew D. McCubbins, *Setting the Agenda: Responsible Party Government in the U.S. House of Representatives* (New York: Cambridge University Press, 2005). See also Nolan McCarty, Keith T. Poole, and Howard Rosenthal, *Polarized America: The Dance of Inequality and Unequal Riches* (Cambridge, MA: MIT Press, 2006).

23 Jonathan Miller, "Party Unity on Congressional Votes Takes a Dive: CQ Vote Studies," Roll Call, February 28, 2019, www.rollcall.com/news/congress/party-unity-congressional-votes (accessed 6/11/20).

24 For a discussion of third parties in the United States, see Daniel A. Mazmanian, *Third Parties in Presidential Elections* (Washington, DC: Brookings Institution, 1974).

25 See Duverger, *Political Parties*.

CHAPTER 12

1 Quinnipiac, "Majority of Voters Say Climate Change Is an Emergency, Quinnipiac University Poll Finds; 72% Say Congress Needs to Act to Reduce Gun Violence," August 29, 2019, https://poll.qu.edu/national/release-detail?ReleaseID=3639 (accessed 6/11/20).

2 Thomas Ferguson, *Golden Rule: The Investment Theory of Party Competition and the Logic of Money-Driven Political Systems* (Chicago: University of Chicago Press, 1995).

3 Clinton L. Rossiter, ed., *The Federalist Papers; Alexander Hamilton, James Madison, and John Jay* (New York: New American Library, 1961), no. 10 (James Madison), p. 78.

4 Rossiter, *Federalist Papers*, no. 10, p. 83.

5 Rossiter, *Federalist Papers*, no. 10.

6 Benjamin Ginsberg, "Administrators Ate My Tuition," *Washington Monthly* (September/October 2011), www.washingtonmonthly.com/magazine/septemberoctober_2011/features/administrators_ate_my_tuition031641.php?page=all (accessed 6/11/20).

7 Mancur Olson, *The Logic of Collective Action: Public Goods and the Theory of Groups* (Cambridge, MA: Harvard University Press, 1971).

8 Kay Lehman Schlozman, Sidney Verba, and Henry E. Brady, *The Unheavenly Chorus: Unequal Political Voice and the Broken Promise of American Democracy* (Princeton, NJ: Princeton University Press, 2012); and Martin Gilens, *Affluence and Influence: Economic Inequality and Political Power in America* (Princeton, NJ: Princeton University Press, 2012).

9 Federal Election Commission, "Number of Federal PACs Increases," www.fec.gov/updates/number-of-federal-pacs-increases-slightly/ (accessed 6/11/20).

10 John Herbers, "Special Interests Gaining Power as Voter Disillusionment Grows," *New York Times*, November 14, 1978.

11 Andrea Louise Campbell, *How Policies Make Citizens: Senior Political Activism and the American Welfare State* (Princeton, NJ: Princeton University Press, 2003).

12 U.S. House of Representatives, Office of the Clerk, "Lobbying Disclosure Act Guidance," effective January 1, 2008, revised January 31, 2017, https://lobbyingdisclosure.house.gov/amended_lda_guide.html#section4 (accessed 6/11/20).

13 For discussions of lobbying, see John R. Wright, *Interest Groups and Congress: Lobbying, Contributions, and Influence* (New York: Longman, 2009).

14 Geoff West, "Revolving Door: Former Lobbyists in Trump Administration," The Center for Responsive Politics, OpenSecrets News, July 16, 2018, www.opensecrets.org/news/2018/07/revolving-door-update-trump-administration/ (accessed 6/11/20).

15 Jacob R. Straus, *Lobbying the Executive Branch: Current Practices and Options for Change*, CRS Report no. R40947 (Washington, DC: Congressional Research Service, 2011), pp. 3–4.

16 Frederick J. Boehmke, Sean Gailmard, and John W. Patty, "Business as Usual: Interest Group Access

and Representation Across Policy-making Venues," *Journal of Public Policy* 33 (2013): 3–33.

17 For an excellent discussion of the political origins of the Administrative Procedure Act, see Martin Shapiro, "APA: Past, Present, Future," *Virginia Law Review* 72, no. 2 (March 1986): 447–92.

18 Statista, "Number of Registered Active Lobbyists in the United States from 2000 to 2019," www.statista.com/statistics/257340/number-of-lobbyists-in-the-us/ (accessed 3/2/2020).

19 *Griswold v. Connecticut*, 381 U.S. 479 (1965); *Eisenstadt v. Baird*, 405 U.S. 438 (1972); *Roe v. Wade*, 410 U.S. 133 (1973).

20 *Webster v. Reproductive Health Services*, 492 U.S. 490 (1989).

21 *Brown v. Board of Education of Topeka, Kansas*, 347 U.S. 483 (1954).

22 *Scheidler v. National Organization for Women et al.*, 547 U.S. 9 (2006).

23 E. Pendleton Herring, *Group Representation before Congress* (1928; repr., New York: Russell & Russell, 1967). See also Kenneth W. Kollman, *Outside Lobbying: Public Opinion and Interest Group Strategies* (Princeton, NJ: Princeton University Press, 1998).

24 Natasha Singer, "Harry and Louise Return, with a New Message," *New York Times*, July 16, 2009, www.nytimes.com/2009/07/17/business/media/17adco.html (accessed 6/11/20).

25 Jane Fritsch, "The Grass Roots, Just a Free Phone Call Away," *New York Times*, June 23, 1995, pp. A1, A22.

26 See Stephen Ansolabehere, John M. de Figueiredo, and James M. Snyder, Jr., "Why Is There So Little Money in U.S. Politics?" *Journal of Economic Perspectives* 17, no. 1 (Winter 2003): 105–30.

27 *Buckley v. Valeo*, 424 U.S. 1 (1976).

28 *Citizens United v. Federal Election Commission*, 558 U.S. 310 (2010).

29 Donald P. Green and Alan S. Gerber, *Get Out the Vote: How to Increase Voter Turnout*, 2nd ed. (Washington, DC: Brookings Institution Press, 2008).

30 Elisabeth R. Gerber, *The Populist Paradox* (Princeton, NJ: Princeton University Press, 1999).

31 Ansolabehere et al., "Why Is There So Little Money in U.S. Politics?"

32 John M. de Figueiredo and Brian S. Silverman, "Academic Earmarks and the Returns to Lobbying," *Journal of Law and Economics* 42 (October 2006): 597–626. Also see Deniz Igan, Prachi Mishra, and Thierry Tressel, "A Fistful of Dollars: Lobbying and the Financial Crisis," NBER Macroeconomics Annual 26 (2012): 195–230.

33 Frank R. Baumgartner, Jeffrey M. Berry, Marie Hojnacki, David C. Kimball, and Beth L. Leech, *Lobbying and Policy Change: Who Wins, Who Loses, and Why* (Chicago: University of Chicago Press, 2009).

CHAPTER 13

1 Lester M. Salamon, "Economic Regulation," in *The Tools of Government: A Guide to the New Governance*, ed. Lester M. Salamon (New York: Oxford University Press, 2002), p. 146.

2 See Margaret Weir, *Politics and Jobs: The Boundaries of Employment Policy in the United States* (Princeton, NJ: Princeton University Press, 1992).

3 See David M. Hart, *Forged Consensus: Science, Technology and Economic Policy in the United States, 1921–1953* (Princeton, NJ: Princeton University Press, 1998).

4 U.S Food & Drug Administration, "Coronavirus (COVID-19) Update: FDA Takes Action to Warn, Protect Consumers from Dangerous Alcohol-Based Hand Sanitizers Containing Methanol," July 2, 2020, www.fda.gov/news-events/press-announcements/coronavirus-covid-19-update-fda-takes-action-warn-protect-consumers-dangerous-alcohol-based-hand (accessed 7/16/20).

5 Kevin G. Hall, "Bernanke to Stay on Greenspan Path, but Not All the Way," *Seattle Times*, November 16, 2005, p. C1.

6 John Cassidy, "Nine Things We Learned on Tuesday about the Next Fed Chairman," *New Yorker*, November 28, 2017, www.newyorker.com/news/our-columnists/nine-things-we-learned-on-tuesday-about-the-next-fed-chairman (accessed 7/16/20).

7 Jeanna Smialek, "Trump Called Powell an 'Enemy.' 'Ugh' Was a Response Inside the Fed," *New York Times*, January 30, 2020, https://www.nytimes.com/2020/01/30/business/economy/fed-trump-powell-ugh.html (accessed 7/17/20).

8 Congressional Budget Office, "Monthly Budget Review: Summary for Fiscal Year 2019," www.cbo.gov/publication/55824#:~:text=In%20fiscal%20year%202019%2C%20the,and%203.5%20percent%20in%202017 (accessed 7/27/20).

9 The U.S. Treasury Department has a website that is updated daily with the current national debt: TreasuryDirect, "The Debt to the Penny and Who Holds It," www.treasurydirect.gov/NP/debt/current (accessed 7/16/20).

10 Office of Management and Budget, "Budget of the U.S. Government: Fiscal Year 2011," www.gpo.gov/fdsys/pkg/BUDGET-2011-BUD/pdf/BUDGET-2011-BUD.pdf (accessed 7/17/20).

11 Office of Management and Budget, Historical Tables, table 2.2, "Percentage Composition of Receipts by Source: 1934–2023," www.whitehouse.gov/wp-content/uploads/2018/02/hist02z2-fy2019.xlsx (accessed 7/17/20).

12 For a systematic account of the role of government in providing incentives and inducements to business, see C. E. Lindblom, *Politics and Markets* (New York: Basic Books, 1977), chap. 13. For a detailed account of the dramatic Reagan tax cuts and reforms, see Jeffrey Birnbaum and Alan Murray, *Showdown at Gucci Gulch: Lawmakers, Lobbyists, and the Unlikely Triumph of Tax Reform* (New York: Random House, 1987).

13 U.S. Department of the Treasury, "Remarks of Under Secretary of the Treasury Peter R. Fisher to the Columbus Council on World Affairs, Columbus, Ohio, Beyond Borrowing: Meeting the Government's Financial Challenges in the 21st Century," November 14, 2002, www.treasury.gov/press-center/press -releases/Pages/po3622.aspx (accessed 7/17/20).

14 The Office of Management and Budgets, "Historical Tables," Table 3.1, www.whitehouse.gov/omb /historical-tables/ (accessed 7/14/20).

15 Congressional Budget Office, "Historical Budget Data, 2020," https://www.cbo.gov/system/files /2020-01/51134-2020-01-historicalbudgetdata.xlsx (accessed 8/14/20).

16 Pew Research Center, "How Republicans and Democrats View Federal Spending," April 11, 2019, www.people-press.org/2017/04/24/how-republicans -and-democrats-view-federal-spending (accessed 7/17/20).

17 Martin Gilens and Benjamin I. Page, "Testing Theories of American Politics: Elites, Interest Groups, and Average Citizens," *Perspectives on Politics* 12, no. 3 (2014): 564–81.

18 Christopher Howard, *America's Hidden Welfare State* (Princeton, NJ: Princeton University Press, 1999).

19 Social Security Administration, "OASDI and SSI Program Rates & Limits, 2020," www.ssa.gov/policy /docs/quickfacts/prog_highlights/RatesLimits2020 .html (accessed 5/12/20).

20 Martin Gilens, *Why Americans Hate Welfare: Race, Media, and the Politics of Antipoverty Policy* (Chicago: University of Chicago Press, 1999), chaps. 3–4.

21 U.S. Department of Health and Human Services, Office of the Assistant Secretary for Planning and Evaluation, "U.S. Federal Poverty Guidelines Used to Determine Financial Eligibility for Certain Federal Programs," https://aspe.hhs.gov/poverty-guidelines (accessed 7/17/20). See also Center on Budget and Policy Priorities, "State Fact Sheets: Trends in State TANF-to -Poverty Ratios," www.cbpp.org/research/state-fact -sheets-trends-in-state-tanf-to-poverty-ratios (accessed 7/17/20).

22 There were a couple of minor precedents. First, the Smith-Hughes Act of 1917 made federal funds available to the states for vocational education at the elementary and secondary levels. Second, the Lanham Act of 1940 made federal funds available to schools in "federally impacted areas"—that is, areas with an unusually large number of government employees and/or areas where the local tax base was reduced by a large amount of government-owned property.

23 For a critique of the act's provisions, see Thomas Toch, "Bush's Big Test," *Washington Monthly*, November 2001, pp. 12–18.

24 Congressional Budget Office, "CBO's March 2016 Baseline Projections for the Student Loan Program," www.cbo.gov/sites/default/files/recurringdata /51310-2016-03-studentloan.pdf (accessed 7/17/20).

CHAPTER 14

1 Rupert Smith, *The Utility of Force: The Art of War in the Modern World* (New York: Vintage, 2008).

2 D. Robert Worley, *Shaping U.S. Military Forces: Revolution or Relevance in a Post–Cold War World* (Westport, CT: Praeger Security International, 2006).

3 This was done quietly in an amendment to the Internal Revenue Service Restructuring and Reform Act of 1998. But it was not accomplished easily. See Bob Gravely, "Normal Trade with China Wins Approval," *Congressional Quarterly Weekly Report*, July 25, 1998; and Richard Dunham, "MFN by Any Other Name Is . . . NTR?" *Business Week* online news flash, June 19, 1997.

4 USAID, "Fact Sheet: U.S. Assistance for the People of Syria," January 26, 2018, www.usaid.gov/news -information/press-releases/jan-26-2018-fact-sheet -us-assistance-people-syria (accessed 5/8/2020).

5 U.S. Agency for International Development, "United States Announces More Than $364 Million Dollars in Additional Humanitarian Assistance for the Syria Response," July 14, 2020, https://www.usaid.gov /syria#:~:text=At%20the%20Third%20Brussels %20Conference,Resilience%20Plan%20for%20 2019%2D2020. (accessed 8/10/20).

6 Alexander Hamilton and James Madison, *Letters of Pacificus and Helvidius* (New York: Scholars Facsimiles and Reprints, 1999).

7 For example, under President Clinton, Senator Lloyd Bentsen and Representative Les Aspin left Congress to become the secretaries of the Treasury and Defense, respectively.

8 A very good brief outline of the centrality of the president in foreign policy can be found in Paul E. Peterson, "The President's Dominance in Foreign Policy Making," *Political Science Quarterly* 109, no. 2 (Summer 1994): 215, 234.

9 One confirmation of this can be found in Theodore J. Lowi, *The End of Liberalism*, 2nd ed. (New York: Norton, 1979), pp. 127–30; another can be found in Stephen Krasner, "Are Bureaucracies Important?" *Foreign Policy* 7 (Summer 1972): 159–79. However, it should be added that Krasner was writing his article in disagreement with Graham T. Allison, "Conceptual Models and the Cuban Missile Crisis," *American Political Science Review* 63, no. 3 (September 1969): 689–718.

10 See Theodore J. Lowi, *The Personal President: Power Invested, Promise Unfulfilled* (Ithaca, NY: Cornell University Press, 1985), pp. 167–69.

11 James Dao and Patrick E. Tyler, "U.S. Says Military Strikes Are Just a Part of Big Plan," *Alliance*, September 27, 2001; Joseph Kahn, "A Nation Challenged: Global Dollars," *New York Times*, September 20, 2001, p. B1.

12 "Official Says Turkey Is Advancing in Drive for I.M.F. Financing," *New York Times*, October 6, 2001, p. A7.

13 The Warsaw Pact was signed in 1955 by the Soviet Union, the German Democratic Republic (East Germany), Poland, Hungary, Czechoslovakia, Romania, Bulgaria, and Albania. Albania later dropped out. The Warsaw Pact was terminated in 1991.

GLOSSARY

administrative legislation Rules made by regulatory agencies that have the force of law.

affirmative action A policy or program designed to correct historical injustices committed against specific groups by making special efforts to provide members of these groups with access to educational and employment opportunities.

agency representation The type of representation in which representatives are held accountable to their constituents if they fail to represent them properly. That is, constituents have the power to hire and fire their representatives.

agenda-setting effect The power of the media to focus public attention on particular issues.

amicus curiae "Friend of the court," an individual or group that is not a party to a lawsuit but has a strong interest in influencing the outcome.

Antifederalists Those who favored strong state governments and a weak national government and who were opponents of the constitution proposed at the Constitutional Convention of 1787.

antitrust policy Governmental regulation of large businesses that have established monopolies.

appeasement The effort to avoid war by giving in to the demands of a hostile power.

Articles of Confederation and Perpetual Union The United States' first written constitution. Adopted by the Continental Congress in 1777, the Articles were the formal basis for America's national government until 1789, when they were superseded by the Constitution.

Australian ballot An electoral format that presents the names of all the candidates for any given office on the same ballot.

authoritarian government A system of rule in which the government's power is not limited by law, though it may be restrained by other social institutions. Compare *constitutional government* and *totalitarian government*.

autocracy A form of government in which a single individual rules. Compare *democracy* and *oligarchy*.

bicameral legislature A legislative body composed of two chambers, or houses.

bilateral treaty A treaty made between two nations.

Bill of Rights The first 10 amendments to the U.S. Constitution, adopted in 1791. The Bill of Rights ensures certain rights and liberties to the people.

block grants Federal funds given to state governments to pay for goods, services, or programs, with relatively few restrictions on how the funds may be spent.

brief A written document in which an attorney explains—using case precedents—why a court should rule in favor of his or her client.

budget deficit The amount by which government spending exceeds government revenue in a fiscal year.

bureaucracy The complex structure of offices, tasks, rules, and principles of organization that large institutions use to coordinate the work of their personnel.

bureaucratic drift The tendency of bureaucracies to implement laws in ways that tilt toward the bureaucrats' policy preferences and possibly away from the intentions of the elected officials who created the laws.

Cabinet The heads of the major departments of the federal government.

casework Efforts by members of Congress to gain the trust and support of constituents by providing personal services. One important type of casework is helping constituents to obtain favorable treatment from the federal bureaucracy.

categorical grants-in-aid Funds given to states and localities by Congress that are earmarked by law for specific policy categories, such as education or crime prevention.

caucus A meeting of a political or legislative group, normally closed to nonmembers, to select candidates, plan strategy, or make decisions about legislative matters.

checks and balances The ways in which each branch of government is able to influence the activities of the other branches.

chief justice The justice on the Supreme Court who presides over the Court's public sessions.

civil law Cases involving disputes among individuals or between the government and individuals that do not involve criminal penalties.

civil liberties The protections of citizens from improper governmental action. Compare *civil rights*.

civil rights The rules that government must follow in the treatment of individuals, especially concerning participation in political and social life. Compare *civil liberties*.

class-action suit A lawsuit in which a large number of persons with common interests join together under a representative party to bring or defend a lawsuit.

clientele agency A department or bureau of government whose mission is to promote, serve, or represent a particular interest. Compare *regulatory agency*.

closed primary A primary election in which only those voters who have registered their affiliation with the party by a specified time before the election can participate. Compare *open primary*.

closed rule The provision by the House Rules Committee that restricts the introduction of amendments during debate. Compare *open rule*.

cloture A procedure by which three-fifths of the members of the Senate can set a time limit on debate over a given bill.

Cold War The period of struggle between the United States and the Soviet Union, occurring from the late 1940s to about 1990.

comity clause Article IV, Section 2, of the Constitution, which prohibits states from enacting laws that treat the citizens of other states in a discriminatory manner.

commander in chief The president's role as commander of the national military and of the state National Guard units (when they are called into service).

commerce clause The clause, found in Article I, Section 8, of the Constitution, that delegates to Congress the power "to regulate Commerce with foreign Nations, and among the several States and with the Indian Tribes."

concurrence An opinion agreeing with the decision of the majority in a Supreme Court case but with a rationale different from the one provided in the majority opinion. Compare *dissenting opinion*.

concurrent powers Authority possessed by both state and national governments, such as the power to levy taxes.

conference committee A joint committee created to work out a compromise between House and Senate versions of a bill.

conservative A person who generally believes that social institutions (such as churches and corporations) and the free market solve problems better than governments do, that a large and powerful government poses a threat to citizens' freedom, and that the appropriate role of government is to uphold traditional values. Compare *liberal*.

constituency The citizens who reside in the district from which an official is elected.

constitutional government A system of rule that establishes specific limits on the powers of the government. Compare *authoritarian government* and *totalitarian government*.

containment A policy designed to limit the political and military expansion of a hostile power.

contracting power The power of government to set conditions on companies seeking to sell goods or services to government agencies.

contributory program A social program financed in whole or in part by taxation or other mandatory contributions by its present or future recipients. The most important example is Social Security, which is financed by a payroll tax. Compare *noncontributory program*.

cooperative federalism The system of government that has prevailed in the United States since the New Deal era (beginning in the 1930s), in which grants-in-aid have been used strategically to encourage states and localities to pursue nationally defined goals. Also called *intergovernmental cooperation. Compare dual federalism.*

court of appeals A court that hears the appeals of lower court decisions. Also called *appellate court*. Compare *trial court* and *supreme court*.

criminal law Cases arising out of actions that allegedly violate laws protecting the health, safety, and morals of the community. Compare *civil law* and *public law*.

de facto segregation Racial segregation that is not a direct result of law or governmental policy but a reflection of residential patterns, income distributions, or other social factors. Compare *de jure segregation*.

de jure segregation Racial segregation that is a direct result of law or official policy. Compare *de facto segregation*.

delegated powers Constitutional powers that are assigned to one branch of the government but exercised by another branch with the permission of the first. Compare *expressed powers* and *inherent powers*.

delegates Legislators who vote according to the preferences of their constituents. Compare *trustees*.

democracy A system of rule that permits citizens to play a significant part in government, usually through the selection of key public officials. Compare *autocracy* and *oligarchy*.

deregulation The policy of reducing the number of rules issued by federal regulatory agencies.

descriptive representation The type of representation in which representatives are trusted to make decisions on their constituents' behalf because they share the religious, gender, philosophical, or ethnic identities of their constituents. Compare *agency representation*.

deterrence The development and maintenance of military strength as a means of discouraging attack.

devolution The policy of delegating a program or passing it down from one level of government to a lower level, such as from the national government to state and local governments.

diplomacy The representation of a government to other foreign governments.

discretionary spending Federal spending on programs that are controlled through the regular budget process. Compare *mandatory spending*.

dissenting opinion A decision written by a justice who voted with the minority opinion in a particular case, in which the justice fully explains the reasoning behind his or her opinion. Compare *concurrence*.

divided government The condition in American government in which one party controls the presidency, while the opposing party controls one or both houses of Congress.

dual federalism The system of government that prevailed in the United States from 1789 to 1937, in which most fundamental governmental powers were shared between the federal and state governments, with the states exercising the most important powers. Compare *cooperative federalism*.

due process The requirement that citizens be treated according to the law and be provided adequate protection for individual rights.

earned income tax credit (EITC) A tax benefit that is designed to supplement the earnings of lower-income workers. The EITC lowers the total taxes the worker must pay—providing a cash refund on most recipients' tax returns.

economic policy A governmental policy aimed at improving economic performance and outcomes.

EITC *See earned income tax credit.*

Electoral College An institution established by the Constitution for the election of the president and vice president of the United States. Every four years, voters in each state and the District of Columbia elect electors who, in turn, cast votes for the president and vice president. The candidate receiving a majority of the electoral vote for president or vice president is elected.

eminent domain The right of the government to take private property for public use, with reasonable compensation awarded to the owner.

entitlement program A social program that guarantees benefits to a category of people defined by law.

equal protection clause The provision of the Fourteenth Amendment guaranteeing citizens the "equal protection of the laws." This clause has served as the basis for the civil rights of African Americans, women, and other groups.

equal time rule An FCC requirement that broadcasters provide candidates for the same political office an equal opportunity to communicate their messages to the public.

establishment clause The First Amendment clause that says, "Congress shall make no law respecting an establishment of religion."

exclusionary rule The requirement that courts exclude evidence obtained in violation of the Fourth Amendment.

executive agreement An agreement between the president and another country that has the force of a treaty but does not require the Senate's "advice and consent."

executive order A rule or regulation issued by the president that has the effect of law.

executive privilege The claim that confidential communications between a president and close advisers should not be revealed without the president's consent.

expressed powers Powers that the Constitution explicitly grants to the federal government. Compare *delegated powers* and *inherent powers*.

Fed See *Federal Reserve System*.

federal funds rate The interest rate on loans between banks; the Federal Reserve Board uses its powers to influence this rate.

Federal Reserve System (Fed) The system of 12 Federal Reserve banks that facilitates exchanges of cash, checks, and credit; regulates member banks; uses monetary policy to fight inflation and deflation in the United States.

federalism The system of government in which a constitution divides power between a central government and regional governments.

Federalists Those who favored a strong national government and supported the constitution proposed at the Constitutional Convention of 1787. Compare *Antifederalists*.

fighting words Speech that directly incites damaging conduct.

filibuster A tactic in which members of the Senate prevent action on legislation they oppose by continuously holding the floor and speaking until the majority abandons the legislation. Once given the floor, senators have unlimited time to speak, and a cloture vote by three-fifths of the Senate is required to end a filibuster.

fiscal policy Regulation of the economy through taxing and spending powers.

formula grants Grants-in-aid for which a formula is used to determine the amount of federal funds a state or local government will receive. Compare *project grants*.

framing The influence of the media over how events and issues are interpreted.

free exercise clause The First Amendment clause that protects the right of citizens to believe and practice whatever religion they choose.

free riding Enjoying the benefits of some good or action while letting others bear the costs.

full faith and credit clause The provision in Article IV, Section 1, of the Constitution, requiring that each state normally honors the governmental actions and judicial decisions that take place in another state.

GDP See *gross domestic product*.

gender gap A distinctive pattern of voting behavior reflecting the differences in views between women and men.

gerrymandering The drawing of electoral districts in such a way as to give advantage to one political party.

going public Trying to influence public opinion for or against some proposed action by the government.

governance The process of governing, which involves making official decisions about a nation's affairs and having the authority to put them into effect.

government The institutions through which a land and its people are ruled.

grand jury A jury that determines whether sufficient evidence is available to justify a trial. Grand juries do not rule on the accused's guilt or innocence.

grants-in-aid Funds given by Congress to state and local governments on the condition that they be used for a specific purpose.

grassroots lobbying Mobilizing an interest group's membership to contact government officials in support of the group's position.

Great Compromise An agreement reached at the Constitutional Convention of 1787 that gave each state an equal number of senators regardless of the size of its population, but linked representation in the House of Representatives to population size. Also called the *Connecticut Compromise*.

gridlock A situation where legislation cannot move forward, typically resulting from strong polarization between groups.

gross domestic product (GDP) The total value of goods and services produced within a country.

home rule The power delegated by a state to a local unit of government to manage its own affairs.

ICJ See *International Court of Justice*.

IMF See *International Monetary Fund*.

impeachment Charging a government official (president or other) with "Treason, Bribery, or other high Crimes and Misdemeanors," and bringing that official before Congress to determine guilt.

implementation The development of rules, regulations, and bureaucratic procedures to translate laws into action.

implied powers Powers derived from the necessary and proper clause (Article I, Section 8) of the Constitution. Such powers are not specifically expressed in the Constitution but are implied through the interpretation of delegated powers.

incumbent A current officeholder.

inflation A consistent increase in the general level of prices.

inherent powers Powers claimed by a president that are not expressed in the Constitution but are said to stem from "the rights, duties and obligations of the presidency." Compare *delegated powers* and *expressed powers*.

initiative A process by which citizens may petition to place a policy proposal on the ballot for public vote.

in-kind benefits Goods and services provided to eligible individuals and families by the federal government, as contrasted with cash benefits.

institutions A set of formal rules and procedures, often administered by a bureaucracy, that shapes politics and governance.

interest group An organized group of people that attempts to influence governmental policies. Also called *lobby*.

Intergovernmental cooperation See *cooperative federalism*.

intermediate scrutiny The test used by the Supreme Court in gender discrimination cases, which places the burden of justifying a law or policy's use mainly on the government. Compare *strict scrutiny*.

International Court of Justice (ICJ) The UN's chief judicial agency, located in The Hague, Netherlands. The ICJ settles legal disputes submitted by UN member states.

International Monetary Fund (IMF) An institution, established in 1944, that provides loans and facilitates international monetary exchange.

isolationism The desire to avoid involvement in the affairs of other nations.

issue voting An individual's tendency to base the decision of which candidate or party to vote for on the candidate's or party's position on specific issues.

judicial activism The judicial philosophy that the Court should see beyond the text of the Constitution or a statute to consider the broader societal implications of its decisions. Compare *judicial restraint*.

judicial restraint The judicial philosophy whose adherents refuse to go beyond the text of the Constitution in interpreting its meaning. Compare *judicial activism*.

judicial review The power of the courts to determine whether the actions of the president, the Congress, and the state legislatures are consistent with the Constitution.

jurisdiction The types of cases over which a court has authority.

legislative initiative The president's inherent power to bring a policy agenda before Congress.

legislative supremacy The preeminent position within the national government that the Constitution assigns to Congress.

Lemon **test** A rule, articulated in *Lemon v. Kurtzman*, that says governmental action with respect to religion is permissible if it is secular in purpose, does not lead to "excessive entanglement" of government with religion, and neither promotes nor inhibits the practice of religion. The *Lemon* test is generally used in relation to government aid to religious schools.

libel A written statement made in "reckless disregard of the truth" and considered damaging to a victim because it is "malicious, scandalous, and defamatory." Compare *slander*.

liberal A person who generally believes that the government should play an active role in supporting social and political change and generally supports a strong role for the government in the economy, the provision of social services, and the protection of civil rights. Compare *conservative*.

line-item veto The power of the president to veto specific provisions (lines) of a bill passed by the legislature (declared unconstitutional by the Supreme Court in 1998).

lobby See *interest group*.

lobbying An attempt by a group to influence the policy process through persuasion of government officials.

logrolling Agreements among members of Congress to vote for one another's bills.

majority leader The elected leader of the party holding a majority of the seats in the House of Representatives or in the Senate. In the House, the majority leader is subordinate in the party hierarchy to the Speaker. Compare *minority leader*.

majority party The party that holds the majority of seats in a legislative chamber, such as the U.S. House or Senate.

majority rule A type of electoral system in which, to win an office, a candidate must receive a majority (50 percent plus one) of all the votes cast in the relevant district. Compare *plurality rule*.

mandatory spending Federal spending that is made up of "uncontrollables," budget items that cannot be controlled through the regular budget process. Compare *discretionary spending*.

means testing A procedure that determines eligibility for governmental public-assistance programs. A potential beneficiary must show need as well as income and assets below a defined level.

Medicaid A federally financed, state-operated program for medical services to low-income people. Compare *Medicare*.

Medicare National health insurance for the elderly and the disabled. Compare *Medicaid*.

minority leader The elected leader of the party holding less than a majority of the seats in the House of Representatives or Senate. Compare *majority leader*.

Miranda rule The requirement, derived from the Supreme Court's 1966 ruling in *Miranda v. Arizona*, that persons under arrest must be informed of their legal rights, including the right to counsel, before undergoing police interrogation.

monetary policy Regulation of the economy through manipulation of the supply of money, the price of money (interest rates), and the availability of credit.

money bill A bill concerned solely with taxation or government spending.

monopoly A situation in which a single firm dominates a market, controlling the supply of a particular good or service; the absence of competition.

moot No longer requiring resolution by the courts, typically because the facts of the case have changed or been resolved by other means.

most favored nation status The status that a country bestows on a trading partner in which it offers that partner the lowest tariff rate that it offers any of its trading partners.

NAFTA See *North American Free Trade Agreement*.

national debt The accumulation of each year's budget deficits or surpluses; the total amount owed by the U.S. government.

National Security Council (NSC) A presidential foreign policy advisory council made up of the president, the vice president, the secretary of state, the secretary of defense, and other officials invited by the president.

NATO See *North Atlantic Treaty Organization*.

necessary and proper clause The last paragraph of Article I, Section 8, which gives Congress the power to make all laws needed to exercise the powers listed in Section 8. Also called the *elastic clause*.

nomination The process by which political parties select their candidates for election to public office.

noncontributory program A social program that assists people on the basis of demonstrated need rather than contributions they have made. Also called *public-assistance program*. Compare *contributory program*.

non-state actor A group, other than a nation-state, that attempts to play a role in the international system.

North American Free Trade Agreement (NAFTA) An agreement by the United States, Canada, and Mexico to lower and eliminate tariffs among the three countries.

North Atlantic Treaty Organization (NATO) A treaty organization comprising the United States, Canada, and most of western Europe, formed in 1949 to address the perceived threat from the Soviet Union.

NSC See *National Security Council*.

oligarchy A form of government in which a small group of landowners, military officers, or wealthy merchants control most of the governing decisions. Compare *autocracy* and *democracy*.

open-market operations The buying and selling of government securities (such as bonds) by the Federal Reserve System to help finance governmental operations and to reduce or increase the total amount of money circulating in the economy.

open primary A primary election in which voters can choose on the day of the primary which party's primary to vote in. Compare *closed primary*.

open rule The provision by the House Rules Committee that permits floor debate and the addition of amendments to a bill. Compare *closed rule*.

opinion The written explanation of the Supreme Court's decision in a particular case.

oral argument The stage in Supreme Court proceedings in which attorneys for both sides appear before the Court to present their positions and answer questions posed by the justices.

oversight The effort by Congress, through hearings, investigations, and other techniques, to exercise control over the activities of executive agencies.

PAC See *political action committee*.

party activist A person who contributes time and energy beyond voting to support a party and its candidates.

party caucus or party conference A nominally closed party meeting to select candidates or leaders, plan strategy, or make decisions regarding legislative matters. Termed a *caucus* in the Democratic Party and a *conference* in the Republican Party.

party identification An individual's attachment to a particular political party, which may be based on issues, ideology, past experience, upbringing, or a mixture of these elements.

party vote A roll-call vote in the House or Senate in which at least 50 percent of the members of one party take a particular position and are opposed by at least 50 percent of the members of the other party.

patronage Direct services and benefits that members of Congress provide to their constituents, especially making partisan appointments to offices and conferring grants, licenses, or special favors to supporters.

pluralism The theory that all interests are and should be free to compete for influence in the government.

plurality rule A type of electoral system in which victory in an election goes to the individual who gets the most votes, but not necessarily a majority of the votes cast. Compare *majority rule*.

pocket veto A veto that occurs automatically when Congress adjourns during the 10 days that a president has to approve a bill and the president takes no action on it.

polarization Strong ideological divisions between groups that makes compromise and progress difficult.

political action committee (PAC) A private group that raises and distributes funds for use in election campaigns.

political party An organized group that attempts to control the government by electing its members to office.

politics Conflict and cooperation over the leadership, structure, and policies of government.

pork-barrel legislation Appropriations that members of Congress use to provide government funds for projects benefiting their home district or state.

PR See *proportional representation*.

precedents Past cases whose principles are used by judges as the bases for their decisions in present cases.

preemption The willingness to strike first in order to prevent an enemy attack.

preventive war The policy of striking first when a nation fears that a foreign power is contemplating hostile action.

priming The use of media coverage to make the public take a particular view of an event or a public figure.

principal-agent relationship The relationship between a principal (such as a citizen) and an agent (such as an elected official) in which the agent is expected to act on the principal's behalf.

prior restraint An effort by a government agency to block publication of material by a newspaper or magazine; censorship.

privatization The act of moving all or part of a program from the public sector to the private sector.

progressive tax A tax in which the proportion of income paid goes up as income goes up. Also called *graduated tax*. Compare *regressive tax*.

project grants Grants-in-aid for which state and local governments submit proposals to federal agencies, which provide funding for them on a competitive basis. Compare *formula grants*.

proportional representation (PR) A multiple-member district system that awards seats to political parties in proportion to the percentage of the vote that each party won.

prospective voting Voting based on the imagined future performance of a candidate. Compare *retrospective voting*.

public good A good that, first, may be enjoyed by anyone if it is provided and, second, may not be denied to anyone once it has been provided. Also called *collective good*.

public law Cases involving the powers of government or rights of citizens. Compare *civil law* and *criminal law*.

public opinion Citizens' attitudes about political issues, personalities, institutions, and events.

public policy A law, rule, statute, or edict that expresses the government's goals and often incorporates rewards and punishments to incentivize their attainment.

recall The removal of a public official by popular vote.

redistribution A tax or spending policy that changes the distribution of income, usually to create greater equality between the rich and the poor in a society.

Referendum (pl. referenda) A direct vote by the electorate on a proposed law that has been passed by the legislature or on a specific governmental action. Compare *initiative*.

regressive tax A tax that is applied uniformly, such that people in low income brackets pay a higher proportion of their income toward the tax than do people in high income brackets. Compare *progressive tax*.

regulated federalism A form of federalism in which Congress imposes legislation on state and local governments that requires them to meet national standards.

regulatory agency A department, bureau, or independent agency whose primary mission is to make rules governing a particular type of activity. Compare *clientele agency*.

regulatory review The Office of Management and Budget's function of reviewing all agency regulations and other rule making before they become official policy.

representation An arrangement in which citizens select individuals to express their views when decisions are made.

reserve requirement The minimum amount of liquid assets and ready cash that the Federal Reserve requires banks to hold in order to meet depositors' demands for their money.

reserved powers Powers that are not specifically delegated to the national government or denied to the states by the Constitution. Under the Tenth Amendment, these powers are reserved to the states.

retrospective voting Voting based on the past performance of a candidate or party. Compare *prospective voting*.

right of rebuttal An FCC requirement that broadcasters give individuals the opportunity to respond to the airing of personal attacks on them.

right to privacy The right to be left alone, which has been interpreted by the Supreme Court to entail individual access to birth control and abortions.

ripeness The requirement that a case must involve an actual controversy between two parties, not a hypothetical one.

roll-call vote Voting in which each legislator's yes or no vote is recorded.

Securities and Exchange Commission (SEC) The agency charged with regulating the U.S. securities industry and stock exchanges.

senatorial courtesy The practice whereby the president, before formally nominating a person for a federal district judgeship, finds out whether the senators from the candidate's state support the nomination.

seniority The priority or status ranking given on the basis of how long an individual has served on a congressional committee.

"separate but equal" rule The legal principle that public accommodations could be segregated by race but still be equal.

separation of powers The division of governmental power among several institutions that must cooperate in decision making.

signing statement An announcement made by the president when signing a bill into law, sometimes presenting the president's interpretation of the law, as well as remarks predicting the benefits it will bring to the nation.

single-member district An electoral district that elects only one representative—the typical method of representation in the United States.

slander An oral statement made in "reckless disregard of the truth" and considered damaging to a victim because it is "malicious, scandalous, and defamatory." Compare *libel*.

SNAP See *Supplemental Nutrition Assistance Program*.

social policy Governmental social insurance, welfare, health, and education programs aimed at protecting against risk and insecurity, reducing poverty, and/or expanding opportunity.

Social Security A contributory welfare program into which working Americans must place a percentage of their wages and from which they receive cash benefits after retirement.

socialization A process in which individuals take on their communities' perspectives and preferences through social interactions.

sovereignty Independent political authority.

Speaker of the House The chief presiding officer of the House of Representatives. The Speaker is elected at the beginning of every Congress on a straight party vote and is the most important party and House leader.

speech plus Speech accompanied by activities such as sit-ins, picketing, and demonstrations.

standing The requirement that anyone initiating a court case must show a substantial stake in the outcome.

standing committee A permanent legislative committee that considers legislation within a designated subject area.

state sovereign immunity A legal doctrine holding that states cannot be sued for violating an act of Congress.

states' rights The principle that states should oppose the increasing authority of the national government. This view was most popular before the Civil War.

strict scrutiny The strictest standard of judicial review of a government's actions, in which the government must show that the law serves a "compelling state interest." Compare *intermediate scrutiny*.

subsidy A government grant of cash or other valuable commodities, such as land, to an individual or an organization. Subsidies are used to promote activities desired by the government, to reward political support, or to buy off political opposition.

Supplemental Nutrition Assistance Program (SNAP) An in-kind benefits program that provides eligible individuals and families with debit cards that can be used to buy food at most retail stores.

supremacy clause A clause of Article VI of the Constitution stating that all laws and treaties approved by the national government are the supreme laws of the United States and superior to all laws adopted by any state or other subdivision.

supreme court The highest court in a particular state or in the country. Compare *trial court* and *court of appeals*.

TANF See *Temporary Assistance for Needy Families*.

tariff A tax on imported goods.

tax expenditure A benefit to an individual or business in the form of relief from taxes that would otherwise be owed to the government.

Temporary Assistance for Needy Families (TANF) Federal cash assistance for children in families that fall below state standards of need.

Three-Fifths Compromise An agreement reached at the Constitutional Convention of 1787, stating that for the purpose of distributing congressional seats on the basis of state populations, only three-fifths of enslaved people would be counted.

totalitarian government A system of rule in which the government's power is not limited by law and in which the government seeks to eliminate other social institutions that might challenge it. Compare *authoritarian government* and *constitutional government*.

trial court The first court to hear a criminal or civil case. Compare *court of appeals* and *supreme court*.

trustees Legislators who vote according to what they think is best for their constituents. Compare *delegates*.

turnout rate The number of people who vote in a given election divided by the number of people who would have been allowed to vote in it.

UN See *United Nations*.

unfunded mandates National standards or programs imposed on state and local governments by the federal government without accompanying funding or reimbursement.

United Nations (UN) An organization of nations founded in 1945 to be a channel for negotiation and a means of settling international disputes peaceably.

United States-Mexico-Canada Agreement Renegotiated free-trade agreement between the United States, Mexico, and Canada that was signed in 2020.

veto The president's constitutional power to reject acts of Congress.

War Powers Resolution A 1973 resolution by Congress declaring that the president can send troops into action abroad only if Congress authorizes the action or if U.S. troops are already under attack or seriously threatened.

welfare state A set of national public policies by which the government takes a central role in promoting the social and economic well-being of its citizens.

whip system A party communications network in each house of Congress. Whips poll their party's members to learn the members' intentions on specific bills and also convey the leadership's views and plans to members.

World Trade Organization (WTO) The international trade agency that promotes free trade. The WTO grew out of the General Agreement on Tariffs and Trade (GATT).

writ of *certiorari* A formal request to have the Supreme Court review a decision of a lower court.

writ of *habeas corpus* A court order demanding that an individual in custody be brought into court and shown the cause for detention. Habeas corpus is guaranteed by the Constitution and can be suspended only in cases of rebellion or invasion.

WTO See *World Trade Organization*.

CREDITS

INDEX

due process of law, 85, 98, *98*, 235
due process rights, *98*
Dunlap, Riley E., 284

early voting, 309, *310*
earmarks, 137, 407
earned income tax credit (EITC), *438*, 445
East India Company, 25
ecclesia, 9
economic aid, international, 473–74
economic benefits, 389
economic interests, 266
economic policy, 412–32
 federal budget deficits and surpluses, *424*
 goals of, 415–19
 influencing, 432–34
 tools of
  fiscal policies (*see* fiscal policies)
  monetary policies and, 419–32
  subsidies and contracting, 432
economic prosperity, 460–61
economic sanctions, 473–74
Economist, 287
Economist/YouGov, 441
economy
 influence on presidential elections, 321, *322–23*
education
 in party identity, *353*
 political parties and, *363*
 schools and lobbying, 407–8
 segregation in, 107–13, *108, 112*
 voting and, 318
 women and, 111–13
Education Act, 112–13
Education Department, U.S., 95, 112, 208
education programs, 446–49
EEOC (Equal Employment Opportunity Commission), 114, 116
E.E.O.C. v. Abercrombie and Fitch Stores, 90
Egypt, 473
Eighteenth Amendment, 42, 45
Eighth Amendment, 43, *44*, 84, 98, 100
Eisenhower, Dwight D., 111
 presidential powers of, 171
EITC (earned income tax credit), *438*, 445

elastic clause. *see* necessary and proper clause
Election Day registration, 308, 318
elections, 298–343. *see also* voter turnout; voting
 of 1800, 369
 of 1824, 370
 of 1828, 370
 of 1832, 370
 of 1840, 370
 of 1856, 370–71
 of 1860, 371
 of 1892, 372
 of 1896, 372
 of 1928, 372
 of 1932, 372
 of 1948, 376
 of 1964, 373
 of 1968, 373, 377
 of 1980, 373
 of 2000, 377
 2000-2020 results, *335, 336*
 of 2006, 77
 of 2008, 77, 298, 300
 of 2010, 78, 299
 of 2014, 78
 of 2016, 78, 128, 159, 274, 298, 299, 319, 324, 357, *358–59*, 365, 375
 of 2018, 78, 128, 274, 289, 290, 341
 of 2020, 319, *320*, 321, 324, 325, 332–40, 341, *341, 375, 375*
 accountability and, 356
 campaigns and, 307, 325–30
 candidate characteristics and, 321–25
 economic influence on Presidential, *322–23*
 issues and policy preferences in, 320–21
 partisan loyalty in, 271, 319, *320*
 primary, 348
 recall, 317
 rules governing, 302
  ballots, 308–9
  electoral districts, 309–13, *312*
  plurality rule, 313–15
  referendum and recall, 315–17
  voter eligibility, 303, 305–8
 runoff, 314–15
 state, 331
 voters' decisions in, 317–25, *320, 322–23*
Electoral College, 23, 33, 35, 46, 168, 310–11, 314

growth, *302–303*
electoral districts, 309–13, *312*
electoral system, 135–39, *139,* 140
electoral votes, *376–79*
electricity, *59*
Elementary and Secondary Education Act, *446,* 447
elementary education policy, 445–49
Eleventh Amendment, 45, *47,* 70
Emergency Economic Stabilization Act, 397
emergency power, presidential, 73, 169
Emergency Price Control Act, 244
eminent domain, 56, 85, *86*
employment, 113–14, 117, 416–17
 in the government, *222*
Endangered Species Act, 395
enemy combatant, 245
Energy, Department of (DOE), 208
England, 183. *see also* United Kingdom
Entertainment Software Association, 396
entitlement, 437, 444
 programs and their cost, *438*
Environmental Defense Fund, 394
environmental interest groups, 468
Environmental Protection Agency (EPA), 177, 198–99, *199,* 205, 208, 213, 214, *225,* 431
EOP (Executive Office of the President), 185
EPA (Environmental Protection Agency), 177, 198–99, *199,* 205, 208, 213, 214, *225,* 431
Episcopalians, 362
Epsy, Mike, 313
Equal Employment Opportunity Commission (EEOC), 90, 114, 116
equal opportunity principle, 268
equal protection clause, 106
equal rights amendment (ERA), 114
equal time rule, 292
ERA (equal rights amendment), 114
Era of Good Feeling, 370
Escobedo v. Illinois, 86
establishment clause, 87–88
Estonia, 476
ethnicity
 political parties and, 361, *363*
 public opinion and, 272–74

Evangelical Protestants, 362

Evans, Romer v., 243

Every Student Succeeds Act, *446, 447,* 448

excessive fines, freedom from, *86*

exchanges, property, 413

excise taxes, 425, *426–27*

exclusionary rule, *86,* 98–99

executive agreements, 160–61, 173, 467

executive branch, *74,* 198–227. *see also* bureaucracy; presidency
  Congress *vs.,* 195
  in Constitution, 34–35, 43, *44,* 84, 168–81
  judicial branch *vs., 40, 74*
  legislative branch *vs., 40, 74*
  lobbying of, 397–98
  organization of, 205–11, *206*

executive-congressional agreement, 467

Executive Office of the President (EOP), 185, 429

executive orders, 166, 180–81, 191–94, *192,* 228, *229*

executive privilege, 75, 76, 173–74

expressed powers, 34, 40, 55, 169, 170–76

expressive speech, 92–93, 95

Facebook, 281, 291
  importance of news on, *291*
  interest groups and, 394
  Obama and, 281

"failed states," 6

Fair Credit Reporting Act, 419

family laws, 266

farmers in colonial America, 29

farm subsidies, 417–18, 432

Farook, Syed, 99

fascism, 270

"Fast and Furious" program, 174

Faubus, Orval, 111

FBI (Federal Bureau of Investigation), 170, 205, 208, 209

FCC (Federal Communications Commission), 207, 208, 289

FDA (Food and Drug Administration), 77, 190–91, 210, 418–19, *419*

FDIC (Federal Deposit Insurance Corporation), 423

FEC (Federal Election Commission), 207

FECA (Federal Election Campaign Act), 327–29, 403, 407

federal appellate courts, 235–36

Federal Bureau of Investigation (FBI), 170, 205, 208, 209

Federal Communications Commission (FCC), 207, 208, 289

federal courts. *see* courts; judicial branch; Supreme Court

Federal Deposit Insurance Corporation (FDIC), 423

Federal Election Campaign Act (FECA), 327–29, 403, 407

Federal Election Commission (FEC), 207, 327

Federal Election Commission, Citizens United v., 92, 329, 433

Federal Emergency Management Agency (FEMA), *202*

federal funds rate, 423

federalism, 22, 33, 40, 52–70, 182
  in Constitution, 55–60
  cooperative, 64–66, *66, 67*
  definition of, 39, 54
  dual, 60–63, *66,* 69, 76
  grants-in-aid, 64–66, *65, 67*
  layer cake *vs.* marble cake, 66
  new, 67–71
  regulated, *66,* 68
  separation of powers and, 71–76, *74*

Federalist Papers
  No. 51, 53

Federalist Party, *368,* 369, 370, 375

Federalists, 41–42

federal jurisdiction, 234–41

Federal Lobbying Disclosure Act, 395, 398

federal outlays, *221*

Federal Register, 204

Federal Regulation of Lobbying Act, 395

Federal Reserve Board, 211, 421, *422*

Federal Reserve System, 211, 421–23

federal service, 217, 220, *222*

Federal Trade Commission (FTC), 61, 96, 210, 431

Federal Trade Commission Act, 431

Feingold, Russell, 327

FEMA (Federal Emergency Management Agency), *202*

females on federal judiciary, *238*

Ferguson, Missouri shooting, 110

Ferguson, Plessy v., 106, *107*

Fifteenth Amendment, *45,* 105, *302*

Fifth Amendment, 43, *44,* 83, 85, 87, 99, 121, 232

fifth party system, *372–73*

fighting words, 95–96

filibuster, 147, 258

Filipino
  party identity of, 361

financial bailout, 180

financial crisis of 2008, 415, 422, 433

Financial Stability Oversight Council, 207, 208

fire alarm oversight, 217

First Amendment, 43, *44,* 81, 83, 84, 87, 90, 94–95, 293, 395, 402
  establishment clause of, 87–88
  freedom of religion and, 87–90
  freedom of speech and, 90–96
  freedom of the press and, 85, *86,* 90–96, 292
  free exercise clause of, 87, 89–90
  libel, slander, obscenity, pornography, and, 93–94
  national government and, 81

First Continental Congress, 25

first party system, 369

fiscal and monetary policy agencies, 210–11

fiscal policies, 423–30
  raising the debt ceiling, 425
  spending and budgeting, *424,* 424–25, 429, *429*
  taxation, 425–27, *426–27*
  welfare system and, 435–45, *440–41*
    growth of, *446*
    income support programs, 443–45
    Medicare, 434, *438,* 442
    reform, 444
    Social Security, 211, 220, *426–27,* 437–39, *438, 440–41*
    spending, *437*

Fisher, Louis, 96

Fisher, Peter, 428

flag burning, 92–93

Flint Michigan drinking water contamination, *216*

floor time in Congress, 155, 156

Florida, 70
  elections in, 331

Floyd, George, 2–3, *170*, 171, 276, *345*, 402, *402*
FOIA (Freedom of Information Act), 204
Food and Drug Administration (FDA), 190–91, 210, 418–19, *419*
Food Safety and Inspection Service, 205
food stamps, 211, 443, 445, *446*
Ford, Gerald, 172
Foreign Affairs Committee, 467
foreign imports, *461*
foreign policy, 129, 454–82
  arbitration and, 480
  bureaucracy and, 466–67, 469
  collective security and, 474–76
  Congress and, 129, 467
  diplomacy and, 470–71
  economic aid and sanctions, 473–74
  goals of, 456–64
    economic prosperity, 460–61
    international humanitarian policies, 462–64
    security, 456–60
  interest groups and, 468
  military force and, *474–75*, 476–80
  president and, 172–73, 464, 466, 469
  role of America in world politics, 480–81
  United Nations and, 471–72
Foreign Relations Committee, 467
Foreign Service Act, 470
Forest Service, 203, 205
formula grants, 65
fossil fuel companies, 153
Fourteenth Amendment, *45*, 46, 47, 83–87, 99, 106–8, 242, 351
  Bill of Rights and, 83–87, *86*
  Brown v. Board of Education of Topeka and, 106–8
  Plessy v. Ferguson and, 106, *107*
  racial discrimination after, 106–10, *108–9*
Fourth Amendment, 43, *44*, 84, 87, 98, 99
fourth party system, 371–72
Fox, 285
Fox News, 286
framing, 293
France, 457
  aiding American Revolutionary War, 27
  United Nations and, 472
  World War I and, 457

Frankfurter, Felix, 236, 252, 255
franking privilege, 137
Franklin, Benjamin, 25
Frazier, Lynn, 317
Frederick, Joseph, 94
freedom. *see* liberty
Freedom Act, 172
Freedom Caucus, 144
freedom from excessive fines, *86*
Freedom from Religion Foundation, 88
freedom of assembly, 85, *86*, 92–93
Freedom of Information Act (FOIA), 204
freedom of petition, 92–93
freedom of religion, 85, *86*, 87–90
freedom of speech, 84, 85, *86*, 90–96. *see also* First Amendment
freedom of the press, 85, *86*, 90–92, 292
free exercise clause, 87, 89–90
free rider problem, 5, 349, 387
Free-Soilers, *368*
free trade, 460–62
Friends of the Earth, 283
FTC (Federal Trade Commission), 61, 96, 210, 431
full faith and credit clause, 56–57

Gailmard, Sean, 398
Gallup polls, 280, 284, 324
gambling, sports, 70
Garland, Merrick, 239, 258
gatekeeping, 151
GATT (General Agreement on Tariffs and Trade), 461
gay and lesbian movement, 120–21. *see also* same-sex marriage
gay marriage. *See* same-sex marriage
GDP (gross domestic product), *221*, 416, *437*
gender
  partisan loyalty and, 319, 361, *363*
  in party identity, *353*
  political engagement of, 358–59
  Presidential candidate and, 324
  public opinion and, 274–75, *277*
gender discrimination, 114–15
gender gap, 274–75, 319, 361
gender identity, 116
gender identity-based discrimination, 114–15

gender-nonconforming individuals, 115
General Accounting Office, 119, 144
General Agreement on Tariffs and Trade (GATT), 461
Genêt, Edmond, 172
Geneva Conventions, 245
geography and public opinion, 276–77
George III, 168
Georgia, 56–57
  ratification of Constitution, 41
  slavery in, 31
  sodomy laws in, 101
  voting in, 314
Gerber, Alan, 405
Gerry, Elbridge, 311
gerrymandering, *70*, 70–71, 138, 311, 313
Gibbons, Thomas, 61
Gibbons v. Ogden, 61
GI Bill of Rights, *446*, 447, 448
Gideon, Clarence Earl, 100
Gideon v. Wainwright, *86*, 87, 99–100
Ginsburg, Ruth Bader, 239, *239*, 254, *256*, *257*
girls
  engagement with politics, *358–59*
Gitlow v. New York, *86*
GNP (gross national product), 416
going public strategy, 400–1, 407
Goldwater, Barry, 373
Gonzales v. Oregon, 69–70
Google, 288, 385, 396
  Democratic Party and, 392–93
  partisanship of, *392*
  political action committees and, 392–93
  Republican Party and, 392–93
Google News, 285
Gore, Al, 377
Gorsuch, Neil, 135, 160, 237, 240, *240*, 254, *256*
governance, 3–4, 22
  tension between representation and, 12–13
government, 6–7, 412. *see also* bureaucracy; federalism; *specific branches of government*
  balance of power, *56*
  complexity of, 52–54

New Politics of the 1960s, 391, 394

New Republic, 287

news

importance of Twitter and Facebook, *291*

source of by age, *290*

sources of, *286,* 290–91, *292–94*

newspaper industry, *286,* 287–88

newspapers, 290

news source, *286*

New York, 56

Gibbons v. Ogden and, 61

impact of Three-Fifths Compromise, 48

ratification of Constitution, 42

renewable energy policy, *58–59*

representation in the Senate, 48

third-party candidates in, 375

voting rights in, 104

New York, Gitlow v., 86

New York Convention, 480

New York Times, 287, 391

New Zealand, 475

Nineteenth Amendment, *45,* 105, 113, *303*

Ninth Amendment, 43, 44, *44,* 84, 102

Niskanen, William, 212

Nixon, Richard, 67, 76, 177, 321, 373, *374,* 403, 410

Congress and, 173

judicial appointees of, 237

pardon of, 172

"southern strategy" of, 373

Nixon, United States v., 173–74, 244

NLRB (National Labor Relations Board), 63, 182, 204, 418

No Child Left Behind Act, *446,* 447–48

nomination of candidates, 347–48, *348*

noncontributory programs, 437, 444–45

non-state actors, 456

nonvoters, 318

North American Free Trade Agreement (NAFTA), 352, 461, 468

North Atlantic Treaty Organization (NATO), 475

North Carolina, 115, 116

elections in, 331

ratification of Constitution, 42

slavery in, 31

Virginia Plan and, 30

North Dakota, 101, 317

impact of Three-Fifths Compromise, 48

representation in the Senate, 48

Northern Ireland, 468

Northern Marianas, 234

North Korea, 6, 455, 459, 470, 473

Northrop Grumman, 465

Northwest Ordinance, 446, *446*

NOW (National Organization for Women), 114, 283, 390, 394, 400

NRA (National Rifle Association), *150,* 382, *383,* 385, 405

NRCC (National Republican Congressional Committee), 325–26, 365

NRSC (National Republican Senatorial Committee), 325, 365

NSA (National Security Agency), 93, 170

NSC (National Security Council), 170, 183, 466, 469

NSF (National Science Foundation), 418

NWSA (National Woman Suffrage Association), 104

OAS (Organization of American States), 475

Obama, Barack, 49, 72, 93, 135, 160, 187, 215–16, 284, 288, *323,* 354–55, 356, 431, *447*

appointments by, *218–19*

approval rating of, 189

banning transgender discrimination, 115, 116

Biden and, 185

BP oil spill and, 171

campaign financing, 328

Deferred Action for Childhood Arrivals Act, 119

election of 2008 and, 77–78, 281, 324, 326

environmental rules and, 203

executive orders of, 194

executive privilege claimed by, 174

federal budget deficits, 425

financial bailout, 180

foreign policy and, 174, 459, 464, 470

health care reform and, 68, 150, 254, 352, 401, 410

Hillary Clinton and, 324, 470

House request refused by, 174

ideological gap between political parties, 154

immigrant deportation executive order, 194, 245, *245,* 251–52

Iran's nuclear ban agreement, 470

judicial appointees of, 237, 239, *240,* 254, 258

judicial nominees, 160

legislative results of, 180

lobbying and, 397, 398

national health insurance, 352

"netroots" campaign, 326

principal-agent problem, 213, 214

regulated federalism and, 68

regulatory review, 191

repealing Don't Ask, Don't Tell policy, 121

signing statements and, 194

social media used by, 187, 281

undocumented immigrants, 194

USA Freedom Act, 172

veto and, 174–75, 176, 178

Obamacare. *see* Affordable Care Act (ACA)

Obergefell v. Hodges, 121, 242, 243, 316

O'Brien, United States v., 92

O'Brien test, 92

obscenity, 93–94

Ocasio-Cortez, Alexandria, 330

Occupational Safety and Health Administration (OSHA), 210, 431

O'Connell, Anne Joseph, 218

O'Connor, Sandra Day, 254, *257*

Office of Financial Research, 207

Office of Management and Budget (OMB), 185, 427

Office of the United States Trade Representative, 467

Office of Tribal Justice, 208

office seekers, 346

Ogden, Aaron, 61

Ohio, 91

Ohio, Brandenburg v., 91

Ohio, Mapp v., 86, 87

oligarchy, 6

Olson, Mancur, 387

O'Malley, Martin, 328

OMB (Office of Management and Budget), 185, 427

online media, *286*

online news, *286*

"separate but equal" rule, 106–7, *107*
separation between church and state, 87–89
separation of powers, 22, 34, 39, *40, 52*–53, 71–76, *74*. *see also* checks and balances
September 11, 2001, terrorist attacks, 171, 188, 456, 458, 466, 472, *478*
Service Employees International Union (SEIU), 405
Sessions, Jeff, 72
Seventeenth Amendment, 33, *46*, 134
Seventh Amendment, 43, *44*, 84
sexual harassment, 95, 114–15
sexual orientation, 116
Shanghai Daily, 288
Shays, Daniel, 29
Shays's Rebellion, 29
Shelby County v. Holder, 105
Shelley v. Kraemer, 106–7
Shell Oil, 385
Sherman, Roger, 25
Sidanius, James, 277
Sierra Club, 283, 394, 395
signing statements, 194–95
single-issue interest groups, 468
single-member-districts, 310–11, 314, 378
Sixteenth Amendment, 45, *47*, 425
Sixth Amendment, 43, *44*, 84, 99–100
sixth party system, 373–74
slander, 93
Slate.com, 288
slavery, *32*, 83, 272
  in Constitution, 48
  prohibition of, *47*
Smith, Al, 276
Smith v. Allwright, 105, 252–53
SNAP (Supplemental Nutrition Assistance Program), *438, 445, 445,* 451
SNCC (Student Nonviolent Coordinating Committee), *109*
Snowden, Edward, 93
social groups, 268–69
social insurance taxes, 425
Socialist Party, *368*
socialization, political, 267, 268–69
social media, 287, 288
  interest groups and, 394
  Obama and, 187, 281
social policy, 435–45, 440–41. *see also* public policy
  income support programs, 443–45
  Medicare, 434, *438,* 442
  reform, 444

Social Security, 211, *426–27, 437–39, 438, 440–41*
  support for, 450–51
Social Security, 211, 220, 425, *426–27,* 428, 433, 434, 435, 437–39, *446*
  cost *vs.* expected tax revenue, *440*
  increasing cost of, *438, 440–41*
  reforming, 439
Social Security Act, 63, 182, 410, 437, 439
Social Security Administration (SSA), 211
Social Security Disability Insurance (SSDI), *446*
Social Security Disability Program (SSDI), *438, 438*
Social Security Trust Fund, 439
Society Security reform, 163
soft money, 367
soft news, 287
software industries, 468
sole executive agreement, 467
Soleimani, Qasem, 454
solicitor general, 249–50
Sondland, Gordon, *160*
sophomore surge, 137
Sotomayor, Sonia, 239, *240,* 254, *256*
Souter, David, 239, 254, *257*
South Carolina
  ratification of Constitution, 42
  slavery in, 31
Southeast Asia Treaty Organization (SEATO), 475
Southern Christian Leadership Conference (SCLC), *108,* 109
sovereignty, 55
Soviet Union, 456, 457–58
Speaker of the House, 140, *142,* 353
  floor time, 155, 157
special assistant, 184
speech, freedom of, 85, *86,* 90–96
speech plus, 93
speed limits, 77, *77*
split-ticket voting, 309
sports gambling, 70
Sputnik, 447
SSA (Social Security Administration), 211
SSDI (Social Security Disability Insurance), *446*
SSDI (Social Security Disability Program), *438, 438*
SSI (Supplementary Security Income), 211, 445, *446*
stable markets, 415
staff agencies, 144

staffers
  advising their party, *152*
  perceptions of constituent preferences, *153*
staff system, 143–44
Stalin, Joseph, 6
standing committees, 141–43, *142, 216. see also* committee system
standing criterion for Supreme Court cases, 246–47
standing in court cases, 247
State Department, 209–10, 462, 466, 470
state legislatures, *57*
State of the Union, 174
states, U.S.
  obligations among, 56–57
  powers of, 55–56, 82–83 (*see also* federalism)
  renewable energy policies, *58–59*
  representation in Congress, *30–31*
  rights of, 60–63, 68–71
  spending, *62–63*
state sovereign immunity, 70
states' rights, 60–63, 68–71
States' Rights Party, *368*
Steel Caucus, 144
Stein, Jill, 328
Stenberg v. Carhart, 101
Stevens, John Paul, 97, 254, *257*
Stewart, Potter, *257*
Steyer, Tom, 280
Stone, Harlan Fiske, 252–53
Stoneman Douglas High School shooting, 98
strict scrutiny, 85, 90
student loan program, 449
Student Nonviolent Coordinating Committee (SNCC), 109, *109*
students as an interest group, 394
student speech, 94–95
subsidies, federal, 417–18, 431–32
substantive limits in government, 6
Super PACs, 329
Supplemental Nutrition Assistance Program (SNAP), 445, *445,* 451
Supplementary Security Income (SSI), 211, 445, *446*
supremacy clause, 39, 55, 61, 242
Supreme Court, 60, 160, 166, 228–29, 232, 233, 234, 235, 236, 433. *see also* judicial review; *specific cases*
  abortion and, 101, 247, 255, 259, 399–400
  affirmative action and, 122–23, 247–48, 259

Voter Registration Information

STATE	REGISTRATION DEADLINE BEFORE ELECTION	EARLY VOTING PERMITTED?	IDENTIFICATION REQUIRED TO VOTE?*	MORE INFORMATION
Alabama	15 days	No	Photo ID required	alabamavotes.gov
Alaska	30 days	Yes	ID requested; photo not required	elections.alaska.gov
Arizona	20 days**	Yes	ID required; photo not required	azsos.gov/elections
Arkansas	30 days	Yes	Photo ID required	sos.arkansas.gov
California	15 days; Election-Day registration permitted	Yes	No	sos.ca.gov
Colorado	8 days by mail or online; no in-person deadline	Yes (all voting by mail)	ID requested; photo not required	sos.state.co.us
Connecticut	7 days by mail or online; no in-person deadline	No	ID required; photo not required	portal.ct.gov/sots
Delaware	Fourth Saturday prior to election	No	ID requested; photo not required	elections. delaware.gov
District of Columbia	21 days by mail or online; no in-person deadline	Yes	No	dcboee.org
Florida	28 days**	Yes	Photo ID requested	dos.myflorida. com/elections
Georgia	28 days	Yes	Photo ID required	sos.ga.gov
Hawaii	30 days; no in-person deadline	Yes (all voting by mail)	Photo ID requested	hawaii.gov/elections
Idaho	25 days; Election-Day registration permitted	Yes	Photo ID requested	idahovotes.gov
Illinois	28 days by mail; 16 days online; no in-person deadline	Yes	No	elections.il.gov
Indiana	29 days	Yes	Photo ID required	in.gov/sos/elections
Iowa	10 days; Election-Day registration permitted	Yes	Photo ID required	sos.iowa.gov
Kansas	21 days	Yes	Photo ID required	kssos.org
Kentucky	29 days	Yes	Photo ID required	elect.ky.gov
Louisiana	30 days; 20 days online	Yes	Photo ID required	sos.la.gov
Maine	15 days by mail**; no in-person deadline	Yes	No	maine.gov/sos
Maryland	21 days	Yes	No	elections.state.md.us
Massachusetts	10 days**	No	Photo ID requested	sec.state.ma.us
Michigan	15 days online or by mail; no in-person deadline	No	Photo ID required	michigan.gov/sos
Minnesota	21 days; Election-Day registration permitted	Yes	No	mnvotes.org
Mississippi	30 days	No	Photo ID required	sos.ms.gov
Missouri	Fourth Wednesday prior to election	No	ID requested; photo not required	sos.mo.gov
Montana	37 days by mail**; no in-person deadline	Yes	ID requested; photo not required	sos.mt.gov
Nebraska	Third Friday prior to election by mail; second Friday prior to election in person; 10 days online	Yes	No	sos.nebraska.gov
Nevada	28 days by mail; 21 days in person; 19 days online	Yes	No	nvsos.gov